GOSPEL PERSPECTIVES

The Miracles of Jesus

Volume 6

Edited by
David Wenham
and Craig Blomberg

jsot press
1986

ISBN 1 85075 008 4
1 85075 009 2 Pbk

Published by
JSOT Press
Department of Biblical Studies
The University of Sheffield
Sheffield S10 2TN
England

Printed in Great Britain
by Redwood Burn Limited
Trowbridge, Wiltshire

British Library Cataloguing in Publication Data

Gospel perspectives.
Vol. 6 : The miracles of Jesus.
1. Bible. N.T. Gospels——Evidences,
authority, etc.
I. Wenham, David II. Blomberg, Craig
226'.01 BS2555.5

ISBN 1-85075-008-4
ISBN 1-85075-009-2 Pbk

CONTENTS

PREFACE

The purpose of the *Gospel Perspectives* series has been to examine the question of the historicity of the gospels from a number of angles. The first two volumes ranged over a variety of questions; the later volumes have each had a specific focus: volume 3 looked at the question of midrash and Jewish historiography; volume 4 was a detailed study of a particular passage, the eschatological discourse; and volume 5 moved outside the gospels, examining the Jesus tradition in other parts of the New Testament and in other early Christian and non-Christian writings. This volume returns to the gospels themselves, and in looking at the miracles of Jesus tackles one of the most important and difficult historical questions which the gospels raise.

The question of the miracles of Jesus is important for the consideration of gospel historicity, since the miracle stories are the element in the gospel tradition which tends to be regarded with most historical suspicion by scholars. (By the 'miracles of Jesus' we mean those actions of Jesus which, as they are described in the gospels, appear to have involved the exercise of supernatural power.) As they are such a sizeable and significant element in the tradition, this suspicion inevitably extends to the gospels as a whole. The question of the miracles is difficult, because it involves an interplay of historical, scientific and philosophical considerations more complex than most other historical questions surrounding the gospels. The conviction that Jesus of Nazareth spoke the parables ascribed to him in the gospels, for example, raises no great problems for the modern scientific historian; but that he walked on water or turned water into wine seems to many unthinkable, or at least highly improbable. The historical evidence for such miracles may be no weaker than for Jesus's parables, but they seem improbable because they are unparalleled in our experience and because they are difficult to square with the secular world-view that is dominant at least in the West today.

To dismiss the miracle stories simply on the grounds that they are strange to our contemporary outlook would, of course, be unsatisfactory. On the one hand, some would argue that miracles such as the gospels portray are not unknown today in certain parts of the world. On the other hand, the evangelists portray the miracles as signs of the supernatural rule of God which were utterly astonishing at the time when they occurred.

Traditional Christian apologetic has appealed to the unprecedented nature of the miracles as evidence for Christian belief. The miracles have thus been seen as a positive asset to Christian faith rather than as a historical liability, as they are often viewed today.

But, although an over-simple dismissal of the miracles because of their strangeness is unacceptable, it remains the case that miracles do pose particular philosophical and historical problems for the modern scholar. Factors such as our scientific understanding of natural cause and effect, our increased knowledge of different religious traditions (some with sophisticated, some with unsophisticated ideas about the supernatural), and our growing appreciation of the power of the human mind, all encourage us to look at miracle stories of any sort (including claimed Christian miracles) critically not credulously. It is not fair or historically accurate to suppose that all societies before the time of the Enlightenment were gullible with regard to miracles; but it is true that some people before and after the Enlightenment have been gullible, and that miracle stories cannot and should not always be taken at face value.

Faced with the complexity of the issue, this volume looks at the question of Jesus' miracles from various angles: we look back at the recent history of scholarly discussion of miracles and seek to analyse some of the methodological and philosophical issues. We look at the Mediterranean world of Jesus' day, examining possible parallels to the traditions of Jesus' miracles and trying to establish whether the Jesus tradition reflects a common mythological way of thinking or whether it is significantly distinctive. We look at the gospels themselves, seeking to review and contribute to the ongoing scholarly debate about the historicity of the miracle stories.

There are numerous omissions in the volume. For example, we have no articles specifically on Jesus' resurrection, even though this is the most important New Testament miracle of all and historically the best attested. In earlier volumes a number of essays did discuss the resurrection traditions, and it was a deliberate decision not to cover them again in this volume. Earlier volumes also included essays on the infancy narratives; this volume does not. This volume leaves undiscussed a range of other interesting questions: for example, have the gospel miracles apologetic significance (for the evangelists and for Christians today)? How, if at all, do the gospel miracles relate to modern 'miracles', if they are correctly so described? What are we to make of non-Christian miracle-workers (in New Testament times and today)? What of Rudolf Bultmann's demythologization? But, although this volume is something of a miscellany of articles and in no way a comprehensive discussion, we hope that between them the articles add up to a significant and useful examination of many of the historical issues raised by the miracle traditions of the gospels. We conclude the volume with a brief summing-up considering what the volume has achieved and in what directions it points.

This volume is the last in the *Gospel Perspectives* series (except for a planned popularization of the findings of the volumes), and it marks the end for the time being of the Tyndale House Gospels Research Project. We are very grateful to all who over the past ten years or so have contributed to the Project and the series. In particular, thanks are due to the Council of Tyndale House in Cambridge who planned and have supported the Project throughout, to Dr. Dick France who set the Project in motion, to all the contributors to the six volumes and to the large number of other people who have contributed very significantly by reading and commenting on articles at various stages of their production. Special thanks are also due to the directors and staff of the JSOT Press, whose consistent helpfulness and encouragement have been so important for the success of the Project.

In explaining the purpose of the Project in volume 1 we spoke of our 'desire to provide answers to the questions of historicity which will stand up to serious academic scrutiny and will provide some help for those perplexed by scholarly disagreement'. It is perhaps too early to say how far we have achieved what we hoped for; but we have been encouraged by the positive reactions to the series from a broad spectrum of reviewers. We hope and pray that the series will continue to be read and to be found useful by theological students and scholars. In the preface to volume 2 we expressed the opinion that 'the cumulative effect of our studies has been to show that serious historical and literary scholarship allows us to approach the gospels with the belief that they present an essentially historical account of the words and deeds of Jesus. As editors we are convinced that a recovery of that belief will prove liberating both in the scholarly enterprise. . . and also within the church, which needs to hear, to see and to follow the Jesus of the gospels.' This continues to be our opinion and conviction, as the *Gospel Perspectives* series is concluded.

THE PROBLEM OF MIRACLES: A HISTORICAL AND PHILOSOPHICAL PERSPECTIVE

William Lane Craig
Trinity Evangelical Divinity School
2065 Half Day Road
Deerfield, IL 60015

Nineteenth Century Collapse of Belief in Miracles

There are two steps to follow in establishing that a miracle has occurred, according to the Göttingen Professor of Theology Gottfried Less in his *Wahrheit der christlichen Religion* (1758): first, one must determine the historicity of the event itself and, second, one must determine the miraculous character of that event./1/ During the ensuing century, the viability of both of these steps came to be regarded with scepticism, resulting in the general collapse within German theology of the credibility of the gospel miracle stories.

Denial of the Miraculous Nature of Gospel Miracles

First to go was the second step. German Rationalists of the late seventeenth/early eighteenth centuries were willing, indeed, sometimes eager, to grant the historicity of the event itself, as called for in step one. But they were at pains to provide a purely natural explanation for the event, thus undercutting step two. Given that events with supernatural causes do not occur, there simply had to be some account available in terms of merely natural causes. Thus Karl Bahrdt, in his *Ausführung des Plans und Zwecks Jesu* (1784-92) explains the feeding of the 5000 by postulating a secret store of bread which Jesus and his disciples distributed to the multitude; Jesus' walking on the water was effected by a platform floating just beneath the surface; his raising the dead was actually reanimation from a coma, thus preventing premature burial. This last explanation provided the key to explaining Jesus' own resurrection. By the end of the eighteenth century, the theft hypothesis, so dear to Deism, had apparently pretty much lost conviction, and a new explanation was needed. This German Rationalism found in the apparent death (*Scheintod*) theory. According to Bahrdt, Jesus' death and resurrection were a hoax engineered by Jesus himself to convince people that he was the Messiah.

But the dean of the natural explanation school was certainly H. E. G. Paulus, professor of theology at Heidelberg. In his *Philologisch-kritischer und historischer Kommentar über das Neue Testament* (1800-02), *Das Leben Jesu, als Grundlage einer reinen Geschichte des Urchristentums* (1828), and *Exegetisches Handbuch über die drei ersten Evangelien* (1830), he perfected the art of explaining naturalistically the miraculous elements in the gospels while retaining a close adherence to the letter of the text. A pantheist who accepted Spinoza's dictum, '*Deus sive Natura*,' Paulus rejected all miracles *a priori*. Although he staunchly insisted that the main point of his *Leben Jesu* was not to explain away miracles,/2/ it is nevertheless true that he expended a great deal of effort doing precisely this, and it is chiefly for this effort that he is remembered. According to Paulus, miracles are not the important thing, but rather the spirit of Jesus as seen in his thought and actions./3/ It is the person of Jesus in his moral character and courage that is truly miraculous. '*Das Wunderbare von Jesus ist Er selbst*.'/4/ The true meaning of Christianity is to be found in the teachings of Jesus, which, Paulus says, are self-evidently true, as demonstrated by their inner spirituality. In any case, literal miracles, even if they had occurred, would contribute nothing toward grounding the Christian truth. 'The main point is already certain in advance, that the most inexplicable changes in the course of Nature can neither overturn nor prove any spiritual truth, since it cannot be seen from any event of Nature for what spiritual purpose it should so happen and not otherwise.'/5/ Once a person has grasped the spiritual truth of Jesus' person and teaching, miracles become superfluous anyway. 'The proof from miracles itself always demands first, as it must, that the claims should be worthy of God and not contrary to reason. If this be the case, then a miracle is no longer necessary as a proof for them.'/6/ Paulus's *a priori* rejection of the miraculous is perhaps best seen in his response to the objection, why all this effort to explain away the extraordinary as something within the order of nature?/7/ He answers, in order to find the more probable explanation; and, he adds, the more probable explanation is that which can be made easier to believe. Since for post-Enlightenment thinkers, miracles had ceased to be believable, a natural explanation would always be preferred. When Paulus states further that probability always depends on whether an effect can be derived from the causes at hand,/8/ then the presuppositional nature of his anti-supernaturalism becomes clear. For now the most probable explanation is seen by definition to be a purely natural explanation; hence, his efforts to explain away the miraculous.

It is noteworthy that Schleiermacher, the father of modern theology, followed Paulus's lead in these regards. Schleiermacher remained rationalistic with respect to the denial of miracles, and he attached no religious importance to the resurrection of Jesus. In his lectures of 1832, *Der Christus des Glaubens und der Jesus der Geschichte*, he passively accepts Paulus's theory of Jesus' merely apparent death, stating that it is unimportant whether the death and resurrection were real or apparent. Schleiermacher himself believed that Jesus' resurrection was only a resuscitation and that he continued to live physically with the disciples for a time after this event.

Denial of the Historicity of Gospel Miracles

Just three years after Schleiermacher's lectures, however, a work appeared which sounded the death knell for the natural explanation school and also served to undercut the first step of Less's procedure: David Friedrich Strauss's *Das Leben Jesu*. In its consistent application of mythological explanations to the New Testament, Strauss's work obviated any need to concede the historicity of the gospel miracles even *qua* events. Strauss rejected the conspiratorial theories typified by the Deist Hermann Samuel Reimarus as characteristic of the eighteenth century's simplistic, naive approach to matters of religious belief. In his helpful treatise, *Hermann Samuel Reimarus und seine Schutzschrift für die vernünftigen Verehrer Gottes* (1861), Strauss describes the prior century's reductionistic attitude toward revealed religion: 'All positive religions without exception are works of deception: that was the opinion that the eighteenth century cherished within its heart, even if it did not always pronounce it as frankly as did Reimarus.'/9/ Thus, whenever miraculous events were encountered in the Scriptures, these were facilely explained away as lies or hoaxes deliberately perpetrated by the persons involved. This sort of explanation completely misunderstands the nature of religious commitment and devotion, charges Strauss. Only the eighteenth century could have conjoined deliberate deception with the apostles' religious zeal; for these are two incompatible things. The nineteenth century considers it a foregone conclusion that no historically permanent religion was ever founded through deception, but that all were founded by people who were themselves convinced. Christianity cannot, therefore, be passed off as simply a hoax. When Reimarus says that Christianity is not a divine revelation, but a human fraud, we know today that this is an error, that Christianity is not a fraud. But the rejection of Reimarus's hypothesis does not entail embracing the supernaturalists' explanation. Reimarus's 'Nein' to the traditional view remains 'Nein,' but his 'Ja' to deception must yield to a better answer.

That answer was not to be found in the natural explanation school epitomized by Paulus. The contrived and artificial character of so many of these explanations was painfully apparent, and the proffered explanations were no more believable than the miracles themselves. Moreover, the natural system of interpretation, while it sought to preserve the historical certainty of the narrative, nevertheless lost its ideal truth. For example, if the transfiguration were, as Paulus claimed, an accidental, optical phenomenon and the two men either images of a dream or simply unknown persons, then what, asks Strauss, is the significance of the narrative? What was the motive for preserving in the church's memory a story so void of ideas and barren of inference, resting upon a delusion? Strauss believed that the natural explanation school abandoned the substance to save the form, whereas his alternative would, by renouncing the historical facticity of the narrative, rescue and preserve the idea which resides in it and which alone constitutes its vitality and spirit.

This alternative Strauss found in the mythological interpretation of the gospels. According to this view, the miraculous events recorded in the gospels never occurred, but are the product of religious imagination and legend, and, hence, require no historical explanation as the Supernaturalists, Deists, and Rationalists assumed. Although Strauss had his predecessors in employing the concept of myth to explain particular elements in the Scriptural narratives, he was the first to compose a wholesale account of the life of Jesus utilizing mythological explanation as the key hermeneutical method. According to Strauss himself, up until the time of his writing, myth had been applied to the childhood and ascension stories of Jesus' life, but not the life of Jesus itself; this yielded a framework in which '. . .the entrance to the gospel history was through the decorated portal of mythus, and the exit was similar to it, whilst the intermediate space was still traversed by the crooked and toilsome paths of natural interpretations.'/10/ In his *Leben Jesu*, Strauss sought to show in detail how all supernatural events in the gospels can be explained as either myth, legend, or redactional additions.

Strauss claimed to operate without any religious or dogmatic presuppositions; he ascribed this neutrality to the influence of his philosophical studies. Nevertheless, it is clear that Strauss did operate on the basis of certain philosophical (if we wish not to call these religious or dogmatic) presuppositions, such as the impossibility of miracles. As an acknowledged pantheist and in later life a materialist, Strauss proceeded, like the Rationalists before him, from the assumption that miracles are impossible in principle. According to Strauss, this is not a presupposition requiring proof; on the contrary, to affirm that miracles are possible is a presupposition which requires proof./11/ God acts immediately on the universe only as a whole, but not on any particular part; on any particular part he acts only mediately through the causal laws of all other parts of nature. Hence, with regard to the resurrection, God's interposition in the regular course of nature is 'irreconcilable with enlightened ideas of the relation of God to the world.'/12/ Thus, any purportedly historical account of miraculous events must be dismissed out of hand; 'indeed no just notion of the true nature of history is possible, without a perception of the inviolability of the chain of finite causes, and of the impossibility of miracles.'/13/ Thus, although Strauss rejected the Rationalist hermeneutic of natural explanation in favor of the mythological, he remained rationalistic in his rejection of the miraculous.

Strauss's application of the category of myth to the miraculous element in the gospels proved a decisive turning point. According to Schweitzer in his history of the Life of Jesus movement *Von Reimarus zu Wrede* (1906), the critical study of the life of Jesus falls into two periods with Strauss. 'The dominant interest in the first is the question of miracle. What terms are possible between a historical treatment and the acceptance of supernatural events? With the advent of Strauss, this problem found a solution, viz., that these events have no rightful place in history, but are simply mythical elements in the sources.'/14/ By the mid-1860's the question of miracles had lost all importance. Schweitzer explains,

> That does not mean that the problem of miracle is solved. From the historical point of view it is really

> impossible to solve it, since we are not able to reconstruct the process by which a series of miracle stories arose, or a series of historical occurrences were transformed into miracle stories, and these narratives must simply be left with a question mark standing against them. What has been gained is only that the exclusion of miracle from our view of history has been universally recognised as a principle of criticism, so that miracle no longer concerns the historian either positively or negatively. Scientific theologians of the present day who desire to show their 'sensibility,' ask no more than that two or three little miracles may be left to them--in the stories of the childhood perhaps, or in the narratives of the resurrection. And these miracles are, moreover, so far scientific that they have at least no relation to those in the text, but are merely spiritless, miserable little toy-dogs of criticism, flea-bitten by rationalism, too insignificant to do historical science any harm, especially as their owners honestly pay the tax upon them by the way in which they speak, write, and are silent about Strauss./15/

Until Strauss it had been pretty generally agreed that the events in question had actually occurred--it was just a matter of explaining how they took place. But with Strauss, the miraculous events recorded in the gospels never in fact happened: the narratives are unhistorical tales determined by myth and legend.

Strauss's work completely altered the whole tone and course of German theology. By rejecting on the one hand the conspiratorial theory of Reimarus and on the other the natural explanation theory of Paulus, and by proposing a third explanation of the gospel narratives in terms of myth, legend, and redaction, Strauss in effect dissolved the central dilemma of eighteenth century orthodoxy's argument for the miracles of Jesus: that if the miracles be denied, then the apostles must be written off as either deceivers or deceived, neither of which is plausible. The evangelists were now seen to be neither deceivers nor deceived, but rather they stood at the end of a long process in which the original events were re-shaped through mythological and legendary influences. The dissolution of the orthodox dilemma did not logically imply that the Supernaturalist view was therefore false. But this Strauss not only took to have been shown by Reimarus-inspired objections concerning contradictions and inconsistencies in the narratives, but for him this was simply given by definition in his criteria for discerning mythological motifs, which were in turn predicated upon the *a priori* presupposition of the impossibility of miracles. Any event which stood outside the inviolable chain of natural causes and effects was *ipso facto* unhistorical and therefore to be mythologically accounted for. In Strauss's later *Glaubenslehre*, he explains in some detail *die Auflösung des Wunderbegriffs*, recounting the arguments of Spinoza, Hume, and Lessing to show that the concept has now become obsolete./16/ This was the legacy which Strauss bequeathed to his successors. The same naturalistic assumption that guided Strauss's historical investigations also determines, for example, the influential work of Rudolf Bultmann in our own century./17/ Bultmann's approach to the New Testament was guided by, among others, two underlying presuppositions: (1) the existence of a full-blown pre-Christian Gnosticism and (2) the impossibility of miracles. While he sought to present evidence in support of (1), he simply assumed (2). Like Strauss he seemed to regard the impossibility of miracles as a presupposition not requiring proof, and many contemporary scholars would also appear to accept a similar position. Pesch asserts that the central task of dogmatic theology today is to show how Jesus can be the central figure of God's revelation without presupposing 'a "theistic-supernaturalistic model of revelation and mediation," which is no longer acceptable to our thought.'/18/ According to Hans Frei, reasons for rejecting as unhistorical reports which run contrary to our general experience of natural, historical, or psychological occurrences 'have become standard explanation of the criteria that go into making unprejudiced ("presuppositionless") assessments of what is likely to have taken place in the past, and what is not.'/19/ Such a perspective makes it impossible even to regard the gospel miracles as events of history, much less to establish them as such.

The Eighteenth Century Crucible

The scepticism of the last and present centuries concerning miracles grew out of what Burns has called 'the Great Debate on Miracles' during the Deist controversy of the seventeenth and especially eighteenth centuries./20/ It would be well, therefore, to return to that great divide in order to rediscover and assess the rational foundations of contemporary criticism's rejection of the miraculous.

The Newtonian World-Machine

The backdrop for the eighteenth century debate was the

widespread world-view of Newtonian mechanism. Under Newton's pervasive influence, the creation had come to be regarded as the world-machine governed by eternal and inexorable laws. Indeed, this complex and harmoniously functioning system was thought to constitute the surest evidence that God exists. Diderot wrote,

> It is not from the metaphysician that atheism has received its most vital attack. . . . If this dangerous hypothesis is tottering at the present day, it is to experimental physics that the result is due. It is only in the works of Newton, of Muschenbroeck, of Hartzoeker, and of Nieuwentit, that satisfactory proofs have been found of the existence of a reign of sovereign intelligence. Thanks to the works of these great men, the world is no longer a God; it is a machine with its wheels, its cords, its pulleys, its springs, and its weights./21/

Given such a picture of the world, it is not surprising that miracles were characterized as violations of the laws of nature. For the same evidence that pointed to a cosmic intelligence also served to promote belief in a Deity who master-minded the great creation but who took no personal interest in the petty affairs of men. It simply seemed incredible to think that God would intervene on this tiny planet on behalf of some people living in Judea. Voltaire exemplified this incredulous attitude. In his *Dictionary* article on miracles, he asserts that a miracle is, properly speaking, something admirable; hence, 'The stupendous order of nature, the revolution of a hundred millions of worlds around millions of suns, the activity of light, the life of animals, all are grand and perpetual miracles.'/22/ But according to accepted usage, 'A miracle is the violation of mathematical, divine, immutable, eternal laws'/23/;therefore, it is a contradiction in terms. But, it is said, God can suspend these laws if he wishes. But why should he wish so to disfigure this immense machine? It is said, on behalf of mankind. But is it not 'the most absurd of all extravagances' to imagine that the infinite Supreme Being would on behalf of three or four hundred emmets on this little atom of mud 'derange the operation of the vast machinery that moves the universe?'/24/ Voltaire's God, indeed the God of all Deists, was the cosmic architect who engineered and built the machine, but who would not be bothered to interfere in the trivial affairs of man. In this light miracles simply became unbelievable.

Benedict de Spinoza

The philosophical attack on miracles, however, antedated

Newton's *Principia* (1687). As early as 1670 Benedict de Spinoza in his *Tractatus theologico-politicus* had argued against the possibility of miracles and their evidential value./25/ He attempts to establish four points: (1) nothing happens contrary to the eternal and unchangeable order of nature; (2) miracles do not suffice to prove God's existence; (3) biblical 'miracles' are natural events; and (4) the Bible often uses metaphorical language concerning natural events so that these appear miraculous. I shall leave (3) and (4) to my colleagues in biblical studies, but the first two contentions merit closer exposition here. (1) Spinoza argues that all that God wills or determines is characterized by eternal necessity and truth. Because there is no difference between God's understanding and will, it is the same to say God knows or wills a thing. Therefore the laws of Nature flow from the necessity and perfection of the divine nature. So should some event occur which is contrary to these laws, that would mean the divine understanding and will are in contradiction with the divine nature. To say God does something contrary to the laws of Nature is to say God does something contrary to his own nature, which is absurd. Therefore, everything that happens flows necessarily from the eternal truth and necessity of the divine nature. What is called a miracle is merely an event that exceeds the limits of human knowledge of natural law. (2) Spinoza maintains, in rationalist tradition, that a proof for the existence of God must be absolutely certain. But if events could occur to overthrow the laws of Nature, then nothing is certain, and we are reduced to scepticism. Miracles are thus counter-productive; the way in which we are certain of God's existence is through the unchangeable order of Nature. By admitting miracles, which break the laws of Nature, warns Spinoza, we create doubts about the existence of God and are led into the arms of atheism! And at any rate, an event contrary to the laws of Nature would not warrant the conclusion to God's existence: the existence of a lesser being with enough power to produce the effect would suffice. Finally, a miracle is simply a work of Nature beyond man's ken. Just because an event cannot be explained by us, with our limited knowledge of Nature's laws, does not mean that God is the cause in any supernatural sense.

David Hume

If Spinoza attacked the possibility of the *occurrence* of a miracle, Hume attacked the possibility of the *identification* of a miracle. In his essay 'Of Miracles,' which constitutes the tenth chapter of his *Enquiry*, Hume presses a two-pronged attack against the identification of a miracle in the form of an 'Even if. . . , but in fact. . .' counterfactual judgment./26/ That is to say, in the first portion of the essay, he argues against the identification of any event as a miracle while granting certain concessions, then in the second half he argues on the basis of what he thinks is in fact the case. We may differentiate the two prongs of his argument by referring to the first as his 'in principle' argument and to the second as his 'in fact' argument. The wise man, he begins, proportions his belief to the evidence. To decide between two hypotheses, one must balance the experiments for each against those for the other in order to determine which is probably true; should the results be one hundred to one in favor of the first hypothesis, then it is a pretty safe bet that the first is correct. When the evidence makes a conclusion virtually certain, then we may speak of a 'proof,' and the wise man will give whole-hearted belief to that conclusion. When the evidence renders a conclusion only more likely than not, then we may speak of a 'probability,' and the wise man will accept the conclusion as true with a degree of confidence proportionate to the probability. So it is with human testimony. One weighs the reports of others according to their conformity with the usual results of observation and experience; thus, the more unusual the fact reported, the less credible the testimony is. Now, Hume argues, even if we concede that the testimony for a particular miracle amounts to a *full proof*, it is still in principle impossible to identify that event as a miracle. For standing opposed to this proof is an equally full proof, namely the evidence for the unchangeable laws of nature, that the event in question is not a miracle. 'A miracle is a violation of the laws of nature, and as a firm and unalterable experience has established these laws, a proof against a miracle, from the very nature of the fact, is as entire as any argument from experience can possibly be imagined.'/27/ Thus the testimony of the uniform experience of mankind stands on one side of the scales against the testimony in any particular case that a transgression of that experience has occurred. Thus, proof stands against proof, and the scales are evenly balanced. Since the evidence does not incline in either direction, the wise man cannot believe in a miracle with any degree of confidence. Indeed, Hume continues, no testimony could establish that a miracle has taken place unless the falsehood of that testimony would be an even *greater* miracle than the fact it seeks to establish. And even then the force of the evidence would only be the difference between the two.

But in fact the evidence for miracles does not amount to a

full proof. Indeed, the evidence is so poor, it does not amount even to a probability. Therefore, the decisive weight falls on the side of the scale containing the full proof for the regularity of nature, a weight so heavy that no evidence for a purported miracle could hope to counterbalance it. Hume supplies four reasons, which are a catalogue of typical Deist objections to miracles, why in fact the evidence for miracles is so negligible: (1) No miracle in history is attested by a sufficient number of men of good sense and education, of unimpeachable integrity so as to preclude deceit, of such standing and reputation so that they would have a good deal to lose by lying, and in sufficiently public a manner. (2) People crave the miraculous and will believe absurd stories, as the multitude of false miracles shows. (3) Miracles only occur among barbarous peoples. (4) All religions have their own miracles and therefore cancel each other out in that they support irreconcilable doctrines. Hume adduces three examples: Vespasian's healing of two men as related by Tacitus, a healing reported by Cardinal de Reutz, and the healings at the tomb of the Abbé Paris. The evidence for miracles, therefore, does not even begin to approach the proof of the inviolability of nature's laws. Hume concludes that miracle can never be the foundation for any system of religion.

The Defense of Miracles

Orthodox defenders were not lax in responding to the objections of Spinoza and Hume, as well as to the popular Newtonian world view in general. Let us consider first some of the replies to Spinoza's arguments against the impossibility of miracles and then some of the responses to Hume's case against the identification of miracles.

1. Response to Spinoza

In his *Sentimens de quelques théologiens* (1685) Jean Le Clerc attempted to present an apologetic for Christianity that would be invulnerable to Spinoza's criticisms. He not only tried to answer Spinoza's biblical criticism but also his philosophical objections. Against these Le Clerc maintains that the empirical evidence for the miracles and the resurrection of Christ is more perspicuous and evidently true than Spinoza's abstract reasoning./28/ Le Clerc's point would seem to be that the back of this *a priori*, philosophical speculation is simply broken under the weight of the evidence. For Le Clerc empirical argument takes precedence over speculative argument. But he also rebutts Spinoza's specific tenets. Against the allegation that miracles are simply natural events, Le Clerc insists that no one will be convinced that Jesus' resurrection and ascension could happen as naturally as a man's birth. Nor is it convincing to say Jesus' miracles could be the result of unknown natural laws, he continues, for why, then, are not more of these effects produced and how is it that at the very instant Jesus commanded a paralyzed man to walk 'the Laws of Nature (unknown to us) were prepared and ready to cause the. . . Paralytic Man to walk'?/29/ Both of these considerations show that the miraculous facts of the gospel, which can be established historically, are indeed of divine origin.

Considerable analysis was brought to the concept of miracle by Samuel Clarke in his Boyle lectures *A Discourse concerning the Unchangeable Obligations of Natural Religion and the Truth and Certainty of the Christian Revelation* (1705). He points out that to the power of God all events--miraculous or not--are alike. Furthermore, it is possible that created beings including angels and demons, may have the power to produce any event, with the sole exception of *creatio ex nihilo*./30/ Reflecting Newtonian influence, Clarke asserts that matter has only the power to continue in its present state, be it rest or motion. Anything that is *done* in the world is done either by God or by created intelligent beings. The so-called natural forces of matter, such as gravitation, are properly speaking the effect of God's acting on matter at every moment. The implication of this is that the so-called 'course of nature' is a fiction; what we discern as the course of nature is nothing else than God's will, producing certain effects in a continual and uniform manner./31/ Thus, a miracle is not against the course of nature, which really does not exist, except only insofar as it is an unusual event which God does./32/ Thus, the regular 'works' of nature prove the being and attributes of God, and miracles prove the interposition of God into the regular order in which he acts./33/ Now from the miracle itself as an isolated event, it is impossible to determine whether it was performed immediately by God or by an angel or by a demonic spirit. Clarke insists that miracles done by demonic spirits are 'true and real' miracles that occur because God does not restrain the demonic spirit from acting at that point./34/ The means of distinguishing between demonic miracles and miracles wrought mediately or immediately by God is the *doctrinal context* in which the miracle occurs:

If the doctrine attested by miracles, be in itself *impious*,

> or manifestly *tending to promote Vice*; then without all question the Miracles. . .are neither wrought by God himself, nor by his Commission; because our natural knowledge of the Attributes of God, and of the necessary difference between good and evil, is greatly of more force to prove any such doctrine to be false, than any Miracles in the World can be to prove it true. . . ./35/

Should the doctrine be neutral in itself, but another person performs greater miracles within a context of doctrine contrary to the first, then the latter is to be accepted as the miracle of divine origin./36/ Thus, the correct theological definition of a miracle is this: 'a work effected in a manner unusual, or different from the common and regular method of Providence, by the interposition either of God himself, or of some intelligent Agent superior to Man, for the proof or Evidence of some particular Doctrine, or in attestation to the Authority of some particular Person.'/37/ The relationship between doctrine and miracle is that miracle proves that a higher power is involved, and the doctrinal context of the miracle enables us to discern the source of the miracle as either God or Satan. Thus, the miracles prove the doctrine, but '. . .at least the *indifferency* of the Doctrine, *[is]* a necessary Condition or Circumstance, without which the *Doctrine* is not capable of being proved by any Miracles.'/38/ When applied to Jesus' miracles, this criterion proves that Jesus was 'a Teacher sent from God' and that he has 'a Divine Commission.'/39/

In his *Traité de la vérité de la religion chrétienne* (1730-88), Jacob Vernet also seeks to answer the objection that any miracle is impossible because it is contrary to the order of Nature./40/ He defines a miracle as 'a striking work which is outside the ordinary course of Nature and which is done by God's all-mighty will, such that witnesses thereof regard it as extraordinary and supernatural.'/41/ Vernet does not, like Clarke, deny that there is a course of nature, but he does insist that the so-called course or order of nature is really composed of incidental states of events, not necessary or essential states. They depend on the will of God, and it is only the constant and uniform procession of the normal course of nature that leads us to think it is invariable. God does not change nature's course entirely, but can make exceptions to the general rules when he deems it important. These miracles serve to show that the course of nature 'is not the effect of a blind necessity, but of a free Cause who interrupts and suspends it when he pleases.'/42/ It might also be objected that the miracles are the result of a yet undiscovered operation of Nature itself./43/ Vernet replies that when the miracles are diverse and numerous, this possibility is minimized because it is hardly possible that all these unknown, marvelous operations should occur at the same time. Perhaps a single, isolated miracle might be so explained away, but not a series of miracles of different sorts.

In Claude François Houtteville's *La religion chrétienne prouvée par les faits* (1740), the Abbé argues against Spinoza that miracles are possible./44/ A miracle he defines as 'a striking action superior to all finite power,' or more commonly, as 'a singular event produced outside the chain of natural causes.'/45/ Given the existence of God, one sees immediately that miracles are possible, for a perfect Being who created the world also conserves it in being, and all the laws of its operation are directed by his sovereign hand. Against Spinoza's charge that miracles are impossible because natural law is the necessary decree of God's nature and God's nature is immutable, Houtteville rejoins that natural law is not necessary, that God is free to establish whatever laws he wills. Moreover, God can change his decrees when He wishes. And even if he could not, miracles could be part of God's eternal plan and decree for the universe just as much as natural laws, so that the occurrence of a miracle in no way represents a change of mind or decree on God's part. Houtteville even suggests that miracles are not contrary to nature, but only to what we know of nature. From God's perspective, they may conform to certain laws unknown to us.

Thus, the orthodox response to Spinoza's objections was quite multi-faceted. Hume's objections also elicited a variegated response.

2. Response to Hume

Although it was against Woolston's attacks on miracles that Thomas Sherlock wrote his *Tryal of the Witnesses of the Resurrection of Jesus* (1729), the counsel for Woolston presents an argument against miracles that is anticipatory of Hume. Woolston's attorney argues that because Jesus' resurrection violates the course of Nature, no human testimony could possibly establish it, since it has the whole witness of nature against it. To this Sherlock replies: (1) If testimony is admitted only when the matter is deemed possible according to our conceptions, then many natural matters of fact would be excluded./46/ For example, a man living in a hot climate would never believe in that case testimony from others that water could exist in a solid state as ice./47/ (2) The resurrection is simply a matter of sense perception./48/ If we met a man who claimed to have been dead, we would be suspicious. But of what? --not that he is now alive, for this contradicts all our senses, but that he was ever dead. But would we say it is impossible to prove by human testimony that this man died a year ago? Such evidence is admitted in any court of law. Conversely, if we saw a man executed and later heard the man had come to life again, we would suspect, not that he was dead, but that he was alive again. But would we say that it is impossible for human testimony to prove that a man is alive? The reason we are suspicious in these cases is not because the matter itself does not admit of being proved by evidence, but only because we are more inclined to believe our own senses rather than reports of others which go contrary to our pre-conceived opinions of what can and cannot happen. Thus, considered as a fact, the resurrection requires no greater ability in the witnesses than to be able to distinguish between a dead man and a living man. Sherlock does admit that in such miraculous cases we may require more evidence than usual, but it is absurd to say that such cases admit of no evidence. (3) The resurrection contradicts neither right reason nor the laws of nature./49/ Sherlock takes yet a third course from Clarke and Vernet. The so-called course of Nature arises from the prejudices and imaginations of men. Our senses tell us what the usual course of things is, but we go beyond our senses when we conclude that it cannot be otherwise. The uniform course of things runs contrary to resurrection, but that does not prove it to be absolutely impossible. The same Power that gave life to dead matter at first can give it to a dead body again; the latter feat is no greater than the former.

Gottfried Less in his *Wahrheit der christlichen Religion* (1758) discusses at length Hume's objections to miracles. Less defines a miracle as a work beyond the power of all creatures./50/ Of course, a miracle is such only in a context; healing itself, for instance, is not necessarily a miracle unless no natural means are employed. Also there are two types of miracles: (1) first degree miracles, which are wrought by the immediate power of God, and (2) second degree miracles, which are above any human power but are wrought by finite spiritual beings such as angels. First degree miracles are incapable of being proved because we never know whether a finite spiritual being might not be at work. Thus, only second degree miracles can be proved to have occurred.

So understood, miracles are possible./51/ Because God is the Lord of nature and can make events happen, it follows that miracles are physically possible. And because miracles are a part of God's eternal plan to confirm his teaching, they are morally possible. But did the gospel miracles occur? Although Hume discounts the testimony of the apostles because they were unlearned men, it is clear that to prove merely that something happened (for example, a disease's being healed by sheer verbal command) one need be no scholar but simply have five good senses and common sense. In fact, the New Testament witnesses fulfill even Hume's conditions for credibility of reports of miracles./52/ Thus, Hume should concede the historical certainty of the gospel miracles *qua* events.

But were these events miracles? Less now turns to a refutation of Hume's objections to establishing miracles by historical testimony./53/ Hume's principal argument is that testimony to miracles has the experience of the world and the centuries against it. In response, Less argues: (1) Because nature is the freely willed order of God, a miracle is just as possible as any event. Therefore, it is just as believable as any event. (2) Testimony to an event cannot be refuted by experiences and observations. Otherwise we would never be justified in believing anything outside our present experience; no new discoveries would be possible. (3) There is no contradiction between experience and Christian miracles. Miracles are different events (*Contraria*) from experience in general, but not contradictory events (*Contradictoria*) to experience in general./54/ The contradiction to the testimony that under the reign of Tiberius Caesar, Jesus raised certain persons from the dead and himself so rose three days after his death must necessarily be the exact opposite of this statement, namely, that Jesus never raised anyone from the dead and never himself so rose. This latter has to be proved to destroy the gospel testimony. It is hardly enough to assert that experience in general says that dead men do not rise, for with this the Christian testimony is in full agreement. Only when the exact opposite is proved to be true can Christian testimony be said to contradict experience. Hume's other objections are easily dismissed: (1) No miracle has a sufficient number of witnesses. This is false with regard to the gospel miracles, for they were publicly performed. (2) People tend to believe and report miraculous stories without proper scrutiny. This shows only that our scrutiny of such stories ought to be cautious and careful. (3) Miracles originate among ignorant and barbaric peoples. This cannot be said to describe Jesus' miracles, which took place under Roman civilization in the capital city of the Jews. (4) All religions have their miracles. This is in fact not true, for no other religion purports to prove its teachings through miracles, and there are no religious miracles outside Jewish-Christian miracles. Less later examines in considerable detail the miracles alleged by Hume to have equal footing with Christian miracles, particularly the miracles at the tomb of the Abbé Paris./55/ In all these cases, the evidence that miracles have occurred never approaches the standard of the evidence for the gospel miracles. Therefore, none of Hume's objections can overturn the evidence for the gospel miracles.

William Paley's *A View of the Evidences of Christianity* (1794) is primarily a studious investigation of the historical evidence for Christianity from miracles, and Paley's preliminary considerations to his investigation aim at an across-the-board refutation of Hume's objections. Paley makes it clear from the beginning that he presupposes the existence of the God proved by the teleological argument./56/ Given the existence of God, miracles are not incredible./57/ For why should it be thought incredible that God should want to reveal Himself in the natural world to men, and how could this be done without involving a miraculous element? Any antecedent improbability in miracles adduced in support of revelation is not such that sound historical testimony cannot surmount it. This, says Paley, suffices to answer 'a modern objection to miracles,' which he later identifies as that of David Hume./58/ The presupposition of Hume's argument, he continues, is that '. . .it is contrary to experience that a miracle should be true, but not contrary to experience that testimony should be false./59/ Like Less, Paley argues that the narrative of a fact can be said to be contrary to experience only if we, being at the time and place in question, were to see that the alleged event did not in fact take place. What Hume really means by 'contrary to experience' is simply the want of similar experiences. (To say a miracle is contrary to universal experience is obviously question-begging.) But in this case, the improbability arising from our want of similar experiences is equal to the probability that, given the event as true, we should also have similar experiences. But suppose Christianity was inaugurated by miracles; what probability is there then that we today must also have such experiences? It is clear that any such probability is negligible; hence, any improbability arising from our lack of such experience is also negligible. A miracle is not like a scientific experiment capable of being subsumed under a law and repeated, for then it would not be contrary to nature as such and would cease to be a miracle. The objection to miracle from want of similar experiences presupposes either (1) that the course of nature is invariable or (2) that if it can be varied, these variations must be frequent and general. But if the course of nature be the agency of an intelligent Being, should we not expect him to interrupt his appointed order only seldom on occasions of great importance? As to the cause of miracle, this is simply the volition of Deity, of whose existence and power we have independent proof. As to determining whether a miracle has in fact occurred, Paley considers Hume's account of the matter to be a fair one: which in any given case is more probable, that the miracle be true or that the testimony be false? But in saying this, Paley adds, we must not take the miracle out of the theistic and historical context in which it occurred, nor can we ignore the question of how the evidence and testimony arose. The real problem with Hume's scepticism becomes clear when we apply it to a test case: suppose twelve men, whom I know to be honest and reasonable persons, were to assert that they personally saw a miraculous event in which it was impossible that they had been tricked; further, the governor called them before him for an inquiry and told them that if they did not confess the imposture they would be tied up to a gibbet; and they all went to their deaths rather than say they were lying. According to Hume, I should still not believe them. But such incredulity, states Paley, would not be defended by any skeptic in the world.

Paley maintains against Hume's 'in fact' argument that no parallel to the gospel miracles exists in history./60/ Paley examines closely Hume's three examples and concludes that it is idle to compare such cases with the evidence for the miracles of the gospels./61/ In none of these cases is it unequivocal that a miracle has occurred. Even in other unexplained instances, it is still true that there is no evidence that the witnesses have passed their lives in labor, danger, and suffering voluntarily undergone in attestation to the truth of the accounts they delivered. Thus, the circumstance of the gospel history is without parallel.

Spinoza's arguments for the impossibility of miracles and Hume's arguments against the identification of miracles were thus contested from various standpoints. It is noteworthy that virtually all of the Christian thinkers presupposed the existence of God in their arguments. It was not a case of theism versus atheism, but of Christian theism versus Deism. In that sense they did not try to found a system of religion on miracles; rather they argued that given the existence of God, miracles are possible and that no *a priori* barrier exists to the discovery of actual miracles on the basis of historical testimony.

Assessment of the Debate

Natural Law and Miracles

It will be remembered that the world view that formed the backdrop to the Deist controversy was a model of the universe as a Newtonian world-machine that bound even the hands of God. So ironclad a view of natural law is, however, untenable. Natural law is today understood essentially as *description*, not *prescription*. This does not mean that it cannot serve as a basis for prediction, for it does; but our formulation of a natural law is never so certain as to be beyond reformation under the force of observed facts. Thus an event cannot be ruled out simply because it does not accord with the regular pattern of events. The advance of modern physics over the Newtonian world-machine is not that natural law does not exist, but that our formulation of it is not absolutely final. After all, even quantum physics does not mean to assert that matter and energy do not possess certain properties, such that anything and everything can happen; even indeterminacy occurs within statistical limits and concerns only the microscopic level. On the macroscopic level, firm natural laws do obtain./62/ But the knowledge of these properties and laws is derived from and based on experience. The laws of nature are thus not 'laws' in the rigid, prescriptive sense, but inductive generalizations.

This would appear to bring some comfort to the modern believer in miracles, for now he may argue that one cannot rule out *a priori* the fact that a certain event has occurred which does not conform to known natural law, since our formulation of natural law is never final and so must take account of the fact in question. It seems to me, however, that while this more descriptive understanding of natural law re-opens the door of possibility to certain anomalous events in the world, it does not help much in settling the question of miracles. The advantage gained is that one cannot rule out the occurrence of a certain event *a priori*, but that the evidence for it must be weighed. The defender of miracles has thus at least gained a hearing. But one is still operating under the assumption, it would appear, that if the event really *did* run contrary to natural law, then it would be impossible for it to have occurred. The defender of miracles appeals to the fact that our natural laws are only inductive generalizations and so never certain, in order to gain admittance for his anomalous event; but presumably if an omniscient mind knew with certainty the precise formulations of the natural laws describing our universe, then he would know *a priori* whether the event was or was not actually possible, since a true law of nature could not be violated.

As Bilynskyj argues, whether one adopts a regularity theory of natural law (according to which laws are simply descriptive of events and have no special modal quality) or a necessitarian theory (according to which natural laws are not merely descriptive of events but possess a special sort of modality determining nomic necessity/possibility), still so long as natural laws are conceived of as universal inductive generalizations the notion of a 'violation of a law of nature' is incoherent./63/ For on the regularity theory, since a law is a generalized description of *whatever* occurs, it follows that an event which occurs cannot violate a law. And on the necessitarian theory, since laws are universal generalizations which state what is physically necessary, a violation of a law cannot occur if the generalization is to remain truly universal. So long as laws are conceived of as universal generalizations, it is logically impossible to have a violation of a true law of nature.

Suppose that one attempts to rescue the notion of a 'violation' by introducing into the law certain *ceteris paribus* conditions, for example, that the law holds only if either (1) there are no other causally relevant natural forces interfering, or (2) there are no other causally relevant natural or supernatural forces interfering. Now clearly, (1) will not do the trick, for even if there were no natural forces interfering, the events predicted by the law might not occur because God would interfere. Hence, the alleged law, as a purportedly universal generalization, would not be true, and so a law of nature would not be violated should God interfere. But if, as (2) suggests, we include supernatural forces among the *ceteris paribus* conditions, it is equally impossible to violate the law. For now the statement of the law itself includes the condition that what the law predicts will occur only if God does not intervene, so that if He does the law is not violated. Hence, so long as natural laws are construed as universal generalizations about events, it is incoherent to speak of miracles as 'violations' of such laws.

The upshot of Bilynskyj's discussion is that either natural laws ought not to be construed as universal generalizations about events or that miracles should not be characterized as violations of nature's laws. He opts for the first alternative, arguing that laws of nature are really about the dispositional properties of things based on the kinds of things they are./64/ He observes that most laws today, when taken as universal generalizations, are literally not true. They must include certain *ceteris paribus* clauses about conditions which seldom or perhaps never obtain, so that laws become subjunctive conditionals concerning what would occur under certain idealized conditions. But that means that laws are true counterfactuals with no application to the real world. Moreover, if laws are merely descriptive generalizations, then they do not really explain anything; rather than telling *why* some event occurs, they only serve to tell us how things are. Bilynskyj therefore proposes that natural laws ought to be formulated as singular statements about certain kinds of things and their dispositional properties: things of kind *A* have a disposition to manifest quality *F* in conditions *C*, in virtue of being of nature *N*./65/ Laws can be stated, however, as universal dispositions, for example, 'All potassium has a disposition to ignite when exposed to oxygen.' On this understanding, to assert that an event is physically impossible is not to say that it is a violation of a law of nature, since dispositional laws are not violated when the predisposed behaviour does not occur; rather an event *E* is not produced at a time *t* by the powers (dispositions) of the natural agents which are causally relevant to *F* at *t*./66/ Accordingly, a miracle is an act of God which is physically impossible and religiously significant./67/ On Bilynskyj's version of the proper form of natural laws, then, miracles turn out to be physically impossible, but still not violations of those laws.

I have a great deal of sympathy for Bilynskyj's understanding of natural law and physical impossibility. So as not to create unnecessary stumbling blocks, however, the defender of miracles might ask whether one might not be able to retain the standard necessitarian theory of natural laws as universal generalizations, while jettisoning the old characterization of miracles as 'violations of the laws of nature' in favor of 'events which lie outside the productive capacity of nature.' That is to say, why may we not take a necessitarian theory of natural law according to which laws contain *ceteris paribus* conditions precluding the interference of both natural and supernatural forces and hold that a miracle is not, therefore, a violation of a law of nature, but an event which cannot be accounted for wholly by reference to relevant natural forces? Natural laws are not violated by such events because they state what will occur only if God does not intervene; nevertheless, the events are still naturally impossible because the relevant natural causal forces do not suffice to bring about the event. Bilynskyj's objections to this view do not seem insuperable./68/ He thinks that on such a view it becomes difficult to distinguish between miracles and God's general providence, since according to the latter doctrine every event has in a sense a supernatural cause. This misgiving does not seem insurmountable, however, for we might construe God's providence as Bilynskyj himself does, as God's conservation of (and, we might add, concurrence with) all secondary causes and effects in being, while reserving only His immediate and extra-concurrent causal activity in the world for inclusion in a law's *ceteris paribus* conditions. Bilynskyj also objects that the physical impossibility of a miracle is the reason we attribute it to supernatural causation, not *vice versa*. To define physical impossibility in terms of supernatural causation thwarts the motivation for having the concept of physical impossibility in the first place. But my suggestion is not to define physical impossibility in terms of supernatural causation, but, as Bilynskyj himself does, in terms of what cannot be brought about wholly by natural causes. One may argue that some event *E* is not a violation of a natural law, but that E is naturally impossible. Therefore, it requires a supernatural cause. It seems to me, therefore, that even on the necessitarian theory of natural law, we may rid ourselves of the incoherent notion of 'violation of the laws of nature' and retain the concept of the naturally impossible as the proper characterization of miracle.

So although an initial advantage has been won by the construal of natural laws as descriptive, not prescriptive, this advantage evaporates unless one abandons the incoherent characterization of a miracle as a 'violation of a law of nature' and adopts instead the notion of an event which is naturally impossible. Now the question which must be asked is how an event could occur which lies outside the productive capacity of natural causes. It would seem to be of no avail to answer with Clarke that matter has no properties and that the pattern of events is simply God's acting consistently, for, contrary to his assertion, physics does hold that matter possesses certain properties and that certain forces such as gravitation and electro-magnetism are real operating forces in the world. Bilynskyj points out that Clarke's view entails a thorough-going occasionalism, according to which fire does not really burn nor water quench, which runs strongly counter to common sense./69/ Nor will it seem to help to answer with Sherlock and Houtteville that nature may contain within itself the power to produce events contrary to its normal operation, for this would not seem to be the case when the properties of matter and energy are sufficiently well-known so as to preclude to a reasonably high degree of certainty the occurrence of the event in question. Moreover, though this might secure the possibility of the event, so as to permit a historical investigation, it at the same time reduces the event to a freak of nature, the result of pure chance, not an act of God. It seems most reasonable to agree with modern science that events like the feeding of the 5000, the cleansing of the leper, and Jesus' resurrection really do lie outside the capability of natural causes.

But that being admitted, what has actually been proved? All that the scientist conceivably has the right to say is that such an event is naturally impossible. But with that conclusion the defender of miracles may readily agree. We must not confuse the realms of logical and natural possibility. Is the occurrence of a miracle logically impossible? No, for such an event involves no logical contradiction. Is the occurrence naturally impossible? Yes, for it cannot be produced by natural causes; indeed, this is a tautology, since to lie outside the productive capacity of natural causes is to be naturally impossible.

The question is: what could conceivably make miracles not just logically possible, but really, historically possible. Clearly the answer is the personal God of theism. For if a personal God exists, then He serves as the transcendent cause to produce events in the universe which are incapable of being produced by causes within the universe (that is to say, events which are naturally impossible). But it is to such a personal, transcendent God that the orthodox defenders of miracles appealed. Given a God who conserves the world in being moment by moment (Vernet, Houtteville), who is omnipotent (Clarke), and free to act as He wills (Vernet, Less), the orthodox thinkers seem to be entirely justified in asserting that miracles are really possible. The question is whether given such a God miracles are possible, and the answer seems obviously, yes. It must be remembered that even their Deist opponents did not dispute God's existence, and Clarke and Paley offered elaborate defenses for their theism. But more than that: if the existence of such a God is even *possible*, then one must be open to the historical possibility of miracles. Only an atheist can deny the historical possibility of miracles, for even an agnostic must grant that if it is possible that a transcendent, personal God exists, then it is equally possible that He has acted in the universe. Hence, it seems that the orthodox protagonists in the classical debate argued in the main correctly against their Newtonian opponents and that their response has been only strengthened by the contemporary understanding of natural law.

Spinoza

1. First Objection

With regard to Spinoza's objections to miracles, the orthodox thinkers seem to have again argued cogently. Turning to his first objection, that nothing happens contrary to the eternal and unchangeable order of nature, it must be remembered that Spinoza's system is a pantheistic one, in which God and nature are interchangeable terms. When we keep this in mind, it is little wonder that he argued against miracles on the basis of the unchangeable order of nature, for, there being no ontological distinction between God and the world, a violation of nature's laws is a violation of the being of God. But, of course, the question is not whether miracles are possible on a pantheistic basis, but whether they are possible on a theistic basis. If God is personal and ontologically distinct from the world, there seems to be no reason why even a total alteration of the laws of nature should in any way affect God's being. There would seem to be no reason why God could not have established a different set of laws for this universe nor why He could not now change them. Vernet correctly argues against Spinoza that nature's laws are freely willed by God and are therefore subject to change. Contrary to Spinoza, the properties of matter and energy do not flow from the being of God with inexorable necessity, but are the result of his choice. Hence, he does not violate his own nature should he choose to produce an event in the world which is not the result of the immanent causes operating in the universe. Houtteville and Less also argued soundly against Spinoza that if God willed from eternity to produce a miracle at some point in time, then there is no change on God's part, either in his being or decrees. Thus, Spinoza's objection to miracles on the basis of the unchangeableness of nature is system-dependent upon his pantheism.

2. Second Objection

Spinoza's second objection, it will be remembered, was that miracles do not suffice to prove God's existence. So stated, the objection found no foothold in the apologies of most orthodox thinkers, for virtually all of them used miracles, not as a proof for the existence of God, but as a proof of his action in the world. Thus, the objection was strictly speaking irrelevant. But Spinoza's supporting reasoning was pertinent to their arguments. His main point appears to have been that a proof for God's existence must be absolutely certain. Since, therefore, we conclude to the existence of God on the basis of the immutable laws of nature, anything that impugned those laws would make us doubt God's existence. Underlying this reasoning would appear to be two assumptions: (1) a proof for God's existence must be demonstratively certain and (2) God's existence is inferred from natural laws. The Christian thinkers denied respectively both of these assumptions. The first is based on Spinoza's rationalism, which prevents him from recognizing the cogency of an argument unless he can affix his *Q. E. D.* at the argument's conclusion. His more empirically minded opponents, however, saw no reason to think that an argument which was not deductively demonstrative could not provide sufficient warrant for theism. Paley, for example, tried to give overwhelming empirical evidence in his *Natural Theology* for God as the designer of the universe; though not achieving demonstrative certainty, the argument's aim was to make it much more plausible to believe in God than not. The demise of Spinozistic rationalism seems to be sufficient testimony that subsequent generations have not shared Spinoza's concern for geometric certainty. The second assumption, for its part, would not have relevance for someone who argued for God's existence by other means. For example, Clarke, while espousing the same concern for demonstrative certainty as Spinoza, based his theism on cosmological and ontological arguments. Hence, the objection that miracles rendered natural law uncertain, even if true, would not strike against Clarke.

But is the objection in fact true? Spinoza seemed to think that the admission of a genuine miracle would serve to overthrow the natural law pre-empted by the miracle. If one retains the old 'violation' concept of miracle, this is certainly true. But if we abandon that notion, as I have suggested, in favor of the naturally impossible, then we can see that Clarke and Paley were correct in arguing that a miracle does not serve to abrogate the regularity of nature in general; it only shows the intervention of God at that point in the natural causal nexus.

As Swinburne has argued, a natural law is not abolished because of one exception; the counter-instance must occur repeatedly whenever the conditions for it are present./70/ If an event occurs which is contrary to a law of nature and we have reasons to believe that this event would not occur again under similar circumstances, then the law in question will not be abandoned. One may regard an anomalous event as repeatable if another formulation of the natural law better accounts for the event in question, and if it is no more complex than the original law. If any doubt exists, the scientist may conduct experiments to determine which formulation of the law proves more successful in predicting future phenomena. In a similar way, one would have good reason to regard an event as a non-repeatable counter-instance to a law if the reformulated law were much more complicated than the original without yielding better new predictions or by predicting new phenomena unsuccessfully where the original formulation predicted successfully. If the original formulation remains successful in predicting all new phenomena as the data accumulate, while no reformulation does any better in predicting the phenomena and explaining the event in question, then the event should be regarded as a non-repeatable counter-instance to the law. Hence, a miraculous event would not serve to upset the natural law:

> We have to some extent good evidence about what are the laws of nature, and some of them are so well-established and account for so many data that any modifications to them which suggest to account for the odd counter-instance would be so clumsy and *ad hoc* as to upset the whole structure of science. In such cases the evidence is strong that if the purported counter-instance occurred it was a violation of the laws of nature./71/

Swinburne unfortunately retains the violation concept of miracle, which would invalidate his argument; but if we conceive of a miracle as a naturally impossible event, he is on target in reasoning that the admission of such an event would not lead to the abandonment of a natural law. Spinoza's fear, therefore, that miracles would destroy natural laws seems unjustified. In fact Spinoza's argument, if taken seriously, would prove a positive impediment to science, for on his principles not even repeatable counter-instances to a natural law could be allowed, since these would impugn the present natural law. In other words, Spinoza assumes we have the final formulation of the natural laws known to us. While he will admit that there may be unknown natural laws, he cannot permit the revision of known laws. But such a position is unscientific. If one adjusted Spinoza's position to admit the possible revision of a natural law by repeatable counter-instances, then any argument for miracles based on those laws would, of course, share in the uncertainty of our formulations. If, however, we were confident that a particular formulation of a law were genuinely descriptive of reality, then the occurrence of an event shown by the law to be naturally impossible could not overthrow this law. Rather than lead us away from God, such a situation could lead us to see the hand of God in that event, for there would be no other way it could be produced. And that was precisely the position of the orthodox defenders of miracles.

Spinoza's sub-contention that a miracle need not prove God's existence, but only the existence of a lesser being was not effective against most defenders of miracles quite simply because they were not trying to prove the existence of God. Having either proved or presupposed the existence of God, they used miracles chiefly to prove Christian theism was true. On the other hand, the protagonists in the classical debate over miracles were greatly concerned about the possibility of demonic miracles and how to identify a truly divine miracle. Their answer to this problem constitutes one of their most important and enduring contributions to the discussion of miracles. They argued that the doctrinal context of the miracle makes it clear whether the miracle is truly from God. Thus, they drew attention to the context in which the miracle occurred as the basis for the interpretation of that miracle. This is extremely important, for a miracle without a context is inherently ambiguous. But in the case of Jesus' miracles and resurrection the context is religiously significant: they occur in the context of and as the climax to Jesus' own unparalleled life, teaching, and personal claim to authority, and served as signs of the inbreaking of the Kingdom. Here is a context of events that, as Paley rightly emphasized, is unique in the history of mankind. It ought, therefore, to give us serious pause, whereas some isolated scientific anomaly might occasion only curiosity. In this way the religious context of a miracle furnishes us with the proper interpretation of that miracle.

Spinoza's concern with lesser divine beings, such as angels and demons, would probably not trouble too many twentieth century minds. It would be very odd, indeed, were an atheist to grant the miracles and resurrection of Jesus as historical and miraculous events and yet assert that perhaps only an angel wrought them. Finite spirit beings are usually conceived to exist only within a wider theistic framework, such that to infer directly that God is responsible for such events would not appear to many to be an unwarranted inference. In this way, then, contrary to Spinoza's allegation, miracles *taken within their religious context* could, it seems, provide an adequate justification for a Christian theism.

Spinoza's final sub-point, that a miracle may simply be the effect of an unknown cause in nature, does not properly strike against the possibility of the *occurrence* of a miracle, but against the *identification* of the occurrence of a miracle. Granted that miracles are possible, how can we know when one has occurred? This is admittedly a very thorny problem, and undoubtedly most of our reserve over against purported miracles stems from an underlying suspicion that the event is somehow naturally explicable, even though we do not know how. The problem has been persuasively formulated in modern times by Antony Flew:

> Protagonists of the supernatural, and opponents too, take it for granted that we all possess some natural (as opposed to revealed) way of knowing that and where the unassisted potentialities of nature (as opposed to a postulated supernature) are more restricted than the potentialities which, in fact, we find to be realized or realizable in the universe around us.
>
> This is a very old and apparently very easy and tempting assumption. . . . Nevertheless, the assumption is entirely unwarranted. We simply do not have, and could not have, any natural (as opposed to revealed) criterion which enables us to say, when faced with something which is found to have actually happened, that here we have an achievement which nature, left to her own unaided devices, could never encompass. The natural scientist, confronted with some occurrence inconsistent with a proposition previously believed to express a law of nature, can find in this disturbing inconsistency no ground whatever for proclaiming that the particular law of nature has been supernaturally overridden./72/

The response of Sherlock and Houtteville that an unknown law of nature may be God's means of acting is surely inadequate, for it may equally be the case that the event in question is no act of God at all, but a product of entirely natural but unknown causes. Le Clerc and Vernet have taken a better tack: when the miracles occur precisely at a momentous time (say, a man's leprosy vanishing when Jesus spoke the words, 'Be clean') and do not recur regularly in history and when the miracles in question are various and numerous, the chance of their being the result of unknown natural properties seems negligible. If the miracles were naturally caused, one would expect them to occur repeatedly and not by coincidence at just the proper moments in Jesus' ministry. And though an isolated miracle might be dismissed as the effect of an unknown operation of nature, Vernet seems to be correct in regarding this possibility as minimal when the entire scope of Jesus' miracles is surveyed.

A final remark on Spinoza's reasoning ought to be made. The objection does not, like Hume's, spring from the nature of historical investigation; rather it could be pressed by witnesses of Jesus' miracles and resurrection appearances themselves. But in this case, the objection loses all conviction: for can we imagine, say, doubting Thomas, when confronted with the risen Jesus, studiously considering whether some unknown natural cause might have produced what he experienced? There comes a point when the back of scepticism is broken by the sheer reality of a wonder before us. At any rate, had Jesus himself been confronted with such scepticism, would he not have attributed it to hardness of heart in his opponent? Having shown the historical credibility of the gospel accounts of Jesus' miracles, should that be possible, a defender of miracles might simply leave the question of their miraculous nature to be settled between his hearer and God. Perhaps Pascal was right in maintaining that God has given evidence sufficiently clear for those with an open heart, but sufficiently vague so as not to compel those whose hearts are closed.

Hume

1. 'In principle' argument

Hume's 'in principle' argument against the identification of a miracle, for its part, seems either question-begging or mistaken./73/ To say that uniform experience is against miracles is implicitly to assume that the miracles in question did not occur. Otherwise the experience could not be said to be truly uniform. Thus, to say uniform experience stands against miracles begs the question. If, however, we relax the term 'uniform' to mean simply 'general' or 'usual,' then the argument fails of cogency. For then it is no longer incompatible that general experience be that miracles do not occur and that the gospel miracles did occur. Hume seems to confuse the realms of science and history: the general experience of mankind has allowed us to formulate certain laws which describe the physical universe. That dead men do not rise is, for example, a generally observed pattern in our experience. But at most this only shows that a resurrection is naturally impossible. That is a matter of science. But it does not prove that such a naturally impossible event has never occurred. That is a matter of history. As Less and Paley pointed out, the testimony in history for the general pattern of events cannot overturn good testimony for any particular event. Since they are not *contradictoria*, they cannot even be weighed in the same scale. Thus, Hume's argument, if it is not simply question-begging, rests on a sort of category mistake.

Moreover, as Sherlock argued, since a miracle is just as much a matter of sense perception as any other event, it is, in principle, provable by historical testimony in the same way as a non-miraculous event. *Qua* history, they stand exactly on a par. It is contrary to sound historical methodology to suppress particular testimony out of regard for general testimony. In the case of the resurrection, for example, if the testimony which we have in the New Testament makes it probable that Jesus' tomb was really found empty on the first day of the week by some of his women followers and that he later appeared to his disciples in a non-hallucinatory fashion, then it is bad historical methodology to argue that this testimony *must* be somehow false because historical evidence shows that all *other* men have always remained dead in their graves. Nor can it be argued that the testimony must be false because such an event is naturally impossible, for it may well be the case that history proves that a naturally impossible event has, in fact, occurred. As Paley contended, Hume's argument could lead us into situations where we would be led to deny the testimony of the most reliable of witnesses to an event because of general considerations, a situation which results in an unrealistic scepticism. In fact, as Sherlock and Less correctly contended, this would apply to non-miraculous events as well. There are all sorts of events which make up the stuff of popular books on unexplained mysteries (such as levitation, disappearing persons, spontaneous human combustions, and so forth) which have not been scientifically explained, but, judging by their pointless nature, sporadic occurrence, and lack of any religious context, are probably not miracles. It would be folly for a historian to deny the occurrence of such events in the face of good eyewitness evidence to the contrary simply because they do not fit with known natural laws. Yet Hume's principle would require the historian to say that these events never actually occurred. The fact is, the historian does, in certain cases, seem able to determine the facticity of a historical event without knowing how or whether it accords with natural laws.

Finally, it might be urged against Hume's 'in principle' argument, if God's existence is possible, then as Paley argued, He may have chosen to reveal himself decisively in history at one point, and there is no probability that we should experience the same events today. Hence, the occurrence of those events uniquely in the past cannot be dismissed because such events are not experienced at other times. As long as God's existence is possible, then it **is** equally possible that he has acted uniquely at a point in history, in which case the question simply becomes whether such an event did take place. But then it is a question of evidence, not of principle, as Hume maintained.

Antony Flew, while acknowledging the failure of Hume's argument, has sought to reformulate a successful version of the argument against the identification of a miracle:

> . . .it is only and precisely by presuming that the laws that hold today held in the past and by employing as canons all our knowledge--or presumed knowledge--of what is probable or improbable, possible or impossible, that we can rationally interpret the detritus of the past as evidence and from it construct our account of what actually happened. But in this context, what is impossible is what is physically, as opposed to logically, impossible. And 'physical impossibility' is, and surely has to be, defined in terms of inconsistency with a true law of nature. . . .
>
> . . .Our sole ground for characterizing *[a]* reported occurrence as miraculous is at the same time a sufficient reason for calling it physically impossible./74/

Now this objection actually seems to be inconsistent with the final point of Spinoza's second objection against miracles, which Flew also sought to defend. There, it will be remembered, it was asserted that our knowledge of nature is so incomplete that we can never regard any event whatsoever as miraculous, since it could be the effect of an unknown law of nature. This would compel us to take a totally open attitude toward the possibility of any given event, for virtually anything would be possible in nature. We should never be entitled to say an event is naturally impossible. But now Hume's objection asserts precisely the opposite, namely, that our knowledge of natural law is so complete that we can not only determine which events would be naturally impossible, but we are able to impose this over the past to expunge such events from the record. The two positions are incompatible. Flew thus seems to have worked himself into a dilemma: either naturally impossible events can be specified or not. If they can, then such an event's occurring could be identified as a miracle. If they cannot, then we must be open to anything's happening in history. Flew cannot have it both ways: he cannot line up behind both Spinoza and Hume. Now I have contended that naturally impossible events can sometimes be specified and that an event such as Jesus' feeding the 5000 ought to be regarded as naturally impossible. Does that mean therefore, as Flew alleges, that it must be regarded *a priori* as unhistorical? Not at all; Flew has made an unjustifiable identification between natural (or in his terms, physical) possibility and actual, historical possibility. The assumption here is that naturally impossible events cannot occur, or in other words, that miracles cannot happen, which is question-begging, since this is precisely the point to be proved. Flew's argument really boils down to the assertion that in order to study history, one must assume the impossibility of miracles. To this question we shall now turn.

In recent times the classical debate over the identification of miracles has continued in the dispute over principles of historical methodology. It has been contended that the historical method is inherently restricted to non-miraculous events; for example, D. E. Nineham asserts,

> It is of the essence of the modern historian's method and criteria that they are applicable only to purely human phenomena, and to human phenomena of a normal, that is non-miraculous, non-unique, character. It followed that any picture of Jesus that could consistently approve itself to an historical investigator using these criteria, must *a priori* be of a purely human figure and it must be bounded by his death./75/

On what basis can it be said that the historical method applies only to non-miraculous phenomena? According to Carl Becker, it is because that method presupposes that the past is not dissimilar to our present experience:

> History rests on testimony, but the qualitative value of testimony is determined in the last analysis by tested and accepted experience. . . . the historian knows well that no amount of testimony is ever permitted to establish as a past reality a thing that cannot be found in present reality. . . . In every case the witness may have a perfect character--all that goes for nothing. . . .
>
> . . .We must have a past that is the product of all the present. With sources that say it was not so, we will have nothing to do; better still, we will make them say it was so./76/

Becker's historical relativism allows him to reshape the past with impunity so that it is made to accord with our experience of the present. The result is that miracles must be expunged by the historian, for these are not found in the experience of his own generation./77/ According to this outlook, historians must adopt as a methodological principle a sort of 'historical naturalism' that excludes the supernatural.

This viewpoint is simply a restatement of Ernst Troeltsch's principle of analogy./78/ According to Troeltsch, one of the most basic of historiographical principles is that the past does not differ essentially from the present. Though events of the past are of course not the same events as those of the present, they must be the same *in kind* if historical investigation is to be possible. Troeltsch realized that this principle was incompatible with miraculous events and that any history written on this principle will be sceptical with regard to the historicity of the events of the gospels.

Pannenberg, however, has persuasively argued that Troeltsch's principle of analogy cannot be legitimately employed to banish from the realm of history all non-analogous events./79/ Properly defined, analogy means that in a situation which is unclear, the facts ought to be understood in terms of known experience; but Troeltsch has elevated the principle to constrict all past events to purely natural events. But that an event bursts all analogies cannot be used to dispute its historicity. When, for example, myths, legends, illusions, and the like are dismissed as unhistorical, it is not because they are unusual, but because they are analogous to present forms of consciousness having no objective referent. When an event is said to have occurred for which no analogy exists, its reality cannot be automatically dismissed; to do this we should require an analogy to some known form of consciousness lacking an objective referent that would suffice to explain the situation. Pannenberg has thus upended Troeltsch's principle of analogy such that it is not the *want* of an analogy that shows an event to be unhistorical, but the *presence* of a positive analogy to known thought forms that shows a purportedly miraculous event to be unhistorical. Thus, he has elsewhere affirmed that if the Easter traditions were shown to be essentially secondary constructions analogous to common comparative religious models, the Easter appearances were shown to correspond completely to the model of hallucinations, and the empty tomb tradition were evaluated as a late legend, then the resurrection would be subject to evaluation as unhistorical./80/ In this way, the lack of an analogy to present experience says nothing for or against the historicity of an event. Troeltsch's formulation of the principle of analogy attempts to squeeze the past into the mold of the present without providing any warrant for doing so. As Richard Niebuhr has protested, Troeltsch's principle really destroys genuine historical reasoning, since the historian must be open to the uniqueness of the events of the past and cannot exclude *a priori* the possibility of events like the resurrection simply because they do not conform to his present experience./81/ But Pannenberg's formulation of the principle preserves the analogous nature of the past to the present or to the known, thus making the investigation of history possible, without thereby sacrificing the integrity of the past or distorting it.

This means that there seems to be no *in principle* philosophical objection to establishing the occurrence of a miracle by means of historical research. According to Pannenberg, a theological interpretation of history will be tested positively by 'its ability to take into account all known historical details' and negatively by 'the proof that without its specific assertions the accessible information would not be at all or would be only incompletely explicable.'/82/ More exactly, Bilynskyj proposes four criteria for identifying some event *E* as a miracle: (1) the evidence for the occurrence of *E* is at least as good as the evidence for other acceptable but unusual events similarly distant in space and time from the point of inquiry; (2) an account of the natures and/or powers of the causally relevant natural factors necessary to explain *E* would be clumsy and *ad hoc*; (3) there is no evidence for one or more of the natural causes which could produce *E* except for the inexplicability of *E* itself; and (4) there is some justification for a supernatural explanation of *E*, apart from the inexplicability of *E*./83/ The historian ought first perhaps, as a methodological principle, to seek natural causes of the events under investigation; but when no natural causes can be found that plausibly account for the data and a supernatural hypothesis presents itself as part of the historical context in which the events occurred, then it would not seem to be illicit to prefer the supernatural explanation.

2. 'In fact' arguments

If, then, there seems to be no 'in principle' argument against establishing miracles by means of the historical method, what may be said concerning Hume's four 'in fact' arguments against miracles? All of Hume's arguments have force; but the fact remains that these general considerations cannot be used to pronounce on the historicity of any particular miracle. They only serve to make us cautious in our investigation. Hume's fourth point does seek to preclude any investigation by asserting that the miracles of various religions cancel each other out. Less, Campbell, and Paley argued fairly convincingly, however, against his three specific examples of purported miracles, but limits of space require that I simply refer the reader to their extended discussions. In any case, it still remains an *empirical* question whether a miracle supporting a counter-Christian claim is equally or better attested than Jesus' miracles and resurrection. There is no way to settle the issue apart from an investigation.

Conclusion

It seems to me, therefore, that the lesson to be learned from the classical debate over miracles, a lesson that has been reinforced by contemporary scientific and philosophical thought, is that the presupposition of the impossibility of miracles should, contrary to the assumption of nineteenth and for the most part twentieth century biblical criticism, play no role in determining the historicity of any event. While many scholars still operate under such an assumption, there seems now to be a growing recognition that such a presupposition is illegitimate. The presupposition against the possibility of miracles survives in theology only as a hangover from an earlier Deist age and ought to be once for all abandoned./84/

Notes

/1/ Gottfried Less, *Wahrheit der christlichen Religion*, 4th ed. (Göttingen & Bremen: Georg Ludewig Forster, 1776) 260-62.
/2/ Heinrich Eberh. Gottlob Paulus, *Das Leben Jesu, als*

Grundlage einer reinen Geschichte des Urchristentums, 2 vols. (Heidelberg: C. F. Winter, 1828) 2.2, xl.
/3/ Ibid., 2.2, xlv.
/4/ Ibid., 2.2, xl.
/5/ Ibid.
/6/ Ibid., 2.2, xlv.
/7/ Ibid., 1, 283-84.
/8/ Ibid., 1, 284.
/9/ David Friedrich Strauss, *Hermann Samuel Reimarus und seine Schutzschrift für die vernünftigen Verehrer Gottes* (Leipzig: F. A. Brockhaus, 1862) 271.
/10/ Idem, *The Life of Jesus Critically Examined*, trans. George Eliot, ed. with an introduction by Peter C. Hodgson (London: SCM, 1973) 64.
/11/ Ibid., 80.
/12/ Ibid., 736.
/13/ Ibid., 75.
/14/ Albert Schweitzer, *The Quest of the Historical Jesus*, 3rd ed., trans. W. Montgomery (London: Adam & Charles Black, 1954) 10.
/15/ Ibid., 110-11.
/16/ David Friedrich Strauss, *Die christliche Glaubenslehre in ihrer geschichtlichen Entwicklung und im Kämpfe mit der modernen Wissenschaft* (Tübingen: C. F. Osiander, 1840) 224-53.
/17/ Rudolf Bultmann, 'New Testament and Mythology,' in *Kerygma and Myth*, 2 vols., ed. Hans-Werner Bartsch, trans. R. H. Fuller (London: SPCK, 1953) 2, 1-44. Bultmann's *a priori* assumption of history and the universe as a closed system is especially evident in idem, 'Bultmann Replies to his Critics,' in ibid., 1, 197. According to Niebuhr, Bultmann retained uncriticized the nineteenth century idea of nature and history as a closed system. (Richard R. Niebuhr, *Resurrection and Historical Reason* [New York: Charles Scribner's Sons, 1957] 60-61.)
/18/ Rudolf Pesch, 'Die Entstehung des Glaubens an den Auferstandenen,' *ThQ* 153 (1973) 227.
/19/ Hans Frei, *The Eclipse of the Biblical Narrative: A Study in Eighteenth and Nineteenth Century Hermeneutics* (New Haven: Yale University Press, 1974) 240.
/20/ Three helpful discussions of this debate are John S. Lawton, *Miracles and Revelation* (New York: Association Press, 1959); R. M. Burns, *The Great Debate on Miracles* (London: Associated University Presses, 1981); Colin Brown, *Miracles and the Critical Mind* (Grand Rapids: Eerdmans, 1984).
/21/ Denis Diderot, 'Philosophical Thoughts,' in *Diderot's Early*

Philosophical Works, trans. Margaret Jourdain (Chicago: Open Court, 1916) pensée 18.
/22/ Marie François Arrouet de Voltaire, *Dictionnaire philosophique* (Paris: Garnler, 1967) s.v. 'Miracles'.
/23/ Ibid.
/24/ Ibid.
/25/ Benedict de Spinoza, *Tractatus theologico-politicus* 6.
/26/ David Hume, 'An Enquiry concerning Human Understanding,' in *Enquiries concerning Human Understanding and concerning the Principles of Morals*, ed. L. A. Selby-Bigge, 3rd ed. rev. P. H. Nidditch (Oxford: Clarendon Press, 1975) 10.1, 90; 10.11, 92 (pp. 114, 116). For a lengthy discussion of this essay, see Burns, *Debate*, 131-75. Remarkably, Burns does not see the counterfactual nature of Hume's argument, so that on Burns's exposition the essay tends to fall into two unconnected halves, with far too much emphasis by Burns on the second half. The same oversight hampers the discussion by Brown, *Miracles*, 79-100.
/27/ Hume, 'Enquiry,' 10.11, 101 (p. 131).
/28/ Jean Le Clerc, *Five Letters Concerning the Inspiration of the Holy Scriptures* (London: 1690) 235. The *Sentimens* was translated into English under this title.
/29/ Ibid., 235-36.
/30/ Samuel Clarke, *A Discourse concerning the Unchangeable Obligations of Natural Religion and the Truth and Certainty of the Christian Revelation* (London: W. Botham, 1706) 351-52.
/31/ Ibid., 354-55.
/32/ Ibid., 356-57.
/33/ Ibid., 359.
/34/ Ibid., 361.
/35/ Ibid., 362-63. Notice that Clarke does not arbitrarily exclude certain doctrines as incapable of being proved, but he presupposes what he has already argued concerning natural theology and ethics. Cf. ibid., 369-70.
/36/ Ibid., 363-64.
/37/ Ibid., 367.
/38/ Ibid., 368-69.
/39/ Ibid., 368. The foregoing exposition makes evident how gross a distortion of Clarke's view is presented by Burns, *Debate*, 96-103, who ascribes to Clarke an 'extreme evidentialism' whereby miracles divorced from their doctrinal context are proof of Christianity. In fact, Clarke is entirely one with the typical orthodox response to Deism. Following Burns in his misinterpretation of Clarke is Brown, *Miracles*, 56-57.
/40/ J. Alph. Turrettin, *Traité de la vérité de la religion chrétienne*, 2nd ed., 7 vols., trans. J. Vernet (Genève: Henri-

Albert Gosse, 1745-55) 5, 235. Vernet translated the first volume written by Turretin in Latin and proceeded to add several volumes of his own. Vernet has Spinoza particularly in mind here.
/41/ Ibid., 5, 2-3.
/42/ Ibid., 5, 240.
/43/ Ibid., 5, 272.
/44/ Claude François Houtteville, *La religion chrétienne prouvée par les faits*, 3 vols. (Paris: Mercler & Boudet, 1740) 1, 32-50.
/45/ Ibid., 1, 33.
/46/ Thomas Sherlock, *The Tryal of the Witnesses of the Resurrection of Jesus* (London: J. Roberts, 1729) 60.
/47/ Originally mentioned by John Locke, *An Essay concerning Human Understanding*, 4.15, 5 and taken up by Hume in a footnote in his essay on miracles, this example was regarded as the Achilles heel of Hume's argument, for Hume had to admit that on his principles the man in the tropics should not in fact believe the testimony of travellers concerning ice.
/48/ Sherlock, *Tryal*, 60-62.
/49/ Ibid., 63-64.
/50/ Less, *Wahrheit*, 243.
/51/ Ibid., 254-60.
/52/ Ibid., 280-84.
/53/ Ibid., 366-75.
/54/ Campbell in his *Dissertation on Miracles* (1762) makes the same point: 'The two thousand instances formerly known, and the single instance attested, as they relate to different facts, though of a contrary nature, are not contradictory. There is no inconsistency in believing both.' (George Campbell, *The Works of George Campbell*, 6 vols. [London: Thomas Tegg, 1840] 1, 23.)
/55/ Less, *Wahrheit*, 471-549; see also discussion in Campbell, *Dissertation*, 88-116).
/56/ William Paley, *A View of the Evidences of Christianity*, 2 vols., 5th ed. (London: R. Faulder, 1796; repr. Westmead: Gregg International Publishers, 1970) 1, 2-3. Cf. 2, 409. For Paley's classic exposition of the teleological argument, see his *Natural Theology* (1802).
/57/ Idem, *Evidences*, 1, 3-15.
/58/ Ibid., 1, 5,7.
/59/ Ibid., 1, 6.
/60/ Ibid., 1, 329-83.
/61/ Ibid., 1, 369-83.
/62/ Even with regard to quantum laws, one may plausibly speak of events which are naturally impossible. See Mary Hesse, 'Miracles and the Laws of Nature,' in *Miracles*, ed. C. F. D. Moule (London: Mowbray, 1965) 38.

/63/ Stephen S. Bilynskyj, 'God, Nature, and the Concept of Miracle' (Ph.D. Diss.: Notre Dame, 1982) 10-42.
/64/ Ibid., 46-53.
/65/ Ibid., 117.
/66/ Ibid., 138.
/67/ Ibid., 146.
/68/ Ibid., 43-44.
/69/ Ibid., 86-97; for further criticism see 97-101.
/70/ R. G. Swinburne, 'Miracles,' *PQ* 18 (1968) 321.
/71/ Ibid., 323.
/72/ *Encyclopedia of Philosophy*, s.v. 'Miracles,' by Antony Flew.
/73/ For a penetrating critique of Hume's reasoning see George I. Mavrodes, 'Testimony and the Resurrection,' paper read at 'Christianity Challenges the University,' Dallas, TX; Feb. 7-10, 1985. He points out that the propositions 'Miracles are not common in the world' and 'Jesus performed miracles' are not epistemological alternatives, so that the evidence for each may amount to a full proof and each be simultaneously believed by a rational person. Of course, 'There are no miracles in the world' is an epistemological alternative to 'Jesus performed miracles,' but we have no grounds for assuming the former to be true. My lack of experiencing a miracle first-hand does not serve to make the universal statement probable because there is no probability that I should experience a miracle myself. In his comment on Mavrodes's paper, Antony Flew admitted the failure of Hume's argument, but pressed the objection from his *Encyclopedia of Philosophy* article discussed below concerning historiographical naturalism.
/74/ *Encyclopedia of Philosophy*, s.v. 'Miracles'.
/75/ D. E. Nineham, 'Some Reflections on the Present Position with regard to *The Jesus of History*,' *CQR* 166 (1965) 6-7.
/76/ Carl Becker, 'Detachment and the Writing of History,' in *Detachment and the Writing of History*, ed. Phil L. Snyder (Ithaca: Cornell University Press, 1958; Westport, CT: Greenwood, 1972) 12-13.
/77/ Ibid., 14. For an incisive critique of historical relativism and its dictum that 'the past is the product of the present,' see Maurice Mandelbaum, *The Problem of Historical Knowledge* (New York: Harper & Row, 1967).
/78/ Ernst Troeltsch, 'Über historische und dogmatische Methode in der Theologie,' in idem, *Gesammelte Schriften* (Tübingen: J. C. B. Mohr, 1913) 2, 729-53. Cf. Bradley's principle of uniformity (F. H. Bradley, *The Presuppositions of Critical History*, ed. Lionel Rubinoff [Chicago: J. M. Dent & Sons, 1968], 100) and its critique at the hands of R. G. Collingwood, *The*

Idea of History, ed. T. M. Know (Oxford: University Press, 1956) 139.
/79/ Wolfhart Pannenberg, 'Redemptive Event and History,' in idem, *Basic Questions in Theology*, 2 vols., trans. G. H. Kehm (Philadelphia: Fortress, 1970) 1, 40-50.
/80/ Idem, cited in James M. Robinson, 'Revelation as Word and History,' in *New Frontiers in Theology*, ed. James M. Robinson & John B. Cobb, Jr. (New York: Harper & Row, 1967) 3, 33.
/81/ Niebuhr, *Resurrection*, 170.
/82/ Pannenberg, 'Redemptive Event and History,' 1, 78.
/83/ Bilynskyj, 'Miracles,' 222.
/84/ Portions of this research were carried out at Cambridge University and the Ludwig-Maximilians-Universität München under a fellowship from the Alexander von Humboldt Foundation. For a fuller and more meticulously documented account, see my *The Historical Argument for the Resurrection of Jesus during the Deist Controversy* (Toronto: Edwin Mellen, 1986).

ZUR NEUTESTAMENTLICHEN WUNDEREXEGESE IM 19. UND 20. JAHRHUNDERT

Gerhard Maier
Albrecht-Bengel-Haus,
Ludwig-Krapf-St. 5,
7400 Tübingen,
West Germany

Vorbemerkung

Die folgende Darstellung hat das Ziel, einige wichtige Entwicklungen der Wunderexegese im Verlaufe des 19. und des 20. Jh. aufzuzeigen. Sie will ausserdem treibende Motive und weltanschauliche Prämissen sichtbar machen, die der ntl. Wunderexegese zugrundelagen bzw. zugrundeliegen.

Dabei kann es aus Mangel an Raum nicht um eine umfassende oder gar erschöpfende Darstellung gehen. Letztere würde mehrere Bände umfassen. Ferner bleibt unsere Darstellung konzentriert auf den kontinentalen Bereich, jedoch zugleich im Bemühen, auch über dessen Grenzen hinauszublicken.

I. Die Problematik ist allseits bewusst

Um die weltanschauliche Problematik der modernen Wunderexegese einsichtig zu machen, bedarf es keines langwierigen Verfahrens. Wer immer über diesen Gegenstand sorgfältig schreibt, gibt seine eigenen und die Probleme anderer freimütig zu.

Wir wählen als Beispiel den abgewogenen Vortrag von Karin Bornkamm über "Wunder und Zeugnis" aus, der 1968 in der "Sammlung gemeinverständlicher Vorträge" erschien und der mit der Feststellung beginnt, dass die Wunderfrage "für uns Menschen der Neuzeit schwieriger zu beantworten ist als für Menschen früherer geschichtlicher Epochen, die noch nicht wie wir durch naturwissenschaftliche und historische Erkenntnisse zu kritischen Anfragen an die uns vorliegenden Texte angeleitet wurden"./1/ Als zweiter Zeuge in dieser Richtung sei Günther Klein gennant: die moderne "intellektuelle Not. . .tritt nirgendwo deutlicher an den Tag als dort, wo diese Verkündigung. . .von Wundern zu reden wagt"./2/

Es ist nur ein kleiner Trost, dass sich die altchristliche Apologetik manchmal in ähnlichen Nöten sah. Auch diese frühchristliche Apologetik führte gegen Celsus, Porphyrius u.a. einen Kampf um die "historische Sicherstellung" des Wunders und um seine Denkbarkeit. "Als eine der ersten steht die historische Frage bei den Apologeten auf"./3/ Ja, es kommt vor, dass frühchristliche Theologen heidnische Wunder "als nicht mit den wissenschaftlichen Erkenntnissen. . .vereinbar" angreifen./4/

Dennoch liegt klar auf der Hand, dass unsere modernen Nöte erheblich grösser sind. Gegenüber der alten Kirche und nicht weniger gegenüber Luther und Calvin ereignete sich geradezu ein "Abbruch der Traditionen"./5/ Es kam zu einer radikalen Wandlung in der herrschenden theologischen Meinung, wie allseits zugegeben wird./6/ Um es mit den Worten von Humphrey Hamilton in B. Marshalls "Malachias" zu formulieren: "nach der vorherrschenden Meinung unserer angesehensten Wissenschaftler liegt es gänzlich ausserhalb jeder Möglichkeit, dass sich Wunder ereignen oder je ereignet haben"./7/

Wo liegen die Wurzeln dieser Veränderung?

II. Die Wurzeln der Problematik/8/

Dem Betrachter der Kirchen- und Geistesgeschichte drängen sich vor allem zwei Ursachen der Veränderung auf: die Überzeugung vom lückenlosen Kausalzusammenhang, auf die sich besonders der Rationalismus stützte,/9/ und die Überzeugung von der Selbständigkeit des religiösen Erlebnisses, wie sie uns bahnbrechend bei Schleiermacher entgegentritt.

(1) Die Überzeugung vom lückenlosen Kausalzusammenhang trug mindestens bei ihrem Aufkommen starke religiöse Züge. Das wird vor allem an Spinozas "Theologisch-politischen Traktat" von 1670 deutlich. Die vorfindliche Natur und ihr erkennbarer Zusammenhang wird hier mit Gottes Willen in eins gesetzt. Gottes Fürsorge und Ordnung finden ihren Ausdruck im natürlichen Kausalzusammenhang: "Alles, was geschieht, geschieht nach Gesetzen und Regeln, die ewige Notwendigkeit und Wahrheit in sich schliessen"./10/ Dann aber wird das Wunder contra naturam verdächtig. Es erweist sich sogar als Glaubenshindernis: "Wenn daher in der Natur etwas geschehen würde, das mit ihren allgemeinen Gesetzen in Widerspruch stünde, so würde es auch dem Ratschluss, dem Verstand und der Natur Gottes notwendig widersprechen; oder wenn jemand behaupten wollte, Gott tue etwas entgegen den Naturgesetzen, so müsste er

zugleich auch behaupten, Gott tue etwas seiner eigenen Natur entgegen, was höchst widersinnig ist"./11/

Überdies ist das Wunder also vernunftwidrig. Schon Spinoza hat der Vernunft das Vertrauen geschenkt, dass sie der gottgestifteten Natur entspricht und dem Menschen als zuverlässiges naturgemässes Erkenntnisorgan gegeben ist. Deshalb kommt er zu dem Urteil: "was gegen die Natur ist, das ist auch gegen die Vernunft, und was gegen die Vernunft ist, ist widersinnig und darum zu verwerfen"./12/

Doch was ist mit den biblischen Wunderberichten? a) Zuerst ist zu prüfen, ob sie tatsächlich den Naturgesetzen widersprechen. b) Lassen sie sich nicht aus den Naturgesetzen herleiten, dann können die betreffenden Berichte eine zeitbedingte Akkommodation (dichterische oder uneigentliche oder angepasste Redeweise) darstellen. c) Im äussersten Falle muss man annehmen, dass der betreffende Bericht "von Frevlerhänden in die Heilige Schriften eingefügt worden ist", d.h. er muss eliminiert werden./13/

Der spätere Rationalismus hat die Forderung der Vernünftigkeit noch schärfer herausgestellt. Dabei ging er ebenfalls von der Voraussetzung aus, dass die Naturgesetze **alles** Geschehen ohne Ausnahme bestimmen. "Die Geseze der Natur", sagte Carl Friedrich Bahrdt (1741-1792), "sind ewig und unveränderlich. Wunder heben sie auf. Also sind Wunder unmöglich"./14/ Bereits wird neben dem Prinzip der Kausalität das Prinzip der Korrelation sichtbar, das alle Vorgänge in gegenseitiger Verknüpfung auffasst. Auch die Heilige Schrift macht hier keine Ausnahme: "Die heilige Geschichte unterliegt keinen anderen Gesetzen, als alle übrigen Ansichten der Vergangenheit"./15/ Sogar das Prinzip der Analogie meldet sich hier schon von ferne.

Nun muss man allerdings sehen, dass die Vernunft für die Theologen unter den Rationalisten mehr ist als nur ein instrumentales Organ der Erkenntnis. Sie ist nämlich ausserdem zur Verwirklichung der Wahrheit und des Guten fähig, oder, wie man sich öfters ausdrückte, zum Erreichen der "moralischen Vollkommenheit"./16/ Deshalb prüft man, ob und inwieweit Wunder als historische Begegenheiten diese moralische Vollkommenheit fördern können. Die Antwort ist negativ. Um noch einmal C. F. Bahrdt zu zitieren: "tausend Wunder mögen einen falschen Lehrsaz (sic!) nicht wahr und einen wahren nicht falsch machen". /17/

Was ist dann mit den biblischen Wundern? a) Zuerst ist der Versuch zu machen, sie auf natürlich-vernünftige Weise zu erklären. So erklärte Heinrich Eberhard Gottlob Paulus 1828 den Jüngling zu Nain und Lazarus für scheintot./18/ b) Wie Spinoza muss man damit rechnen , dass die Jünger als zeitverhaftete und geistesschwache Zeugen eben nach ihrer beschränkten Auffassungsgabe erzählen./19/ c) Jesus hat sich seinen damaligen Zeitgenossen akkommodiert./20/ Ingesamt hat der theologische Rationalismus das Wunder als miraculum, weil nicht in den vernunftmässig erkannten Kausalzusammenhang passend und weil für die moralische Vollkommenheit unerheblich, als unmöglich und unnötig hinwegerklärt. "Den Rationalisten", urteilte Reginald H. Fuller ein wenig schroff, "erschien das Wunder als eine Beleidigung der Vernunft, es musste sich also natürlich erklären lassen, oder es konnte nicht geschehen sein"./21/

Es gehört zu den Seltsamkeiten jener Zeit, dass manche Rationalisten für Apollonius von Tyana schwärmen und sogar über die "Gewissheit der Beweise des Apollinismus" schreiben konnten . /22/

(2) Bei Friedrich Schleiermacher (1768-1834), dessen Name "eine Epoche bezeichnet",/23/ verliert die ratio ihre Mittelpunktstellung. Zugleich öffnet sich Schleiermacher, der ursprünglich von Herrnhut geprägt war, den Gedankengängen Spinozas./24/ Bei ihm rückt nun das religiöse Erlebnis in die Mitte. Damit ist zugleich gesagt, dass das fromme Bewusstsein zum Ansatzpunkt und zum Massstab der christlichen Theologie wird.

Was ergibt sich daraus für das Wunder? Weil das Universum von Gott geschaffen und erfüllt ist, muss alles Geschehen als ein Handeln Gottes vorgestellt werden. Würde Gott "contra naturam" handeln, dann würde in sein eigenes Wesen der Widerspruch hineingetragen. Daher lehnt auch Schleiermacher eine Durchbrechung des Naturzusammenhangs ab. In seiner Glaubenslehre (§ 47) formuliert er: "Aus dem Interesse der Frömmigkeit kann nie ein Bedürfnis entstehen, eine Tatsache so aufzufassen, dass durch ihre Abhängigkeit von Gott ihr Bedingtsein durch den Naturzusammenhang schlechthin aufgehoben werde". Diese Feststellung lautet-wie Fascher bemerkte-so, "wie es Spinoza nicht besser sagen konnte"./25/

Dennoch redet Schleiermacher postiv vom Wunder. Und zwar so, dass "Wunder" der religiöse Name wird, der eine Begebenheit als Ergebnis göttlichen Handeln ausdrückt. Alles, was Gott tut und was vom Menschen als von ihm bewirkt aufgefasst wird, ist also ein "Wunder". Oder, um es mit seinen eigenen Worten zu sagen: "jede auch die allernatürlichste (= Begebenheit), sobald sie sich dazu eignet, dass die religiöse Ansicht von ihr die herrschende sein kann, ist ein Wunder"./26/ Wenn auf diese Weise praktisch alles zum Wunder wird, hat das Wunder im traditionellen Sinne freilich aufgehört, zu existieren. Das miraculum ist im mirabile auf- und untergegangen. Der Ort des Wunders hat sich vom Objektiven, das der orthodoxen Dogmatik wichtig war,/27/ ins Subjektive verlagert. Wer nach dem Wunder fragt, fragt jetzt im Grunde nach dem menschlichen Subjekt.

Allerdings, und das sollte nicht übersehen werden, hat Schleiermacher der Theologie einen Wunderbegriff vermittelt, der auch durch das Kausaldenken des 19. Jh. nicht zu zerstören war. Er hat während eines kritischen Zeitalters ein jahrzehntelanges "Überwintern" des Wunderbegriffes möglich gemacht. Denn das religiöse Erlebnis als solches konnte als Realität nicht geleugnet werden. Nur auf der äussersten Linken, bei Karl Marx und seinen Nachfolgern, endete die Überzeugungskraft der Schleiermacherschen Position.

III. Liberale Wunderexegese im 19. Jh.

Wir verdeutlichen uns einigen Grundlinien liberaler Wunderexegese an zwei ausgewählten Beispielen, an F. C. Baur und an A. von Harnack. Zuvor werfen wir noch einen Blick auf D. F. Strauss.

(1) D. F. Strauss wurde im Gebiet der Theologie als ein "Revolutionär" empfunden./28/ Nach der Vorrede zum "Leben Jesu" (1835/36) wollte er "an die Stelle der veralteten supranaturalistischen. . .Betrachtungsweise" eine neue setzen. Diese sollte die "mythische" sein./29/ Ausführlich behandelt er "Die Wunder Jesu" (251 Seiten im zweiten Band). Liest man die betreffenden Seiten aufmerksam, dann wird deutlich, dass seine Wunderkritik grossenteils dem Rationalismus verhaftet bleibt. So sind beispielsweise die Dämonenaustreibungen "aus natürlichen Ursachen abzuleiten", die Ereignisse "mit aufgeklärten. . . Augen" zu betrachten./30/ Der evangelische Wunderbericht ist noch lange kein "Faktum" oder historisch./31/ Zum Seewandel bemerkt Strauss: "Ein Jesus, der im Wasser nicht einsänke, wäre ein Gespenst"./32/ Wenn wir also trotz seiner Bestrebungen, sich vom Rationalismus eines H. E. G. Paulus und anderer abzusetzen, Strauss bei seiner Wunderkritik im Gefälle des Rationalismus sehen, dann sollte dennoch nicht übersehen werden, dass er der Wunderexegese wichtige Impulse vermittelt hat: die

evangelischen Wundererzählungen sind teilweise der damaligen Erwartung entsprungen, dass der Messias Wunder tun müsse./33/ "Psychologisch erklärbare Heilungen" sind in der Überlieferung gesteigert worden./34/ In anderen Fällen wurde eine Gnome "zur Parabel erweitert, und endlich zur Geschichte realisiert"./35/ Alttestamentliche Erzählungen haben neutestamentliche hervorbringen helfen, z. B. die Speisung der 5000/36/--alles Gedanken, die wir bei Harnack, Bultmann, u.a. wiederfinden werden. Sogar formgeschichtliche Einteilungen sind bei Strauss vorweggenommen, wie z. B. "Sturm-, See- und Fischgeschichten" oder "Speisungsgeschichten" im Unterschied zu den Heilungswundern./37/

(2) Ferdinand Christian Baur, nach E. Hirsch "Der eigentliche Urheber der historisch-kritischen Theologie",/38/ will die Geschichte in ihrer Einheit begreifen. Seine Zielvorstellung ist das "Nachdenken der ewigen Gedanken des ewigen Geistes, des Werk die Geschichte ist"./39/ Wie man sieht, steht Baur unter dem Einfluss der Hegel'schen Philosophie. Als Aufgabe für den christlichen Theologen ergibt sich daraus, "das Christenthum schon in seinem Ursprung als eine geschichtlich gegebene Erscheinung aufzufassen und als solche geschichtlich zu begreifen"./40/ Wiederum liegt auf der Hand, dass Baur von einem Kausalzusammenhang allen Geschehens und von der Korrelation aller geschichtlichen Erscheinungen ausgeht.

Das Geschichtsbild, welches auf diese Weise entsteht, bleibt ein rationalistisches. An Karl Hase schreibt Baur 1855, ein wirkliches Wunder sei "nicht für möglich (zu) halten". "Lazarus kann somit nicht wirklich todt gewesen sein"./41/ Diesselbe Scheintod-Erklärung hatte uns 1828 H. E. G. Paulus angeboten. Noch grundsätzlicher äussert Baur seine Meinung im selben Schreiben an Karl Hase: "am Ende kann sich doch nur diejenige Ansicht behaupten, die in unsere Weltanschauung, in unsere Auffassung der evangelischen Geschichte, in unser ganzes Bewusstsein Einheit, Zusammenhang und vernünftige Consequenz bringt". Der Begriff "Bewusstsein" mag das Schleiermacher'sche Erbe andeuten. Die "vernünftige Consequenz" schliesst ein Wunder als widervernünftig aus./42/

(3) Wie die gesamte Ritschl'sche Schule, der er in vielem verbunden ist, lehnt auch Adolf von Harnack jede Durchbrechung der Naturgesetze ab./43/ Er geht soweit, zu sagen, "dass schwerlich ein Gebildeter unter uns sich selbst durch den Augenschein davon überzeugen lassen würde, ein solches Wunder und nicht bloss etwas ihm zur Zeit noch Unbegreifliches erlebt

zu haben"./44/ Das heisst mit dürren Worten: hätten wir die biblischen Wunder mit eigenen Augen erlebt, wären es doch für uns keine Wunder. Sie wären lediglich im Augenblick noch unerklärbar. Und woran liegt das alles? An unserer Bildung. D. h. an der zum Dogma gewordenen "modernen" Weltanschauung, die mit einem undurchbrechbaren Kausalzusammenhang rechnet.

In seinen berühmten Vorlesungen über "Das Wesen des Christentums" (Leipzig 1913 veröffentlicht) hat Harnack noch einmal zum Wunder Stellung genommen. "Dass die Erde in ihrem Lauf je stille gestanden, dass eine Eselin gesprochen hat, ein Seesturm durch ein Wort gestillt worden ist, glauben wir nicht und werden es nie wieder glauben"./45/ Wie man sieht, konnte Bruce Marshall die Grundlinien für sein "Wunder des Malachias" ohne weiteres A. v. Harnack entnehmen.

Wie sollen wir dann mit den Wundern der Bibel umgehen? Eine Antwort gibt Harnack, indem er auf folgende Entstehungsmöglichkeiten der biblischen Berichte hinweist: a) Es handelt sich um "Steigerungen natürlicher, eindrucksvoller Vorgänge"; b) sie sind "aus Reden und Gleichnissen oder aus der Projektion innerer Vorgänge in die Aussenwelt" entstanden (Lk 5,1ff!); c) in ihnen wirkt das Interesse, "alttestamentliche Berichte erfüllt zu sehen"; d) Heilungen und dgl. lassen sich als tatsächliche Vorgänge aufgrund von Suggestion z. B. festhalten/46/ (Suggestionshypothese); e) wir müssen freilich ein "Undurchdringliches" in Anschlag bringen, das in heutigen Zeiten noch keine Erklärung finden kann./47/

Insgesamt ergibt sich, dass für die liberalen Exegeten eigentliche Wunder unmöglich waren, nämlich Wunder im Sinne unnatürlicher Begebenheiten. Was die biblischen Wunderberichte anbetrifft, so sind sie nur insoweit "historisch", als sich "natürliche" Ursachen ausfindig machen lassen. So kam es mehr und mehr zu einer Unterscheidung von (historisch möglichen) "Heilungswundern" und (historisch unmöglichen) "Naturwundern"--eine Unterscheidung, die z. B. noch das monumentale Werk von van der Loos (1965) bestimmt./48/

Freilich sollten wir beachten, dass diese Zeilen der damaligen Exegese gelten, und deshalb die Frage der Historizität in den Vordergrund rückte. Unter VI. wird das Bild, wie wir hoffen, umfassender werden.

IV. Der Beitrag der Religionsgeschichtlichen Schule

Der hauptsächliche Beitrag der Religionsgeschichtlichen Schule zur ntlichen Wunderexegese lässt sich in zwei Sätzen zusammenfassen: a) Wundergeschichten gibt es überall, nicht nur in der Bibel, b) nur solche Wunder sind historisch, die wir aus dem Naturzusammenhang erklären können. Die beiden Sätze stehen in einer gewissen Spannung zueinander. Denn was nach a) möglich ist, kann nach b) wieder ausgeschlossen werden. Ausserdem wird die Historizitätsfrage abhängig gemacht von der naturwissenschaftlichen Denkbarkeit. Zugespitzt formuliert: Vieles, was die Religionsgeschichtliche Schule für die Zeit des NT erarbeitet hat, weist sie für die moderne Systematik zurück. So wird der grosse Reichtum, den uns die Religionsgeschichtliche Schule erschloss, nur teilweise genutzt.

(1) Wenden wir uns dem ersten der beiden Sätze zu. Die vielen Untersuchungen, die O. Pfleiderer, H. Gunkel, W. Bousset, P. Fiebig, R. Reitzenstein, O. Weinreich u.a. zusammentrugen--um nur einige Namen aus dem deutschsprachigen Bereich zu nennen --, zeigen, dass Wunder in ntlicher Zeit "etwas Geläufiges waren", wie es Fiebig formulierte./49/ Die Folgerung lautete, dass die Wunder als Beweise der Messianität untauglich sind: Jesus war nicht mehr der einzigartige Wundertäter./50/ Eine weitere Beobachtung war die, dass die ntlichen Wunderberichte im "Stil" eine "Verwandtschaft" mit ausserbiblischen Wundern aufwiesen./51/ Konnte man daraus schliessen, dass ntliche Wunder aus nichtchristlichen Quellen stammten, "Leihgut" waren? Auch dieser Schritt wurde vollzogen. Bei einem Vergleich der Apostelakten mit hellenistischen Wundererzählungen kam Reitzenstein zu dem Ergebnis, "dass ganze Stücke der christlichen Missions-Aretalogien einfach aus ägyptisch-griechischen Erzählungen übernommen sind"./52/ Pfleiderer und Gunkel gingen noch weiter. Für sie war "Das Christentum. . .eine synkretistische Religion"./53/ Im Hintergrund steht die Anschauung, dass auch das Christentum in einen immanent erkennbaren Kausalnexus der allgemeinen menschlichen Geschichte hineingehört. Noch in der Formgeschichtlichen Schule schlagen diese Gedankengänge durch, so wenn Bultmann annimmt, "dass volkstümliche Wundergeschichten und Wundermotive in die mündliche (sc. christliche) Tradition eingedrungen sind"./54/

Nun ist ja mit der Festellung, dass man Wundergeschichten ähnlichen Stils auch ausserhalb des NT antrifft, die Frage nach der Historizität noch nicht beantwortet. Logischerweise sind mindestens vier Antworten möglich: a) Die Wunderberichte stimmen überall mit der Realität überein. b) Die Wunderberichte stimmen nur teilweise (im NT oder auch ausserhalb!) mit der Realität überein. c) Die Wunderberichte sind samt und sonders unhistorisch. d) Die Wundergeschichten wollen überhaupt nichts Historisches erzählen, sondern drücken nach einem antiken Konsensus etwas ganz anderes aus.

(2) Für welche Antwort hat sich die Religionsgeschichtlichen Schule entschieden? Wir konkretisieren wieder an drei Beispielen.

(a) In einem Buch über "Jüdische Wundergeschichten" im Jahre 1911 teilt Paul Fiebig die ntlichen Wunder in Heilungswunder und Naturwunder auf. Erstere können historisch sein (z. B. die Exorzismen Jesu). Warum? "Der Heilungsvorgang gehört zu denjenigen Wunderberichten, die wir am ehesten verstehen und wahrscheinlich finden können"./55/ Fiebig verweist auf die "Suggestionswirkung"./56/ Hier weiss er sich mit dem Dogmatiker (J. Weiss) und dem Mediziner (W. Ebstein) einig./57/ Dagegen haben die Naturwunder, wozu er "Speisungswunder" und "Seegeschichten" rechnet, "m.E. nichts Historisches". Warum? Wir kennen "die unbedingte Zuversicht zu Gottes Allmacht und zu der Macht des Gebetes" heute nicht mehr, da sie "unserer heutigen, normalen Frömmigkeit nicht entspricht". "Wir weichen an diesem Punkte mit Bewusstsein von Jesus und seiner Zeit ab"./58/ D.h. die heutige "Frömmigkeit" hat eine andere Stufe erklommen, als diejenige zur Zeit Jesu. Sie steht zwar in einem Zusammenhang mit der Bibel, aber sie ist nicht mehr ganz und ausschliesslich biblisch bestimmt. Zwischen der Bibel und dem modernen Ausleger stehen die Grundüberzeugungen der Vernunft und der Naturwissenschaft, steht die abendländische Geschichte, wie sie sich seit Spinoza, dem Rationalismus, Kant und Schleiermacher entfaltet hat. Ist es ein Verlust, wenn uns damit eine Reihe von biblischen Wundern historisch abhanden kommt? Fiebig verneint dies. Denn "das für uns heutzutage Wertvollste in den Evangelien liegt nicht in den Wundergeschichten, sondern in den Worten Jesu"./59/ Und zusammen mit G. Traub erklärt er in Aufnahme der Schleiermacherschen Tradition: die Seele zu Gott führen lassen, sei *"das"* eigentliche Wunder./60/

(b) G. Traubs Abhandlung über "Die Wunder im Neuen Testament" (1905) erschien in der Reihe "Religionsgeschichtliche Volksbücher" und war von vornherein für einen breiten Leserkreis bestimmt. U.a. sollte dem durch die wissenschaftliche Theologie beunruhigten Publikum eine Beruhigung und eine positive Gesamtanschauung vermittelt werden: "man ist nervös geworden in der Behandlung der Wunderfrage"./61/ Traub bemüht sich zunächst um eine Definition. Aus dem Wunderbegriff wird das "Mirakel" als "das reine Verstandeswunder" ausgegrenzt. Fur dieses "Mirakel" ist wesentlich, dass es "die Durchbrechung des Naturzusammenhangs als unentbehrliche Voraussetzung" hat./62/ Traub lässt keinen Zweifel daran, dass das Mirakel dem modernen christlichen Glauben widerspricht. Wir müssen heraus "aus der eingebildeten (!) Welt der Mirakel". /63/ Dass dies tatsächlich möglich ist, zeigt uns Paulus. Paulus konnte, wie Traub meint, auf Mirakel verzichten./64/ Anders, sagt Traub, liegt es allerdings bei den Evangelien: "die Schreiber der Evangelien wollten Mirakel erzählen"; sogar ein "grosser Teil" der Evangelien ist voll davon./65/

Bevor wir Traubs Lösungsvorschläge weiterverfolgen, sei ein kurzer Hinweis angebracht. Die Unterscheidung eines mirakelfeindlichen Paulus von mirakulösen Evangelien hat in der Folgezeit einen wesentlichen Einfluss genommen. Sie hat u.a. den "Paulinismus" des deutschen Nachkriegsprotestantismus gefördert. Man muss aber sehen, dass Gunkel und Bousset einen ganz anderen Weg gegangen waren. Ihr Bestreben war es, "das einfache Evangelium Jesu" als Kernpunkt festzuhalten und der religionsgeschichtlichen Einebnung zu entziehen. Umgekehrt war es in ihren Augen Paulus, der wegen seines Synkretismus verdächtig erschien. So ordneten sie die Synoptiker vor./66/

Kehren wir zurück zu Traub. Wie bahnen wir uns den Weg zum richtigen Verständnis der evangelischen Wunder/67/? Unser Weg kann allein der wissenschaftliche sein. Diesbezüglich gilt: "die Wissenschaft kennt als einziges Werkzeug den Verstand, Sinn und Vernunft." Die Vernunft aber bleibt an den Naturzusammenhang gebunden : "gross ist das Natürliche. . .das Widernatürliche ist Theologen-traum"./68/ Diese an den Kausalnexus allen Geschehens gebundene Vernunft vermag "Heilungen aller Art" anzuerkennen./69/ Psychologie und Medizin lehren uns ja, die "Heilkraft der Suggestion" in Rechnung zu setzen, Dämonenaustreibungen mit hysterischer "Neurose" zu erklären, "besondere Bildungen des Nervensystems" zu berücksichtigen./70/ Anders steht es mit den Naturwundern ("Seeanekdoten, Speisungsgeschichten")./71/ Sie sind grundsätzlich unhistorisch. Hier urteilt Traub bei der Sturmstillung: "eine ursächliche Verbindung zwischen dem Wort Jesu und dem Aufhören des Sturmes ist ausgeschlossen"--"eine derartige physische Machtenfaltung (ist) nach heutigen

Kenntnissen unmöglich"./72/ Der Bericht vom Stater im Fischmaul (Mt 17,24ff) ist "haltlos", "aus den Sagen und Gedanken der späteren Gemeindeentwicklung" entstanden usw./73/ Immer wieder sind es die "heutigen (modernen) Kenntnisse", die zum bindenden Dogma erhoben werden und zur Verneinung der Historizität führen. Doch kombiniert Traub damit in der Art Harnacks historisch-theologische Argumente: "Wundergeschichten, wie sie in der Bibel vorliegen", werden "überall erzählt" (religionsgeschichtliches Argument); das damalige "dogmatische Bild des Messias" habe vorgeschrieben, dass er Wunder tun müsse (dogmatisches Argument); Wundererzählungen werden abgewandelt, gesteigert oder aus Worten Jesu herausgesponnen (Lk 5,1ff!-- literarisches Argument)./74/ Schliesslich, und damit partizipiert auch Traub am Erbe Schleiermachers, bleibt dem Christen das "Wunder des Glaubens". Es ist einmal "der lebendige Gott", ein andermal das Führen der Seele zu Gott./75/

(c) Nachdem die populäre Abhandlung G. Traubs verhältnismässig viel Raum beansprucht hat, soll noch ein kurzer Hinweis auf Troeltsch folgen, dessen Position ja weithin bekannt ist. Ernst Troeltsch, der von Stuhlmacher als "der führende protestantische Systematiker des sog. Liberalismus und Historismus" bezeichnet wird,/76/ hat die historische Methode in der Theologie an die Prinzipien der Analogie, der Kausalität und der Korrelation gebunden. Wunder sind nach der Konzeption Troeltschs durch "die von der Naturwissenschaft aufgewiesene Eigengesetzlichkeit und Regelmässigkeit des Naturwirkens unmöglich gemacht". Daneben wehrt sich Troeltsch aus religiösen Gründen gegen ein Wunder als "Sonderkausalität". Es wäre ihm "metaphysisch unerträglich". Denn seine Gottesauffassung verlangt ein einheitliches Universum, das sich nicht in "natürlich" und "supranatural" aufspalten lässt./77/ Wenngleich modifiziert, erkennen wir auch in diesen Überlegungen das rationalistische Kausalprinzip und den Schleiermacherschen Universalismus wieder./78/

Die Religionsgeschichtliche Schule hat der Wunderexegese den Horizont geweitet. Sie blieb aber wie die vorausgehende liberale Exegese in den Stiefeln des ererbten Rationalismus und der Schleiermacher-Tradition stecken. Der ererbte Rationalismus führte dazu, die Historizität durch den naturwissenschaftlichen Kausalgedanken zu entscheiden. Schleiermacher half auf das "Wunder des Glaubens", das mirabile, auszuweichen, oder unterstützte durch seinen Pantheismus den Gedanken eines unentrinnbaren geschlossenen Universums. Suggestionshypothese, Scheintodhypothese, Visionhypothese, Undurchdringlichkeits- oder

Zufallshypothese sind es, die sich auf diesem Boden immer wieder finden./79/

V. Der Beitrag der Formgeschichtlichen Schule

Die "Formgeschichtliche Schule" hat sich in Deutschland, wie man weiss, nicht auf die Untersuchung von "Formen" beschränkt. Sie wollte vielmehr einen Weg eröffnen, auf dem die Entstehung des NTs, mindestens jedoch die Entstehung der Evangelien, verständlich wurde.

Wie sieht nun ihr Beitrag zur Wunderexegese aus? Die wirkungsgeschichtlich wichtigste Untersuchung hat Rudolf Bultmann (1884-1976) geliefert. In seiner "Geschichte der synoptischen Tradition" leitet er uns an, streng zwischen dem vorliegenden Evangelium und der hinter ihm liegenden, älteren Tradition zu unterscheiden.

Was das vorliegende Evangelium betrifft, so gehört es zu seinem "Wesen. . ., Wundergeschichten zu enthalten". Die evangelischen Wunder dienen zum "Erweise seiner (sc. Jesu) messianischen Kraft bzw. seiner göttlichen Macht" und sind als "Beweise für die Messianität Jesu besonders wichtig"./80/

Aber wie sieht es mit den älteren Traditionen aus? Hier wandelt sich das Bild. Oft beobachten wir eine "Steigerung des Wunderbaren",/81/ eine Beobachtung, auf die sich auch Harnack, Traub u.a. stützen. Das kann nur bedeuten, dass geringere oder zahlenmässig weniger Wunder am Anfang der christlichen Überlieferung standen. Eine weitere Beobachtung lautet, "dass volkstümliche Wundergeschichten und Wundermotive in die. . . Tradition eingedrungen sind"./82/ Die Konsequenz dieser Beobachtung ist dieselbe wie eben zuvor: die älteste Christenheit kannte weniger Jesuswunder, nahm sie evtl. gar nicht so wichtig. Gibt es vielleicht sogar ein ältestes Stratum, das ohne Wunder auskommt? Bultmann verweist auf Q, wo "die Wundergeschichten fast ganz fehlen"./83/ Weil Markus sie aber zahlreich hat, ist Bultmann der Überzeugung, dass der Hellenismus den hauptsächlichen Ursprungsort der synoptischen Wundergeschichten darstellt. Ohne in Abrede zu stellen, dass "schon in der palästinischen Gemeinde Wunder von Jesu berichtet" wurden, ergibt sich historisch "ein Vorurteil für die Entstehung der synoptischen Wundergeschichten auf hellenistischem Boden". /84/ Der Hellenismus, der bei Markus zum Zuge kommt, will Jesus werbewirksam als den "theios anthropos" darstellen./85/

An dieser Entwicklung ist abzulesen, dass *viele* Wunder nicht historisch sind. Allerdings leugnet Bultmann nicht, dass den Heilungswundern gewisse historische Elemente zugrundeliegen können./86/ Ähnliches kann aus dem religionsgeschichtlichen Vergleich geschlossen werden. Denn auch die "Parallelen zum Stil der synoptischen Wundergeschichten" aus der Umwelt des NT deuten auf die Ahistorizität./87/

Haben wir oben unter IV. vier mögliche Antworten genannt, die angesichts der religionsgeschichtlichen Parallelen auf die Frage nach der Historizität des Wunders gegeben werden können, dann ist jetzt deutlich, dass Bultmann die unter c) erwähnte Antwort bevorzugt: die religionsgeschichtlichen Parallelen dienen dem Erweise, dass die berichteten Wunder nicht historisch sind.

Insgesamt hat sich mit der Formgeschichtlichen Schule, trotz ihrer teilweisen Anlehnung an die Religionsgeschichtliche Schule, die Situation der Wunderexegese verändert. Der grösste Wandel besteht darin, dass die Entscheidung mit Energie im Gebiet der Geschichtswissenschaft gesucht wird. Die naturwissenschaftliche Argumentation tritt zurück./88/ Aber dieser Wandel lässt zunächst ein Ergebnis unberührt: die Ungeschichtlichkeit des Wunders bleibt als ein rocher de bronce bestehen.

Von der hier eingenommenen Position aus öffneten sich verschiedene Weiterwege. Man konnte z. B. das ursprüngliche Evangelium ohne Wunder wiederherzustellen versuchen. In dieser Richtung hat später W. Schmithals einige Schritte getan. Wir erinnern uns dabei an Traub, der allerdings nicht das älteste Evangelium, sondern Paulus als mirakelfremd betrachtet hatte. Man konnte z. B. auch die "quaestio facti" für gleichgültig erklären und sich ganz auf die Frage nach der Bedeutung der Wundergeschichten konzentrieren. Diese Richtung haben z. B. Fridrichsen,/89/ später Bultmann und die sog. existentiale Interpretation eingeschlagen./90/

Bevor wir uns aber den weiteren Entwicklungen zuwenden, müssen wir im Fortgang unserer Betrachtung für einige Augenblicke innehalten. Wir haben nämlich zu registrieren, dass von Baur zu Bultmann keine gerade Linie verläuft, dass noch weniger eine einfache Abfolge exegetischer Schulen oder Entwicklungen existiert, sondern dass die Theologie gerade an der Wunderfrage bis in ihre Fundamente hinein gespalten wurde. Es lohnt sich, den Streit um das Wunder, der sich vor allem am Anfang des 20 Jh. abspielte, ins Auge zu fassen.

VI. Der Streit um die Aufrechterhaltung des Wunders

Dieser Streit, bei dem es um die Aufrechterhaltung oder Rückgewinnung des Wunders ging, beschäftigte die verschiedensten Richtungen der Theologie. Zwar stellte K. Bornkamm einmal fest: der Widerspruch gegen den Rationalismus "erfolgte nicht zuletzt im Zeichen eines orthodoxen Biblizismus"./91/ Aber die Verteidiger des Wunders blieben keineswegs auf eine neulutherische Orthodoxie oder den sog. Biblizismus beschränkt. Allerdings waren die Ergebnisse sehr verschiedenartig.

(1) Beginnen wir mit der Ritschl'schen Schule. Hier hat sich Wilhelm Herrmann, u.a. einer der einflussreichsten Lehrer Bultmanns,/92/ intensiv mit dem Thema "Offenbarung und Wunder" befasst (1908). Für ihn steht fest: alle Wissenschaft ist an das Kausalitätsprinzip gebunden: "was in dieser Welt als wirklich nachgewiesen wird, enthält immer eine Gesetzmässigkeit des Geschehens"./93/ Für Gott als "übernatürliche" Ursache ist in dieser Wissenschaft kein Platz./94/ Aber--und damit drängt W. Herrmann "die" Wissenschaft zurück--es gibt jenseits des wissenschaftlich Feststellbaren noch eine andere Wirklichkeit--Gott. Diese ist mit den Mitteln der Wissenschaft nicht zu erfassen. Sie wird nur im Erlebnis zugänglich und nur in Bekenntnis und Bezeugung ausgesprochen und weitervermittelt. Damit bekommt die Religion einen eigenen, unzerstörbaren Raum neben dem wissenschaftlichen, kausal bedingten. Der Theologe aber kann die Kausalität und Korrelation, denen die Wissenschaft folgt, anerkennen. Der Preis, der dafür bezahlt wird, ist das Auseinanderfallen von Gotteserkenntnis und Welterkenntnis, von Glauben und Wissen. Was bedeutet das für das Wunder? Es behält seinen Platz in jener "anderen", metawissenschaftlichen Wirklichkeit. Es ist erlebbar, aber nicht beweisbar. Und dabei konzentriert es sich auf die sittliche Tat. Weil diese sittliche Tat die Kraft des Einzelnen übersteigt, weist sie auf ein göttliches Eingreifen hin. Marquardt nennt es das "ethische Wunder"./95/

Damit ist Schleiermacher, was die Selbständigkeit des religiösen Erlebnisses anlangt, konsequent zur Anwendung gebracht. Damit hat die Theologie auch gegenüber einer scheinbar alles beherrschenden Kausalität das Wunder behauptet. Aber zugleich ist die Geschichte dem Kausalitätsprinzip und der Wunderfeindlichkeit ausgeliefert. Wer die Frage stellt: sind die biblischen Wundergeschichten reale Ereignisse? erhält die Antwort: nur, insofern sie immanent-kausal erklärbar sind.

(2) Johannes Wendland hat die Schwächen bei W. Herrmann deutlich erkannt. In seiner 1910 erschienenen Abhandlung "Der Wunderglaube im Christentum" wendet er sich gegen den "schneidenden Widerspruch", den Herrmann zwischen Wunderglauben und Welterkennen aufrichtet./96/ Der Hauptfehler Herrmanns liege darin, dass er den Begriff "Wissenschaft" von der "Naturwissenschaft" her bestimme und deshalb mit einem unzulänglichen Wissenschaftsbegriff arbeite: "Herrmann identifiziert fälschlich Wissenschaft und Naturwissenschaft: er macht die letztere zur Richterin über das, was wissenschaftlich erkennbar ist. Sein Wissenschaftsbegriff ist viel zu eng"./97/

Wenn man mit Wendland den "Wissenschafts"-Begriff weiter fasst, so hat das unmittelbare Konsequenzen für das Historische. Der "Dualismus zwischen Natur und Geist", der der Ritschl'schen Richtung anhaftet, muss fallen./98/ Gott wirkt nicht nur in der sittlichen Tat, sondern in den Gesamtbereich des menschlichen Lebens hinein: "dass Gott. . .nur in das geistige Leben des Menschen Neues hineinwirken könnte, ist widersinnig". Gebete verändern den Weltlauf. Im Gegensatz zu F. C. Baur, zu Zeller und Herrmann gibt es Wunder auch im Bereich des Historischen./99/

Damit ist eine Tür weit aufgestossen. Es fragt sich allerdings: was wird nun für den Wirklichkeits- und Wissenschaftsbegriff konstitutiv? Etwa die Offenbarung? Wer damit rechnet, wird enttäuscht. Konstitutiv ist für Wendland vielmehr die "religiöse Erfahrung"./100/ Wir beobachten also, dass derselbe Autor, der sich mit Schleiermacher, Troeltsch, Herrmann u.a. auseinandersetzten wollte,/101/ einen halben Schritt zurückgeht und doch wieder der Bannkraft Schleiermacherscher Traditionen erliegt./102/

Die menschliche "Erfahrung" also ist der Ansatzpunkt, der es ermöglicht, Gotteserkennen und Welterkennen, Natur und Geist, Naturwissenschaft und Theologie in ein Ganzes zu integrieren. Dabei wird der Rationalismus dahin korrigiert, dass er mit dem Beharren auf Naturgesetz und Kausalzusammenhang nur eine Teilwahrheit ausspricht: diese Begriffe "erschöpfen nicht den Bestand des Daseins"./103/ Troeltsch wird dahin korrigiert, dass das Weltganze und das einheitliche Erkennen dieses ganzen Wunder nicht aus-, sondern einschliesst. Schleiermacher und Herrmann werden dahin korrigiert, dass man das Wunder nicht in ein subjektives Erlebnis zurückverlegen darf; vielmehr gilt: "wir brauchen einen objektiv-metaphysischen Wunderbegriff"./104/ Wendland meint, dass er dies "Objektiv-Metaphysische" berücksichtigt hat, wenn er definiert: "Wunder sind religiös bedeutsame *Ereignisse*" (Hervorhebung vom Verfasser)./105/ Wenn Wendland ein andermal sagt, es handle sich beim Wunder um Gottes "schöpferisches Neuwirken",/106/ dann lenkt er tatsächlich zur altkirchlichen Auffassung zurück./107/

Was heisst das nun bei der Anwendung auf die Wunder des Neuen Testaments? Heilungen sind tatsächlich geschehen. Denn sie entsprechen den "Analogien der religiösen Erfahrung". Übrigens gilt das auch von Blumhardt und Lourdes./108/ Naturwunder dagegen sind nicht geschehen. Denn das "erleben wir nicht"./109/ An die Stelle der naturwissenschaftlichen Kausalität tritt also die moderne religiöse Erfahrung als Unterscheidungsmerkmal: "wir müssen. . .die biblischen Wunder nach Analogie heutigen religiösen Erlebens verstehen"./110/ Damit ist auch das Analogieprinzip wieder aufgetaucht. Allerdings handelt es sich um das Analogieprinzip der Erfahrung. Es ist eigenartig, wie Wendland mit Hilfe *dieses* Analogieprinzips zu gleichen Ergebnissen kommen kann, wie sie das kausalitätsverhaftete ebenfalls erzeugt hat: "Jesus hilft für gewöhnlich, ohne die Naturordnungen aufzuheben; also ist anzunehmen, dass er nicht drei oder viermal die Ordnungen Gottes durchbrochen hat, die in seinem ganzen Leben auch für ihn galten"./111/ Der Fortschritt bei Wendland ist also im Grundsätzlich-Systematischen grösser als in der praktischen Exegese.

(3) Auf einer anderen Linie operieren die sog. Biblizisten, wie z. B. Paul Feine, Hermann Cremer oder Hans Emil Weber. Sie wollen den gewöhnlichen Kausalzusammenhang nicht durch eine "andere" Wirklichkeit ergänzen, sondern von einer anderen Wirklichkeit her durchbrechen. Am stärksten hat sich dies wohl bei Hermann Cremer ausgeprägt, für den die Durchbrechungen in Form des Wunders "für die Verwirklichung der Erlösung schlechthin notwendig" sind (1900)./112/ Weil unser gegenwärtiger Naturzusammenhang durch den Sündenfall böse geworden ist! Er kann uns deshalb nicht mehr zum Heil dienen. Will Gott uns retten, dann muss er Wunder als "Gegenwirkungen gegen die Wirksamkeit der kreatürlichen Kausalitäten" benutzen./113/ Von daher kann Cremer das Wunder als ein Ereignis definieren, das "durch eine nicht im natürlichen Kausalzusammenhange vorhandene Kraft" bewirkt wurde./114/

Dieser soteriologische Ansatz H. Cremers ist hochinteressant. Ähnliches werden wir übrigens bei J. Kallas wiederfinden. Er kann damit die ntlichen Wunder als historische, reale Ereignisse stehen lassen. Er vermeidet damit sogar einen Dualismus, den man zuerst befürchten mag. Denn die von Gott abgefallene Welt bleibt in Gottes Verfügungsmacht. Nur liegt die Einheit nicht mehr in ihr oder in unserer Erkenntnis, sondern allein in Gott. Es ist also ein ganz und gar theistischer Wunderbegriff, dem wir hier begegnen.

(4) Nur wenn man diesen theistischen Ansatz im Auge behält, lässt sich auch Hans Emil Weber verstehen. In Gott finden Natur und Wunder ihre Einheit: "Gott wirkt sowohl in der Natur wie im Wunder"/115/ (1914). Es hebt diese letzte Einheit nicht auf, wenn man das Wunder als "praeter naturam", "supra naturam" oder sogar als "contra naturam" bezeichnen kann./116/ Weber definiert: "das Wunder ist die Selbstbekundung des welterhabenen Gottes in der Welt"./117/ Damit sind zwei weitere Aussagen gegeben : die Natur ist nur eine Teilbekundung Gottes, und der "welterhabene Gott" kann nicht "natürlichen" Gesetzen unterworfen werden. So können Natur- und Geschichtswissenschaft nur Teilwahrheiten aussprechen und der naturgesetzliche Kausalzusammenhang ist lediglich ein "Arbeitsprinzip". Als "konstitutives Wirklichkeitsprinzip" kommt allein Gott in Frage. Deshalb brauchen die Geschichts- und die Naturwissenschaft die Ergänzung durch eine Wissenschaft, die das "Übergeschichtliche" aufnehmen kann, d.h. sie sind auf die "theologische Geschichtsbetrachtung" angewiesen./118/ Im Gebiet der Wunderexegese wird also jene Revision des Wirklichkeits- und Geschichtsverständnisses vollzogen, die dann in der hermeneutischen Debatte der 70er Jahre eine solche Rolle spielen sollte.

(5) Da man Cremer und Schlatter oft nebeneinander zu stellen pflegt, ist man überrascht, wenn man sich in unserem Zusammenhang mit Adolf Schlatter (1852-1938) beschäftigt. Schlatter setzt bei der "natürlichen" Erkenntnis an. Der Mensch kann, wenn er sich nicht blind und taub stellt, Gott als den Schöpfer aus der Natur erkennen. Der Sündenfall hat diese gottgeschenkte Fähigkeit nicht zerstört. Mit diesem Ansatz gerät Schlatter in eine solche Nähe zur thomistisch-katholischen Erkenntnislehre, dass er in Marquardts Untersuchung als der am meisten katholische bezeichnet wird./119/ Wahrscheinlich hat ihm Franz Baader diese Nähe vermittelt.

Andrerseits ist es "der eine Gott. . ., der sowohl Wunder tut als auch die Natur erhält"./120/ Ganz ähnlich wie H. E. Weber kommt also Schlatter von seinem andersartigen Ansatz her zu einer Einheit von Natur und Geschichte, von Gottes- und

Welterkenntnis, ohne dem Pantheismus zu verfallen. Es ist bei Schlatter noch viel weniger als bei Wendland nötig, ein vom natürlichen Kausalgeschehen getrenntes eigenes religiöses Erleben anzunehmen--um ganz davon zu schweigen, dass Schlatter die Aufspaltungen der Ritschl'schen Schule nie akzeptieren konnte. Im Unterschied zu Weber jedoch meint Schlatter, das Wunder stehe "nicht gegen die Natur". "Der Streit um die Durchbrechung der Naturgesetze ist also sinnlos"./121/ Und zwar eben deshalb, weil der eine Gott im Wunder wie in der Natur handelt. Damit hat Schlatter aber auch einen völlig anderen Weg gewählt als Cremer, für den ja die Wunder "Gegenwirkungen" gegen das natürliche, verderbte Geschehen darstellten. In diesem Gegensatz von Schlatter und Cremer dürfte ein Gegensatz von Täufertum und Luther auferstehen.

Wir interessieren uns für die Konsequenzen im Bereich des Neuen Testaments. Da ist nun zu sagen, dass Schlatter keine dogmatischen Hindernisse kennt, die ihn von der Annahme eines realen Wundergeschehens abhielten. In seiner "Geschichte des Christus" (2. Aufl. 1923) geht er als ein historisch Beobachtender vor. Er hat da vermutlich schon Bultmann im Auge, wenn er feststellen muss, dass "der Christenheit die Erzählung von Jesus nie anders als so vorlag, dass sie über seine Zeichen berichtete". "Der Versuch, ein wunderfreies Evangelium als die erste Gestalt der christlichen Überlieferung aufzufinden", ist also vergeblich. Der innere Grund liegt darin, dass "der königliche Wille" Jesus sich im Wunder kundtun wollte und sollte. /122/ Gerade die Realität der Geschichte hindert uns daran, die Wunderberichte zu eliminieren oder umzuinterpretieren: "je mehr wir den Wunderbericht umdeuten oder aus dem Geschichtslauf entfernen, um so weiter werden wir uns von den wirklichen Vorgängen entfernen"./123/ Aber nun beobachtet der Historiker noch ein anderes. Gerade weil die ersten Christen Jesus nur als den wundermächtigen kannten, "sind Steigerungen des wunderbaren Hergangs in einzelnen Fällen möglich und wahrscheinlich" (so z. B. Mk 5,1; Mt 21,39; 17,27)./124/ Aber nicht nur "Steigerungen", sondern auch "Einzelne Angleichungen der evangelischen Erzählungen an die alttestamentlichen Geschichten sind wahrscheinlich" (so z. B. in Mt 4,2; 21,7; 27,34)./125/ Damit treffen wir zwei Harnack'sche Argumente bei Schlatter wieder, und es bleibt im Einzelfall offen, wieviel tatsächlich historisch ist, wenn Schlatter auch betont,/126/ "die Substanz der Berichte" bleibe erhalten./127/

(6) Hat uns Schlatter schon ein Stück weit ins 20. Jh. hineingeführt, so tritt uns in dem Heidelberger Theologen Robert

Jelke noch einmal ein Autor entgegen, der einen originellen Weg sucht und dabei dogmatische und exegetische Überlegungen miteinander verbindet (1922). Zuerst geschieht eine scharfe Abgrenzung gegen den Rationalismus: "es ist gerade der irrationale Charakter des Wunders, auf den es uns ankommt."/128/ Sodann erfolgt eine ebenso entschiedene Hinwendung zum Historischen, die ja überhaupt die Wunderexegese seit dem 1. Weltkrieg charakterisiert. Wie Schlatter beobachtet Jelke eine " unlösliche Verbindung von Wundertat und Rede Jesu". Ein wunderfreies Evangelium hat es nie gegeben: "wir kennen Jesum als Wundertäter oder wir kennen ihn überhaupt nicht"./129/ Jelke tritt hier bereits in eine Auseinandersetzung mit Bultmanns "Geschichte der synoptischen Tradition" ein und bemerkt: "Bultmann hat hier viele Urteile gefällt, die sich sehr apodiktisch ausnehmen, aber keinerlei beweisende Kraft haben." /130/ Ist es aber so, dann müssen wir auch als Historiker annehmen, "dass Jesus wirklich Wunder getan hat"./131/ Und ganz im Gegensatz zu liberalen Exegeten wie Heitmüller, Keim und Knopf, will Jelke nicht nur Heilungen anerkennen, sondern auch Naturwunder./132/ Hier argumentiert Jelke ein Stück weit dogmatisch. Denn "Ohne den Glauben" an wunderbare Hilfe in jeder äusserlichen Not "hätte jedenfalls das christliche Bittgebet keinen Sinn"./133/ Am Ende kommt alles auf die historische Bezeugung an. Wir können mit der Historizität der Wunder, gleich ob "Heilungswunder" oder "Naturwunder", rechnen, "insoweit, als ihre historische Bezeugung eine einwandfreie ist"./134/ Damit ist die ausschliessliche Kompetenz dem Historiker übergeben.

(7) Eine eigenartige und selbständige Lösung vertritt Karl Heim. In der Abhandlung "Zur Frage der Wunderheilungen" (1929) /135/ stellt er fest: "das Wunder der Bibel steht nicht im Gegensatz zur Natur"./136/ Warum nicht? Weil das moderne "mechanistische Naturbild" dem biblischen Menschen noch unbekannt war. Das biblische Wunder gehört in einen ganz anderen Bezugsrahmen, nämlich in den Kampf zwischen der Macht Gottes und den antigöttlichen Gewalten. Heim schliesst sich dieser biblischen Sicht an. Hier bildet "das gegenständliche Naturgeschehen", das "Physische", nur die eine Hemisphäre "einer und derselben Wirklichkeit". Die andere Hemisphäre jener einheitlichen Wirklichkeit bildet "das Ethische". In der verborgenen Hemisphäre des Ethischen spielt sich ein Geisterkampf zwischen göttlichen und widergöttlichen Gewalten ab. Entscheidend ist das Zweite, die "Innenseite". Die Aussenseite stellt nur den "Niederschlag" jener Geistesmächte dar, die Heim auch "Willensmächte" nennt. Von da aus wird es begreiflich, dass die Wunder Jesu auf die Natur einwirken und sie verändern: sie

sind Siege über die feindlichen Willensmächte./137/ Mit dieser Konzeption gelingt es Heim, a) die Einheit des Geschehens festzuhalten, b) die Ergebnisse der modernen physikalischen Forschung mit den biblischen Aussagen zu vereinen, und c) die Realität und Historizität des biblischen Wunders generell zu bejahen.

(8) Eine der intensivsten historischen Untersuchungen, die wir aus der 1. Hälfte des 20. Jh. kennen, entstammt der Feder von Alan Richardson. Sein Buch über "The Miracle-Stories of the Gospels" ist 1941 in 1. Auflage erschienen. Merkwürdigerweise ist dies dasselbe Jahr, in dem Bultmann in seinem Alpirsbacher Vortrag über "Neues Testament und Mythologie" das Wunder erneut unter vermeintliche naturwissenschaftliche Gesetze beugte und damit eher einen Schritt rückwärts auf Wilhelm Herrmann zu tat. Aber das berührt den Wert der Richardson'schen Auseinandersetzung mit der Formgeschichtlichen Schule nicht.

Richardson unterstreicht zunächst, dass Wunder allein die Messianität Jesu in ntlicher Zeit nicht begründen konnten./138/ Das bedeutet ein Argument gegen die traditionelle Meinung, wonach Wunder die Göttlichkeit Jesu beweisen könnten. Das bedeutet aber auch ein Argument gegen die Meinung von Harnack, Traub, Bultmann u.a., wonach man mittels fingierten Wunder besonders gut für Jesus werben konnte. Denn wenn die Rabbinen oder Simon Magus Ähnliches vollbrachten, was konnte es dann Jesus nützen? Sodann richtet Richardson an die Adresse von Bultmann und Dibelius den Vorwurf, sie würden Jesus in die Religionsgeschichte einebnen, wenn sie ihn nach Analogie der antiken theioi anthropoi behandelten./139/ Es geht hier darum, dass die Formgeschichtler die Wunder Jesu gelegentlich als "gleichsam etwas von seinem individuellen Wollen Losgelöstes, automatisch Funktionierendes" betrachteten./140/ Richardson hält ihnen entgegen, dass die Wundergeschichten nicht weniger als die Paradigmen den Zweck haben, "to awaken saving faith in the person of Christ"./141/ Drittens geht Richardson auf die frappierenden Parallelen in der Form ein, die auf eine Übernahme ausserchristlicher Wundergeschichten im NT hindeuten sollen. Richardsons ebenso verblüffende wie einfache Lösung: man kann z. B. Heilungen gar nicht anders erzählen, als indem man--normalerweise!--den Ablauf von Exposition, Heilungsvorgang und Approbation einhält: "it is impossible to tell the story of a cure in any other way"./142/ Weiterhin macht Richardson darauf aufmerksam, welch hoher Anteil der Evangelienberichte dem Wunder gewidmet ist./143/ Dabei kann man nicht mit der Formgeschichtlichen Schule auf eine ältere Tradition ausweichen, die angeblich wunderfrei oder wundersprõde war. Nein, "the miracle-stories are a part of the Gospel itself"./144/ Wir erinnern uns, dass Schlatter und Jelke dasselbe feststellten. So wird es zur eigentlichen Aufgabe, zu erklären, warum die Evangelien so viel mit dem Wunder befasst sind. Hier gibt Richardson eine doppelte Antwort. Einmal sind die Wunder die prophetischen Zeichen des kommenden Gottesreiches, das die Evangelien verkünden./145/ Zweitens sind die Wunder Zeichen dafür, dass Gottes Macht in Jesus Christus wirkt: Christus ist "the manifestation of the power of God in the world"./146/ Von daher wird die Unterscheidung von "Heilungswundern" und "Naturwundern" belanglos. Denn Jesus teilt ja die Macht Gottes über die Schöpfung, die bereits das AT verkündigt hat./147/ Als A. Schlatter vom "königlichen Willen Jesu" sprach, hatte er Ähnliches gemeint. So stellen uns die Evangelien/148/ letzlich vor die christologische Frage: "whether the power of God was or was not revealed in the person and work of Jesus Christ". Weil auf diese Frage aber nur der Glaube Antwort geben kann, haben wir lediglich die Alternative, diesen Jesus anzunehmen oder ihn abzulehnen. Nimmt ihn der Glaube als den Christus Gottes an, dann gilt auch: "the miracles did happen"./149/ Richardson lässt keinen Zweifel über seinen eigenen Standpunkt: "The miracles of the Gospels are not the figments of a legend-loving Christian community; they are the hard facts which underline man's rejection of God's salvation and which bring history to a climax and the purpose of God to its fulfilment"./150/

Damit hat der Historiker die Kompetenz über die Wirklichkeit des Wunders, die ihm soeben übergeben worden war--an den Glauben weitergereicht. Das Erregendste an der historischen Untersuchung Richardsons ist der Schluss, wo der Historiker die Entscheidung, ob die Wunder historisch sind, dem Glauben überlässt.

Wir haben eine Reihe von Bemühungen verfolgt, den Streit um das Wunder zu schlichten. Jeder der Beteiligten hat auf seine Weise versucht, das Wunder aufrechtzuerhalten. Aber wir sind in einer gewissen Verwirrung gelandet. Wer hat denn nun die Kompetenz, uns zu sagen, ob Wunder möglich, ob sie tatsächlich geschehen sind? Der Naturwissenschaftler? Das religiöse Erleben? Der Historiker? Der Glaube? Die Offenbarung? Die Philosophie?

VII. Einige jüngere Tendenzen

Bei der Fülle der nach dem 2. Weltkrieg erschienenen Literatur zum "Wunder" ist hier die Auswahl besonders schwierig.

Die Bandbreite der Anschauungen reicht von A. Ficarras Satz: "Gesù non operò miracoli"/151/ bis zur Überzeugung von J. Kallas, dass es gerade der wundervollbringende Jesu als "The Conquering Christ. . .the Stronger One, the Victorious, the Triumphant Foe of evil who battled Satan" ist,/152/ der in der Mitte des Evangeliums steht. Wir sind weiter von einem Konsens entfernt als je.

(1) Ein breiter Strom kontinentaler Theologie schloss sich Bultmanns existentialer Interpretation an. Bultmann hat zunehmend historische Erwägungen mit dogmatisch-philosophischen verschränkt, wobei u.E. der Rückgriff auf W. Herrmann immer stärker zu Tage trat./153/ Schon 1933 schrieb er in einer Art, die an Troeltsch und Traub erinnert: "der Gedanke des Wunders als Mirakels ist für uns heute unmöglich geworden, weil wir das Naturgeschehen als gesetzmässiges Geschehen verstehen, also das Wunder als eine Durchbrechung des gesetzmässigen Zusammenhang des Naturgeschehens"./154/ Ist er hier der These vom lückenlosen Kausalzusammenhang verhaftet, so tritt das Schleiermacher-Herrmann'sche Erbe dort hervor, wo er *ein* Wunder gelten lässt, nämlich das der "Vergebung". Auf die Vergebung reduziert sich das Werk Christi in so starkem Masse, dass die Wunder Jesu im NT "keine Werke Christi" mehr sind, "sofern wir unter dem Werk Christi das Werk der Erlösung verstehen". Deshalb sind die Wunder Jesu als Ereignisse der Vergangenheit "restlos der Kritik preiszugeben, und es ist mit aller Schärfe zu betonen, dass schlechterdings kein Interesse für den christlichen Glauben besteht, die Möglichkeit oder Wirklichkeit der Wunder Jesu als Ereignisse der Vergangenheit nachzuweisen, dass im Gegenteil dies nur eine Verirrung wäre"./155/ Denn es ist das gottlose Streben nach eigener Gerechtigkeit, das nach Wundern verlangt./156/ 1941 unterstreicht Bultmann noch einmal, dass a) "vom naturwissenschaftlichen Weltbild" her und b) "aus dem Selbstverständnis des modernen Menschen" (d.h. aus der Philosophie) Kritik am ntlichen Wunder geübt werden muss./157/ Stattdessen will Bultmann existential interpretieren. D.h. er will die Wundergeschichten unter der Leitfrage nach dem hier "zum Ausdruck kommenden Verständnis der menschlichen Existenz" auslegen./158/

Leider ist hier nicht der Raum, um den Zusammenhang dieser Art von Interpretation mit philosophischen Strömungen näher zu diskutieren. Die Diskussion darüber ist allerdings schon längst im Gange./159/

Bei denen, die sich Bultmann anschlossen, wird wie bei

Bultmann selbst immer wieder betont, dass wir unser Weltbild nicht selber wählen, sondern dass es uns mit unserer Existenz unentrinnbar gegeben ist. So formuliert Karin Bornkamm: "dem geistigen Schicksal, dem wir durch das Aufbrechen solcher Erkenntnisse und Anfragen unterliegen, kann sich keiner entziehen"./160/ Zweitens wird hier betont, dass der naturgesetzliche Kausalzusammenhang kein Wunder supra oder contra naturam erlaube./161/ Drittens ergibt sich aus dem gewandelten Weltbild, dass man Wunder "nicht als historisch anerkennen kann"; man könne sich ja "nicht. . .einfach ausserhalb des allgemeinen Wahrheitsbewusstseins. . .stellen"./162/ Viertens wird die Wundergeschichte vor allem als Predigt und nicht als historischer Bericht gelesen. Die ntl. Wundergeschichten sind "nicht historisch mehr oder weniger einwandfreie Berichte, sondern Predigten. . ., die Jesus als den Christus bezeugen wollen"./163/ Man glaubt sich im Einverständnis mit Luther, wenn man die historische Frage auf diese Weise zugunsten des Kerygmas relativiert./164/

Übrigens hat die englische Forschung teilweise diese Interpretationsrichtung aufgenommen. So hat C. F. D. Moule (1965) in einem anregenden Essay von der Frage: "what actually happened?" abgeraten. Besser sollter man an die Wundergeschichten die Frage richten: "what ideas did the narrator intend to convey?"/165/ Wir erinnern uns an ähnliche Überlegungen bei Fridrichsen (1925).

(2) Walter Schmithals unternahm dann 1970 den Versuch, ein wunderfreies Christentum herauszuarbeiten. Er vollzieht in seinem Buch "Wunder und Glaube" vier Schritte: 1) Die Historizität der neutestamentlichen Wunder stösst auf schwere Bedenken, weil damals Wunder "eine gewöhnliche Erscheinung waren" (cf. die durchgängigen Thesen der Religionsgeschichtlichen Schule!), ja "nur eine Sprechweise", die der damalige Christ "um der Verständlichkeit der Glaubenssprache" (sic!) willen wählen musste./166/ Die Frage nach dem Ereignis wird von Schmithals gar nicht eigentlich gestellt. 2) Nur Teile des NT enthalten Wunder. Andere Teile sind wunderfeindlich oder gleichgültig (cf. Traub und ähnliche Thesen der Formgeschichtlichen Schule!). "Paulus beispielweise. . .polemisiert" gegen Wunder und setzt ihnen "die Predigt des gekreuzigten Christus entgegen"./167/ Denn nach seiner Auffassung entspricht die Forderung nach Wundern "dem Streben nach Werken des Gesetzes"/168/ (cf. Bultmann!). Ähnliches gilt für das Heidenchristentum, Matthäus, Johannes, und das palästinische Judenchristentum. Sogar bei den Rabbinen sind die "Wunderrabbinen" "minderen Ranges" und "führen

ein Winkeldasein"./169/ Es bleibt offen, wie dann Wunder "eine gewöhnliche Erscheinung" gewesen sein sollen. Am Ende haben nur Markus und Lukas "ein unmittelbares Interesse an Wundergeschichten"; "hellenistisch -judenchristliche Kreise" also haben das Wunder ins NT hineingebracht./170/ 3) Wunder sind dem modernen Menschen nicht mehr zuzumuten. Die sind "für die moderne wissenschaftliche Denkweise überholt", "undenkbar", und "wir rechnen. . .nicht mehr. . .mit der Wirklichkeit von Wundern." "Die Einstellung zum Wunder wurde seit der Aufklärung geradezu zum Schibboleth der Weltbildfrage"./171/ Statt nach damaligen Ereignissen sollten wir nach dem fragen, "was heute durch diese Geschichten passiert"./172/ So trennen sich "Wahrheit" und "Wirklichkeit", Ereignis und Verkündigung (im Sinne Herrmanns und Bultmanns!). 4) Sollten wir da nicht überhaupt auf Wunder bzw. Wundergeschichten verzichten? Schmithals antwortet: "die Möglichkeit sollte ernsthaft erwogen werden"; das wäre "eine verantwortbare Entscheidung"./173/ Doch widerraten dieser Entscheidung pragmatische und pädagogische Überlegungen: a) die Wundergeschichten sind nun einmal da, b) das christliche Bewusstsein will sie nicht hergeben, c) Kinder können sie "unmittelbar. . .verstehen, da für sie existentielle Wahrheit und geschichtliche Wirklichkeit noch nicht auseinanderfallen."/174/

(3) Es ist reizvoll, dem Entwurf von W. Schmithals die Ausführungen von Reginald H. Fuller zu kontrastieren. Wie dessen Titel "Die Wunder Jesu in Exegese und Verkündigung" (dt. 1967) ausweist, geht es ja auch ihm um die praktische Bedeutung der Wunderexegese für das kirchliche Leben.

Für Fuller ist im Gegensatz zu Schmithals und anderen existentialen Interpreten die Frage: hat Jesus Wunder getan? berechtigt. Denn "schliesslich erhebt das Evangelium den Anspruch, dass Gott sein eschatologisches Heilshandeln im historischen Leben Jesu von Nazareth geoffenbart hat"./175/ Der christliche Offenbarungsgedanke erzwingt also die historische Frage. Zweitens fordert Fuller: Weg mit allen Apriorismen! "Es ist. . .ein unwissenschaftlicher Apriorismus, Wunder grundsätzlich auszuschliessen"./176/ Damit ist die Freiheit der Theologie vom naturwissenschaftlichen Kausalprinzip postuliert. Dann aber geht es bei der Wunderfrage allein "um eine historische Frage, die nur mit den Methoden historischer Kritik geprüft werden kann"./177/ Damit sind die Wunder wieder der Kompetenz des Historikers übergeben (die Parallele zu Richardson ist unübersehbar). In religionsgeschichtlicher Hinsicht spricht sich Fuller gegen die Meinung aus, "dass alle Wundergeschichten im hellenistischen Raum entstanden sind"./178/ Fuller argumentiert, das Schema solcher Wundergeschichten "könne" uns überall begegnen (cf. Richardson!) und die Sprache deute öfters auf das Aramäische. Was ergibt nun die historische Untersuchung? Zunächst, dass Jesus Exorzismen und Krankenheilungen bewirkt hat./179/ Sodann, dass Naturwunder höchstwahrscheinlich nicht historisch sind. Zwar zweifelt Fuller daran, ob man "Naturwunder" zu einer besonderen Gattung erheben darf./180/ Aber gegen ihre Historizität sprechen: "ihre theologische Symbolträchtigkeit, das Fehlen jeder Anspielung auf Naturwunder in Q und im übrigen Redenstoff. . . . Die Seltenheit der Naturwunder. . .sowie die Tatsache, dass nur die Jünger als Zeugen genannt werden"./181/ Fuller ist hier exegetisch leicht zu widerlegen: auch Heilungen sind "theologisch symbolträchtig"; die Seltenheit ist kein Argument, sonst wäre auch die Auferstehung unhistorisch; die Speisungen z. B. wurden auch von Nicht-Jüngern erlebt. Äussert sich dann bei Fuller doch ein weltanschauliches Vorurteil, wenn er ausgerechnet die sog. "Naturwunder" als wenig oder gar nicht historisch bewertet?/182/ --wie soll man, so fragt Fuller schliesslich, Wunder heute verkündigen? Er gibt dazu eine spannungsvolle Antwort. Einerseits will er die Faktizität nicht ausklammern: "schliesslich hat es keinen Sinn, von der Bedeutung der Wunder Jesu zu sprechen, wenn er niemals welche gewirkt hat!"/183/ Hierin grenzt er sich also von der existentialen u.a. Interpretationen ab. Doch zugleich betont er: "Hauptanliengen des Predigers und Katecheten muss. . .die Bedeutung des Wunders für uns. . .sein"./184/ Beispiel ist wieder (wie bei Wellhausen, Bultmann, Klein u.a.) Lk 5,1-11. Im Endergebnis dominiert also eine Tendenz zur Spiritualisierung, wie man sie ähnlich bei Grant, Richardson u.a. beobachten kann./185/

(4) In einer Vielzahl von Untersuchungen wird eine Reihe von Ausgangspunkten der existentialen Interpretation in Frage gestellt bzw. widerlegt und das Ringen um das Wunder, das im ersten Drittel des 20. Jh. vorwiegend *dogmatisch* geführt wurde, nun verstärkt *historisch* fortgesetzt.

Ein breiter Konsens zeichnet sich ab, dass Jesus tatsächlich "Wunder" getan hat, wie immer man das "Wunder" definiert. Nicht das ist das Neue, dass man Jesus überhaupt als Wundertäter sieht, sondern die Selbstverständlichkeit, mit der man jetzt Heilungen u. dgl. anerkennt./186/ Mit Recht wird davor gewarnt, "dass. . .die Analogien (sc. in der Religionsgeschichte) automatisch eine Faktizität fraglich werden lassen"./187/ Allerdings besteht Streit über den Umfang der Wunder Jesu. Handelt es sich nur um ein "Minimum" in Gestalt von

Krankenheilungen und Exorzismen?/188/ Oder um mehr?

Immer stärker zeigte sich auch, dass man im Neuen Testament nicht einfach mirakulöse und mirakelfeindliche Schichten voneinander trennen kann. Ausleger wie Schille, Theissen oder Kertelge beharren darauf, dass auch Paulus positiv vom Wunder reden konnte./189/ Für Johannes wies z. B. K. H. Rengstorf darauf hin, dass die Zeichen Jesu "auch der Begründung des Glaubens an Gott dienen" und das "Christussein Jesu" anziegen sollen./190/ Ja, es wird erneut und verstärkt eine Erkenntnis aufgegriffen, die wir z. B. bei Schlatter und Jelke fanden, dass nämlich die Wunderüberlieferung zu den ältesten Schichten des NT gehört. Das Wunder bildet demnach einen unablösbaren Bestandteil des Evangeliums./191/

Ist es aber auch so, dass die Evangelisten mit ihren Wunderberichten eine historische Intention verfolgten? Waren sie nicht nur kerygmatisch interessiert? Karl Kertelge stellte in seiner Untersuchung über "Die Wunder Jesu im Markusevangelium" 1970 fest: "Jesu Heilungstätigkeit ist für Markus fraglos geschichtliche Wirklichkeit"./192/ Theissen ging 1974 noch weiter. In seiner Abhandlung über "Urchristliche Wundergeschichten" konstatierte er, diese hätten "eine 'historische' Intention. Sie (= die Evangelisten) sind sich der Einzigartigkeit der erzählten Wunder bewusst"./193/

Dass es den Evangelisten um eine einzigartige und geschichtlich reale Wirklichkeit ging, wird noch von anderer Seite her unterstützt. Neuere Untersuchungen zeigen nämlich, dass die Vorstellung, hellenistischer Einfluss habe aus Jesus einen wundertätigen theios aner gemacht, korrigiert werden muss. Offensichtlich--so D. L. Tiede (1973)/194/--ist der theios aner kein "fixed concept in the Hellenistic world" gewesen. Ebensowenig ist eine Gleichsetzung von theios aner und Wundertäter erlaubt./195/ C. H. Holladay (1977) geht noch einen Schritt weiter. Er glaubt zeigen zu können, dass das Judentum gerade in hellenistischer Umwelt die thaumaturgischen Züge Moses und anderer "Heroen" eher heruntergespielt hat, und kommt für die Evangelien zu dem Schluss: "to account, therefore, for the presence of miracles and miracle traditions within the Gospels on the basis of a Hellenistic Sitz im Leben, particularly that of missionary preaching, as the earlier form critics did, seems to be a highly dubious exercise"./196/ Scheidet aber der "Hellenismus" als Quelle der evangelischen Wunderberichte aus, und werden die Wunder Jesu wieder in das jüdisch-palästinische Milieu zurückversetzt, dann ergibt sich daraus auch ein *indirektes* Argument *für* ein tatsächliches Geschehensein./197/

Nimmt man an, dass Jesu Wunder zum Sieg über Satan und Dämonen dienen (Kallas, 103ff), dass sie "Zeichen der anbrechenden Gottesherrschaft" (Kertelge, 201; Baltensweiler, 256) oder eine "Offenbarung des Heiligen" darstellen sollen, ja geradezu seine "Macht, das normale Weltgeschehen zu durchbrechen" (Theissen, 287),/198/ dann müssen die Evangelisten von ihrem Geschehensein, d.h. ihrer Faktizität und geschichtlichen Bedeutung, überzeugt gewesen sein.

Theissen wehrt sich gegen die "innere Relativierung des Wunders", die besagt: "die Wunder selbst seien nicht ihre Pointe"./199/ Nein, gerade von der darin offenbarwerdenden Macht Jesu will die Urchristenheit erzählen; "von seiner Macht" eben, "das normale Weltgeschehen zu durchbrechen--von nichts anderem"./200/ "Wer sich als Bibelleser etwas Unbefangenheit bewahrt hat, steht oft ratlos vor den Interpretationen 'moderner' Exegeten", die den Eindruck erwecken, "das Wunder sei des Glaubens illegitimes Kind, dessen Existenz man verlegen zu entschuldigen sucht", auf dessen Bestreitung oder Relativierung ("religionsgeschichtliche"--"redaktionsgeschichtliche"--"traditionsgeschichtliche"--"historische"--"innere") viel exegetische Mühe verwandt werde./201/

Freilich sucht Theissen eine Lösung auf einem religionssoziologischen Wege, der unser Vertrauen in die historische Glaubwürdigkeit der Wunder nicht gerade stärken kann.

Eine der festen Voraussetzungen der existentialen Interpreten war die des uns unverbrüchlich gegebenen modernen Weltbildes. Nun aber mehren sich die Stimmen, die vor jeder weltanschaulichen Bindung warnen. Der Schlüssel, mit dem man kausalgesetzlichem und sonstigem weltanschaulichen Denken entkommen will, heisst: "historische" Forschung. Eine dezidierte Feststellung trifft Rudolf Pesch in seinem Buch "Jesu ureigene Taten?" (1970): "weltanschauliche Vorentscheidungen darüber, was möglich sei, sind keine Kriterien historischen Urteils. . . . Die Frage nach der Historizität des in den Wundergeschichten Erzählten. . .muss historisch. . . beantwortet. . .werden"./202/ Alfred Suhl geht in diesselbe Richtung: "man darf nicht bestreiten, dass das Berichtete tatsächlich geschehen sei, nur weil man heute so etwas nicht für möglich hält"./203/ Unterstützung findet diese Tendenz durch Veröffentlichungen von naturwissenschaftlicher Seite, etwa von

Günter Ewald oder Mary Hesse. Sie legen Wert darauf, dass von einer lückenlosen Determiniertheit des Naturlebens nicht mehr die Rede sein kann. Deshalb ist es *nicht* die Naturwissenschaft, die über die Tatsächlichkeit der ntlichen Wunder zu entscheiden hat. Vielmehr sei die gesamte Frage, wie Ewald meint, "eine theologische Frage"./204/

Eine grundsätzliche Auseinandersetzung mit der "Kritik am Wunder" hat Erich Fascher schon 1960 in seinem gleichnamigen Buch zu führen versucht. Gegenüber Bultmanns Entmythologisierung bemerkte er: "es gibt Millionen von Menschen, die einer naturalistischen Weltansicht mit vollem Bewusstsein eine religiöse entgegensetzen"./205/ Der sog. "moderne Geschichtsbegriff", "ein modernes Natur- und Geschichtsverständnis" darf nicht "zum Richter über das Urchristentum und seine Geschichte gemacht werden"./206/ Ähnlich wie 1961 James Kallas erblickt Fascher darin eine Preisgabe des biblischen Gottesglaubens./207/ Leider gibt Fascher nur wenige Andeutungen von dem, was er sich stattdessen positiv vorstellt./208/ So bleibt eigentlich nur sein Protest gegen den modernen Geschichts- und Naturbegriff übrig.

Wie wir gesehen haben, ist der Prüfstein für eine neue weltanschauliche Freiheit die Behandlung der sog. "Naturwunder". Vermutlich hat Bruce Marshall deshalb die Versetzung eines Tanzpalastes auf einen Felsen als Exempel für ein Wunder gewählt. Es war ein wesentlicher Beitrag, dass C. F. D. Moule 1965 klarstellte, dass sich das "Naturwunder" eigentlich nicht klassifizieren lässt./209/ Die Konsequenz daraus müsste sein, dass sog. Naturwunder nicht anders behandelt werden als die übrigen Wunder. Eigenartigerweise ist das aber nicht der Fall. Greifen wir als Beispiel noch einmal Rudolf Pesch heraus. Er war es ja, der die Zuständigkeit des Historikers betont hatte. Wir sind erstaunt, dass er über das zugestandene "Minimum" hinaus, nämlich über Jesu Heilungen hinaus, eine "besonders kritisches Prüfung" der Wunder verlangt./210/ Warum? a) Totenerweckungen und "Naturwunder" seien "nicht durch Jesu Wort gedeckt"; das kann er nur sagen, weil für ihn Mt 11,2ff par ein "sekundäres Wort" darstellt./211/ b) Zudem seien "die bezeichneten Wundergeschichten (sc. Totenerweckungen und Naturwunder) selbst nicht dazu angetan, Vertrauen zu wecken". /212/ Weshalb nicht? Ist da nicht doch eine weltanschauliche Vorentscheidung im Spiel? c) Der "offen zutage liegende Einfluss alttestamentlicher Texte und Motivbilder", die "sekundären" Orts- und Personennamen und die "kerygmatische Prägung fast aller Einzelzüge" dieser Wundergeschichten deuteten ebenfalls auf "sekundäre", d.h. letzlich unhistorische Überlieferung./213/ Im Ergebnis bleibt also das sog. "Naturwunder" weiterhin unter dem Verdacht, unhistorisch zu sein./214/

(5) Werfen wir noch kurz einen Blick auf phänomenologische Untersuchungen. In seinen "Traditionen über Apollonius von Tyana und das Neue Testament" machte G. Petzke 1970 den Versuch, an Philostrats Vita Apollonii dieselbe "historisch-kritische Methode" anzulegen wie an das Neue Testament./215/ Ausserdem wollte er "bewusst" "im Bereich des Phänomenologischen" bleiben. /216/ Wie 40 Jahre vorher H. Schlingensiepen machte er darauf aufmerksam, dass man schon zu Eusebs Zeiten die Sonde der "Wissenschaftlichkeit" benutzte, um angebliche Wunder zu bejahen oder zu verneinen./217/ Solche Beobachtungen widerraten der pauschalen Annahme früherer Wundergläubigkeit. Im Ergebnis anerkennt Petzke bei Apollonius wie bei Jesus die Möglichkeit von Wundern, vor allem gewisse "magische Fähigkeiten"./218/ Die historisch-kritisch angewandte Phänomenologie führt also im Grundsätzlichen zu keinen anderen Ergebnissen als die aufs NT beschränkte, historisch-kritische Wunderexegese.

(6) Auffallenderweise wird in der Diskussion--sehen wir richtig--dem Problem des vaticinium ex eventu weniger Aufmerksamkeit geschenkt, als es verdient. Zwar wird das vaticinium ex eventu mit grosser Selbstverständlichkeit gehandhabt und z. B. bis in neueste Zeit als Datierungsmerkmal angewandt./219/ Aber dies geschieht in der Regel ohne grundsätzliche Erörterungen--obwohl man bei einem wundervollbringenden Jesus ja auch die Gabe des vaticinium voraussetzen sollte.

(7) Der letzte Blick in diesem Zusammenhang gilt C. S. Lewis/220/ Lewis stellt uns mit Entschiedenheit vor die grundsätzliche Alternative: "muss die philosophische Frage zuerst kommen" oder müssen wir zuerst "nach den üblichen Regeln historischer Untersuchung" vorgehen?/221/ Mit anderen Worten: ist für die Wunderfrage in erster Linie der Philosoph (Dogmatiker) zuständig oder der Historiker? Lewis meint das erstere. Denn Erfahrung und Glaube sind zweierlei: "sehen ist nicht glauben. Darum kann die Frage, ob Wunder geschehen, niemals einfach durch Erfahrung beantwortet werden"./222/ Wir erinnern uns an Harnacks Ausspruch, dass wir selbst dann nicht an ein "Wunder" glauben würden, wenn wir dessen Augenzeugen wären. "Was wir aus der Erfahrung lernen, hängt von der Philosophie ab"./223/ Deshalb muss zuerst die Philosophie entscheiden, ob und inwieweit Wunder möglich sind. Dann erst

können wir zum historischen Handwerkzeug greifen und uns vom historischen "Beweismaterial" überzeugen lassen.

VIII. Folgerungen

(1) Überblickt man die ntliche Wunderexegese im 19. und 20. Jh., so zeigt sich eine generelle Verschiebung vom Dogmatisch-Philosophischen zum Historischen. Die Forderung nach *historischer* Forschung nimmt geradezu den Charakter einer Befreiungsbewegung an, die sich aus den Fesseln weltanschaulicher Prämissen lösen will. In diesem Zusammenhang stellt die Bultmann'sche Schule mit ihrer Weltbild-Verhaftung eher ein retardierendes Element dar.

(2) Die Vorstellung, dass ein lückenloser Naturzusammenhang die Annahme eines Wunders im Sinne eines miraculum verbiete, ist mehr und mehr fragwürdig geworden. Auch und gerade Naturwissenschaftler weisen darauf hin, dass von einem geschlossenen Weltbild oder einer durchgängigen Determiniertheit des Geschehens keine Rede mehr sein kann. Naturwissenschaftliche, weltbildhafte Kriterien sollten also dort ausscheiden, wo es um die Möglichkeit und Wirklichkeit des Wunders geht.

(3) Als nicht weniger fragwürdig erweist sich heute der Ansatz beim religiösen Erlebnis. Gerade der historischen Forschung enthüllt sich, dass die Eigenart der biblischen Wundergeschichten eine Aufspaltung in miraculum und mirabile nicht zulässt. Im NT liegt beides ineinander: das miraculum und das mirabile. Das NT wehrt sich gegen eine Trennung von Wahrheit und Wirklichkeit, von Ergebnis und Deutung. Wunder sind auffallende Ereignisse, die in der immanenten Welt in Erscheinung treten, aber in der Regel des deutenden Wortes bedürfen.

(4) In der Historizitätsfrage sind erhebliche Fortschritte erzielt worden. Dass Jesus Wunder tat, steht heute den meisten fest. Ebenso, dass sie mit seinen Worten einen unlösbaren Zusammenhang bilden, Teil seines "Christusseins" sind. Eine Reihe von Einwänden gegen die Historizität ist erschüttert: so, dass religionsgeschichtliche Parallelen die Historizität der ntlichen Wunder aufhöben; oder dass Jesus bzw. die ältesten Traditionen auf Wunder keinen Wert legten; oder dass das Neue Testament lediglich an der kerygmatischen Bedeutung der Wundergeschichten interessiert sei; oder dass in der Antike ausnahmslos eine unkritische Wundergläubigkeit geherrscht habe. Natürlich müssen wir offen

hinzufügen, dass die genannten Punkte nach wie vor umstritten sind.

(5) Einen Problemfall stellt das sog. "Naturwunder" dar. Fast alle Exegeten, die wir bei unserer Übersicht berücksichtigt haben, lehnen Naturwunder ab. Und dies trotz der wachsenden Unsicherheit, ob es überhaupt eine besondere formgeschichtliche Klasse der "Naturwunder" geben kann. Dass weltanschauliche Motive und Prämissen die Wunderexegese in besonderem Masse beeinflussen, wird hier noch einmal deutlich.

(6) Insgesamt lässt sich als Ergebnis festhalten: historische Forschung kann heute mit guten Gründen sagen, dass Jesus damals Wunder getan hat. Es gehört zu den bemerkenswertesten Entwicklungen, dass eine grosse Zahl historisch forschender Exegeten von der Skepsis zu einer vorsichtigen oder zuversichtlichen Bejahung seiner Wunder fortgeschritten ist.

Anmerkungen

/1/ K. Bornkamm, *Wunder und Zeugnis* (Tübingen: Mohr, 1968) 5.
/2/ G. Klein, *Wunderglaube und Neues Testament* (Wuppertal-Barmen: Jugenddienst, 1960) 5.
/3/ H. Schlingensiepen, *Die Wunder des Neuen Testaments* (Gütersloh: Bertelsmann, 1933) 33. Cf. dort insbesondere 47, 76-77.
/4/ So Euseb in der Auseinandersetzung mit Philostrat bezüglich der Wunder des Apollonius. Cf. G. Petzke, *Die Traditionen über Apollonius von Tyana und das Neue Testament* (Leiden: Brill, 1970) 7.
/5/ Schlingensiepen, *Wunder*, 220.
/6/ Cf. neben Schlingensiepen a.a.O. auch Bornkamm, *Wunder*, 29-30; R. H. Fuller, *Die Wunder Jesu in Exegese und Verkündigung* (Düsseldorf: Patmos, 1967) 19--Eng. or. *Interpreting the Miracles* (London: SCM, 1963); E. u. M.-L. Keller, *Der Streit um die Wunder* (Gütersloh: Gerd Mohn, 1968) 18--ET *Miracles in Dispute* (London: SCM, 1969); A. Richardson, *The Miracle-Stories of the Gospels* (London: SCM, 1948) 20.
/7/ B. Marshall, *Das Wunder des Malachias* (Köln: Hegner, 1951) 55.
/8/ Cf. zu diesem Teil meiner Darstellung den Artikel von W. L. Craig in diesem Band.
/9/ Dabei kann man die Frage stellen, ob nicht der Rationalismus der Moderne eine Art Renaissance philosophischer Strömungen der griechisch-römischen Welt darstellte. Cf. A. E.

Harvey, *Jesus and the Constraints of History* (London: Duckworth, 1982) 101ff. Den Hinweis verdanke ich E. E. Ellis.
/10/ Zitiert noch Keller, *Streit*, 40.
/11/ A.a.O.
/12/ A.a.O., 42.
/13/ A.a.O., 42ff.
/14/ A.a.O., 65.
/15/ A.a.O., 67.
/16/ Cf. J. S. Semlers *Abhandlung von freier Untersuchung des Canon usw.* (1771) I, 87, 115-16; F. A. Stroths *Freymüthige Untersuchungen usw.* (1771) 238-9; H. Corrodis *Kritische Geschichte des Chiliasmus* (1781) I, xviii, vii; II, 445; III, xi, xiii, 218.
/17/ Zitiert nach Keller, *Streit*, 68. Cf. noch einmal Humphrey Hamilton bei Marshall, *Wunder*, 55.
/18/ Bornkamm, *Wunder*, 32-33. Über die haarsträubende Erklärung des Seewandels Jesu bei Bahrdt cf. Keller, *Streit*, 62.
/19/ A.a.O., 66.
/20/ A.a.O., 59.
/21/ Fuller, *Wunder*, 19. In der Sache ähnlich E. Fascher, *Kritik am Wunder* (Stuttgart: Calwer, 1960) 9.
/22/ So Cotta (1787). Cf. Petzke, *Apollonius*, 11-12, der ausserdem Legrand d'Aussy erwähnt.
/23/ O. Kirn, in F. Schleiermacher, *RE* 17 (1906) 589.
/24/ Cf. A.a.O., Sp. 593ff.
/25/ Fascher, *Kritik*, 26.
/26/ Cf. hierzu G. Marquardt, *Das Wunderproblem in der deutschen protestantischen Theologie der Gegenwart* (München: Hueber, 1933) 48.
/27/ Cf. C. E. Luthardt, *Kompendium der Dogmatik* (Leipzig: Dörffling und Franke, 1886) 135ff.
/28/ Cf. Kümmel, 147 und Anm. 157 (Th. Ziegler bzw. St. Neill) sowie Keller, *Streit*, 86ff.
/29/ D. F. Strauss, *Das Leben Jesu, kritisch bearbeitet*, 2 Bde. (Tübingen: Osiander, 1835-36) I, iii bzw. iv--ET *The Life of Jesus Critically Examined* (London: SCM, 1973).
/30/ A.a.O. II, 14-15.
/31/ A.a.O. II, 177.
/32/ A.a.O. II, 181.
/33/ A.a.O. II, 1ff.
/34/ A.a.O. II, 50.
/35/ A.a.O. II, 250-1.
/36/ A.a.O. II, 215ff.
/37/ Cf. a.a.O., ix, 173, 215.
/38/ E. Hirsch, *Geschichte der neuern evangelischen Theologie*, V (Gütersloh: Gerd Mohn, 1975) 518.

/39/ A.a.O., 520.
/40/ F. C. Baur, *Das Christentum und die christliche Kirche der ersten drei Jahrhunderte* (Tübingen: Fues, 1860) viii.
/41/ *An Herrn Dr. Karl Hase usw.* (Tübingen: Fues, 1855) 20-21.
/42/ A.a.O., 22. Vgl. J. Wendland, *Der Wunderglaube im Christentum* (Göttingen: Vandenhoeck und Ruprecht, 1910) 101ff. und meine Untersuchung *Die Johannesoffenbarung und die Kirche* (Tübingen: Mohr, 1981) 480-1.
/43/ Cf. Marquardt, *Wunderproblem*, 71ff.
/44/ Zitiert nach a.a.O., 73.
/45/ Zitierung nach a.a.O.
/46/ Cf. Fuller, *Wunder*, 19; Fascher, *Kritik*, 10.
/47/ Cf. Marquardt, *Wunderproblem*, 75-76.
/48/ Cf. aber auch R. M. Grant, *Miracle and Natural Law in Graeco-Roman and Early Christian Thought* (Amsterdam: North Holland, 1952) 168. Siehe Fuller, *Wunder*, und Marquardt, a.a.O.
/49/ P. Fiebig, *Jüdische Wundergeschichten des neutestamentlichen Zeitalters* (Tübingen: Mohr, 1911) 72.
/50/ A.a.O. Cf. H. Baltensweiler, "Wunder und Glaube im Neuen Testament," *TZ* 23 (1967) 244; Keller, *Streit*, 113.
/51/ Fiebig, *Wundergeschichten*, 74; Baltensweiler, "Wunder," 245.
/52/ R. Reitzenstein, *Hellenistische Wundererzählungen* (Leipzig: Tuebner, 1906) 35.
/53/ Gunkel nach W. G. Kümmel, *Das Neue Testament, Geschichte der Erforschung seiner Probleme* (München: Karl Alber, 1970) 326-27--ET *The New Testament: The History of the Investigation of Its Problems* (London: SCM, 1973); Pfleiderer nach a.a.O., 265-66.
/54/ R. Bultmann, *Die Geschichte der synoptischen Tradition* (Göttingen: Vandenhoeck und Ruprecht, 1964) 246--ET *The History of the Synoptic Tradition* (Oxford: Blackwell, 1968).
/55/ Fiebig, *Wundergeschichten*, 91.
/56/ A.a.O., 87, 91.
/57/ A.a.O.
/58/ A.a.O., 94, 97.
/59/ A.a.O., 97-98.
/60/ A.a.O., 98.
/61/ G. Traub, *Die Wunder im Neuen Testament* (Halle: Gebauer-Schwetschke, 1905) 1.
/62/ A.a.O., 7, 24.
/63/ A.a.O., 70.
/64/ A.a.O., 11ff.
/65/ A.a.O., 22.
/66/ Cf. W. Bousset, "Die Religionsgeschichte und das neue Testament," *ThRu* 7 (1904) 311; H. Gunkel, *Zum religionsgeschichtlichen Verständnis des Neuen Testaments* (1903) dazu Kümmel, *Neue Testament*, 326-27.

/67/ Praktisch geht es nur um die Synoptiker. Traub nimmt "ein wissenschaftliches Recht" in Anspruch, "die johanneische Berichte auf die Seite zu schieben" (*Wunder*, 33).
/68/ A.a.O., 23, 25-26.
/69/ A.a.O., 24.
/70/ A.a.O., 41, 35, 25.
/71/ Zu dieser Gliederung, angeblich "nach sachlichen Gesichtspunkten", cf. a.a.O., 33.
/72/ A.a.O., 61.
/73/ A.a.O., 63-64.
/74/ A.a.O., 26ff.
/75/ A.a.O., 10 bzw. 72.
/76/ P. Stuhlmacher, *Vom Verstehen des Neuen Testaments, Eine Hermeneutik* (Göttingen: Vandenhoeck und Ruprecht, 1979) 22.
/77/ Zitate nach Marquardt, *Wunderproblem*, 32-33.
/78/ Interessant ist, dass W. Bousset ganz ähnliche Gedankengänge aufweist, cf. a.a.O., 38-39.
/79/ Cf. hier Fuller, *Wunder*, 19ff.
/80/ Bultmann, *Geschichte*, 233-34, 241.
/81/ A.a.O., 243.
/82/ A.a.O., 246
/83/ A.a.O., 256.
/84/ A.a.O., 254-55.
/85/ A.a.O., 256.
/86/ A.a.O., 244 (eine teilweise anders begründete Skepsis bei A. Fridrichsen, *Le problème du miracle dans le christianisme primitif* (Strasbourg/Paris: Istra, 1925) 10-11--ET *The Problem of Miracle in Primitive Christianity* (Minneapolis: Augsburg, 1972).
/87/ A.a.O., 244; cf. Keller, *Streit*, 131-32; O. Betz und W. Grimm, *Wesen und Wirklichkeit der Wunder Jesu* (Frankfurt/Bern/Las Vegas: Peter Lang, 1977) 26-27.
/88/ In Bultmanns berühmten Entmythologisierungsaufsatz von 1941 ist sie wieder da.
/89/ Cf. insbesondere Fridrichsen, *Miracle*, 10-11.
/90/ Cf. Keller, *Streit*, 160.
/91/ Bornkamm, *Wunder*, 33.
/92/ Cf. nur R. Bultmann, "Das Problem der Hermeneutik," in *Glauben und Verstehen*, II (Tübingen: Mohr, 1958) 232ff.--ET *Faith and Understanding*, ed. R. W. Funk (London: SCM, 1969) aber nicht dieser Band.
/93/ Zitiert nach Marquardt, *Wunderproblem*, 50-51.
/94/ Cf. den Streit über atheistische Methoden in der Theologie zwischen Jäger und Schlatter in *Beiträge zur Förderung christlicher Theologie* 9, 4 (1905).

/95/ Cf. überhaupt Marquardt, *Wunderproblem*, 50ff, speziell, 55.
/96/ Wendland, *Wunderglaube*, 51.
/97/ A.a.O., 54.
/98/ A.a.O., 77.
/99/ A.a.O., 77, 91ff., 101ff.
/100/ Cf. a.a.O., v , 105ff.
/101/ A.a.O., v.
/102/ Allerdings ist Marquardts Kritik an Wendland (*Wunderproblem*, 88ff.) zu hart.
/103/ Wendland, *Wunderglaube*, 7.
/104/ A.a.O.
/105/ A.a.O., vi.
/106/ A.a.O., 6.
/107/ Cf. Marquardt, *Wunderproblem*, 88ff.; Schlingensiepen, *Wunder*, 151ff.
/108/ Wendland, *Wunderglaube*, 105.
/109/ A.a.O., 107-8.
/110/ A.a.O., 109.
/111/ A.a.O., 111.
/112/ Zitiert nach Marquardt, *Wunderproblem*, 266.
/113/ A.a.O., 265.
/114/ Wieder nach a.a.O., 264. Für P. Feine, cf. a.a.O., 263.
/115/ Zitiert nach a.a.O., 247.
/116/ A.a.O.
/117/ A.a.O.
/118/ A.a.O., 255-56.
/119/ A.a.O., 322, cf. 271.
/120/ A.a.O., 273-74.
/121/ A.a.O.
/122/ A. Schlatter, *Die Geschichte des Christus* (Stuttgart: Calwer, 1923) 224-25.
/123/ A.a.O., 249.
/124/ A.a.O., 226 mit Fussnote 3.
/125/ A.a.O., 229 mit Fussnote 1.
/126/ A.a.O.
/127/ Cf. die Kritik Marquardts, *Wunderproblem*, 276.
/128/ R. Jelke, *Die Wunder Jesu* (Leipzig/Erlangen: A. Deichert, 1922) 21.
/129/ A.a.O., 23-24.
/130/ A.a.O., 33.
/131/ A.a.O., 29.
/132/ A.a.O., 44, 70.
/133/ A.a.O., 74.
/134/ A.a.O., 83.
/135/ In *Die neue Welt Gottes* (Berlin: Furche, 1929) 13ff.
/136/ A.a.O., 28.

/137/ A.a.O., 28-31. Teilweise parallele Gedanken entdecken wir bei Betz-Grimm, *Wesen und Wirklichkeit*, 29, 152.
/138/ Richardson, *Miracle-Stories*, 21.
/139/ A.a.O., 22ff.
/140/ Cf. Bultmann, *Geschichte*, 244.
/141/ Richardson, *Miracle-Stories*, 26.
/142/ A.a.O., 28. Bei der Anwendung von Dr. Browns Serum bei Heufieber würde ebenso erzählt!
/143/ A.a.O., 36.
/144/ A.a.O., 126.
/145/ A.a.O., 38ff.
/146/ A.a.O. 126.
/147/ A.a.O. 90.
/148/ Deren Einheit (Mt, Mk, Lk und Joh !) Richardson darzulegen versucht (a.a.O., 109ff.).
/149/ A.a.O., 126-28.
/150/ A.a.O., 135.
/151/ A. Ficarra, *Miracoli e miracolati nelle Sacre Scritture* (Milano: Sugar, 1972) 101. Auf 168 erklärt er z. B. Mk 5,1-20 parr für "pura fantasia".
/152/ J. Kallas, *The Significance of the Synoptic Miracles* (London: SPCK, 1961) 115.
/153/ Cf. R. Bultmann, "Zur Frage des Wunders," in *Glauben und Verstehen*, I (Tübingen: Mohr, 1958) 215--ET "The Question of Wonder," in *Faith and Understanding*, 247-61.
/154/ A.a.O., 214.
/155/ A.a.O., 221, 227.
/156/ A.a.O., 221.
/157/ R. Bultmann, "Neues Testament und Mythologie," in *Kerygma und Mythos*, I, ed. H.-W. Bartsch (Hamburg-Volksdorf: Herbert Reich, 1951) 18--ET "New Testament and Mythology," in *Kerygma and Myth* (London: SPCK, 1953) 1-44.
/158/ R. Bultmann, "Das Problem der Hermeneutik," in *Glauben und Verstehen*, II, 232. Der ganze Aufsatz (zuerst 1950 in der *ZTK* 47-69, erschienen) ist grundlegend für die sog. existentiale Interpretation. Zur Kritik cf. B. Schilling, "Die Frage nach der Entstehung der synoptischen Wundergeschichten in der deutschen neutestamentlichen Forschung," *SvExAr* 35 (1971) 66ff.
/159/ Cf. beispielsweise P. L. Berger, *A Rumor of Angels* (Garden City: Doubleday, 1969) *passim*; idem, *The Heretical Imperative* (Garden City: Doubleday, 1979) 101ff.
/160/ Bornkamm, *Wunder*, 5, 34; cf. Keller, *Streit*, 67; Klein, *Wunderglaube*, 6.
/161/ Bornkamm, *Wunder*, 31; Keller, *Streit*, 72; Klein, *Wunderglaube*, 5-6.
/162/ Bornkamm, *Wunder*, 31, 34.

/163/ A.a.O., 36, cf. 43; Keller, *Streit*, 160; Klein, *Wunderglaube*, 11.
/164/ Bornkamm, *Wunder*, 36, 43-44; cf. Klein, *Wunderglaube*, 18.
/165/ C. F. D. Moule, ed. *Miracles* (London: Mowbray, 1965) 13.
/166/ W. Schmithals, *Wunder und Glaube* (Neukirchen-Vluyn: Neukirchener Verlag, 1970) 9, 16 (cf. Klein, *Wunderglaube*, 12).
/167/ A.a.O., 16 (cf. Klein, *Wunderglaube*, 14ff.).
/168/ A.a.O., 17.
/169/ A.a.O., 18.
/170/ A.a.O., 20 (cf. Klein, *Wunderglaube*, 32.)
/171/ A.a.O., 26-27.
/172/ A.a.O., 28.
/173/ A.a.O., 29-30.
/174/ A.a.O., 30.
/175/ Fuller, *Wunder*, 25.
/176/ A.a.O., 26-27.
/177/ A.a.O., 27.
/178/ A.a.O., 41.
/179/ A.a.O., 38: dies "könnte kaum besser bezeugt sein".
/180/ A.a.O., 44: "keinem Evangelisten wäre es in den Sinn gekommen, die 'Naturwunder' in eine besondere Klasse einzureihen" (cf. auch Moule, *Miracles*, 240).
/181/ A.a.O., 45-46.
/182/ Auch Grant, *Miracle*, 168 u.a. führen ja immer wieder solche Unterscheidungen durch. Fullers Einwände gegen die "Fundamentalisten", 128 (*Wunder*, 128) lassen das Vorurteil durchscheinen.
/183/ A.a.O., 121.
/184/ A.a.O.
/185/ R. M. Grant, *The Problem of Miraculous Feedings in the Graeco-Roman World* (Berkeley: Center for Hermeneutical Studies in Hellenistic and Modern Culture, 1982) 15.
/186/ Cf. Baltensweiler, "Wunder," 256; Kallas, *Miracles*, 103ff.; R. Pesch, *Jesu ureigene Taten* (Freiburg/Basel/Wien: Herder, 1970) 17; G. Schille, *Die urchristliche Wundertradition* (Stuttgart: Calwer, 1967) 54; A. Suhl, *Die Wunder Jesu* (Gütersloh: Gerd Mohn, 1968) 42; G. Theissen, *Urchristliche Wundergeschichten* (Gütersloh: Gerd Mohn, 1974) 248, 274--ET *The Miracle Stories of the Early Christian Tradition* (Edinburgh: T & T Clark, 1983); D. L. Tiede, *The Charismatic Figure as Miracle Worker* (Missoula: SBL, 1973) 266ff.
/187/ Baltensweiler, "Wunder," 245.
/188/ Cf. Pesch, *Jesu*, 17 unter Verweis auf W. Trilling und R. Bultmann.
/189/ Cf. Röm 15,18f; 1 Kor 12,9f.29; 2 Kor 12,12; Apg 16,13ff; 13,6ff; 14,7ff; 16,16ff; 20,7ff; 28,2ff und Schille,

Wundertradition, 15ff.; Theissen, *Wundergeschichten*, 291; K. Kertelge, *Die Wunder Jesu im Markusevangelium* (München: Kösel, 1970) 209.
/190/ K. H. Rengstorf, "σημεῖον," in *ThWNT* VII (1964) 249, 251--ET in *TDNT* VII, 200-69; anders z. B. Tiede, *Charismatic Figure*, 283; Schille, *Wundertradition*, 20.
/191/ Cf. Fascher, *Kritik*, 11; Kallas, *Miracles*, 1ff.; Suhl, *Wunder*, 31; Betz-Grimm, *Wesen und Wirklichkeit*, 26ff.; Schilling, "Entstehung," 62ff.; anders noch Schille, *Wundertradition*, 18ff.; D.-A. Koch, *Die Bedeutung der Wundererzählungen für die Christologie des Markusevangeliums* (Berlin/New York: de Gruyter, 1975) 2ff.
/192/ Kertelge, *Wunder*, 37; cf. a.a.O., 53; anders Suhl, *Wunder*, 51, 54.
/193/ Theissen, *Wundergeschichten*, 273.
/194/ Tiede, *Charismatic Figure*, 289; cf. C. H. Holladay, *Theios Aner in Hellenistic Judaism* (Missoula: SBL, 1977) 237ff.; H. C. Kee, *Miracle in the Early Christian World* (New Haven/London: Yale, 1983) 297ff.
/195/ Cf. Holladay, *Theios Aner*, 236-37, 238-39, 241.
/196/ A.a.O., 239.
/197/ Cf. hier das letzte Kapitel von C. Brown, *Miracles and the Critical Mind* (Grand Rapids: Eerdmans, 1984).
/198/ Cf. Kee, *Miracle*, 156ff. und J. D. Kingsbury, *The Christology of Mark's Gospel* (Philadelphia: Fortress, 1983) 25ff der sich mit der "korrektiven Christologie" auseinandersetzt.
/199/ Theissen, *Wundergeschichten*, 293.
/200/ A.a.O., 287.
/201/ A.a.O., 294-95, 287.
/202/ Pesch, *Jesu*, 142.
/203/ Suhl, *Wunder*, 7; cf. 48.
/204/ G. Ewald, B. Klappert, H. Demmer, *Das Ungewöhnliche* (Wuppertal-Aussaat-Verlag, 1969) 8, cf. 10ff.; Hesse bei Moule, *Miracles*, 33ff.; Klappert bei Ewald *et al.*, *Ungewöhnliche*, 29; Betz-Grimm, *Wesen und Wirklichkeit*, 28.
/205/ Fascher, *Kritik*, 8.
/206/ A.a.O., 18.
/207/ A.a.O.; cf. Kallas, *Miracles*, 112-13.
/208/ Fascher, *Kritik*, 42, z. B. sagt er: "das Wunder schlechthin ist die von Gott geschaffene Welt". Aber was bedeutet dies?
/209/ Moule, *Miracles*, 240. Dasselbe später z. B. bei Betz-Grimm, *Wesen und Wirklichkeit*, 29.
/210/ Pesch, *Jesu*, 141.
/211/ Cf. a.a.O. mit 44 sowie Suhl, *Wunder*, 51-52.
/212/ Pesch, *Jesu*, 141.

/213/ A.a.O., 141-42.
/214/ Cf. hierzu auch Suhl, *Wunder*, 47ff.; Klein, *Wunderglaube*, 28.
/215/ Petzke, *Apollonius*, ix.
/216/ A.a.O., 231.
/217/ Cf. a.a.O., 7 mit Schlingensiepen, *Wunder*, 47, 76ff., 104ff., 112; sowie Kee, *Miracle*, 265ff.
/218/ Petzke, *Apollonius*, 157, 233.
/219/ Cf. M. Hengel in *Markus-Philologie*, ed. H. Cancik (Tübingen: Mohr, 1984) 21-22 und Fussnote 86.
/220/ Cf. wieder den Artikel von W. L. Craig in diesem Band.
/221/ C. S. Lewis, *Wunder* (Köln/Olten: Hegner, 1952) 13-14--Eng. or. *Miracles* (London: Geoffrey Bles, 1947).
/222/ A.a.O., 13.
/223/ A.a.O.

MAGIC OR MIRACLE?
DISEASES, DEMONS AND EXORCISMS*

Edwin Yamauchi
History Department
Miami University
Oxford, OH 45056
U.S.A.

I. Introduction
A. Perspectives on Magic and Jesus' Miracles

1. Christian Perspectives

During the early history of the church Christians regarded God's supernatural intervention through Jesus and His followers in healings and exorcisms as miracles. Rival claims of wonders by pagans were dismissed as 'magic', a word which was consistently used by Christian writers as a pejorative term./1/ In opposition to writers like Celsus, who accused Jesus of magic, Origen responded that Jesus unlike sorcerers called his followers to lives of moral transformation./2/ According to Eusebius sorcery was incompatible with Christ's moral character./3/

Other church fathers stressed the idea that Christ performed his miracles without the usual magical materials. According to Arnobius (*Adv. Nat*. I.44): 'But it is agreed that Christ did all He did without any paraphernalia, without the observance of any ritual or formula but only through the power of His name, and as was proper, becoming, and worthy of a true god'./4/ Similarly Lactantius (*Divin. Inst.* iv.15.9) asserted: 'And He performed all these things not by His hands, or the application of any remedy, but by His word and command'.

In like manner contemporary Christian apologists still stress the moral dimensions of Christ's miracles. According to Norman Geisler: 'Unlike miracles, magic as such is amoral. It does not bring glory to God (it really brings honor to the magician), and there are usually no divine truth claims connected with it./5/ Moule asks, 'Why do we universally refuse to believe in the miracles in the Infancy Narratives of Thomas?' and answers, 'Surely because they are all out of character with a Jesus who, as we have reason on other ground to believe, took seriously the meaning of "sonship"...'./6/

In his massive study on the subject of miracles, H. van der Loos declares that: '...in the lowest forms of religion magic and miracles cannot be separated, but that at the level of religion with a God-given law the miracles which the godhead performs either directly or through the agency of specially designated persons must be distinguished from magic as a profane art. Magic uses the underworld, demons. Magic is always a kind of art, it is the Ars magica'./7/

2. Pagan Perspectives

Even among the pagan classical writers magic, which was associated with the Persian magi, was held in low repute./8/ The Hippocratic work, 'On the Sacred Disease', denounced magic as opposed to religion. Plato (*Laws* 933a-c) condemned magic tricks, incantations, and binding spells. Pliny the Elder regarded magic as detestable, vain and idle. Apuleius defended himself against the charge of magic.

When Celsus therefore described Jesus as a magician, he was impugning his moral character as a charlatan. According to Gallagher: 'Thus, the accusation that someone believed in or practised magic was scarcely the result of a dispassionate perception of the magicians, such accusations were most often the vehicles for social, moral, and intellectual invective'./9/ In Alan Segal's analysis, 'The early charge of magic against Jesus is not so much clear proof that Jesus was a magician as a clear example of the social manipulation of the charge of magic'./10/

3. Jewish Perspectives

According to the Gospels Jesus was accused by his Jewish contemporaries of many things, but never explicitly called a 'magician'./11/ A later Tannaitic tradition preserved in the Talmud (b. Sanh. 43a) attributes Jesus' miracles to magic: 'He is going forth to be stoned because he has practised sorcery and enticed Israel to apostasy'./12/ Other references include Tos. Hulin 2.22f., which speaks about an attempt to heal a snake bite in the name of Yeshua ben Pantera, i.e. Jesus the illegitimate son of the soldier Pantera and Mary.

The accusation that Jesus was a sorcerer was elaborated in the slanderous medieval work, the *Toledoth Jeshu*, which dates as a whole from the ninth century. A recently published manuscript of this genre speaks of Jesus' healing as the result of magic: 'Then he whispered an incantation over this lame man, with only his lips moving while his voice was not heard'./13/

4. Social Science Perspectives

The social sciences--anthropology, psychology, and sociology--have contributed numerous studies analyzing such phenomena as magic, possession, and healing and have provided insights which have at times been applied to the biblical texts. Since the pioneering anthropological comparisons of Sir James Frazer's classic, *The Golden Bough*, parallels--which are not always congruous--have been drawn between biblical phenomena and observations made among primitive tribes./14/ Anthropological surveys indicate that 'possession' is a wide-spread phenomenon:

> Spirit possession, in one form or another, is reported throughout the world. Bourguignon (1973) has found that in a sample of 488 societies in all parts of the world, 437 (90%) are reported to have one or more institutionalized, culturally patterned forms of altered states of consciousnes; 251 (52%) of these societies associate such experiences with spirit possession./15/

Some psychologists have suggested that the possessed seek to escape from conflict by the projecting of guilt upon the intruding spirit./16/ Other psychologists have studied the psychosomatic aspects of the healing process./17/ A major sociological study of magic concludes: 'Magic is the expropriation of religious collective representations for individual or subgroup purposes--to enable the individual ego to resist psychic extinction or the sub-group to resist cognitive collapse'./18/

On the basis of such analyses Hollenbach declares: 'the question of the miraculous need no longer be a serious issue because the phenomena of possession and exorcism are now examined and understood via the social sciences as common world-wide phenomena throughout most of history'./19/ One might even suggest that such sociological applications are now the vogue in biblical studies.

There are, however, inherent limitations in the sociological enterprise, at least as practiced in the functionalist/structuralist mode which reduces phenomena to social relationships and recurring patterns./20/ Segal points out these deficiencies:

> As for the definitional problems in the study of magic, this survey has tried to show that functionalist definitions (and to some degree certain structuralists as well) have brushed over several crucial factors 'internal' to the situation. These approaches tend to produce definitions of concepts for analytical use but they often miss the subtleties and dramatic presentiment of the term in the situation itself or in their drive for taxonomic clarity fail adequately to distinguish between social perspectives./21/

B. Recent Provocative Publications

1. Otto Böcher

The most recent extensive examination of the demonological background of the Bible has been the trilogy of studies by Otto Böcher:

a) *Dämonenfurcht und Dämonenabwehr* [hereafter *DD*];/22/

b) *Das Neue Testament und die dämonischen Mächte* [hereafter *NTDM*];/23/

c) *Christus Exorcista* [hereafter *CE*];/24/

These works have been widely cited by such scholars as Hollenbach, Smith, and Faus./25/

Böcher adopts what I would call a pan-demonological interpretation of a belief in demons as the cause of illnesses, disasters, etc. He makes the categorical statement that this demonological aetiology of diseases was generally true for antiquity,/26/ including as a matter of course the biblical writers./27/ As proof of this view he cites the fact that healings and exorcisms are mentioned in the same breath in the Synoptic Gospels and in Acts./28/

From the belief that some demons were *succubi* and *incubi* like the 'lilith' (see below II.A.2) who appeared as seductive spirits in dreams,/29/ Böcher suggests that the belief in demons has an originally sexual origin./30/ He interprets circumcision as originally an apotropaic sanguinary rite against sexual demons./31/

Böcher admits that there is not much explicit evidence in the Old Testament to support his general thesis, but he interprets Psalm 91:5 f. as Yahweh redeeming one from the 'sickness demons' of the night and of the midday, and the purity restrictions against leprosy in Lev. 13 as betraying the demonological aetiology of that disease./32/

Assuming that ancient peoples attributed all diseases to demons, Böcher consequently maintains that the consensus of heathen, Jewish and early Christian antiquity held that the curing of such ailments could only come with the exorcism of demons./33/ Böcher goes to extreme lengths to interpret everything in the Bible as either an instance of demonic influence or conversely as a prophylactic against demons. Böcher interprets Paul's description of sin personified (Rom. 6-7) as a demonic power./34/ Since some peoples believe that demons enter through the orifices of the body, he suggests that clothing functioned to protect the genitalia against demons, citing I Cor. 12:23./35/ As keeping awake was a protection against demons, the sleep which overcame the disciples in Gethsemane was a victory of the demons./36/ As pagans sometimes depicted demons in theriomorphic guise, i.e. as animals, Böcher finds a hidden demonic significance in all kinds of fauna mentioned in the Bible from the devil as a roaring lion to the locusts of Rev. 9:7 ff. /37/

2. John M. Hull

In 1974 John M. Hull, an Australian who is a professor of education in England, published his important monograph, *Hellenistic Magic and the Synoptic Tradition* [hereafter *HM*]. /38/ Though he, like Morton Smith (see 3. below), based his work on the Greco-Egyptian papyri, Hull was evidently quite unaware of Smith, whose works he does not cite at all.

Though Hull concedes that 'Jesus did not think of himself as a magician, any more than he thought of himself as pre-existent Logos or as metaphysical Son of God',/39/ he believes that 'by the time the earliest gospel was written the tradition of the acts of Jesus had already been saturated with the outlook of Hellenistic magic'./40/ This 'magical' view of Jesus, which is most prominent in Mark and Luke-Acts may have been reduced by Matthew and John./41/

Hull's primary conviction is his view that exorcisms are inextricably linked with magic./42/ He asserts: 'Above all, the two earliest of all the sets of collected materials, Q and Mark, make it clear that Jesus entered without reserve into the central conflict of the magician's art, the struggle with evil powers, directly confronted in the persons of the possessed'./43/ In other words Hull seems to reason: 1) Exorcisms are inextricably linked with magic; 2) Jesus practiced exorcisms; 3) Therefore Jesus was depicted as a magician. We shall examine later the validity of his first premise (see II.G)./44/

3. Morton Smith

The renowned professor of ancient history at Columbia University, Morton Smith, has long been fascinated with ancient magic./45/ But it was his discovery of an 18th-century manuscript at the Mar Saba Monastery south of Jerusalem in 1958, which inspired him to write a trilogy of works that argue that Jesus was a 'magician' and that the essence of early Christianity was libertine magic:

a) *Clement of Alexandria and a Secret Gospel of Mark* [hereafter *CA*];/46/

b) *The Secret Gospel* [hereafter *SG*];/47/ and

c) *Jesus the Magician* [hereafter *JM*]./48/

The Mar Saba manuscript contained a two-and-a-half page letter ascribed to Clement of Alexandria (A.D. 150-211). Like Hull, whom Smith cites in his latest work, Smith relies primarily on the Greek magical papyri which date from the third century A.D. and later, but which he believes contains materials as early as the Gospels./49/

Though W. Völker, J. Munck and even A. D. Nock, to whom Smith dedicated the *CA*, doubted the authenticity of the ascription to Clement, a dozen other distinguished scholars whom Smith consulted were convinced by him that he had indeed discovered a new text by Clement. Most of the reviewers also seem impressed by Smith's presentation of the evidence for Clement's authorship./49a/ If this was the extent of Smith's claims, all would wish to congratulate him.

But Smith has utilized the new document to lend support to his view that Jesus was indeed a magician as hostile Jewish and pagan sources depicted him. The manuscript refers to an alleged 'secret' Gospel of Mark and quotes a short passage from it, which describes a nude youth covered with only a linen cloth who stays with Jesus overnight, as Jesus conveys to him the 'mystery' of the kingdom./50/ Smith contends that this 'Secret' Gospel of Mark contains materials which reveal an independent and earlier account of the Lazarus account in John 11./50a/

What are the traits which convince Smith that Jesus was a magician? He asks: 'What then were the marks of a magician? First of all, he had to do miracles. He was primarily a miracle worker'./51/ Second, 'Even when not directly connected with miracles the claim to be divine is, by itself, taken as evidence that he was a magician ....'/52/ Third, 'Prayer was a specialty of ancient magicians.'/53/ Moreover like a demoniac Jesus was characterized with compulsive behavior as when the Spirit drove him out into the wilderness (Mark 1:12)./54/

Smith's most important argument to support his view that Jesus was a magician and not a rabbi or Messiah is the 'magical' nature of the Eucharist: 'That a man should undertake to identify *his own* blood with wine and give it to his followers to drink in order to unite them with himself--this goes far beyond the mysteries; its only close parallels are in magic'./55/ More specifically Smith suggests a derivation from the genre of erotic magic./56/

Smith concedes that as a matter of fact the canonical Gospels do not represent Jesus as a magician or as one who used magical rites, but this is an understandable 'cover-up' because 'magician' was a dirty word./57/ We therefore have to infer the originally libertine nature of Christianity as its original writings were destroyed, perhaps by new converts under the leadership of James:/58/ 'Accordingly, *the picture of early Christianity given by the New Testament has constantly to be supplemented by pictures of the parties it opposes, and has frequently to be explained by reference to factors it attempts to conceal* './59/ Smith maintains: 'Consequently, the elements in them [the Gospels] that could be used to support the charge of magic are probably only the tips of the iceberg of suppressed traditions, while elements that counter the charge must be viewed with suspicion as probably exaggerated, if not wholly invented'./60/

Not surprisingly, the radical views of Smith have been sharply criticized by numerous reviewers./61/ His penchant for parallels with the life of Apollonius by Philostratus and the Greek Magical Papyri of the third-fourth century is criticized as historically anachronistic in a major monograph by H. C. Kee, whose observations deserve to be quoted at length. Speaking both of the monograph by Hull and the recent work by Smith, Kee concludes:

> Both books overlook the fact that phenomena perceived as miracle or magic must be analyzed by the historian in relation to the life-world of the writer (and his community in which they appear) and to the social functions which they serve. Both writers in these studies reason backward from third- and fourth-century evidence to posit historical conditions from which they draw conclusions about the first century. For that period no adequate documentation exists. The authors assume that, because demons were dealt with by magical means in the later Roman empire, wherever demons appear in the text the appropriate way to describe such phenomena is as magic. The consequence of this methodological confusion is that Hull, for example, simply dumps all the evidence into one undifferentiated heap .... But for Smith, the real Jesus was a demoniac, who engaged in such magical acts as eating flesh, drinking blood, and participating in nocturnal lustrations in the nude with his circle of male followers .... The circularity of what passes for argument and the prejudices that shape the reconstruction of the figure of Jesus will be apparent to any careful reader of these

works./62/

4. David Aune

David Aune, a highly respected evangelical scholar, has contributed a major study on 'Magic in Early Christianity' for the reference work, *Aufstieg und Niedergang der römischen Welt.* /63/ On the one hand, Aune dismisses studies like those of H. van der Loos as 'theologically and apologetically motivated',/64/ and on the other hand, regards Hull's monograph as 'an important contribution to a seriously neglected subject'./65/ As for Morton Smith's works, Aune has nothing but the words of highest praise: in the *CA* Smith devoted 'a short but superb discussion to affirming the widespread influence of ancient magic on Jesus and earliest Christianity',/66/ and *JM* is 'an important book' in which Smith 'analyzes the New Testament evidence in the light of Graeco-Roman magical traditions, and concludes that Jesus is best understood in the role of a magician or sorcerer'./67/

Aune himself is persuaded that: 'The rise of the structural-functional method in sociology and anthropology and the phenomenological method in comparative religions have provided scholars with theoretical frameworks in which the value judgements of the observers are regarded as an improper intrusion into the subject matter'./68/ He believes that the structural-functional sociological framework is 'the most satisfying theoretical perspective from which to analyze magic in Graeco-Roman religions'./69/

Since magic is 'universally regarded as a form of deviant behavior', Aune defines magic as 'that form of religious deviance whereby individual or social goals are sought by means alternate to those normally sanctioned by the dominant religious institution'./70/ A second criterion is that: 'goals sought within the context of religious deviance are magical when attained through the management of supernatural powers in such a way that results are virtually guaranteed'./71/

Aune would agree with those authors who stress the similarity between Jesus' exorcistic commands and magic, rather than with those who would emphasize the differences./72/ Operating with his sociologically derived definition of a magician, Aune concludes: 'The wonders performed by Jesus are magical because they occur within a context of social deviance in which widely accepted but generally unattainable goals highly valued in Judaism are thought to be accomplished for particular individuals through the application of generally successful management techniques'./73/ But he stops short of Morton Smith's conclusion that Jesus was a magician: 'However, it does not seem appropriate to regard Jesus as a magician. ... it would be problematic to categorize Jesus as a magician, since those magical activities which he used can be more appropriately subsumed under the role of messianic prophet'./74/

Aune seems to have accepted certain assumptions:

1) The view that it is clearly the conservative theologians and biblical scholars who are biased and have an apologetic aim. Are the views of Morton Smith unbiased?

2) The view that certain miracles of Jesus are incredible. Aune shares the view of many critics when he writes, 'The nature miracles, however, are generally regarded as legendary embellishments of the Jesus tradition'./75/

3) The view that sociological analyses may provide us with a 'value-free' objective insight as to Jesus' relation to magic. He relies on a structuralist/functonalist model which does not take seriously the supernatural aspects of Christianity./76/ Aune has not taken heed of the criticisms of such reductionist modes of sociology which have been expressed especially since 1969 by such prominent sociologists as Robert Bellah, Peter Berger, and David Moberg. Sociological models are inherently incapable of dealing with an individual who is unique. As Robert Friedrichs observes: 'The epistemology of a sociology which focuses only on "the inter-subjective, the recurrent, and the relational" rules out ipso facto "the existential, the unique, and the absolute"'./77/

II. Diseases, Demons and Exorcisms

In order to evaluate these perspectives on magic and miracle I will survey the subject of diseases, demons and exorcisms in antiquity. The evidence of paleopathology derived from mummies in Egypt and from skeletal remains elsewhere indicate that men were subject to disease from time immemorial./78/ The evidence for cancer is relatively rare, and there is some question as to whether we have any physical evidence of true leprosy (Hansen's Disease)./79/

How was the aetiology, i.e. the cause, of diseases regarded in antiquity? As noted above Böcher believes that all the peoples of the past, including the biblical writers, either explicitly or implicitly regarded demons as the source of their illnesses. While this was a prominent motif in some ancient societies, especially in Mesopotamia, Böcher's assertion is too broad a generalization, based on a very limited and one-sided reading of the evidence.

We may isolate four main sources of illness, which were not mutually exclusive: 1) a divine source which sent illness as a punishment for sin; 2) a demonic source which indwelt or tormented the individual; 3) a magical source sent from a sorcerer or practitioner of black magic; and 4) a natural source as discerned by experience. The modes of treatment would include: 1) prayer, sacrifice and repentance; 2) the exorcism of demons; 3) counter magic; and 4) empirical applications of medicine, drugs, or surgery. Quite frequently different kinds of treatment were combined.

A. Mesopotamia

1. Diseases

We have about a thousand cuneiform texts dealing with diseases and their treatment by magico-medical methods from Mesopotamia./80/ An interesting variety of ills are recorded including: impotency,/81/ infant mortality and childhood diseases,/82/ migraine headaches,/83/ ear infections,/84/ nose bleeds, toothaches, difficult breathing,/85/ stomach ailments, /86/ indigestion, /87/ jaundice, an insatiable appetite,/88/ and even falling hair. /89/

2. Demons

We also have many thousands of texts which refer to the elaborate demonology of the Mesopotamians./90/ As in the case of the later Greeks, the Mesopotamians had 'good' as well as 'evil' spirits. These protected individuals, and in the form of the *šedu* and the *lamassu*, represented as colossal figures, protected the palaces of Assyria./91/

Among the evil spirits were: the *ahhazu* 'seizer'; the *alû* a demon who hid in dark corners, waiting for the unwary; *asakku* death; the *ekimmu* a departed spirit; the *etimmu* a ghost; the *gallû* a spirit of the Underworld; the *ilu limnu* an evil god; the *labasu* a ghoul; the *lamashtu* (previously read as *labartu*), who threatened women in childbirth and snatched suckling infants from their mothers' breasts;/92/ *lilû*, an incubus; the *lilîtu*, a succubus /93/ (cf. *ardat lilî* —'*ardat*'=marriageable woman);/94/ the *namtaru* a plague demon, who was the messenger of Nergal, the god of the Underworld; the *pazuzu*, a mighty SW wind /95/; the *rabitsu* a lurking demon; the *utukku*, originally a ghost.

As even the gods themselves could be attacked by the demons,/96/ all kinds of efforts were made to defend against these ubiquitous dangers. These included great collections of magical texts such as the *Utukki Limnuti* 'Evil Spirits'/97/ and the Namburbi series, and other incantations./98/ Also apotropaic figures were placed aound the homes, including those of armed warriors and of dogs, which in one case from Nineveh has the the inscription: 'Don't stop to think, bite him (i.e. the demon)'./99/

The most common forms of amulets were made in the form of bronze pazuzu figures, a winged figure with a deformed head and legs in the form of eagle claws, or in the form of the lamashtu, a female figure with the head of a lioness. Several lamashtu amulets depict a patient lying on a bed, arms upraised, surrounded by exorcists dressed in fish costumes./100/ The *kubum*, an amulet of a divinized premature birth, may have served as a counter-demon against the lamashtu./101/

3. Demonic Aetiology of Diseases

Many ailments and diseases were ascribed to demons by the ancient Mesopotamians./102/ It was when a man's own protective šedu abandoned him that he was vulnerable to attack from evil demons./103/ Pregnant women and newborn infants were especially in danger from the attack of the pazuzu./104/

Different demons were thought to attack different parts of the body:

The ashakku attacks the head of the man.
The namtaru attacks the life of the man.
The bad utukku attacks the neck of the man.
The bad alû attacks the breast of the man.
The bad gallû attacks the hand of the man.

> The bad ekimmu attacks the stomach of the man.
> The bad god attacks the foot of the man.
> These seven together are found upon him!/105/

We have the description of a vivid case of psychotic epilepsy, which was attributed to the attacks, literally 'hand' (*qat*), of a god, of a ghost, of the power of an oath, etc.:

> If a man is currently suffering from major or minor epileptic attacks ..., and an alû limnu then begins to inflict him with (ideas of) persecution so that the finger of condemnation is being pointed at him behind his back and that god or goddess is angry with him; ... if he engages in periodic outbursts of anger against god or goddess, is obsessed wth delusions of his own mind ... if all his muscles are subject to paralysis, if his eyes exhibit (visual sensations of) red, yellow, and black, if he has a condition of aphasia such that he forgets what he wants to say ..../106/

To cure these ailments the demons had to be exorcised by such formulas as 'In the name of the great god Ea ... be ye exorcised!' or 'Depart, Namtar, black demon! I am the beloved of Bel, depart from me!' Or if the name of the demon was not known, the exorcist commanded, 'Whatever be thy name, depart!' /107/. In place of the demon, the protective spirit is invited back: 'As for the man, the son of his god, may the evil demon who has seized him stand aside. May the favourable spirit stand at his head ....'./108/

4. Non-Demonic Aetiology of Diseases

Even among the Mesopotamians who were especially conscious of demons, not all illnesses were attributed to demons. The cause of diseases are divided by Ritter into three categories: 1) Supernatural causes, including the 'hand' or 'attack' of a god or demon; 2) Retribution for sins or transgressions; and 3) 'Natural' causes such as stroke, jaundice, gastritis, etc./109/ A few cases were attributed to magical curses./110/

According to Saggs: 'Not all afflictions befalling a man were, however, the result of witchcraft, or of ill-disposed demons. The affliction might be brought upon the man by his own action in violating a taboo'./111/ The *Shurpu* texts include a nearly exhaustive list of 95 sins which may have angered the gods against a man./112/ Lambert summarizes the focus of the series 'Incantation for Appeasing an Angry God', which is found in both Sumerian and Akkadian versions, as follows.

> Occasionally the sins of parents or other relatives are suggested as the cause (I 115-18). More commonly the sufferer assumes that he himself must be at the root of the trouble. Sometimes he simply confesses his many sins in the hope that confession alone will appease the angry god, as in I 121ff. especially. This confession often invokes the excuse that man is naturally sinful and so inevitably so./113/

Even mental or psychological ills were not always attributed to demons with cures to be effected by exorcisms. An interesting Old Babylonian text vividly describes neurotic/psychotic symptoms, which are attributed to the anger of the god:

> If he has frequent nervous breakdowns, and from constantly giving orders with no(one) complying, calling with no(one) answering ... he shakes with fear in his bedroom and his limbs have become 'loose' *to an extreme degree* ; if he is filled with anger against god and king; if his limbs often hang limp, and he is sometimes so frightened that he cannot sleep by day or night and consistently sees disturbing dreams ....

The cure in this case was to be effected by the burial of substitute clay figures./114/

Nor were the aetiology and the cure of illnesses always based on supernatural explanations. According to Biggs:

> It is incorrect to assume, as has often been done, that all illness was attributed to witches, demons, and other malevolent beings (against which one might consider a magical treatment particularly appropriate) or to divine displeasure, since the effects of heat, cold, indigestion, etc. were recognized./115/

Biggs cites the Old Babylonian letters of Mari which refer to illnesses and doctors without any reference to magical practice. These letters reveal an acquaintance with the principles of infection and of quarantine. King Zimri-Lim in a letter to Shibtu, the queen, says that he has heard that Dame Naname has been struck with illness. 'Now then, give strict orders that no one drink from the cup from which she drinks, that no one sits on the seat where she sits, and that no one lies on the couch on which she lies. ... This evil is contagious'./116/

5. Magicians and Physicians

The *šsipu*, usually translated 'magician' or 'exorcist', who was also a priest, was not so much involved in exorcizing demons as in offering a diagnosis and prognosis of the illnesses./117/ For example, in 'The Poem of the Righteous Sufferer', we read: 'The exorcist (ašipu) has not diagnosed the nature of my complaint'./117a/ Some practitioners would perform acts of sympathetic magic including the peeling of an onion or tearing apart of dates which were then thrown into the fire to rid the patient of illness./118/ In a charm against 'gall' (perhaps indigestion), which was copied over a millennium, salt was placed in the patient's mouth with the injunction: 'Let it (the ailment) come out like breaking wind, let it come out in little pieces, let it come out of his anus like the wind!'/119/

A common magical praxis was to place a clay figure or an animal, such as a suckling-pig or kid, upon the patient in order to transfer the illness to the substitute, which was then destroyed./120/ Or, the statue of the sick was placed in a grave./121/

On the other hand the *asû* or physician specialized in 'pharmaceutical medicine'./122/ He cooperated with the magician but used various medications rather than incantations. According to Biggs: 'The magician attempted to effect his cures through incantations, prayers, libations and the laying on of hands, while the physician employed a great variety of potions, bandages, cataplasms, lotions, suppositories, enemas, purgatives, etc., but never himself resorted to magic'./123/ Though the Hammurabi Law Code does refer to magic (e.g. #2), laws ## 215-25 regarding surgeons simply deal with their liabilities without any reference to demons or magic./124/

B. Egypt

1. Diseases

Thanks to their well-preserved mummies,/125/ we have an excellent knowledge of the kinds of diseases prevalent among ancient Egyptians,/126/ and especially of dental disorders./127/ There is a continuing controversy over the alleged pathology of the famous monotheistic pharaoh Akhnaton as he is depicted with an elongated skull and effeminate features in art. The mummy often identified with him has now been identifed as that of Smenkhare instead./128/

For our knowledge of Egyptian medicine we are also fortunate in possessing eight major papyri: 1) the Kahun (1900 B.C.); 2) the Edwin Smith (1600 B.C.); 3) the Ebers (1550 B.C.); 4) the Hearst (1550 B.C.); 5) the Erman (1550 B.C.); 6) the London (1350 B.C.); 7) the Berlin (1350 B.C.); and 8) the Chester Beatty (1200 B.C.)./129/ Some of these contain magical prescriptions as well as medical diagnoses and prognoses./130/ Other papyri such as the Berlin Papyrus 3027 published by A. Erman are wholly devoted to magical prescriptions./131/ The fragmentary Kahun Papyrus contains no incantations. The Edwin Smith Papyrus contains only one magical treatment out of 48 cases. The Ebers Papyrus includes only 12 out of 879 prescriptions which are magical, whereas the London Papyrus has 36 out of 61 which may be deemed magical./132/

The identification of various diseases in texts is sometimes problematic. For example the malady *nsj.t.*, which occurs in Hearst 206-10 and Ebers 751-54, has been translated 'epilepsy' by Ebbell. Leake, noting that the disease in Ebers 751 is located in the eyes, suggests that 'fever' is a better translation./133/

The main types of diseases listed in the Hearst Papyrus are as follows:

a) Internal disorders, treated by oral administration: constipation, stomach disorders, heart disease, urinary disorders, dropsy, fevers, malaise.

b) Cutaneous disorders, treated by local application: pruritus, insect bites, boils, burns, contusions, animal bites, wounds.

c) Orthopedic conditions, treated by local application: fracture, pain in the limbs, head injuries, diseases of joints, fingers, and toenails.

d) Cosmetic matters, handled by local application: teeth, dandruff, lice, body odor, hair and skin disorders./134/

2. Demons

Demons played such a relatively insignificant role in Egyptian religion that major studies of Egyptian religion by J. H. Breasted, Henri Frankfort, and Jacques Vandier devote at best a few lines to them. Demons or spirits of the dead are prominent in the magical texts.

3. Demonic Aetiology of Diseases

It was especially internal diseases which had no obvious aetiology which were ascribed to demons or spirits by the Egyptians. Amundsen notes, 'Spirits were thought to be sent through the malevolent magic of one's enemies .... Spirit intrusion caused by magic or by the dead would be countered by magical means'./135/ According to Dawson,

> In the numerous medico-magical texts which have come down to us, the leading idea is possession, for diseases are treated as if personified and are harangued and addressed by the magician. It is generally stated or implied that disease or suffering is due to the actual presence in the patient's body of the demon itself, but frequently it is implied that the suffering is due to some poison or other evil emanation that the demon has projected into the body of his spirit./135a/

As the demons came unobtrusively, one incantation declares: 'You will break out, you who have come in the darkness, who have entered stealthily--his nose turned backwards, his face averted--having failed in what he came for!'/136/ In addition to the intrusion of demons or spirits, we also have the *mt* or *mt.t* , male or female ghosts of the dead, who also had the power to enter into one's body. Affliction by the spirits of the dead was considered one of the chief causes of disease in Egypt./137/ Bloody urine was blamed on the presence of a god or a ghost in the abdomen of an individual./138/

According to Ghalioungui,

> These evil spirits had a chief who introduced them into the body and guided them in its interior. The Egyptians called him the 'Great Slanderer'.... These devils, these envoys of Sekhmet, carried with them 'the wind of the pest of the year'. They masqueraded under different disguises, and hid in the corners of the houses. The windows and doors had to be exorcized to protect the beds, furniture and food against their mischief./139/

The most notable example of possession is the story of the daughter of the Prince of Bekhten inscribed at Thebes from the reign of Ramses II.

> The god Khonsu went to the place where Bent-ent-resht was, and, having performed a magical ceremony over her, the demon departed from her and she was cured straightway. Then the demon addressed the Egyptian god, saying, 'Grateful and welcome is thy coming unto us, O great god, thou vanquisher of the hosts of darkness!'/140/

4. Non-Demonic Aetiology of Diseases

Apart from the intrusion of spirits, diseases in Egypt were attributed to the gods, especially Sekhmet. 'There is little evidence to suggest that in Egypt the idea of sin as a moral failing was viewed as a cause of disease', according to Amundsen./141/

The evidence of the major medical papyri shows that the Egyptians were accurate observers and were aware of natural factors in the progress of injuries and diseases. Leake concludes: 'It is surprising that there is not more evidence of supernaturalism in the medical papyri. ... Taken as a whole the evidence from the papyri indicates a relatively high standard of medical practice in old Egypt'./142/ In fact, if one were to view only the medical papyri rather than the magical texts, one would conclude that demonic aetiology played an insignificant role--at least as far as the doctors were concerned. Leake observes:

> On the other hand, since the medical papyri deal chiefly with internal diseases, one might expect, with an assumed demoniacal etiology, to find an irrational hodgepodge of magical and demoniacal therapy. But this is not the case; nor is demoniacal etiology suggested, except so rarely as to be startling by its implied presence. On the contrary, the various prescriptions recommended seem to be quite rational and natural applications to the alleviation of symptom complexes of empirical knowledge of the general physiological properties of plant, animal, and mineral materials./143/

5. Magicians and Physicians

The Berlin Papyrus (3027) published by Erman is a charm to protect an infant from demons. The text reads: 'Comest thou to kiss this child? I will not let thee kiss him. ... I have made his protection against thee out of Efet-herb, it makes pain; out of onions, which harm thee'./144/ Nibamon of Thebes, a famous exorcist, cured migraine headaches which he diagnosed as caused by a ghost which visited the afflicted every night./145/ One common magical method was an incantation identifying oneself as a god:

> Withdraw, ye disease demons. The wind shall not reach me, that those who pass by may pass by to work disaster against me. I am Horus who passes by that diseased one of Sekhmet, [even] Horus, Horus, healthy despite Sekhmet. I am the unique one, son of Bastet, I die not through thee./146/

Sorensen analyses the logic of Egyptian incantations as follows:

> The narrative and dramatic arguments, the partial mythological identifications, the monstrosity of demons, the impossible, anticosmic character of enemies and the threats of cosmic breakdown--all these are ... tools of the same ritual logic, which reduces the situation to its cosmological significance in order to subject it to ritual control./146a/

Magicians would also draw circles around the patient's bed

and about his house. Magical herbs and prescriptions (e.g. Pap. Ebers 211, 592) were also used to conjure, for example the 'akhu demon'./147/ Pap. Ebers 209 is a magical prescription for *nśyt*, possibly 'epilepsy'./148/ To drive out a 'seizure' from the body the Hearst Papyrus III:6-7 prescribes a potion of date stones, frankincense and juniper berries (cf. Ebers 165)./149/ Hearst III:IX:8-9 prescribes garlic and fat for local application to expel the 'devouring of blood' in any member./150/ Some of the doses contained such noxious elements as animal dung to induce the possessing spirit to depart.

Magic was used along with medicine to enhance the power of the remedies. For example, the Ebers Papyrus directs:

> Beginning of the recital for applying a remedy on any part of the body of a man. I know charms that the Almighty wrought to chase away the spell of a God, or a Goddess, of a dead man, of a dead woman ... to punish the Accuser, the Master of Those who allow decay to seep into this mine flesh, numbness into these mine limbs as Something entering into this mine flesh .... Spoken while applying remedies to any sick part of the body of a man. Really outstanding, millions of times./151/

As in Mesopotamia pain could be transferred to a substitute. Ebers 250 relates: 'To cure a migraine, the aching side of the head was rubbed with the head of a fried fish to transfer the pain from the head of the sick person to the head of the fish'.

According to Jayne, 'The sacerdotal methods of healing consisted in magico-religious rites (*hike'*), ... which centered about the idea of exorcism, or expelling the unseen, malicious spirits which caused disease'./152/ But this is a very broad generalization which does not take into account significant exceptions. For example, symptoms of mental disturbances in seven cases are ascribed to vascular rather than supernatural causes, leading Ghalioungui to comment: 'It is significant that, in an allegedly demoniac system of medicine, illnesses that are pre-eminently and traditionally attributed to possession by evil spirits should have been systematically traced to organic disease'./153/

Medical experts were renowned in Egypt almost from the beginning of its recorded history. Imhotep, the architect of King Djoser of the IIIrd Dynasty (c. 2700 B.C.), was famed for his medical knowledge and was indeed later immortalized as a healing divinity. Niqmad, the king of Ugarit, wrote to Amenhotep: 'Please send me a palace physician. There is no doctor present here'. Egyptian physicians were also welcomed by the Hittites of Anatolia and the Kassites of Mesopotamia. /154/ Herodotus (5th cent. B.C.), who mistakenly believed that the Babylonians had no doctors, was deeply impressed by the medical specialists of Egypt.

Almost all diseases except those of the eyes were treated by priests of the goddess Sekhmet./155/ These priest-physicians, the *wabw*, ranked highest and were entitled to examine patients./156/ Next were the *swnw* or lay physicians, whose name is formed by the signs of a lancet and a pot. Their patron was the god of wisdom, Thoth. Jonckheere's prosopographical study has catalogued the names of about one hundred individuals who can be identified as physicians./157/ Of these 42 are from the Old Kingdom, 16 from the Middle Kingdom, 29 from the New Kingdom, and 11 from the Late Empire. Some of these are identified as specialists, e.g. *Swnw ir.tj*,'doctor of the two eyes'; *Swnw h-.t* , 'doctor of the stomach'; *'Ibh.j*, 'dentists'./158/

A minority of these doctors were also interested in magic, judging from the appended titles. Two are also identified as *h-rj-h.b* 'magician'; six are associated with the scorpion goddess Selkis, a patroness of magic; four are associated with the goddess of magic personified./159/ There were also magicians, who used only incantations rather than medicine to attempt cures./160/

Even in some of the magical prescriptions there was some empirical basis for the praxis, as in the following spell for a bone which was stuck in a man's throat:

> You make invocation to a little oil. You put the face of the man upwards and place your finger and your nail (to the?) two muscles (?) of his throat; you make him swallow the oil and make him start up suddenly, and you eject the oil which is in his throat immediately; then the bone comes up with the oil./161/

Most remarkable is the empirical approach to fractures found in the cases described in the Edwin Smith Papyrus./162/ In only one of the 48 cases is there a reference to a magical cure. In case 9 for a compound fracture of the skull one is advised to grind up the egg of an ostrich, mix it with grease, and apply it as a poultice with an invocation to the god Horus and the goddess Isis. According to John Wilson's interpretation, case 8 specifically rejects a demoniacal aetiology for a patient with a partial paralysis of the body./163/

C. Greece and Rome

1. Diseases

The dedication of *simulacra*, models of terra cotta or other materials representing the parts of the bodies which have been healed, is a custom which dates from the prehistoric caves of Crete to Greek Orthodox circles today. Numbers of such replicas have been found at various shrines of Asclepius, such as those at Epidaurus and Corinth./164/

Modern medical authorities are divided as to the identity of the celebrated plague, so vividly described by Thucydides who caught but survived the disease, which struck Athens at the beginning of the Peloponnesian War (431-404 B.C.). Among the candidates suggested have been bubonic plague, typhus, small pox, ergot, and measles./165/ Diseases described in the Hippocratic Corpus include mumps, pneumonia, gangrene, dropsy, tetanus, and malaria.

The Roman writer Celsus (floruit A.D. 14-37) devoted much space to malaria. Celsus also seems to have been familiar with diabetes, liver abscesses and kidney stones. He describes about 50 cutaneous disorders, including *elephantiasis Graecorum* =leprosy./166/ We have an extensive range of ailments from the encyclopedic work of Pliny the Elder (*Natural History*XX-XXXII), which lists hundreds of remedies for dropsy, leprosy, ulcers, erysipelas, toothaches, headaches, epilepsy and insanity.

2. Demons

The Greek word δαίμων, from which we derive the English

word 'demon', did not always signify an evil being. In Homer the word stands for God five times in the Iliad and once in the Odyssey./167/ It also occurs as an evil being ten times in the Iliad, and about twenty in the Odyssey. Δαίμων is used in Hesiod of heroes of the past who have been transformed into supernatural beings. It is found in the dramatists, e.g. Sophocles (*Ajax* 1214-15), as the equivalent of Fate. Later δαίμονες were conceived as intermediaries between gods and men, perhaps about 500 B.C. in the Pythagorean school, according to Jensen./168/

Socrates had his personal δαιμόνιον./169/ Plato maintained that δαίμονες as well as gods were worthy of worship (*Laws* IV.717; cf. *Apology* 27E-28A). It was through the race of δαίμονες that all intercourse took place between gods and men according to Plato's *Symposium* 202E-203A./170/ Though Plutarch quotes those who speak of evil demons, Brenk has argued that Plutarch himself adhered to Plato's view of the δαίμων as the higher part of the soul./171/ The Greeks and Romans also venerated beings which are sometimes designated as 'angels'./172/

Whether the δαιμόνιον feared by the δεισιδαίμων or Superstitious Man caricatured by Theophrastus, was a fear of the 'divine' or 'supernatural' in general or of the 'demonic' in particular is a matter of dispute./173/ The hellenistic orator Isocrates (V.117) contrasted gods responsible for blessings and the gods set over punishments. A. D. Nock suggests that in the latter category the Greeks may have included: Hecate, the Erinyes, ἀλάστορες the 'avenging' spirits, the κῆρες, a night bird, and the evil eye./174/ Plutarch (*D.O.* 14. II,417d) cited the ἀλάστορες as examples of evil demons. Creatures such as the Empusa and Lamia were not called demons by the Greeks but would correspond to demons in other traditions. The Empusae were succubi who lay with men in their sleep, sucking up their vital forces until they died (cf. Aristophanes, *Frogs* 293; *Eccles.* 1056). Lamia was a creature whose children by Zeus were killed by Hera. In revenge she destroyed the children of others. The Keres were the bringers of death and other ills, including old age and illness. According to Rose, 'Therefore they are about as near to being devils as any native Greek figure ever came ...'./175/

Roman beliefs in ghosts and spirits were of great antiquity./176/ In order to placate the Lemures or spirits of the dead, the Romans celebrated the festival of Lemuria in May. But it was not until the period of the Empire as evidenced especially in the Greek Magical Papyri that we have very well developed beliefs in evil demons./177/ The concept of the νεκυδάμιον, for example, is restricted to these post-Christian Greek papyri from Egypt./178/

3. Demonic Aetiology of Diseases

Prior to the classical period a widespread belief existed that disease was caused by κῆρες and ἀλάστορες./179/ In the Archaic Greek period madness was attributed to possession by a god or more often by a nymph./180/ The chthonic spirits of the underworld, such as spirits of the dead and the hounds of Hecate, were feared particularly as those who caused mental and nervous disorders such as madness, hysteria, and epilepsy./181/

4. Non-Demonic Aetiology of Diseases

Before the dawn of the Classical era, most Greeks probably attributed illnesses to the wrath of the gods such as Apollo (cf. Homer's *Iliad* I.43 ff.). The illness of Philoctetes was divinely sent (Sophocles, *Philoc.* 192). In the fifth cent. B.C. Hippocrates, 'The Father of Medicine', established a famed medical school on the island of Cos. Physicians still today swear the 'Hippocratic Oath'. The rationalist author of the Hippocratic treatise 'On the Sacred Disease' denounced as superstitious such supernatural ideas about the cause of diseases. It is worth noting that these were divine not demonic causes.

> If the patient imitate a goat, if he roar, or suffer convulsions in the right side, they say that the Mother of the Gods is to blame. If he utter a piercing and loud cry, they liken him to a horse and blame Poseidon. ... If he foam at the mouth and kick, Ares has the blame. When at night occur fears and terrors, delirium, jumpings from the bed and rushings out of doors, they say that Hecate is attacking or that heroes are assaulting./182/

'On the Sacred Disease' suggests that epilepsy was caused by a phlegmatic discharge which blocked the vessels to the brain, and notes that this was more apt to occur when there was a change in the winds. Most of the Hippocratic corpus ascribed diseases to maladjustments of the four humors in the body: blood, phlegm, yellow bile, and black bile (or water)./182a/

From the late fifth century B.C. one of the most popular healing gods was Asclepius, who was worshiped at many healing centers./183/ The usual recourse when one was ill was to seek guidance through dreams obtained through incubation, i.e. sleeping in temples of Asclepius, such as at Epidauros/184/ and Pergamum./185/

After a plague the Romans invited the god Asclepius (Roman Aesculapius) to come to Rome in 293 B.C./186/ The god was given a temple on the island in the Tiber River. The dreams sent by Asclepius usually prescribed bleedings, purgatives, diets, fasts, baths, and rubbings with oil sometimes accompanied by incantations. Our best first-hand evidence comes from the second-century A.D. orator Aelius Aristides, who was afflicted with smallpox, respiratory ills and intestinal ailments./187/

With the development of philosophy and a rationalistic approach to phenomena, supernatural causes for diseases were replaced by natural causes, at least among the intelligentsia. The Hippocratic school declared that psychotic behavior was due to brain disease and not demon possession./188/ The naturalistic aetiology of disease became the dominant attitude of both Greek physicians and philosophers./189/ The physician applied his science and was held liable for his failures. According to Amundsen, 'It is well known that Greek physicians hesitated to take on cases that they considered as hopeless'./190/

This same rationalistic approach was conveyed to the Romans by the Greek physicians. The medical writer Celsus wrote: 'Diseases were [in olden times] ascribed to the anger of the immortal gods, and from them help used to be sought ...'. According to Plutarch (2nd cent. A.D.) only the superstitious man believed that the indispositions of his body were due to the afflictions of God or attacks of an evil spirit./191/

5. Magicians and Physicians

As early as the Homeric epics there are numerous

references to surgeons, for example in the *Iliad* XIII.210-14. The divine patron of the healing arts was the centaur Chiron. In Homer Asclepius was a mortal physician who was taught the use of medicinal herbs by Chiron. He became divine only after his death.

In Archaic Greece (800-500 B.C.) the expulsion of the god or spirit who caused illness was sought through the aid of the ἰατρομάντεις, wandering physician-seers, who employed herbs, spells, charms, and exorcisms./192/ The Homeric Hymn to Demeter (II.229-30) speaks of a charm against the 'Woodcutter', the worm thought to cause toothache. Otherwise there is very little evidence to indicate that magic played much of a role in medicine from Homer to Galen (2nd cent. A.D.)./193/ Sophocles (*Ajax* ll.581-82) notes that a good physician does not sing incantations over pains that should be cured by surgery. The author of 'On the Sacred Disease' disparaged 'magicians, purifiers, charlatans, and quacks' who resorted to incantations to treat epilepsy.

In the early Roman Republic Cato (3rd cent. B.C.) suggested that remedies using *brassica* 'cabbage' were especially effective for a variety of ailments including the healing of sleeplessness, wounds, and cancerous ulcers. He also recommended magic for dislocated joints: 'However, go through the form of incantation daily over the man who has suffered the dislocation. Or use this form: *huat haut haut istasis tarsis ardannabou dannaustra*./194/

Prior to their contact with the Greeks, the Romans had no indigenous medical tradition./195/ Cato the Censor warned his son Marcus about the wiles of the Greek physicians. But the prestige and influence of Greek medicine remained undiminished in the early Roman Empire. Pliny the Elder (*N.H.* XXIX.viii.17) observed:

> Medicine is the only one of the arts of Greece that serious Romans have not yet begun to practice. Even though it is lucrative, very few Roman citizens have touched it; and those who do at once become deserters to the Greeks. Nay, even more than this, if they treat of it

in any other language than Greek, they lose authority even with laymen.

In the late Roman Republic physicians were mainly Greek slaves or freedmen. Julius Caesar granted citizenship to foreign physicians and Augustus exempted them from public taxes./196/ It is in Roman sources that we hear of the first major amputations, mastectomies, and operations for goiter, hernia and bladder stone./197/ It was the Roman army which developed the first effective hospitals./198/

D. Ancient Israel

1. Diseases

There are many passages in the Bible which are translated as references to 'leprosy', but which may also be references to infectious skin diseases distinct from true leprosy or Hansen's disease./199/ There are also numerous references to the plague, which at least in 1 Samuel 5-6 was no doubt a reference to the bubonic plague ('emerods'='buboes')./200/ Other ailments described in the Old Testament may possibly include cerebral hemorrhage (1 Sam. 25:37f.), cataplectic paralysis (1 Kings 13:4ff.), meningitis? (2 Kings 4:18ff.), ophthalmia (Lev. 26:16), staphylococcal infection (Deut. 28:27, 35; 2 Kings 20:7), scabies (Deut. 28:27), ringworm (Lev. 13:30), favus (Isa. 3:17), bacillary dysentery (2 Chron. 21:18f.), and boils (Job 2:7,8)./200a/

2. Demons

The name Satan occurs but three times in the Old Testament. He appears as Satan or 'the accuser' in Job 1:6 and Zech. 3:1-2./201/ In 1 Chron. 21:1 Satan appears as a proper name without the article. Various speculative attempts have been offered to explain Satan's origins./202/ He is not yet depicted as the ruler of evil spirits.

Böcher sees demons everywhere in the Old Testament. In his view Jacob's wrestlng with the angel at Jabbok (Gen. 32) is in reality an Israelite superstition about the conflict with a nocturnal 'Flussdämon', which may be compared to motifs from Germanic fairy tales./203/ Animals, fire, water, the midday, etc. all represent demonic dangers according to

Böcher's understanding./204/ The 'unclean' animals of Lev. 11 and Deut. 14 are in reality demonic animals./205/ But he has to admit that these conclusions must be inferred on the basis of extra-biblical parallels.

To be sure, there are some explicit references to demons in the Old Testament. The *shedim*, which were considered to be protective genii by the Babylonians and Assyrians, were worshiped by the apostate Israelites (Deut. 32:17; Ps. 106:37-38). In Psalm 106:37 the LXX translated the word as 'demons'./206/ Another word which some have considered to represent demons is *se'irim*. The LXX translates the word in 2 Chron. 11:15 as 'idols and worthless things' (cf. Lev. 17:7). The word which also occurs in Is. 13:21 and 34:14 (RV 'satyrs'; LXX δαιμόνια) and in 2 Chron 11:15 (RV 'he-goats') represents 'hairy demons' rather than animals according to Langton./207/ Gruenthaner comments:

> From the name, which means 'hairy ones' or 'goats', we conjecture that the Israelites imagined them to be goat-like in appearance or in their attributes; hence, for want of a better name, they may be termed satyrs. We do not know whether they had some objective reality or existed only in the mind of their worshippers; in either supposition they were demons, for their cult was abhorrent to Yahweh./208/

An interesting case of the appearance of a Mesopotamian demon in Israel is the reference to the *lilith* in Isaiah 34:14, where the King James Version translators rendered the word as 'screech owl' with 'nightmonster' in the margin./209/ The Revised Standard Version has rendered the word 'night hag'. In post-biblical magic texts such as the Aramaic, Syriac, and Mandaic incantation bowls the liliths are quite prominent./210/ In Rabbinic literature Lilith was portrayed as a creature with long flowing hair and with wings. She was considered to be the first wife of Adam, who left him as the result of a quarrel. Lilith was feared by the Jews down through the Middle Ages /211/.

One problem with interpreting the *se'irim* and the *lilith* in Isaiah 34:14 is the association of a number of real animals which also occupy the ruins of Edom with them./212/ Langton's solution is to interpret all of the animals as demonic manifestations./213/ The other consistent solution would be to regard the *se'irim* and the *lilith* as animals./214/ Others accept the mixture of animals with demonic beings./215/

E. A. Speiser interpreted the word *rabitsu* (RV 'coucheth') in Gen. 4:7 as a reflection of the Babylonian demon with the same name, and translated the phrase: 'sin is the demon at the door'./216/ Other possible demons may include *Deber* and *Keteb* in Psalm 91:5 and *Alukah* in Proverbs 30:15./217/

On the Day of Atonement (Lev. 16) the priest took two scapegoats. The first was sacrificed to the Lord. The second, bearing all of the sins of the people, was sent free to Azazel. The NEB translates the word as 'precipice'. Following the LXX, which calls the scapegoat itself 'Azazel', R. de Vaux, B. Levine, and other scholars identify Azazel with a demonic being inhabiting the desert./218/ This is based on later Midrashic interpretation. The oldest source for the interpretation of Azazel as a fallen angel is found in the Ethiopic Book of Enoch. This identification of Azazel as a demon on the basis of such late tradition is rejected by Kaupel./219/ Tawil suggests that the name is derived from an epithet for Mot, the Ugaritic god of the dead. The scapegoat, according to this interpretation, was being sent to the netherworld./220/

In contrast especially to the extravagant demonology of the Mesopotamians, the demonology of the Old Testament is quite restrained./221/ Langton speculates that this may have been due to a kind of censorship:

> Traces of these beliefs are comparatively few in the literature of the Old Testament, and it is not difficult to conceive of the reasons for this paucity of reference. ... The same influences, therefore, which availed to suppress nearly all references to such traditional beliefs and customs as those associated with ancestor worship, necromancy, and the like, tended also to exclude, to a very large degree, allusions to the rampant demonology which certainly existed among the early Hebrews, as among the surrounding peoples./222/

The development of demonology in the later period of the

Old Testament is often attributed to Iranian influences./223/ The conquest of Mesopotamia in 539 B.C. by Cyrus certainly did expose the Jewish exiles to Iranian culture. One specific case which can be attributed to Iranian influence is the name of the demon Asmodaios in the book of Tobit, which seems clearly to be derived from the Iranian Aešma./224/

The difficulty, however, is that most of our sources on Iranian religion are very fragmentary and extremely late, with the notable exception of the Gathas of Zoroaster. We do have the famous *daiva* text of Xerxes, but scholars disagree as to what kinds of gods the king suppressed./225/ We have virtually nothing, however, from the crucial Parthian period (250 B.C.-A.D. 225)./226/ Whether Sasanian and post-Islamic Zoroastrian sources can be used to recreate the alleged pre-Christian demonology of Israel is highly debatable./227/ We have a wealth of data on demons from late Zoroastrian texts such as the Vendidad and Manichaean sources./228/ According to the later Avesta diseases with the exception of trauma were attributable to demons./229/

The development of demonology in the Intertestamental period is reflected in the Apocrypha and the Pseudepigrapha. Quite striking is the story of Tobit, which describes how the evil demon Asmodeus killed the seven successive bridegrooms of Sarah, each on their wedding night (Tob. 3.7 f.)./230/ Though some scholars assert that Sarah was possessed by the evil spirit,/231/ others point out that the text does not really say this. As Gruenthaner notes: 'None of the recensions of the Book of Tobias contains the least intimation that Sara was obsessed by Asmodaeus. His power was restricted to her prospective bridegroom'./232/ The demon was frightened off by the burning of the liver and the heart of a fish (Tob. 8.3)./233/

By the first century B.C. or earlier the books of Enoch and of Jubilees were interpreting the 'Sons of God' of Genesis 6 as fallen angels, the Watchers, who corrupted men with their own sexual passions./234/ According to 1 Enoch 6:2, 'And the angels, the children of heaven saw them and desired them; and they said to one another, "Come, let us choose wives for ourselves from among the daughters of man and beget us children"'./235/ The view that demons originated from the fall of angels was accepted subsequently by Origen, Aquinas, and Calvin./236/

3. Demonic Aetiology of Diseases

Böcher maintains that Israel like Babylon attributed disease to demonic possession./237/ But while demons are mentioned in the Old Testament, demon possession is not clearly attested. According to 1 Sam. 10 and 19 Saul was tormented from time to time by an evil spirit. McCasland comments, 'Saul is the only close approach to possession in the Old Testament, and it does not clearly present the change of personality demanded, although that may possibly have been present'./238/ M. Unger regards 1 Samuel 16:18-21 as a case of demonic influence, if not of possession; Berends denies that Saul's mania is a case of demonic possession./239/ We may conclude that possession by demons is not given as a cause of disease in the Old Testament./240/

4. Non-Demonic Aetiology of Diseases

According to Neufeld:

> It is clear that the understanding of the differences between acute, chronic, and contagious illness were well known. ... Many of those ritual purification laws and their techniques reflect for their time a remarkable understanding of hygiene, and closely related subjects, which was acquired empirically. They presuppose a fairly well developed system of hygiene./241/

It was, to be sure, as a by-product rather than as an explicit goal of their purity laws that the Israelites practiced hygienic principles of quarantine which kept infectious disease from spreading.

5. Magicians and Physicians

According to the pan-demoniacal interpretation of Böcher, not only is the Old Testament pervaded with demonic dangers, but almost every rite and activity has an anti-demoniacal function. These would include not only the rites of cleansing,/242/ but also the sacrifices,/243/ nakedness or the rending of garments (citing Isaiah 20:2; Job 22:6; Matt. 25:36; 1 Cor. 4:11),/244/ fasting,/245/ continence,/246/ and sleeplessness./247/

There are no references in the Bible to remedies similar to the magical 'dung pharmacopeias' of Egypt./248/ According to Harrison's monograph, 'the ancient Hebrews appear to have employed herbs and vegetable substances of reputed medicinal virtue independently of magic or systematised medicine purely for general therapeutic or culinary purposes'./249/

The Old Testament has but few references to physicians. An unfavorable reference is found in 2 Chron. 16:12, describing how Asa resorted to a physician rather than to the Lord and then died. Gen. 50:2 refers to Egyptian 'physicians' who embalmed Jacob. Job calls his friends 'worthless physicians' (Job 13:4). Jeremiah (8:22) asks: 'Is there no balm in Gilead? Is there no physician there?' Jubilees 10:10-15 describes how the angels revealed the secrets of medicine to Noah. Ecclesiasticus (Ben Sira) 38:1 contains a striking encomium to physicians:

> Give a physician due honour. ... The Lord has created medicine out of the earth and a wise man does not despise them. ... Do not neglect your sickness, but pray to the Lord and he will cure you .... They (the physicians) shall also pray to the Lord that He will let them succeed in bringing relief and healing to save life.

E. Qumran

1. Demons and Diseases

Several texts from Qumran have been interpreted as providing evidence for a demonic aetiology for disease, together with exorcistic methods of healing. An apocryphal Psalm from Qumran declares, 'Let not Satan rule over me nor an unclean spirit, neither let pain nor the evil inclination take possession of my bones'./250/

Avigad and Yadin in their 1956 translation of the *Genesis Apocryphon* XX:28 f. translated the Aramaic words *ruh' d' bysht'* as the 'evil wind'./251/ Fitzmyer in his 1966 translation more correctly rendered the words as 'evil spirit'./252/ In the somewhat broken text of 1QGA 20:28-29, we read that the pharaoh asked Abraham to pray that the evil spirit might be rebuked. Abraham obliged by laying his hands upon the pharaoh's head,/253/ whereupon the plague was removed and the evil spirit was rebuked./254/

A word *gzr* in the Aramaic Prayer of Nabonidus (4QOrNab) has been interpreted by Dupont-Sommer as 'exorcist' on the basis of a study by G. Furlani./255/ In the text king Nabunai (i.e. Nabonidus) is afflicted with *shehîn* a kind of ailment for seven years (cf. Job 2:7). Vermes, who accepts Dupont-Sommer's interpretation, observes:

> It is worth noting that although the devil, sin and sickness are logically combined in the Qumran picture, the story is told ellipticlly. The narrator mentions the king's illness without referring to its cause; and the exorcist is credited, not with the expulsion of a demon, but with the remission of the sufferer's sins./256/

2. Exorcism at Qumran?

Upon closer examination we find that the Genesis Apocryphon passage does not speak explicitly of demon possession or of exorcism. Fitzmyer supplies the words 'to depart' from his association of the Aramaic verb *g'r* 'to rebuke' with the Greek ἐπιτιμάω to suggest that an exorcism is involved./257/ In contrast to Dupont-Sommer's idiosyncratic rendering of *gzr* as 'exorcist' the lectionaries and all other translations except one render the word as 'diviner'./258/ Because of these considerations other scholars have expressed doubts that either a demonic aetiology of disease or healing by the expulsion of demons was current at Qumran/259/.

F. Later Judaism

1. Demons and Diseases

Surprisingly there is but one reference to evil spirits in the Mishnah (c. A.D. 200). Pirke Aboth 5.6 reports that some rabbis listed them among the ten things created on the eve of Sabbath between the suns at nightfall. The fear of demons is well attested from late rabbinic sources as the Talmud/260/ and the Aramaic magic bowls./261/ Aune concludes: 'In general, it may be stated that the belief in demons and their effect upon mankind increased in Judaism from A.D. 150 to 450'./261a/ According to Carr: 'By the third century AD Judaism was swamped with demons. Rabbi Johanan (died 279) knew of three hundred varieties of demons, ...'./262/ The whole world was full of such *mazzigin* (Tanch. Mish. 19). R. Hanina mentioned that there were one thousand at the left hand, ten thousand at the right. Among the most feared was Lilith, the queen of female demons, with eighteen myriads accompanying her (Pes. 112b). Lilith was depicted with luxuriant hair (Nidd. 24b; Erub. 100b). One was not culpable if he put out a lamp on the Sabbath for fear of evil spirits (Shab. 2.5).

According to rabbinic traditions numerous diseases were ascribed to demons./263/ The following were affected by demons:

> Sick women, at and after childbirth; also brides, bridegrooms, mourners, and the pupils of the Rabbis, are specially obnoxious to the demons of darkness (Ber. 54b). To demons are ascribed leprosy (Horayoth 10a), rabies (Yoma 83b), coup (Yoma 77b; Taanith 20b), asthma (Bekhoroth 44b), cardiac disease (Gittin 67b). Nervous diseases are the specialty of evil demons, such as epilepsy (Shab. Bab. 67a; Jos. Ant. VI.viii.2; VIII.ii.5)./264/

But as Foerster points out, 'not all sicknesses are traced back to demons' in the rabbinic traditions./265/

The New Testament itself bears witness to the activity of Jewish exorcists (Mark 9:38f., Matt. 12:27//Luke 11:19; Acts 19:13-17). According to Josephus (*Antiq*. 8.46-49) Eleazar exorcised a demon in the presence of Vespasian./266/ Justin, in his dialogue with the Jew Trypho (2nd cent.), declared: 'Now assuredly your exorcists, I have said, make use of craft when they exorcise, even as the Gentiles do, and employ fumigations and incantations'./267/ Belief in exorcisms continued in the later Jewish circles./268/

2. Non-Demonic Aetiology of Diseases

According to the Talmud sickness was not only sent as a punishment for sin (Sabbath 32b), but could be inherited (Yebamoth 64b). The rabbis also recognized natural causes as Kagan summarizes:

> The Babylonian Talmud states that the causes of disease are uncleanliness, cold wind, improper food,

excesses, worry, fear, trauma, hereditary weakness and infections. The Palestinian Talmud emphasizes also, that most deaths are caused by cold, heat and neglect./268a/

The rabbis stressed cleanliness as necessary to health (Erubin 65a), and were aware of the importance of nutrition (Erubin 83b). They banned marriages into families with epilepsy (Yebamoth 64b). Though physicians were generally held in high esteem, there were debates as to the value of the physician (Berachoth 60a).

3. Miracles

A number of wonder-working rabbis have been celebrated in later Jewish traditions./269/ For example there was Honi (1st cent. B.C.), who was able to perform miracles by his powerful prayers./270/ There was also Hanina Ben Dosa (1st cent. A.D.), who was famed for his healing miracles./271/ From their similarities to Jesus as miracle workers Vermes concludes: 'It would appear, rather, that the logical inference must be that the person of Jesus is to be seen as part of first-century charismatic Judaism and as the paramount example of the early Hasidim or Devout'./272/

Kee, however, notes the different emphasis of the rabbinic stories: 'An analysis of the intention of the rabbinic miracle stories leads to an important conclusion: the exorcisms of the rabbinic literature were told in order to exalt the person of the performer'./273/ Since the rabbis' 'miracles' were typically in answer to their prayers in contrast to Jesus' 'miracles', Achtemeier concludes: 'It ought to be fairly clear that Jesus was not pictured in terms with which the rabbinic wonder-worker was described'./274/

Fiebig's major study, *Jüdische Wundergeschichten im Zeitalter Jesu* (Tübingen: J. C. B. Mohr, 1911), which sought to demonstrate that in Palestine miracle stories attributed to Jewish teachers were not extraordinary, has been criticized by Morton Smith for using the later strata of the rabbinic traditions./275/ Neusner's comprehensive studies of the Pharisees before 70 have revealed a virtually total absence of miracle stories./275a/ Tannaitic literature contains almost no stories of miracles performed by the Tannaim except for the story of Honi the circle maker. Green believes that Honi was originally a magician, who was transformed into a pious rabbi by later traditions./276/

4. Magic

Though some magical practices were condemned, magic enjoyed a considerable popularity among the Jews, and Jewish magicians were notorious in the Roman Empire./277/ Hillel used to say, 'The more flesh, the more worms; the more property, the more anxiety; the more wives, the more witchcraft (Pirke Aboth 2.8). The Talmud repeated the assertion that the most pious of women were engaged in sorcery./278/ Rab attributed 99% of all diseases to the evil eye./279/

An important new document of Jewish magic is the *Sepher ha-Razim*, which comes from the late Byzantine era. As against the third-century date proposed by the original editor, Gruenwald suggests a fifth-sixth century date./280/ The document reveals a belief in the use of black magic to cause someone's enemy to become bedridden, blind or lame./281/ One very interesting magico-medical prescription found in it reads:

> If you wish to cure a headache (affecting) half the head or to bind or rebuke the spirit causing blindness, take fat that covers the brain of a black ox, and while in (a state of) purity, write on it the names of these angels and place it in a silver tubular case, then bind the tube with seven colors and place it beside the pain. (In order to succeed) abstain from meat, from wine, from (contact with) the dead, from menstruating women, and from every unclean thing./282/

Such popular remedies as the milk of a white goat over three cabbage stalks, and excrement of white dog mixed with balsam were also prescribed among the Jews./283/ Various amulets were used by them as protective measures against demons and disease./284/

III. THE NEW TESTAMENT

A. Satan

In the New Testament the central place of Satan or however he is variously called can hardly be gainsaid./285/ Jesus is portrayed as in mortal conflict with him./286/ Jeffrey Burton Russell, the medieval historian who has most thoroughly researched the subject of Satan's image in history, remarks:

> Generations of socially oriented theologians dismissed the Devil and the demons as superstitious relics of little importance to the Christian message. On the contrary, the New Testament writers had a sharp sense of the immediacy of evil. The Devil is not a peripheral concept that can easily be discarded without doing violence to the essence of Christianity. He stands at the center of the New Testament teaching that the Kingdom of God is at war with, and is now at least defeating, the Kingdom of the Devil./287/

In a personal aside, Russell confesses, 'All reservations considered, however, I do believe in the existence of a personification and principle of evil, call it what you will'./288/

This has been the position of Catholicism and of conservative Protestantism down through the ages./289/ As Sabourin stresses: 'From all this it is clear that the existence of a personal hostile power, whether called Satan or any other name, forms an essential element in the teaching of the New Testament and that all attempts to 'demythologize' the New Testament in this matter or to eliminate the figure of Satan from it on psychological ground runs counter to the whole spirit of the New Testament'./290/

The question of whether one accepts the biblical view of a personal evil being is an issue of faith. His existence can be denied, however, only at the cost of bargaining away much of the supernatural basis of Christianity itself. Baudelaire once quipped, Satan's 'cleverest wile is to convince us that he does not exist'./291/

B. Evil Spirits

The 'sons of God' who lusted after the daughters of men (Gen. 6:2) were interpreted as fallen angels by the LXX./292/ References to fallen angels appear in the New Testament in 2

Pet. 2:4 (cf. Jude 6) and Rev. 20:2-3./293/ Demons are mentioned in the Pauline corpus only at 1 Cor. 10:20f. (cf. Deut. 32:17) and 1 Tim. 4:1./294/ A popular view of Paul's injunction for women to veil themselves in 1 Cor. 11:10 is to interpret the veil as a protective device against fallen angels./295/ J. A. Fitzmyer, however, has shown that the Qumran evidence would indicate that the angels whose presence was to be respected by the women were probably conceived of as holy rather than as fallen angels./296/

The significance of the στοιχεῖα, which is translated by the KJV as 'elements' in Gal. 4:3, 9 and as 'rudiments' in Col. 2:8, 20, is disputed. They are conceived of as hostile spirits by Böcher and most scholars./297/ According to the post-Christian *Testament of Solomon* 8 the στοιχεῖα were the 'cosmic rulers of darkness'. Recently, however, Carr in a monograph on the subject has argued that all 'the principalities and powers are angel figures of the heaven of God, not demonic beings or fallen angels'./298/ That hypothesis, however, founders on Eph. 6:12, which describes at least some of the principalities and powers as hostile. Carr's response is to argue that this is an interpolation:

> The letter to the Ephesians presents particular problems. It was the thought contained especially in Eph. 6:12 that became prominent in the Church and affected all other interpretations. We have attempted to show, however, that this verse is unlikely to have been part of the original text, and that if it was, it represents a considerable move away from the Pauline notion of the Christian life, and of the nature of the world./299/

The word δαιμόνιον is used about 50 times and the verb δαιμονίζομαι 'to be possessed' is found 12 times in the Synoptic Gospels. Other synonyms are 'unclean spirits' and 'evil spirits'. It is striking that the Gospel of John does not recount any exorcism of demons by Jesus,/300/ but does report several accusations that Jesus had a 'demon' (John 7:20; 8:48-52; 10:20-21).

C. Demonic Aetiology of Diseases

As noted before, Böcher conceives of all diseases as

attributed to demons, and all healings as originally exorcistic./301/ According to Böcher, with the exception of John 9:1-3 and Gal.4:13f., 'An der Annahme dämonischer Ursache der Krankheiten hält das Neue Testament gleichfalls im allgemeinen fest'./302/ Some would infer that madness and demon possession were associated in the New Testament (cf. Mark 3:21 and 30)./303/

In a general sense it is true that illness as well as many other ills are attributed to Satan (Luke 13:16; Acts 10:38). But even when a particular ailment is sent from Satan, it is God who is ultimately in control (2 Cor. 12:7). In rebuttal of Böcher's position, Sabourin responds:

> It is often stated also in good faith, that the New Testament writers, being of their time, did not distinguish clearly illness and possession, healing and exorcism. Acts 10:38 is sometimes quoted in that sense, because Peter says there that Jesus 'went about doing good and healing all that were oppressed by the devil, for God was with him'. But this text simply reflects the belief that diseases and other natural calamities are effects of the evil influence attributed to the devil as incarnation of rebellion and mischief./304/

D. Non-Demonic Aetiology of Diseases

John 9:3 denies a necessary connection between sin and sickness. Sometimes, however, sickness is viewed as a punishment from God (Acts 12:23; cf. 1 Cor. 11:30).

Most scholars would agree that the New Testament does not attribute all illnesses to demons./305/ As Amundsen summarizes the New Testament data: 'We have already seen that disease was sometimes said to be from Satan. In such cases healing did not involve exorcism. ... That the apostles distinguished between demon possession and disease generally is clear from Acts 5:16. ... It is clear from the New Testament that most disease was not, however, attributed to a demonic causality'./306/ As noted by many scholars, Jesus healed with a touch but exorcized simply with a word./307/

E. Jesus' Exorcisms

1. Exorcisms in Jesus' Ministry

One can hardly do justice to Jesus if one ignores his miracles. It has been estimated that 209 out of the 666 verses of Mark's Gospel are occupied with his miracles./308/ Moreover of the thirteen healing stories in Mark, four deal with exorcisms./309/ The six exorcisms in the Synoptic Gospels include: 1) the demoniac in the synagogue (Mark 1:21-27//Luke 4:33-36), 2) the Gerasene demoniac (Mark 5:1-20//Matt. 8:28-34//Luke 8:26-39), 3) the daughter of the Syrophoenician woman (Mark 7:24-30//Matt. 15:21-28), 4) the epileptic boy (Mark 9:14-29//Matt. 17:14-20//Luke 9:37-43), 5) the dumb demoniac (Matt. 9:32-34), and 6) the dumb and blind demoniac (Matt. 12:22-28). The healing of the woman with the spirit of infirmity (Luke 13:10-17) has sometimes been considered an exorcism, but Wilkinson demonstrates that this is a case of healing./310/

It is acknowledged by even otherwise sceptical critics that the traditions of exorcisms are particularly convincing. As summarized by Aune: 'However, there is also general consensus among critical New Testament scholars that there is overwhelming evidence that Jesus did in fact perform exorcism and healings. ... The historicity of the exorcisms is particularly emphasized by a number of prominent critical scholars'./311/

As similar as some of the features of Jesus' exorcisms appear to the practices of contemporary exorcists, they were but a single aspect of his larger ministry of healing and teaching. It would be a distortion to view him as simply or primarily an exorcist. The stories of his exorcisms had a transcendent significance, announcing the advent of the Kingdom of God (Matt. 12:28//Luke 11:20). As Kee remarks, 'They were told ... to identify his exorcism as an eschatological event which served to prepare God's creation for his coming rule'./312/

2. The Healing of the Epileptic Boy

a. Epilepsy in Antiquity

Of all the disorders of antiquity the one which seemed

most susceptible of interpretation as caused by demon or spirit possession was probably epilepsy. Akkadian texts speak of a malady sent by the 'hand of Sin' which caused a man's neck to turn, his hands and feet to become tense, and foam to flow from his mouth./313/ Several Egyptian magical texts such as Ebers Pap. 209-210 and Kahun Pap. 33 ('to prevent a woman from biting her tongue') may refer to epilepsy./314/ The popular Greek view did not believe that the 'sacred disease' was caused by the actual possession of a demon or a spirit but believed that it was sent by the gods./315/ On the other hand, the author of the Hippocratic treatise, 'On the Sacred Disease', attributed epilepsy to the diversion of phlegm to the veins and the heart./316/ The association of the malady with demonic influence was maintained through the Middle Ages,/317/ largely through the influence of Origen./318/

b. Epilepsy in the New Testament

The Greek word (σεληνιάζω) which appears in Matt. 17:15 (cf. Matt. 4:24) is etymologically similar to the Latin word 'lunatic', i.e. moon-struck, and in this context means 'epileptic' from the popular belief that the incidence of the disease was influenced by the waxing and waning of the moon--a view expressed by Galen and accepted by many later writers including Calvin./319/ The Curetonian Syriac has *bar egara*, a name 'apparently derived from a custom of worshipping a lunar demon on the flat roofs of houses'./320/

The word 'moon-struck' did not always mean 'epileptic' as the moon was believed to have other effects. That in later Christian texts those who were 'moon-struck' were not necessarily identical with epileptics may perhaps be shown by a Christian magical text against both ἐπιλημψέως and [σ]εληνι[ι]ασμοῦ./321/ According to Ross, σεληνιασμός means epilepsy in modern Greek, though the word ἐπιληψία is now more common./322/

The symptoms of the suffering lad--convulsions, foaming at the mouth, falling into fire and water, gnashing the teeth, and a state of rigidity--have convinced translators/323/ and commentators that a case which corresponds with *grand mal* epilepsy is being described./324/ These seem to correspond with the following stages of epilepsy: 1) aura or premonitory stage, 2) unconsciousness, 3) tonic stage of muscular rigidity,

4) clonic stage of muscular jerking, 5) flaccid stage of unconsciousness, and 6) recovery.

c. Epilepsy and Demon Possession

The association of demon possession and a clear case of epilepsy in the Gospels presents a particularly acute problem of interpretation and application, now that we are more fully if not perfectly aware of the physiological bases of epilepsy./325/

First, I know of no responsible Christian interpreter who would wish to maintain that all cases of epilepsy have a demonic aetiology, though this position was maintained by the church fathers after Origen./326/ Some literalistic minded Fundamentalist sects do serious damage by insisting that such cases need to be exorcized.

Second, secular scientists would deny any supernatural aetiology of this or any disease. Christian authors, who adopt this position, must maintain that Christ accommodated himself to the ignorance of his contemporaries./327/ Dunn and Twelftree, for example, are willing to concede that a naturalistic explanation rather than a demonic aetiology should be accepted in the case of the epileptic boy:

> Some of the cases of demon-possession in the Gospels can be 'demythologized', at least to some extent. In particular, in the case of Mark 9:14-26 it may well be that we should recognize the signs of epilepsy and recategorize it accordingly. That is to say, Mark 9 is probably a good example of 'pre-scientific' man attributing to demon-possession a malady whose physical mechanism we have since learnt to identify and largely control./328/

Third, there are some authors who would maintain that in this particular case of epilepsy a demonic influence cannot be excluded. Wilkinson, for example, argues that epilepsy is a symptom rather than a disease: 'Therefore to arrive at a diagnosis of epilepsy does not automatically exclude demon possession as the cause of his disease as some commentators maintain'./329/ Citing the concept of idiopathic epilepsy whose causes are not yet known, Richards argues that if the boy had suffered from symptomatic epilepsy rather than one associated with a demon, Jesus would have cured him by an act of healing rather than of exorcism./330/

F. Techniques of Exorcism and Healing

1. Incantations

We have numerous examples of incantations and the accompanying praxis for the exorcism of demons from Mesopotamia./331/ According to Lucian (*Philopseudes* 16) Syrian and Palestinian exorcists used incantations and spells to threaten the demons out of the afflicted. Such incantations were ordinarily whispered or uttered in an abnormal voice (cf. Sanh. 11.1). Often the incantations had to be recited carefully word for word, with prescribed procedures exactly followed./332/ As summarized by O'Keefe:

> Magic speech is not like ordinary speech. It is often extremely odd speech, full of mumbo-jumbo words, archaisms, neologisms and nonsense syllables; it is repetitious, alliterative and full of figures. It may be said in a peculiar tone of voice: chanted or sung or mumbled or sing-songed. Above all, it is usually scripted speech, said in a certain way and that way only, often using fixed expressions handed down./333/

Or as Seligmann remarks of Egyptian magic: 'To accomplish its full effect the word must be spoken correctly. Magic conjuration prescribed the intonation, the secret rhythm which Thoth, god of magic and inventor of language, had taught to the wise men. Success depended on the exact delivery of the formula'./334/ The same point is made by Ghalioungui: 'It consists of the words to be uttered by the exorcist, and these must be rendered with the utmost fidelity. Otherwise, the spell loses all its efficiency, for its power lies in its verbal form, in the sound and rhythm of its words, and has no connection with the intentions of the utterer or with the subject'./335/

Burris enumerates the following characteristics of Roman incantations:

> (1) It was in the form of a command; (2) it was

> chanted; (3) it was uttered in an undervoice; (4) in order to be effective it must be repeated; (5) the wording of the incantation must be exact; (6) the usual purpose of the incantation was secretly to secure evil ends; (7) no god was involved in the incantation./335a/

Vermes observes of Jewish exorcists: 'Contemporary sources also suggest that the exorcist's success was believed to depend on a literal and precise observance of all the prescribed rules and regulations; the correct substances were to be employed possessing the right supernatural properties and the appropriate conjurations uttered.'/336/

Sometimes the incantation had to be repeated./337/ Often incantations included incomprehensible syllables such as an Egyptian spell: 'Bekes, Gs, Gs, Gs, Gs, Ianian, Eren, Eibs, Ks, Ks, Ks, Ks',/338/ or 'Paparouka, paparaka, paparoura'./339/ In a Roman incantation we have the words: 'Huat haut haut istasis tarsis ardannabou dannaustra'./340/

2. Jesus' Words

The spoken word was powerful, some would say even magical./341/ The word was also imbued with power in the Old Testament/Jewish traditions./342/ That this was a magical conception is denied by Lauterbach: 'Viewed in the light of these explanations this belief in the potential effectiveness of the uttered word does not ascribe any magic power to the human voice as such and is certainly not incompatible with Jewish teachings. On the contrary, it rather stems from generally accepted Jewish doctrines and orthodox beliefs'./343/

Some parallels, particularly to the Greek Magical Papyri, have prompted some scholars to speak of Jesus' exorcistic words to the demon as 'incantations'. It has also been alleged that the few words of Jesus preserved in Aramaic/344/ such as *talitha koum* (Mark 5:41) and *ephphatha* (Mark 7:34) are like the Latin *nomina barbarica* (Greek: ῥῆσις βαρβαρική) of magical incantations/345/ but this is not a persuasive explanation. /346/ As Melinsky notes: '*Ephphatha*, of course, was not a foreign word when originally spoken, and in any case Mark is careful to provide a translation into the vernacular for his readers'./347/

The words of Jesus, except for parallels to exorcistic commands, such as 'Get out', certainly do not resemble the elaborate magical incantations which are known from pre-Christian Mesopotamian, Egyptian, or Greco-Roman magic. If one looks diligently enough, one can find instances of ἐξέλθε as an imperative (PGM IV, 1243, 1245, 3013; V, 158), but these commands are seen to be similar only when extracted from their respective contexts. One may see the difference in settings by comparing the occurrence of the word in the Paris Magical Papyrus and the Gospels./348/

Jesus exorcised by his word of command (Mark 1:25, 5:8, 9:25). Aune comments, 'Jesus' own use of the authoritative word of command was perhaps the most characteristic technique which he used to effect both exorcisms and healings'./349/ According to Davies, 'He utters no incantation: He simply speaks the word'./350/ Sabourin concludes:

> Jesus does not work his miracles by magical means or through iatromantic, which we have mentioned. He performs them by the sole power of his word, even if occasionally accompanying gestures indicate or underline the effects it produces. The personality of Jesus remains in every case the decisive factor./351/

3. Appeal to an Authority

Solomon was famed for his wisdom in his lifetime./352/ In later ages his reputation grew. According to Josephus (*Ant.* VIII.45f.): 'Solomon composed incantations by which illnesses are relieved, and left behind forms of exorcisms with which those possessed by demons drive them out, never to return'. Josephus recounts that a certain fellow Jew, Eleazar, exorcised a demon in the presence of Vespasian by using a ring which had one of the roots prescribed by Solomon and by invoking Solomon's name./353/ At Qumran Solomon's name was inserted in Psalm 91 (11QPsA), a psalm which was interpreted as a protection against demons and insanity. The image of Solomon riding on horseback and spearing a demon was a popular motif in Syriac amulets./354/ The Nag Hammadi text, *The Testimony of Truth* (CG IX.3, 70f.), preserves the tradition that Solomon built the temple with the aid of demons, whom he then imprisoned./355/

Duling has edited and retranslated the important pseudepigraphical work *The Testament of Solomon*./356/ This is dated between the first and the third century A.D. The Testament describes how Michael granted Solomon a magic seal ring to call up the demons./357/ The author was keenly interested in the healing of diseases and ills by the exorcisms of demons./358/

The name of 'Jesus' was invoked by later magicians./359/ This has led Loren Fisher to wonder if the reference to Jesus as 'the Son of David' in Matthew 22:42 is not an allusion to Jesus as healing in the name of Solomon./360/ Duling also holds that the Solomonic tradition is possibly behind such references: 'In short, it would appear that Solomon-as-exorcist, who *may* be called 'Son of David' in a more or less casual way, could have had an effect on early Christian tradition in so far as Mark modified the conception for its own purposes'./361/ I would say that such conclusions are rather remote possibilities which have been retrojected from later evidences.

Though others even in his lifetime appealed to the name of Jesus (Mark 9:38-39; cf. Acts 19:13-17) in their exorcisms, what is striking about Jesus' exorcisms is that he does not appeal to Solomon or any similar authority. According to van der Loos, 'It strikes us that, though the pagan exorcists made such frequent use of some name or the other, this was never the case with Jesus'./362/ Foerster declares: 'The crucial thing is that demons are expelled by a word of command issued in the power of God and not by the invocation of a superior but essentially similar spirit, nor by the use of material media'./363/

4. The Name of the Demon

The knowledge of names was important to magicians in general, and the names of demons essential to the work of exorcists. According to Langdon:

> To use words, especially the names of gods, demons and sacred things without knowing their meaning and their history was mere vocal exercise. ... Only by knowing the real name and character of a demon could the magician hope to place him fully in the power of those divine forces whose names he wielded with equal skill./364/

In Egyptian mythology Isis tricked Re into revealing his secret name./365/ In an Egypto-Hellenistic text the god is threatened, 'Give me grace for I have pronounced your hidden name'./366/

Jesus' asking for the name of the demoniac, whose name was 'Legion' (Mark 5:9//Luke 8:30), indeed parallels this practice. /367/ Yet it should be noted that an explicit reference to the demon's name does not seem to be a *sine qua non* as it is not mentioned in all of the other passages on exorcisms by Jesus.

5. Jesus' Touch

The use of the hand and of touch has played a variety of roles from time immemorial in not only magical and religious rites but also in acts of healing in many different cultures./368/ An Egyptian magical text (Berlin Papyrus 3027) reads: 'My hands rest on this child and the hands of Isis rest on him, as she rests her hands on her son Horus'./369/ After having exorcised a demon, an Egyptian magician declared, 'My hand is on thee and my seal is thy protection'./370/

In opposition to those who regard Jesus as working his miracles, his exorcisms in particular, by the simple authority of the word, Remus protests: 'To say that the Jesus of the Synoptics worked his wonders simply by a word is erroneous. Many of them simply happen, and in others he employs manipulations and material objects. These manipulations and *materia* can be paralleled from the magical papyri and from texts describing magicians ...'./371/

By 'manipulations' I understand Remus to be referring to those cases of healing in which Jesus touched those who were ill (e.g. Matthew 9:29; Mark 6:5, Luke 4:40), and by 'materia' I understand him to refer to Jesus' use of spittle (see below). Though Jesus evidently did not use his hand in exorcisms, Böcher nonetheless interprets all laying on of hands in the New Testament as having the power of expelling the evil powers of sickness./372/

Morton Smith, in arguing that Jesus was a magician, notes: 'Besides prayer, magicians might--and Jesus did--resort to physical means. Most common was touching the patient, either fingering the affected area, or taking hold of the person; Jesus/the magician's hand was his most potent instrument'./373/

Hull believes that the Gospel writers struggled with the possible magical implications of Jesus' touch. According to his analysis, 'It is clear that although Matthew did not seek to add the touch he has no objection to the idea of touching except when an impersonal automatic magical idea is implied, as it is in Mark 3.10 and 5.28ff.'./374/ He uses some rather contorted arguments to sustain his thesis with regard to Luke: 'Luke, who was certainly aware of the struggle with Hellenistic magic, actually multiplies the touching incidents, but that is because it is his aim to show not that Christianity has nothing to do with magic, but that Christians can outdo magicians at their own game'./375/

Was Jesus' touch a necessarily magical act? Or are other explanations more likely? When he touched the lepers, for example, was he not defying the ban on contact with the unclean and manifesting his compassion for such untouchables?/376/ Indeed anyone who attempts to heal can hardly avoid touching his patients. According to Majno: 'Physical contact is reassuring; when a doctor touches the patient, both parties have the feeling that something is being done. Touching also means taking part; it means that matters are being taken in hand'./377/

Modern doctors are being encouraged to be aware of the importance of how they touch their patients: 'From the first handshake to heart massage, healers touch their patients, and patients expect to have hands laid on them in one form or another. ... In fact, clinical literature points to the therapeutic potential of touch in nearly every branch of medicine from psychiatry to gerontology'./378/

Not only the touch of Jesus but also touching Jesus has been widely regarded as magical. Aune believes that the incident of the woman with the hemorrhage, who is healed when she touches the hem of Jesus' garment (Mark 5:28; cf. 6:56), and other episodes 'do not border on magic, they are of the essence of Graeco-Roman magical notions'./379/ Other incidents which have been interpreted as conferring healing by magical contact are those involving Peter's shadow (Acts 5:15) and the handkerchiefs and aprons which had touched Paul (Acts 19:12). Commentators have regarded these incidents as either extraordinary miracles or as superstitious practices which were described without being commended./380/

Though these incidents no doubt encouraged a superstitious belief in the healing powers of relics in the Middle Ages, in the Gospels the spiritual basis of the healing of the woman who touched his hem as Jesus himself explained was not the touch itself but the individual's faith (Mark 5:34)./381/ Derrett comments: 'Because Jesus works silently the divine *dunamis* (Matt 28,18) comes from him .... It does not follow that he was unaware of it. It was not magical as was supposed about the middle of the second century and since'./382/ Or as Erasmus paraphrased Mark 6:56:

> Those who touched the hem of Jesus' garment were healed of their diseases, but observe that those who smote him, scourged him, nailed him to the cross, touched his very naked flesh but no one of them was cured of anything. The physical contact achieves nothing without faith. There is no profit in touching Jesus to one who has not first been touched by him./383/

6. Spittle

In many cultures spittle was more than expectorated fluid. It was widely used both for benevolent and for malevolent purposes. As Contenau describes the uses of spit in Mesopotamia:

> Tantôt elles sont bénéfiques: protection contre le mauvais oeil, création d'un lien indissoluble entre deux personnes par échange de salive; tantôt elles son maléfiques, le jet de salive indique le mépris et accompagne une maléfiction./384/

Spit was used, for example, in black magic. One counter charm commanded: 'That the magic which mingleth with the spat-forth spittle may be turned back'./385/ A Mandaic text reads: 'The spit has been spat, and bitter are (the curses) which we have cursed'./386/

But in other cases spittle was believed to have prophylactic power, i.e. the power to repulse evil. According to Trachtenberg, 'Human saliva, especially that of a fasting man, was believed to possess anti-demonic and anti-magical, that is, generally protective powers'./387/ Among the Romans spit was used to protect against the 'evil eye'. According to Persius (*Satires* II.31-34): 'See how a granny, or an auntie who fears the gods, takes baby out of his cradle: skilled in averting the evil eye, she first, with her rebuking middle finger, applies the charm of lustrous spittle to his forehead and slobbering lips'. According to other classical writers spitting in one's bosom was a safeguard against not only the evil eye but against epileptics. Pliny (*N.H.* XXVIII.4,7) wrote: 'We guard ourselves against epilepsy by spitting,--that is, we hurl back the plague. In like manner we repel the evil eye, and the lame man who jostles us on the right-hand side. We also ask pardon from the gods for any overbold hope by spitting into the bosom.' Likewise Theophrastus' *Superstitious Man* related: 'And, if he sees a maniac or an epileptic man, he will shudder and spit into his bosom'. Reference to 'the disease which is spit upon' (Plautus, *The Captives* III.4.550) was understood as a reference to epilepsy./388/

There is a clear allusion to the 'evil eye' in Gal. 3:1. /389/ The Greek verb ἐξεπτύσατε in Gal. 4:14 translated 'rejected', literally means 'spat out' or 'spat at'. If Paul was afflicted with an eye ailment (cf. Gal. 4:15) when he preached to the Galatians and was therefore a trial to them, the normal reaction would be to spit in order to protect oneself from the evil eye.

The prophylactic use of spit survives in some regions today. Ebon reports:

> The use of spit, like blowing or breathing on a person or a possessing demon, is an exorcism method of long standing. I have seen it, to this day, often enough in modern Greece, where a woman will admire a pretty child, for example, and immediately make spitting sounds in order to keep away demons, the evil eye, or other influences that might be jealous of the child and seek to do it harm./390/

On a number of occasions Jesus used his spittle in healing the blind or the deaf (Mark 7:33, 8:23; John 9:6). In a widely reported incident (Tacitus, *Histories* 4.81; Suetonius, *Vespasian* 7; Dio Cassius 65.8) the emperor Vespasian is reported to have restored the sight of a blind man at Alexandria by use of his spittle./391/

Morton Smith concludes: 'Fluid could help to make the contact closer; the readiest form of fluid was spittle, and both spittle and the act of spitting were commonly believed to have magical powers; so we find Jesus, like other magicians, smearing spittle on his patients or using a salve made with spittle'./392/ Böcher also cites the passages which mention spittle to support his conviction that the New Testament authors understood illnesses as caused by demons and healing as the result of exorcisms. For him spittle is evidence of 'die homöopathisch-magische Verwendung der Elemente'./393/

While it is clear that spittle was and is widely used both for black magic and for white or protective magic, it does not necessarily follow that Jesus' use of spittle in healing was therefore magical./394/ There is also considerable evidence that spittle was commonly used to treat eye diseases. Benjamin Gordon notes: 'Spittle was among popular therapeutic agents used in ocular practice by ancient physicians. ... The cure of inflammatory diseases of the eye with spittle was also popular among the Romans and Egyptians. ... In Egypt, spittle was used as a solvent for disturbing films in the eye'./395/ The use of spittle for healing purposes is also attested in rabbinical sources (BB 126b; Shab. 14,14d; 18; Sotah. 16d,37)./396/ Vermes comments, 'Even in regard to healing, the closest he (Jesus) came to the Noachic, Solomonic and Essene type of cure was when he touched the sick with his own saliva, a substance generally thought to be medicinal'./397/

Now as spittle was used both by magicians and by physicians, the use of spittle cannot ipso facto define Jesus as a magician. This would be true only if the spittle itself had been regarded as *ex opere operato* magically effective. If the spittle had been believed to have curative powers its use would have been medicinal. But in any case as reported in the Gospels themselves the miracles of healing are not ascribed to the means used but to Jesus himself: 'He even makes the deaf hear and the dumb speak' (Mark 7:37); 'He opened my eyes' (John 9:30).

G. Was Jesus an Exorcist/Magician?

1. Exorcism as Magical

For scholars who regard exorcism as inherently magical, the fact that Jesus exorcised is sufficient reason to regard Jesus as a magician. Hull declares 'that Jesus entered without reserve into the central conflict of the magician's art, the struggle with evil powers, directly confronted in the persons of the possessed'./398/ Smith also declares: 'Curiously, the first miracles reported are of the most credible sorts, and occur in the most plausible succession: winning disciples, exorcisms, and cures. ... Whatever their historicity, these miracles are all familiar feats of the magician's repertory. /399/ O'Keefe, who is influenced by Smith, declares: 'The clearest case (of religious magic) is exorcism, which is religion's own medicine man magic to fight black magic'./400/

Benko, commenting on the early church, maintains: 'Quite often, however, in the writings of the church fathers their belief in the principles of magic surfaces. For example, they firmly believed in the existence of demons as intermediary beings and that is one of the preconditions for any system of magic'./401/

2. Exorcism as Not Always Magical

Though many exorcists used magic, I would hold that exorcism per se is not necessarily a magical act unless one defines it as such. Knox also declares, 'exorcism in itself cannot justly be regarded as a branch of magic, except on the assumption that the ancient world ought to have possessed a scientific knowledge of psychology'./402/

Moreover in contrast to Benko's assessment Weltin analyzes the Christian church's exorcisms as follows:

> It is surprising that in exorcism, where offhand one would somehow naturally expect 'magical' doings to be at a

> premium, there appears to be no independent virtue attached to any distinct verbal formula or particular rite. ... This informality to which no magical efficacy could adhere is probably explained by the fact that in exorcism the effect sought is sensible; obvious failures of exorcists to produce immediate or even eventual results conclusively demonstrated that no *ex-opere-operato* power resided in any particular 'magical' formula./403/

Few question any longer the accounts that report Jesus' exorcisms. But to characterize him as simply an exorcist would overlook the many other aspects of his ministry./404/ An examination of Jesus' exorcisms does indicate that in some respects they resembled the exorcisms of his contemporaries, such as the stress on the demon's names in one case and the commands to come out of the possessed. However, to designate his commands as 'incantations ' is to distort the customary understanding of the word 'incantation'. To regard his touch and use of spittle as magical is to ignore their therapeutic intention in favor of inexact magical parallels. Jesus' exorcisms transform him into a magician only for those who believe that exorcisms are unavoidably magical.

3. The Kingdom of Beelzebub

Though Jesus accepted the reality of demons, he did not share the general magical view of conflicting demonic powers. In ancient Mesopotamia the amulet of the demon Pazuzu was worn to protect women against the demon Lamashtu. One Akkadian text reads, 'May the bad demons depart! May they seize upon one another!'/405/ In an Old Babylonian text one demon is described as biting another./406/

Speaking of Greco-Roman magic, Lowe observes: 'Certain charms were employed on the principle that the demon of the disease could be frightened away by being told that a more powerful demon was on his track'./407/ In later Mandaic texts we read of the expulsion of curses by the head of the powers of darkness, Adonai Yorba, and of a lilith counteracting the evil workings of the witch./408/

This background may underly the accusation that Jesus exorcised demons by Beelzebul or Beelzebub, the prince of demons (Matt. 12:24; Mark 3:22; Luke 11:15)./409/ In his response to the Pharisees, Jesus equated Beelzebub with Satan, and asked, 'If Satan drives out Satan, he is divided against himself. How then can his kingdom stand? And if I drive out demons by Beelzebub, by whom do your people drive them out?' (Matt. 12:26-27) . In place of a world of demons competing with each other, Jesus regarded all demons as belonging to the kingdom of Satan--a radically new conception./410/

Yates concludes: 'The whole approach to the powers of evil is transposed into a different key. As compared with the demon-riddled world of contemporary belief we witness in the Synoptic Gospels a simplification of these ideas, and a stress on the close connection between the operation of the demons and Satan'./411/ According to Kallas, 'Jesus, instead of merely accomodating himself to contemporary thought, deepens the concepts of the day regarding demons'./412/

IV. CONCLUSIONS

Our study has demonstrated that Böcher's pan-demonological view that the ancients, including the biblical writers, believed that all diseases were caused by demons and that they could be cured only be exorcisms is patently false./413/ Our survey of the evidences indicate that non-demonic aetiologies were maintained both in Mesopotamia, Egypt, Greece, Rome, Judaism, as well as in the Old and New Testaments.

We have also argued that the characterization of Jesus as a magician by Hull, Smith, and Aune often relies on either hostile or inappropriate sources, and on the debatable assumptions that touch is necessarily a magical act, that spittle is always materia magica, and that exorcism inevitably involves magic. The answer to the further question of whether the exorcisms and healings of Jesus were miracles or not depends largely upon the presuppositions of the reader. We may examine some of the possible options.

V. THE CREDIBILITY OF EXORCISMS

A. Anti-Supernaturalism.

Especially since the development of rationalism in the

17th and 18th centuries many distinguished scholars have flatly denied the possibility of miracles. For example, David Hume (1711-76) argued that it was always more reasonable to reject testimonies about miracles than to accept them. Matthew Arnold (1822-88) declared: '*miracles do not happen*'./414/

Rudolf Bultmann's dicta have often been quoted:

> Now that the forces and the laws of nature have been discovered, we can no longer believe in spirits, *whether good or evil*.
>
> Sickness and the cure of disease are likewise attributable to natural causation: they are not the result of daemonic activity or of evil spells.
>
> It is impossible to use electric light and the wireless and to avail ourselves of modern medical and surgical discoveries, and at the same time to believe in the New Testament world of spirits and miracles./415/

As Brown has pointed out in his recent work on miracles, this skeptical view depends not only upon the evidences but also upon a certain philosophical or theological view of reality./416/ Alan Richardson concludes:

> Thus, the answer to the question, Did the miracles happen? is always a *personal* answer. It is not the judgment of an historian *qua* scientific investigator, or the verdict of a school of theologians, or the pronouncement of an authoritative council of churchmen. It is the 'Yes' of faith to the challenge which confronts us in the New Testament presentation of Christ--the only Christ we can know./417/

According to Mortimer Adler: 'The materialist assumption that spiritual substances do not exist is as much an act of faith as the religious belief in the reality of angels. The latter is an act of religious faith; the former, it might be said, is an act of anti-religious faith'./418/

As a specific illustration of this consideration, we may take Morton Smith's attitude to the supernatural. In his words, that Christ 'should be represented as a supernatural being is the first suspicious item, for his was a common claim of magicians and result of magical operations'./419/ Smith accepts the authenticity of Jesus' exorcisms but explains them as the 'sudden cessation of hysterical symptoms and cognate psychological disorders'./420/ Reviewers have underscored Smith's approach. For example, William A. Beardslee, commenting on Smith's *SG*, writes: 'This perspective is more a product of his enlightenment rationalism than of his sources'./421/ Walter Wink analyzes Smith's goal as follows:

> Make no mistake. Smith's is a theological and not just an historical program. He is engaged in a systematic effort to undermine the very ground on which Christian faith rests. His tools are the familiar ones: historical revision and psychological reduction./422/

B. Rationalistic Reinterpretations

1. Advocates of Rationalistic Reinterpretations

Medical research into the implications of psychosomatic illness have persuaded many of the credibility of Jesus' healing miracles. For example, John T. McNeill declares:

> Modern research into comparable phenomena of spiritual healing makes it necessary to concede the possibility of genuine cures by the impact of spiritual and personal forces; and when we add to this the evidence of Jesus' unique power of personality, we must become incredulous of the incredulity that would reject the fact of His 'miraculous' healing./423/

On the other hand, a less sympathetic attitude prevails toward Jesus' miracles of exorcisms. Understandably uncomfortable with the ramifications of ancient beliefs in demons, many interpreters have sought to reinterpret the biblical accounts. David Strauss, the 19th-century critic, explained the exorcisms as Jesus' helping the victims overcome their neurotic obsessions. As to the phenomena of possession, Sigmund Freud in a celebrated essay on 'A Neurosis of Demoniacal Possession in the Seventeenth Century' wrote: 'What in those days were thought to be evil spirits to us are base and evil wishes, the derivatives of impulses which have been rejected and repressed'./424/

In 1975 a group of 65 academic theologians advised the Church of England against giving official recognition to the rite of exorcism as it was based on a pre-scientific outlook./425/ Liberal Catholic scholars, Cortés and Gatti assert: 'We do believe in the Devil, but not in demons'./426/ They argue that only illnesses with imperceptible causes were attributed out of ignorance to demons:/427/

> We contend that the illnesses of the demon-possessed were real illnesses, caused at least in some instances by brain disorders or cerebral organic impairments, but that their attribution to demons was a mode of expression common to those times. The sick were not really possessed. The language of possession was their way of explaining the unknown causes that produced what were then looked on as very strange symptoms and manifestations. /428/

Others such as Macgregor also regard such beliefs as 'simply part of the religious symbolism and ideology of the times ...'./429/ Reginald Fuller notes that many biblical scholars interpret the exorcisms and healings psychologically. /430/ He suggests:

> Of course, we no longer believe in demons .... But we are bound to believe in what the demons of the New Testament signify. We need not *eliminate* the devil from the catechism but we must *interpret* what he stands for. He stands for the supra-personal reality of evil, something outside ourselves which gets us in its grip. The old mythology may still be used, but it must be understood as a symbolic expression of the realities of human experience./431/

2. The Weaknesses of Such Reinterpretations

But such a rationalizing, anti-supernaturalistic approach to religion in general and to Scriptures in particular has resulted in diminishing if not self-destructive results./432/ A recent critique by J. G. Davies cautions:

> To commit oneself uncritically to the historical-critical approach is to forget its own historical

conditioning. In an age when science is dominant, the method appears to provide a basis for understanding that is equivalent to the objectivity extolled by scientists, but faith in such a method can lead to a denial by an exegete of his own historicality. After all, hermeneutics, since it is an activity of the historical consciousness, cannot be absolute; it is unable to conform to the natural sciences' ideal of objectivity./433/

Moreover, the social sciences--such as anthropology, sociology, and psychology--which have informed many of the modern attempts to reinterpret the Scriptures are themselves involved in subjective perspectives./434/ For example, the psychoanalytic approach involves the acceptance of dubious postulates of Freud, whereas a behavioristic attitude involves the acceptance of a starkly reductionist view of what constitutes reality. Crapanzaro asks:

> To emphasize 'pathology,' 'mental disorder,' 'psychosis,' and 'neurosis' in cases of spirit possession, as Devereaux (1956) and Silverman (1967) have done, is to raise what is essentially a misleading, though culturally expectable, response to an 'uncanny' encounter. However 'ego-syntonic' they may be to the investigator, such diagnoses may well blind us to the dynamics of spirit possession. The question that must be asked is this: What, besides a protective shield, do we gain from calling a shaman a schizophrenic (Silverman, 1967), an individual possessed by a spirit a paranoid (Ortigues, 1966), a neurotic (Freud, 1963a; Wallace, 1966), or an hysteric (Freed, 1964)?/435/

In a noteworthy admission the prominent sociologist of religion, Robert N. Bellah, confessed:

> But what came through in my lectures, I am afraid, was the assumption that social scientists understood what people are doing when they are being religious in ways deeper than they do. Those poor benighted religious people down there are sort of blindly going through their religious practices but we social scientists with our conceptual frameworks and our functional analyses really know what is going on. ... What I have come to see in

> the past five years ... is that I was not only offering an alternative religious view of my own, but a peculiarly dessicated one, because utterly conceptual, that was designed to cope with the great issues of religion mainly by screening them out in a maze of intellectualization. /436/

The prominent sociologist, Peter Berger, has pointed out that contemporary theologians and biblical critics have been conditioned by modern secularism to 'demythologize' the supernatural elements of Scriptures. Berger criticizes the tacit assumption that the modern anti-supernaturalist view is superior to that of the supernaturalist:

> Even if it is conceded (which ought not to be conceded) that, the moment one starts using an electric toothbrush or watching the CBS news, the world of the gods recedes into implausibility, is this necessarily an advance over the author of the Gospel of John (not to mention Socrates, Aeschylus, and the Buddha)?/437/

Berger points out that it is a fallacy to believe that 'what is' is necessarily 'what ought to be'--a view which seems to be encouraged by a facile reading of sociology. For example, the fact that people in the western world are conditioned so that they are not conscious of angels or demons, does not thereby demonstrate that angels or demons do not exist./438/ Berger also points out that liberal reinterpretations of Christianity like Bultmann's are ultimately self-defeating:/439/ 'In other words, the theological surrender to the alleged demise of the supernatural defeats itself in precisely the measure of its success. Ultimately, it represents the self-liquidation of theology and of the institutions in which the theological tradition is embodied'./440/

C. Qualified Supernaturalism

1. The Implications of Jesus' Exorcisms

The Old Testament assumes not only the existence of God but also of opposing spirits. In the New Testament Christ is depicted as exorcising demons as an important part of his ministry./441/ So much is clear. Christians, who accept the Scriptures as authoritative, accept these data as given./442/

But how are these data to be interpreted?

As Loos succinctly summarizes the alternative responses to these accounts: 'A number of investigators say that Jesus "erred". Others are of the opinion that He "adapted" Himself. A third group assumes that Jesus did in fact expel unclean spirits'./443/

We should be aware of the implications of explaining away all cases of alleged possession as psychoses or schizophrenia, though many may indeed be correctly analysed as such./444/ To those like Rudolf Otto, who insist that the exorcisms of Jesus were central to Jesus' message, but that these were related to 'non-organic psychological phenomena', Kallas protests: 'Thus to call the exorcisms of demons on the one hand the central message of Jesus, and then on the other hand to deny the strength or evil effects of these demons, is to reduce Jesus to a rather befuddled do-gooder who spent all his time chasing harmless spectres who existed only in the imagination of the self-styled afflicted'./445/ Sabourin declares:

> Yet it seems easier to accept the existence of demons, as independent entities, than to explain, if this is denied, that Jesus is represented as having expelled them from the possessed. It is hardly possible, both to safeguard his honesty and to say that he simulated to act according to the common belief, or else to propose that he was invincibly immersed as man in the mistaken persuasions of his age and country./446/

2. The Reality of Possession

We are not bound to believe--as the pagans did then and as many primitive tribes believe today--in the ubiquity of demons and their unbridled power. We may affirm the reality of the exorcisms, while conceding that they were couched in the 'jargon' of the day./447/ I. Howard Marshall suggests:

> The biblical teaching is making the same point, that there is an evil force in the universe of cosmic dimensions. Maybe, therefore, we should see the biblical teaching as testifying to the existence of real, evil forces in the universe without necessarily being committed to sharing all of the popular language and

> conceptualisation which is used to express this belief. To say this is not to deny the possibility of such powers affecting individuals in the way described in the Gospels; modern Western man would be ill-advised to deny this possibility./448/

The famous psychologist Carl Jung was raised in the rationalism and materialism of the early twentieth century. But he found that these conceptual frameworks did not explain for him the evil of the Nazi atrocities nor 'the data that were forcing themselves on him from the unconscious depths of his patients'./449/ Accoring to Melinsky: 'The vast psychic world with which man is presented through unconscious contents and meanings, Jung found, is as objectively real, and as meaningful and possible to experience, as the physical world of space and time'./450/

Missionaries and anthropologists alike attest to frequent cases even today of possession most commonly in the non-western world./451/ Occasionally there are celebrated cases of possession in the western world also, such as the notorious episode of the German girl Anneliese Michel, who died in 1976. A noted anthropologist, Felicitas D. Goodman,/452/ has examined the case in detail. The poor girl was incorrectly diagnosed as an epileptic./453/ Neither priests, nor psychologists, nor doctors were able to help her. Drugs given to her may have hastened her death.

Who can say that chemical possession by drugs such as heroin and cocaine in the western world is any less destructive or diabolical than demonic possession? The enduring message of the Gospel is that Christ died and rose to triumph over all principalities and powers, and that He can deliver us from all demons and obsessions, whether chemical or psychological or spiritual./454/

Notes

*I am indebted to the Institute for Advanced Christian Studies for a fellowship to pursue further studies in ancient magic. My interest in the subject of magic goes back to the research for my dissertation which was published as *Mandaic*

Incantation Texts [hereafter *MIT*] (New Haven: American Oriental Society, 1967). See also my articles: 'Aramaic Magic Bowls', *JAOS* 85 (1965) 511-23; 'Magic in the Biblical World', *Tyn Bul* 34 (1983) 169-200.

In addition to the abbreviations listed in the *JBL* : I have also used the following:

ANRW	*Aufstieg und Niedergang der römischen Welt*
BHM	*Bulletin of the History of Medicine*
CSR	*Christian Scholars Review*
JASA	*Journal of the American Scientific Affiliation*
JETS	*Journal of the Evangelical Theological Society*
JHMAS	*Journal of the History of Medicine and Allied Sciences*

/1/ See Harold Remus, 'Does Terminology Distinguish Early Christian from Pagan Miracles?', *JBL* 101 (1982) 531-51; idem, '"Magic or Miracle"? Some Second Century Instances', *Second Century* 2 (1982) 127-56; idem, *Pagan-Christian Conflict over Miracles in the Second Century* (Cambridge, MA: Patristic Foundation, 1983); R. M. Grant, *Eusebius* (Oxford: Clarendon Press, 1980) 150. R. M. Grant, *Miracle and Natural Law in Graeco-Roman and Early Christian Thought* (Amsterdam: North Holland Pub., 1952) 173, does not believe that a thoroughgoing distinction can be made between Christian and non-Christian stories: 'The contexts are different; the phenomena are somewhat similar'. But is not the context the most important determining hermeneutical factor?

/2/ Henry Chadwick, *Origen, Contra Celsum* (Cambridge: Cambridge University, 1980); Eugene V. Gallagher, *Divine Man or Magician? Celsus and Origen on Jesus* (Chico: Scholars Press, 1982); S. Benko, 'Pagan Criticism of Christianity During the First Two Centuries A.D.', *Aufstieg und Niedergang der römischen Welt*, ed. H. Temporini and W. Haase (Berlin: Walter de Gruyter, 1980) II.23.2 1085-1118.

/3/ G. Lampe, 'Miracles and Early Christian Apologetic', in C. F. D. Moule, ed., *Miracles: Cambridge Studies in Their Philosophy and History* (London: Mowbrays, 1965) 213.

/4/ See A. Fridrichsen, *The Problem of Miracle in Primitive Christianity* (Minneapolis: Augsburg, 1972) 90.

/5/ Norman L. Geisler, *Miracles and Modern Thought* (Grand

Rapids: Zondervan, 1982) 120-21. Cf. P. Samain, '"L'accusation de magie contre le Christ dans les Evangiles"', *ETL* 15 (1938) 471.

/6/ C. F. D. Moule, 'Introduction', in Moule 17.

/7/ H. van der Loos, *The Miracles of Jesus* (Leiden: Brill, 1965) 142.

/8/ See Pliny, *Natural History* XXX.1; Catullus XC; cf. my article, 'Christmas Metamorphoses: How the Magi Became Melchior, Gaspar and Balthasar', *BA* (forthcoming).

/9/ Gallagher 47.

/10/ Alan F. Segal, 'Hellenistic Magic: Some Questions of Definition', *Studies in Gnosticism and Hellenistic Religions*, ed. R. Van den Broek and M. J. Vermaseren (Leiden: Brill, 1981) 369.

/11/ See, however, the views of Morton Smith described below.

/12/ See E. Bammel, 'Christian Origins in Jewish Tradition', *NTS* 13 (1967) 317-35; W. Horbury, 'The Trial of Jesus in Jewish Tradition', *The Trial of Jesus*, ed. E. Bammel (London: SCM Press, 1970) 106-21; D. R. Catchpole, *The Trial of Jesus* (Leiden: Brill, 1971) 1-7. The recent attempt to deny the authenticity of all Talmudic references to Jesus by Johann Maier, *Jesus von Nazareth in der talmudischen Überlieferung* (Darmstadt: Wissenschaftliche Buchgesellschaft, 1978), is criticized by David Goldenberg, 'Once More: Jesus in the Talmud', *JQR* 73 (1982) 78-86.

/13/ G. Schlichting, *Ein jüdisches Leben Jesu* (Tübingen: J. C. B. Mohr, 1982) 100-101.

/14/ Such anthropological studies are, of course, invaluable for missionaries. See Miriam Adeney, 'What Is "Natural" about Witchcraft and Sorcery?' *Missiology* 2 (1974) 377-95.

/15/ Vincent Crapanzaro and Vivian Garrison, *Case Studies in Spirit Possession* (New York: John Wiley & Sons, 1977) 7.

/16/ Michael A. Beaubrun and Colleen Ward, 'The Psychodynamics of Demon Possession', *JSSR* 19 (1980) 202-207. For the views of Christian psychologists see: Walter C. Johnson, 'Demon Possession and Mental Illness', *JASA* 34 (1982) 149-54; and articles in John W. Montgomery, ed., *Demon Possession* (Minneapolis: Bethany Fellowship, 1976).

/17/ Jerome D. Frank, *Persuasion and Healing* (New York: Schocken Books, 1974); Ari Kiev, ed., *Magic, Faith and Healing* (New York: Free Press, 1974).

/18/ Daniel L. O'Keefe, *Stolen Lightning: The Social Theory of Magic* (New York: Continuum, 1982) 14. O'Keefe 140-41,

accepts Morton Smith's magical interpretation of Jesus.
/19/ Paul W. Hollenbach, 'Jesus, Demoniacs, and Public Authorities', *JAAR* 49 (1981) 567. For an example of an anthropological analysis of demon possession see J. Duncan M. Derrett, 'Legend and Event: The Gerasene Demoniac ...', *Studia Biblica* 2 (1978) 67-68.
/20/ See my 'Sociology, Scriptures and the Supernatural', *JETS* 27 (1984) 169-92.
/21/ Segal 375.
/22/ (Stuttgart: Kohlhammer, 1970).
/23/ (Stuttgart: Katholisches Bibelwerk, 1972).
/24/ (Stuttgart: Kohlhammer, 1972).
/25/ Hollenbach 584: 'The most complete work on demonology was written by Böcher'; M. Smith in his latest work discussed below; J. I. González, 'Jesús y los demonios', *EstEcl* 52 (1977) 487-519.
/26/ Böcher, *DD* 152: 'Ganz allgemein aber gilt für die Antike, dass man keine natürliche Ätiologie der Krankheiten gekannt hat, sondern alle Krankheiten auf die Einwirkung von Dämonen aufrückführte'. See also p. 18 and *passim*. A similar generalization was made earlier by F. C. Conybeare, 'The Demonology of the New Testament', *JQR* 8 (1896) 588: 'They (the demons) cause in man all sin and disease and death. ... To be sick is to have a devil inside one. To be cured is to have it cast out'.
/27/ Böcher, *DD* 316-17; *CE* 16, 70.
/28/ Böcher, *NTDM* 20.
/29/ This is the etymological background of the English word 'nightmare'.
/30/ Böcher, *DD* 124-26. As proof of the fear of the demons of sexuality he cites the biblical passages which denounce idolatry as 'whoredoms'. See Böcher, *NTDM* 18.
/31/ Böcher, *DD* 129.
/32/ Ibid. 155.
/33/ Böcher, *NTDM* 9.
/34/ Ibid. 15.
/35/ Ibid. 14.
/36/ Ibid. 126.
/37/ Ibid. 27-29. Leopold Sabourin, 'The Miracles of Jesus II: Jesus and the Evil Powers', *BTB* 4 (1974) 170 comments: 'Böcher's efforts ... to link New Testament exorcisms and healings with the kathartic, anti-demonic means of protection and purification (sympathetic magic, light, water, blood, oil,

breath, salt and other elements) are largely unsuccessful, relying as they do on parallels which appeared to me often singularly irrelevant'.

/38/ (London: SCM, 1974).

/39/ Hull, *HM* 144.

/40/ Ibid. 142-43.

/41/ John M. Hull, 'Exorcism in the NT', *The Interpreter's Dictionary of the Bible, Supplementary Volume*, ed. Keith Crim (Nashville: Abingdon, 1976) 313.

/42/ Hull, *HM* 158, n. 102; idem, 'Exorcism in the NT' 313: 'Almost every reference to exorcism in pre-Christian and first-century literature is associated with magic'.

/43/ Hull, *HM* 143.

/44/ John W. Drane, 'The Religious Background', in *New Testament Interpretation*, ed. I. Howard Marshall (Exeter: Paternoster Press, 1977) 122 seems to echo Hull, when he writes: 'This does not necessarily mean that Jesus actually thought of himself as a magician after the Hellenistic model, though we can have no doubt that the early Christians were being faithful to their Lord and Master when they so portrayed him'.

/45/ E.g. Morton Smith, 'Comments on Taylor's *Commentary on Mark*', *HTR* 48 (1955) 23.

/46/ (Cambridge, MA: Harvard University, 1973).

/47/ (New York: Harper and Row, 1973).

/48/ (San Francisco: Harper and Row, 1978).

/49/ On the Greek Magical Papyri see my 'Magic in the Biblical World', 173. Eugene N. Lane, 'On the Date of *PGM* IV', *The Second Century* 4 (1984) 27, places the terminus post quem of PGM IV at A.D. 380.

/49a/ M. Smith, 'Clement of Alexandria and Secret Mark: The Score at the End of the First Decade', *HTR* 75 (1982) 450, tallies up the 'score' as follows: 'Of the scholars listed in the bibliography here following, twenty-five have agreed in attributing the letter to Clement, six have suspended judgment or have not discussed the question, and only four have denied the attribution, namely, Kümmel, Murgia, Musurillo, and Quesnell'. H. Musurillo, 'Morton Smith's Secret Gospel', *Thought* 48 (1974) 327-31, suggests the possibility of either a modern or more likely an ancient forgery.

/50/ Smith, *CA* 251; *SG* 114.

/50a/ But R. E. Brown, 'The Relation of "The Secret Gospel of Mark" to the Fourth Gospel', *CBQ* 36 (1974) 509, concludes: 'I do not regard my study as probative, but I hope I have made a reasonable case for maintaining that Morton Smith is wrong when he contends that the author of SGM [The Secret Gospel of Mark] could not have drawn upon the Fourth Gospel'. P. W. Skehan in his review of Smith's *CA* in *CHR* 60 (1974-75) 452, makes the same point: 'Despite Smith's efforts to detach the passages quoted by Clement from any secondary relationship to the canonical gospels, a dependence on the canonical John is, in the reviewer's judgment, unmistakable ...'.

/51/ Smith, *JM* 81; ibid. 107: 'Cures are also a major concern of magic'.

/52/ Ibid. 82.

/53/ Ibid. 130. Contrast, however, Martin Nilsson's comment on the Greek Magical Papyri in his *Greek Piety* (NY: W. W. Norton, 1969) 175: 'Magicians do not pray but compel gods or daimones by their potency, and the potency (δύναμις) which the operator assumes is called divine power or spirit (πνεῦμα), or divine effluence (ἀπόρροια); sometimes the magician identifies himself with a god'.

/54/ Smith, *JM* 143.

/55/ Smith, *CA* 218-19; *JM* 123.

/56/ Smith, *SG* 102-103, 140.

/57/ Smith, *CA* 235.

/58/ Ibid. 254, 257, 263; *SG* 121.

/59/ Smith, *CA* 252; *SG* 131.

/60/ Smith, *JM* 93, cf. 129.

/61/ See for example: P. J. Achtemeier, *JBL* 93 (1974) 625-28; Per Beskow, *Strange Tales about Jesus* (Philadelphia: Fortress, 1983) ch. 14; F. F. Bruce, *The 'Secret' Gospel of Mark* (London: Athlone, 1974); J. A. Fitzmyer, *America* (June 23, 1973) 570-72; R. M. Grant, *ATR* 56 (1974) 58-64; R. P. C. Hanson, *JTS* n.s. 25 (1974) 513-21; H. C. Kee, *JAAR* 43 (1975) 326-29; H. Merkel, *ZTK* 71 (1974) 123-44; P. Parker, *ATR* 56 (1974) 53-57; Q. Quesnell, *CBQ* 37 (1975) 48-67; W. Wink, *USQR* 30 (1974) 3-14; E. Yamauchi, *CSR* 4 (1975) 238-51. See also R. H. Fuller et al., *Longer Mark: Forgery, Interpolation, or Old Tradition?* (Berkeley: Center for Hermeneutical Studies, 1976). E. P. Sanders, *Jesus and Judaism* (Philadelphia: Fortress, 1985), who is otherwise appreciative of Smith's analysis, disagrees with his conclusion (170): 'Nor do we understand Jesus by calling him "a magician"'.

/62/ Howard Clark Kee, *Miracle in the Early Christian World: A Study in Sociological Method* (New Haven: Yale University,

1983) 211; also 288: 'But to offer Philostratus or the Greek Magical Papyri as historical evidence for events reported by writers of the Gospels and Acts, is historiographically irresponsible'. In the current study I will concentrate on pre-Christian materials, but will quote some post-Christian examples as illustrations.

/63/ (Berlin: Walter de Gruyter, 1980) II.23.2, 1507-57.

/64/ Ibid. 1524.

/65/ Ibid. 1508.

/66/ Ibid.

/67/ Ibid. 1509.

/68/ Ibid.

/69/ Ibid. 1514.

/70/ Ibid. 1515.

/71/ Ibid.

/72/ Ibid. 1532.

/73/ Ibid. 1539.

/74/ Ibid.

/75/ Ibid. 1524.

/76/ See my 'Sociology, Scriptures and the Supernatural', 169-92.

/77/ Robert Friedrichs, 'Sociological Research and Theology', *Review of Religious Research* 15 (1974) 120.

/78/ See Calvin Wells, *Bones, Bodies and Disease* (New York: Praeger, 1964); Paul A. Janssens, *Palaeopathology of Disease and Injury of Prehistoric Man* (London: John Baker, 1970); Srboljub Živanović', *Ancient Diseases* (New York: Pica Press, 1982); P. B. Adamson, 'Human Diseases and Deaths in the Ancient Near East', *WO* 13 (1982) 5-14. James Mellaart, *The Neolithic of the Near East* (NY: Charles Scribner's Sons, 1975) 98-100, reports that the very early site of Catal Hüyük in Anatolia, the largest Neolithic site in the Near East, yielded skeletons with evidence of anaemia, possibly caused by malaria. The average height of men was 5'7", of women 5' 2"; the average longevity was from 30 to 34 years.

/79/ J. V. Kinnier Wilson, 'Leprosy in Ancient Mesopotamia', *RA* 60 (1966) 47-58; Calvin Wells, 'Pseudopathology', *Diseases in Antiquity* [hereafter *DIA*], ed. D. Brothwell and A. T. Sandison (Springfield, IL: Charles C. Thomas, 1967) 17, points out that the Greek word λέπρα 'embraced a wide range of skin diseases such as psoriasis, eczema, dermatoses, etc. and possibly never true leprosy'; Robert Biggs, 'Medicine in Ancient Mesopotamia', *History of Science* 8 (1969) 101-102; E. V. Hulse, 'Leprosy and Ancient Egypt', *Lancet* 2 (1972) 1024-25.

/80/ Guido Majno, *Healing Hand: Man and Wound in the Ancient World* (Cambridge, MA: Harvard University, 1975) 36. Franz Köcher has been publishing these cuneiform texts in copies in the series, *Die Babylonisch-assyrische Medizin in Texten und Untersuchungen* (Berlin: Walter de Gruyter, 1963-80) I-V. His footnotes refer to earlier translations of some of the texts. See A. Leo Oppenheim, 'Mesopotamian Medicine', *BHM* 36 (1962) 97-108.

/81/ Robert D. Biggs, *ŠÀ.ZI.GA; Ancient Mesopotamian Potency Incantations* (Locust Valley, NY: J. J. Augustin, 1967).

/82/ J. Van Dijk, 'Une incantation accompagnant la naissance de l'homme', *Or* 42 (1973) 502-07; idem, 'Incantations accompagnant la naissance de l'homme', *Or* 44 (1975) 52-79.

/83/ R. Labat, 'Remèdes assyriens contre les affections de l'oreille ...', *RSO* 32 (1957) 110.

/84/ Ibid.; also R. C. Thompson, 'Assyrian Prescriptions for Diseases of the Ears', *JRAS* (1931) 1 ff.

/85/ Köcher, VI, vii.

/86/ R. C. Thompson, 'Assyrian Medical Prescriptions for Disease of the Stomach', *RA* 26 (1929) 47-70.

/87/ B. Alster, 'A Sumerian Incantation against Gall', *Or* 41 (1972) 349-58.

/88/ J. V. Kinnier Wilson, 'Two Medical Texts from Nimrud', *Iraq* 18 (1956) 130-46.

/89/ R. Labat, 'Le premier chapitre d'un précis médical assyrien', *RA* 53 (1959) 1-18.

/90/ P. Weber, *Dämonenbeschwörung bei den Babyloniern und Assyrern* (Leipzig: J. C. Hinrichs, 1906); R. C. Thompson, *The Devils and Evil Spirits of Babylonia* (= *DESB*) (London: Luzac, 1903-04) 2 vols.; idem, *Semitic Magic* (New York: KTAV, 1971 repr. of the 1908 ed.) 40 ff.; E. Unger, 'Dämonenbilder', *Reallexicon der Assyriologie*, ed. E. Ebeling & B. Meissner (Berlin: W. de Gruyter, 1938) 113-15; J. L. Llarri, 'Demonologia Mesopotámica', *Semana Bíblica Española* 27 (1967, pub. 1970) 143-59.

/91/ H.W.F. Saggs, *The Greatness That Was Babylon* (NY: Hawthorn, 1962) 313.

/92/ D. W. Myrhman, 'Die Labartu-Texte', *ZA* 16 (1902) 141-200; F. Thureau-Dangin, 'Rituel et amulettes contre Labartu', *RA* 18 (1921) 162-98; C. Frank, *Lamaštu, Pazuzu und andere Dämonen* (Leipzig: Harrassowitz; Osnabrück:

O. Zeller, 1941 repr. 1972); L. J. Krušina-Černý, 'Three New Amulets of Lamashtu', *AO* 18 (1950), 297-303; Wolfram von Soden, 'Eine altbabylonische Beschwörung gegen die Dämonin Lamaštum', *Or* 23 (1954) 337-47; H. Klengel, 'Neue Lamaštu-Amulette aus dem Vorderasiatischen Museum zu Berlin und dem British Museum', *MIO* 7 (1959-60) 334-55; idem, 'Weitere Amulette gegen Lamaštum', *MIO* 8 (1961-63) 24-29; J. Nougayrol, 'La Lamaštu à Byblos', *RA* 65 (1971) 173-74; M. V. Tonietti, 'Un incatesimo sumerico contro la Lamaštu', *Or* 48 (1979) 301-23; G. Wilhelm, 'Ein neues Lamaštu-Amulett', *ZA* 69 (1979) 34-40. Indeed, among the most ancient Akkadian texts, i.e. Old Assyrian and Old Babylonian, are charms against the Lamashtu. See W. Farber, 'Zur älteren akkadischen Beschwörungs-literatur', *ZA* 71 (1981) 51-72.

/93/ Israel Zoller, 'Lilit', *Filologische Schriften* 3 (1929) 121-42.

/94/ S. Lackenbacher, 'Note sur l'ardat-lilî', *RA* 65 (1971) 119-54.

/95/ H. W. F. Saggs, 'Pazuzu', *AfO* 19 (1960) 123-27; P. R. S. Moorey, 'A Bronze "Pazuzu" Statuette from Egypt', *Iraq* 27 (1965) 33-41; R. Ghirshman, 'Le Pazuzu et les fibules du Louristan', *MUSJ* 46 (1970) 119-27.

/96/ Ibid. 302.

/97/ Cf. G. Castellino, 'Rituals and Prayers against "Appearing Ghosts"', *Or* 24 (1955) 240-74.

/98/ Erich Ebeling, 'Beiträge zur Kenntniss der Beschwörungsserie Namburbi', *RA* 48 (1954) 1-15, 76-85, 130-41, 178-91; idem, *RA* 49 (1955) 32-41, 137-48, 178-92; W. G. Lambert, 'An Address of Marduk', *AfO* 17 (1956) 310-21; idem, 'An Address of Marduk to the Demons; New Fragments', *AfO* 19 (1959-60) 114-19.

/99/ M. Mallowan, *Twenty-five Years of Mesopotamian Discovery* (London: British School of Archaeology/Iraq, 1956) 57; O.R. Gurney, 'Babylonian Prophylactic Figures and Their Ritual', *Annals of Archeology and Anthropology* 22 (1935) 31-96.

/100/ Thureau-Dangin; G. Contenau, *La médicine en Assyrie et en Babylonie* (Paris: Maloine, 1938) 90, 154, 180; E. Leichty, 'Demons and Population Control', *Expedition* 13 (1971) 22-26; Majno 40. For other representations see: Woldemar G. Schileico, 'Tête d'un démon Assyrien', *RA* 11 (1914) 57-59; R. Borger, 'Zu einigen Dämonenkopf-Inschriften', *AfO* 17 (1954-56) 358-59.

/101/ W. H. Ph. Römer, 'Einige Bemerkungen zum dämonischen

Gotte d. Kubu(m)', *Symbolae biblicae et mesopotamicae F. M. Th. de Liagre Böhl Dedicatae* (Leiden: Brill, 1973) 310-19.
/102/ C. Fossey, *La Magie Assyrienne* (Paris: Leroux, 1902) 21; G. Contenau, *La Magie chez les Assyriens et les Babyloniens* (Paris: Payot, 1947) 213; D. Goltz, *Studien zur altorientalischen und griechischen Heilkunde* (Wiesbaden: F. Steiner, 1974) 8; René Labat, 'Geisteskrankheiten', *Reallexicon der Assyriologie*, ed. E. Weidner and W. von Soden (Berlin: W. de Gruyter, 1957-71) III, 196-97.
/103/ Contenau, *Medicine*, 87; A. L. Oppenheim, *Ancient Mesopotamia* (Chicago: University of Chicago, 1964) 199.
/104/ Leichty 23.
/105/ Contenau, *Medicine* 86; cf. Thompson, *DESB* II, 29.
/106/ Cited by J. V. Kinnier Wilson, 'An Introduction to Babylonian Psychiatry', *Studies in Honor of Benno Landsberger*, ed. H. G. Güterbock and T. Jacobsen (Chicago: University of Chicago, 1965) 291. The word *antashubbû* is translated as the major epileptic attack, and the phrase *bēl ūri* as minor epileptic attack; the latter phrase literally means 'lord of the roof top', possibly referring to a demon who caused the victim's eyes to roll upwards. See J. V. Kinnier Wilson, 'Organic Diseases of Ancient Mesopotamia', *DIA*, 201-202; idem, 'Mental Diseases of Ancient Mesopotamia', *DIA* 725.
/107/ Walter A. Jayne, *The Healing Gods of Ancient Civilization* (New York: University Books, 1967 repr. of 1925 ed.) 107.
/108/ M. J. Geller, 'A Middle Assyrian Tablet of Utukku Lemnûtu, Tablet 12', *Iraq* 42 (1980) 35.
/109/ Edith K. Ritter, 'Magical-Expert (=Ašipu) and Physician (=Asû); Notes on Two Complementary Professions in Babylonian Medicine', *Studies in Honor of Benno Landsberger*, 305-307. René Labat, 'Ordonnances medicales ou magiques', *RA* 54 (1960) 169 ff.
/110/ See Goltz 9; Jayne 103.
/111/ Saggs, *Babylon*, 318.
/112/ Erica Reiner, *Shurpu: A Collection of Sumerian and Akkadian Incantations* (Graz: Ernst Weidner, 1958) 1-4; M. J. Geller, 'The Šurpu Incantations and Lev. V.1-5', *JSS* 25 (1980) 182.
/113/ W. G. Lambert, 'Dingir. sa.dib.ba Incantations', *JNES* 33 (1974) 270.
/114/ E.K. Ritter and J.V. Kinnier Wilson, 'Prescription for an Anxiety State: A Study of *BAM* 234', *AS* 30 (1980) 25.

/115/ Biggs, 'Medicine', 95-96.

/116/ A. Finet, 'Les médicins au Royaume de Mari', *Annuaire de l'Institut de Philologie et d'Historie Orientales et Slaves (Brussels)* 14 (1954-57) 129. For other examples of the empirical aspects of Mesopotamian medicine, see Martin Levey, 'Some Objective Factors of Babylonian Medicine in the Light of New Evidence', *BHM* 35 (1961) 61-70. Levey 61, comments, 'In the past, the magical and exorcistic nature of medicine in Babylonia has been unduly accented'.

/117/ Erica Reiner, 'Medicine in Ancient Mesopotamia', *Journal of the International College of Surgeons* 41 (1964) 544; S. Parpola, *Letters from Assyrian Scholars IIA* (Kevalaer: Butzon & Bercker, 1971) 14-15.

/117a/ W. G. Lambert, *Babylonian Wisdom Literature* (Oxford: Clarendon Press, 1960) 44-45.

/118/ Saggs, *Babylon*, 306-307.

/119/ Piotr Michalowski, 'Carminative Magic: Towards an Understanding of Sumerian Poetics', *ZA* 71 (1981) 4; cf. Alster 349-58.

/120/ Thompson, *DESB* II, 21, 32ff., 69 and 100 ff.; S. H. Hooke, *Babylonian and Assyrian Religion* (Oxford: Blackwell, 1962) 35-36; Saggs, *Babylon*, 311-2. The illness of the Ugaritic King Kret was treated by *h.rš* 'magic'. Unfortunately the exact praxis is unclear as the text at that point (Kret V:25 ff.) is broken and the translation of the word *rt* is disputed: Cyrus H. Gordon, *Ugaritic Literature* (Rome: Pontificium Institutum Biblicum, 1949) 81: 'clay'; H. L. Ginsberg in *ANET* (1955): 'clay (?)'; G. R. Driver, *Canaanite Myths and Legends* (Edinburgh: T. & T. Clark, 1956) 45: 'dung'; Michael D. Coogan, *Stories from Ancient Canaan* (Philadelphia: Westminster Press, 1978) 72: leaves out the broken line in his excerpt. Our limited evidence from Hittite sources indicates that the cure of illness was based on magic--not on exorcisms, but rather ablutions, passing through a magic gate, and symbolic acts. See Hans G. Güterbock, 'Hittite Medicine', *BHM* 36 (1962) 111.

/121/ W. Farber, *Beschwörungsrituale an Ištar und Dumuzi* (Wiesbaden: Franz Steiner, 1977) 237.

/122/ The commonly given etymology of the Sumerian *azu*, Akkadian *asu* 'physician' as 'one who knows water' is incorrect as pointed out by Biggs, *Incantations*, 23.

/123/ Ibid. 95; see especially Ritter 299-321; D. W. Amundsen

and G. B. Ferngren, 'Medicine and Religion: Pre-Christian Antiquity' *Health/Medicine and the Faith Traditions*, ed. M. E. Marty and K. L. Vaux (Philadelphia: Fortress, 1982) 58.
/124/ R. Labat, 'À propos de la chirurgie babylonienne', *JA* 243 (1954) 207-18 summarizes the little that is known about Mesopotamian surgery apart from the Hammurabi Code.
/125/ J. E. Harris and K. R. Weeks, 'X-Raying the Pharaohs', *Natural History* 81.7 (1972) 54-63; idem, *X-Raying the Pharaohs* (NY: Charles Scribner's, 1973); M. Zimmerman, 'Pathology of Ancient Egyptian Mummies' (Ph.D. Dissertation, University of Pennsylvania; Ann Arbor: University Microfilms, 1976); D. A. Rosalie, ed., *Manchester Museum Mummy Project* (Manchester: Manchester University, 1979); J. E. Harris and E. F. Wente, *An X-Ray Atlas of the Royal Mummies* (Chicago: University of Chicago, 1980); A. & E. Cockburn, eds., *Mummies, Disease and Ancient Cultures* (NY: Cambridge University, 1980).
/126/ Paul Ghalioungui, 'Parasitic Disease in Ancient Egypt', *Bulletin de l'Institut d'Egypte* 48-49 (1969) 13-26; G. S. El-Assal, 'Ancient Egyptian Medicine', *The Lancet* (Aug. 5, 1972) 273.
/127/ F. Filce Leek,'Reputed Early Egyptian Dental Operation, An Appraisal', *DIA* ch. 54; idem, 'Dental Pathology in Ancient Egyptian Skulls', *JEA* 52 (1966) 59-64; idem, 'The Practice of Dentistry in Ancient Egypt', *JEA* 53 (1967) 51-57; idem, 'A Technique for the Oral Examination of a Mummy', *JEA* 57 (1971) 105-109.
/128/ R. G. Harrison, 'An Anatomical Examination of the Pharaonic Remains Purported to be Akhenaten', *JEA* 52 (1966) 95-115; Cyril Aldred, *Akhenaten* (NY:McGraw-Hill, 1968) ch. viii; Guenter B. Risse, 'Pharaoh Akhenaton of Ancient Egypt: Controversies among Egyptologists and Physicians ...',*JHMAS* 26 (1971) 3-17; P. Costa, 'The Frontal Sinuses of the Remains Purported to be Akhenaten', *JEA* 64 (1978) 76-79.
/129/ Chauncey D. Leake, *The Old Egyptian Medical Papyri* (Lawrence, KS: University of Kansas, 1952) 7.
/130/ Leake 36, questions whether the Egyptian word *r'* 'mouth' should be translated as 'incantation' in the Ebers, Berlin and Hearst Papyri.
/131/ Leake 14. For the Ebers Papyrus, see: H. Joachim, *Papyros Ebers: Das älteste Buch über Heilkunde* (Berlin: W. de Gruyter, 1973 repr. of 1890 ed.); B. Ebbell, *The Papyrus Ebers, The Greatest Egyptian Medical Document* (London: Oxford University, 1973); Cyril Bryan, *Ancient*

Egyptian Medicine: The Papyrus Ebers (Chicago: Ares, 1975).
/132/ Paul Ghalioungui, *Magic and Medical Science in Ancient Egypt* (London: Hodder & Stoughton, 1963) 40, 50.
/133/ Leake 37. See Hassan Kamal, *Dictionary of Pharaonic Medicine* (Cairo: National Publication House, 1967).
/134/ Leake 58. El-Assal 272-73, lists also: erysipelas, dysentery, mumps, bubonic plague, tuberculosis, tetanus, appendicitis, and asthma.
/135/ Amundsen in Marty 57. Cf. Jayne 39; T. K. Oesterreich, *Possession: Demoniacal and Other* (NY: Gateway Books, 1974 repr. of 1921 ed.) 149-51.
/135a/ Warren R. Dawson, 'The Egyptian Medical Papyri', *DIA* 106.
/136/ J. F. Borghouts, *Ancient Egyptian Magical Texts* (Leiden: Brill, 1978) 41.
/137/ Henry E. Sigerist, *A History of Medicine I: Primitive and Archaic Medicine* (NY: Oxford University, 1961) 274.
/138/ Gustave Lefebvre, *Essai sur la médecine égyptienne de l'époque pharaonique* (Paris: Presses Universitaires de France, 1956) 154, citing Pap. Ebers 225.
/139/ Ghalioungui, *Magic*, 79.
/140/ E. A. W. Budge, *Egyptian Magic* (New Hyde Park, NY: University Books, 1958 repr. of 1899 ed.) 212; Loos 394.
/141/ Amundsen in Marty 57. From the late New Kingdom on, however, prayers to personal gods do indicate a concern for guilt and punishment as well as for a life without illness. See Eberhard Otto, 'Gott als Retter in Ägypten', *Tradition und Glaube*, ed. G. Jeremias et al. (Göttingen: Vandenhoeck & Ruprecht, 1971) 9-22.
/142/ Leake 17.
/143/ Ibid. 35.
/144/ J. H. Breasted, *Development of Religion and Thought in Ancient Egypt* (NY: Harper & Brothers, 1959 repr. of the 1912 ed.) 291.
/145/ Benjamin L. Gordon, *Medicine Throughout Antiquity* (Philadelphia: F. A. Davis, 1949) 121.
/146/ Bob Brier, *Ancient Egyptian Magic* (NY: William Morrow, 1980) 61.
/146a/ Jorgen P. Sorensen, 'The Argument in Ancient Egyptian Magical Formulae', *Acta Orientalia* 45 (1984) 17.
/147/ Borghouts 21.
/148/ Lefebvre 132. The verso of the Chester-Beatty Papyrus contains spells and incantations for epilepsy. See Dawson, in

DIA 103.
/149/ Leake 8.
/150/ Leake 88.
/151/ Majno 125; cf. Borghouts 44-45:1, spells for applying or drinking medicine.
/152/ Jayne 42-43.
/153/ Ghalioungui, *Magic*, 129.
/154/ Elmer Edel, *Ägyptische Ärzte und ägyptische Medizin am hethitischen Königshof* (Opladen: Westdeutscher Verlag, 1976).
/155/ Ghalioungui, *Magic*, 31.
/156/ Ibid. 105.
/157/ F. Jonckheere, *Les médecins de l'Egypte pharaonique*, (Bruxelles: Fondation égyptologique Reine Elizabeth, 1958) 17.
/158/ Ibid. 99.
/159/ Ibid. 126-28.
/160/ Brier 59.
/161/ F. Griffith and H. Thompson, *The Leyden Papyrus: An Egyptian Magical Book* (NY: Dover, 1974 repr. of 1904 ed.) 125-27. Some prescriptions in the Ebers Papyrus may have had the desired effects: e.g. the *shepen* (opium) plant to quiet a screaming child, figs to cure a surfeit of food, and an emetic to arouse a 'woman who likes to lie in bed'. Many other prescriptions using such noxious substances as centipede fat and crocodile dung were popular through the centuries for such purposes as contraception. See William A. Ward, *The Spirit of Ancient Egypt* (Beirut: Kayats, 1965) 145; John Noonan, *Contraception* (Cambridge, MA: Harvard University, 1965) 9.
/162/ J. H. Breasted, *The Edwin Smith Surgical Papyrus* (Chicago: University of Chicago, 1930).
/163/ John A. Wilson, 'A Note on the Edwin Smith Surgical Papyrus', *JNES* 11 (1952) 76-80; idem, *The Culture of Ancient Egypt* (Chicago: University of Chicago, 1959) 57; idem, 'Medicine in Ancient Egypt', *BHM* 36 (1962) 114-23.
/164/ A. E. Hill, 'The Temple of Asclepius: An Alternate Source for Paul's *Body* Theology', *JBL* 99 (1980) 437-39, suggests that Paul may have been inspired to write about the unity of the body of Christ by the sight of these *disjecta membra*.
/165/ William McArthur, 'The Athenian Plague: A Medical Note', *CQ* 48 (1954) 171-74; E. Watson Williams, 'The Sickness at Athens', *Greece and Rome* 4 (1957) 98-101; F. W. Mitchel, 'The Athenian Plague: New Evidence Inviting Medical Comment', *GRBS* 5 (1964) 101-12; Adam Patrick, 'Disease in Antiquity: Ancient

Greece and Rome', *DIA* 238-39.
/166/ Patrick, 240-45.
/167/ See, e. g., Mario Untersteiner, 'Il concetto di daimôn in Omero', *Atene e Roma* 7 (1939) 93-134. In general see W. Foerster, 'δαίμων, δαιμόνιον', in *TDNT* (1964) II, 1-19; M. Nilsson, *Geschichte der Griechischen Religion* [hereafter *GGR*] (Munich: C. H. Beck'sche Verlagsbuchhandlung, 1967) I, 216 ff.; cf. also Ramsay MacMullen, *Paganism in the Roman Empire* (New Haven: Yale University, 1981) 79-83.
/168/ Soren Skovgaard Jensen, *Dualism and Demonology: The Function of Demonology in Pythagorean and Platonic Thought* (Copenhagen: Munksgaard, 1966) 13.
/169/ Pierre Boyance , 'Les deux démons personnels dans l'antiquité grecque et latine', *Revue de Philologie* 61 (1935) 189-202.
/170/ A. D. Nock, *Conversion* (London: Oxford University, 1961) 221-24; see P. Merlan, 'Greek Philosophy from Plato to Plotinus', *The Cambridge History of Later Greek and Early Medieval Philosophy*, ed. A. H. Armstrong (Cambridge: Cambridge University, 1967) 33-35.
/171/ F. E. Brenk, '"A Most Strange Doctrine", *Daimon* in Plutarch', *CJ* 69 (1973) 1-11. Cf. J. A. Smith, 'Towards Interpreting Demonic Powers in Hellenistic and Roman Antiquity', *ANRW* II.16.1 (1978) 425-39.
/172/ F. Sokolowski, 'Sur le culte d'angeles dans le paganisme grec et romain', *HTR* 53 (1960) 225-29. Cf. angel worship in the area of Colosse.
/173/ J. M. Edmonds, *The Characters of Theophrastus* (London: Heinemann, 1929) 78-79, translates 'divine'. Warren Anderson, *Theophrastus: The Character Sketches* (Kent, OH: Kent State University, 1970) 67, 69, renders the word as 'supernatural' and doubts that it refers to demons as some have maintained.
/174/ A. D. Nock, 'The Cult of Heroes', *HTR* 37 (1944) 171; reprinted in *Essays on Religion and the Ancient World*, ed. Zeph Stewart (Cambridge, MA: Harvard University, 1972) II, 600.
/175/ H. J. Rose, 'Keres and Lemures', *HTR* 41 (1948) 225; W. K. C. Guthrie, *The Greeks and Their Gods* (Boston: Beacon, 1955) 276; M. Nilsson, *Greek Folk Religion* (NY: Harper, 1961) 91.
/176/ Eli Burriss, *Taboo, Magic, Spirits . . . in Roman Religion* (NY: Macmillan, 1931); Jacques Puiggali, 'Remarques sur δαιμόνιον et δαίμων chez Artémidore', *Prudentia* 15 (1983) 117-22.

/177/ Hans Herter, 'Böse Dämonen im Früh-griechischen Volksglauben', *Rheinisches Jahrbuch für Volksglauben* 1 (1950) 114.
/178/ K. Preisendanz, 'Nekydaimon', *PW* XXXII, 2241.
/179/ Nilsson, *GGR* 222 ff. Only once in the Odyssey is a demon associated with illness; see Nilsson, *GGR* 220.
/180/ Nilsson, *Greek Piety*, 172.
/181/ Jayne 223. The early Romans also believed that hostile spirits sent maladies.
/182/ *The Sacred Disease* IV.21-34.
/182a/ G. E. R. Lloyd, ed., *Hippocratic Writings* (Harmondsworth: Penquin Books, 1983) 26 ff.
/183/ Nilsson, *Greek Folk Religion*, 93. See also S. V. McCasland, 'The Asklepios Cult in Palestine', *JBL* 58 (1939) 221-27.
/184/ See Werner Peek, 'Fünf Wundergeschichten aus dem Asklepieion von Epidauros', in *Inschriften der Griechen: Epigraphische Quellen zur Geschichte der antiken Medizin*, ed. G. Pfohl (Darmstadt: Wissenschaftliche Buchgesellschaft, 1977) 66-78; A. Charitonidou, 'Epidaurus: The Sanctuary of Asclepius', *Temples and Sanctuaries of Ancient Greece*, ed. Evi Melas (London: Thames and Hudson, 1973) 89-99.
/185/ See my *The Archeology of New Testament Cities in Western Asia Minor* (Grand Rapids: Baker, 1980) 45-49.
/186/ C. Kerényi, *Asklepios* (NY: Pantheon Books, 1959) 9.
/187/ See C. A. Behr, *Aelius Aristides and the Sacred Tales* (Amsterdam: Hakkert, 1968) 164-68; E. D. Phillips, 'A Hypochondriac and His God', *Greece and Rome* 21 (1952) 23-36.
/188/ Goltz, 267, speaking of 'Der Krankheitsbegriff der griechischen therapeutischen Schriften', declares: 'Zunächst ist festzuhalten, dass keine der Krankheiten auf eine übernatürliche Ursache, auf ein Eingriefen fremder Mächte von aussen zurückgeführt wird'.
/189/ Edelstein, *AM* 220.; cf. G. E. R. Lloyd, *Early Greek Science* (NY: W. W. Norton, 1970), 55.
/190/ Darrel W. Amundsen, 'The Liability of the Physician in Classical Greek Legal Theory and Practice', *JHMAS* 32 (1977) 202.
/191/ Cf. Edelstein, *AM* 224.
/192/ Amundsen in Marty 71.
/193/ Ibid. 80.
/194/ E. Brehaut, tr., *Cato the Censor on Farming* (NY: Columbia University, 1933) 143; see also citations of Cato, *On Agriculture* in F. C. Grant, ed., *Ancient Roman Religion* (NY: Liberal Arts Press, 1957) 37-38; and in N. Lewis & M.

Reinhold, eds., *Roman Civilization Sourcebook I: The Republic* (NY: Harper & Row, 1966) 446.
/195/ J. F. Schulze, 'Die Entwicklung der Medizin in Rom. . .' *Živa Antika* 21 (1971) 500, 'Eine eigene römische Heilkunde und Ärtzteschaft gab es nicht'. Cf. T. C. Allbutt, *Greek Medicine in Rome* (London: Macmillan, 1921); J. Scarborough, *Roman Medicine* (Ithaca: Cornell, 1969); R. W. Davies, 'Medicine in Ancient Rome', *History Today* 21 (1971) 770-78.
/196/ S. Treggiari, *Roman Freedmen During the Late Republic* (Oxford: Clarendon, 1969) 129-32; V. Nutton, 'Archiatri and the Medical Profession in Antiquity', *Proceedings of the British School at Rome* 45 (1977) 207-208; for inscriptional references to doctors in the Roman Empire, see G. H. R. Horsley, *New Documents Illustrating Early Christianity*, 2 (North Ryde: Macquarie University, 1982) 2-25.
/197/ Lawrence J. Bliquez, 'Greek and Roman Medicine', *Archaeology* 34.2 (1981) 15.
/198/ Scarborough 76-79.
/199/ See John Wilkinson, 'Leprosy and Leviticus', *SJT* 30 (1977) 153-69; R. K. Harrison, *Leviticus* (Downers Grove: Inter-Varsity Press, 1980) 136 ff.; and n. 79 above.
/200/ On the general subject of plagues in history see: Hans Zinnser, *Rats, Lice and History* (NY: Bantam Books, 1960); William H. McNeil, *Plagues and Peoples* (Garden City, NY: Doubleday & Co., 1976).
/200a/ R. K. Harrison, 'Disease', *The International Standard Bible Encyclopedia*, ed. G. W. Bromiley (rev. ed.; Grand Rapids: Eerdmans, 1979) I, 953-60.
/201/ Edward Langton, *Essentials of Demonology* (London: Epworth, 1949) 9; H. H. Rowley, *Job* (London: Nelson, 1970) 31. Satan's role in the Old Testament is quite limited. See F. I. Andersen, *Job* (Downers Grove: Inter-Varsity Press, 1976) 82-83.
/202/ A. Lods, 'Les origines de la figure de Satan, ses fonctions à la coure céleste', *Mélanges syriens offerts à M. R. Dussaud* (Paris: Geuthner, 1939) II, 649-66, suggested an origin in the accusatory espionage system of the Persian King. A. Brocke-Utne, 'Der Feind--Die alttestamentliche Satansgestalt im Lichte der sozialen Verhältnisse des nahen Orients', *Klio* 28 (1945) 220-27, speculated that he was patterned after the denouncer mentioned in the Amarna Letters of Amenhotep III and IV. R. S. Kluger, *Satan in the Old Testament* (Evanston: Northwestern University, 1967) uses Jungian psychology to argue that Satan was differentiated from the Godhead itself!

/203/ Böcher, *DD* 54, 75.
/204/ Ibid. 30, 78, 83, passim.
/205/ Ibid. 118.
/206/ The LXX rendering of Psalm 95:5 [Heb. 96:5] demotes all heathen gods to the status of demons.
/207/ Langton 21.
/208/ Michael J. Gruenthaner, 'The Demonology of the Old Testament', *CBQ* 6 (1944) 23; W. O. E. Oesterley and T. H. Robinson, *Hebrew Religion, Its Origin and Development* (2nd ed.; NY: Macmillan Co., 1937) 112-13; S. M. Lehman, 'The Book of Leviticus', in A. Cohen, ed., *The Soncino Chumash* (London: Soncino Press, 1947) 713; N. H. Snaith, 'II Kings', in *The Interpreter's Bible*, ed. G. A. Buttrick (NY: Abingdon, 1954) III, 322.
/209/ The Vulgate translated the word as *lamia*. The Romans regarded the *strix* (plural *striges*) 'owl' as a bird with supernatural characteristics. See F. Boehm, 'Striges', *PW* IInd series, VII (1931) 356-63.
/210/ See Yamauchi, *MIT* 17:6-10; 24:5; idem, 'Aramaic Magic Bowls', 517. See also Hans Duhm, *Die bösen Geisten im alten Testament* (Tübingen: J. C. B. Mohr, 1904) 51-52; Zoller, 'Lilit', 121-42; H. Torczyner, 'A Hebrew Incantation against Night-demons from Biblical Times', *JNES* 6 (1947) 18-29.
/211/ Moses Gaster, 'Lilith und die drei Engel', *MGWJ* 29 (1880) 553-65.
/212/ G.R. Driver, 'Once Again: Birds in the Bible', *PEQ* 86 (1955) 5-20; 87 (1955) 129-40.
/213/ Langton 43.
/214/ Cf. J. A. Alexander, *Commentary on the Prophecies of Isaiah* (Grand Rapids: Zondervan, 1962 repr. of 1847 ed.) 28ff.
/215/ Saggs, *Babylon*, 485; E. J. Young, *The Book of Isaiah II* (Grand Rapids: Eerdmans, 1969) 440.
/216/ E. A. Speiser, *Genesis* (Garden City, NY: Doubleday, 1964) 29, 33.
/217/ Langton 21. See also Andre Caquot, 'Sur quelques démons de l'Ancien Testament (Reshep, Qeteb, Deber)', *Semitica* 6 (1956) 53-68. Cf. K. J. Cathcart, 'The "Demons" in Judges 5:8a', *BZ* 21 (1977) 111-12.
/218/ Roland de Vaux, *Ancient Israel* (NY: McGraw-Hill, 1961) 509; Bamberger, ch. 2; Benjamin Mazar, *The Mountain of the Lord* (Garden City, NY: Doubleday & Co., 1975) 110.
/219/ H. Kaupel, *Die Dämonen im alten Testament* (Augsburg: B.

Filser, 1930) 91. Baruch Levine, *In the Presence of the Lord* (Leiden: Brill, 1974) 55-59, interprets the Levitical purity laws as having had an apotropaic function against demonic forces.

/220/ H. Tawil, 'Azazel, The Prince of the Steppe', *ZAW* 92 (1980) 43-49.

/221/ Duhm, 63: 'In der alten Zeit begegnen uns auffallend wenig böse Wesen bei den Israeliten. ... Es fehlen durchweg solche dämonische Wesen, die bei andern Völkern, vor allem bei den Babyloniern, ihre Entstehung einer starken kosmologischen Phantasie verdanken'. Cf. also W. Foerster, *TDNT* ll, 'In general we may say the Old Testament knows no demons with whom one may have dealings in magic even for the purpose of warding them off'.

/222/ Langton 10; cf. Böcher, *DD* 30, 'Der Dämonismus, welcher mit Sicherheit auch für die israelitische Volksfrömmigkeit postuliert werden kann, ist nur in verschwindend geringen Spuren in den Kanon der alttestamentlichen Literatur eingedrungen, etwas, wenn von Jahwes Hilfe gegen die (dämonischen!) Elemente Feuer und Wasser gesprochen wird (Jes. 43,2; Ps 66,12)'.

/223/ Alexander Kohut, 'Über die jüdischen Angelologie und Dämonologie in ihrer Abhängigkeit von Parsismus', *Abhandlungen für die Kunde des Morgenlandes* 4.3 (1866); G. Vermes, *Jesus the Jew* (London: Collins, 1973) 61; J. Bright, *A History of Israel* (Philadelphia: Westminster, 1959) 444; R. N. Frye, *The Heritage of Persia* (Cleveland: World, 1962) 122; D. S. Russell, *The Method and Message of Jewish Apocalyptic* (Philadelphia: Westminster, 1964) 254-62, 385-87; Mary Boyce, *A History of Zoroastrianism* (Leiden: Brill, 1982) II, 194-95. A rare expression of doubt is found in Gruenthaner 19; Kluger 156-57, points out the fundamental differences between Angra Mainyu and Satan.

/224/ Shaul Shaked, 'Iranian Influence on Judaism: First Century B.C.E. to Second Century C.E.', *The Cambridge History of Judaism I: Introduction; The Persian Period*, ed. W. D. Davies and L. Finkelstein (Cambridge: Cambridge University, 1984) 318.

/225/ See R. G. Kent, *Old Persian* (New Haven: American Oriental Society, 1953) 151; H. W. Bailey, 'The Persian Language', in A. J. Arberry, ed., *The Legacy of Persia* (Oxford: Clarendon Press, 1953) 180; W. Th. in der Smitten, 'Xerxes und die Daeva', *BO* 30.5-6 (1973) 368-69; R. Ghirshman,

'Les Daivadâna', *Acta Antiqua Hungarica* 24 (1976) 3-14.
/226/ See my review of *The Cambridge Ancient History of Iran III: The Seleucid, Parthian and Sasanian Periods*, ed. Ehsan Yarshater (Cambridge: Cambridge University, 1983) in *The American Historical Review* 89 (1984) 1055-56.
/227/ See my *Pre-Christian Gnosticism* (2nd ed.; Grand Rapids: Baker, 1983) ch. 5, and 206-209; M. J. Dresden, 'Mythology of Ancient Iran', in S. N. Kramer, ed., *Mythologies of the Ancient World* (Garden City, NY: Doubleday, 1961) 357-58.
/228/ Werner Sundermann, 'Namen von Göttern, Dämonen und Menschen in iranischen Versionen des manichäischen Mythos', *Altorientalische Forschungen* 6 (1979) 95-133.
/229/ B. Gordon, 300.
/230/ Böcher, *DD* 129.
/231/ E. g. Vermes 61; J.D.G. Dunn & G. Twelftree, 'Demon-Possession and Exorcism in the New Testament', *Churchman* 94 (1980) 216, who call this story 'unique' in B.C.E. Judaism.
/232/ Gruenthaner 25; cf. also McCasland 23.
/233/ Wolfram Von Soden, 'Fischgalle als Heilsmittel für Augen', *AfO* 21 (1966) 81-82; Paul E. Dion, 'Raphaël l'exorciste', *Biblica* 57 (1976) 399-413.
/234/ J. T. Milik, *The Books of Enoch* (Oxford: Clarendon, 1976) 4. For an account of these developments see D. Aune, 'Demon', *The International Standard Bible Encyclopedia* I, 920-21.
/235/ James H. Charlesworth, ed., *The Old Testament Pseudepigrapha: I. Apocalyptic Literature and Testaments* (Garden City, NY: Doubleday, 1983) 15; cf. Bamberger chs. III-XI; John Lust, 'Devils and Angels in the Old Testament', *Louvain Studies* 5 (1974) 115-20.
/236/ M. A. H. Melinsky, *Healing Miracles* (London: Mowbray, 1968) 27.
/237/ Böcher, *DD* 154.
/238/ S. V. McCasland, 'Religious Healing in First-Century Palestine', *Environmental Factors in Church History*, ed. J. McNeil, et al. (Chicago: University of Chicago, 1939) 23. We may cf. David's feigning madness by foaming at the mouth.
/239/ M. Unger, *Biblical Demonology* (9th ed.; Wheaton: Scripture Press, 1971) 80; William Berends, 'The Biblical Criteria for Demon-Possession', *WTJ* 37 (1975) 36-37. Cf. also Gruenthaner 24, 'The fact that Saul behaved like a prophet does not prove that he was possessed'.
/240/ Adam Patrick, 'Diseases in the Bible and Talmud', *DIA*

218. S. Mowinckel, *The Psalms in Israelite Worship* (NY: Abingdon, 1962) II, 2, believed otherwise, citing the 'destroyer' of Exod 12:23, 'the firstborn of death' of Job 18:13, and other 'terrific beings'. He also interpreted references to 'evil workers' in such Psalms as 35, 38, 42-45, 63, and 109, as references to sorcerers who caused illnesses by their spells.
/241/ Edward Neufeld, 'Hygiene Conditions in Ancient Israel (Iron Age)', *JHMAS* 25 (1970) 437. Cf. S. Levin, 'Bacteriology in the Bible', *ET* 76 (1964-65) 154-57.
/242/ Cf. M. Noth, *Leviticus* (London: SCM Press, 1965) 107.
/243/ Böcher, *DD* 162.
/244/ Ibid. 247.
/245/ Ibid. 274-78.
/246/ Ibid. 288.
/247/ Ibid. 296. J. G. Plöger, *'adhamah'*, in *The Theological Dictionary of the Old Testament*, ed. G. J. Botterweck and H. Ringgren (Grand Rapids: Eerdmans, 1974) I, 90, suggests that the placing of dust and ashes as signs of mourning was originally apotropaic in function.
/248/ Fred Rosner, *Medicine in the Bible and the Talmud* (NY: KTAV, 1977) 8.
/249/ R. H. Harrison, *Healing Herbs of the Bible* (Leiden: Brill, 1966) 3.
/250/ J. A. Sanders, *The Psalms Scroll of Qumran Cave II* (Oxford: Clarendon Press, 1965) 77-78.
/251/ Nahman Avigad and Yigael Yadin, *A Genesis Apocryphon* (Jerusalem: Magnes Press, 1956) 44.
/252/ J. A. Fitzmyer, *The Genesis Apocryphon of Qumran Cave I* (Rome: Pontifical Biblical Institute, 1966) 58-59, 123.
/253/ D. Flusser, 'Healing through the Laying-on of Hands in a Dead Sea Scroll', *IEJ* 7 (1957) 107-108, points out that healing by the laying on of the hands is unknown in the Old Testament and in rabbinic literature.
/254/ See A. Dupont-Sommer, 'Exorcismes et guérisons dans les écrits de Qumran', *VT Supplement* 7 (Leiden: Brill, 1960) 246-61; Vermes 66; W. H. Brownlee, 'Jesus and Qumran', in F. Thomas Trotter, ed., *Jesus and the Historian* (Philadelphia: Westminster, 1968) 69-70.
/255/ A. Furlani, 'Aram. GAZRIN=scongiuratori', *Atti della Accademia nazionale dei Lincei* 4 (1948) 177-96.
/256/ Vermes 68; cf. H. C. Kee, 'The Terminology of Mark's Exorcism Stories', *NTS* 14 (1967-68) 239.

/257/ Fitzmyer, *Genesis Apocryphon*, 123.
/258/ The only scholar who agrees with Dupont-Sommer's rendering is: Florentino Garcia, '4Q Or Nab. Nueva Sintesis', *Sefarad* 40 (1980) 8, 'exorcista'. All others maintain the etymological sense of 'one who divides', that is, a diviner. Marcus Jastrow, *Dictionary of the Talmud Babli, Yerushalmi, Midrashic Literature and Targumim* (New York: Pardes, 1950) I, 231-32; J. T. Milik, 'Prière de Nabonide', *RB* 73 (1956) 407, 'devin'; Werner Dommershausen, *Nabonid im Buche Daniel* (Mainz: Matthias-Grünewald, 1964) 70, 'Seher'; M. Delcor, 'Le Testament de Job, la prière de Nabonide et les traditions targoumiques', *Beiträge zur Erforschung der Beziehungen zwischen Bibel- und Qumranwissenschaft* (Berlin: Evangelische Haupt-Bibelgesellschaft, 1958) 61, 'conjureur'; Alfred Martens, *Das Buch Daniel im Lichte der Texte vom Toten Meer* (Echter: KBW Verlag, 1971) 35, 'Seher'; B. Jongeling, C. J. Labuschagne, and A. S. van der Woude, *Aramaic Texts from Qumran* (Leiden: Brill, 1976) 129, 'diviner'; P. Grelot, 'La prière de Nabonide (4 QOrNab)', *RB* 36 (1978) 485, 'devin'; A. S. Van der Woude, 'Bemerkungen zum Gebet des Nabonid', *Qumran: sa piété, sa théologie et son milieu*, ed. M. Delcor (Gembloux: Duculot, 1978) 125: 'Weil kein Exorzist aramäisch 'ašaph heisst, *gzr* aber "teilen", "zerlegen" und assyr. *parisu* "Traumdeuter", "Weissager" bedeutet, haben wir keinen objektiven Grund, der von Furlani und Dupont-Sommer vorgeschlagenen Erklärung von *gzr* als "Exorzist" zu folgen'. See most recently F. M. Cross, 'Fragments of the Prayer of Nabonidus', *IEJ* 34 (1984) 264, 'diviner'.
/259/ Helmer Ringgren, *The Faith of Qumran* (Philadelphia: Fortress, 1963) 90-91; Walter Kirschläger, 'Exorzismus in Qumran?' *Kairos* 18 (1976) 135-53; Wesley Carr, *Angels and Principalities* (Cambridge: Cambridge University, 1981) 196.
/260/ See in general: Hermann L. Strack and Paul Billerbeck, *Kommentar zum Neuen Testament aus Talmud und Midrasch* (Munich: C. H. Beck'sche Verlagsbuchhandlung, 1928) IV.1, 501-35; Bernard J. Bamberger, *Fallen Angels* (Philadelphia: Jewish Publication Society, 1952) chs. XVI-XIX; Leo Jung, *Fallen Angels in Jewish and Christian and Mohammedan Literature* (NY: KTAV, 1926); for later developments, see G. Scholem, 'Some Sources of Jewish-Arabic Demonology', *JJS* 16 (1965) 1-14.
/261/ See my 'Aramaic Magic Bowls'; J. Neusner and J. Smith, 'Archaeology and Babylonian Jewry', in J. A. Sanders,

ed., *Near Eastern Archaeology in the Twentieth Century* (Garden City, NY: Doubleday, 1970); M. J. Geller, 'Jesus' Theurgic Powers; Parallels in the Talmud and Incantation Bowls', *JJS* 28 (1977) 140-55.

/261a/ Aune, 'Demon', 922.

/262/ Carr 27.

/263/ See esp. Strack-Billerbeck; Alfred Edelsheim, *The Life and Times of Jesus the Messiah* (5th ed.; New York: Randolph, 1886) II, 774.

/264/ W. M. Alexander, *Demonic Possession in the New Testament* (Grand Rapids: Baker, repr. of the 1902 ed.) 32.

/265/ Foerster 13.

/266/ L. Hermann, 'Les premiers exorcismes juifs et judéo-chrétiens', *Revue de l'Université de Bruxelle* II, 7 (1954-55) 305-308.

/267/ Justin Martyr, *Dialogue* # 8, 205; cf. Irenaeus, *Against Heresies* 2.6.2; Origen, *Contra Celsum* 1.24f.; 5:45; cf. 2.51.

/268/ Wilfred L. Knox, 'Jewish Liturgical Exorcism', *HTR* 31 (1938) 191-203; Salcia Landmann, 'Exorzismen in der jüdischen Tradition', *ZRGG* 28 (1976) 357-66.

/268a/ Solomon R. Kagan, 'Etiology, Pathology and Prognosis According to Ancient Hebrew Literature', *New England Journal of Medicine* 202 (1930) 334. See idem, 'Medicine in Ancient Hebrew Literature', *Medical Life* 117 (1930) 312, 317, 321. For other medical traditions in the Talmud see Rosner, *Medicine*.

/269/ See J. Neusner, *A History of the Jews in Babylonia* II, 147-50; III,110-26; IV, 324-69; V, 174-96, 217-43; Leopold Sabourin, 'Hellenistic and Rabbinic "Miracle"', *Bible and Theology Bulletin* 2.3 (1972) 281-307.

/270/ Vermes 69 f.

/271/ Ibid. 72 ff.

/272/ Ibid. 79.

/273/ H. C. Kee, 'Terminology', 239. Kee admits to no wider meaning for these deeds, although miracles were sometimes cited by rabbis in favor of their interpretation of legal disputes, but were generally rejected as decisive halakhic arguments by the statement 'the Torah is not in heaven'. See A. I. Baumgarten, 'Miracles and Halakah in Rabbinic Judaism', *JQR* 73 (1983) 238-53.

/274/ P. Achtemeier, 'Gospel Miracle Tradition and the Divine Man', *Int* 26 (1972) 185.

/275/ Morton Smith, *Tannaitic Parallels to the Gospels*

(Philadelphia: JBL, 1951) 81-84.
/275a/ Jacob Neusner, *The Rabbinic Traditions about the Pharisees before 70* (Leiden: Brill, 1971) III, 86: 'We find no reference to demons or exorcisms (except Hanina and Igrath--Babylonian and late) ... Except for Honi's rain-making, all the rabbinic nature-miracles ... pertain to late masters'.
/276/ W. S. Green, 'Palestinian Holy Men: Charismatic Leadership and Rabbinic Tradition', *ANRW* II.19.2 (1979) 647.
/277/ Joshua Trachtenberg, *Jewish Magic and Superstition* (Philadelphia: Jewish Publication Society, 1961); Geller, 'Jesus' Theurgic Powers', 140-55.
/278/ Salo W. Baron, *A Social and Religious History of the Jews* (2nd ed.; Philadelphia: Jewish Pub. Soc., 1952) II, 21.
/279/ Ithamar Gruenwald, *Apocalyptic and Merkavah Mysticism* (Leiden: Brill, 1980) 71.
/280/ Michael A. Morgan, tr., *Sepher ha-Razim: The Book of the Mysteries* (Chico: Scholars Press, 1983) 26.
/281/ See Baron II, 21.
/282/ Morgan 59.
/283/ Edersheim 774. See Kagan 329-30.
/284/ W. L. Nash, 'A Hebrew Amulet Against Disease', *Proceedings of the Society of Biblical Archaeology* 28 (1906) 182-84; Pierre Benoit, 'Fragment d'une prière contre les esprits impurs?' *RB* 58 (1951) 549-65; for other examples see my 'Magic in the Biblical World', *TynBul* 34 (1983) 197. For medieval Jewish magic see: Moses Gaster, *Studies and Texts in Folklore: Magic, Medieval Romance, Hebrew Apocrypha and Samaritan Archaeology* (NY: KTAV, 1928 repr.).
/285/ Morton Kelsey, *Discernment: A Study in Ecstasy and Evil* (NY: Paulist Press, 1978) 60: 'he is called by one name or another in fifty places in the gospels and Acts'.
/286/ Langton 31.
/287/ Jeffrey B. Russell, *The Devil: Perceptions of Evil from Antiquity to Primitive Christianity* (Ithaca: Cornell University, 1977) 222; cf. 249. See Richard H. Hiers, 'Satan, Demons, and the Kingdom of God', *SJT* 27 (1974) 35-47; James Kallas, *The Real Satan* (Minneapolis: Augsburg, 1975).
/288/ J. Russell, 266; Melinsky 29.
/289/ Paul M. Quay, 'Angels and Demons: The Teachings of IV Lateran', *TS* 42 (1981) 20-45; Mortimer Adler, *The Angels and Us* (NY: Macmillan, 1982) 85.
/290/ Leopold Sabourin, 'Jesus and the Evil Powers', 153. Cf. H. Kruse, 'Das Reich Satans', *Bib* 58 (1977) 29-61;

Kelsey 61.
/291/ Karl Barth, *Church Dogmatics* (Edinburgh: T & T Clark, 1960) III.3, 445: 'Demons are only the more magnified if they are placed in the framework of the conflict between a modern and an ancient system, and called in question in this exalted company (of God and His angels). The demythologisation which will really hurt them as required cannot consist in questioning their existence. Theological exorcism must be an act of the unbelief which is grounded in faith. It must consist in a resolute denial that they belong to this exalted company'.
/292/ See Carr 25.
/293/ See M. Takahashi, 'An Oriental's Approach to the Problem of Angelology', *ZAW* 78 (1966) 348-50; C. F. Dickason, *Angels, Elect and Evil* (Chicago: Moody Press, 1975).
/294/ See Carr 3; Jung Young Lee, 'Interpreting the Demonic Powers in Pauline Thought', *NovT* 12 (1970) 54-69. Böcher, *CE* 172, following Martin Dibelius, conceives of sin personified in Romans 6 and 7 as a demonic power.
/295/ N. Brox, 'Magie und Aberglaube an den Anfängen des Christentums', *Trierer Theologische Zeitschrift* 83 (1974) 159.
/296/ J. A. Fitzmyer, 'Qumran Angelology and I Cor 11:10', *NTS* 4 (1957-58) 48-58; reprinted in J.Murphy-O'Connor, *Paul and Qumran* (London: Geoffrey Chapman, 1968) 31-47; also reprinted in J. A. Fitzmyer, *Essays on the Semitic Background of the New Testament* (Missoula: Scholars Press, 1974) ch. 9.
/297/ Böcher, *CE* 20; cf. Heinrich Schlier, *Principalities and Powers in the New Testament* (NY: Herder and Herder, 1961); E. G. Rupp, *Principalities and Powers* (London: Epworth, 1964); Michael Green, *I Believe in Satan's Downfall* (London: Hodder & Stoughton, 1981) 86.
/298/ Carr 77.
/299/ Ibid. 175.
/300/ Melinsky 166-67, suggests, 'He recognised the demonology of his day to be a variable, and to some extent deceptive, frame of reference, and since the aim of his gospel was to be as universal as possible, this was the one element which he deliberately excluded'.
/301/ Böcher, *CE* 79.
/302/ Ibid. 160-61.
/303/ See G. Twelftree's article elsewhere in this volume.
/304/ Sabourin, 'Jesus and the Evil Powers', 164-65.
/305/ Smith, *JM* 195, comments, 'The attempt of Böcher,

Christus 70 ff., to represent all healings as exorcisms, is refuted by the fact that the gospels do not do so'.

/306/ M. Kelsey, *Healing and Christianity* (NY: Harper and Row, 1973) 77; H. Bietenhard, 'Demon', Colin Brown, ed., *The New International Dictionary of New Testament Theology* (Grand Rapids: Zondervan, 1975) I, 453: 'But not all illness is attributed to them'; J. R. Michaels, 'Jesus and the Unclean Spirits', in J. W. Montgomery, ed., *Demon Possession* (Minneapolis: Bethany Fellowhip, 1976) 48: 'Sickness and demon possession are here closely associated, yet kept distinct'; Dunn and Twelftree (n. 231) 217: 'Moreover, by no means all illnesses were attributed to demons and demon-possession'; Peder Borgen, 'Miracles of Healing in the New Testament', *Studia Theologica* 35 (1981) 98: 'It is worth noting that in the Gospel of John cases of sickness are at no point directly connected with demons'; M. Green 87.

/307/ Amundsen and Ferngren 97. See also Foerster, esp. 18: 'First, with respect to demons as the cause of sickness, it should be noted that in the New Testament not all sicknesses are attributed to demons even in older strata of the Synoptic tradition. ... Thus, while not all sicknesses are the work of demons, they may all be seen as the work of Satan'.

In the Gospels the word for physician ἰατρός appears in two proverbial statements: 'They that are whole have no need of the physician' (Mark 2:17//Matt. 9:12//Luke 5:31), and 'Physician heal thyself' (Luke 5:31). The woman with the flux of blood had spent all her savings on physicians in vain (Mark 5:26). Luke is called 'the beloved physician' (Col. 4:14). Ignatius in his letter to the Ephesians (7:2) speaks of Christ as the 'one physician, both fleshly and spiritual, begotten and unbegotten, come in flesh'. See G. Dumeige, 'Le Christ médecin dans la littérature chrétienne des premiers siècles', *Rivista di archeologia cristiana* 48 (1972) 115-41.

/308/ Vermes 66.

/309/ Melinsky 15.

/310/ J. Wilkinson, 'The Case of the Bent Woman in Luke 13:10-17', *EvQ* 49 (1977) 195-205. In addition to the explicit exorcism stories, scholars such as Böcher, *CE* 22, also interpret such healings as that of Peter's mother-in-law's fever as actually an exorcism of the demon Fever. Cf. also M. Green 127. Smith, *JM* 107, cites this incident as further evidence of Jesus' role as a magician inasmuch as 'cures for fever are particularly frequent in the magical material ...'.

/311/ Aune, 'Magic', 1524; Reginald Fuller, *Interpreting the Miracles* (Philadelphia: Westminster, 1963) 29: 'The evidence in favour of the general tradition of Jesus' exorcisms is little short of overwhelming'; Hull 143; Smith, *JM* 14.

/312/ Kee, 'Terminology', 245. This widely held view is challenged by E. P. Sanders 122-41.

/313/ See Owsei Temkin, *The Falling Sickness* (2nd ed.; Baltimore: Johns Hopkins University, 1971) 3. See also the texts published by Kinnier Wilson cited above (n. 106), and Farber, *Beschwörungsrituale*, 64-65.

/314/ Kamal 154-55.

/315/ McCasland, 'Healing', 25; Edelstein, *AM* 219.

/316/ Edwin B. Levine, *Hippocrates* (NY: Twayne, 1971) 108. The Jewish rabbis emphasized the hereditary factor in epilepsy. J.Snowman, *A Short History of Talmudic Medicine* (London: John Bale, Sons & Danielsson, 1935) 40: 'They emphasised the urgency of calling in a qualified physician, and protested against the method of exorcising the evil spirit which, in the popular view, was the cause of the disease'.

/317/ Stanley W. Jackson, 'Unusual Mental States in Medieval Europe: I. Medical Syndromes of Mental Disorder 400-1100 A.D.', *JHMAS* 27 (1972) 292.

/318/ F. J. Dölger, 'Der Einfluss des Origenes auf die Beurteilung der Epilepsie und Mondsucht im christlichen Altertum', *Antike und Christentum* 4 (1934) 95-109.

/319/ Melinsky 135; W. Alexander 62-63.

/320/ T. C. Falla, 'Demons and Demoniacs in the Peshitta Gospels', *Abr-Nahrain* 9 (1969-70) 44.

/321/ See I. Proulx and J. O'Callaghan, 'Papiro Mágico Cristiano (P. Yale inv. 989)', *Studia Papyrologica* 13 (1974) 84.

/322/ J. M. Ross, 'Epileptic or Moonstruck?' *Bible Translator* 24 (1978) 126.

/323/ "Epileptic" is the translation of the RV, RSV, Weymouth, Moffatt, Schonfield, NEB, JB; following the KJV 'lunatick', Knox and Phillips render the word 'lunatic', and Williams opts for 'mad'. The Latin *lunaticus* was also used of epileptics.

/324/ Loos 401.

/325/ The known causes include birth defects, brain tumors, and head injuries.

/326/ Dölger 103: 'Auch das christliche Abendland kannte also im fünften Jahrhundert keine natürliche Krankheit, Epilepsie oder Mondsucht, sondern dämonische Besessenheit'.
/327/ E.g. J. Cortés and F. M. Gatti, *The Case Against Possessions and Exorcisms* (NY: Vantage, 1975) 108.
/328/ Dunn & Twelftree 222. In his important new *Christ Triumphant* (London: Hodder & Stoughton, 1985) 170, the latter author writes: 'But even if all sicknesses were to be accounted for by natural explanations, the "demonic" dimension to sicknesses would not necessarily be eliminated. For example, because a sickness is labelled, understood and cured in terms of "epilepsy" it may not mean that there is not a demonic aspect to the sickness which also needs to be discerned and dealt with'. For an attempt to explain all New Testament exorcisms in terms of hysteria, multiple personality, catatonic schizophrenia, etc., see J. Keir Howard, 'New Testament Exorcism and Its Significance Today', *ExpTim* 96 (1985) 105-109.
/329/ J. Wilkinson, 'The Case of the Epileptic Boy', *ExpTim* 79 (1967-68) 42; so also William Barclay, *And Jesus Said* (Edinburgh: The Church of Scotland Youth Committee, 1952) 188. Cf. Colin Brown, *Miracles and the Critical Mind* (Grand Rapids: Eerdmans, 1984) 265.
/330/ John Richards, *But Deliver Us from Evil* (London: Darton, Longman & Todd, 1974) 103. See Twelftree 155.
/331/ Werner Mayer, *Untersuchungen zur Formensprache der babylonischen Gebetschwörungen* (Rome: Biblical Institute, 1976); Michalowski 1-18.
/332/ Sigerist I, 274.
/333/ O'Keefe 62.
/334/ Kurt Seligmann, *Magic, Supernaturalism and Religion* (NY: Pantheon Books, 1973) 39.
/335/ Ghalioungui, *Magic*, 21.
/335a/ Burriss 181. According to J. E. Lowe, *Magic in Greek & Latin Literature* (Oxford: Basil Blackwell, 1929) 15: 'These incantations were made in a sort of barking howl, like the cry of a dog or wolf, and were usually unintelligible to the uninitiated'.
/336/ Vermes 64.
/337/ Farber, *Beschwörungsrituale*, 155.
/338/ Griffith and Thompson 65.
/339/ Ghalioungui, *Magic*, 40.

/340/ Cato, cited in Naphtali Lewis and Meyer Reinhold, ed., *Roman Civilization; Sourcebook I: The Republic* (New York: Harper & Row, 1966) 446.
/341/ Entralgo Lain, *The Therapy of the Word in Classical Antiquity* (New Haven: Yale University, 1970).
/342/ O. Grether, 'Name und Wort Gottes im AT', *ZAW* 64 (1934) 59 ff.
/343/ Jacob Z. Lauterbach, The Belief in the Power of the Word', *HUCA* 14 (1939) 301-302. See the criticisms of A. C. Thiselton, 'The Supposed Power of Words in the Biblical Writings', *JTS* n.s. 25 (1974) 283-99.
/344/ See my article on 'Aramaic', *The New International Dictionary of Biblical Archaeology*, ed. E. M. Blaiklock and R. K. Harrison (Grand Rapids: Zondervan, 1983) 38-41.
/345/ Böcher, *NT* 35, 90, even regards such words in the liturgy as Hosanna, Maranatha, and Amen as magical! See also R. Grant, *Miracle*, 172; Smith, *JM* 95; D. L. Tiede, *The Charismatic Figure as Miracle Worker* (Missoula: Scholars Press, 1972) 267; Gerard Mussies, 'The Use of Hebrew and Aramaic in the Greek New Testament', *NTS* 30 (1984) 127.
/346/ J. S. Wright in C. Brown 260.
/347/ Melinsky 132.
/348/ C. K. Barrett, ed., *The New Testament Background* (NY: Harper & Brothers, 1961) 31-34; Georg Luck, *Arcana Mundi* (Baltimore: Johns Hopkins University, 1985) 190-91.
/349/ Aune, 'Magic', 1529.
/350/ Davies, *MDD* 105; Loos 324; cf. C. Brown 242-43, citing Barth: 'He made pronouncements, but these do not have the character of incantations'. My main disagreement with Twelftree's scholarly and helpful book is his use of the term 'incantations' (68) for Jesus' exorcistic commands.
/351/ L. Sabourin, *The Divine Miracles Discussed and Defended* (Rome: Catholic Book Agency, 1977) 54; Dunn & Twelftree 214.
/352/ See my article on 'Solomon', *IDBA* 419-22; also M. Seligsohn, 'Solomon', in I. Singer, ed., *The Jewish Encyclopedia* (NY: Funk & Wagnalls, 1909) XI, 435-37.
/353/ See Martin Hengel, *Judaism and Hellenism* (Philadelphia: Fortress, 1974) I,130; II, 88.
/354/ H. Gollancz, *The Book of Protection* (London: A. Froude, 1912). Cf. P. Perdrizet, 'Sphragis Solomônos', *Revue des études grecques* 16 (1903) 42-61; C. C. McCown, 'The Christian Traditions to the Magical Wisdom of Solomon', *JPOS* 2 (1922) 1-24.

/355/ J. M. Robinson, ed., *The Nag Hammadi Library* (NY: Harper & Row, 1977) 415. See S. Giversen, 'Solomon und die Dämonen', *Essays on the Nag Hammadi Texts in Honor of Alexander Böhlig*, ed. M. Krause (Leiden: Brill, 1972) 16-21.
/356/ D. Duling in Charlesworth 935-87.
/357/ Ibid. 934.
/358/ Ibid. 954.
/359/ Cf. Karl Preisendanz, *Papyri Graecae Magicae* (Leipzig: B. G. Teubner, 1928) I, 170; E. S. Drower, 'A Mandaean Book of Black Magic', *JRAS* (1943) 159-60.
/360/ Fisher in Trotter 89.
/361/ Dennis Duling, 'Solomon, Exorcism, and the Son of David', *HTR* 68 (1975) 252.
/362/ Loos 324; cf. Vermes 64; Dunn and Twelftree 214.
/363/ Foerster 19. Among other distinctives Twelftree (69) notes that Jesus unlike Jewish holy men is not reported as praying in the course of his exorcisms.
/364/ S. Langdon, 'Babylonian Magic', *Scientia* 15 (1914) 233; cf. Georges Contenau, 'De la valeur du nom chez les Babyloniens et de quelques-unes de ses consequences', *RHR* 81 (1920) 316-32.
/365/ *ANET* 12-14; Ghalioungui, *Magic* 23; E. Lefébvre, 'La vertu et la vie du nom en Egypte', *Mélusine* 8 (1897) 217-35.
/366/ Campbell Bonner, *Studies in Magical Amulets, Chiefly Graeco-Egyptian* (Ann Arbor: University of Michigan, 1950) 23.
/367/ Hull, *HM* 69.
/368/ See S. Morenz, H.-D. Wendland, W. Jannasch, 'Handauflegung', *RGG* (Tübingen: J. C. B. Mohr, 1959) III, 52-55; E. Lohse, 'Laying on of Hands', *TDNT* (Grand Rapids: Eerdmans, 1974) IX, 424-37.
/369/ J. Behm, *Die Handauflegung im Urchristentum* (Leipzig: A. Deichert, 1911) 104.
/370/ Cited by Sigerist I, 281.
/371/ Remus, '"Magic or Miracle"?' 138.
/372/ Böcher, *NT* 37.
/373/ Smith, *JM* 128.
/374/ Hull, *HM* 141.
/375/ Ibid. 169, n. 32.
/376/ Richards, *Deliver* 13.
/377/ Majno 105. Cf. Jayne 411; Loos 314.

/378/ Jules Older, 'Teaching Touch at Medical School', *Journal of the American Medical Association* 252 (Aug. 17, 1984) 931.
/379/ Aune, 'Magic' 1536.
/380/ For the former position see: J. A. Alexander, *Commentary on the Acts of the Apostles* (Grand Rapids: Zondervan, 1956 reprint of 1875 ed.) 210, 656-57; William Barclay, *The Acts of the Apostles* (Philadelphia: Westminster, 1955) 156. For the latter position, see E. M. Blaiklock, *The Acts of the Apostles* (Grand Rapids: Eerdmans, 1959) 71, 156-57.
/381/ Berends 62.
/382/ J. Duncan M. Derrett, 'Mark's Technique: The Haemorrhaging Woman and Jairus' Daughter', *Bib* 63 (1982) 494.
/383/ For the original English translation of Erasmus' work, see *The First Tome or Volume of the Paraphrase of Erasmus upon the Newe Testamente [1548]* (Delmar: Scholars' Facsimiles & Reprints, 1975) fol. xliii.
/384/ Contenau, *Magie* 140.
/385/ Thompson *DESB* II, 108 f.; cf. Thompson *DESB* I, LIII, 'Spittle had great power in Babylonian sorcery, particularly in bewitching men or casting spells upon them'.
/386/ Yamauchi, *MIT* 73.
/387/ Trachtenberg 120.
/388/ Temkin 8.
/389/ See my 'Magic in the Biblical World', 187-92.
/390/ Martin Ebon, *The Devil's Bride: Exorcism, Past and Present* (NY: Harper & Row, 1974) 25.
/391/ For comments by Hume, see C. Brown 87.
/392/ Smith, *JM* 128; cf. Aune, 'Magic' 1537; Hull, *HM* 143. A contrasting position is taken by Dunn with regard to these verses: 'The counter evidence--that Jesus used magical techniques--is scanty (Mark 7:33,35; 8:23) ... and can hardly overthrow the weightier evidence cited above. Within the context of Jesus' ministry these actions have more charismatic than magical significance'. J. D. G. Dunn, *Jesus and the Sprit* (London: SCM, 1975) 380, n. 37.
/393/ Böcher, *CE* 219.
/394/ Kee, *Miracle* 214-15: 'Although commentators have sought to find traces of magic in the healing stories of Jesus (such as his use of spittle) or of the Apostles (such as their invocation of the name of Jesus), the world-view of the writers of the Gospels and Acts is fundamentally religious rather than magical'. There is no indication that it was intended as a

prophylactic against demons or the evil eye.
/395/ B. Gordon, 772-73.
/396/ As Böcher himself notes, *DD* 219.
/397/ Vermes 65.
/398/ Hull, *HM* 143.
/399/ Smith, *JM* 106.
/400/ O'Keefe 5; cf. 140-41; Luck 8: 'Exorcism is the ancient magical technique of driving out daemons from patients who are thought to be possessed'.
/401/ Stephen Benko, 'Early Christian Magical Practices', *SBL Seminar Papers 1982* (Chico: Scholars Press, 1982) 10.
/402/ Knox, 203. Cf. Kirschläger 152: 'Exorzismus ist kein geheimnisvoll-magisches Geschehen, letzlich wird er auf Gott berückgeführt, der Heilung wirkt'.
/403/ E. G. Weltin, 'The Concept of Ex-Opere-Operato Efficacy in the Fathers as an Evidence of Magic in Early Christianity', *Greek, Roman, Byzantine Studies* 3 (1960) 84-85.
/404/ Loos 371. On the question of whether Jesus' exorcisms would have characterized Jesus as a magician Twelftree (77) concludes:

> *First*, if the *life style* of a miracle worker revealed him to be a cheat, liar or murderer (etc.) he was deemed to be a magician. *Second*, of most importance was the *reality and longevity of a person's work*. But so far as we can see from the Gospels none of Jesus' detractors, not even in connection with the exorcisms, drew attention to either his life style or the reality of his miracles--including the exorcisms. It is only legitimate to conclude that in observing Jesus as an exorcist no one would have considered him to be a magician.

/405/ Lenormant 34.
/406/ F. M. Böhl, 'Zwei altbabylonisch Beschwörungstexte', *BO* 11 (1954) 82.
/407/ Lowe 48.
/408/ Yamauchi, *MIT* 54 f.
/409/ Hebrew *Baal-zebub* 'Lord of flies'was a derisive distortion of *Baal-zebul* 'Prince Baal', the god of Ekron (2 Kings 1:1-6).
/410/ Foerster 18. Even Böcher, *CE* 17, 161, acknowledges that this is a novel viewpoint. Cf. A. Fridrichsen, 'The Conflict of Jesus with the Unclean Spirits', *Theology* 22 (1931)

126-27; idem, *The Problem of Miracle* 105: 'It is interesting, then, to observe how the defense in Mark 9:23ff. opposes to this naive pluralism a rigorously *monistic* view of the spirit-world'.

/411/ Roy Yates, 'Jesus and the Demoniac in the Synoptic Gospels', *ITQ* 44 (1977) 45, 'Thus throughout the Beelzebul controversy the point is made in several different ways that the exorcisms of Jesus are not wrought by magic or by any other alien power, but by the power of God'.

/412/ J. C. Kallas, *The Significance of the Synoptic Miracles* (London: SPCK, 1961) 67.

/413/ Even so careful an exegete as I. Howard Marshall, *Biblical Inspiration* (Grand Rapids: Eerdmans, 1982) 101, sets up a straw man when he writes: 'To quote the hackneyed example, when somebody falls ill, those who claim to follow the New Testament should probably attribute the cause to demon-possession and seek out a person with spiritual powers of healing rather than go to a doctor ...'. This would only be true if the New Testament itself attributed all illnesses to demon possession, a false assumption.

/414/ Cited by C. Brown 150.

/415/ R. Bultmann, *Kerygma and Myth* (New York: Harper, 1961) 4-5. For discussions that argue that scientific discoveries have not eliminated the concept of miracle, properly defined and understood, see: David L. Dye, *Faith and the Physical World* (Grand Rapids: Eerdmans, 1966); Werner Schaaffs, *Theology, Physics, Miracles* (Washington, DC: Canon Press, 1974); J. W. Montgomery, 'Science, Theology and the Miraculous', *JASA* 30 (1978) 143-53; D. and R. Basinger, 'Science and the Concept of Miracle', ibid. 664-68.

/416/ C. Brown 195.

/417/ A. Richardson, *The Miracle Stories of the Gospels* (London: SCM, 1941) 127.

/418/ Adler 106.

/419/ Smith, *CA* 221.

/420/ *JM* 8.

/421/ *Int* 28 (1984) 235.

/422/ Wink 11.

/423/ In O. H. Mowrer, ed., *Morality and Mental Health* (Chicago: Rand McNally, 1967) 209; cf. Ann Lodge, 'Satan's Symbolic Syndrome', in ibid. 494-96; Frank 48. For criticisms of this rationalizing type of explanation, see Kelsey, *Healing* 76; Richardson, *The Problem of Miracle* 63; Loos 110.

/424/ Cited by O. Hobart Mowrer, *The Crisis in Psychiatry and Religion*.
/425/ M. Green 116 comments, 'Ironically, the church may well prove to be the last sector in the community which comes to believe in the supernatural'.
/426/ J. Cortés and F. Gatti, 'Exorcising "The Exorcist"', *Human Behavior* (May, 1974) 22; idem, *Exorcisms* 252; cf. Henry A. Kelly, *The Devil, Demonology and Witchcraft* (Garden City, NY: Doubleday & Co., 1968) 1, 131.
/427/ Cortés and Gatti, *Exorcisms* 251.
/428/ Ibid. 138. See Alan H. Jones, 'A Psychological and Theological Response to a Case of Demon Possession', Ph. D. Dissertation (Claremont: 1977; Ann Arbor: University Microfilms, 1980).
/429/ G. H. C. Macgregor, 'Principalities and Powers: The Cosmic of Paul's Thoughts', *NTS* 1 (1954) 28.
/430/ Fuller, *Interpreting* 19.
/431/ Ibid. 120.
/432/ See the remarkable article of Reginald Fuller, 'What Is Happening in New Testament Studies?' *St. Luke's Journal of Theology* 23 (1980) 95: 'It is undeniable, however, that not all is well in the relation between NT studies and the church. The malaise has been voiced impressively by Walter Wink in his book, *The Bible in Human Transformation*. ... Wink is convinced of the bankruptcy of a purely historical-critical approach to the NT. It results in the yawning gap between the study of the Bible and our religious experience.'
/433/ J. G. Davies, 'Subjectivity and Objectivity in Biblical Exegesis', *BJRL* 66 (1983) 51.
/434/ On subjectivity in the social sciences, see: Stanley E. Lindquist, 'Psychology' and David O. Moberg, 'Social Science', chs. 9 & 10 in Richard Bube, ed., *The Encounter between Christianity and Science* (Grand Rapids: Eerdmans, 1968); Ian G. Barbour, *Issues in Science and Religion* (NY: Harper & Row, 1971) ch. 7.
/435/ Crapanzano 14.
/436/ Robert N. Bellah, 'Confessions of a Former Establishment Fundamentalist', *Council on the Study of Religion Bulletin* 1 (1970) 3-4.
/437/ Peter L. Berger, *The Heretical Imperative* (Garden City, NY: Doubleday & Co., 1979) 109; cf. idem, *A Rumor of Angels* (Garden City, NY: Doubleday & Co., 1970) 41.
/438/ Berger, *The Heretical Imperative* 9-10; idem, *A Rumor of*

Angels 42.
/439/ Berger, *The Heretical Imperative* 93-107.
/440/ Berger, *A Rumor of Angels* 21.
/441/ Hiers 47: 'There is no reason for us to suppose that Jesus did not view the demons in the same way as did his contemporaries and the synoptic evangelists: realistically and seriously'.
/442/ J. Lhermitte, *True and False Possession* (NY: Hawthorn, 1963) 8.
/443/ Loos 204. F. C. Conybeare, 'Christian Demonology', *JQR* (1897) 602 declares:

> According as we take one or the other view, we must or must not attribute to Jesus himself the belief that tempests and fevers were demons, and that rheumatism, madness, deafness, and dumbness and all other physical weaknesses were due to demoniacal possession. I myself am convinced that he did so regard them. Anyhow he regarded madness as such. Indeed if we are to credit the gospels at all, we must believe that he was thoroughly immersed in all the popular superstitions of his age concerning evil spirits.

/444/ Jackson in Montgomery, *Demon Possession* 263, 'It is, therefore, not surprising that most cases referred to me as "typical" cases of demon possession are clinically seen to be schizophrenic in nature ...'.
/445/ Kallas, *Significance* 87.
/446/ Sabourin, 'Jesus and the Evil Powers' 175.
/447/ J. B. Phillips, *The Ring of Truth* (London: Hodder and Stoughton, 1967) 72.
/448/ Marshall, 109-10.
/449/ Melinsky 30, 289.
/450/ Ibid. 324.
/451/ See J. L. Nevius, *Demon Possession and Allied Themes* (Chicago: Revell, 1895); Oesterreich; Crapanzano.
/452/ The author of *Speaking in Tongues* (Chicago: University of Chicago, 1972).
/453/ Felicitas D. Goodman, *The Exorcism of Anneliese Michel* (Garden City, NY: Doubleday & Co., 1981) 52-53.
/454/ Barth, *Church Dogmantics* III.3, 530.

'MIRACLE WORKING ΘΕΙΟΙ ΑΝΔΡΕΣ' IN HELLENISM (AND HELLENISTIC JUDAISM)

Barry L. Blackburn
Michigan Christian College
800 W. Avon Road
Rochester, Michigan 48063
U.S.A.

Study of the Gospel miracle stories has long been heavily influenced by the belief that early Greek-speaking Christians, whether Jewish or Gentile,/1/ formulated these accounts so as to assimilate Jesus to the typical miracle-working *divine man* (θεῖος ἀνήρ) with which the Hellenistic world was familiar./2/ To support this thesis of assimilation adherents have argued that the Gospel miracle stories (1) betray reflection upon Jesus' θεία φύσις, (2) contain themes and motifs having parallels in traditions associated with various miracle-working θεῖοι ἄνδρες, and (3) exhibit a literary form which was also employed by the devotees of certain θεῖοι ἄνδρες in order to publish their masters' miracles and win adherents to their cults or sects./3/ This theory of assimilation, if adopted, naturally has rather profound implications for *traditions-geschichtliche* study of the Gospel miracle traditions, for features which bear the impress of the θεῖος ἀνήρ will hardly be judged to have originated in the early Aramaic-speaking church, much less in the life of Jesus./4/

To embark upon a comprehensive and systematic evaluation of these arguments is forbidden by the spacial confines of this essay; I do propose, however, to contribute toward such an evaluation by making use of the legends surrounding human figures in Hellenism (and Hellenistic Judaism) to whom both miracles and divinity were ascribed in order to address three basic questions: How far is it justifiable to speak of "the typical miracle-working *divine man* with which the Hellenistic world was familiar", i.e., do these figures, known through reports and legends, constitute a type? To what extent are various themes and motifs in the Gospel miracle stories paralleled in miracle traditions associated with these divine miracle workers? And finally, to what extent were the miracles of these divine men narrated in a literary form analogous to that assumed by most of the Gospel miracle narratives? In order to assess the significance of the answers to the last two questions it will be necessary to make reference to certain Jewish miracle traditions.

The preliminary task, however, is to identify the individuals, mythical or historical, who qualify as miracle-working θεῖοι ἄνδρες. 'Miracle-working' here implies no attempt to discern between miracle and magic; the difficulties in such a distinction are well known./5/ However, deeds performed by men of extraordinary strength or military prowess, e.g., the labors of Heracles, fall out of consideration.

Defining just who qualifies as a θεῖος ἀνήρ is not as easy as it is sometimes assumed. I follow the conventional practice of excluding the gods,/6/ except for those regarded as having lived a human life (during which they performed supernatural deeds) prior to death and apotheosis or assumption into heaven. Asclepius is an obvious example of such. In reality, however, classical piety does not offer us sharp, clear criteria for distinguishing between θεοί and θεῖοι ἄνδρες. Pythagoras, for example, who is often recognized as the most significant pre-Christian miracle-working θεῖος ἀνήρ, was revered by some Pythagoreans as nothing less than the Hyperborean Apollo, one of the Olympian gods in human form!/7/

Furthermore, θεῖοι ἄνδρες will be taken to encompass those miracle workers to whom their legends more or less explicitly attribute, in some fashion, divinity. Since the author of Joseph and Asenath allows Joseph to be called 'son of God', and since Artapanus, Philo, and Josephus describe Moses in particular as ἰσόθεος or θεῖος, these two biblical figures will also be included./8/ But as we will see, it is debatable whether these authors intended to promote Joseph and Moses to an 'order of being' fundamentally superior to that enjoyed by ordinary mortals.

Finally, we are primarily concerned with those divine miracle workers whose lives and miraculous deeds were already objects of interest within the Mediterranean world by the mid-first century A.D. Nevertheless, second century figures (e.g., Alexander Abonuteichos) will not be ignored insofar as they may reflect earlier patterns and beliefs.

Within these parameters the following list emerges:

I. Pre-Christian Figures
  Seers
    Amenophis/9/
    Amphiaraus
    Amphilochus
    Tiresias
    Idmon
    Mopsus (son of Chloris)
    Phineus
    Cassandra (θεία γυνή!)
    Calchas
    Mopsus (son of Manto)
    Parnassus
    Telemus
    Democritus/10/
  Healers
    Asclepius
    Machaon
    Podalirius
    Polemocrates
    Nicomachus
    Gorgasus
    Alexanor
    Aristomachos
    Amunos
    Ἰατρὸς Ἥρως
    Oresinios
    Menecrates of Syracuse
  Other Miracle Workers
    Aethalides
    Amphion
    Melampus
    Aristaeus
    Orpheus
    Musaeus
    Argonauts
      Calais and Zetes
      Euphemus
      Periclymenus
    Abaris
    Aristeas of Proconnesus
    Hermotimus of Clazomenae
    Epimenides
    Pythagoras
    Empedocles
    Zalmoxis
    Sophocles/11/
    Socrates
    Nectanebus
    Joseph
    Moses
II. Post-Christian Figures
  Simon Magus
  Menander
  Apollonius of Tyana
  Iarchas and Indian Sages/12/
  Vespasian
  Hadrian
  Alexander Abonuteichos
  Peregrinus
  A Hyperborean Magician/13/

With these figures/14/ before us we are now in a position to find answers for the questions that we have set for ourselves.

I. The Miracle-Working θεῖος Ἀνήρ: A Type?

Those who write about the θεῖος ἀνήρ in the context of Gospel studies often leave the impression of a more or less fixed 'type' whose individual members share a set of common traits and characteristics. Suspicion, however, that this impression, whether intentional or not, is erroneous is initially raised, as I indicated above, as soon as one attempts to draw a clear boundary between divine men and anthropomorphic gods. As it turns out, this lack of conceptual precision proves to be a forerunner of more serious objections to this 'miracle-working divine man type'.

In the first place, the ancient sources yield no standard or customary designation, including θεῖος ἀνήρ, for these miracle workers. Thus my research has confirmed W. von Martitz's position that θεῖος ἀνήρ was not employed as a *technicus terminus* at the time of the Gospels' composition./15/ θεῖος ἀνήρ is applied once to Epimenides, once (perhaps twice) to Moses, and four times to Apollonius./16/ Moreover, only in the case of Apollonius, whose extant biography was not composed until the early part of the third Christian century, is it likely that this epithet (1) denotes the possession of a θεία φύσις/17/ against the background of a polytheism which knows several distinct 'orders of being' (e.g., men, heroes, daemons, gods), /18/ and (2) is awarded, partially at any rate, on the basis of miracles which go beyond divination. Epimenides' mantic abilities and his priestly expiation of Athens' pollution are the grounds upon which Plato calls him a θεῖος ἀνήρ, but as Tiede has shown, one cannot--especially in the case of Plato --simply equate divination with miracle working in general./19/ With respect to Moses, Tiede and, more recently, C. Holladay have emphasized that neither Philo nor Josephus, in those passages where θεῖος ἀνήρ occurs or in those passages containing the 'language of deification', betrays a 'visible tendency to authenticate such claims by appeals to miracles or miracle traditions'./20/ There is moreover, reason to question whether it is not misleading to attribute belief in Moses' divinity to Philo and Josephus. Whatever these authors mean when they apply θεῖος to Moses, the term, because of their Jewish, monotheistic heritage, will necessarily bear a distinctive and characteristic connotation *vis-à-vis* its application to pagan heroes by Gentiles./21/ In light of the above evidence, scholars who state or imply that in the Hellenistic environment of early Christianity θεῖος ἀνήρ functioned as a technical term for human figures who manifested their θεία φύσις through miraculous deeds do so without adequate warrant.

What is true for θεῖος ἀνήρ is likewise valid for another designation frequently assumed to have been applied to divine miracle workers: (ὁ) υἱὸς τοῦ θεοῦ./22/ It is true that several, but by no means all, miracle workers were believed to have been fathered by a god (e.g., Zeus, Apollo, Poseidon), but I found no examples of a pagan miracle worker called, or confessed as, (ὁ) υἱὸς τοῦ θεοῦ./23/ Nor do I know of any case where the miracle worker's divine paternity (or maternity) is deduced from his miraculous deed(s). The only really close parallel appears in Iamblichus who says that the young Pythagoras was regarded by many as θεοῦ παῖς, but even here the basis for this opinion is his virtuous deportment, not miraculous power./24/ The author of Joseph and Asenath allows Joseph, on the basis of his superior beauty and wisdom, to be called 'son of God' by the Egyptians,/25/ but Hengel is probably correct when, on the basis of texts like Wis. 5:5 and T. Ab. 12:4-5, he connects this usage with the Jewish habit of describing angels as sons of God./26/

But if the ancient sources offer no standard classifying label for these divine miracle workers, neither do they offer a uniform way of viewing the nature of their divinity. Some regarded themselves or were regarded as θεοί: Amenophis, Amphiaraus, Cassandra (θεά), Democritus, Asclepius, Menecrates of Syracuse, Aristaeus, Orpheus, Epimenides, Pythagoras, Empedocles, Zalmoxis, Nectanebus, Simon Magus, Menander, Apollonius of Tyana, Hadrian, and Peregrinus./27/ Of these, Pythagoras, Apollonius, and Peregrinus were sometimes held to be δαίμονες./28/ The status of 'hero' was ascribed to most of the figures listed as 'Seers' and 'Healers'./29/ Some of these θεοί, δαίμονες, and ἥρωες, as well as some miracle workers who were never accorded these honors, enjoyed the reputation of divine paternity or maternity. Thus we not only encounter sons of Re or Amon-Re (Amenophis, Nectanebus), /30/ Zeus (Amphion, Epimenides, Apollonius of Tyana),/31/ Apollo (Idmon, Mopsus, son of Chloris, Mopsus, son of Manto, Asclepius, Pythagoras),/32/ Poseidon (Phineus, Parnassus, Euphemus, Periclymenus),/33/ Hermes (Aethalides),/34/ Proteus (Telemus),/35/ Boreas (Calais and Zetes),/36/ and the goddess Selene (Musaeus),/37/ but also sons of Muses (Orpheus)/38/ and nymphs (Tiresias, Parnassus)./39/ Finally the exalted status of a few of the figures in question is expressed in less precise ways: Socrates, Moses, and Iarchas and the Indian sages were θεῖοι, Joseph was called a 'son of God', Vespasian was a Roman emperor and his miracles gave him a certain *maiestas*, Alexander was ὅῖος and received worship, and Abaris and Lucian's magician were Hyperboreans./40/

If the miracle workers' divinity can be expressed in a variety of (sometimes conflicting) ways, no less diversity is apparent with respect to their miracle-working activity. The most common form of miraculous power is some form of divination. In addition to those figures listed under the heading 'Seers', mantic skills (usually prediction) are also known to have been claimed for Melampus, Aristaeus, Orpheus, Musaeus, Abaris, Hermotimus, Epimenides, Pythagoras, Zalmoxis, Nectanebus, Moses, Iarchas, Peregrinus, and especially Apollonius./41/ Besides the 'Healers' the power to heal was attributed to Melampus, Aristaeus, Musaeus, Abaris, Pythagoras, Empedocles, Apollonius, Iarchas, Vespasian, Hadrian, and Alexander Abonuteichos, although the connection with healing is quite tenuous in the cases of Aristaeus, Musaeus, and Abaris./42/ It is certainly fair to conclude that divination and healing are fairly common miraculous powers among our figures, but neither encompasses all, and what is more, divination, the most prevalent power, plays a comparatively minor role in the miracle traditions associated with Jesus in the Gospels.

The miracle traditions that fall outside divination and healing are too numerous for exhaustive recitation, but some examples will illustrate their variety: (1) Resuscitations of the dead were associated with Asclepius, Empedocles, Apollonius, and Alexander Abonuteichos, (2) control of the elements (wind, hailstorms, or violent seas or rivers) was ascribed to Orpheus (by his music), Abaris, Epimenides, Pythagoras, Empedocles, and Apollonius, (3) Amphion and Orpheus could charm rocks, animals, and (in Orpheus' case) trees, by their music, (4) Pythagoras persuaded animals to do his bidding, (5) Musaeus, Calais and Zetes, Abaris (riding on Apollo's arrow), and Lucian's Hyperborean magician had the ability to fly, (6) Pythagoras was seen teaching in two cities on the same day and hour, (7) the power to walk (or run) upon water was associated with Euphemus and the Hyperborean magician, (8) Periclymenus and Nectanebus sometimes assumed different (usually animal) forms, (9) a *katabasis* to and *anabasis* from Hades was achieved by Orpheus, Pythagoras, and Zalmoxis, (10) Hermotimus, and in later tradition Aristeas and Epimenides, could send their souls on journeys, (11) the

Hyperborean practiced love-magic, (12) Abaris engaged in a continual fast, (13) Epimenides took a 57 year nap, (14) Apollonius exorcised or chased away demons and ghosts, (15) Nectanebus caused another to have a deceptive dream, (16) Melampus understood bird language, and Apollonius all animal and human languages, (17) Epimenides and Pythagoras knew the former incarnations of their souls, (18) Pythagoras recognized human souls in animals, and (19) he could hear the cosmic music./43/

We are now in a position to draw an important conclusion: the figures included in our survey have only two things in common, viz., all are reputed to have accomplished miraculous deeds and to have been, in some sense, divine. It is therefore illegitimate to imply that these figures constitute anything like a fixed type whose individual members are bound together by a number of common features./44/ The expression θεῖος ἀνήρ is associated with only three of them./45/ There is, moreover, certainly no uniform way of expressing the nature of their divinity: within their ranks appear sons of gods (or other superhuman beings), heroes, daemons, and even gods. We have also seen the diversity which exists with respect to their miraculous activities; in fact, by looking at the types of miracles performed one can isolate two more or less homogeneous groups of miracle workers which are in turn fairly distinct from one another e.g., the old Greek seers and the Hero physicians. A more amorphous group consists of Pythagoras, the older shamanlike figures (Abasis, Aristeas, Hermotimus, Epimenides, Empedocles, and Zalmoxis) who were absorbed in Pythagorean legend,/46/ and the Neopythagoreans, Apollonius and Alexander Abonuteichos.

In view of this situation it is misleading to ask: 'Do the Gospel miracle stories assimilate Jesus to the typical miracle-working θεῖος ἀνήρ?' What *is* the typical miracle-working θεῖος ἀνήρ? By posing this latter question I do not mean to imply that the Gospel miracle stories are automatically freed from the suspicion of Hellenistic influence, but the question that inquires concerning this influence needs to be modified in a manner similar to this: 'Do the Gospel miracle stories (or some of them), in their Christology, their themes and motifs, and their general structure, betray having been influenced by various Hellenistic ideas and concepts which were associated, rarely or more frequently, with miracle-working and miracle workers and which would have been alien to the culture and possibly to the religious sensibilities of the early Jewish church?' This question, though too broad to be answered comprehensively in the present discussion, has the merit of not implying that the various putative θεῖος ἀνήρ features in the Gospel miracle traditions can be frequently documented in the legends of several divine-human miracle workers whose common characteristics bind them together into a type.

II. Themes and Motifs

Part of the argument for advocating that the Gospel miracle stories were influenced and perhaps even inspired by similar traditions associated with miracle-working divine men rests upon parallelism in themes and motifs./47/ Hence we must now ask, first with respect to themes (e.g., exorcisms, healings, miraculous supply of food, etc.), and then with respect to motifs, 'To what extent does this parallelism in fact exist?'

Exorcisms, which are relatively prominent among Jesus' miracles, would be completely absent from the repertoire of our pagan wonder workers were it not for Philostratus, who in his early third century *Vita Apollonii* relates one executed by Apollonius (4.20) and one by the Indian sage, Iarchas (3. 38). /48/ Recipients of healing include the blind (by Asclepius), epileptics (Menecrates), the lame (Vespasian, Iarchas), one with a crippled hand (Vespasian), one with dropsy (Apollonius), and one paralyzed (Iarchas)./49/ Power to raise the dead was credited to Asclepius, Empedocles, Apollonius, and, apparently, Alexander Abonuteichos./50/

Earlier we had occasion to note that the power to control the winds and waves was imputed to Orpheus (by his music), Abaris, Epimenides, Pythagoras, Empedocles, and Apollonius. With respect to Pythagoras and Apollonius, there are traditions which suggest that their presence on board a ship would guarantee the safety of the voyage,/51/ but there are no miracle stories which tell how a miracle worker saved a ship from storm, as in Mark 4:35ff. Euphemus, like his father Poseidon, could run over the sea without getting his feet wet, and Lucian's Hyperborean magician could walk on water,/52/ but again walking on water never figures in an actual miracle *story*. Philostratus provides us with the only account reminiscent of the two miraculous feedings and the changing of water to wine: the Indian sages whom Apollonius visited entertained King Phraotes by miraculously providing wine, food, and soft grass upon which to lie./53/

As was pointed out above, supernatural knowledge of the past, present, or future is by far the most common form of miracle attributed to the miracle-working divine men of the Greco-Roman world, and therefore it is surprising, on the assumption that Jesus' miracles were heavily influenced by such traditions, that this element is not more dominant in the Gospels. Not only predictions of the future, but also miracles similar to Jesus' 'seeing' Nathanael under the fig tree (John 1:47-49) and his complete knowledge of the Samaritan woman's life (4:16-29) are easily paralleled in the relevant literature./54/

To Jesus' epiphanies during his earthly life--Walking on Water and Transfiguration--our comparative material offers a few limited analogies. The ability to walk on water, as we just saw, was attributed to Euphemus and a Hyperborean magician, but in neither case does this action figure in an epiphany narrative. With respect to the Transfiguration, Periclymenus could transform himself into various insects and animals, and Nectanebus into a snake and the forms of certain gods, but surely the context and purpose of these latter transformations put considerable distance between them and Jesus' metamorphosis./55/ Perhaps a closer parallel is the account of how Pythagoras and Alexander Abonuteichos revealed their golden thighs, but here there is no talk of a transformation. /56/ Post-mortem appearances were made by Aristeas, possibly Pythagoras, and Apollonius./57/ Noteworthy is Philostratus' story of a meeting between Apollonius and two of his disciples who are afraid that he has already been executed. To confirm that he is indeed alive and in the body, and not a ghost, he invites them to grasp hold of him./58/ The links with Luke 24:36ff. and John 20:19ff. are obvious, but there is the difference that while Apollonius proves that he has not been killed, Jesus proves his bodily life after death./59/

In addition to these thematic parallels, older *religionsgeschichtliche* scholars pointed to various motifs present in the Gospel miracle stories and in similar traditions with a divine miracle worker as the subject. There are, for example, motifs which function to glorify the miracle worker by underscoring the difficulty or apparent impossibility of the deed undertaken. Thus Pythagoras was ridiculed when he asked an oxherd to tell an ox to abstain from eating beans./60/ The woman Empedocles healed or raised was 'Panthea . . . who had been given up by the physicians'./61/ In two healing accounts in the *Vita Apollonii* the duration of the illness is noted./62/

Apollonius' exorcism of a young man is glorified by describing the demoniac's behavior: he is licentious and irrational, 'for he would laugh at things that no one else laughed at, and then he would fall to weeping for no reason at all, and he would talk and sing to himself'./63/ The demon which Iarchus exorcised threatened to kill his host--a boy--by casting him down 'steep places and precipices'./64/

In spite of the immense difficulty of the feat required and the gravity of the situation, the miracle worker can act with confidence. Thus Apollonius and Iarchas speak the encouraging θάρσει./65/ The miracle itself can be effected by various means: touching with the hand or some other part of the body is fairly common and occasionally we encounter 'words of power' which accompany the physical gesture./66/ To heal a blind man Vespasian made use of spittle./67/ To overcome a demon Apollonius gazed on him and 'addressed him with anger, as a master might a shifty, rascally, and shameless slave and so on, and he ordered him to quit the young man'./68/ The demon, speaking through the mouth of the youth, responded with cries of fear and rage and promised to depart./69/ In several stories the miracle is explicitly said to have occurred immediately./70/

Finally, there are those motifs which occur in the conclusion of a miracle story. Having raised a dead woman, Empedocles 'dismissed' her./71/ Occasionally information is supplied which proves the reality of the miracle: the rampaging bear which Pythagoras stroked and admonished 'was never again seen attacking any animal at all'./72/ Similarly, after he whispered in the ear of a bean-eating ox, the beast 'not only left the beanfield at that moment but never again touched beans'./73/ The reality of Apollonius' resuscitation of a dead bride is demonstrated when she awakes and speaks, while a dual demonstration appears in the account of his exorcism: the demon knocks over a nearby statue as he exits and the demoniac, previously so irrational, came to his senses, 'for he no longer showed himself licentious, nor did he stare madly about, but he . . . returned to his own self'./74/ Those who witnessed this exorcism 'clapped their hands with *wonder*' (my emphasis). Likewise, the Argonauts were amazed when in response to Orpheus' prayers, the Dioscori immediately calmed a threatening sea storm./75/ The witnesses, however, sometimes draw specific conclusions about the miracle worker: sailors on board ship with Pythagoras conclude that he is really a δαίμονα θεῖον when they reflect on his miraculous and mysterious conduct and 'how, contrary to their expectations, their voyage had been continued and uninterrupted'./76/ Apollonius' divine nature is deduced from his miraculous power on several occasions: (1) Damis, having learned that Apollonius not only knew all human languages but also 'all the secrets of human silence', 'worshipped (προσηύξατο) him, . . . , and regarded him as a demon (δαίμονα)'; (2) when Tigellinus, Nero's minister, unrolled the scroll that contained charges against Apollonius and found it completely blank, 'he came to the conclusion that he had to do with a demon (δαίμονος)'; (3) when Damis saw Apollonius unfetter himself, he 'for the first time . . . really and truly understood the nature of Apollonius, to wit that it was divine (θεία) and superhuman (κρείττων ἀνθρώπου)'; and (4) when Hellas learned of Apollonius' miraculous escape from Domitian its attitude came near to that of worship./77/ Lastly, we should not fail to observe that two miracle stories end with the notice that the person delivered henceforth devoted himself to the philosophy of the miracle worker./78/

In light of the foregoing one can hardly deny that a number of parallels with respect to both themes and motifs certainly exist between the Gospel miracle traditions and those with a divine-human miracle worker as their subject. The crucial question, however, is 'What do these parallels signify?' Specifically, do they reveal a process of assimilating, consciously and/or unconsciously, Jesus the miracle worker to various divine-human miracle workers native to the Hellenistic world? And, assuming that such a process would have seen little progress among the earliest Jewish Christians, do they then yield firm information as to the relative date and provenance of the present form, and perhaps even the origin, of various Gospel miracle stories?

Before one quickly moves from the parallels to an affirmative answer to these two questions, several considerations need to be taken into account. In the first place, some of the parallel themes and motifs which appear in traditions associated with Hellenistic divine miracle workers are only attested in authors as late as Philostratus and Iamblichus. /79/ In the case of these themes and motifs, therefore, it remains uncertain whether they had been firmly associated with one or more divine-human miracle worker(s) in the pre-Christian period. Additional considerations affect even those cases where there is an undeniable pre-Christian association. Thus with respect to parallel themes, it is almost universally recognized that the tradition of Jesus' exorcistic and healing ministry is ultimately rooted in his own activity./80/ In other words, practices associated with divine miracle workers did not transform an originally non-exorcising and non-healing Jesus into an exorcist and healer. Neither, of course, was the belief that the risen Jesus had appeared to some of his disciples a secondary development in the early church. Naturally, this does not preclude the notion that other activities (e.g., raising the dead, exercising power over the elements) were later ascribed to Jesus largely because other divine-human miracle workers were believed to have performed such. But the parallelism between pagan and Jesuan miracle traditions with respect to exorcisms, healings, and post-mortem appearances demonstrates that parallelism alone does not prove the type of assimilation at issue here, and one must at least allow for the possibility that what is true for these three themes *may* be true for others as well.

In assessing the significance of the parallel motifs, one needs to bear in mind that, as we observed, many of these motifs function to emphasize and accentuate the miraculous power of a revered miracle worker. Given this fact, therefore, one would expect similar motifs to surface independently in different cultures which sought to praise their miracle-working men and gods by reciting their marvelous deeds./81/

Be this as it may, however, one thing is certain, almost all of the parallel themes and motifs in question *can also be documented in OT, Palestinian Jewish, and/or rabbinic literature* where the miracle worker is God or, more significantly from the perspective of this study, one of His authorized and divinely-endowed human representatives. As substantiation of this claim I offer the following list which in some cases only offers a few of the more significant examples; other texts are cited in the appropriate footnotes.

Themes

1. Exorcism (Tob 3:7-17; 6:1-17; 8:1-3;/82/ 1QapGen 20.16-29; 4QPrNab; Ps-Philo *Bib. Ant.* 60; Jos. *Ant.* 8.46-49). /83/
2. Healing (1 Kgs 13:4-6: withered hand; 2 Kgs 5:1-14: leprosy; Isa 35:5f: blind, deaf, lame, dumb; *b. Ber.* 34b: fever)./84/
3. Raising the dead (1 Kgs 17:17-24; 2 Kgs 4:18-37)./85/
4. 'Nature Miracles'
    a. Miraculous production of food and drink (2 Kgs 4:42-44)./86/

b. Stilling of sea storms (Ps 107:23-32; Jonah 1:4-16; *p. Ber.* 9.1 [13b])./87/

c. Walking or treading on the sea (Job 9:8; Ps 77:19).

5. Supernatural knowledge (in addition to the many predictions in Jewish literature see 2 Kgs 4:27; 5:26; 6:8-12; b. *Ber.* 34b)./88/
6. Epiphany (in addition to the various theophanies and angelophanies of the OT see Exod 34:29-35; 1 Sam 28:11-14).

Motifs

1. Incredulity toward the possibility of a miracle (Gen 17:15-17; 18:9-15; 2 Kgs 4:16; 5:7, 11-12; 7:2; Dan 2:10f.).
2. Unsuccessful attempts at miracle by physicians, magicians, or idols (Exod 8:18f; 2 Chr 16:12; Dan 2:1-49; 5:8-29; Jonah 1:5; Tob 2:10; 1QapGen 20. 18-21; 4QPrNab; *p. Ber.* 9.1 [13b]).
3. Duration of the illness or calamity (1 Kgs 18:1f.; 1QapGen 20. 17f.; 4QPrNab; 4 Ezra 9:43-45; cf. T. Reub. 1:7f.; T. Gad 5:9-11).
4. The wild, irrational, and dangerous character of demoniacs or demons (1 Sam 18:10f.; 19:9f. in light of Ps.-Philo *Bib. Ant.* 60; Tob 3:7-9; 8:9-14; 1QapGen 20. 20f.; *b. Pesaḥ.* 112b-113a; *b. Meʿil.* 17b; *b. Qidd.* 29b).
5. The miracle-worker's word of assurance (Exod 14:13; 1 Kgs 17:13; 2 Kgs 6:16; Tob 11:11).
6. The miracle-working touch (1 Kgs 17:21; 2 Kgs 4:29, 34; 13:20f.; 1QapGen 20.22, 29; *p. Ketub.* 12 [35a]).
7. Miracle-working words (see next paragraph).
8. Use of spittle (*t. Sanh.* 12. 10 [433]; *ʾAbot R. Nat.* 36; *p. Sanh.* 10 [28b, 2]; *p. Šabb.* 14 [14d, 18]; *p. Sota* 1 [16d, 37]; *b. Sanh.* 101a; *b. B. Bat.* 126b)./89/
9. Dialogue between exorcist and demon (*b. Pesaḥ.* 112b-113a; *b. Ḥul.* 105b; *b. Meʿil.* 17b).
10. A demon is 'rebuked' (1QapGen 20. 28f.; Ps.-Philo *Bib. Ant.* 60).
11. Immediacy of the miraculous occurrence (Num 16:31; Dan 4:33; Tob 8:3 [S]; *Mek.* Beshallah 1.98, 107; *Mek.* Kaspa 3. 41; *b. Taʿan* 19b-20a, 23a; *b. Ber.* 34b).
12. Dismissal (2 Kgs 4:7; 5:19; cf. 1 Kgs 17:13; 2 Kgs 4:36).
13. Demonstration (1 Kgs 17:15; 2 Kgs 4:35, 44; Jos. *Ant.* 8.48; *m. Taʿan.* 3. 8; *b. Ber.* 34b,)./90/
14. Fear or amazement (Gen 43:33; Exod 14:31; 1 Sam 12:18; Dan 3:24; 6:26; Jonah 1:16; Tob 11:16; Sir 48:14; *Mek.*

Beshallah 1. 98).
15. Prostration (2 Kgs 2:15; 4:37; Dan 2:46).
16. Acclamation (1 Kgs 17:24; 2 Kgs 5:15; Dan 2:47; 3:28; 6:26f.)./91/
17. 'Conversion' of the recipients or the witnesses of a miracle (2 Kgs 2:4-18; 5:14-19; Jonah 1:15f.).

At this point it might be instructive to discuss briefly an issue entailed in Jesus' use of miracle-working words or commands (see motif # 7). It is sometimes argued that the θεῖος ἀνήρ influence on the Gospel miracle stories clearly manifests itself in that Jesus, unlike the Old Testament prophets and rabbis, does not accomplish his miracles through prayer, through the use of God's name, through the formula 'Thus says the Lord . . .', or at least by the execution of some action directed by God, but rather, using a miracle-working command and/or gesture, he acts 'autonomously'. While this distinction is valid in general, one should note that 'autonomous' miracle-working is by no means absent from Jewish literature. I located seven miracle stories in the Old Testament--mostly in the Elijah/Elisha cycles--where the miracle worker performed his deed with no mention of God's name, His direction, or His role in the miraculous event./92/ In addition there are examples, in the Old Testament and in later Jewish literature, of a miracle performed by a powerful commanding word: (1) Joshua says: 'Sun, stand thou still at Gibeon, and thou Moon in the valley of Aijalon', (2) according to Pseudo-Philo, David addressed Saul's demon: 'Now therefore, *be not injurious, whereas thou art a second creation*, but if not, thou *remember Hell wherein thou walkest*' (my italics), (3) R. Joshua rebuked the walls of a schoolhouse, saying, 'When scholars are engaged in a *halachic* dispute, what have ye to interfere?' (4) R. Simeon b. Yohai exorcised a demon by commanding, 'Ben Temalion leave her, Ben Temalion leave her', and (5) the son of R. Jose provided food for his father's laborers by commanding the fig tree: 'Fig tree, fig tree, bring forth thy fruit . . . .' /93/ These examples *plus independent reasons for believing that the exercise of direct authority in Jesus' miracle-working harks back to the historical Jesus himself*/94/ should caution us against hastily assuming that a foreign, specifically θεῖος ἀνήρ, ideology has intruded itself here.

The considerations of the immediately preceding paragraphs, when taken seriously, militate against *confidently* concluding that themes and motifs present both in Gospel miracle traditions and in Hellenistic traditions with a divinized human miracle worker as their subject demonstrate that a substantial number of the relevant Gospel themes and motifs entered the tradition only when more hellenized Jewish and Gentile Christians began to assimilate Jesus to various divine-human miracle workers familiar to them. While the possibility that this process occurred cannot be denied, it is at the same time difficult to conclude with confidence that any given theme or motif in the Gospel pericopae is a result of such a process.

III. Form

Just as certain themes and motifs of the Gospel miracle stories also appear in miracle traditions associated with various divine men, so it is that the basic literary form which most of the canonical miracle traditions exhibit is likewise attested in this stratum of Hellenistic tradition. The stories in question are generally more or less self-contained units, though some are rather closely interwoven into larger literary units (e.g., John 9:1-7 in 9:1-41). As for length, they are normally longer than one sentence, but generally contain less than 400 words (in Greek). Finally, these stories evince a threefold pattern, i.e., they (1) describe the plight which requires the miracle worker's assistance, (2) narrate the miracle-producing action, (3) testify to the occurrence and reality of the miracle./95/

The presence of such stories in both the Gospels and in the legends of certain divine-human miracle workers has, in conjunction with other evidence, been interpreted as evidence for the view that later, Greek-speaking tradents of the Jesus narratives assimilated him to his counterparts in the wider Greco-Roman world./96/ In view of this interpretation we shall wish to ascertain to what extent this basic miracle story 'form' manifests itself in the traditions of the figures listed in the introduction of this article.

In the vast majority of cases, the author only makes a passing reference to the miraculous deed(s) in question. Even in Aristotle's list of Pythagoras' marvels, each item is described in only one sentence./97/ Certain miracles are narrated in more detail, but because they do not describe a miraculous action which resolves a problem or an unsatisfactory state of affairs, they naturally do not exhibit the same basic structural features of the Gospel stories./98/ In fact, among the undoubtedly pre-Christian traditions I can adduce only three stories formally reminiscent of the Gospel accounts. The first comes to us from Timaeus (*c.* 356-260 B.C.) by way of Diogenes Laertius:

> When the etesian winds once began to blow violently and to damage the crops, he [Empedocles] ordered asses to be flayed and bags to be made of their skin. These he stretched out here and there on the hills and headlands to catch the wind and, because this checked the wind, he was called the 'wind-stayer.'/99/

From Dionysius Scytobrachion (second or first century B.C.) *via* Diodorus Siculus we learn how Orpheus the Argonaut (like R. Gamaliel according to *b. B. Mes*. 59b, and the Jewish lad of *p. Ber*. 9.1 [13b]) calmed a sea storm through prayer:

> But there came on a great storm and the [Argonaut] chieftains had given up hope of being saved, when Orpheus, they say, who was the only one on shipboard who had ever been initiated in the mysteries of the deities of Samothrace, offered to these deities the prayers for their salvation. And immediately the wind died down and two stars fell over the heads of the Dioscori, and the whole company was amazed at the marvel which had taken place and concluded that they had been rescued from their perils by an act of Providence of the gods./100/

The third account, firmly embedded in the poetry of Ovid's *Fasti* has the mortal, pre-apotheosized Asclepius as its subject:

> Hippolytus fell from the car, and, his limbs entangled by the reins, his mangled body was whirled along, till he gave up the ghost, much to Diana's rage. 'There is no need for grief,' said the son of Coronis [Asclepius], 'for I will restore the pious youth to life all unscathed, and to my leech-craft gloomy fate shall yield.' Straightway he drew from an ivory casket simples that before had stood Glaucus' ghost in good stead, what time the seer went down to pluck the herbs he had remarked, and the snake was succoured by a snake. Thrice he touched the youth's breast, thrice he spoke the healing words; then Hippolytus lifted his head, low laid upon the ground./101/

When we move to traditions whose earliest attestation postdates the ministry of Jesus, we discover more examples. The following two Pythagorean stories can probably be traced back as far as Nicomachus of Gerasa (*c.* A.D. 50-150):

> Moreover, if the ancient and reputable authors who wrote accounts of his life are to be credited, his admonitions extended even to irrational animals. For catching the Daunian bear, that is said to have wounded many of those who lived in its country, he stroked it for a long time and fed it with barley cake and acorns, and having sworn it never again to touch living creatures, let it go. Thereupon it went off into the mountains and thickets, and was never again seen attacking any animal at all. Again, when he saw an ox in Tarentum eating green beans in a pasture that contained many sorts of food, he went up to the oxherd and advised him to tell the ox to abstain from beans. The oxherd answered him with ridicule and said that, himself, he didn't speak ox language. So Pythagoras went near and whispered in the ear of the ox. It not only left the beanfield at that moment but never again touched beans. It lived to an extreme old age in Tarentum, staying near the temple of Hera, and was called the sacred ox and ate such food as the passers-by offered it./102/

At least nine stories which are formally, if not materially, similar to these two find their repository in Philostratus' *Vita Apollonii*./103/ Of these I have selected for quotation two which are not only formally but also thematically similar to certain Gospel stories. The subject of the first account is Apollonius; in the second, the Indian wise men./104/

> Here too is a miracle which Apollonius worked: A girl had died just in the hour of her marriage, and the bridegroom was following her bier lamenting as was natural his marriage left unfulfilled, and the whole of Rome was mourning with him, for the maiden belonged to a consular family. Apollonius then witnessing their grief, said:'Put down the bier, for I will stay the tears that you are shedding for this maiden.' And withal he asked what was her name. The crowd accordingly thought that he was about to deliver such an oration as is commonly delivered as much to grace the funeral as to stir up lamentation; but he did nothing of the kind, but merely touching her and whispering in secret some spell over her, at once woke up the maiden from her seeming death; and the girl spoke out loud, and returned to her father's house, just as Alcestis did when she was brought back to life by Hercules.

> There also arrived a man who was lame. He already thirty years old was a keen hunter of lions; but a lion had sprung upon him and dislocated his hip so that he limped with one leg. However when they massaged with their hands his hip, the youth immediately recovered his upright gait.

Besides these stories which have Pythagoras, Apollonius, or Philostratus' Indian sages as their subject, the remaining miracle stories are apportioned to Empedocles (one), Vespasian (one), Hadrian (two), and Lucian's Hyperborean (one). /105/

Therefore, by combing through pre- and post-Christian sources one can find several accounts of miracles allegedly performed by various divine-human figures which have been transmitted in a form very much like that which characterizes the Gospel miracle stories. Since all but three of these Hellenistic stories are found in post-Christian texts, it is more difficult to determine how accustomed the early Christian tradents were to hearing the miracles of divine-human figures recited in the form under consideration. Perhaps the scarcity of pre-Christian examples of this phenomenon is a result of our lack of direct access to popular, oral traditions and/or the survival of only a portion of classical and Hellenistic literature. On the other hand, is it perhaps possible that the recitation of miracle stories formally similar to those in the Gospels in order to glorify and/or to win adherents to a divine-human thaumaturge was not as prevalent as is sometimes supposed?

Even assuming, however, that the answer to this question is 'no', it is still necessary, as in the previous section, to inquire as to the significance of the parallelism observed. Specifically does it mean that the Gospel miracle stories were first formulated by Greek-speaking Christians under the influence of similar Hellenistic stories with divine men as their subjects? Here again it is necessary to note several relevant facts. In the first place, even in the Hellenistic sphere divine-human miracle workers had no monopoly on the miracle story form in question; the single most abundant collection of (healing) miracle stories was discovered inscribed upon the Asclepieion in Epidaurus (4th cent. B.C.). /106/ But neither did Hellenistic culture as a whole possess a monopoly on such stories./107/ Miracle stories structurally similar to those in the Gospels are easily attested in pre- and post-Christian Jewish literature. Doubters are advised to begin by reviewing the miracle stories of the Elijah/Elisha cycle, e.g., 2 Kings 6:1-7:

> Now the sons of the prophets said to Elisha, 'See, the place where we dwell under your charge is too small for us. Let us go to the Jordan and each of us get there a log, and let us make a place for us to dwell there.' And he answered, 'Go.' Then one of them said, 'Be pleased to go with your servants.' And he answered, 'I will go.' So he went with them. And when they came to the Jordan, they cut down trees. But as one was felling a log, his axe head fell into the water; and he cried out, 'Alas, my master! It was borrowed.' Then the man of God said, 'Where did it fall?' When he showed him the place, he cut off a stick, and threw it in there, and made the iron float. And he said, 'Take it up.' So he reached out his hand and took it./108/

Also worthy of special mention is the miracle story which the author of 1QapGen created of Genesis 12:17-20. This story, closely tied into the larger narrative of 1QapGen, does admittedly exhibit two rather unusual features: it is told in the first person (from Abram's perspective) and the biblical basis of the story requires that the patient (Pharaoh) perform a specified action (restore Sarai to Abram) before receiving the miraculous healing that he desires. But the basic three-fold pattern of most of the Gospel stories is easily discernible in it, and as an added bonus it exhibits several motifs that were mentioned in the previous section:

> And during that night the Most High God sent a spirit to scourge him [Pharaoh], an evil spirit to all his household; and it scourged him and all his household. And he was unable to approach her [Sarai], and although he was with her for two years he knew her not.
>
> At the end of those two years the scourges and afflictions grew greater and more grievous upon him and all his household, so he sent for all [the sages] of Egypt, for all the magicians, together with all the healers of Egypt, that they might heal him and all his household of this scourge. But not one healer or magician or sage could stay to cure him, for the spirit scourged them all and they fled.
>
> Then Harkenosh came to me [Abram], beseeching me to go to the king and to pray for him and to lay my hands

> upon him that he might live, for the king had dreamt a dream . . . . But Lot said to him, 'Abram my uncle cannot pray for the king while Sarai his wife is with him. Go, therefore, and tell the king to restore his wife to her husband; then he will pray for him and he shall live.'
>
> When Harkenosh had heard the words of Lot, he went to the king and said, 'All these scourges and afflictions with which my lord the king is scourged and afflicted are because of Sarai the wife of Abram. Let Sarai be restored to Abram her husband, and this scourge and the spirit of festering shall vanish from you.'
>
> And he called me and said, 'What have you done to me with regard to [Sarai]? You said to me, She is my sister, whereas she is your wife; and I took her to be my wife. Behold your wife who is with me; depart and go hence from all the land of Egypt! And now pray for me and my house that this evil spirit may be expelled from it.'
>
> So I prayed [for him] . . . and I laid my hands on his [head]; and the scourge departed from him and the evil [spirit] was expelled [from him], and he lived./109/

The fact that this threefold pattern exists in the Jewish instances just cited, and also in other biblical, pseudepigraphical, and rabbinic miracle stories,/110/ surely means that one should not automatically assign the formulation of the Gospel miracle stories to Greek-speaking Christians./111/ Even Bultmann judged that a Palestinian origin was probable for Mark 1:40-45, 2:1-12, 4:35-41, 5:25-34, and 6:34-44/8:1-9,/112/ and more recent interpreters usually admit that some of the Gospel miracle stories were circulated within the early Aramaic-speaking church./113/ Thus on the basis of form alone, a given Gospel miracle story should not be denied a place among the Jesus tradition which was current within the early Aramaic-speaking church prior to the Gentile mission.

Conclusion

As stated in the introduction, this study does not purport to analyze and evaluate all of the arguments used to justify talk of a θεῖος ἀνήρ ideology in the Gospel miracle traditions. A thorough evaluation, for example, would have to grapple with data within the miracle traditions which appear to assimilate Jesus to Yahweh. On the other hand, the data presented in the foregoing discussion strongly suggests that the relatively large degree to which assimilation to 'the miracle-working θεῖος ἀνήρ' has been called upon to account for the origin of various features in the Gospel miracle tradition is without justification. The impression that such pervasive assimilation to the alleged type in question has occurred can only be maintained if *every* feature in the Jesuan miracle traditions which can be paralleled *at least once* in the legends associated with 'the miracle-working θεῖοι ἄνδρες of Hellenism' is regarded as a typical 'θεῖος ἀνήρ' motif or feature. But it hardly seems legitimate to so regard those Gospel features which rarely surface in the aforementioned Hellenistic traditions (e.g., exorcism, miraculous production of food/drink, walking on water, metamorphosis, *proskynesis* before the wonder-worker, use of spittle, use of ῥήσεις βαρβαρικαί, sighing, etc.). In fact, it is questionable whether it is useful to speak of the known divine-human miracle workers of Hellenism as constituting a type, unless one simply means to say that they were all regarded as both divine and in possession of miraculous powers. Over a decade ago D. Tiede taught us to discriminate between moral virtue/wisdom and miracle-working as (usually conflicting) criteria for authenticating the divinity of exceptional individuals in Hellenistic antiquity. In view of this dichotomy we were told that it was 'in the hues of the divine *miracle worker* [my emphasis]' that the novelistic (Gospel) miracle stories painted Jesus./114/ Our study, however, has shown that precious little homogeneity exists among the motley assortment of figures to whom Hellenistic sources attribute both divinity and miraculous power. Even among those specific miracle workers who were linked together and revered by the Neopythagoreans, there are few typical features which can be paralleled in the Gospel traditions.

These observations, of course, do not preclude the possibility of Hellenistic influence upon the Gospel miracle traditions. Indeed we have had the opportunity to note several parallels, specifically with respect to themes, motifs, and literary form, between the Jesuan miracle traditions and those associated with *specific* divine-human miracle workers known in Greco-Roman antiquity. One can thus hardly deny the possibility that at least in some cases the Hellenistic traditions in question may have, by means of hellenized Jewish and/or Gentile Christians, influenced the Gospel miracle stories. Yet the ability to prove that such has occurred in any given instance is questionable since, as we have seen, those features present in the Gospel miracle traditions *and* in those associated with various divine men of the Hellenistic sphere are also rarely absent from Palestinian Jewish literature, even though the quantity of this literature is miniscule compared with classical and Hellenistic literary and inscriptional remains.

The burden of this article has not been to demonstrate positively the historicity of this or that element of the Gospel miracle tradition, but my conclusions are relevant to the historicity issue insofar as they place a question mark beside one of the most common attempts to relegate a significant portion of the Gospel miracle tradition to a secondary (or tertiary) stage in its development. While of course it would be possible to argue that there are individual features within the Gospel miracle stories or even entire stories which were known to the early, Aramaic-speaking church, *and yet are not historical*,/115/ certainly with all other things equal the case for historicity is enhanced if the features and stories in question are conceivable in a Jewish, Aramaic-speaking milieu; conversely, the case is demolished unless they can be traced back to this early period.

NOTES

/1/ Over against the rather common view that the θεῖος ἀνήρ ideology was mediated to the early church by Hellenistic Judaism (H. Windisch, *Paulus und Christus* [Leipzig: Hinrichs, 1934] 101-14; L. Bieler, ΘΕΙΟΣ ΑΝΗΡ [Vienna: Oskar Höfels, 1935-36] vol. 2, 25-36; D. Georgi, *Die Gegner des Paulus im 2. Korintherbrief* [Neukirchen: Neukirchener Verlag, 1964] 145-67), see C. Holladay, *Theios Aner in Hellenistic Judaism* (Missoula: Scholars Press, 1977) 22-43.

/2/ It has long been recognized that on the whole the distinction between god and man was much more fluid for the Hellenistic world than for those whose theology was primarily rooted in the OT. Thus in Hellenistic thought one encounters not only gods, daemons, and heroes, but also humans whose abilities, achievements, and feats lift them head and shoulders above the common rank of humanity, and therefore distinguish them as being in some sense divine. In his classic work, ΘΕΙΟΣ ΑΝΗΡ, Bieler studied such figures, ranging from pre-classical Greece to the church's hagiography, and amassed a catalogue of features associated with them in an effort to set before his readers 'den Gesamttypus, gewissermassen die platonische Idee des antiken Gottmenschen' (vol. 1., 4). Many NT scholars have interpreted (wrongly says E. Gallagher, *Divine Man or Magician? Celsus and Origen on Jesus* [Chico: Scholars Press, 1982] 10-18) Bieler's work as an attempt to portray *the* divine man type (consisting of many component features) which exercised the minds of Greek-speaking pagans in the first century A.D. and, in turn, exerted a formidable influence upon early Christian traditions pertaining to Jesus' life. Recently Tiede (*The Charismatic Figure as Miracle Worker* [Missoula: SBL, 1972]) and Gallagher (*Divine Man*) have called attention to evidence which suggests that antiquity, at least during the first Christian century (Tiede), was not agreed upon the criteria for judging the divinity of a really exceptional figure. See also the recent contribution of H. D. Betz, 'Gottmensch II', *RAC*, vol. 12, 234-88.

/3/ E.g., see M. Dibelius, *From Tradition to Gospel* (New York: Scribner's, 1965) 70-97; R. Bultmann, *History of the Synoptic Tradition* (New York: Harper & Row, 1963[2]) 218-41; Bieler, ΘΕΙΟΣ ΑΝΗΡ; H. D. Betz, *Lukian von Samosata und das Neue Testament* (*TU* 76 [1961]) 100-103; idem, 'Jesus as Divine Man', in *Jesus and the Historian*, ed. F. T. Trotter (Philadelphia: Westminster, 1968) 114-33; G. Petzke, *Die Traditionen über Apollonius von Tyana und das Neue Testament* (Leiden: Brill, 1970); G. Theissen, *The Miracle Stories of the Early Christian Tradition* (Philadelphia: Fortress, 1983) 265-76; U. Luz, 'Das Jesusbild der vormarkinischen Tradition', in *Jesus Christus in Historie und Theologie*, ed. G. Strecker (Tübingen: J. C. B. Mohr, 1975) 355-67; Betz, 'Gottmensch II', 288-90; 296-300.

/4/ Some of these implications can be discerned, for example, in the studies of K. Kertelge, *Die Wunder Jesu im Markusevangelium* (Munich: Kösel-Verlag, 1970), and L. Schenke, *Die Wundererzählungen des Markusevangeliums* (Stuttgart: Katholisches Bibelwerk, 1974).

/5/ Cf. J. Hull, *Hellenistic Magic and the Synoptic Tradition* (London: SCM, 1974) 54-61; D. Aune, 'Magic in Early Christianity', *Aufstieg und Niedergang der römischen Welt* 23.2, ed. W. Haase (Berlin: de Gruyter, 1980) 1510-16; A. Segal, 'Hellenistic Magic: Some Questions of Definition', *Studies in Gnosticism and Hellenistic Religions*, ed. R. van den Broek and M. J. Vermaseren (Leiden: Brill, 1981) 349-75.

/6/ See Bieler ΘΕΙΟΣ ΑΝΗΡ, 5-6; Betz, 'Jesus as Divine Man', 116; T. Weeden, *Traditions in Conflict: The Aretalogy Used by Mark* (Berkeley: Center for Hermeneutical Studies, 1975) 48.

/7/ Ael. *Var. Hist.* 2. 26; D. L. 8. 11.; Iamb. *Vit. Pyth.* 30, 140 (see N.G.L.Hammond and H.H.Scullard, eds., *The Oxford*

Classical Dictionary [Oxford: Clarendon Press, 1970[2]] ix-xxii, for help in deciphering the abbreviations for classical authors and their works which appear in this article). This Pythagoras = Apollo equation is probably at least as old as (pseudo?) Aristotle's Περὶ τῶν Πυθαγορείων, part of which is quoted by Apollonius Paradox (*Mir.* 6) in the second century B.C.

If we treat as a θεῖος ἀνήρ Pythagoras, whom some of his disciples regarded as Apollo, is it not a bit arbitrary to exclude (as is customarily done) Dionysus, who was involved in numerous earthly travels and exploits which included miracle-working? To object that Dionysus was only a 'mythical' figure is anachronistic.

/8/ Although Moses and Joseph are often viewed as two of the more obvious examples of Old Testament heroes transformed into θεῖοι ἄνδρες by Hellenistic Judaism, there are other prophets and miracle workers for whom this claim has been made E.g., see Bieler, ΘΕΙΟΣ ΑΝΗΡ, vol. 2, 28-29: (1) Solomon, whose wisdom enabled him to exorcise demons (Jos. *Ant.* 8. 45-49) was regarded ὡς θείαν ἔχοντι διάνοιαν (*Ant.* 8. 34; cf. 8. 187); (2) Jeroboam, rebuked by the prophet Jadon, called him a θεῖον ἀληθῶς καὶ προφήτην ἄριστον (*Ant.* 8.243); (3) Elijah was ἔνθεος (Philo *Deus Imm.* 138); (4) Elisha during his life and after his death possessed a δύναμιν θείαν (*Ant.* 9. 183); (5) Isaiah's predictions qualified him as a prophet ὁμολογουμένως θεῖος καὶ θαυμάσιος (*Ant.* 10. 35); (6) Daniel, on account of his beneficent and true predictions, received δόξαν θειότητος παρὰ τοῖς ὄχλοις (*Ant.* 10. 268); and (7) the prophets as a whole are θεῖοι προφῆται (*Ant.* 18. 64).

/9/ Jos. *Ap.* 1. 232.

/10/ D. L. 9. 39.

/11/ Philostr. *Vit. Ap.* 8. 7.

/12/ Ibid., 3. 11-50.

/13/ Lucian *Philops.* 13-14.

/14/ Individuals who performed miracles but to whom divine status was not explicitly ascribed include Thales, Phormion and Leonymus, Polyidos, Pherecydes of Syros, Anaxagoras of Clazomenae, Pyrrhus, and Eunus; perhaps reference should also be made to some of the better known astrologers and magicians, such as Zoroaster, Ostanes, Hystaspes, Nechepso-Petosiris, Thessalos, Bolus-Democritus, Nigidius Figulus, Anaxilaus, Thrasyllus, Pachrates/Pancrates, Apuleius, and some of the figures mentioned in Lucian's *Philopseudes*.

/15/ W. von Martitz, 'υἱός (in Greek)', *TDNT* 8 (1972) 339.

/16/ Plat. *Leg.* 1. 642d; Philo *Virt.* 177 (?); Jos. *Ant.* 3. 180; Apollonius Ty. *Epist.* 48; Philostr. *Vit. Ap.* 2. 17, 40; 8. 15.

/17/ Philostr. *Vit. Ap.* 7. 38.
/18/ Cf. Pind. *Olymp.* 2. 1; Plat. *Crat.* 397c, 398e; Plut. *Def. Orac.* 10 (415B).
/19/ Tiede, *The Charismatic Figure*, pp. 36-37: 'In the philosophical schools of the Hellenistic world, particularly in the Stoa after Poseidonius, divination frequently held a special place as an intellectually respectable art, even among many of those who were skeptical about other popular beliefs and practices which were regarded as superstitious.' On Plato see 30-34. Later, as an example of this attitude, Tiede (128-9) cites Philo, who did not view divination of the future and 'magical-miraculous performances' as inextricably bound together, for in the case of Moses he emphasized and enhanced the former but not the latter.
/20/ Holladay, *Theios Aner*, 237; esp. see Tiede, *The Charismatic Figure*, 101-37; 207-40.
/21/ Thus even if one accepts Georgi's (*Die Gegner*, 140-67) elucidation of the meaning of θεῖος ἀνήρ in these authors, it quickly becomes apparent that Moses 'divinity' is not as straightforward as one might expect. For example, (according to Georgi) Moses' divinity consists in the fact that he, in a singularly advanced way, has apprehended in himself, and has become a participant in, the cosmic δύναμις or ἀρετή of God. But since all men are granted 'die Gegenwart der göttlichen Kraft in Gestalt der Seele' (143), the mode of existence which Moses actualizes is potentially present for all men (145-6). But with this we have moved out of the sphere of popular piety with its belief in more or less fixed 'orders of being' which various creatures occupy, as it were, by nature. Furthermore Jewish monotheism, accompanied as it was by the desire to see in God the ultimate subject of reality, meant that the virtue and power which Moses displayed remained, at bottom, God's virtue and power, and thus there could be no thought that Moses, either before or after his death, was worthy of a cult (i.e., temples, priests, sacrifices, prayers).

In Artapanus (*FGrHist* 726F3; Eng. trans. of frag. 3 in Tiede, *The Charismatic Figure*, 317-8), however, it is more difficult to deny that Moses was divinized, for this author states that Moses (1) was called Musaeus by the Greeks (3. 3), (2) appointed the (animal) god that each Egyptian Nome should worship (3. 4), and (3) was judged by the Egyptian priests as being worthy of ἰσόθεου τιμῆς. See Georgi, *Die Gegner*, 148-51; Tiede, *The Charismatic Figure*, 146-77; and from a different perspective Holladay, *Theios Aner*, 199-232.
/22/ Cf. Holladay, *Theios Aner*, 9-11.
/23/ As M. Hengel, *The Son of God* (Philadelphia: Fortress, 1976)

30, n. 57, has said: 'A fundamental distinction must be drawn between the numerous παῖδες or υἱοὶ Διός and υἱὸς θεοῦ as a title.'
/24/ Iamb.*Vit. Pyth.* 10.
/25/ 6:2-6; 13:13; cf. 23:10. Joseph, however, retains his human paternity (7:5; 22:4).
/26/ *The Son of God*, 43 and n. 87. Cf. E. Schweizer, 'υἱός', *TDNT* 8 (1972) 356, n. 134.
/27/ Amenophis: incarnation of Horus (cf. W. Schottroff, 'Gottmensch I', *RAC*, vol. 12, 181); Amphiarius: Paus. 1. 34. 4; Cassandra: Lycophron *Alex*. 1128-30; Democritus: D. L. 9. 39; Asclepius: see numerous texts in E. and L. Edelstein, *Asclepius*, vol. 1 (Baltimore: Johns Hopkins, 1945); Menecrates: Ephippus, Frag. 17 (T. Kock, *Comicorum Atticorum Fragmenta* [= *CAF*], vol. 2), Plut. *Ages*. 21; Aristaeus: Diod. S. 4. 82. 5; Orpheus: A. Boeckh, *Corpus Inscriptionum Graecarum*, vol. 3, no. 5970; Epimenides: D. L. 1. 114; Pythagoras: Aristotle Περὶ τῶν Πυθαγορείων, Frag. 191 (V. Rose); Kranz, *Die Fragmente der Vorsokratiker* (= *DK*) 31B112; D. L. 8. 69-70; Zalmoxis: Hdt. 4. 94-95; Hellanicus (F. Jacoby, *Die Fragmente der griechischen Historiker* [=*FGrHist*] 4F73); Nectanebus: incarnation of Horus; Simon Magus: Justin M. *Apol*. 1.26.3; Menander: Justin M. *Apol*. 1.26.1,4; Apollonius: Philostr. *Vit. Ap*. 1.4,19; 3.50; 4.31,44; 5.24,33; 6.39; 7.11,20-21; 8.5-7; Hadrian: a 'god' as emperor; Peregrinus: Lucian *Peregr*. 1,6.11.
/28/ Pythagoras: Iamb.*Vit. Pyth*. 10, 16; Apollonius: Philostr. *Vit. Ap*. 1. 19; 4. 44; 7. 32; Peregrinus: Lucian *Peregr*. 27. Additionally, Socrates was believed to have possessed a δαιμόνιον (Plat. *Ap*. 31C, 40A-B; *Euthyd*. 272E; Xenoph. *Mem*. 1.1. 3). Here of course δαίμων and δαιμόνιον do not bear a 'demonic' connotation.
/29/ Amphiaraus: Paus. 3. 12. 5; Amphilochus: Paus. 1. 34. 3; Tiresias: an oracle in Orchomenus (Plut. *Def. Orac*. 44 [434C]); Idmon: Apoll. Rhod. 2. 844-50; Mopsus (son of Chloris): Amm. Marc. *Res Gestae* 14. 8. 3; Calchas: Strabo 6. 3. 9 (284); Mopsus (son of Manto): Pluto. *Def. Orac*. 45 (434D-F); Machaon and Podalirius: Aristotle, Frag. 640. 20 (V. Rose), Lycoph. *Alex*. 1047-55, Paus. 3. 26. 9; Polemocrates: Paus. 2. 38. 6 Nicomachus and Gorgasus; Paus. 4. 3. 10; 4. 30. 3; Alexanor: Paus. 2. 11. 6; Aristomachus: *Lexicon Rhetoricum* (I. Bekker, *Anecdota Graeca*, vol. 1, 262); Amunos: inscriptional evidence in A. Körte, 'Die Ausgrabungen am Westabhange der Akropolis IV. Das Heiligtum des Amynos', *Mittheilungen des kaiserlich Deutschen archaeologischen Instituts: Athenische Abtheilung* 21 (1896) 295; Ἰατρὸς Ἥρως: Demosth. *Fal. Leg*. 249; Oresinios: *Lexicon Rhetoricum* (Bekker, *Anec. Graeca*, vol. 1,

263); Melampus: Paus. 1. 44.5; Orpheus: cf. J. A. R. Munro, 'Epigraphical Notes from Eastern Macedonia and Thrace', *JHS* 16 (1896) 321; Aristeas: Apollonius Para. *Mir.* 2; Hermotimus: Apollonius Para. *Mir.* 3; Sophocles: Ister *Vit. Soph.* 17.

/30/ Cf. Schottroff, 'Gottmensch I', 181-2.

/31/ Hom. *Od.* 11. 260-62; D. L. 1. 114; Philostr. *Vit. Ap.* 1. 6.

/32/ Pherecydes *FGrHist* 3F108; Valerius Flaccus *Argon.* 1. 383-4; Conon *FGrHist* 26F1. 6; Hom. *Hym.* 16. 1-2; Iamb. *Vit. Pyth* 7.

/33/ Apollod. *Bibl.* 1. 9. 21; *Paus.* 10. 6. 1; Pind. *Pyth.* 4. 43-46; Sen. *Med.* 635-6 (cf. K. Scherling, 'Periklymenos', PW, 19:792-3).

/34/ Heraclides Pont., Frag. 89 (F. Wehrli).

/35/ Hyginus *Fab.* 128.

/36/ Pind. *Pyth.* 4. 181-83.

/37/ Plato *Resp.* 2. 7 (364e).

/38/ Apoll. Rhod. 1. 23-4.

/39/ Callim. *Hymn.* 5. 57-67; Paus. 10. 6. 1.

/40/ Socrates: Plat. *Phaedr.* 238c, etc.; Moses: Philo *Vit. Mos.* 1. 27; 2. 188 (perhaps *Virt.* 177; *Quaest. in Ex.* 2. 54 is preserved only in Armenian); Jos. *Ant.* 3. 180; ἰσόθεος is applied to Moses in Artapanus (*FGrHist* 726F3. 6); Iarchas and sages: Philostr. *Vit. Ap.* 6.3; 7. 14; Joseph: *Jos. Asen.* 6. 2-6; 13. 13; but cf. 7.5; 22. 4; 23. 10; Vespasian: Suet. *Vit. Caes.* 8. 7. 2; Alexander: Lucian *Alex.* 11, 24, 39; Abaris and Lucian's magician: *Hdt.* 4. 36; Lucian *Philops.* 13 (on Hyperboreans cf. Pind. *Pyth.* 10. 41-2; Strabo 15. 1. 57 [711]).

/41/ Apollonius' divination often takes the form of recognizing or perceiving present reality which for some reason is hidden to ordinary people.

/42/ Melampus: Ovid *Meta.* 15. 322-28; Aristaeus: Apoll. Rhod. 2. 510-12; Musaeus: Aristoph. *Ra.* 1033; Abaris: Plat. *Charm.* 158b; Pythagoras: Antonius Diogenes (in Porph. *Vit. Pyth.* 32-33; Iamb. *Vit. Pyth.* 110-11); Empedocles: Emped., Frag. 102 (Wright) = DK 31B112; Apollonius: Philostr. *Vit. Ap.* 6. 43; Iarchas: Philostr. *Vit. Ap.* 3. 39; Vespasian: Tac. *Hist.* 4. 81; Suet. *Vit. Caes.* 8. 7; Dio Cass. 65. 8. 1; Hadrian: Ael. Spart. *Vit. Had.* 25; Alexander: Lucian *Alex.* 5.

/43/ (1): Ovid *Fasti* 6. 743-62; D. L. 8. 60-62, 67; Philostr. *Vit. Ap.* 4. 45; Lucian *Alex.* 24; (2): Apoll. Rhod. 1. 26-27; Nicomachus of Gerasa (in Porph. *Vit. Pyth.* 29 and Iamb. *Vit. Pyth.* 135); Timaeus *FGrHist* 566F30=D. L. 8. 60; Philostr. *Vit. Ap.* 4. 13, 15; 7. 26; 8. 13; (3): Verg. *Ecl.* 2. 23-4; Eur. *Phoen.* 823-4; Apoll. Rhod. 1. 26-31, 569-79; (4): Nicomachus (in Porph. *Vit. Pyth.* 23-25 and Iamb. *Vit. Pyth.*

60-62, 36); (5): Paus. 1.22.7; Pind. *Pyth.* 4. 181-83; Nicomachus (in Porph. *Vit. Pyth.* 29 and Iamb. *Vit. Pyth.* 136); Lucian *Philops.* 13; (6): Apollonius Para. *Mir.* 6; (7): Apoll. Rhod. 1. 179-84; Lucian *Philops.* 13; (8): Apoll. Rhod. 1. 156-60; Pseud.-Callisth. 1. 6-7; cf. Hdt. 4. 14; (9): Verg. *Culex* 268-93; D. L. 8. 21, 41; Hdt. 4. 94-5; (10): Apollonius Para. *Mir.* 3; Max. Tyr. 10. 2; *Suda* s.v. ''Επιμενίδης'; (11): Lucian *Philops.* 14; (12): Hdt. 4. 36; (13): Apollonius Para. *Mir.* 1; (14): Philostr. *Vit. Ap.* 2. 4; 4. 20; (15): Pseud.- Callisth. 1. 5; (16): Apollod. *Bibl.* 1. 9. 11; Philostr. *Vit. Ap.* 1. 19-21; 4. 3; (17): D. L. 1. 114; Heraclides Pont., Frag. 89 (Wehrli); (18): Xenophanes DK 21B7; (19): Porph. *Vit. Pyth.* 30; Iamb. *Vit. Pyth.* 65.

/44/ For the diversity among divine beings (men and gods) in general, irrespective of whether they were famous as miracle workers, see M. Smith, 'Prolegomena to a Discussion of Aretalogies, Divine Men, the Gospels and Jesus', *JBL* 90 (1971) 179-88.

/45/ Cf. above, sec. 1.

/46/ Cf. W. Burkert, *Lore and Science in Ancient Pythagoreanism* (Cambridge: Harvard Univ. Press, 1972) 147-59.

/47/ In this regard, Bultmann, *History of the Synoptic Tradition*, pp. 220-40, has been very influential.

/48/ The expulsion of demons from humans was certainly practiced before the third century A.D. (cf. the article by E. Yamauchi in the present volume), but to my knowledge no Hellenistic text earlier than Philostratus attributes the work of exorcism to a human miracle worker who is explicitly regarded as divine.

/49/ Blind: Phylarchus *FGrHist* 81F18; Tac. *Hist.* 4. 81; Suet. *Vit. Caes.* 8. 7; Dio Cass. 65. 8. 1; Ael. Spart. *Vit. Had.* 25; Philostr. *Vit. Ap.* 3. 38-9; insane: Ovid *Meta.* 15. 322-28; Polyanthus *FGrHist* 37F1; epileptics: Ephippus, Frag. 17 (*CAF*, vol. 2); Alexis, Frag. 136 (*CAF*, vol. 2); Plut. *Ages.* 21; the lame: Suet. *Vit. Caes.* 8. 7.; Philostr. *Vit. Ap.* 3. 39; crippled hand: Tac. *Hist.* 4. 81; Dio Cass. 65. 8. 1; dropsy: Philostr. *Vit. Ap.* 1. 9 (not a miracle in the usual sense); paralyzed: Philostr. *Vit. Ap.* 3. 39.

/50/ Pind. *Pyth.* 3. 55-58; Aesch. *Ag.* 1019-24; Heraclides Pont., Frag. 83 (Wehrli); Philostr. *Vit. Ap.* 4. 45; Lucian *Alex.* 24.

/51/ Pythagoras: Iamb. *Vit. Pyth.* 14-17; Apollonius: Philostr. *Vit. Ap.* 4. 13, 15; 7. 26; 8. 13.

/52/ Apoll. Rhod. 1. 179-84; Hyginus *Fab.* 14; Lucian *Philops* 13.

/53/ *Vit. Ap.* 3. 27.

/54/ Supernatural knowledge of past or present reality which is beyond the ken of ordinary mortals is abundantly manifested in

Apollonius' life; cf. Philostr. *Vit. Ap*. 1. 23; 4. 34; 2. 40; 3. 23-4; 4. 10, 25, 28, 34; 5. 5, 24-5, 30, 42; 6. 3, 5, 38-9; 8. 26.

/55/ Apollod. *Bibl*. 1. 9. 9; Pseud.-Callisth. 1. 6-7.

/56/ Apollonius Para. *Mir*. 6; Lucian *Alex*. 40.

/57/ Hdt. 4. 14-5; Apollonius Para. *Mir*. 2; D. L. 8. 14; Philostr. *Vit. Ap*. 8. 30-1.

/58/ *Vit. Ap*. 8. 12.

/59/ Also in the Philostratean story Apollonius does not suddenly and miraculously appear before his disciples' eyes. As it turns out his presence there is due to miraculous transport, but they did not know this until he informs them.

/60/ Nicomachus (in Porph. *Vit. Pyth*. 24 and Iamb. *Vit. Pyth*. 61). Pythagoras then whispered in the ox's ear and persuaded it to cease eating beans.

/61/ Hermippus, Frag. 27 (Wehrli) = D.L. 8. 69.

/62/ 3. 38 (cf. 3. 39); 6. 43.

/63/ Philostr. *Vit. Ap*. 4. 20.

/64/ Ibid., 3. 38.

/65/ Ibid., 3. 38; 4. 10.

/66/ Touching: Ovid *Fasti* 6. 749-54; Nicomachus (in Porph. *Vit. Pyth*. 23 and Iamb. *Vit. Pyth*. 60) (stroking); Pseud.-Plat. *Theag*. 130d-e; Philostr. *Vit. Ap*. 3. 39 (massaging); 4. 45; 6. 43 (stroking); Tac. *Hist*. 4. 81; Suet. *Vit. Caes*. 8. 7; Dio Cass. 65. 8. 1; Ael. Spart. *Vit. Had*. 25; the word: Ovid *Fast*. 6. 749-54; Nicomachus (in Porph. *Vit. Pyth*. 24 and Iamb. *Vit. Pyth*. 61), idem (in Porph. *Vit. Pyth*. 30-1 and Iamb. *Vit. Pyth*. 64-6); Iamb. *Vit. Pyth*. 113; Philostr. *Vit. Ap*. 4. 45 .

/67/ Tac. Hist. 4. 81; Suet. *Vit. Caes*. 8. 7; Dio Cass. 65. 8. 1.

/68/ Philostr. *Vit. Ap*. 4. 20. Likewise Apollonius and his party chased away hobgoblins by heaping abuse upon them (2. 4), and Iarchas gave a letter containing 'treats' (ξὺν ἀπειλῇ καὶ ἐκπλήξει) to a woman who was demon-possessed that she might deliver it to the demon (3. 38).

/69/ When Apollonius heaped abuse on the hobgoblins, they fled shrieking (2. 4).

/70/ Nicomachus (in Porph. *Vit. Pyth*. 24 and Iamb. *Vit. Pyth*. 61); idem (in Porph. *Vit. Pyth*. 29 and Iamb. *Vit. Pyth*. 135); Tac. *Hist*. 4. 81; Iamb. *Vit. Pyth*. 112; Philostr. *Vit. Ap*. 3. 39; 4. 45.

/71/ Heraclides Pont., Frag. 83 (Wehrli) = D.L. 8.67.

/72/ Nicomachus (in Porph. *Vit. Pyth*. 23 and Iamb. *Vit. Pyth*. 60).

/73/ Idem (in Porph. *Vit. Pyth*. 24 and Iamb. *Vit. Pyth*. 61).

/74/ Philostr. *Vit. Ap*. 4. 45; 4. 20.
/75/ Diod. S. 4. 43. 1-2.
/76/ Iamb. *Vit. Pyth*. 16-17.
/77/ (1): Philostr. *Vit. Ap*. 1. 19; (2): 4. 44; (3): 7. 38; (4): 8. 15.
/78/ Ibid., 4. 20; Iamb. *Vit. Pyth*. 113.
/79/ *Themes*: exorcism, healing of dropsy, miraculous production of food and wine; *motifs*: all motifs pertaining to exorcism; duration of the illness, the miracle worker's word of assurance, the conversion of the person healed.
/80/ See, e.g., G. Bornkamm, *Jesus of Nazareth* (New York: Harper & Row, 1960) 130-1; N. Perrin, *Rediscovering the Teaching of Jesus* (New York: Harper & Row, 1976) 130-140; Theissen, *Miracle Stories*, 277-78.
/81/ Thus Bultmann, *History of the Synoptic Tradition*, 221-26, found parallels to various Gospel miracle motifs in literature culturally and temporally far removed from first century Palestine. Now examine the miracle stories in A. Feldhaus' English translation of *The Deeds of God in Ṛddhipur* (New York: Oxford, 1984), a religious biography about Guṇḍam Rāūḷ, a madman whom the Mahānubhāva sect of Western India (founded in the late thirteenth century A.D.) worshipped as the incarnation of the supreme God.
/82/ Although Tobit was perhaps written in Egypt, it may not on this account be disqualified as evidence of the Palestinian-Jewish background against which the early Christian miracle stories originated, for not only do many scholars favor the idea of an Aramaic original, but also Aramaic and Hebrew fragments (4QTob ar^{a-d}; 4QTob hebr^{a}) of Tobit were found among the literary remains of Qumran.
/83/ Cf. 1 Sam 16:14-23; Matt 12:27/Luke 11:19; Lucian *Philops*. 16 (a Syrian exorcist from *Palestine*); *b. Pesaḥ*. 112b-113a; *b. Meʿil* 17b.
/84/ Cf. Gen 20:17; Num 12:9-15 (leprosy); 2 Kgs 20:1-7 (boil); Ps 107:17-22; 146:8 (blind and those bowed down); *Jub*. 23:29-30; 1QapGen 20. 16-29 (scourging?); 4QPrNab (ulcer); 1QS 4.6; 1QH 9. 25, 27; 11. 22; *CD* 8.4; *1 Enoch* 96:3; *2 Apoc. Bar*. 73:2; *m. Ber*. 5. 5; *b. Ḥag*. 3a.
/85/ Cf. 2 Kgs 13:20-21; Dan 12:2 and all texts which anticipate an eschatological resurrection; perhaps *Mek*. Amalek 1. 68-85; H. Strack and P. Billerbeck, *Kommentar zum Neuen Testament aus Talmud und Midrasch*, vol. 1 (Munich: C. H. Beck, 1922) 557, 560.
/86/ Gen 21:15-19 (water); Exod 16:1-36 (quail and manna); 17: 1-6 (water); Num 11:1-32 (quail); 20:1-11 (water); 21:16-18 (water); Judg 15:18-19 (water); 1 Kgs 17:1-6 (bread and meat);

17:8-16 (meal and oil); 19:4-8 (bread and water); 2 Kgs 3:9-20 (water); 4:1-7 (oil); *2 Apoc. Bar.* 29:5-8 (wine and manna); *b. Taʿan* 24a (grain, figs); 24b-25a (bread); *b. Yoma* 39a (bread); *b. Šabb.* 33b (water and carobs).

/87/ Cf. Ps 89:9; *b. B. Meṣ.* 59b; Strack and Billerbeck, *Kommentar*, 4:555f. Also in connection with 'stilling of sea storms' and 'walking on the sea' see those texts which attest: (1) God's power over the waters in Creation (Job 26:11-13; Ps 89:10), (2) God's rebuke and division of the Red Sea (Exod 14:16-31; Ps 77:16-20; 106:9; 114:1-8; Isa 51:9f), (3) the parting of the Jordan (Josh 3-4; 2 Kgs 2:8, 14; cf. Jos. *Ant.* 20.97-98; *b. B. Mes.* 59b), (4) God's power over the waters in general (Ps 93:3-4; Nah 1:2-6; Hab 3:3-15; *1 Enoch* 191:4-9), and (5) the eschatological David's authority over the sea and rivers (Ps 89:25).

/88/ Cf. Luke 7:39; 22:64; *Lev. Rab.* 21. 8, and also those texts which present God as the knower of hearts (1 Sa 16:7; 1 Kgs 8:39; 1 Chr 28:9; Ps 7:9; Jer 11:20; 17:10; *Pss. Sol.* 14:5) or the knower of past, present and future (Sir 42:18-20).

/89/ For the use of other healing substances see 2 Kgs 20:7 and Tob 6:8; 11:11-14.

/90/ Cf. Exod. 7:24; 8:14; 2 Kgs 2:22; perhaps 1QapGen 20. 29.

/91/ Cf. Exod 4:5, 31; 7:5, 9; 8:10, 19; 9:14, 29; 10:2; 14:4, 18, 31; 18:11; Josh 3:7; 4:14 24; 2 Kgs 5:8; *m. Taʿan.* 3. 8; *b. Ber.* 33a.

/92/ Exod 17:8-13; 2 Kgs 2:6-8; 4:1-7, 38-41; 5:1-14, 19-27; 6:1-7.

/93/ (1): Josh 10:12; (2): Ps.-Philo *Bib. Ant.* 60; (3): *b. B. Meṣ.* 59b; (4): *b. Meʿil.* 17b; (5): *b. Taʿan* 24a. Also see *b. Yoma* 39b, which along with *b. B. Meṣ.* 59b, contains the word גער, the Hebrew equivalent of ἐπιτιμάω, which occurs in some Gospel miracle stories.

The Jewish and apostolic miracle stories (or at least some of them) apparently do not presuppose that 'prayer' miracles are of a completely different order than those performed by decree or command of the miracle worker. Josh 10: 12-14 clearly interprets Joshua's command to the sun and moon as a prayer heeded by God. According to 2 Kgs 2:6-8, Elijah divided the Jordan by simply striking it with his mantle, but when Elisha attempts the same feat he cries, 'Where is the Lord, the God of Elijah?' (2:13-14). Peter prays *and* commands (Acts 9:40). R. Joshua's rebuke of the schoolhouse walls is set over against the R. Eliezer's more prayerlike, 'If the *halachah* agrees with me, let the walls . . . prove it' (*b. B. Meṣ.* 59b). The words of R. Ḥanina b. Dosa, 'If I am of any account in Heaven, . . .

I order you [demon] never to pass through settled regions' (*b. Pesaḥ.* 112b), correspond to the Sanhedrin's interpretation of the activity of Honi the Circle Drawer, i.e., Honi decrees on earth, and because he is especially pious and dear to God, God honors his command with a miracle (*b. Taʿan.* 23a). Likewise, R. Jose chides his son for commanding the fig tree to yield fruit in these words: 'My son, you have troubled your Creator to cause the fig tree to bring forth its fruit before its time . . .' (*b. Taʿan.* 24a). Cf. also Mark 11:20-24; John 11:40-43.

/94/ The Gospels' presentation of Jesus' direct manner of performing miracles neatly coheres with that striking degree of authority which the historical Jesus undeniably exercised. Cf. J. Jeremias, *The Parables of Jesus* (London: SCM, 1972[3]) 132; E. Fuchs, *Studies of the Historical Jesus* (Naperville: Allenson, 1964) 20-21, 36; E. Käsemann, *Essays on New Testament Themes* (Naperville: Allenson, 1964) 37-40, 46; Bornkamm, *Jesus*, 56-63, 67-69, 96-100, 169-70; E. Schweizer, *Jesus* (Richmond: John Knox, 1971) 14.

/95/ Recent discussion of this pattern, at least with respect to healings, can be located in W. Kelber, *The Oral and the Written Gospel* (Philadelphia: Westminster, 1983) 46. Theissen, *Miracle Stories*, 72-74, finds four major divisions in the NT miracle stories: Introduction, Exposition, Middle, Conclusion.

/96/ See, e.g., Dibelius, *From Tradition to Gospel*, 79-97; Bultmann, *History of the Synoptic Tradition*, 220-26, 240; E. Käsemann, 'Wunder IV. Im NT', *RGG*[3] 6 (1962) 1835-36; H. Koester, 'One Jesus and Four Primitive Gospels,' *Trajectories through Early Christianity*, ed. J. Robinson and H. Koester (Philadelphia: Fortress, 1971) 187-88.

/97/ Aristotle Περὶ τῶν Πυθαγορείων, Frag. 191 (Rose).

/98/ See, e.g., the story of Epimenides' long sleep in Apollonius Para. *Mir.* 1.

/99/ Timaeus *FGrHist* 566F30=D.L. 8. 60. Eng. trans. by R. D. Hicks (LCL).

/100/ Dionysius Scytobrachion *FGrHist* 32F14=Diod. S. 4. 43. 1-2. Eng. trans. by C. H. Oldfather (LCL).

/101/ Ovid *Fasti* 6. 743-54. Eng. trans. by J. G. Frazer (LCL).

/102/ In Porph. *Vit. Pyth.* 23-24 and Iamb. *Vit. Pyth.* 60-61. Eng. trans. of Porph. *Vit. Pyth.* 23-24 by M. Smith in M. Hadas and M. Smith, *Heroes and Gods* (New York: Harper & Row, 1965).

/103/ 1. 9; 2. 4; 3. 38-9; 4. 20, 45; 6. 41, 43.

/104/ 4. 45; 3. 39. Eng. trans. by F. C. Conybeare in LCL. As has long been recognized, the former story is remarkably similar to Lk. 7:11-17, although the really striking parallels are only two: (1) the dead person is raised *while being carried on a bier*, and (2) the miracle worker indicates that weeping should or will cease. Nevertheless, the parallelism between those and other Gospel and Philostratean stories raises the issue of whether Philostratus or his sources were influenced by the Christian stories. M. J. Lagrange, 'Les légendes pythagoriennes et l'évangile', *RB* 46 (1937) 18, is representative of several older scholars who felt that such influence had occurred, but more recent scholars generally agree with G. Petzke, *Die Traditionen über Apollonius von Tyana und das Neue Testament* (Leiden: Brill, 1970), 65-66: 'Von einer auch nur versteckten Polemik gegen Jesus und das Christentum ist schlechterdings gar nichts zu bemerken. Die im Text angestellten Vergleiche zeigen immer in dieselbe Richtung: es werden griechische Vorbilder genannt, die Apollonius übertrifft.' See, however, E. Jones, 'The Concept of the θεῖος 'Ανήρ in the Graeco-Roman World with Special Reference to the First Two Centuries A.D.' (Ph.D. Thesis: Durham, 1973) 197-205.

/105/ Empedocles: Iamb. *Vit. Pyth.* 113; Vespasian: Tac. *Hist.* 4. 81; Suet. *Vit. Caes.* 8. 7; Dio Cass. 65. 8. 1; Hadrian: Ael. Spart. *Vit. Had.* 25; Hyperborean: Lucian *Philops.* 14.

/106/ For Gk. text and Eng. trans. see Edelstein and Edelstein, *Asclepius*, vol. 1, 221-37.

/107/ For medieval Indian parallels to this form see Feldhaus, *The Deeds of God*, 64, 79, 92, 133-34, 149, 154.

/108/ Cf. also 1 Kgs 17:17-24; 2 Kgs 2:19-22; 2 Kgs 4:18-37, 38-41, 42-44; 5:1-19. See the observations of R. Brown, 'Jesus and Elisha', *Perspective* 12 (1971) 85-99.

/109/ 1QapGen 20. 16-29. Eng. trans. by G. Vermes, *The Dead Sea Scrolls in English* (Harmondsworth: Penguin Books, 1975[2]) 219-20.

/110/ Cf. Judg 15:18-19; Ps 107: 4-9, 10-16, 17-22, 23-32; Jonah 1:1-16; *4 Ezra* 9:43-45; *Mek.* Kaspa 3. 35-41; *Mek.* Beshallaḥ 1. 85-108; *m. Taʿan.* 3. 8; *p. Ber.* 9. 1; *b. B. Meṣ.* 59b; *b. Ber.* 34b; *b. Pesaḥ.* 112b-113b; *b. Taʿan.* 19b, 23a, 23b.

/111/ These stories, some of which underscore the miracle worker's true prophetic office, his divine authorization, or his filial status before God, form part of the basis on which H. C. Kee (*Community of the New Age* [Philadelphia: Westminster, 1976] 22-29; cf. also the main thrust of his recent *Miracle in the Early Christian World* [New Haven: Yale, 1983]) has argued (correctly, I believe) that miracle stories are not inherently bound up with the desire to document the divine nature of the thaumaturge.

/112/ Bultmann, *History of the Synoptic Tradition*, 240.

/113/ The following stories, more or less in their present form, have been traced back at least as far as the early, Aramaic-speaking church: *1:21-28* (J. Gnilka, *Das Evangelium nach Markus*, vol. 1 [Zurich: Benziger , 1978] 77-78); *1:29-31* (Kertelge, *Die Wunder Jesu*, 61; Schenke, *Wundererzählungen*, 20-21; R. Pesch, *Das Markusevangelium*, Vol. 1 [Freiburg: Herder, 1976] 129, 131; Gnilka, vol. 1, 85); *2:1-12* (Schenke, 155; Pesch, vol. 1, 157-58; Gnilka, vol. 1, 98); *5:21-24, 35-43* (Pesch, vol. 1, 312); *5:25-34* (Pesch, vol. 1, 306); *6:30-44* (Schenke, 230; Pesch, vol. 1, 355-56; Gnilka, vol. 1, 258); *8:22-26* (Pesch, vol. 1, 420); *9:14-27* (Pesch, vol. 2 [1977] 95; Gnilka, vol. 2 [1978] 45); *10:46-52* (Schenke, 364; Pesch, vol. 2, 174; Gnilka, vol. 2, 109). In addition, see the specific accounts of healing and exorcism in Q (Matt 8:5-13/Luke 7:1-10 and Matt 12:22-23/ Luke 11:14).

/114/ Tiede, *The Charismatic Figure*, 290.

/115/ Cf. e.g. O. Betz, 'The Concept of the So-called "Divine Man" in Mark's Christology', in *Studies in the New Testament and Early Christian Literature*, ed. D. Aune (Leiden: Brill, 1972) 234-39.

THE COIN IN THE FISH'S MOUTH

Richard Bauckham
Faculty of Theology
University of Manchester
Manchester M13 9PL

Although the main purpose of this study is to clarify the origin and significance of Matt. 17:27, in relation to other Gospel miracles, much of the argument will involve the claim that this verse and the question of its historical authenticity must be studied in close connexion with the preceding verses. Consequently a fairly full study of the whole pericope (Matt. 17:24-27) will be necessary.

1. Preliminary Exegesis

The aim of this section is to establish an exegesis of Matt. 17:24-27 as a basis for the investigation of its source and historical value. Although questions relevant to authenticity will inevitably arise in this section, they will not be systematically discussed until later in the study.

As almost all recent exegetes agree,/1/ the pericope concerns the payment of the Temple tax, which was an annual payment of a half shekel due from every adult male Jew, to finance sacrificial worship in the Temple. That this is the tax referred to is clear for two reasons. (1) As we shall see, Jesus' argument in vv. 25-26 presupposes a tax levied in the name of God, as the Temple tax was./2/ (2) The monetary references in vv. 24, 27 precisely fit the requirements of the Temple tax./3/ It had to be paid in 'Temple shekels' (Exod. 30:13), for which in New Testament times the Tyrian silver *tetradrachmon*, known as a stater (v. 27), was used. The amount payable by each individual, the half shekel, was therefore a *didrachmon* (Josephus, *Ant.* 18:312), and the reference to the tax collectors as those who collected the *didrachma* (v. 24) would have been readily understood as a reference to those appointed in each locality to collect the Temple tax before forwarding it to Jerusalem./4/ On payments in *didrachmon* coins, which might not be exactly equivalent in weight to half a shekel and which had to be changed into shekels, surcharges were required (*m. Shek.* 1:6). If the regulations in the Mishna accurately reflect pre-70 practice, it seems that the one case in which payment outside Jerusalem could be made without any surcharge was if one man paid a stater on behalf of himself and someone else, as a matter of charity (*m. Shek.* 1:7). Thus in the case of Peter's payment on behalf of Jesus and himself (v. 27) the stater alone would suffice. As far as the tax collectors were concerned, the payment was by Peter on behalf of himself and his teacher, and this sufficiently explains why the pericope is not concerned with the tax payments of the other disciples, whom the tax collectors would expect to pay for themselves.

The financial sums involved were quite large, since a shekel or stater was equivalent to four denarii, and a denarius is usually reckoned, on the basis of Matt. 20:1-15, to have been a labourer's daily wage./5/ This is sufficient alone to refute the suggestion, taken seriously by some scholars,/6/ that v. 27 in either its original or present form meant that Peter was to sell the fish for a stater. It is unlikely that any fish would have been worth a stater./7/ Had Peter wished to earn the money, he would have taken his partners out in the boats with a net, rather than fishing with a hook and line./8/

The Temple tax has been discussed in detail by several writers,/9/ and some further details will be mentioned as they become relevant later in this study. At this point we should notice that the tax was probably of comparatively recent origin, /10/ but in current interpretation, as advocated by the Pharisees and accepted in practice by the Sadducean priestly aristocracy, it was regarded as a tax instituted by Moses (Exod. 30:11-16; cf. 38:25-26; 2 Chron. 24:5-7). However, this interpretation was debatable, and there is some evidence of opposition to the current view./11/ The best evidence of such opposition is 4Q 159 (4Q Ordinances) 2:6-7, in which Exod. 30:11-16 is interpreted as requiring a half shekel payment only once in a man's lifetime./12/

That the legitimacy of the annual Temple tax was debated may explain why the tax collectors' question (v. 24), though expecting the answer Peter gives, envisages the possibility that Jesus might not pay the tax. As a religious teacher known to disagree with Pharisaic halakhah on other issues, Jesus could not be assumed to agree on this. Alternatively, since Jesus was supported by charity, the question may be an enquiry whether he paid the tax himself or had it paid by a patron./13/ On the other hand, the conversation between the tax collectors and Peter may be no more than a narrative device to introduce the topic of the pericope, so that to press the implication of the question may be inappropriate.

The key to the pericope as a whole, including the significance of the miracle, is to appreciate the reason why Jesus holds at least himself and Peter to be exempt from the Temple tax. Misunderstandings of this point are at the root of widespread objections to the historical authenticity of the tradition.

V. 25 is a metaphorical or parabolic saying in which Jesus follows the practice, widely attested in rabbinic and other Jewish literature, of comparing God's activity to that of an earthly king. 'The kings of the earth' are so called by contrast with the heavenly King, God. Since the Temple tax was regarded as a tax levied by God on his people, Jesus asks, for comparative purposes, a question about the taxes levied by earthly kings. The phrase τέλη ἢ κῆνσον (v. 25) refers to indirect and direct taxes respectively, and is therefore a comprehensive term for all taxes. 'The kings of the earth' (an OT phrase: Ps. 2:2 etc.) should not be restricted to the Romans: the reference is to the general practice of earthly kings./14/

For the interpretation of the saying, the two essential questions, which should not be confused, are: (1) Who are the 'sons' and the 'strangers' (ἀλλότριοι) on the literal level of the parable, in relation to the earthly kings? (2) Whom do the 'sons' and the 'strangers' represent, in the implied application of the parable, in relation to God? In answer to the first of these questions, there are three views: (a) The 'sons' are the king's own nation, while the 'strangers' are foreign subject peoples./15/ (b) The 'sons' are the king's household, his employees and top administrators, while the 'strangers' are the rest of his subjects./16/ (c) The 'sons' are the royal family, the king's physical sons, while the 'strangers' are the rest of his subjects./17/

View (a) has two difficulties. In first place, those who advocate it give no evidence that a king's nation could be called his sons. Allen's comment that 'τῶν υἱῶν αὐτῶν in Oriental idiom, means not relatives, but members of one's own race',/18/ is typical in being an assertion for which no evidence is given. Expressions of the idea that the king is the father of his nation could probably be found in ancient literature,/19/ but we need strong evidence to justify us in assuming that a reference to a king's sons could be naturally understood, without further explanation, as a reference to his nation.

The second difficulty in this view is that it was not generally true in the ancient world that kings exempted their own nation from taxes, collecting them only from subject foreigners./20/ Even if the reference were to Roman practice, Roman citizens, while exempt from κῆνσος, certainly paid τέλη.

The second view, (b), avoids this second difficulty, but it is still problematic in relation to the terminology used. Again, Derrett, who advocates this view, cites no evidence that a king's whole household could be called his sons. There is some evidence that in the OT period the title 'king's son' sometimes designated a very high ranking government official, not actually a member of the royal family./21/ But even this usage would not meet the requirements of this view of our passage, and we should in any case need to know that it was sufficiently current in the first century A.D. to be the natural sense of Jesus' words.

In view of these difficulties, it seems best to take (c) as the natural meaning of the passage. It is true that ἀλλότριοι can mean 'foreigners', but its meaning in this context must be determined by the preceding reference to the 'sons'. After a reference to the king's own family, there is no difficulty in taking ἀλλότριοι to mean 'strangers,' i.e. members of other families (for the very general sense of ἀλλότριος, cf. John 10:5; LXX Job 19:13; Ps. 108:11; Prov. 5:10, 17; 27:2; Sir. 8:18). The point of the saying, as Jesus draws the conclusion in v. 26b, is that kings do not levy taxes on their own sons.

In answer to question (2), it must first be said that, as with all parabolic sayings, the application should not be pressed too far. The point of the saying is that of v. 26b, which, in terms of the comparison, means that God does not tax his 'sons'. Whether there are other people whom God does tax is not the point of the saying, and so we need not ask whom the 'strangers' represent. But whom do the 'sons' represent?

Of course, they represent at least Jesus and Peter. The general scholarly view is that for Matthew and/or the Jewish Christian community from whom he received the tradition, the 'sons' would be Jesus' disciples, and therefore Christians, who have God as their Father, rather than Israel in general. There is however considerable cogency in Horbury's argument that the saying is plausibly understood as an authentic saying in which Jesus refers to God as the Father of his people Israel./22/ In some other sayings Jesus assumes the *status* of Israel as a nation to be that of sonship to God (Mark 7:27 par.; Matt. 8:12 par.), while regarding his mission as one of calling Israel to *fulfil* that status in a renewed Israel of which his disciples are the nucleus. Since Matthew himself elsewhere retains sayings which imply God's fatherhood of Israel (especially 15:26; cf. 8:12), even at the redactional level the significance of our saying need be no different. A formal status of sonship for Israel as such, during Jesus' ministry, is not inconsistent with Matthew's view that in the end it is the church which proves to be God's faithful sons and inherits Israel's destiny, while non-Christian Jews do not (cf. 21:28-32).

Jesus' argument is therefore that God does not tax his own people. Jesus takes up the common Jewish belief that God is both King and Father to his people,/23/ a belief which is everywhere presupposed in his own preaching, and points out an implication of this belief by making a comparison with earthly kings *who are also fathers*. In the matter of taxation, the father-son relation takes precedence over the king-subject relation. Kings do *not* treat their sons as liable to taxation, like subjects, but exempt them from taxation, because they are sons. Similarly, because God is a father to his people, as well as a king, he does not tax them. In this matter he treats them as sons rather than as subjects.

The implication is that the Temple tax is illegitimate, but it is important to notice that this illegitimacy has nothing to do with the religious status of the Temple as such or the legitimacy of its worship. The *argument* of vv. 25-26 in no way presupposes later Jewish Christian discussion of the continuing validity of Temple worship or the Christian's relation to it. The argument establishes only that to raise money for the Temple worship by means of *taxation* is inappropriate in view of God's fatherhood./24/

The fact that vv. 25-26 are not aimed against the Temple as such also helps to explain v. 27a, the instruction that the tax be paid in order not to offend the tax collectors (αὐτούς must be the tax collectors, especially because αὐτοῖς at the end of v. 27 undoubtedly refers to the tax collectors)/25/ or to cause them to sin (σκανδαλίσωμεν). The Temple tax was widely regarded as an expression of support for and a means of participating in the daily sacrificial worship, and the tax collectors were presumably local people who undertook the task as an act of piety. They would take Jesus' refusal to pay as an act of critical dissociation from the Temple worship, perhaps all the more so since the Qumran community's support for an alternative interpretation of the tax law was associated with their critical attitude to the existing Temple worship. Jesus' objection to the tax is, in a sense, more radical than theirs, in that he objects to the very principle of theocratic taxation, but he does not share their critical attitude to the Temple worship./26/

With this exegesis of the rest of the pericope, we are now in a position to understand the significance of the miracle in its context (without yet raising historical questions about it). Jesus' desire not to offend the tax collectors means that, even though God does not require the tax, it must in this instance be paid. But the miracle does not simply provide a means of paying the tax. If that were the case, it would surely be an unnecessarily exotic means and would have to be attributed to a storyteller's delight in the marvellous for its own sake. In fact, however, the miracle has a much closer connexion with the message of the whole pericope. It is not simply a way of paying the tax; it is a way of paying the tax which strongly reinforces the argument of vv. 25-26. It demonstrates, in a remarkable way, that God does not exact taxation from his people, but *on the contrary provides* for his people, as a father provides for his children. The whole point is the contrast between the view of God implied by a Temple tax and the view of God implied by the miracle. The actual form of the miracle, which enables Peter to receive a coin, so to speak, from the hand of God, is essential to this point. Instead of demanding a Temple shekel *from* Peter, God actually *provides* him with one.

This exegesis of the whole pericope therefore has the advantage of not leaving the miracle as a somewhat exotic and redundant addendum to the main point, nor even treating it as simply a supernatural happening which confirms Jesus' ruling on the tax question,/27/ comparable to what Theissen calls the 'justificatory rule miracles' in some rabbinic stories./28/ In those stories, the point is simply that something miraculous happens. In this case, though Theissen's classification of it as a rule miracle is broadly correct, the *kind* of miracle which occurs serves to continue the argument of vv. 25-26 and is integral to the teaching content of the whole pericope.

The complaint of some commentators that Jesus performs a miracle for his own benefit/29/ can now be seen to have missed the point. Jesus foresees the miracle; he does not perform it. The miracle itself is the Father's provision for his children.

Of course, Matthew leaves us to presume that the miracle occurred. He records Jesus' instructions and prediction, but not the event. This curious feature of the pericope makes it, as a miracle story, unique among the Gospel miracle stories, and study of the form of the pericope does not much help to explain this feature. Though the story is not easy to classify formally, it seems most comparable with those controversy stories whose climax is a miracle: the healing of the paralytic (Mark 2:1-12 par.) and the healing of the man with the withered hand on the Sabbath (Mark 3:1-6 par.)./30/ In common with Matt. 17:25, the argument in these two stories takes the form of an either-or question (Mark 2:9; 3:4; cf. Luke 14:3), the answer to which is demonstrated by the miracle. But in distinction from Matt. 17:27, in both stories the miracle is recounted as the climax of the story (Mark 2:12; 3:4), and this is also true of Matthew's versions (9:7; 12:13), despite his tendency to abbreviate. In view of these parallels it is not easy to sustain the argument that in Matt. 17:27 the miracle itself is omitted because the interest is in the teaching rather than the miracle./31/ The puzzle of the ending of the story can probably only be solved by a fuller study of the pericope at the redactional level than is possible here.

2. Place in Matthew's Gospel

Within the scope of this study, a full treatment of the pericope at the redactional level, within its context in Matthew's Gospel, is unfortunately not possible. But some consideration of Matthew's redactional interest in and treatment of this pericope is indispensable in our attempt to move back from the Matthean text to the historical Jesus. In the present section we shall consider the pericope's connexions with its context in Matthew, in order to suggest that Matthew's reasons for placing the pericope at this point in his Gospel and his interest in it, insofar as the context reveals this, are consistent with the view that Matthew is substantially reproducing an existing tradition which he has done little to adapt to its context in his Gospel./32/ Then in the next section we shall ask more directly about the existence and nature of Matthew's source.

2.1 Geographical and Temporal Connexions

If Matthew here follows a pre-existing tradition, it was a tradition which had to be located in Galilee in general and in Capernaum in particular. A location in Galilee was required by Peter's fishing in the sea of Galilee, and a location at Capernaum was required by the fact that a man's Temple tax was collected at the local centre closest to his place of residence. In Jesus' case this would probably have been Capernaum, which Matthew regards as Jesus' home town during the period of the ministry (9:1). Thus, whether or not Capernaum was explicitly named in the tradition as Matthew knew it, he would have had to place the tradition at a point in his narrative when Jesus was in Capernaum.

In chapters 16-21 Matthew follows Mark's geographical indications of Jesus' movements from Caesarea Philippi to Jerusalem, and his mention of the disciples' arrival at Capernaum in 17:24 corresponds to Mark 9:33. Thus Matthew takes advantage of Mark's geographical notice to insert a non-Markan tradition which had to be located at Capernaum, before continuing to follow Mark in 18:1 (cf. Mark 9:34).

Matthew could have placed the pericope earlier in the Gospel, when Jesus is frequently in Capernaum. Part of the reason why he did not might be a chronological consideration, since this is a tradition which not only locates itself but also dates itself. The collection of the Temple tax in Palestine outside Jerusalem began four weeks before Passover (15 Adar). Admittedly, this allows an improbably short period for Jesus' journey through Perea to Jerusalem (Matt. 19-20), but if Matthew envisaged Jesus' ministry as lasting no more than a year, he had to place this pericope during Jesus' last visit to Capernaum. Matthew's Gospel shows little evidence of interest in chronology, but the fact that this pericope occurs at the only chronologically plausible point in the narrative is striking and may not be accidental. However, if this suggestion is not accepted, a strong reason why Matthew placed this pericope during Jesus' last visit to Capernaum, rather than during an earlier visit, will be found in the next section (*2.2*).

2.2 The Petrine Interest

Matthew has five non-Markan passages in which Peter is named (14:28-31; 15:15; 16:17-19; 17:24-27; 18:21). It is striking that these all occur in the relatively short space of four chapters (14-18), in which Markan material giving prominence to Peter also occurs (16:16, 22-23; 17:1, 4), and that they constitute Matthew's major additions to Markan material in chapters 14-17. It seems clear that Matthew deliberately grouped his special Petrine traditions together,/33/ and the reason why he placed them in this part of the Gospel is not far to seek. Matt. 14:28-31 had to be linked to the Markan passage Matt. 14:22-27, and Matthew then found the earliest suitable opportunities to insert his other special Petrine traditions into the Markan framework which he follows in these chapters.

Of the two minor special Petrine passages (15:15; 18:21), in which Peter plays the role of spokesman for the disciples (as in many parts of the Gospel tradition), one (15:15) is almost certainly redactional,/34/ and the other may be. But the three major Petrine passages (14:28-31; 16:17-19; 17:24-27) do not really offer any consistent theological intepretation of the figure of Peter, such as would suggest a major redactional contribution. Attempts to force them into some pattern of Matthean thinking about Peter, to which 16:17-19 would be the key, do violence to the other passages. 16:17-19 (cf. 10:2) may account for Matthew's interest in traditions in which Peter is prominent, but no more. It seems that Matthew simply knew some such traditions, linked thematically only by the prominence of Peter, and considered this common characteristic sufficient reason to group them in one part of his Gospel.

2.3 Other Thematic Connexions

There are two possible thematic links between 17:24-27 and the Markan material which follows in Matt. 18:1-9 (par. Mark 9:33-48). (1) The prominence of Peter in 17:24-27 may provoke the disciples' question in 18:1. However, this is not a very convincing connexion, since one would have expected Matthew to make it more explicitly in 18:1, where he has in any case had to rewrite his source (Mark 9:34) in order to allow for his non-Markan insertion (17:24-27). (2) The concern not to give offence (σκανδαλίζειν) in 17:27 is taken up again in 18:6-9./35/ If Matthew intended these connexions they would have reinforced his other reasons for placing 17:24-27 at this point, but they are likely to be connexions which he saw in his sources, not connexions which he created by his redaction or composition of 17:24-27. This follows from the facts that (1) while Matt. 17:24-27 acknowledges Peter's leadership of the group of disciples (especially in v. 24, where the tax collectors ask Peter about 'your *[ὑμῶν]* teacher'), this is not the point which the passage has been composed to make; (2) the link between 'offending' the tax collectors (17:27) and the kinds of 'offence' discussed in 18:6-9 is more verbal than material.

3. Matthew's Source

There are good reasons for supposing that Matt. 17:24-27 is based on a tradition which Matthew has redacted no more freely than he customarily redacts Mark and which was not of recent origin when Matthew wrote.

3.1 If Matthew wrote after A.D. 70, he must have derived this material from a source representing pre-70 Gospel tradition. After the destruction of the Temple, the Temple tax as such no longer existed. The Romans continued to collect it (as the *fiscus judaicus*), but diverted it to the use of the temple of Jupiter Capitolinus in Rome./36/ Our pericope could not possibly have been understood by its redactor as an argument about liability to the *fiscus judaicus*,/37/ still less could it have been composed as such, since the argument *hangs* on the fact that the Temple tax was levied in God's name for God's purposes. It makes no sense with reference to a Roman tax./38/

This point is J.A.T. Robinson's most cogent argument for dating Matthew's Gospel before A.D. 70, when the story would still have had relevance to the question whether Jewish Christians should pay the Temple tax./39/ But Robinson neglects the fact that Matthew characteristically preserves traditions which have become, in this sense, anachronistic. This applies not only to other sayings which presuppose the existence of the Temple (e.g. 5:23-24), but also to those which restrict the disciples' mission to Israel (10:5-6; cf. 15:24). Whether or not the latter originated or were preserved in Jewish Christian circles opposed to the Gentile mission, it is clear that Matthew, whatever the date of his Gospel, understands them as appropriate to the period of Jesus' ministry, but superseded thereafter. Sayings which presume the existence of the Temple were probably understood by him in the same way.

Of course, this is not to imply that Matthew preserved the Temple tax tradition out of merely historical interest; he must have seen some contemporary relevance in it, a meaning which survived when the issue of the Temple tax itself no longer existed. But this does suggest that Matthew derived the story, with relatively little adaptation, from an earlier tradition in which the central issue of the story--the payment of the Temple tax--was still the reason for its preservation.

Epistle of the Apostles 5 (in which the story no longer concerns the Temple tax: see section *5.3* below) shows what could have happened to this Gospel tradition, if it survived at all, in a community for which the issue of the Temple tax no longer had any relevance. That Matthew has preserved this tradition as a story about the Temple tax results, not from Matthew's writing before A.D. 70, but from Matthew's remarkably conservative treatment of his traditions. Moreover, it is not at all surprising that this tradition, which could easily seem of interest only to Jewish Christians before A.D. 70, has not survived in other branches of the Gospel tradition. Its attestation only in Matthew's special material should not weigh too heavily against its historical value.

3.2 Arguments concerned with the presence of characteristically Matthean vocabulary and style in this pericope can demonstrate its Matthean composition only for those who use such arguments in a recklessly unprincipled way./40/ Arguments that regard as characteristically Matthean the word ναί (of which Matthew has nine of the thirty-four NT occurrences), the phrase ἄρα γε (which, elsewhere in the NT, occurs in Matt. 7:20 and Acts 17:27), and the verb σκανδαλίζειν (eleven of whose other thirteen occurrences in Matthew have Synoptic parallels)/41/ are statistically worthless and ought not to need refutation.

Convincing cases of Matthean style and vocabulary are in fact largely limited to the narrative framework/42/ and, with one exception, do not appear in the words of Jesus. The one exception is the phrase τί σοί δοκεῖ, which is typically Matthean (cf. 18:12; 21:28; 22:17, 42)/43/. But since in two of its other four occurrences in Matthew it is a redactional addition to Markan material, its presence here in 17:25 cannot detract from the traditional character of the rest of Jesus' words in vv. 25-27.

3.3 There is good reason to suppose that much of Matthew's special material derives from the oral tradition of the church at Antioch,/44/ and in view of Peter's association with Antioch, the Petrine character of this pericope makes that an appropriate source in this case./45/ Although Matthew's special material (or at least the special narrative material) tends to be regarded as the least historically valuable part of the Synoptic tradition, there is no reason to let this judgment prejudice one's view of any particular passage. It would be surprising if the oral tradition of the church at Antioch did not include some very primitive Gospel traditions. Nor should we dismiss too quickly the possibility that a Petrine tradition could go back to Peter's own preaching at Antioch./46/

3.4 It is possible that evidence for knowledge of this tradition in the church at an early date can be found in Paul's discussions of his collections for the Jerusalem church. Nickle's study of the collection argued that the parallels between it and the Temple tax collected in the diaspora are too numerous to be coincidental,/47/ but that, on the other hand, there are significant differences which suggest that, although to some extent Paul had the Temple tax in mind as a model for his collection, he was also careful to observe distinctions at certain points./48/ The most important points of principle involve Paul's rather evident concern to avoid giving any impression that the collection was a *tax*. Instead of a specific amount, prescribed by law in the case of the Temple tax, Paul, while encouraging liberal giving, goes out of his way to insist that inner motivation must determine how much is given, that each must decide the amount of his gift for himself (2 Cor. 9:7), and that Paul's own expectations are not relevant (2 Cor. 8:5). The voluntary character of the contributions is repeatedly stressed, both in Rom. 15:26-27 and throughout the long discussion in 2 Cor 8-9./49/ That Jesus was known to have objected in principle to theocratic taxation could partly explain this emphasis.

4. Verses 25-26 as an Authentic Saying of Jesus

Although the principal objections to the authenticity of these verses are removed by the exegesis proposed in section 1, several further considerations will help to make the ministry and teaching of Jesus appear the most natural context for the origin of the saying.

4.1 In order to appreciate the plausibility of the view that Jesus objected to the Temple tax on the grounds indicated in these verses, we need to think rather concretely about how the average Galilean Jew would have perceived the tax. The Pharisaic ideal was that the tax enabled every adult male Jew to *participate* in the daily sacrificial worship of the Temple by helping to finance it./50/ Doubtless prosperous Jews, who could well afford half a shekel a year, readily shared this view. The prosperous diaspora Jews, about whose Temple tax contributions Philo and Josephus tell us,/51/ no doubt contributed (as Philo says) 'cheerfully and gladly' (*Spec. Leg.* 1:77), both for the personal religious reasons which Philo mentions and as an expression of loyalty to the religious heart of the nation.

However, it is important to remember that the Temple tax was a tax, legally required at the same rate from all adult males, with no allowance for poverty (except that a poor man's tax could be charitably paid by another). The Mishna's regulations about it may be idealized, and the powers it grants the tax collectors to distrain the goods of those who could not pay (*m. Shek.* 1:3) may not have been exercised very consistently, /52/ but there is some pre-70 evidence of enforcement,/53/ and the Mishna surely preserves accurately enough the pre-70 *concept* of the tax, as a legal imposition which could in principle be enforced at law./54/ Jesus' comparison of the tax with the taxes of earthly kings was quite justified by current conceptions of the tax.

There is evidence that taxation in general in Palestine in Jesus' time was perceived as burdensome. Whether or not civil taxes were *objectively* excessive, or were perceived as such partly because they were paid to the Romans or to the unpopular Herodian dynasty, is unimportant in this context./55/ Taxation by unpopular despotic rulers is almost always perceived as exploitative, and first-century people could not easily regard taxes as contributions to the benefit of their own communities. /56/ The Romans built fine bridges (said the Jews) simply in order to collect the tolls (*b. Shab.* 33b).

For Palestinian *Jews* there were religious (theocratic) taxes on top of the burden of civil taxation: the annual tithe and other forms of priestly dues, the 'poor tithe' payable every third year, and the Temple tax. To the ordinary person struggling to meet these demands, the Temple theocracy could easily appear just another level of oppressive government, and there is good evidence that the conspicuous wealth of the high priestly families was resented and connected with their control of the Temple finances, of which the Temple tax was the major source./57/

Finally, it should be remembered that the Temple tax was conceived very directly as a tax levied by and paid to God./58/ Both Josephus (*Ant.* 18:312)/59/ and a saying ascribed to Yohanan b. Zakkai/60/ speak of it as paid 'to God,' which was doubtless a common way of speaking. Thus the implication of the Temple tax, perceived as oppressive and comparable to the exploitative taxes of the 'kings of the earth,' was that God was an oppressive despot, extorting taxation from his people. It is this implication which Jesus sees and counters in vv. 25-26.

The objection that Jesus could not have opposed the Temple tax unless he 'meant to let the Temple fall into ruin and its services cease'/61/ is easily answered. Jesus approved of voluntary giving to the Temple, as the story of the widow's offering (Mark 12:41-44) makes clear./62/ Such a distinction between the tax and voluntary giving is not a quibble, but corresponds to the felt reality of the tax.

4.2 Jesus' attitude to the Temple tax in these verses is coherent with and also helps to explain the so-called 'cleansing of the Temple,' which has been something of a puzzle in recent discussion./63/ The moneychangers, whose tables Jesus overturned, changed money into the coinage required for payment of the Temple tax. Our pericope enables us to see that Jesus objected to their presence, not because they were making a dishonest profit or because the trade should have been conducted outside the Temple, but because of his fundamental objection to the Temple tax. By making the Temple worship a pretext for financial exaction in God's name, the tax distorted the whole character of the worship of God for which the Temple existed. Although this point cannot be further developed here, it is one which deserves extended discussion elsewhere.

4.3 Jesus' attitude to the Temple tax is consistent with his reply to the question about the tribute money (Mark 12:13-17 par.), which I understand to mean that Caesar's right to taxation (as one of the kings of the earth) does not conflict with a Jew's duty to God. Those who argued that it did conflict were believers in theocratic taxation. The taxes paid to Caesar, they thought, should rightfully be paid to God. Jesus rejects this argument because he rejects the principle of theocratic taxation.

4.4 An argument against the Temple tax which is based, not on any criticism of the Temple or its worship, but on the character of God as Father and King, seems much more likely to come from Jesus than from the Jewish Christian church. The way in which Jesus here gives priority to God's fatherhood over his kingship, as a model for God's relationship to his people, coheres with a prominent and distinctive feature of Jesus' authentic teaching, i.e. the fact that, while Jesus repeatedly speaks of God's kingdom, his portrayal of the way God exercises his rule is usually in terms of fatherhood rather than kingship.

By comparison with rabbinic parables, in which God is very frequently represented by a king, Jesus' parables are notable for their infrequent use of a king as a figure for God and their preference for other figures such as masters, landowners, and fathers. The fathers, however, act in character, whereas the other figures, like the astonishingly generous king in the parable of the Unmerciful Servant (Matt. 18:23-34), often act uncharacteristically. Furthermore, Jesus' concern in our verses to distinguish God's treatment of his people from the way earthly kings treat their subjects is comparable with his concern (in Mark 10:42-44 par.) to distinguish the domineering rule of the kings of the Gentiles from the way things should be done among his followers./64/

5. Verse 27 and the Historical Jesus

The aim of this section is to show that v. 27 is not, as many scholars have thought, an anomalous and presumably late accretion to the Jesus tradition, but on the contrary coheres very well with central and primitive features of the Jesus tradition.

5.1 I have argued that the miracle is one of divine provision, which (by contrast with the idea that God exacts taxes) illustrates or demonstrates that God provides for his people in the way that a father provides for his children. The notion that God's fatherhood entails his provision for his children is characteristic of Jesus (cf. especially the Q passages: Matt. 6:25-34 par. Luke 12:22-32; Matt. 7:7-11 par. Luke 11:9-13). Jesus argues that if earthly fathers provide for their children, how much more will God (Matt. 7:11), and certainly includes the everyday needs of God's people in his fatherly provision for them (Matt. 6:31-32)./65/ Of course, the coin in the fish's mouth is an exceptional instance of this, but should be understood in this context. As an exceptional instance it calls attention to what Jesus expects to be ordinarily the case.

5.2 Once the miracle has been recognized as one of divine provision, it can be seen to be, not a unique kind of miracle in the Gospel tradition, but one of a recognizable class of miracles. Other miracles of divine provision are the feeding miracles, the miraculous draughts of fish, and the turning of water into wine. Theissen correctly groups these others together as 'gift miracles' and has much to say that illuminates them as a class,/66/ but he fails to note that the coin in the fish's mouth is another of this class./67/

An interesting feature of these miracles is that *as a class* they are remarkably well attested in the tradition. At least one occurs in each of the major strands of the Gospel tradition except Q (which is notoriously short of narratives): Mark has two feeding miracles (6:34-44; 8:1-10), Luke's special material has the draught of fish (Luke 5:4-10), Matthew's special material has the coin in the fish's mouth, and the Johannine tradition has no less than three of these miracles: the turning of water into wine (2:1-11), the feeding of the five thousand (6:1-15) and the draught of fish (21:1-14). It should also be noted that there are apocryphal traditions of the feeding of the five thousand (*Sib. Or.* 1:356-359; 8:275-278)/68/ and of the draught of fish (*Gos. Pet.* 14:60), which may be substantially independent of the canonical Gospels, while *Acts of John* 93 preserves an apocryphal tradition of a feeding miracle which should not be identified with those of the canonical Gospels. The latter is especially significant in view of the fact that, whereas apocryphal sayings of Jesus are plentiful, apocryphal miracles of Jesus are surprisingly rare (apart from those in the infancy Gospels). The fact that miracles of divine provision are so well attested across the various strands of the Gospel tradition indicates that this type of miracle belongs to a primitive stage of the Gospel tradition, and should be considered a third major category of miracles alongside healings and exorcisms.

When we consider these miracles as a class, in the way that Theissen does, we can see that their basic significance lies in being divine provision for ordinary needs: the need of a hungry crowd when no food is available, the need of fishermen who have toiled long and fruitlessly at their daily occupation, the need of a host faced with the embarrassment of being shown up as too poor to be able to provide enough wine for a celebration,/69/ the need for money to pay the tax collector. However, this basic feature of divine provision for everyday kinds of need, which is what unites these miracles as a class, was evidently not sufficient to enable them to survive in the tradition, perhaps partly because, unlike healings and exorcisms, such miracles did not, so far as we know, occur in the early church./70/ Consequently, in the tradition, they have acquired various types of further significance: in terms of new Exodus and Elisha typologies, divine Shepherd Christology,/71/ eucharistic interpretation, symbolic significance (the new wine of the Gospel, the draught of fish as a parable of mission).

The coin in the fish's mouth escaped such secondary interpretation at first, probably because it survived in the tradition for the sake of its relationship to the preceding saying, but eventually, in the Fathers, it too succumbed to the process, when the fish became an allegory of Christ./72/

The very variety of these secondary interpretations suggests, again, that the original stories, which behind their secondary interpretations exhibit a common type, belong to a very early stage of the tradition. Whether or not we can accept that things of this kind happened in Jesus' ministry, as historians we should accept that *reports* of this type of miracle probably go back to the time of Jesus' ministry.

5.3 Although the original significance of the miracles of divine provision is overlaid, in the canonical Gospels, with further levels of significance, it did not disappear, because in each case it is embodied in the actual character of the miracle, and so could always be reappropriated. This is what happened in *Epistle of the Apostles* 5, which is of some interest as much the earliest extra-canonical reference to the miracle of Matt. 17:27./73/

Not only the *Epistle of the Apostles* as a whole, but also chapter 5 in particular, shows evidence of dependence on the specifically Matthean redaction of the Gospel tradition,/74/ and so it is unlikely that its account of the miracle of the coin in the fish is an independent variant of Matt. 17:24-27,/75/ especially since it shares with Matt. 17:24-27 the peculiarity of failing to relate the occurrence of the miracle. In the version in *Epistle of the Apostles* 5, which is not interested in the tax question for its own sake and has nothing corresponding to Matt. 17:25-26, this feature is even stranger than it is in Matthew, and so probably results from dependence on Matthew.

However, even though dependent on Matthew, the *Epistle of the Apostles* belongs to the period, in the early second century, when the Gospels were known in the context of continuing oral tradition, and it is probable that chapter 5 reproduces an existing, traditional summary of the miracles of Jesus, based on the Gospel accounts but exhibiting features of continuing development in oral tradition. Like similar summaries elsewhere (cf. *Sib. Or.* 1:351-359; 6:13-16; 8:272-278), it ends with the feeding of the five thousand as the climactic miracle, but, uniquely, it pairs that miracle with the miracle of the coin in the fish, plainly considering these two miracles of the same type. Their character as miracles of divine provision is strongly emphasized in the parallel introductions to both, indicating a situation of need ('when we had no denarii'; 'when we had no bread') for which the miracle provides. That the writer of the *Epistle of the Apostles* is here following a traditional summary of the Gospel miracles can be seen from the fact that, like most other early Christian writers, he himself was not satisfied with understanding the feeding of the five thousand as a simple miracle of divine provision, but added an allegorical interpretation of the five loaves (cf. his allegorical interpretation of the ten virgins in chapter 43), which is rather obviously secondary to the account.

Thus it is likely that the account of the miracle of the coin in the fish and its pairing with the feeding miracle exhibit the development of oral tradition after Matthew. A definite tendency of the tradition in the post-70 period can be seen in the fact that all trace of connexion with a particular tax, the Temple tax, has disappeared, along with Matt. 17:25-27a, and the coin found in the fish is now a denarius (perhaps owing to Mark 12:15 par.)./76/ Peter is no longer named, and the tax is to be paid on behalf of the disciples in general (for these features, cf. also *Acts of Thomas* 143). That the coin was found in the fish's *mouth*, a feature which distinguishes Matt. 17:27 from the usual form of the folklore motif of the finding of an object in a fish (see section 6 below), has been forgotten, and the miracle has in this respect been conformed to the common folklore motif. All these features serve to highlight, by comparison, the relatively primitive character of Matthew's account.

However, in the tradition behind *Epistle of the Apostles* 5, *one* primitive feature of the tradition has surfaced more prominently than in Matthew, i.e. the character of the miracle as one of divine provision and its kinship with other such miracles. /77/ Precisely because attention is focussed exclusively on the miracle, and not on the teaching of Matt. 17:25-27a, which has disappeared, the tradition has had to clarify the character of the miracle, and, with the instinct of a period in which such miracle stories were known and understood, it has done so correctly. This may serve as a minor, though only a minor, confirmation of our argument.

5.4 We are now in a position to combine points *5.1* and *5.2*, and to show how the miracles of divine provision fit into Jesus' understanding of his miracles.

In the case of the healings and exorcisms, Jesus' understanding of their significance can be gathered from probably authentic sayings in the sayings tradition (e.g. Matt. 11:4-5; 12:28-29; Luke 10:18). Although other people also performed healings and exorcisms, in the context of Jesus' ministry his healings and exorcisms were signs of the healing and victorious power of God's kingdom. At these points where the bounds of ordinary experience were broken through, the coming kingdom became visible.

Unfortunately we lack such interpretation of the miracles of divine provision in the Synoptic tradition of Jesus' sayings. In fact, the Gospel tradition has no way of referring to these miracles as a class. In one case, however, the coin in the fish's mouth, we have already seen how the saying about the Temple tax (Matt. 17:25-26) enables us to connect it with a major theme of Jesus' teaching: the Father's provision for his children's needs. The coin in the fish's mouth is an extraordinary instance of and therefore also a *sign* of God's fatherly care for his people. If we extend this significance to all the miracles of divine provision, we can see them as signs of the kingdom, like the healings and exorcisms, but signs in which a different aspect of the kingdom becomes visible: God's fatherly provision. That Jesus should have seen the extraordinary provision of ordinary, daily needs as signs of the kingdom is comparable with his understanding of physical healings as signs of the kingdom. Of course, if we wish, we can also support both notions from Jewish eschatological expectation, which by no means excluded eating and drinking from the kingdom of God./78/

6. Parallels in Folklore and Rabbinic Literature

We have still to consider the precise form which our miracle takes. The finding of a valuable object in a fish is a folklore motif. But before examining our miracle's relationship to other examples of this motif, we should notice, once again, that this relationship does not make our miracle an isolated anomaly in the Gospel tradition, for two reasons: (1) The Gospel miracles of divine provision, as a group, are close to the themes of folklore and folk religion (two fields which overlap in this area). The miraculous draught of fish/79/ and the miraculous increase of food/80/ could equally be regarded as folklore motifs. Many of the best parallels to this whole group of miracles are to be found in the Elijah and Elisha traditions of 1-2 Kings, and in the medieval lives of the saints, in cases where we can be confident that the stories reflect folk religion and are not just literary creations modelled on biblical precedents./81/ Though miracles of divine provision are rare in rabbinic tradition,/82/ it is no accident that one of them, which provides the best clue to the original significance of the Gospel miracle of turning water into wine, is told of the wife of Ḥanina b. Dosa,/83/ the Galilean charismatic who presents many parallels to Jesus, partly because he and Jesus were closer to folk religion than the Pharisees were./84/

(2) Folklore motifs are by no means absent from the probably authentic sayings of Jesus. Of particular interest at this point is the parable of the Treasure in the Field (Matt. 13:44), which, as Crossan's study brilliantly shows,/85/ can be very much illuminated by comparative folklore analysis. The motif of finding hidden treasure and the motif of finding a valuable object in a fish are closely similar motifs, both in content and in their extraordinarily wide distribution through the folk literature of the world. As far as the similarity of content goes, we may note, for the moment, that the motif of finding hidden treasure occurs in a rabbinic story as a miracle of divine provision (*Lev. Rab.* 5:4). Those who wish to argue, as has sometimes been suggested,/86/ that Matt. 17:27 was originally a *parabolic* saying, might find something of a parallel here. In any case, the presence of very similar folklore motifs in a story told about Jesus and a story told by Jesus may warn us against assuming any considerable historical distance between the two. A desire to detach Jesus from the sphere of folklore and folk religion is bound to be disappointed but in any case needs be entertained only by those who despise folklore and folk religion. Jesus, it seems, did not despise them, but raised them to eschatological significance./87/ (This point will be further explained at the end of this article.)

The folktale motif of finding a valuable object in a fish is found in hundreds of versions from India to Ireland, from the fifth century B.C. to the present day./88/ The majority of these versions take the special form of the 'Polycrates' ring' motif (so called after its earliest occurrence in the story of Polycrates' ring in Herodotus 3:42), in which a ring or other valuable object is first lost and then recovered by being found in a fish./89/ But it is not true, as has sometimes been claimed,/90/ that Matt. 17:27 is distinguished from all other occurrences of the motif in being a finding without previous loss. There are other examples of finding only, including the three examples from rabbinic literature given below.

A fullscale comparative study of Matt. 17:27 in relation to all the various forms and functions of the motif in world folklore--on the lines of Crossan's study of the hidden treasure parable--would undoubtedly be worthwhile. As a preliminary step towards this, I offer a comparison with five instances of the motif in rabbinic literature./91/

Finding a valuable object in a fish: Jewish versions

A. *Losing and finding*
Solomon's ring: Jellinek, *Bet Ha-midrash* II, 86-87
(Gaster, *Exempla* no. 404)
(the variant in *b. Giṭ*. 68b lacks this motif)

Summary: God decreed that Solomon be punished for sin. The demon Ashmedai threw Solomon's ring into the sea and a fish swallowed it. Ashmedai removed Solomon four hundred miles away. Eventually Solomon found his ring inside the fish which had been caught from the sea, and was able to return to Jerusalem, with the ring to prove his identity.

Meaning: punishment ended
Object: magic ring/92/
Where found: inside fish

B. *Losing by one man, finding by another*
Joseph-who-honours-the-Sabbath: *b. Shab*. 119a
(Gaster, *Exempla* no. 380)

Summary: Joseph-who-honours-the-Sabbath lived near a very rich Gentile, who was told by soothsayers that Joseph would acquire all his property. In order to prevent this the Gentile sold his property and with the proceeds bought a jewel which he set in his turban. The wind blew it off into a river, a fish swallowed the jewel, and the fish was caught and brought to market on the eve of the Sabbath. Joseph bought it in honour of the Sabbath, found the jewel in it and sold it for a vast sum of money.
Moral: 'he who lends to the Sabbath, the Sabbath repays him.'

Meaning: reward for Sabbath observance
Object: jewel of very great value
Where found: inside fish

C. *Finding*
The man who threw bread in the sea: *Eccl. Rab*. 11:1
(cf. similar stories without this motif: Gaster, *Exempla*

nos. 381, 449)

Summary: Every day a certain man threw a loaf in the sea. One day he bought a fish and found a valuable object in it. People applied to him the text, 'Cast your bread on the waters. . .'

Meaning: illustrates Eccl. 11:1/93/
Object: a valuable object
Where found: inside fish

D. *Finding*
The disinherited son of Joseph b. Joezer: *b. B. Bat.* 133b

Summary: Joseph b. Joezer had a loft full of denarii, which he consecrated to the Temple, instead of leaving it to his disobedient son. The son bought a fish and found a pearl in it. The Temple treasurers valued the pearl at thirteen lofts full of denarii, of which the Temple funds had only seven available. Joseph's son took the seven and consecrated the remaining six to the Temple.

Meaning: good fortune
Object: pearl of very great value
Where found: inside fish

E. *Finding*
The Jewish tailor in Rome: *Gen. Rab.* 11:4; *Pesiq. R.* 23:6 (Gaster, *Exempla* no. 118)
(the finding motif is lacking in some manuscripts of *Gen. Rab.* and may be a secondary addition to the story/94/)

Summary: A poor Jewish tailor, on the eve of Yom Kippur, bargained with the governor's servant for the only fish left in the market. He bought it for the excessive price of twelve denarii. Brought before the governor, he explained that he did it to honour Yom Kippur and was allowed to go free. He later found a valuable pearl in the fish.

Meaning: reward for honouring Yom Kippur
Object: jewel or pearl of very great value
Where found: inside fish
(variant in Gaster no. 118: among the scales)

Without denying a basic kinship between Matt. 17:27 and the motif in these stories, it is also important to notice differences, which occur in each of the elements listed above:

meaning (i.e. the significance of the motif in its narrative context), object, and where the object is found.

(1) The significance of the motif in the stories varies./95/ In D, for example, it seems to be used as a narrative device to explain how a man could suddenly come into a large fortune without inheriting it: there is no particular sense of the providential nature of the finding. In B and E, as in other rabbinic stories of miraculous or providential divine provision, the finding is a reward for distinctively Jewish piety. Accordingly, Dan Ben-Amos, in his study of Jewish haggadic folktales, classifies our stories B and E, along with some other rabbinic stories in which divine provision occurs, as 'exempla,' i.e. stories of exemplary activity which is rewarded./96/ By contrast, in Matt. 17:27, as in all the Gospel miracles of divine provision, the thought is not of reward, but simply of provision for need. Thus, in terms of the significance of the motif in its narrative context, Matt. 17:27 aligns itself with the Gospel miracles of divine provision, rather than with the 'exempla' of rabbinic haggadah.

(2) Apart from the oddly vague little story C, in the Jewish examples the object found is extremely valuable. In B a rich Gentile sells all his property to buy the jewel; in D the pearl is worth thirteen lofts full of denarii; and in E the tailor lives off the proceeds of his find for the rest of his life. This extreme value of the find is also quite typical of the motif in folk literature generally, and shows it to be a parallel to the motif of finding hidden treasure. In B and E the great value of the find is an integral feature of this kind of 'exemplum,' in which the reward for pious activity often effects a change of social status, from a poor or humble condition to riches and respect./97/ In Matt. 17:27 by contrast the find is worth little, just the amount required for the immediate need. Again this is typical of the Gospel miracles of divine provision, which do not turn paupers into rich people, but in every case supply an immediate, everyday kind of need, in accordance with Jesus' teaching that daily needs are met day by day (Matt. 6:11, 34).

(3) The Jewish examples are typical of the motif in folklore generally in that the object is found inside the fish (i.e. in its stomach) and so is discovered only when the fish is being prepared for cooking. Peter, on the other hand, finds the coin in the fish's mouth./98/ Like the variant in Gaster's version of E (found among the fish's scales)/99/, this variation

probably arises from observation. Those who have studied the natural history of the matter, while not agreed on the species of fish most likely to be in question in Matt. 17:27, do agree that to find a small object like a coin in the *mouth* of a fish from the sea of Galilee would not be especially surprising./100/ That Galilean fishermen talked about finding such objects as coins in fishes' mouths is likely enough.

From this comparative study two general conclusions can be drawn, representing two different aspects of the relation between Matt. 17:27 and the folklore motif:

(1) The relation to folklore does not settle the historical question.

The Jewish stories, of course, can have no serious claim to historicity in the eyes of the modern historian, and it is hard to tell how far they were ever taken seriously as history. Their function in rabbinic teaching is as illustrative haggadah, which make a teaching point in a striking and entertaining way. It is possible that Matt. 17:27 should be understood in the same way. In that case the arguments so far presented in this section, including the three important differences between Matt. 17:27 and the Jewish examples of the motif, would indicate that it was Jesus himself who used this folklore motif, in a particular way which coheres with his teaching as a whole, in order to illustrate his point. The saying would be a picturesque, perhaps somewhat humorous, way of expressing Jesus' belief that the Father would provide the means of paying the tax. This interpretation could be supported by the otherwise puzzling fact that Matthew does not record the occurrence of the miracle. This would indicate that in the tradition which Matthew reproduces Jesus' saying was correctly understood as a hyperbolic illustration, rather than a literal command.

On the other hand, the parallel with other miracles of divine provision in the Gospel traditions may suggest that we should entertain more seriously the possibility that the finding of the coin in the fish's mouth in fact occurred in Jesus' ministry, even though the evidence is not likely to permit a firm conclusion to this effect. The second and third of the differences we observed between Matt. 17:27 and the Jewish instances of the motif indicate that such an occurrence is more credible than immediate impressions might perhaps suggest.

The mere fact that Matt. 17:27 is an instance of a common folklore motif does not in itself entail the conclusion that no such event occurred, since the enormous popularity of this motif in world folklore is connected with precisely the fact that such things can happen. Bright objects are occasionally swallowed by fish and found in them, just as buried treasure is occasionally dug up by accident. Precisely because these things lie beyond the bounds of everyday experience, but *only just* beyond, at a point which by luck or providence one could envisage oneself reaching, they appeal to the mentality of the folktale. They are events which, however improbable, observation and experience allow one to think *might* happen.

Peter's find would not constitute a miracle story/101/ if it did not step outside the bounds of regular, everyday experience, but the step taken is very small. He does not find an object he had previously lost; he does not find a priceless jewel. He only finds half a shekel. It is the kind of remarkable occurrence that would nowadays merit a short paragraph in the local newspaper.

(2) The relation to folklore throws light on the significance of the miracle.

As a short paragraph in the local newspaper, such an event today would provide no more than a moment's entertainment. What the relation to folklore highlights for us is the mentality or the approach to reality which finds revelatory significance in such an event. Folklore and folk religion alike delight in the marvellous, i.e. the unexpected, the inexplicable, the improbable coincidence. They focus attention on these events, which break the bounds of everyday experience. They constitute *significant* cracks in ordinary experience through which one may glimpse a different aspect of reality or a more desirable reality than appears in ordinary experience. The point is not that for such a mentality there are no regularities and the world is full of miracles. On the contrary, there is normal experience, which governs expectations to the extent that miracles encounter real doubt and scepticism, but the abnormal, the irregular, is seen as significant.

This approach to reality must be contrasted with an approach in which the regular and the normal are exclusively significant, and the cracks which undoubtedly occur in normal experience are treated as meaningless, random occurrences of no serious interest. This is the case in our dominant culture (though it has subcultures where things are different), not only because we are used to scientific explanation of the world, but also because for our dominant culture the possibilities of different and better life depend on our understanding and control of the *normal* processes of nature, through technology. (Whether this is really sufficient to save even an affluent culture from banality is another question.)

It is easy for modern people to see in folk religion only a naive preoccupation with the marvellous, but at the very least folk religion made life bearable and hopeful for people who experienced the regularities of the world as oppressive, confining and inhuman.

The affinity between Jesus' miracles, especially those of divine provision, and the kind of events to which folk religion attaches significance need not embarrass modern followers of Jesus. It is one of the ways in which Jesus' message of the kingdom of God made contact with his contemporaries' experience of the world. That hope for a reality more friendly to human life than the world of ordinary experience , which folk religion focuses on the unexpected interruptions of normal experience, Jesus took up into his expectation of the kingdom of the fatherly God. In so doing Jesus opened the folk religious mentality to an eschatological prospect. As events which broke the bounds of everyday experience, his miracles were signs of the world's openness to the coming kingdom of God. By making the kingdom of God's fatherly care concrete in remarkable instances, they made it possible to live even everyday experience in faith that that kingdom was coming about. Instead of the closed and banal world in which regularity is exclusively dominant, Jesus combined folk religion and eschatology to enable us to glimpse through the cracks in ordinary experience the dawning of the kingdom of God./102/

Notes

/1/ R. Cassidy, 'Matthew 17:24-27--A Word on Civil Taxes,' *CBQ* 41 (1979) 571-80, argues for a civil tax, but his argument is based on a misunderstanding of vv. 25-26, which he takes to be, not a *comparison* with civil taxes, but an argument directly about the tax in question (pp. 572-73). His argument is easily refuted by asking why Jesus and Peter are in principle exempt from the tax. Cassidy cannot answer this question (p. 575), since he cannot argue that Jesus and Peter are 'sons' of the

/28/ G. Theissen, *The Miracle Stories of the Early Christian Tradition* (Edinburgh: T & T Clark, 1983) 107; cf. A. C. Wire, 'The Structure of the Gospel Miracle Stories and Their Tellers,' *Semeia* 11 (1978) 92-96.
/29/ Van der Loos, *Miracles*, 686 and n. 3; R. E. Brown, K. P. Donfried, J. Reumann, ed., *Peter in the New Testament* (New York: Paulist/Minneapolis: Augsburg, 1973) 102.
/30/ Cf. also Luke 13:10-17, 14:1-6; but in these cases the controversy follows the miracle.
/31/ E.g. R. H. Gundry, *Matthew: A Commentary on His Literary and Theological Art* (Grand Rapids: Eerdmans, 1982) 357.
/32/ Of course, we have no way of knowing whether Matthew abbreviated his source, as he so often does Mark.
/33/ Elsewhere in the Gospel, he emphasizes Peter's leadership role in 10:2, but actually drops four Markan references to Peter (Mark 5:37, 11:21, 13:3, 16:7) and otherwise only reproduces Mark's references to Peter (Matt. 4:18; 8:14; 19:27; 26:33, 37, 40, 58, 69-75).
/34/ With v. 12, it is Matthew's editorial means of inserting vv. 13-14 into a Markan passage.
/35/ Both these points are made by, e.g., Meier, *Matthew*, 197-98.
/36/ On the diversion of the Temple tax to Rome, see E. M. Smallwood, *The Jews under Roman Rule* (Leiden: Brill, 1976) 371-76.
/37/ *Contra* a common opinion: e.g. Montefiore, 'Jesus'; P. Perkins, 'Taxes in the New Testament,' *JourRelEth* 12 (1984) 189-90; W. D. Davies, *The Setting of the Sermon on the Mount* (Cambridge: University Press, 1964) 390-91.
/38/ Many of the Fathers *misunderstood* it as a reference to a Roman tax, but only by ignoring aspects of vv. 25-26 which we cannot suppose Matthew--who never reproduces tradition *mechanically*--to have missed. If Matthew had misunderstood the pericope in this way he would have had to rewrite it accordingly.
/39/ J. A. T. Robinson, *Redating the New Testament* (London: SCM, 1976) 104-5; followed by Gundry, *Matthew*, 357.
/40/ E.g. McEleney, 'Matthew 17:24-27,' 183-84; Gundry, *Matthew*, 355-56; M. D. Goulder, *Midrash and Lection in Matthew* (London: SPCK, 1974) 397. For more sober use of such arguments, see G. Strecker, *Der Weg der Gerechtigkeit* (Göttingen: Vandenhoeck & Ruprecht, 1966) 200-1; W. G. Thompson, *Matthew's Advice to a Divided Community (Mt. 17:22-18:35)* (Rome: BIP, 1978) 51-62; Horbury, 'Temple Tax,' 267-68.
/41/ These examples in McEleney, 'Matthew 17:24-27,' 183.

Many of Gundry's 'Mattheanisms' (*Matthew*, 355-56) are even less convincing.
/42/ Thompson, *Matthew's Advice*, 62.
/43/ Not in Mark or Luke, but cf. John 11:56.
/44/ I hope to argue for this in detail elsewhere. For the time being, see my discussion of Ignatius' relationship to Matthew's special traditions in 'The Study of Gospel Traditions outside the Canonical Gospels: Problems and Prospects,' in *Gospel Perspectives 5: Jesus Tradition outside the Gospels*, ed. D. Wenham (Sheffield: JSOT, 1985) 386-98.
/45/ Ignatius, *Smyrn*. 3:1-3 and the *Gospel of Peter* are later evidence of Peter's association with Antiochene Gospel traditions.
/46/ It is intriguing to notice that in the only record we have of Peter's activity in Antioch (Gal. 2:12) he must have been acting on a principle comparable to the concern of Matt. 17:27a. But I doubt if this observation has any evidential value.
/47/ Nickle, *Collection*, 87-88.
/48/ Ibid., 90-93.
/49/ Cf. also Perkins, 'Taxes,' 193-94.
/50/ Montefiore, 'Jesus,' 68-69.
/51/ Philo, *Leg. Gaium* 156, 315; *Spec. Leg.* 1:76-78; Josephus, *Ant.* 14:110-13; 16:28, 160-73, 312-13.
/52/ There is some evidence to suggest fairly widespread nonpayment: Horbury, 'Temple Tax,' 280; cf. Montefiore, 'Jesus,' 62.
/53/ The series of complaints against the high priestly families (*t. Menaḥ.* 13:21; *b. Pesaḥ.* 57a; quoted in T. Rajak, *Josephus: The Historian and His Society* [London: Duckworth, 1983] 22-23) are surely genuine tradition from the pre-70 period. They conclude: 'For they are high priests and their sons are treasurers, and their sons-in-law are Temple overseers, and their servants smite the people with sticks.'
/54/ E. P. Sanders' comment that 'payment of the tax was voluntary' (*Jesus and Judaism* [London: SCM, 1985] 64) is mistaken and has no support in the Mishnaic passage he cites as evidence (*m. Shek.* 1:3). According to this passage, the tax was voluntary only for those not legally obliged to pay (women, slaves, minors, priests). Cf. Nickle, *Collection*, 79-80.
/55/ Cf. Rajak, *Josephus*, 122-23, on resentment of the taxation of Herod the Great.
/56/ Cf. Perkins, 'Taxes,' 195: 'most tax revenue flowed out of the local communities into imperial or royal coffers.'
/57/ Rajak, *Josephus*, 22-24, and especially the quotation (from *t. Menaḥ.* 13:21; *b. Pesaḥ.* 57a) on pp. 22-23. For archeological finds which help to substantiate this point, see

B. Mazar, *The Mountain of the Lord* (Garden City: Doubleday, 1975) 84-86; N. Avigad, *Discovering Jerusalem* (Nashville: Thomas Nelson, 1983) 129-30.
/58/ This accounts for the outrage Pilate caused by his unauthorized use of the funds to build an aqueduct: Josephus, *BJ* 2:175.
/59/ Cf. also *Ant.* 14:113.
/60/ Quoted in Horbury, 'Temple Tax,' 280.
/61/ McEleney, 'Matthew 17:24-27,' 187.
/62/ Cf. Montefiore, 'Jesus,' 70. But for a different interpretation, see A. G. Wright, 'The Widow's Mites: Praise or Lament? A Matter of Context,' *CBQ* 44 (1982) 256-65.
/63/ A. E. Harvey, *Jesus and the Constraints of History* (London: Duckworth, 1982) 129-34; Sanders, *Jesus*, 61-76.
/64/ B. Lindars, 'Slave and Son in John 8:31-36,' in W. C. Weinrich ed., *The New Testament Age: Essays in Honor of Bo Reicke* (Macon: Mercer, 1984) 278, connects Matt. 17:25-26 with the reconstructed parable of Jesus at the basis of John 8:35 (contrasting the freedom of a son with a slave's lack of freedom). But I doubt whether ἐλεύθεροι in the context of Matt. 17:26 means more than 'exempt' (from tax).
/65/ Cf. also the instructions in Mark 6:8-9 par., which underline the disciples' dependence on divine provision.
/66/ See esp. Theissen, *Miracle Stories*, 103-6, 251-52, and on these miracles as a group, see also Wire, 'Structure,' 96-99.
/67/ He classifies it as a 'rule miracle,' which is also justified up to a point, but just as the healing of the paralytic is *both* a healing miracle and a 'rule miracle,' so the coin in the fish's mouth is both a 'gift miracle' and a 'rule miracle'.
/68/ For the independent value of this tradition, see E. Bammel, 'The Feeding of the Multitude,' in *Jesus and Politics*, 218.
/69/ Theissen, *Miracle Stories*, 252; and cf. the story of the wife of Ḥanina b. Dosa (*b. Ta'an.* 24b-25a), quoted in ibid., 104.
/70/ Ibid., 106. The story about Polycarp in the Pionian *Life of Polycarp* 4-5, is a later (fourth-century?) legend.
/71/ For the influence of Ezek. 34 on the tradition of the feeding miracle, see Bammel, 'Feeding,' 220.
/72/ McEleney, 'Matthew 17:24-27,' mistakenly reads this interpretation back into Matthew's intention.
/73/ Later second-century references are in Melito, *Peri Pascha* 86; Clement of Alexandria, *Paed.* 2:1:14:1; *Quis dives salvetur* 21:4.
/74/ E.g. in the account of the feeding of the five thousand which follows that of the coin in the fish, the words 'besides

women and children' correspond to Matt. 14:21.
/75/ Against M. Hornschuh, *Studien zur Epistula Apostolorum* (Berlin: de Gruyter, 1965) 11, though he admits that the author knew Matthew (p. 12).
/76/ Cf. *Acts of Thomas* 143, which seems to interpret Matt. 17:24-27 as meaning that Jesus paid the types of tax specified in v. 25.
/77/ *Epistle of the Apostles* 5 has not linked the turning of water into wine with the coin in the fish and the feeding miracle, but this is because it has placed the Cana miracle at the head of its catalogue of miracles, following John 2:11. It is possible that the presence of the word 'net' after 'hook' in the account of the coin in the fish is a gloss deriving from another miracle of divine provision (Luke 5:4).
/78/ Cf. R. H. Hiers, *Jesus and the Future* (Atlanta: John Knox, 1981) chap. 5.
/79/ Cf. R. Eisler, *Orpheus--The Fisher* (London: J. M. Watkins, 1921) 109-10, for parallels from the Arabian Nights.
/80/ See P. Saintyves, *Essais de folklore biblique* (Paris: E. Nourry, 1922) chap. 6; R. Bultmann, *The History of the Synoptic Tradition* (Oxford: Blackwell, 1968[2]) 236.
/81/ E.g. the anonymous Life of Cuthbert.
/82/ Bultmann, *History*, 234, lists most of the examples, but add *Pesiq. R.* 23:3; *b. Shab.* 150a (a tree grows as reward for honouring the Sabbath), and the parallels to Matt. 17:27 mentioned below. Many of the rabbinic stories are of divine *reward* (for charity, honouring the Sabbath, etc.) rather than simply divine provision for need, as in the Gospels. This is an important distinction, but the motifs of the provision itself are comparable.
/83/ *b. Ta'an.* 24b-25a (the parallel lies in the notion of divine provision for a need arising from social embarrassment); cf. also the story of Hanina's daughter and the Sabbath lamp (*b. Ta'an.* 25a).
/84/ G. Vermes, *Jesus the Jew* (London: Collins, 1973) chap. 3; cf. also idem, 'Ḥanina ben Dosa,' chap. 12 in *Post-Biblical Jewish Studies* (Leiden: Brill, 1975).
/85/ J. D. Crossan, *Finding is the First Act: Trove Folktales and Jesus' Treasure Parable* (Philadelphia: Fortress/Missoula: Scholars, 1979).
/86/ C. H. Dodd, *Historical Tradition in the Fourth Gospel* (Cambridge: University Press, 1963) 227; followed by Meier, *Matthew*, 197.
/87/ On this see E. Bloch, *Man on His Own* (New York: Herder & Herder, 1970) 232-40, a discussion with more insight into the Gospel miracles than many a more technically expert study.

/88/ Many stories of very varied origins are quoted in Saintyves, *Essais*, chap. 8; and for further references, see Stith Thompson, *Motif Index of Folk-Literature*, 6 vols. (Copenhagen: Rosenkilde & Bagger, 1955-58[2]) 5. 87-88 (N211.1), 113 (N529.2); A. Aarne and S. Thompson, *The Types of the Folktale: A Classification and Bibliography* (Helsinki: Suomalainen Tiedeakatemia, 1961[2]) 253 (nos. 736, 736A). For a modern instance, see Dodd, *Historical Tradition*, 225 n. 7.
/89/ The object may, of course, be, not accidentally lost, but deliberately thrown away, as in the original Polycrates story.
/90/ Derrett, 'Peter's Penny,' 259 n. 2 (who himself cites the example in *Gen. Rab*. 11:4, in which only finding occurs), followed by Horbury, 'Temple Tax,' 274; cf. Gundry, *Matthew*, 357.
/91/ Where these stories occur in M. Gaster, *The Exempla of the Rabbis* (London/Leipzig: Asia Publishing Company, 1924), I have given their numbers, because Gaster provides invaluable lists of parallels. Since I am here interested in synchronic rather than diachronic relationships, the fact that it is virtually impossible to assign dates to most of these rabbinic stories is immaterial.
/92/ The story is a conflation of the two motifs of Solomon's magic ring and 'Polycrates' ring' motif. On the story, see L. Ginzberg, *The Legends of the Jews* (Philadelphia: Jewish Publication Society of America, 1911-38) 6. 299-301; I. Levi, 'L'orgueil de Salomon,' *REJ* 17 (1888) 58-65; and cf. a parallel Muslim story, which similarly combines the two motifs, in ibid., 58-59; Saintyves, *Essais*, 374-75.
/93/ R. Meyer, 'Der Ring des Polykrates, Mt 17,27 und die rabbinische Überlieferung,' *OLZ* 40 (1937) 668, thinks this must have been originally a pagan story, in which the man offered bread to and was rewarded by a sea divinity. But it may be only a literalistic exegesis of the text it is used to illustrate.
/94/ For an argument that it is, see ibid., 667.
/95/ For the very varied significance of the motif in the wider field of world folklore, see Saintyves, *Essais*, chap. 8.
/96/ D. Ben-Amos, *Narrative Forms in the Haggadah: Structural Analysis* (Ph.D. Thesis: Indiana University, 1966) chap. 6 and Appendix D, which is a collection of stories of this type, including our stories B and E as numbers 9 and 10, and other stories which include divine provision as numbers 11 and 12. Ben-Amos gives a version of story E (no. 10) in which the divine provision of the pearl in the fish is omitted, but in fact the inclusion of this motif conforms the story more closely to his analysis of the typical features of this kind of 'exemplum' (see pp. 172-75). If it was not original to the story, it is easy to see why it was added, by analogy with similar stories.

/97/ Ibid., 165-75. The motif of hidden treasure has this function in *Lev. Rab.* 5:4 (no. 11 in Ben-Amos, Appendix D).
/98/ Parallels to finding in the *mouth* of the fish are known to me only in medieval European tales (e.g. those in Eisler, *Orpheus*, 100-1; Saintyves, *Essais*, 373, 376), where the influence of Matt. 17:27 is likely. Cf. Horbury, 'Temple Tax,' 274 n. 52.
/99/ Another variant of the motif occurs in the story of the twelfth-century bishop Benno, who found the lost keys of his cathedral stuck in the *gills* of a fish (Saintyves, *Essais*, 375). Here the nature of the object to be found may have suggested the variant.
/100/ Bishop, 'Jesus and the Lake,' 404; Derrett, 'Peter's Penny,' 258-59 (and n. 3 with references to other literature).
/101/ By 'miracle' in this context I do not mean an event which contravenes natural law (a modern conception), but a significant exception to normal experience. From the modern perspective, there is no physical impossibility, only a statistical improbability, in Peter's find.
/102/ I am indebted to colleagues in the Gospels Project, who made many useful suggestions in response to the first draft of this paper, to members of the Ehrhardt Seminar, in the University of Manchester, who heard a shorter version of the paper and made valuable comments, to Dr. William Horbury, whose own study of this Matthean pericope helped inspire me to begin work on the paper and who kindly read and commented on my work, and especially to Dr. Philip Alexander, whose expert advice on many points was invaluable.

EXORCISM AND HISTORY: MARK 1:21-28

B. D. Chilton
Yale University
The Divinity School
409 Prospect St.
New Haven, CT 06510

The current fashion is to approach the Gospels in a synthetic manner, as literary entities which have insights and fresh perspectives to offer./1/ To a considerable extent, the fashion is a timely corrective of purely analytic approaches, which may give rise to the false impression that the Gospels are merely layers of tradition and redaction. Particularly, a more integrative approach to the scripture may help to correct some forms of the odd notions that only the earliest layer of a text can possibly be historical, and that only historical traditions can possibly be authoritative. Literary criticism permits of the necessary distinction between historicity and authority, because its premise is that texts communicate, quite aside from the question of whether they communicate as history. But while there is a distinction to be made, it should not be pressed to the point of a divorce. Authority is more than a matter of what actually happened, but it would be an odd sort of faith in Jesus, a historical figure, which took no notice of what he actually said and did. Again, literary meaning/2/ is more than a matter of historical content, but one's evaluation of a document in literary terms, and the consequent judgment of the grounds of its authority, will depend to some extent on its historical accuracy. In the present paper, I should like to represent a redaction critical approach which is chastened but not converted, by recent discussion. The attempt will be made to relate a redaction critical with a literary critical orientation; the question of how such a reading influences the perceived authority of a text lies outside the present purpose.

The present approach is 'chastened,' in the sense that a simplistic picture of Mark, as a mechanical compilation of earlier units which are easily distinguished from the Evangelist's theology, will be eschewed. If it is reasonable to speak of 'Mark' at all, the name should refer to the document as a whole, not to the purely hypothetical idea of a final redactor. And any suggestion to the effect that meaning is inherent in redaction alone, or that history is only to be discovered in traditional material, should be avoided as simple prejudice. But the present approach is also 'not converted,' in the sense that, however fiction should be evaluated/3/, the Gospels are palpably not the compositions of single authors./4/ The documents as we read them probably derive from many witnesses, ranging from oral tradents to professional scribes (cf. Luke 1:1-4). To this extent, distinctions within each Gospel are a part of its literary character; to attempt to homogenize such distinctions in the quest for the significance of 'the text as it now stands' may do violence to that character./5/ In the present enquiry, the term 'redaction' is used to speak of those features of Mark 1:21-28 which serve to anchor the story in well-established themes within the Gospel; 'tradition' is used to speak of more unusual features, which do not serve the interests of larger themes, but rather seem to belong to the material which was incorporated into the redactional whole.

These definitions indeed introduce qualifications into current usage, but they appear to be necessary. Normally, redaction is ascribed to 'the Evangelist,' who is understood to have been responsible for the theological meaning of a given Gospel, while his tradition, frequently called 'a kernel,' is held to approximate to a historical datum. What is unfortunate about such a picture is that it misleads. The process of framing an entire Gospel may have required the work of more than one 'redactor', the purpose of redaction may or may not have been primarily theological, and the last person in the process need not have been the most determinative of the result. The material incorporated during the course of redaction, in turn, may be more of theological than of historical interest. Because we have only texts before us, without reliable external evidence of the persons and motives behind them, attention should be directed to the shape of those texts. The consideration of a passage will then begin with seeing how it relates to the Gospel in which it is found. The passage may be found to cohere with the tendencies of redaction, and/or to manifest its own particular tendencies.

The redactional emphases of the first exorcism story in Mark seem evident. It is presented as the first event in a long day of healing at Capernaum (vv. 21-24, inclusive), and the introductory words (καὶ εἰσπορεύονται εἰς Καφαρναούμ) are typically Markan in respect of diction (cf. 5:40) and syntax (cf. 8:22; 11:15, 27)./6/ The day of what we might call authoritative healing at Capernaum/7/ is paradigmatic; Jesus is to preach elsewhere just as he does here (v. 38). But what justification have we for speaking of 'authoritative healing,' and for linking that to preaching? The justification lies in the redactional framework which presents the stories about healing in general, and the exorcism story in particular. The entry into Capernaum is but preliminary to Jesus' entry into the synagogue in order to teach (v. 21b, c). The reference to the sabbath seems superfluous, until it is remembered that within Mark the sabbath is often the time of controversy (cf. 2:23, 24, 27, 28; 3:2), much as the synagogue often is the place of controversy (cf. 3:1; 12:38, 39; 13:9). The time and place are occasions of amazement, just as they later will be when Jesus teaches in his home town (6:2). 'Sabbath,' 'synagogue,' 'teach' and 'amazed' are all shared by 1:22 and 6:2. Although the emphases of the two passages are quite different, it is plain from Markan usage that the verbal form ἐξεπλήσσοντο in the earlier story does not suggest the response of the congregation was unequivocally positive./8/ Those in the synagogue are astounded, and they correctly perceive Jesus' 'authority' as different from that of the scribes; they (implicitly) will tell the tale of what happened in the synagogue (v. 28). But there is room for misunderstanding, as subsequent Markan narrative will demonstrate. For now, however, what is established is the authority of Jesus' teaching. That is the redactional category under which the exorcism is introduced. It is, in this sense, an instance of healing with authority (cf. v. 27), an instance of the ministry which is to be conducted outside Capernaum (v. 38).

It has frequently been observed that 'teaching' in Mark is used to characterize Jesus' ministry in such a way that the emphasis falls more on the one who teaches than on the content of his teaching./9/ That would appear to be the case in 11:18 (which is reminiscent of 1:22), since the paramount issue for the high priests and scribes (again, cf. 1:22) is how to destroy Jesus himself./10/ Verbal usages of διδάσκω would appear to confirm the personal emphasis which Jesus' teaching has within Mark (cf. 2:13; 6:6, 34; 14:49, none of which specify the content of Jesus' teaching)./11/ The point seems to be rather that Jesus taught habitually (cf. 10:1, ὡς εἰώθει), and that he became known in his teaching. One might conclude from 1:15 that Jesus' message is understood to concern the kingdom of God, but v. 22b, c would appear to focus more on the manner of Jesus' teaching (ὡς ἐξουσίαν ἔχων καὶ οὐχ ὡς οἱ γραμματεῖς) than on its matter. The comparison with the scribes invites attention, since scribes feature prominently in the opposition to Jesus (cf. 2:6; 3:22; 11:18; 12:35, 38)./12/ Commentators will, no doubt, insist on trying to discover in what precise way Jesus differed from the scribes./13/ If they succeed, it will not be because of any information which Mark here provides: the focus of v. 22 is the uniqueness of Jesus, not the ground of the comparison with scribes. In contrast with them, Jesus' authority becomes plain; the particulars of the contrast are not at issue.

To some extent, this authority is none other than the power to exorcise demons (cf. v. 27d; 3:15, 6:7)./14/ But far more to the point, ἐξουσία is--directly or indirectly--the basis on which he acts (11:28, 29, 33). V. 27 makes this point evident within the terms of reference of the present story. To general amazement (cf. the wording of 9:10, 15), Jesus' teaching is recognized as new, that is non-scribal (v. 22), because he commands unclean spirits and is obeyed. The recognition of 'teaching' provokes the question: 'what is this?'. It is a primitive sort of question, even less appropriate than the disciples' befuddled 'who then is this?' at 4:41. But these are as yet early days in the literary context of the Gospel. For the moment, the scribes constitute a contrasting group, not an opposition; the teaching does not yet occasion scandal. The sabbath is still kept;/15/ the synagogue is--for the only time on this, the first reported day of Jesus' ministry with disciples--the place where Jesus' ἐξουσία is disclosed without occasioning overt resistance (cf. 3:1-6; 6:1-6)./16/ If the recognition of Jesus is partial, and couched in terms redolent of future conflict, at least for a moment, starting from a single day in Capernaum, his fame can go forth unimpeded (v. 28), just as he himself can (v. 39).

Within its redactional frame (vv. 21, 22, 27, 28), the exorcism therefore raises the question of Jesus' authority in an acute way, and on two levels. At the level of the people in the story, whose identity is never specified, the question concerns both the teaching and the exorcism: taken together, they are altogether new and strangely efficacious in the Markan presentation. Incipient conflict in no way diminishes Jesus' authority; comparison with scribal teaching makes it all the more apparent. There is a partial disclosure of Jesus' identity, even to his contemporaries. At the level of the reader or hearer of the Gospel, the disclosure is more complete. He or she knows whom this story concerns (1:1), and how its principal has been designated by God (1:11). The outline of Jesus' ministry as recounted in the Gospel is perhaps already known to the reader, so that there is some poignancy in the not yet hardened reaction of the congregation in the synagogue: the watershed presented by the crucifixion has not yet been passed. Between those in the synagogue in Capernaum and those in Mark's congregation there is not yet a world of difference. The former are amazed (v. 22), but disciples can be, as well (10:26); the former--all of them (ἅπαντες)--are astounded (v. 27), but an even more emphatic derivative of the same verb, θαμβέομαι, is used of Jesus in Gethsemane (14:33) and of the women at the tomb (16:5). Before a divine epiphany, of whatever sort, composure ceases to be a virtue; the attitude of those in the synagogue is quite appropriate, given the new teaching and healing/17/ authority which confronts them. Within the Markan style of presentation, Jesus is disclosed as wielding a divine but confusing authority, both to his contemporaries and to Mark's readers. The latter enjoy a position of privilege as compared to the former, but it is the relative privilege of knowledge, not an inalienable possession. Those who read the Gospel know more of the story, and yet--in the end--awe such as is shown in the synagogue is the only appropriate response, provisional though it may be./18/ The Gospel represents the disturbing 'new teaching with authority' (v. 27, construed in a manner different from that of the Revised Standard Version) which challenges ordinary expectations of how God operates.

The Markan presentation therefore invites us, in our privileged position as readers or hearers, to participate in the response of Jesus' contemporaries, and thereby to learn and develop our own attitude. But there is also a third level at which the Markan presentation seeks to disclose the authority of Jesus. Within the body of the exorcism story (vv. 23-26), one or two striking features, which are coherent with the tendencies of Markan redaction, are evident. The first oddity is the immediate usage by the demon/19/ in v. 24a, b of the first person plural, 'what have we to do with you. . .have you come to destroy us?' (τί ἡμῖν καὶ σοί. . .ἦλθες ἀπολέσαι ἡμᾶς;). In v. 24c, however, the demon says, '*I* know who you are' (οἶδά σε τίς εἶ), and is addressed by Jesus in the singular of the second person aorist imperative in v. 25b (φιμώθητι καὶ ἔξελθε ἐξ αὐτοῦ). The plurality of the demons might have been an original feature of this story, as in that of the Gerasene demoniac (Mark 5:1-20), but the narrative as we have it (vv. 23, 26) as well as some of the direct discourse of the demon (v. 24c) and of Jesus (v. 25b), tells somewhat against this possibility. The plural usage seems rather more to belong to the Markan scheme, according to which demons or unclean spirits are regularly referred to in the plural when they are spoken of in relation to Jesus (cf. 1:34, 39; 3:11, 12). The usage, of course, interrupts the narrative flow of the passage, which requires only a single demon; but within Mark as a whole, symmetry with 5:1-20, and some allusion to the special knowledge of demons in general, is achieved. The present story is the most specific instance of what the later, summary passages intimate: the knowledge of the demons (1:34) that Jesus is God's son (3:11). To those who know the pattern of the Gospel, a special disclosure of Jesus' authority is here offered. They will know that the demon's (or demons') identification of Jesus as the 'holy one of God' (v. 24d) is insightful, but partial. The demons in Mark serve to keep Jesus' divine identity in the forefront of readers' minds. But even as compared to the demons' knowledge, theirs is more complete.

In another sense, however, the demons' fearful knowledge of Jesus points to an authority even beyond the readers' present experience. The unclean spirit of 1:24 speaks as a representative of a force, or group of forces, which fears for its very existence: 'have you come to destroy us?' (ἦλθες ἀπολέσαι ἡμᾶς;). Generally, it is odd to speak of an exorcist destroying a demon; the verbs 'binding' (δέω) or 'tormenting' βασανίζω, cf. Mark 5:7) would have been more conventional./20/ The demons here seem to tremble before an eschatological destruction/21/ (cf. the use of the verb ἀπόλλυμι at 12:9), not simply a displacement from the person they occupy. While the Markan reference to the temptation of Jesus by Satan (1:13) is so spare as to make any guesses as to its precise outcome largely speculative, the narrative line of 1:21-28, 34, 39; 3:11, 12, 20-27; 5:1-20 presupposes that the rule of the demons has been broken, and that a new era dawns. In that new era, the Markan reader is a stranger. He knows more of it than Jesus' contemporaries in the synagogue, but the new and the unexpected still have the upper hand. Because the disclosure of Jesus' authority in the story is of an eschatological nature, the reader realizes that even his or her knowledge of Jesus as God's son is but an intimation of what is as unknown as it is irresistible. Even for the reader, it is a new teaching which needs to be learned afresh at each moment, as the future comes closer.

Three dimensions of disclosure are therefore realized in the Markan emphasis on Jesus' authority. At the level of past, historical experience, Jesus' contemporaries express an amazement, which may border on scandal, at a new, efficacious 'teaching'. At the level of present, literary experience, the reader is invited to know more than Jesus' contemporaries, to look more to the teacher than to his message. And at the level of future, eschatologically anticipated experience, the broken power of the demons intimates a new reality which otherwise is only a matter of hope. The attentive reader (to whom Mark seems especially addressed *[cf. 13:14]*) need not, of course, be consciously aware of the three dimensions of disclosure as he/she reads. But any reading of the text which excluded one or more of them would be incomplete. To read the text purely historically, or purely literarily, or purely eschatologically, would be one-sided, and unacceptable as an account of what is said. The three dimensions are all involved in appreciating the Markan redaction at the moment one reads.

Particular attention might nonetheless be given to the historical level of the Markan discourse. The literary disclosure of Jesus' authority in the text can be appreciated by placing the story in context; similarly, the eschatological level of address is appreciable as soon as it is placed within the framework of early Christian expectation. But the text as it stands seems to make a categorical statement about the past; in that claim, it places itself at the bar of history. If the text is an historical nonsense, its claim to disclose Jesus' authority is purely theoretical, at least as far as modern readers are concerned. But if the text is historically tenable in the reader's mind, he or she might see even in the literary and eschatological dimensions of the story an assertion about the real world. In any sort of reading, of course, the reader permits his or her own world to be influenced by the world of the text. That is why reading of a serious sort is fundamentally an act of disciplined imagination. In Mark 1:21-28, however, the world of the text claims to be more than imaginary; Jesus' authority is presented, not only as a literary motif and an eschatological hope, but as instanced in an event. Whether one sees that presentation as historically true or false will therefore influence one's reading of the text. That is to say, the issue of historicity is not only a function of an *a priori* historical interest in Jesus; it is also part and parcel of considered literary awareness.

In general terms, there is a good degree of coincidence

between this story in its Markan presentation and the kerygma of the New Testament. The eschatological significance of Jesus' exorcisms is claimed in a saying attributed to Jesus himself (Matthew 12:28/Luke 11:20). More particularly, some of Jesus' parables, including the one about the strong man, make the claim that his exorcisms signify the end of Satan's régime (Mark 3:23-27/Matthew 12:25-29/Luke 11:17-22), which--in effect--is what is implicitly claimed by Mark by virtue of the ordering of 1:21-28 shortly after the temptation story. Even on the supposition that these sayings are authentic, of course, one could not infer immediately that this particular Markan exorcism story is historical. It is possible that the Markan presentation accords with a theological claim which is itself not based on any fact, or--at any rate--which is not based on the understanding that the present story is factual. But at least we should grant that Mark 1:21-28 accords with an early (perhaps, the earliest) understanding of Jesus' exorcisms, as eschatologically redolent. Similarly, the literary emphasis of Mark on the demons' knowledge and disclosure of Jesus' identity is not merely an inventive motif,/22/ but an element in early Christian theology (cf. Acts 19:13-17; and perhaps James 2:19). Within the generally acceptable understanding that Jesus was known among his followers as a successful exorcist whose success was a seal of who he was and an eschatological portent, the Markan story of the exorcism in the synagogue seems at home. It is difficult to imagine how Jesus could have gained the reputation he did unless such stories were circulated, and harder still to understand why Mark begins with the particular story it does unless the story was at least credible. In other words, we should recognize from the outset that, whatever we might make of the story, in its own time it was considered tenable.

The observation of certain features of the text encourages the view that it is far from a composition designed merely to illustrate Markan themes. The story manifests oddities which do not appear to be redactional, but rather suggest it had its own individual character before it was taken up into Mark's Gospel. The first and most striking oddity is found in the opening statement of the demon (v. 24). Except for the first person plural usage, the initial τί ἡμῖν καὶ σοί fits well within the convention of exorcism stories: the demon attempts to put off his antagonist./23/ But the demon in the story goes further. He names the exorcist quite precisely as Ἰησοῦς [ὁ] Ναζαρηνός, a designation which only appears in Mark in direct or indirect discourse./24/ Demons were commonly thought to possess supernatural insight in antiquity, but this one is portrayed as naming Jesus in quite a formal sense: 'I know who you are, the holy one of God' (οἶδά σε τίς εἶ, ὁ ἅγιος τοῦ θεοῦ). In the literature which mentions exorcism, the technique of naming (sometimes with multiple designations) generally appears as the means by which the exorcist gains control over the demon. /25/ That convention is here reversed: the demon, in effect, attempts to exorcize Jesus, much as at 5:7 (cf. Luke 8:28). No doubt, the demon acts with the mere intention of warding Jesus off; the fact remains that it utilizes exorcistic means to do so. Jesus' counter-measure in v. 25/26/ proves effective, but the demon departs only with violence, convulsing (σπαράξαν) the man and screaming (v. 26). Comparison might be made with 9:26, where σπαράσσω is used to describe such a violent seizure that onlookers believe the victim dead when it is over. It is true that exorcism stories sometimes include physical 'evidence' of a demon's departure; the most famous example is probably that of Eleazar in Josephus, who commanded demons to knock over vessels of water as they departed./27/ But the present story is odd in the violence it stresses. (Because the mention of violence occurs just when one might expect a clear statement of the success of the exorcism, to speak of a stress on violence appears appropriate.) Both the attempt of the demon to gain control over Jesus, and its final, furious attempt to injure the demoniac are also, of course, hardly consistent with the Markan emphasis on the magisterial authority of Jesus' exorcism.

Although these features of the story amount to a coherent version (and help to confirm that it is traditional in substance), they are not easily explained as theologically motivated elements. Such christological point that there might be in having a demon in a synagogue call Jesus 'the holy one of God' is dissipated, first of all by the strong resistance of the demon to Jesus, but also by the vagueness of the designation./28/ It has been suggested from time to time that stories about the exorcisms of Jesus might have circulated among those who were interested more in the style of the exorcisms than in the person of the exorcist./29/ But the relative absence of technical detail and practical advice (in the style, say, of the Magical Papyri) would seem to tell against speculation of this kind, at least in the case of the present passage. More to the point, the peculiar features of the story are no better accounted for on the supposition it belonged to an exorcism cycle than they are on the supposition it was transmitted by disciples of Jesus. The question of who the pre-Markan tradents of the story were is best left open, which implies there is something of a mystery as to why it was told. The theological usefulness of the story to the disciples, once it originated, is evident; but the story cannot be explained as a mere reflection of their theology.

In the absence of certainty, or even information, about the story-tellers and their motives, the odd elements of the story are difficult to evaluate. They might conceivably represent theological or typical features of which we are ignorant, but in which the story-tellers (be they disciples, folk exorcists, or whatever) and their audiences delighted. But the presently available evidence concerning conventions of exorcism stories in general lends no support to such an understanding. Moreover, the story is somewhat out of step with what we know of disciples' claims about Jesus' exorcisms in particular. As we have already observed, the Markan redaction presents the point of the story as the manifestation of Jesus' authority, not the struggle of one exorcistic oath against another. The Matthean redaction handles the difficulty in a more dramatic way, by referring to it, if at all, only in respect of Jesus' teaching, and in very summary form (7:28, 29). Although the Lukan parallel of the story (4:31-37) has reference to the demon's adjuration of Jesus (4:34),/30/ the description of the violence done by the demon is weaker than in Mark. Instead of σπαράσσω, ῥίπτω is used to speak of the demon's action, and the reassurance is added that it did no damage (μηδὲν βλάψαν αὐτόν [4:35]). In the end, it would appear most unwise to try to explain the peculiar features of the story with reference to convention of theological tendency.

The understanding that an exorcism of the sort described was believed by the story-tellers to have happened would, on the other hand, adequately account for its presence in the Gospels, and for the relative importance ascribed to it within the Markan redaction. Above all, it would explain the existence of the odd features of the story: Jesus was believed on one occasion to be addressed in a synagogue by a demon who used an earthly name (Ναζαρηνός) and a divine name (ὁ ἅγιος τοῦ θεοῦ) in a vain attempt to exorcize the exorcist and/or kill the demoniac. As the story was told, the ultimate victory of Jesus was stressed more and more, until it came to be seen as a manifestation of his authority. At the end of the day, the aspect of struggle which the story reveals only links in with the Markan outline insofar as it is in proximity to the temptation story. The attempt of the demons to stop Jesus by naming him is submerged in the motif of the demons' knowledge of Jesus' identity (cf. 1:34d). In other words, a tradition history of the story is not difficult to construe on the supposition that it was told originally to speak of an actual event; just those features which suggest it is in *that* sense historical are difficult to account for as secondary elaborations.

Pre-modern readers of Mark would have required no tradition critical consideration to be convinced that the story-tellers intended to speak of an occurrence, and that they accomplished their intention. Even for them, however, an element of unexpected struggle and violence was present, an element which is softened in Luke and expunged in Matthew. Markan readers were invited to perceive Jesus' authority in all its dimensions, historical, literary, and eschatological, as disclosed in continuing combat with the agents of Satan. For them, Jesus had joined combat and begun the long battle for victory, but the fight had still to be waged in his name (cf. 9:38-40).

Modern readers of Mark are put in a different position, not by the text, but by their own understanding of the world. For us, the meaning of Jesus' authority within Mark is still conveyed by the text, and we can appreciate the significance which might be attached to this sort of authority. But among educated Westerners, to think of demons at all, much less of demons uttering exorcistic formulae and convulsing their victims, has long been considered more appropriate within the realm of fantasy, rather than of fact. (The commonly voiced objection that there are certain instances of demoniacal thinking and experience in our culture does not refute the general observation that such instances are not consonant with our normal apprehension.) A critical reading of the evidence will not necessarily resolve our dilemma, because it is not within the province of exegetes or historians to rule on matters of natural science. To say, for example, that the story is true and our view of the world too narrow, is a perfectly respectable philosophical reflection, but it can hardly be commended on purely textual or historical grounds. Similarly, to say that demons do not exist and stories which suppose they do are misleading, has the attractive ring of rational consistency about it, but it would seem to reduce history to *a priori* notions of what is possible.

Within the discipline of historical exegesis, the text is neither an absolute, nor an inconvenience to be overcome: the task of the reader as exegete is to understand what the text he or she is reading offers. In the present case, what is offered is a picture of Jesus' authority based on the report of an exorcism which, in the minds of those who told the story, actually occurred. The claim of actuality, so far as criticism can determine, lies at the very origin of the story; without it, we can understand neither why the story was told, nor why it was incorporated as it now is within Mark. In this sense, the speech of the demon and Jesus' eventual exorcism of it are historical events. History in this case contradicts received notions of ordinary reality. One might easily construct an alternative diagnosis of the demoniac, along the lines, say, of a dissociative reaction./31/ But constructions of that sort would only impose an alien point of view on the text, and are more an exercise in natural philosophy than in exegesis. The story raises in our minds the phenomenological question whether demons exist without settling it; what would have been experienced by a modern observer in ancient Capernaum remains a mystery. If we cannot accept the terms of reference with which the story works, it will not help us to its meaning if we invent new terms of reference for it. Even the attempt to impose the demonic conventions of the story on the modern reader is an exercise in inventing terms of reference, since demons are not a normal part of our world view. The story does not preach the existence of demons; it merely takes them for granted.

Above all, exercises in the alternative reconstruction of the event described do not explain why the text emerged as it has; they sacrifice the study of the text to a general study of the phenomenology of exorcism. In the present case, to say that all alleged instances of possession are really a species of psychological disturbance/32/ might make some readers more comfortable with the story, but it would not account for its impact on those who heard and told it, or for the precise words ascribed to the demon. Rather, the historicity of the text, quite aside from the ontological question of the existence of demons, should be accepted on exegetical grounds as one facet of its effectiveness as a literary whole. History is essentially the study of human events, and of the factors which occasioned and influenced those events./33/ By an act of sympathy historians attempt to understand the recorded impact of events on people; how people perceived events is therefore part of the historical record. The exorcism reported in Mark

1:21-28 should be accepted as one factor in the recognition of Jesus' identity by his followers./34/ Usually, such conditioning factors--such as economic climate, and popular expectations of the time--can be recognized as possible realities in the present, as well as the past. Historians normally speak of the conditioning factors of the past in the comforting knowledge that they would easily be recognized in the present. But there are occasions, and this is one of them, when the historical conditions of the past have no obvious analogies in the present; whether that is because human perceptions have changed over time, or because the actuality perceived has itself altered, no one can say with certainty. An event may be said to be historical without being repeatable in the present. On such occasions, historical enquiry must itself be exorcized of the pretension to speak of what is true for all time, and rest content with a reasoned, exegetical account of how what is written came to be, and how that influences our appreciation of the received form of the text. The historical question centers fundamentally on what people perceived, and how they acted on their perception; the question of how ancient experience relates to modern experience is a distinct, interpretive matter./35/

Notes

/1/ Cf. J. D. Kingsbury, *The Christology of Mark's Gospel* (Philadelphia: Fortress, 1983); R. A. Culpepper, *The Anatomy of the Fourth Gospel: A Study in Literary Design* (Philadelphia: Fortress, 1983). For an attempt to reconcile redaction criticism and the newer movement, cf. R. M. Fowler, *Loaves and Fishes: The Function of the Feeding Stories in the Gospel of Mark* (Chico: Scholars, 1981), and the reviews in *JTS* 34 (1983) 593-96 and *JBL* 103 (1984) 290-92. That Fowler tries to reconcile the approaches is surely to be welcomed at a time when even more experienced scholars appear to believe that the historical dimension can be ignored within literary criticism.
/2/ Cf. W. Ray, *Literary Meaning: From Phenomenology to Deconstruction* (Oxford: Blackwell, 1984), as a readable introduction to more recent theories of meaning.
/3/ Fiction has, for understandable reasons, been the especial interest of literary critics, some of whom would define historical writing as a species of story (cf. J. Barr, 'Story and History in Biblical Theology,' *JR* 56 [1977] 1-17). That is a matter for further discussion, but quite beside the purpose of the present paper. The present point resides purely in the observation that the Gospels are not the compositions of

single authors. To attempt to skirt that reality by using jargon of an 'implied author' (cf. Culpepper, *Anatomy*) simply shows that the paraphernalia of modern literary theory should not be applied unreflectively to the study of the Gospels.

/4/ Cf. 'An evangelical and critical approach to the sayings of Jesus,' *Themelios* 3 (1978) 78-85. The programme of the earlier article was solely developed in respect of the tradition of Jesus' sayings. The present contribution is designed to cope with narrative material. Cf. *A Galilean Rabbi and His Bible: Jesus' Use of the Interpreted Scripture of His Time* (Wilmington: Glazier, 1984), also published (with the subtitle *Jesus' own interpretation of Isaiah*) by SPCK in London, 71-78.

/5/ The phrase is that of J. Barr, 'Reading the Bible as Literature,' *BJRL* 56 (1973) 10-33, 25, and he uses it in discussing the contribution of Meir Weiss in his sympathetic survey of attempts to appreciate the Bible from a literary point of view. In his conclusion, he seems to me at least to approach the very difficulty here at issue (p. 34): 'The literature *is* its own meaning; we cannot expect to identify a set of external realities of which it is the linguistic sign, and nobody approaches other literatures in such a way.' The 'external realities' Barr here has in mind are theological exegeses of the Bible, but he tentatively applies the attitude of the dictum to Jesus' birth and resurrection (p. 16). The last clause in the quotation is in any case an exaggeration; the approach which Barr rather dogmatically excludes is, for good or ill, common among classicists. The statement on the whole is, as a generalization, only applicable to modern fiction, and then only because the post-Enlightenment tendency has been to expunge the historical element from what is called literature, and to de-emphasize the literary element in what is called history.

/6/ Stylistically, the appearance of the clause is infelicitous, in that the use of the two impersonal forms, εἰσπορεύονται (v. 21) and ἐξεπλήσσοντο (v. 22) involves a change in subjects from the disciples to the congregation in the synagogue.

/7/ Cf. R. Pesch, 'Ein Tag vollmächtigen Wirkens Jesu in Kapharnaum (Mk 1, 21-34.35-39),' *BibLeb* 9 (1968) 114-28, 177-95, 261-77; J. Gnilka, *Das Evangelium nach Markus* I (Köln und Neukirchen-Vluyn: Benziger und Neukirchener, 1978) 76. But the observation was already made by E. Lohmeyer, *Das Evangelium des Markus* (Göttingen: Vandenhoeck und Ruprecht, 1967 [from the 1951 edition]) 34.

/8/ In 7:37 and 11:18, the verb indicates a positive response. But 10:26 is ambiguous in this regard.

/9/ Cf. A. M. Ambrozic, *The Hidden Kingdom: A Redaction-Critical Study of the References to the Kingdom of God in Mark's Gospel* (Washington: Catholic Biblical Association, 1972) 84, 85. For a fuller discussion of the phenomenon see R. T. France, 'Mark and the Teaching of Jesus,' in *Gospel Perspectives* I (ed. R. T. France & D. Wenham; Sheffield: JSOT, 1980) 101-36.
/10/ Ἀπόλλυμι is also the language of contention in 1:24, albeit in a different connection (cf. below).
/11/ 12:35f. is something of an exception, in that an instance of teaching is given.
/12/ But cf. 12:28, 34; scribes are not merely enemies in Mark. Cf. M. J. Cook, *Mark's Treatment of the Jewish Leaders* (Leiden: Brill, 1978).
/13/ Cf. E. Haenchen, *Der Weg Jesu: Eine Erklärung des Markus-Evangeliums und der kanonischen Parallelen* (Berlin: de Gruyter, 1966) 86, 87 for an instant identification of the scribes with the later rabbis.
/14/ Cf. J. Starr, 'The Meaning of 'Authority' in Mark 1, 22,' *HTR* 23 (1930) 302-5; and R. Reitzenstein, *Die hellenistischen Mysterienreligionen* (Leipzig: Teubner, 1927) 363. Cf. the translation of J. E. Steely, *Hellenistic Mystery-Religions: Their Basic Ideas and Significance* (Pittsburgh: Pickwick, 1978).
/15/ It is of note in this connection that v. 32 has the populace wait for sundown, the end of the sabbath, before bringing the diseased to Jesus.
/16/ Even at this early stage, however, the synagogue is called 'their synagogue' (v. 23). In that the pronoun refers back to the (merely implicit) subject of ἐξεπλήσσοντο in v. 22, it may be taken to mean 'Jewish synagogue,' as in v. 39. The attitude towards Judaism is similar to what is found at 7:3, 4.
/17/ That the exorcism is seen within the context of healing, whatever its distinctive elements, is suggested by its association with vv. 29-34a. Cf. D.-A. Koch, *Die Bedeutung der Wundererzählungen für die Christologie des Markusevangeliums* (Berlin: de Gruyter, 1975).
/18/ Given that the amazement/astonishment of Jesus' contemporaries can lead to scandal, there is perhaps a certain suggestion that awe is no guarantee that one has understood correctly. It is a necessary, but in itself insufficient, response.
/19/ At first, it is not apparent whether it is the unclean spirit or the demoniac that is speaking, although the masculine participle makes it appear the voice is the man's (cf. R. G. Bratcher & E. A. Nida, *A Translator's Handbook of the Gospel of Mark* [Leiden: Brill, 1961] 49). But v. 25 makes it clear that

Jesus thinks he is addressing the demon in the story. The ambiguity should not be pressed for significance, however. Possession involved the control of the boy by an alien spirit, at least in the understanding of those who told stories such as this. Cf. F. Annen, 'Die Dämonenaustreibungen Jesu in den synoptischen Evangelien,' *Theologische Berichte* 5 (1976) 107-46, 108.

/20/ Cf. O. Bauernfeind, *Die Worte der Dämonen im Markusevangelium* (Stuttgart: Kohlhammer, 1927) 24, 25.

/21/ Cf. V. Taylor, *The Gospel according to St. Mark* (London: Macmillan, 1952) 174, where *1 Enoch* 69:27; Luke 10:18; Rev. 20:10 are cited by way of comparison, and Annen, 'Dämonenaustreibungen,' 126, citing the *Testaments* of *Simeon* 6:6 and *Levi* 18:12. A case has been made against seeing Satan as strictly associated with demons in general by M. Limbeck, 'Jesus und die Dämonen,' *BK* 30 (1975) 7-11. But cf. R. Yates, 'Jesus and the Demonic in the Synoptic Gospels,' *ITQ* 44 (1977) 39-57; J.D. G. Dunn & G. Twelftree, 'Demon-Possession and Exorcism in the New Testament,' *Churchman* 94 (1980) 210-25, 217, 218; Annen, 'Dämonenaustreibungen,' 180-82.

/22/ Cf. H. Räisänen, *Das 'Messiasgeheimnis' im Markusevangelium: Ein redaktionskritischer Versuch* (Helsinki: Länsi-Suomi, 1976) 91-93; and M.-J. Lagrange, *L'Evangile selon Marc* (Paris: Gabalda, 1947) 23.

/23/ Cf. Bauernfeind, *Worte*, 7. As Räisänen, 92, n. 9, observes, Bauernfeind based many of his generalizations on the assumption that texts of a magical nature are immediately relevant to the question of Jesus' exorcisms. To an extent, however, the *religionsgeschichtliche* approach he employed justified such a procedure, although the approach has since been discredited (cf. C. Colpe, *Die religionsgeschichtliche Schule: Darstellung und Kritik ihres Bildes vom gnostischen Erlösermythus* [Göttingen: Vandenhoeck und Ruprecht, 1961]; H. C. Kee, *Miracle in the Early Christian World: A Study in Sociohistorical Method* [New Haven: Yale University Press, 1983]). In any case, Bauernfeind's findings can be checked against more obviously relevant texts. A list of useful analogies to exorcism stories in the Gospels might include Tob. 6-8, 1QapGen. 20:12-32 (J. A. Fitzmyer, *The Genesis Apocryphon of Qumran Cave 1* [Rome: Biblical Institute Press, 1971]), *Antiquities* 8.2.5 pars. 46-48 (H. St.J. Thackeray & R. Marcus, *Josephus V: Jewish Antiquities, Books V-VIII* [London: Heinemann, 1934]), *Life of Apollonius* 3.38; 4.20 (from a later period; F. C. Conybeare, *Philostratus: The Life of Apollonius of Tyana* [London: Heinemann, 1912]). Reference might also be made to K.

Preisendanz, *Papyri Graecae Magicae* (Leipzig: Teubner, 1928) and the revision undertaken by A. Henrichs, *Die griechischen Zauberpapyri* (Stuttgart: Teubner, 1973, 1974), which offers actual instances of the language of exorcism and incantation, but the dates of the documents are too late to permit of a direct comparison with the Gospels. (Cf. also the remarks of Kee, *Miracle*, 214f.) The question of chronology must also be borne in mind when one uses G. A. Deissmann's *Light from the Ancient East* (London: Hodder & Stoughton, 1910). It is also worth noting that there are not many stories of exorcisms in the literature of early Judaism. But the evidence does not suggest that such stories differed entirely from those of Hellenistic literature. Moreover, this is an area in which the chronology of sources may have little to do with the practices they relate. C. Bonner, for example, demonstrates that elements in the narrative of Josephus resemble a contemporary story ('The Violence of Departing Demons,' *HTR* 37 [1944] 334-36). Cf. also Bauernfeind, *Worte*, 13, n.3, which gives a sure indication that the practitioners of *Religionsgeschichte* were not as naive in respect of chronology as is sometimes alleged; and J. M. Hull, *Hellenistic Magic and the Synoptic Tradition* (London: SCM, 1974).

/24/ Cf. H. H. Schaeder, 'Ναζαρηνός, Ναζαραῖος,' *TDNT*, IV, 874-79. The understanding of the term as referring first of all to Jesus' provenience is probably to be preferred.

/25/ Cf. Annen, 'Dämonenaustreibungen,' 121, citing the work of Limbeck; but their supposition that this feature is theologically motivated does not bear examination. Bauernfeind, *Worte*, 3-18, presents the classic form of the observation. His position is attacked by A. Fridrichsen, 'Jesu Kampf gegen die unreinen Geisten,' in *Der Wunderbegriff im Neuen Testament* (ed. A. Suhl; Darmstadt: Wissenschaftliche Buchgesellschaft, 1980), 248-65, 251-52. Fridrichsen's argument that the demon's words amount to a confession is, however, only tenable within the Markan context, not within the context of the tradition. The oddity of the demon's speech is mentioned by C. Bonner, 'The Technique of Exorcism,' *HTR* 36 (1943) 39-49, 44, who in turn ascribes the observation to Loisy. For usage of ἅγιος, cf. *Testament of Solomon* as cited by Bonner. Haenchen, *Weg*, 88, rejects the idea, raised by Lohmeyer, that the naming represents an attempt to control one's adversary, by saying, 'Jesus ist doch für den Dämon kein "Rumpelstilzchen"!' Were this observation couched in the form of an argument, one might respond to it. Cf. R. Pesch, *Der Besessene von Gerasa: Entstehung und Überlieferung einer Wundergeschichte* (Stuttgart: KBW, 1972) 26 (cf. 32, 33), who characterizes Mark 5:7 as a parody of an exorcistic formula. Such words should be distinguished from those in which demons might recognize the power of exorcists (cf. ibid., 34; Annen, 'Dämonenaustreibung,' 120, 121 for examples).

/26/ Cf. Dunn & Twelftree, 'Demon-Possession,' 212; T. A. Burkill, *Mysterious Revelation: An Examination of the Philosophy of St. Mark's Gospel* (Ithaca: Cornell University, 1963) 73.

/27/ Cf. *Antiquities* 8.2.5 pars. 46-48.

/28/ Cf. Lagrange, *Marc*, 22, 23. Although this description might be held to be disappointingly general, it seems more adequate than the attempt to see the phrase in a specifically messianic (so H. B. Swete, *The Gospel according to St. Mark* [London: Macmillan, 1913] 19), high priestly (so Lohmeyer, *Markus*, 37), or charismatic (so Haenchen, *Weg*, 87, n. 5) light.

/29/ Cf. E. Trocmé, *La formation de l'Evangile selon Marc* (Paris: Presses Universitaires, 1963) 42, 43. Pesch, 48, 49 speaks of quite a different cycle in respect of the story of the Gerasene demoniac. But he clearly distinguishes 1:21-28 from this complex, and argues that the earlier exorcism story is to some extent the paradigm of the later (pp. 41f.).

/30/ Cf. also 8:29 as compared to Mark 5:7, and Pesch, *Besessene*, 52, 53. But compare Luke 8:28 with Mark 5:7, and cf. ibid., 61.

/31/ Cf. N. Cameron, *Personality Development and Psychopathology: A Dynamic Approach* (Boston: Houghton Mifflin, 1963) 338-72, who deals with the rather rare occurrence of multiple personality within this category (pp. 358-60). It should be observed that schizophrenia is described quite differently, as regression expressed by the production of delusions and/or hallucinations (p. 584). Cf. also *The Psychiatric Clinics of North America* 7 (1984). On the generally problematic nature of attempts at retrospective diagnosis, cf. R. Hengel und M. Hengel, 'Die Heilungen Jesu und medizinisches Denken,' in *Wunderbegriff*, 338-73.

/32/ Before psychological explanations of such events are accepted, however, it must be appreciated that the entire notion of mental disease has come under attack, both on practical (cf. W. E. Broen, *Schizophrenia: Research and Theory* [New York: Academic, 1968]; T. R. Sarbin & J. C. Mancuso, *Schizophrenia: Medical Diagnosis or Moral Verdict?* [Oxford: Pergamon, 1980])and moral (cf. J. Coulter, *Approaches to Insanity: A Philosophical and Sociological Study* [London: Robertson, 1973]; T. Szasz, *The Myth of Psychotherapy: Mental Healing as Religion, Rhetoric, and Repression* [Oxford: Oxford University, 1979]) grounds.

/33/ Cf. B. J. F. Lonergan, *Method in Theology* (New York: Herder & Herder, 1972) 178-96, 220-24.

/34/ Annen, 'Dämonenaustreibung,' 115-17, puts his finger on a difficulty which has been created for (and by) critical scholarship. Critics are willing to say Jesus exorcized in general, but not which stories are historical (cf. Dunn & Twelftree, 'Demon-Possession'). But general statements cannot possibly do justice to the particularity of texts, in this case, the struggle of the demon and its naming of Jesus. The force of any story lies precisely in its unusual elements; their appreciation as historical, mythical, theoretical, fantastic, or whatever, is part of the reader's task.
/35/ Cf. A. Suhl, 'Die Wunder Jesu: Ereignis und Überlieferung,' in *Wunderbegriff*, 464-509.

THE FEEDING OF THE MULTITUDE IN MARK 6/JOHN 6

P. W. Barnett
Robert Menzies College
Macquarie University
Sydney 2113

Our aim is to explore the relationship between the accounts of the Feeding of the Multitude recorded in Mark 6:30-46 and John 6:1-15. In the course of the paper we will ask: did the Fourth Evangelist derive his data directly from Mark, from his recollection of what Mark had written, from an underlying source common to both writers, or did both authors, Mark and John, edit separate and independent traditions which had come to them? Behind this question of relationship lies the deeper question: does the story of the Feeding of the Multitude have a basis in history? Clearly its historicity is enhanced if the accounts as we have them arose separately and is diminished if one is (ultimately) derived from the other.

Despite all that has been written, the question of the relationship between John and the Synoptics, within which the present study belongs, remains open. In 1964 D. M. Smith spoke of a 'growing consensus' in favour of John's independence of the Synoptics./1/ In 1980, however, Smith/2/ stated that the consensus 'did not rest long,' pointing to a resurgence of the contrary view in particular in the work of F. Neirynck/3/ and C. K. Barrett./4/

The significance of the Feeding incident in relation to the wider question of John and the Synoptics is well-known. It is one of the earliest episodes in John which has points of contact with the Synoptics;/5/ it is the only miracle story found in all four gospels. Clearly the Feeding of the Multitude is a critical test case./6/

Our method will be to discuss the similarities and differences between the two accounts and to this we now turn./7/

I. Similarities

Three kinds of similarity are noted.

1. Arithmetical and other detail

a. the value of bread: δηναρίων διακοσίων (Mark); διακοσίων δηναρίων (John)
b. the numbers of people: πεντακισχίλιοι ἄνδρες (Mark); ἄνδρες. . .ὡς πεντακισχίλιοι (John)
c. the source of the meal: ἄρτους. . .πέντε καὶ δύο ἰχθύας (Mark); πέντε ἄρτους. . .καὶ δύο ὀψαρία (John)
d. the uneaten food: κλάσματα δώδεκα κοφίνων (Mark); δώδεκα κοφίνους κλασμάτων (John)
e. the grass: τῷ χλωρῷ χόρτῳ (Mark); χόρτος πολύς (John)

Whatever else is true of these passages, agreement in specifics of this kind is noteworthy.

2. The Narrative

In both accounts we find:

a. separate journeys by Jesus and the multitude to the *place* (τόπος in both gospels).
b. There Jesus sees a *great crowd* (πολὺς ὄχλος in both gospels).
c. The problem of *purchasing* food for the people is recognised (ἀγοράζειν in both gospels).
d. The disciples refer to five *loaves* (πέντε ἄρτοι in both gospels).
e. The people sit down (ἀναπίπτειν in both gospels).
f. Jesus takes the food, blesses and distributes.
g. The people eat and the left-over food is collected (κοφίνοι in both gospels).
h. Later Jesus goes to a mountain while the disciples cross the lake by boat.
i. At night Jesus comes to the disciples walking on the sea.

Again we are struck by the agreements between the two accounts--the story-line, the sequence and the words used.

3. Verbal agreement

Apart from the words relating to arithmetical detail, the nouns, verbs and adjectives which occur in both accounts are as follows:

	Mark 6	John 6
λέγω	vv. 31,35,37,38^2	vv. 5,6,8,12,14
τόπος	vv. 31,32,35	v. 10
ὄχλος	vv. 34,45	vv. 2,5
πολύς	vv. 31,33, 34^2,35^2	vv. 2,5,10

ὄρος	v. 46	vv. 3,15
μαθητής	vv. 35,41,45	vv. 3,8,12,16
ἀπέρχομαι	vv. 32,36,37	v. 1
ποιέω	v. 30	vv. 2,6,10,14,15
ἔρχομαι	v. 31	vv. 5,14,15
ἐσθίω	vv. 31,36,37^2,42,44	v. 5
κλάσμα	v. 43	vv. 12,13
ἀγοράζω	vv. 36,37	v. 5
ἀποκρίνομαι	v. 37	v. 7
δίδωμι	vv. 37^2,41	v. 11
γινώσκω	vv. 33,38	v. 15
χόρτος	v. 39	v. 10
ἀναπίπτω	v. 40	v. 10^2
λαμβάνω	v. 41	vv. 7,11

These words fall into three groups:

(a) words which are too general to impinge on the question of dependence: λέγω, ἔρχομαι, ἀπέρχομαι, ποιέω, ἀποκρίνομαι, γινώσκω

(b) words which are not in narrative parallel portions and for which alternative words would not be easy to find: τόπος, ὄχλος, πολύς, ὄρος, μαθητής, χόρτος

(c) words found in (roughly) parallel texts in the two accounts: ἐσθίω, κλάσμα, ἀγοράζω, δίδωμι, ἀναπίπτω, λαμβάνω.

These verbal agreements, especially (b) and (c), are impressive and when taken in consideration with the agreement of arithmetical detail and of the narrative add up to a good case in favour of John's knowledge or use of Mark. On the other hand it is possible that these verbal agreements could point to separate traditions which coincidentally employed a dozen or so common words. It is submitted that the verbal similarities, in themselves, are not conclusive either way.

When we turn to investigate phrases common to Mark and John the result is different, especially when we then note the frequency of repetition of Markan phrases in Matthew and Luke. Most of the phrases common to Mark and John relate to arithmetical detail, though the word order and word-endings are different in each case.

Mark 6		John 6	
v. 34	πολὺν ὄχλον	vv. 2,5	ὄχλος πολύς/πολὺς ὄχλος
v. 37	δηναρίων διακοσίων ἄρτους	v. 7	διακοσίων δηναρίων ἄρτοι
v. 41	λαβὼν τοὺς πέντε ἄρτους	v. 11	ἔλαβεν οὖν τοὺς ἄρτους

v. 43	κλάσματα δώδεκα κοφίνων	v. 13	δώδεκα κοφίνους κλασμάτων
v. 44	πεντακισχίλιοι ἄνδρες	v. 10	ἄνδρες...ὡς πεντακισχίλιοι

It is noted that not only are there few phrases in common, and mostly connected with statistics; *these phrases are in no case exactly repeated.* This factor of inexactness is thrown into relief by comparing the (probable?) dependence of Matthew and Luke on Mark as reflected in the frequent repetition of phrases./8/ For example:

	Mark 6		Luke 9
v. 30	καὶ συνάγονται οἱ ἀπόστολοι...καὶ ἀπήγγειλαν αὐτῷ πάντα ὅσα ἐποίησαν	v. 10	καὶ ὑποστρέψαντες οἱ ἀπόστολοι διηγήσαντο αὐτῷ ὅσα ἐποίησαν
v. 35	προσελθόντες αὐτῷ οἱ μαθηταὶ αὐτοῦ	v. 12	προσελθόντες δὲ οἱ δώδεκα εἶπαν αὐτῷ

	Mark 6		Matthew 14
v. 32	καὶ ἀπῆλθον ἐν τῷ πλοίῳ εἰς ἔρημον τόπον κατ' ἰδίαν	v. 13	ἀνεχώρησεν ἐκεῖθεν ἐν πλοίῳ εἰς ἔρημον τόπον κατ' ἰδίαν
v. 34	καὶ ἐξελθὼν εἶδεν πολὺν ὄχλον καὶ ἐσπλαγχνίσθη ἐπ' αὐτούς	v. 14	καὶ ἐξελθὼν εἶδεν πολὺν ὄχλον καὶ ἐσπλαγχνίσθη ἐπ' αὐτοῖς

In these examples the similarities of phraseology, often in exact form, leave little doubt that both Luke and Matthew had access to and in fact depended upon the text of Mark in this story. The similarity of phrases between the Synoptic authors and the dissimilarity at this point between John and Mark suggests that John did not depend upon the text of Mark.

In sum, while agreements in verbal detail, in story-line and in a (small) common vocabulary could support the dependence model, the absence of common phrases, especially when contrasted with the presence of many common phrases in the Synoptics, leaves the question open. Thus, the similarities are inconclusive; they could support either a dependence or an independence model.

II. Differences

The differences between the two accounts are considered under two headings: (1) narrative differences and (2) verbal differences.

1. Narrative Difference

a. Place, Time, People

While Mark does not name the sea/9/ it is identified by John as ἡ θαλάσσα τῆς Γαλιλαίας τῆς Τιβεριάδος. Similarly it is John who notes the time as ἐγγὺς τὸ πάσχα (v. 4), though Mark's χλωρῷ χόρτῳ confirms this detail, which might otherwise be dismissed as purely redactional. The naming of Philip and Andrew by John (vv. 5,8) contrasts also with Mark where no names are given. While the evangelist may have supplied these details to embellish Mark, or a common source, it could equally be argued that this information was embedded within a separate independent tradition upon which John depended.

b. The Journey

In Mark, at the return of 'the apostles,' the πολλοί are in a state of agitation, apparently on account of the recent mission of the twelve to the πόλεις of Galilee (v. 33). The journey to the ἔρημος τόπος is undertaken to get away from the crowd, who, however, anticipate the destination of Jesus, and running together (συνέδραμον--v. 33) arrive beforehand awaiting the arrival of the boat. The gathering of the multitude to meet Jesus in the ἔρημος τόπος (vv. 31,35) clearly arose out of prior incidents, in particular the commissioning of the twelve and their mission to the πόλεις of Galilee. Given John's intense interest in Mosaic-Exodus themes his omission of Mark's twofold ἔρημος τόπος is curious and arguably a point in favour of the separate tradition model.

The narrative of John 6:1-15, by contrast, does not appear to arise out of earlier episodes recorded in the Fourth Gospel. John's version depicts Jesus being constantly followed (ἠκολούθει) by the ὄχλος πολύς on account of the 'signs which he has performed upon the sick' (v. 2; see also Mt. 14:14; Lk. 9:11). Having ascended and sat down upon 'the mountain'/10/ he saw the 'great multitude' *coming* (ἔρχεται) *towards* him. Unlike Mark's account, where Jesus' withdrawal is contingent upon the crowd's presence, in John Jesus is the complete master of the events, having freely taken the initiative to travel to the place, knowing what he will do in the situation (v. 6) and then doing it with abundant oversupply of food (v. 13), even though it was a *great* multitude (vv. 2,5; cf. v. 9).

Since the differences between the stories are so great it is difficult to imagine how John could have been using Mark, or the common source, at this point. The versions appear to be quite independent.

c. The Problem of Purchasing Food

While both authors are united in observing that Jesus, upon arrival at the destination, saw the great multitude, implying by the very statement something of the problem of providing food in an isolated place, the accounts diverge as to when the problem is voiced, how and by whom. In Mark's story, Jesus, on seeing the great crowd and feeling compassion for them, taught them, the problem of food only being raised later in the day and by the disciples who ask that the people be sent off to the surrounding villages to purchase food (v. 35). When Jesus enigmatically commands the disciples to feed the people, the disciples themselves enquire if they should go to purchase bread, specifically to the value of 200 denarii (v. 36). In John's account, however, it is Jesus himself who, (immediately?) on seeing the great crowd, asks where bread may be purchased so that the people may eat (v. 5). Philip, one of the disciples, so far from suggesting going away to purchase 200 denarii of bread as a solution to the problem, ruefully observes that this amount is not sufficient to give each person something (v. 7); Mark affirms that bread to the value of 200 denarii would be needed (v. 37). In similar vein, Andrew helplessly takes stock of the resources of the crowd, a mere five loaves and two fish--which belong to a boy (vv. 8-9).

The divergences at this part of the story-line are capable of several explanations, none of which appears decisive on its own. On the one hand, following the dependence model, John could be altering Mark (or a source common to and depended upon by both authors) so as to highlight the hopelessness of the situation to demonstrate the greatness of the sign, something in keeping with the author's stated objective (Jn. 20:30-31). Alternatively, following the independence model, the divergences could have been part of the separate traditions which the respective authors used.

d. The Feeding

The feeding of the multitude falls into five parts: the sitting down, the blessing, the distributing, the eating, the collecting.

i. The Sitting. In Mark it is Jesus who commands the people to sit, by companies (συμπόσια συμπόσια) upon the 'green grass' whereupon they sat down in groups (πρασιαὶ πρασιαί) of 'hundreds and fifties' (vv. 39-40)./11/ Presumably this was to facilitate the distribution of the food. In John, however, Jesus says (to the disciples?) 'make the people sit down.' The 'men' (οἱ ἄνδρες) then sat down, there being 'much grass in the place' (v. 10).

Although there are significant divergences, Matthew and Luke appear to be depending on Mark. Matthew's κελεύσας τοὺς ὄχλους (14:19) is distinctive but his ἀνακλιθῆναι ἐπὶ τοῦ χόρτου appears to be derived from Mark's ἀνακλῖναι. . .ἐπὶ τῷ χλωρῷ χόρτῳ (v. 39). While Luke, in common with John, has Jesus telling the disciples to seat the people (9:14-15), he does reproduce the detail of the group size (ἀνὰ πεντήκοντα--9:14). Matthew and Luke appear to be depending upon, but adapting, Mark, whereas John's version seems to be either dependent upon a separate and parallel tradition or alternatively an embellishment on a tradition common also to Mark to which he has however added seating details.

ii. The Blessing. In Mark's narrative, followed almost verbatim by Matthew and Luke, a fourfold action is set forth: λαβὼν τοὺς πέντε ἄρτους καὶ τοὺς δύο ἰχθύας ἀναβλέψας εἰς τὸν οὐρανὸν εὐλόγησεν καὶ κατέκλασεν τοὺς ἄρτους (v. 41). John's reference to ἔλαβεν...τοὺς ἄρτους...καὶ εὐχαριστήσας uses εὐχαριστεῖν instead of εὐλογεῖν and is also briefer, omitting the fishes from the blessing and also the verbs ἀναβλέψας and κατέκλασεν. Granted that John uses εὐχαριστεῖν/12/ but not εὐλογεῖν/13/ it may be argued that the omissions signify that separate and independent traditions were being employed by Mark and John.

iii. The Distributing. In Mark's account, Jesus commands the people to sit (in groups) but it is the disciples to whom the bread is given (καὶ ἐδίδου) for distribution to the people (τοῖς μαθηταῖς ἵνα παρατιθῶσιν αὐτοῖς--v. 41), a pattern followed by Matthew and Luke. By contrast, in John the disciples seat the multitude while it is Jesus who distributes the food to the people (διέδωκεν τοῖς ἀνακειμένοις--v. 11). At first it appears that these divergences imply independence of tradition. However it is also possible that the authors have manipulated details from an earlier common source for (differing) redactional motives--Mark to stress the ongoing place of the disciples' ministry; John to emphasise the complete mastery of Jesus.

iv. The Eating. Both authors stress the satiation of the crowd. Mark's καὶ ἔφαγον πάντες καὶ ἐχορτάσθησαν (v. 42) is followed exactly by Matthew (and also by Luke except for the final positioning of πάντες). John writes τοῖς ἀνακειμένοις...

ἐκ τῶν ὀψαρίων ὅσον ἤθελον ὡς δὲ ἐνεπλήσθησαν. Separate and independent traditions appear to be implied by these differences.

v. The Collection. Mark's laconic ἦραν κλάσματα δώδεκα κοφίνων πληρώματα καὶ ἀπο τῶν ἰχθύων (v. 43) is recognisably, but not exactly, followed by Matthew and Luke./14/ John, however, interposes Jesus' command to the disciples that the broken pieces be gathered up so that nothing be lost. John then narrates that συνήγαγον...ἐγέμισαν δώδεκα κοφίνους κλασμάτων ἐκ τῶν πέντε ἄρτων τῶν κριθίνων ἃ ἐπερίσσευσαν τοῖς βεβρωκόσιν (v. 13)./15/ While ἐπερίσσευσαν echoes Matthew (14:20) and Luke (9:17) and the δώδεκα κοφίνους is found in all four accounts (with case and word-order variations), John's account employs such different vocabulary, and for no discernible redactional motive, that his literary dependence upon Mark appears unlikely.

e. The Recognition

The climax of John's account is the recognition, based on the σημεῖον narrated, οὗτός ἐστιν ἀληθῶς ὁ προφήτης ὁ ἐρχόμενος εἰς τὸν κόσμον (v. 14) followed by Jesus' perception μέλλουσιν ἔρχεσθαι καὶ ἁρπάζειν αὐτὸν ἵνα ποιήσωσιν βασιλέα (v. 15)./16/ Possibly the most curious feature in the relationship between the Feeding of the Multitude as related by Mark and John is the absence of this recognition incident from Mark 6:30-45 (and also from Matthew and Luke). How do we explain its presence in John and its absence from Mark? One possibility is that John has created this detail *ex nihilo* for redactional reasons, namely to promote the view of Jesus as Prophet-King./17/ This, however, is unlikely to be the case since the Fourth Evangelist neither here nor elsewhere (see 1:21, 7:40) actively portrays Jesus as ὁ προφήτης ἐρχόμενος εἰς τὸν κόσμον./18/ Since the writer does not describe (Jesus' perception of) the crowd's intentions about kingship with approval, this passage is arguably not redactional. It is quite conceivable that the incident is historically based and that it arises out of a separate and independent tradition known to John, but which for unknown reasons has been omitted from the Gospel of Mark.

f. The Return Journey

Although certain critical details are missing from both accounts it is evident that there is a common underlying story-line. In both versions the disciples having embarked are crossing the sea during the night and encountering strong winds (Mk. 6:45a, 47a-48; Jn. 6:16-18). Prior to this, however, Mark (very closely followed by Mt. 14:22-23) records the following dramatic sequence:

i. Jesus compelled (ἠνάγκασεν) his disciples to get into the boat (Mk. 6:45--ἐμβῆναι εἰς τὸ πλοῖον; Jn. 6:17--ἐμβάντες εἰς πλοῖον) and set out for the other side (v. 45a).
ii. Jesus farewelled (ἀποταξάμενος--v. 46) and dismissed (ἀπολύει--v. 45) the crowd.
iii. Jesus went up to the mountain (τὸ ὄρος--v. 46; see also Jn. 6:15) to pray (προσεύξασθαι).

While Mark has many details not found in John, a basic sequence is implied by the presence in both accounts of τὸ ὄρος, the embarkation and his walking upon the sea (Mk. 6:48--περιπατῶν ἐπὶ τῆς θαλάσσης; Jn. 6:19--περιπατοῦντα ἐπὶ τῆς θαλάσσης). The dramatic sequence in Mark 6:45-46 appears not to be redactionally motivated, either theologically or verbally. In terms of the theological purpose of the passage the details appear to be entirely gratuitous and for this reason we suggest that the story is historically based. John's omission of the more dramatic elements suggests that he was not deriving his tradition from Mark, especially when we note, for example, Matthew's almost complete reproduction of the Markan material.

Mark has narrated Jesus' enforced embarkation of the disciples, his dismissal of the crowd and his own withdrawal to the mountain for prayer but without stating why the Feeding of the Multitude should have finished so abruptly. Apparently something occurred between πεντακισχίλιοι ἄνδρες (v. 44) and καὶ εὐθύς (v. 45) about which the text is silent. The critical missing detail, surely, is to be found in John's account: Ἰησοῦς...γνοὺς ὅτι μέλλουσιν ἔρχεσθαι καὶ ἁρπάζειν αὐτὸν ἵνα ποιήσωσιν βασιλέα ἀνεχώρησεν (v. 15). The crowd's attempt to force the kingship upon Jesus, it seems, provoked his rapid termination of the occasion./19/ Conceivably the action of the Galilean men ἁρπάζειν αὐτὸν...βασιλέα was viewed with displeasure, consistent with his opinion expressed elsewhere in the enigmatic ἡ βασιλεία...βιάζεται καὶ βιασταὶ ἁρπάζουσιν αὐτήν (Mt. 11:12)./20/ Perhaps, too, he regarded the twelve as having shared the crowd's messianic expectation and indeed of having contributed to it during their preaching tour to the towns of Galilee; hence his peremptory despatch of their boat across the sea. His own withdrawal to the mountains to pray may perhaps be understood as reflecting the pressure he felt (by Satanic temptation?/21/) to fulfil his mission as a military-messiah.

John's failure to include the dramatic circumstances by

which Jesus terminated the gathering and, more significantly, his innocent, unmotivated inclusion of the crowd's attempt to impose the kingship is strong evidence that, at this point at least, the Fourth Evangelist is not derived from Mark or a common source but is depending upon a separate and independent tradition.

2. Verbal Differences

In this section we concentrate on differences in those parts of the respective accounts which are clearly parallel.

a. When describing Jesus' sighting of the multitude Mark writes εἶδεν (v. 34; followed by Matthew) whereas John has ἐπάρας... τοὺς ὀφθαλμοὺς ὁ Ἰησοῦς καὶ θεασάμενος (v. 5), which is well explained redactionally as a phrase the Fourth Evangelist uses elsewhere (4:35, 17:1).

b. For Mark's ἄρτους and ἰχθύας (v. 38; followed by Matthew and Luke) John has ἄρτους κριθίνους and ὀψάρια which were brought by the παιδάριον. While ἄρτους, κριθίνους and παιδάριον may have been influenced by 4 Kgs. 4:42 and 12 (LXX), the chapter which recounts the provision of twenty barley loaves for one hundred persons (4 Kgs. 4:42-44), and ὀψάριον is found only in the Fourth Gospel (6:9,11; 21:9,10,13), there is no good reason to believe that the Evangelist by his use of these words is re-wording or re-working Mark's vocabulary. It is more likely either that these words were embedded in the tradition or that they represent the author's re-wording of that tradition./22/

The remaining differences are unremarkable word variations which convey an impression of John's innocent unawareness of the text of Mark.

c. Mark has ἀνακλῖναι (v. 39) whereas John has ἀναπεσεῖν (v. 10).

d. In Mark Jesus takes πέντε (v. 41; followed by Matthew and Luke) loaves whereas John only has the ἄρτους (v. 11).

e. For Mark's εὐλόγησεν (v. 41; followed by Matthew and Luke) John has εὐχαριστήσας.

f. For the satisfaction of the people Mark uses ἐχορτάσθησαν (v. 42; followed by Matthew and Luke); John, ἐνεπλήσθησαν (v. 12).

g. For Mark's ἦραν κλάσματα (v. 43; followed by Matthew; Luke has ἤρθη) John has ἐγέμισαν δώδεκα κοφίνους (v. 13).

At these points where Mark is not followed by John, he is

depended upon by Matthew (in every case) and by Luke (in every case except one). While ἐπάρας, ἄρτους κριθίνους, παιδάριον and ὀψάρια may perhaps (but not necessarily) be explained on redactional grounds, the most probable conclusion for the remainder of the examples is that, unlike Matthew and Luke, John has not depended upon Mark's text.

III. Relationship between Mark 6:30-44 and John 6:1-15

In view of the foregoing examination let us now consider the four main possible explanations which might account for the similarities and differences between the two texts.

1. John's Dependence on the Text of Mark (and of the other Synoptists)/23/

The factors in favour of this model are the agreement of arithmetical details, the dozen or so common words which could point to dependence and the narrative agreement. Against this theory we note that apart from the statistics there is no phrase or sentence of Mark found in John (unlike Matthew and Luke where extensive copying appears to have occurred). Similarly on most occasions where John specifically differs verbally from Mark there is no obvious redactional reason. On every such occasion Mark is followed by Matthew and, in every case except one, by Luke.

The most telling consideration against Johannine dependence is his inclusion of the critical kingship bid, which is apparently underived and whose inclusion cannot satisfactorily be explained logically on redactional grounds. We contend that this detail arose out of the incident as it occurred.

2. John's and Mark's Dependence on a Common Source/24/

This is, at first sight, an attractive explanation since it appears to account for the phenomenon of similarities and differences. Thus the similarities are due to Mark's and John's dependence on a commonly held tradition, which logically would have been fairly simple and unembellished. The differences, on this theory, would be due to the redactional activities of the respective evangelists. The great difficulty with this is to explain why the authors should introduce such gratuitous details as for example in the frenetically described introduction and the abrupt ending of Mark's version or the kingship incident in John's account. In the final analysis this model is the least satisfactory.

3. John's Knowledge of but Independence from Mark/25/

Fundamental to this theory are the twin beliefs that Mark and John arose in independent circles and that the Gospel of John was written later than and knew of the Gospel of Mark. This view does not demand Mark to have been John's sole source; indeed it is likely that he knew and depended more directly upon other sources. Apart from the necessity, as yet unproven, that Mark was written earlier than and known to John,/26/ the problem with this theory is to isolate critically which parts of Mark were influential upon the Fourth Evangelist. In fact, the text of John appears to be coherent and complete, derived from and dependent upon its own tradition with little trace of derivation from the Gospel of Mark./27/

4. John's and Mark's Dependence on Independent, Separate Traditions/28/

The strength of this proposition lies in the significant differences of narrative detail and of vocabulary between the two passages, as previously discussed. While some divergences can be accounted for as due to the editorial activities of the Evangelists, most are not. Given the nature and extent of the dissimilarities, direct textual dependence, distant recollection, or derivation from a common source appear unlikely.

But what of the similarities--of statistics, of the overall narrative and, less impressively, of vocabulary? How would the independence hypothesis explain these? Statistics, it is submitted, perennially create interest and are easy to remember. The broad outline of the story--the separate journey to an isolated place, the lack of provisions, the Lord's thanksgiving for a tiny amount of food, the miraculous satiation of the multitude seated on the ground and the oversupply of the food--is striking and not difficult to recall. The range of words needed for the story is not large and this would explain the dozen or so words in common for which comment is warranted. It is held, therefore, that the phenomenon is consistent with the theory that the two texts as we have them arose out of separate and independent traditions.

Further, it can be argued that many of the distinctive details in the respective versions, being vivid in character, could be accounted for as arising from eyewitness recollection. Mark narrates/29/ the (implied) fatigue of the disciples, the need for privacy and rest, the running Galileans, details which all drop out of Matthew and Luke. Such detail is thoroughly concrete and yet uncontrived. So too is the memorable συμπόσια συμπόσια ἐπὶ τῷ χλωρῷ χόρτῳ/30/ and Jesus' abrupt termination of the proceedings--the ἠνάγκασεν, the ἀπολύει, the ἀποταξάμενος. John's account, though less obviously resting on recollection nevertheless also contains vivid details, for example, the χόρτος πολύς and the μέλλουσιν ἔρχεσθαι...ἁρπάζειν.

Thus while there is, as we shall see, evidence of editorializing by each author, many of the details are gratuitous, unrelated to the writer's redactional interests. Each text, as it stands, contains raw tradition. As one compares the texts of Mark and John one is left with the impression that each author is innocently unaware of the other, but shaping and working up a tradition which has come to him separately./31/

IV. Two Texts: Two Contexts

It remains to examine, briefly, the redactional interests of both authors and to propose a hypothetical context for each.

1. *Mark*

Three major redactional interests may be discerned in Mark 6:30-46, two of them positive, one negative.

a. Mark presents Jesus as the compassionate shepherd who teaches and feeds his people (vv. 34,41-42) in the wilderness/32/ in fulfilment of two Old Testament texts (Num. 27:15-17; Ezek. 34:5,23) in which Jesus could be seen, respectively, as the new Moses and the new David./33/

b. Mark appears to emphasise the role of the disciples as the representatives of Jesus' ministry. In Mark, unlike John, Jesus provided the food but the disciples distributed to the people (v. 41), having taken initiative for their feeding (vv. 35-36). This is in line with the important ministry role the disciples have in Mark's Gospel. Jesus appointed the twelve to be with him and to be sent out to preach and to have authority to cast out demons (3:14-15) and, immediately before the Feeding of the Multitude, to have done these things throughout Galilee (6:7,12-13,30). Their distribution of the food provided by Jesus could be a further example of the role, given by Jesus, to minister to the people as representatives in extension of his ministry./34/

c. Mark's omission of the critical cause which abruptly

terminated the wilderness feeding, namely the attempt to foist the kingship on Jesus, as recorded in John 6:14-15, may reflect a Gentile setting for this gospel. From the time of the crisis in Alexandria (A.D. 38-41) we know that Claudius was deeply concerned over civil unrest precipitated by problems with the Jews and among the Jews. In A.D. 41 Claudius referred to them as 'fomentors of what is a general plague of the whole world' (οἰκουμένη)./35/ In A.D. 49 he expelled the Jews from Rome 'because they were persistently rioting at the instigation of Chrestus'/36/, that is, over Jewish messianism in Rome./37/ It is possible that the nervousness of the politarchs in Thessalonica in A.D. 50 over the Jews, Paul, Silas and Timothy as 'men who turned the world upside down (τὴν οἰκουμένην ἀποστατώσαντες)' and who said there was 'another king (βασιλέα ἕτερον)' was in relationship to Claudius' strong policies directed towards the Jewish problems in the Empire (Acts 17:6-8; cf. v. 3)./38/ Mark's omission of the kingship incident may point to the Gospel having been written during the delicate period of Claudius' principate (A.D. 41-54)./39/ In Nero's time, however, the Christians were evidently recognised as distinct and separate from the Jews since they were able to be seized by the Emperor as scapegoats for the great fire of A.D. 64./40/ While it would be unwise to set the date of writing Mark too specifically it is possible that the absence of the kingship bid, a spectacular redactional omission, may be a pointer to locating the Gospel of Mark within or shortly after Claudius' principate. That this gospel was written in the period between the expulsion of the Jews from Rome in A.D. 49 and Nero's assault on the Christians in A.D. 64 is an attractive hypothesis.

2. John

John's narrative is dominated by the magnitude of the σημεῖον (vv.2,14) indicating as it does the greatness of Jesus in relation to Moses (vv. 31-32). We note such evocative references to τὸ ὄρος (v.3), τὸ πάσχα (v.4), ἄρτους (v.9) and ὁ προφήτης ὁ ἐρχόμενος (v.14). In contrast with the disciples' sense of helplessness (vv. 7-9) Jesus knew what he was about to do (v.6), took the initiative (v.10) and himself distributed as much food as the 5000 men wanted (v.11) and with generous over-supply (v. 13).

In the discourse which follows Jesus declares himself to be the 'bread of life' (v. 35), 'the true bread from heaven,' given by 'my Father' (v. 32). Those who recognised him as the Mosaic Prophet and who attempted to force the kingship upon him merely ate of the loaves; they did not in fact see a 'sign' (v. 30; cf. v. 26).

John's redactional interest, as set out above, may reflect a Palestinian setting during A.D. 40-70 for the writing of his gospel./41/ In the critical and deteriorating period between the death of Agrippa (A.D. 44) and the destruction of the temple (A.D. 70) Josephus records the activities of a number of self-styled prophets who were followed by large numbers of Jews usually to some location which evoked memories of the Exodus-Conquest and where an attempt was made to perform σημεῖα./42/

During Fadus' procuratorship (A.D. 44-46) Theudas attempted to part the Jordan River (*AJ* XX, 97-98). In Felix's incumbency (A.D. 52-60) certain (prophetic?) figures led the multitudes to the ἐρημία where they promised God would give them σημεῖα ἐλευθερίας (*BJ* II, 258). An Egyptian προφήτης led his followers from the ἐρημία to the Mount of Olives where, he claimed, the walls of Jerusalem would collapse at his command for him to establish himself as τοῦ δήμου τυραννεῖν (*AJ* XX, 169-71; *BJ* II, 261-63; Acts 21:38). In Festus' time (A.D. 60-62?) people followed a prophet (?) to the ἐρημία having been promised σωτηρίαν...καὶ παῦλαν κακῶν (*AJ* XX, 188). In A.D. 70 when the temple was on fire a ψευδοπροφήτης promised the people τὰ σημεῖα τῆς σωτηρίας (*BJ* VI, 284-86).

Many scholars have shown how the activities of these prophetic figures call to mind the Exodus-Conquest epoch in Jewish history./43/ M. Hengel has drawn attention to a midrash in Mek. Exodus 14:15 where the people believe and follow Moses as referring to 'the way in which these apocalyptic prophets faithfully interpreted the second eschatological exodus along the lines of the first'./44/ Josephus' description of the crowds 'following after' such prophets corresponds with this midrash.

Although John does not refer specifically to these prophets, it is evident that they are on view in Matthew's Gospel. A comparison of Mark's and Matthew's apocalyptic discourse indicates that Matthew has introduced the warnings: 'many false prophets will arise and lead many astray. And because wickedness is multiplied, most men's love will grow cold' (Mt. 24:11), and 'so if they say to you "Lo he is in the wilderness" do not go out. . . .' (Mt. 24:26). It is likely that these ψευδοπροφῆται, whom we identify with those described by Josephus, were creating urgent problems for Matthew's readers. Why else would he write that 'most men's love will grow cold' and 'do not go out'?

John's unusual use of his keyword σημεῖον may indicate that he has this Palestinian setting in mind. Σημεῖον is rarely used for 'miracle' in classical Greek, the LXX (that is on its own as separate from τέρας) or Philo./45/ While Josephus' use of σημεῖον for 'miracle' is rare it is noteworthy that he does use the word in this connection with the apocalyptic ψευδοπροφῆται of A.D. 40-70 whom, apparently, he specifically contrasts with God's true prophet, Moses./46/ With the sea ahead and the pursuing Egyptians behind, the Israelites turned to Moses 'forgetful of those *miracles* (σημεῖα) wrought by God in token of their *liberation* (ἐλευθερία) insomuch that the words of the *prophet* (προφήτης) who cheered them and promised them *salvation* (σωτηρία) were met with incredulity' (*AJ* II, 327). Josephus' rare use of σημεῖον for miracle is used here, we suggest, to establish a backdrop against which the ψευδοπροφῆται of Josephus' day can be seen for what they are--charlatans and deceivers.

The Synoptic Evangelists do not use σημεῖον for a miracle of Jesus but chiefly for a 'portent' sought by the Pharisees (e.g. Mk. 8:11) or by his own disciples (e.g. Mk. 13:4)./47/ Δύναμις is the word for a 'miracle' of Jesus favoured by the Synoptists. John, however, continually and exclusively uses σημεῖον for a miracle of Jesus, and this is all the more noteworthy in that this usage occurs almost entirely in the evangelist's narrative and not on the lips of Jesus. The critical place of the word is seen in the author's statement of the purpose of the 'book' he has 'written' which is to set forth the σημεῖα of Jesus so that the readers will 'believe that he is the Christ, the Son of God' (Jn. 20:30-31). Earlier the evangelist numbered the 'first,' then the 'second,' of these σημεῖα (2:11, 4:54) which suggests that the reader will continue to notice these striking works and believe in the one who performed them.

While the Fourth Evangelist does not refer directly to these sign-prophets his gospel could have been written, in part at least, with them in mind./48/ John lets his readers know that Jesus is twice recognised as 'the prophet' (6:14, 7:40)/49/ and yet to be greater by far than that figure (e.g. 1:1, 1:49-51, 3:12-14, etc.). Unlike these prophets who presented themselves as a new Moses or a new Joshua but whose promised 'signs' failed to materialize, Jesus effortlessly performed the great σημεῖον of the loaves whereby he fed 5000 men at a mountain in the time of Passover./50/

V. Conclusion

Our conclusion is that the two accounts of the Feeding of the Multitude were, and had been throughout their pre-histories, separate, with each resting in all probability on independent eyewitness recollection. It was, after all, a great miracle and one which created its own testimony with commonly held details relating to numbers of men, amounts of food and grassiness of the place. Such details, especially the statistics, are likely to have been remembered. What we have in Mark and John are two idiosyncratically described accounts of that testimony, which have reached their present form on account of, on the one hand a Gentile, and on the other a Jewish, setting. The major implication is that although the stories have been subjected to editorial redaction in ways which have been mentioned, the underlying traditions are independent, thus enhancing the probable historicity of the incident./51/

Notes

/1/ D. M. Smith, 'The Sources of the Gospel of John: An Assessment of the Present State of the Problem,' *NTS* 10 (1963-64) 349.
/2/ Idem, 'John and the Synoptics: Some Dimensions of the Problem' *NTS* 26 (1980) 426.
/3/ F. Neirynck, 'John and the Synoptics,' in *L'Évangile de Jean: Sources, rédaction, théologie*, ed. M. de Jonge (Leuven: University Press, 1977) 73-106.
/4/ C. K. Barrett, *The Gospel according to St. John* (London: SPCK, 1978[2]).
/5/ See L. Morris, 'The Relationship of the Fourth Gospel to the Synoptics,' in *Studies in the Fourth Gospel* (Exeter: Paternoster, 1969) 15-63.
/6/ For study of other test cases see, e.g., R. Fortna, 'Jesus and Peter at the High Priest's House: A Test Case for the Question of the Relation between Mark's and John's Gospels,' *NTS* 24 (1978) 371-83; B. Lindars, 'John and the Synoptic Gospels: A Test Case,' *NTS* 27 (1981) 287-94.
/7/ For a comparative chart setting out the Johannine and the two Synoptic 'multiplications' see R. E. Brown, *The Gospel according to John*, vol. 1 (Garden City: Doubleday, 1966) 240-43.
/8/ The synoptic relationships can be seen at a glance in A. Barr, *A Diagram of Synoptic Relationships* (Edinburgh: T & T Clark, 1938).
/9/ By mentioning the destination as Bethsaida, Luke 9:10 implies that it is the Sea of Galilee.

/10/ See also Mk. 6:46 where Jesus withdraws to a *mountain* to pray.
/11/ *Contra* S. Masuda, 'The Good News of the Miracle of the Bread,' *NTS* 28 (1982) 191-219, who argues on syntactical grounds that the material is Markan not traditional.
/12/ See also 6:23 and 11:41.
/13/ Except in quotation as in Jn. 12:13.
/14/ See Masuda, 'Good News,' 204, where Mark's words are treated as redactional.
/15/ On Jewish scruples about collecting uneaten food, see R. Bultmann, *The Gospel of John: A Commentary* (Oxford: Blackwell, 1971) 213, n. 3.
/16/ The problem of the virtual identification was recognised and commented on in T. F. Glasson, *Moses in the Fourth Gospel* (London: SCM, 1963) 29. It may be significant that in the anthology of texts found in cave 4 (*4QTest.*) Deut. 18:18-19 ('a prophet like Moses') and Num. 24:15-17 ('a ruler out of Zion') were side by side.
/17/ See further Bultmann, *John*, 213, and for a specialist treatment W. Meeks, *The Prophet-King* (Leiden: Brill, 1967) e.g. 99.
/18/ For the considerable literature on 'the prophet' see e.g. H. Teeple, *The Mosaic Eschatological Prophet* (Philadelphia: SBL, 1957); U. Mauser, *Christ in the Wilderness* (London: SCM, 1963); R. H. Smith, 'Exodus Typology in the Fourth Gospel,' *JBL* 81 (1962) 329-42; *TDNT* IV, 861.
/19/ See H. W. Montefiore, 'Revolt in the Desert?' *NTS* 8 (1961-62) 135-41; H. G. Wood, 'Interpreting this Time,' *NTS* 2 (1956) 262-66.
/20/ See P. W. Barnett, 'Who Were the ΒΙΑΣΤΑΙ? (Matthew 11:12-13)' *RTR* 36 (1977) 65-70.
/21/ Mk. 1:12, 8:33 and synoptic parallels.
/22/ Cf. Bultmann, *John*, 210.
/23/ This was 'the dominant view' until W.W. II (D.M. Smith, 'John & the Synoptics,' 425. C. K. Barrett, 'John and the Synoptic Gospels,' *ExpTim* 85 (1974) 228-33, lists those who have more recently advocated John's dependence on Mark.
/24/ See the interchange: E. R. Goodenough, 'John: A Primitive Gospel,' *JBL* 64 (1945) 145-82; and R. P. Casey, 'Professor Goodenough and the Fourth Gospel,' *JBL* 64 (1945) 535-42; and E. R. Goodenough, 'A Reply,' *JBL* 64 (1945) 543-44.
/25/ According to Barrett, 'John and the Synoptic Gospels,' 231, 'Gardner-Smith, Morris,. . .mean. . .that Mark was not a major source of John, or a determining factor in the writing of the gospel. But this is all they can mean; they cannot mean that John had not read Mark. . .' D. M. Smith, 'John and the

Synoptics,' 443, writes: 'I am beginning to be able to conceive of a scenario in which John knew, or knew of, the synoptics and yet produced so dissimilar a gospel as the one which now follows them in the New Testament.'

/26/ Those who advocate an early dating for the Fourth Gospel include F. L. Cribbs, 'Reassessment of the Date of Origin and the Destination of the Gospel of John,' *JBL* 89 (1970) 38-55; and J. A. T. Robinson, *Redating the New Testament* (London: SCM, 1976) 254-311. See also B. Lindars, *The Gospel of John* (London: Oliphants, 1972) 237: 'John's source represents an earlier stage in the history of the transmission of the sequence than John.'

/27/ For a variation of this theory see Fortna, 'Jesus and Peter,' 379, who comments, with respect to the incident about Jesus and Peter at the high priest's house, that 'John is somehow in contact with Mark's tradition but has no knowledge of, or certainly makes no use of Canonical Mark.'

/28/ Though a lone voice pre-war, P. Gardner-Smith, *Saint John and the Synoptic Gospels* (Cambridge: University Press, 1938) 33, wrote: 'a close study of the four gospels suggests that John knew a popular story. . .but there is no evidence to prove that he had read it in Mark or Luke and considerable reason for concluding that he had not.' The most notable convert to Gardner-Smith's position was C. H. Dodd, *Historical Tradition in the Fourth Gospel* (Cambridge: University Press, 1963), whose advocacy of Johannine independence has been highly influential (See Barrett, 'John and the Synoptic Gospels,' 229). For an extended review of Dodd's work, consult D. A. Carson, 'Historical Tradition in the Fourth Gospel: After Dodd, What?' in *Gospel Perspectives*, vol. 2, ed. R. T. France and D. Wenham (Sheffield: JSOT, 1981) 83-145.

/29/ For examples of and argument for vivid detail in the Gospel of Mark, see T. W. Manson, *Studies in the Gospels and Epistles* (Manchester: University Press, 1962) 29-45.

/30/ However, S. Masuda, 'Good News,' 195, rejects this as redactional, but for syntactical reasons, quite apart from the question of historical probability.

/31/ For a brief study devoted to this incident, see E. D. Johnston, 'The Johannine Version of the Feeding of the Five Thousand--An Independent Tradition?' *NTS* 8 (1961) 151-54.

/32/ R. W. Funk, 'The Wilderness,' *JBL* 78 (1959) 213, argues that ὁ ἔρημος τόπος means no more than 'the country' in contrast to 'the town'.

/33/ So Masuda, 'Good News,' 209.

/34/ Masuda's view (ibid.) that this really refers to the disciples' eucharistic ministry is speculative. There is at least one example in the New Testament where λαβὼν ἄρτον εὐχαρίστησεν τῷ θεῷ...καὶ κλάσας is unlikely to refer to the eucharist, namely Paul's feeding of the pagan crew of the storm-beset ship (Acts 27:35)! Since it is clear Luke is describing a Jewish-style thanksgiving for food we suppose that the synoptic multiplications in Mark 6 and 8 need not necessarily have eucharistic overtones.

/35/ 'Claudius' letter to the Alexandrians,' in N. Lewis and M. Reinhold, *Roman Civilization*, vol. 2 (New York: Harper, 1966) 366-69.

/36/ Suetonius, *Claudius* XXV, 4. Against the view that Suetonius is referring to Jesus, see E. A. Judge and G. S. R. Thomas, 'The Origin of the Church in Rome,' *RTR* 25 (1966) 81-94.

/37/ See further, W. Wieful, 'The Jewish Community in Ancient Rome...,' in *The Romans Debate*, ed. K. P. Donfried (Minneapolis: Augsburg, 1977) 100-19; and R. Penna, 'Les Juifs à Rome au temps de l'Apôtre Paul,' *NTS* 28 (1982) 321-47.

/38/ See further E. A. Judge, 'The Decrees of Caesar at Thessalonika,' *RTR* 30 (1971) 1-7; and idem, 'St. Paul and Classical Society,' *Jahrbuch für Antike und Christentum* 15 (1972) 19-36.

/39/ F. F. Bruce, 'The Date and Character of Mark,' in *Jesus and the Politics of His Day*, ed. E. Bammel and C. F. D. Moule (Cambridge: University Press, 1984) 69-89, argues, on different grounds, for a similar time-frame.

/40/ So J. Munck, *The Acts of the Apostles* (Garden City: Doubleday, 1967) 232.

/41/ Cribbs, 'Reassessment,' argues for a Palestinian setting for the writing of the Fourth Gospel.

/42/ For a general discussion see P. W. Barnett, 'The Jewish Sign Prophets AD 40-70: Their Intentions and Origin,' *NTS* 27 (1981) 679-97; and for an opposing viewpoint, R. A. Horsley, '"Like One of the Prophets of Old": Two Types of Popular Prophets at the Time of Jesus,' *CBQ* 47 (1985) 435-63.

/43/ See n. 18.

/44/ M. Hengel, *The Charismatic Leader and His Followers* (Edinburgh: T & T Clark, 1981) 21.

/45/ See *TDNT* VII, 202-25.

/46/ See the following for references to σημεῖον: *BJ* I, 28; II, 259,579; III, 88,105,404; VI, 285; VII, 438; *AJ* I, 59; II, 274,276,280,283,284,327; V, 12; VI, 57; VIII, 347; X, 28,29, 234; XII, 404; XVIII, 61,211; XIX, 9; XX, 167-68; *Vita* 322. Note that all the references to σημεῖον in *AJ* II refer to Moses.

/47/ Brown, *John*, vol. 1, 'Appendix III: Signs and Works,' 525-32.

/48/ W. Nicol, *The Sēmeia in the Fourth Gospel* (Leiden: Brill,

1972) 84, argues that 'the Jews. . .had many ideas about a (final) prophet authenticated by signs' and that this has conditioned the emphasis on σημεῖα in S, the Signs-Source underlying John. But it could equally be argued that the Fourth Evangelist is not responding to current ideas so much as the activities of the sign-prophets.

/49/ G. Vermes, *Jesus the Jew* (London: Collins, 1973) suggests that there was a primitive 'prophet-christology' among the earliest Christians (as in Acts 3:22, 7:37) but which dropped out of Christian theology due to the rise of Jewish Sign-Prophets in the forties.

/50/ Early Christian preaching, healing and exorcism stimulated imitation, as for example by the sons of Sceva of Paul (Acts 19:11-14) and Simon of Philip and Peter (Acts 8 :9-19). It is possible that Philip's activities and eschatological proclamation served as a catalyst for the Samaritan prophet who promised to locate the missing temple vessels on Mt. Gerizim (*AJ* XVIII, 85-87). Certainly the miracles of Christ were known in Palestine (Acts 2:22, 10:36-38; cf. 24:22, 26:26) and may have provided an impulse for the rise of the Sign-Prophets. See further Barnett, 'Sign Prophets,' 689-93.

/51/ See e.g. Lindars, *John*, 238, who comments: 'concerning the historicity of the feeding miracle, the account is so well attested that there is no need to doubt that a real incident lies behind it.'

'THE DEAD ARE RESTORED TO LIFE': MIRACLES OF REVIVIFICATION IN THE GOSPELS

Murray J. Harris
Tyndale House
36 Selwyn Gardens
Cambridge
CB3 9BA

There are probably no lines anywhere in Greek literature that more aptly epitomise the prevailing Greek attitude towards resurrection than in the *Eumenides* of Aeschylus (647-8), where, on the occasion of the founding of the court of the Areopagus in Athens, the god Apollo observes 'Once a man is slain and the dust has drunk up his blood, there is no coming back to life (ἀνάστασις)'. Yet the Gospels relate three occasions on which Jesus is said to have restored a dead person to life, and Luke could sum up the message of Paul to the Athenians as being 'Jesus and the resurrection (ἀνάστασις)' (Acts 17:18). It is our purpose here to examine the literary setting of these three stories, to analyse them exegetically, and then to discuss their historicity and theological significance.

I THE WIDOW OF NAIN'S SON (Luke 7:11-17)

After describing the birth and childhood of Jesus and the inauguration of his messianic mission, the third Evangelist deals with the Galilean ministry of Jesus (4:14 - 9:50), concentrating particularly on the deeds of the Messiah./1/ The account of the raising of the widow of Nain's son falls within a non-Markan section (Lk 6:12 - 7:50) which elucidates the distinctive character of the Messiah's mission. By including this incident (part of his special source) Luke shows that death (7:11-17), as well as disease (7:1-10), is subject to the Messiah's power: he not only heals the sick but also raises the dead. His mission involves emancipation from the tyranny of death rather than that of Rome. Also the story forms a necessary introduction to 7:18-35 which discusses the distinctive roles of John the Baptist and Jesus, for one aspect of Jesus' distinctive ministry as the Isaianic Servant of

Yahweh was that through him 'the dead are restored to life' (7:22; *cf.* Is. 26:19), which was aptly illustrated by the occurrence at Nain.

A. The Circumstances of the Miracle (Lk 7:11-13)

Soon after healing the centurion's servant at Capernaum, Jesus travelled to Nain, a small village six miles SW of Nazareth, accompanied by his disciples and a large crowd. Near the town gate (πύλη, perhaps here indicating 'the place where the road entered between the houses of Nain' /2/) this procession met another procession, a funeral cortège that was just emerging from the town to bury a young man (νεανίσκος) at a burial-site outside the city. First came the widowed mother along with other women relatives and friends, then the bier on which the dead man was lying, probably with his face uncovered, and finally male relatives and friends, the hired mourners and musicians, and 'a considerable throng of people from the town' (v.12)/3/. Jesus was filled with pity for the mother, recognising or learning that to a widow's loneliness was now added a mother's grief at the premature death of an only child. Once Jesus had told the mother to stop weeping (μὴ κλαῖε, v.13) and had moved forward to halt the procession by touching the bier, the noise of movement and of mourning would have subsided.

In Luke's sketch of the circumstances leading up to the miracle, five points are particularly noteworthy. First, Luke means his readers to regard the concurrence of the two processions at the entrance to the town, not as a happy coincidence but as a divinely designed event. The prince of life confronts a victim of death. Secondly, each procession was composed of a sizeable throng (ὄχλος πολύς, v.11; ὄχλος ... ἱκανός, v.12), who were all to become witnesses of the miracle, both visually and verbally (ἔλαβεν δὲ φόβος πάντας, v.16; καὶ ἐξῆλθεν ὁ λόγος οὗτος, v.17). Thirdly, the four successive uses of αὐτή in vv.12-13 (σὺν αὐτῇ ... ἰδὼν αὐτὴν ... ἐπ' αὐτῇ ... αὐτῇ) focus attention on the plight of the widow, deprived of an only son, and possibly, with his death, of one means of support. Fourthly, the action of Jesus is presented as totally unsolicited. He was not responding to faith shown by the mother or by the dead man's friends, nor to a request for help. Indeed, in normal circumstances his procession would be expected to fall in with the funeral procession. But instead, Jesus takes the initiative, moved with compassion for the widow. Fifthly, there can be no doubt that Luke believed the young man to be dead. Even if we translate v.12a 'there was being carried out dead the only son of a woman who was a widow', τεθνηκώς cannot refer to someone who is comatose or is feigning death, since this would require ὡς (or ὡσάν) τεθνηκώς and v. 15 describes him as ὁ νεκρός.

B. The Performance of the Miracle (Lk 7:14)

Whereas the centurion's servant at Capernaum had been healed at a distance (Lk 7:7,10), in this case Jesus not only went right up to the bier (προσελθών being a prelude to messianic action) but actually touched it and thereby became ritually unclean (Num 19:11,22). His purpose in touching the bier was not to effect the miracle /4/ - that did not happen until the word of command was spoken - but to halt the procession and (probably) indicate to the bearers of the bier that they should set it down. There is no indication that Jesus touched the body or took the dead man's hand (*cf.* Lk 8:54). It was merely by the spoken word that the miracle occurred: 'Young man, get up, I tell you.'

This revival of a dead person is portrayed as effortless. The way is prepared for the display of the potency of 'the word of the Lord' by which the heavens were made (Ps 33:6) by the use of ὁ κύριος in v. 13./5/ Since Luke's account of this miracle at Nain has several clear reminiscences of Elijah's miracle at Zarephath (see below), we should not rule out the possibility that Luke intended a contrast to be drawn between Elijah's expenditure of physical and spiritual effort in performing the miracle and the sublime effortlessness of the new Elijah in performing his. 'Then he [Elijah] stretched himself out upon the child three times, and cried to the Lord [?three times], "O Lord my God, let the breath of life return to this child's body"'(1 Kgs 17:21). Another remarkable feature of the story is that the dominical command is addressed to a corpse. It was not a case of prayer addressed to God on behalf of the dead person (as in 1 Kgs 17:20-22), but just as God 'gives life to the dead and commands the things that do not exist as if they did'(Rom 4:17), so too does 'the Lord' (v. 13).

C. The Outcome of the Miracle (Lk 7:15-17)

By noting that the son sat up and began to speak (v. 15a) Luke indicates that he was fully restored to life, movement and speech being indicators of physical and mental alertness. The cause of death was not specified but it is clearly implied that the miracle involved restoration to health as well as to life. 'He gave him back to his mother' (v. 15b), which alludes to 1 Kings 17:23, must mean that Jesus presented to the mother the young man, alive and well and (presumably) now standing upright.

Verse 16 notes the two effects of the miracle on all the bystanders (including the mother), that is, the sizeable crowd of each procession (vv. 11-12) who had by now doubtless intermingled. 'Everyone was awe-struck' (TCNT). The term φόβος ('awe') here denotes not only the people's natural reaction to an event that was unprecedented in their experience but also their recognition that supernatural power had been displayed in the revivification. All were overcome with awe because they had witnessed a τέρας ('marvel') and a δύναμις ('mighty act'). Their second reaction was to glorify God with the words 'A great prophet has arisen among us', and again,'God has visited his people'. Each statement must be understood in the light of the other. The people hailed Jesus not simply as a prophet or even a 'great prophet', but as a great prophet by whom God had intervened to bring salvation (ἐπεσκέψατο ὁ θεός) to his people. Given the allusions to Elijah found in the story (see below), it seems likely that for Luke, as for the people, the main reference is to a prophet like Elijah./6/ But because God had 'visited' the nation of Israel also through Moses, their 'ruler and deliverer' (Acts 7:35) who was 'mighty in his words and deeds' (Acts 7:22), we should not exclude a reference here to the prophet like Moses of the end time (Deut 18:15-18), especially since Luke later records the description of Jesus as 'a prophet mighty in deed and word' (Lk 24:19). Similarly, the immediate context (Lk. 7:18-23) which deals with 'the deeds of the Messiah' suggests that messianic overtones were present in Luke's understanding of the crowd's acclamation./7/

Verse 17 is transitional. The report that God had visited his people by sending a great prophet who could raise the dead went abroad not only in Galilee where the miracle took place (this is implied) but also in all Judaea (here = Palestine; *cf*. Lk 4:44; 23:5) and surrounding districts - even to the prison at Machaerus in Peraea where John the Baptist was imprisoned (*cf*. Lk 3:20; Jos. *Ant*.18:112, 119). Thus the way is prepared for the following section on 'Jesus and the Baptist' (Lk 7:18-35).

D. The Historicity of the Miracle

There are several pointers to the authenticity of the miracle.

The circumstantial detail is true to fact. In Galilee, as opposed to Judaea, women walked in front of the bier./8/ It was therefore natural that Jesus, coming in the opposite direction, should speak to the mother before approaching the bier

(vv. 13-14). If the whole event were fictitious, the product of Christian imagination working, perhaps, on the Elijah-Elisha sagas, we might have expected the story to be much more widely diffused (it is peculiar to Luke), and it is remarkable on this hypothesis that the evangelist (i) has located the miracle at Nain, a small, insignificant village that is nowhere else mentioned in the Bible;/9/ and (ii) has made no reference to the *post mortem* state or whereabouts of the young man and does not have him speak at all or divulge secrets gained by his passage to the 'other side'. As an account of the instantaneous reanimation of a corpse, the pericope is remarkably restrained and unadorned; sensational detail is conspicuously absent. Such extraordinary sobriety of diction points to its authenticity. Nor should it be forgotten that this is only one of four miracles of 'raising' recorded in the Lukan writings./10/ To explain one miracle naturalistically is not to explain them all.

E. Literary Parallels of the Miracle

1. 1 Kings 17:8-24

J.D. Dubois has shown that in the third Gospel the most obvious allusions to the cycle of Elijah traditions occur in the miracle stories, the transfiguration and the ascension./11/ That there should be at least some resemblances in Luke between the miracles of Jesus and those of Elijah occasions no surprise, given the fact that both were credited with raising the dead and that Jesus alluded to the ministry of Elijah at Zarephath in his announcement of his own forthcoming public ministry (Lk 4:25-26).

How strong, in fact, are the resemblances between the story of Elijah's raising of the son of the widow of Zarephath (1 Kings 17:8-24) and Luke 7:11-17? The principal similarities are these:

(a) the incident involved an only son of a widow,/12/ who was raised from the dead (1 Kgs 17:12,13,15,22; Lk 7:12,15)

(b) the 'deadness' of the son is stressed (1 Kgs 17:17,18,20, 21; Lk 7:12,15)/13/

(c) the raised person speaks, an evidence of the return of his faculties (1 Kgs 17:22 LXX but not MT; Lk 7:15) (*cf*. 2 Kgs 4:31)/14/

(d) the revived son is given to his mother (1 Kgs 17:23; Lk 7:15)

(e) the miracle-worker is recognized as a person of exalted spiritual status (1 Kgs 17:24; Lk 7:16).

The actual verbal similarity is as follows:

	1 Kings 17 (LXX)		*Luke 7*
8,10	καὶ ἐγένετο ... ἐπορεύθη εἰς Σαρεπτά	11	καὶ ἐγένετο ... ἐπορεύθη εἰς πόλιν καλουμένην Ναΐν
10	καὶ ἐπορεύθη ... εἰς τὸν πυλῶνα τῆς πόλεως	12	ὡς δὲ ἤγγισεν τῇ πύλῃ τῆς πόλεως
10	καὶ ἰδοὺ ... χήρα	12	καὶ ἰδοὺ ... χήρα
23	καὶ ἔδωκεν αὐτὸν τῇ μητρὶ αὐτοῦ	15	καὶ ἔδωκεν αὐτὸν τῇ μητρὶ αὐτοῦ

On the other hand, there are fundamental differences in content:

(i) The miracle at Zarephath (Z) was performed in private (1 Kgs 17:19,23), the miracle at Nain (N) in public (Lk 7:11b, 12b, 16).

(ii) In Z, the raising was effected by thrice-repeated action in addition to prayer to God (1 Kgs 17:21; *cf.* 2 Kgs 4: 33-35), in N by a single command apparently unaccompanied by prayer (Lk 7:14).

(iii) The focus in Z is on the mother's plight before the miracle and her reaction after (1 Kgs 17:12,18,23-24), in N on the mother's plight before, and the crowd's reaction after, the miracle (Lk 7:12-13, 16).

(iv) Before and after Z, the widow refers to Elijah as a 'man of God' (1 Kgs 17:18,24), while after N the crowds speak of Jesus as a 'great prophet' (Lk 7:16).

(v) In Z the υἱός is also described as a παιδάριον (1 Kgs 17:21 *bis*, 22; MT, ילד, also v.23) ('little boy'), in N as a νεανίσκος (Lk 7:14) ('young man').

(vi) In Z there is no reference to crowds or followers of Elijah, the widow's weeping, Elijah's compassion, a funeral procession and imminent burial; in N no mention is made of an illness that preceded the son's death or of the widow's household.

From this comparison of the two stories we conclude that although the Elijah story seems to have influenced Luke's language in describing the miracle at Nain,/15/ the differences between the two incidents are so pronounced and significant that it would be improper to claim that Luke actually created this miracle story from the OT narrative in order to portray Jesus as a new Elijah./16/

2. *Pliny,* Natural History *26.15 (c. A.D. 80)*

In the course of describing various new diseases that were afflicting people in Europe at the time and the customary natural remedies that were being prescribed, Pliny the Elder mentions a certain Asclepiades who began a medical career after he found that his gains as a professor of rhetoric were too meagre. He became famous for his attractive and innovative methods of treatment, such as suspended beds (which, by being rocked, could either relieve diseases or induce sleep) and a system of hydropathy 'which accorded with people's greedy love of baths'. The text continues 'His reputation was no less great when, on meeting the funeral procession of a man who was not known to him, he had him taken down from the pyre and saved his life'. Pliny says he recounted this incident lest anyone should imagine that it was merely on slender grounds (*levibus momentis*) that so radical a change in public opinion about the medical profession took place (*tantam conversionem factam*) (*cf.* 26.13).

All that may be said about the thirteen relevant words (written in Pliny's terse, unadorned style: *nec minore fama, cum occurrisset ignoto funeri, relato homine ab rogo atque servato* ...) is that the circumstances of the healing (? through artificial resuscitation) are the same as in Luke 7, except that at Nain the subject was not removed from the funeral bier before the 'cure' was effected. Pliny clearly regards the remarkable incident as explaining or perhaps justifying, at least in part, the dramatic shift in public opinion about medical practice, but he gives no hint as to the means Asclepiades used to effect the cure.

In this episode we have an interesting but insignificant parallel to Luke 7. Much more impressive and important, however, is the detailed and celebrated parallel found in Philostratus.

3. *Philostratus,* Life of Apollonius of Tyana *4.45 (c. A.D. 217)*

There are three notable similarities between the stories

in Philostratus and Luke: the miracle-worker halted a funeral bier that carried a young person who had just died; crowds of mourners were accompanying the cortège to the burial; the subject's immediate speech was the indication of revival.

Much more numerous are the differences.

(a) In Philostratus (P) the person revived was a maiden (κόρη) or young lady (παῖς) who belonged to a consular family; in Luke (L), a young man (νεανίσκος) who was without siblings (an only son, μονογενὴς υἱός, 7:12).

(b) The young lady either had just been married or was on the point of being married (ἐν ὥρᾳ γάμου), with the marriage as yet unconsummated (ἀτελεῖ γάμῳ) (P). The young man was, presumably, unmarried, since mention is made only of his mother, not of his wife (L).

(c) One was only apparently dead (τεθνάναι ἐδόκει, τοῦ δοκοῦντος θανάτου) (P), the other actually dead (τεθνηκώς, 7:12; ὁ νεκρός, 7:15) (L).

(d) In one case, the crowds console the husband (P); in the other, the mother (7:12b) (L).

(e) Apollonius witnesses the crowd's grief and promises to stay their tears (P), while Jesus feels compassion for the mother and tells her to stop weeping (7:13) (L).

(f) The funeral procession stopped: when Apollonius directed the bier (κλίνη) to be set down (P); when Jesus touched the bier (σορός, 7:14; see *MM* 581 s.v.) (L).

(g) The revival was effected by: touching the maiden and whispering a secret formula over her (τι ἀφανῶς ἐπειπών) (P)/17/; addressing the dead man with an audible word of command ('get up', ἐγέρθητι, 7:14) (L).

(h) In P the actual revival is described by a transitive form, 'he woke up the maiden' (ἀφύπνισε τὴν κόρην) from her apparent sleep of death; in L by an intransitive, 'the dead man sat up' (ἀνεκάθισεν ὁ νεκρός).

(i) Upon revival the young person: herself returned to her father's house (P); was returned by Jesus to his mother (7:15) (L).

(j) In one case, the bystanders were mystified by the marvel (θαῦμα), unsure whether the young lady had simply been comatose or whether she had actually been restored to life by the warmth of Apollonius's touch (P). In the other case, the bystanders 'glorified God' (7:16) (L).

We cannot know whether this 'marvel' performed by Apollonius had been recounted in the memoirs that were compiled by his disciple and companion Damis and were used by Philostratus, although in those memoirs the wisdom and extraordinary powers of Apollonius are certainly exaggerated.

On the possible relation between the two accounts, two points may be made. First, it is highly improbable that Philostratus intended his account of Apollonius's exploit to be a direct counterblast to the miracle of Jesus at Nain. While it is true that there are a few verbal reminiscences of the Gospels scattered throughout the *Vita* of Philostratus, /18/ it seems unlikely that this particular incident is even an indirect counterblast to the Lukan account of Jesus' miracle, since Philostratus twice explicitly questions whether the maiden had actually died (τεθνάναι ἐδόκει ... τοῦ δοκοῦντος θανάτου) and neither of his explanations of the 'marvel' is supernatural: he professes (like the bystanders) to be unable to decide whether Apollonius had detected some spark of life in the maiden which had escaped the notice of her attendants or whether it was a case of the restoration of life by the warmth of his touch./19/ The miraculous or 'marvellous' element is far more pronounced in the Gospel narrative. The view, once dominant, that Philostratus aimed to portray Apollonius as a neo-Pythagorean reformer whose supernatural wisdom and powers made him a rival of Jesus, has given place to the more cautious assessment that Philostratus sought to restore the reputation of Apollonius as a divinely-inspired sage and wonder-worker against current claims that he was a charlatan guilty of sinister magical practices./20/ On this interpretation of the general aim of Philostratus, Apollonius is being portrayed in the present episode as a beneficent exorcist driving out an evil spirit by whispering into the victim's ear or over the victim's body a magical formula that included her name./21/ Secondly, the differences between the accounts are so numerous and substantial (see above) that any theory of their interdependence or their dependence on a common tradition may be discounted./22/

II THE DAUGHTER OF JAIRUS

This is the only miracle of Jesus' raising the dead that is recorded by all three synoptic Gospels. Mark's account (5:21-24, 35-43) is slightly longer than that of Luke (8:40-42, 49-56), while Matthew's report (9:18-19, 23-26) is less than half the length of Mark's. Another distinctive feature is that in each Evangelist's narrative the story of the woman with a hemorrhage is interwoven with the story of Jairus's daughter./23/

The historical setting of the miracle is not immediately obvious. According to Mark and Luke it occurred at some point after Jesus had returned to Capernaum on the western shore of the Sea of Galilee (τὸ πέραν, Mk 5:21) following the healing of the demoniac at Gerasa (Mk 5:1-21; Lk 8:26-40). In the first Gospel, however, it takes place immediately after the conversation in Matthew's house regarding Jesus' eating with sinners (Mt 9:9-13) and his disciples' failure to fast (Mt 9:14-17). No serious divergence between the accounts need be postulated, for if we assume (a) that the Gerasa/Gadara incident occurred between the calling of Matthew (Mt 9:9) and the meal held in his house (Mt 9:10-17); and (b) that all three Gospel writers have naturally associated Matthew's call and the meal in his house in topical fashion, placing them either earlier than (thus Mark and Luke) or after (thus Matthew) the Gerasa incident, the apparent difficulty disappears and Matthew's setting for the miracle can be accepted simply as being more precise than that of Mark and Luke./24/

A. *Features Common to all three Evangelists*

From the features common to all the narratives we can reconstruct the following sequence of events.

> A certain ruler approached Jesus with a request that he should come and heal his daughter. Jesus began to follow him but was delayed by an incident involving a woman suffering from a hemorrhage. On entering the ruler's house and hearing the commotion, Jesus rebuked those who were now mourning the young girl's death, and said that she was not dead but sleeping. This prompted their mockery. But he took the girl's hand and she stood up.

Some of these features are worthy of further comment.

1. *The ruler.* All the Evangelists depict him as an ἀρχών,

but while Matthew uses only this term (Mt 9:18,23) Mark introduces him as 'one of the rulers of the synagogue' (εἷς τῶν ἀρχισυναγώγων, Mk 5:22; *cf.* ὁ ἀρχισυνάγωγος, 5; [35], 36, 38) and Luke as 'the ruler of the synagogue' (ἄρχων τῆς συναγωγῆς, Lk 8:41; *cf.* ὁ ἀρχισυνάγωγος, 8:49, of his house). As such, he was both a member of the synagogue board of (usually) seven persons (Mark) and the synagogue president (Mark and Luke), the lay official responsible to the board for the actual administration of the synagogue, especially its services and its maintenance./25/ It must therefore be deemed probable that Jesus was known to this man through his participation in the synagogue services in Capernaum (Mk 1:21-22, 39), although it is unnecessary to view the ruler as one of the 'elders of the Jews' who interceded with Jesus for the centurion at Capernaum (Lk 7:3-5)./26/ Given the acknowledged dignity of the position of synagogue president (it was a special privilege to marry his daughter, Bar. b Pes. 49b), it is significant that in his hour of dire need he sought out Jesus and made his urgent request, assuming the posture of a desperate suppliant (προσεκύνει αὐτῷ, Mt 9:18).

Mark and Luke tell us that his name was Ἰάϊρος (Mk 5:22; Lk 8:41)./27/ This is a Grecized form of the Hebrew name יאיר, which means 'he [Yahweh] will enlighten' or 'May he [Yahweh] enlighten' (Num 32:41; Jos 13:30; Judg 10:3-5; Est 2:5). If the name is traced to the Hebrew יעיר, 'he will awaken', it can scarcely be a purely symbolic name in reference to Jairus himself, for in the story, as C.E.B.Cranfield observes, Jairus does not awaken anyone nor is he himself awakened by God./28/ But if 'he [Yahweh] will awaken' expresses a promise, the word of Jesus to Jairus will mean '"Be confident! Only believe" (Mk 5:36) in the promise which your name already expresses'./29/

2. *The daughter*. Each of the narratives uses the term θυγάτηρ, although Matthew (9:24,25) and Mark (8:41,42) also have κοράσιον ('girl'), while παιδίον is distinctive to Mark (5:39,40,41), παῖς to Luke (8:51,54), both words meaning '(young) child', and θυγάτριον ('little daughter' or 'young daughter') to Mark (5:23). This latter term corresponds closely to the Hebrew נערה, 'young daughter', the term used in a legal sense of a girl aged between twelve and twelve and a half years (see *SB* 2.10, 374). As a θυγάτηρ μονογενής (Lk 8:42), the girl was not merely an only daughter but the only child in the family; she was without siblings.

3. The commotion (θόρυβος). On entering the crowded house of the 'ruler of the synagogue' Jesus saw the commotion and heard a cacophony of sounds - the strident weeping and wailing of the relatives as they beat their breasts over the girl's death, the antiphonal chanting and handclapping of the professional mourners, mingled with the plaintive sound of the flutes (Mk 5:38; Mt 9:23; Lk 8:52)./30/ We do not know the length of the delay to Jesus' arrival at the house that was occasioned by his encounter with the woman with a hemorrhage or the distance he had to travel or route he chose to follow to reach the house. There is therefore insufficient reason to assert that in view of the apparent shortness of time since the girl's death the mourners were more probably members of Jairus's household than professional mourners. The action of Jesus in evicting all these noisy mourners (*cf*. Acts 9:40) was perhaps prompted by this, that those indulging in disorderly grief or simulated grief or callous scorn were not suitable witnesses of the quiet and mysterious act of raising the dead./31/

4. Death and Sleep. All three Evangelists record the enigmatic words of Jesus: οὐκ ἀπέθανεν ἀλλὰ καθεύδει. Only the Markan account leaves open the possibility that the young girl had not actually died but was in a death-like sleep (note τὸ θυγάτριόν μου ἐσχάτως ἔχει, Mk 5:23). Both Matthew and Luke leave us in no doubt that the girl had died (Mt 9:18; Lk 9:42, 53). But it is easier to suppose that Matthew and Luke have rightly understood Mark's account as referring to a restoration to life (note ἡ θυγάτηρ σου ἀπέθανεν, Mk 5:35) than that they have converted a story that illustrated Jesus' medical insight or his healing power into a narrative that described a miracle of revivification./32/ Further reasons for believing that the young girl was in fact dead will be rehearsed below (II.C).

It is true that elsewhere in the NT καθεύδειν generally denotes physical sleep, not the sleep of death, but its use in Daniel 12:2 (LXX), Ephesians 5:14 and 1 Thessalonians 5:10 /33/ shows that the metaphorical sense of the verb was not foreign to Jewish and Christian thought. In affirming that the girl was 'sleeping', Jesus was not denying the reality of death nor teaching that all death is sleep but rather was using picturesque, figurative language to indicate that, in this girl's case, death was like sleep in that it was not permanent and was to be terminated by an awakening (*cf*. Jn 11:11-14). On this view οὐκ ἀπέθανεν is ironic hyperbole and a foil for the main point that follows. Jesus is saying, in effect, 'As far as I am concerned, this young girl did not die in any final sense but is temporarily in the sleep of death'.

5. *The mockery* (καὶ κατεγέλων αὐτοῦ, 'and they started making fun of him', Mk 5:40; Mt 9:24; Lk 8:53). This outburst of scorn was triggered by Jesus' statement 'she is not dead but sleeping' which the bystanders had interpreted literally. Luke adds '(And they began to laugh at him) because they knew (εἰδότες) that she *was* dead.' But they were also jeering at Jesus' sheer folly, as they saw it, for he himself had not yet seen the girl (note Mk 5:40b); and at his presumptuous rashness in imagining that at a distance he could perceive something about the girl that had escaped the notice of the messengers and the professional mourners (viz. that she was merely in a coma). The artificiality of these mourning customs is shown by the ease and speed with which profuse tears could turn into jeering laughter.

6. *The revivification*. Each narrative notes that Jesus took the young girl's hand as a prelude to his word and act of authority (Mk 8:41; Mt 9:25; Lk 8:54). This 'taking of the hand' is reminiscent of the father's request that Jesus should lay his hands on her (Mk 5:23; Mt 9:18). It was not the means of the reanimation - the sentence does not read 'he took her hand and raised the girl up' (καὶ ἤγειρεν τὸ κοράσιον) - but in fact became the occasion of Jesus' ceremonial defilement (*cf*. Num 19:11-16). So effective was the miracle that the girl 'stood up' (ἠγέρθη, Mt 9:25; ἀνέστη, Mk 5:42; Lk 9:55) in her own strength.

B. Features Distinctive of One or More Evangelist

Some of the more significant distinctive features of each Evangelist may now be discussed.

Matthew's account appears to be an abbreviated version of Mark's. Because he omits all reference to the messengers who, according to Mark (5:35) and Luke (8:49), arrive on the scene while Jesus is still talking to the woman healed of her hemorrhage and announce the recent death of Jairus' daughter, he is obliged to have Jairus report at the outset not merely that his daughter is 'at the point of death' (Mk 5:23, where ἐσχάτως ἔχειν = *in extremis esse*) but, proleptically, that she has 'just died' (Mt 9:18, ἄρτι ἐτελεύτησεν)./34/

Mark is unique in retaining the actual words spoken

by Jesus in performing the miracle, ταλιθα κουμ, a transliteration of the Aramaic טליתא קום, which he paraphrases as 'Little girl, I say to you, get up' (τὸ κοράσιον, σοὶ λέγω, ἔγειρε, Mk 5:41)./35/ The Evangelist's retention of the original Aramaic does not prove that he regarded it as a species of magical spell, for (i) Aramaic was the mother-tongue of Jesus and the earliest Christians; (ii) elsewhere Mark retains Aramaic words and supplies a Greek translation;/36/ (iii) he translates (or, more accurately, paraphrases) the Aramaic./37/ More satisfactory is the suggestion that the original words are reproduced because they were the precise words spoken on an unforgettable occasion./38/

In his account Luke is dependent upon Mark, and probably Mark alone,/39/ whom he follows closely, differences being mostly abbreviations, clarifications of meaning (Lk 9:42, 50, 51, 53, 55) or improvements in style (Lk 9:42, 49, 52). A distinctive note is struck in 9:55. After Jesus' command 'get up' (ἔγειρε) and before the statement 'she got up' (ἀνέστη), Luke inserts the phrase 'and her spirit returned' (καὶ ἐπέστρεψεν τὸ πνεῦμα αὐτῆς). Some argue that this indicates that the miracle was essentially a recall (note ἐφώνησεν, 9:54) of the spirit to rejoin the body,/40/ but, 1 Kings 17:21-22 (LXX) notwithstanding, /41/ the expression may mean no more than that signs of life (such as breathing, colour in the cheeks, opened eyes) returned./42/

Four features common to Mark and Luke are worthy of mention. There is the emphasis on faith: when Jesus overhears the announcement of the death of Jairus's daughter, he immediately reassures Jairus ('stop being afraid', μὴ φοβοῦ) and challenges him to even greater faith, now that he has witnessed the healing of the woman ('simply persist in your faith', μόνον πίστευε, Mk 5:36). This emphasis is not absent from Matthew ('Come and lay your hand on her, and she will come to life', καὶ ζήσεται, Mt 9:18). Secondly, those privileged to witness Jesus' acts of resuscitation are named - Peter, James and John (*cf*. Mk 9:2; 14:33), and the girl's parents (Mk 5:37, 40; Lk 8:51). These were also necessary witnesses, since it would have been improper for Jesus to have entered the bedroom alone. Thirdly, both authors note Jesus' address to the girl (τὸ κοράσιον, Mk 5:41; ἡ παῖς, Lk 8:54), the immediate revivification, the command that she should be given food, and the resulting utter amazement. Finally, each records Jesus' injunction to silence (Mk 5:43; Lk 8:56), a somewhat strange directive, given the fact that so many already knew of the child's death (Mt 9:23) and would naturally connect Jesus' presence in the house with her revival. But it was an effort to avoid unnecessary publicity - 'no one was to know about it who need not ... And if immediate publicity were avoided, the news when it was no longer fresh would cause less excitment when it did get round'/43/ (*cf.* Mt 9:26).

C. The Historicity of the Miracle

Not a few commentators explain this 'raising' as an instance of healing rather than of revivification, or of extraordinary knowledge rather than of supernatural power./44/ In reality, it is suggested, the girl was in a death-like coma that might well have led to her death but for Christ's intervention. With skilful medical diagnosis, he recognized certain signs of life in the girl and raised her up either from a terminal coma (a miracle of healing) of from a state of temporarily suspended animation (an example simply of his superior knowledge). 'She is not dead' would then mean 'she is not really dead' or 'she is only apparently dead'.

Now it is true that in the first century AD medical science was inexact so that there was always the danger of an erroneous diagnosis of death. But presumably in the present case many people in addition to the parents had observed the young girl closely after her death and before she was placed in some inner room (Mk 5:38-40), especially in view of the fact that among Jews theological significance was found in the time, manner and posture of a person's death./45/ What is more, professional mourners would not be unaccustomed to recognising - accurately - the signs of death. Moreover, Jairus had set out to find Jesus and enlist his help when his daughter was already 'at death's door' (Mk 5:23, NIV). Before the messengers were dispatched to find Jairus and inform him of his daughter's death, there must have been a consensus that the young girl had in fact died. Finally, nowhere else in the Gospels does Jesus give a medical diagnosis - as if he were saying 'Her death is only apparent; she is merely in a deep coma'.

Nor should we dismiss as insignificant the uniform testimony of the three Evangelists, each of whom clearly believed that the girl was dead. Mark records the unambiguous words of the messengers, 'Your daughter is dead' (ἡ θυγάτηρ σου ἀπέθανεν, Mk 5:35), while Luke's altered wording emphasises the reality and finality of the girl's death (τέθνηκεν ἡ θυγάτηρ σου, Lk 8:49). Also, Luke states that the bystanders mocked

Jesus when he said 'She is not dead', 'because they knew that she had died' (εἰδότες ὅτι ἀπέθανεν, Lk 8:53); 'because they knew (εἰδότες)...' not 'because they imagined (δοκοῦντες)...'. As we have noted, Matthew omits the messenger scene and therefore telescopes Jairus's statement 'My daughter is at the point of death' (Mk 5:23) and the messengers' announcement, 'Your daughter has died' (Mk 5:35) into the one declaration, 'My daughter has just now died (ἄρτι ἐτελεύτησεν). But come and lay your hand on her and she will come to life (ζήσεται)' (Mt 9:18). We have, in effect, three literary witnesses to the fact that the girl had died.

The question therefore becomes 'Was Jairus's daughter restored to life at the command of Jesus?' Sometimes the answers that commentators give to this question depend on considerations broader than the text itself - considerations such as the scholar's view of the possibility of miracle, the nature of Jesus's person and mission, and the historicity and theological tendencies of the Gospels. The texts themselves portray the event as a straightforward revivification. They include a wealth of unexpected and unnecessary circumstantial detail that bespeaks authenticity /46/ - details such as Jairus prostrating himself before Jesus (Mk 5:22; Lk 8:41); the pressing throng hindering Jesus' progress to the house of Jairus (Mk 5:24; Lk 8:42); Jesus overhearing (παρακούσας) the message delivered to Jairus by his servants (Mk 5:36); Jesus' repeated directive (ἔλεγεν) to the professional mourners - 'Out you go!' (Mt 9:24); the outburst of derision (κατεγέλων αὐτοῦ) when Jesus said that the young girl was not dead but asleep (Mk 5:40; Mt 9:24; Lk 8:53); Jesus' order that the reanimated girl should be given food (Mk 5:43; Lk 8:55). Moreover the narratives lack the fantastic features that characterise some of the miracle tales of the apocryphal Gospels.

III LAZARUS (John 11:1-44)

It has become customary to describe the first twelve chapters of the Fourth Gospel as 'The Book of Signs' because they contain six (or seven) signs that Jesus performed in demonstration of his glory (Jn 2:11)./47/ The raising of Lazarus is the final sign in this Book (1:19 - 12:50), but it also forms a prelude to 'The Book of Glory' (13:1 - 20:31) for the Evangelist presents the Lazarus incident as precipitating the climax of Jewish opposition to Jesus (11:46, 53) and as triggering that sequence of events, beginning with the triumphal entry (12:12-18), that finally led to Jesus' death and to his resurrection, the supreme sign of the whole Gospel.

Numerous attempts have been made to isolate the nucleus of the story from the dialogue, to separate 'pure narrative' from redaction,/48/ but it is worth recalling that in the Fourth Gospel theological reflection is inextricably blended with historical reminiscence, or, as C.H.Dodd comments about the present passage, narrative and discourse are inseparably interwoven. 'Nowhere perhaps, in this gospel, have attempts to analyse out a written source, or sources, proved less convincing, and if the evangelist is following a traditional story of fixed pattern, he has covered his tracks'./49/

The narrative falls into three parts.

(1) Setting (11:1-6): the illness of Lazarus

A message is sent to Jesus in the region beyond Jordan that his friend, Lazarus, the brother of Mary and Martha, is ill in Bethany.

(2) Complication (11:7-37): the death of Lazarus

When his 'hour' has come, Jesus proposes to his disciples that they should all go to Judaea so that he can awake Lazarus out of his sleep of death. As Jesus approaches Bethany, on the fourth day after Lazarus's death, he is met first by Martha and then by Mary, both of whom wistfully comment, 'Lord, if you had been here, my brother would not have died'. A sense of anticipation is aroused by Martha's confidence that 'even now I know that whatever you ask from God, God will give you', by Jesus' assurance 'I am the resurrection and the life', and by his question 'Where have you laid him?'

(3) Resolution (11:38-44): the revivification of Lazarus

Jesus orders the stone to be removed from the shaft tomb, prays to God, and addresses Lazarus with the words 'Come out!' Lazarus emerges, bound in graveclothes, and Jesus directs him to be released.

A. The Miracle as History

In his treatment of the miracles of Jesus, H. van der Loos notes that 'around the resurrection of Lazarus the critics are ranked in battle array, like an army round a beleaguered fortress' but he also observes that the army is far from united./50/ Apart from the fact that in the Lazarus episode we are confronted by another ostensible miracle of reanimation - and at that, reanimation four days (not shortly) after death - there are two principal objections to the historicity of the Johannine account.

First, there is the silence of the three Synoptic gospels regarding the miracle. How could such a notable event at this crucial stage of Jesus' career be totally ignored by all three writers, who describe the days leading up to the death of Jesus in such detail? This difficulty should not be minimised.

At least a partial explanation, however, is afforded by several observations.

(i) It is not impossible that Peter was absent from Jerusalem at the time and consequently the episode did not find a place in the Gospel of Mark that, according to tradition, reflects Peter's personal reminiscences, nor in Matthew who seems dependent on Mark at this point in his narrative./51/

(ii) For Mark, 'Galilee is the place of Jesus' ministry, Judaea of his death. A miracle of resurrection in Judaea so soon before the Passion (if he had known about it) might have seemed to him theologically inappropriate'./52/ In any case, Mark, like Matthew, had already recorded a miracle of reanimation (*viz.* Jairus's daughter), while Luke had included a second instance in his Gospel (*viz.* the son of the widow of Nain).

(iii) Assuming that the Synoptic Gospels were written and published before the Fourth Gospel, we may suggest that the story, if known to the Synoptists, may have been suppressed in order to shelter Lazarus and his sisters from reprisal from the Sanhedrin in Jerusalem (*cf.* Jn 12:10-11).

(iv) The silence of three witnesses should not be rated more highly than the testimony of one, if on other grounds that testimony can be shown to be reliable. At numerous points recent discussion has demonstrated the historical value of the Fourth Gospel./53/

The second objection relates to the apparent discrepancy between the Fourth Gospel and the Synoptics concerning the event that precipitated the plan of the chief priests and

Pharisees to destroy Jesus. According to Mark (11:15-18) and Luke (19:45-48), it seems to have been the 'cleansing' of the Temple; according to Matthew (21:32, 45-46; 26:3-5) Jesus' teaching, especially the parable of the vineyard; according to John (11:45-53), the raising of Lazarus.

This objection overlooks several facts. Probably a considerable interval of time elapsed between the Lazarus episode and the final crisis of passion week, for John 11:53-54 indicates that precisely because of (οὖν) the plot to kill him, Jesus avoided publicity by withdrawing to Ephraim (possibly Ain Samieh) on the edge of the desert./54/ Secondly, official opposition to Jesus in Judaea seems to have increased by stages (Jn 5:18; 7:1, 25, 44; 8:59; 10:31; 11:8,16). John may have had access to particularly reliable information about the significance of the Lazarus incident in the intensification of opposition to Jesus. There is no difficulty in believing that the Lazarus incident had the effect of converting the Jewish determination to kill Jesus from being a sporadic and spontaneous outburst into an official policy, and that it was a prelude to further confrontations with the Jewish authorities over the triumphal entry and the temple 'cleansing'./55/ Thirdly, the perturbation of the Sanhedrin arose from the fact that Jesus had performed 'many signs' (Jn 11:47), not simply one 'sign'. Fourthly, the Synoptics are not without a hint that the climax of opposition to Jesus arose from his miraculous acts as well as his teaching and political activities. Luke notes that after the triumphal entry 'the whole multitude of the disciples' began to praise God for the *mighty acts* (δυνάμεις) they had seen, thereby incurring Pharisaic displeasure (Lk 19:37,39)./56/

In favour of the historical trustworthiness of the Evangelist's reporting of this story, we may mention the following points. The author clearly assumed that an actual reanimation had taken place, for he traced the decision of the authorities to try to encompass the death of Jesus to their receipt of news of Lazarus's reanimation (Jn 11:45-53) and on three subsequent occasions (Jn 12:2,9,17) he identifies Lazarus as the person whom Jesus had raised from the dead. Noticeable, too, is the wealth of circumstantial detail (11:6, 12-14, 28, 33, 35, 39, 44), including geographical notes (11:1, 18) and personal references (*cf.* Lk 10:38-42), and the numerous surprising details that would be improbable in a work of fiction or historical romance (11:16, 20b, 37, 42). There are also surprising silences - about the character and *post mortem* experience of Lazarus or the reaction of the bystanders - and the actual raising of Lazarus is reported with remarkable simplicity and brevity (11:44). All this creates not merely an impression of verisimilitude but a presumption of factuality.

Alternative explanations of the origin of the narrative fail to convince:

(i) It sometimes happened, in cases where the dead were buried immediately (*e.g.*, Acts 5:5-6, 10), that a swoon was mistaken for death. Lazarus, it is suggested, recovered from a trance or swoon just as Jesus arrived at the tomb, so that he was rescued from a premature burial.

(ii) In order to confound the enemies of Jesus, Mary and Martha may have concurred in a plan to have Lazarus feign death so that Jesus could effect a simulated reanimation./57/

(iii) The writer created a fictional narrative, perhaps akin to 2 Kings 13:21, composed of assorted Synoptic fabrics. His aim was to illustrate Christ's power over death as 'the resurrection and the life' (Jn 11:25) or his surpassing of his Old Testament prototypes, Elijah (1 Kgs 17:17-24) and Elisha (2 Kgs 4:8-37)./58/ Or else he sought to reinforce the truth of the parable recorded in Luke 16:19-31 that ends 'If they do not hear Moses and the prophets, neither will they be convinced if some one should rise from the dead'.

The first two explanations are patently improbable, involving as they do the evangelist's total misapprehension of the actual course of events or Jesus' concurrence in planned deception. As for the third explanation, we would claim that it remains more difficult to imagine that the narrative with all its circumstantial detail was created by the fertile imagination of the writer as an illustration of a theological truth, than to believe that the story reflects the vivid personal reminiscence of eyewitnesses. Though not created to convey spiritual meaning, the story certainly illustrates many spiritual truths. But it would be incongruous for the author to preface his account of the indubitably historical death of Jesus with an episode of didactic fiction. No more probable is the suggestion that the writer invented the story to dramatise and reinforce the parabolic truth that even a person's return from the grave could not or would not induce faith, for the narrative makes it clear that as a specific result of the raising of Lazarus Jews believed in Jesus in sufficient numbers to incite their leaders to plan the arrest and death of Lazarus (Jn 11:45; 12:9-11). In any case it seems far more likely *a priori* that a narrative would prompt a parable than that a parable would generate a narrative.

B. The Miracle as Theology

For the Fourth Evangelist history and symbolism were not irreconcilable opposites. The reporting of history became the vehicle for the enunciation of theological truths. Nor was such teaching conveyed only through dialogue. For an author who had 'bifocal historical vision'/59/ the narrative itself became didactic history, occurrences of the past shedding light on issues of the present or hopes for the future./60/

Whether they are viewed from the standpoint of content or structure, verses 25-26 are of central importance in John 11. 'I am the resurrection' (v.25a) is expanded in v.25b: 'the person who believes in me, though he should die, shall come to life [through a resurrection effected by me]'. 'I am the life' (v.25a) is developed in v.26a: 'and whoever lives [through that resurrection] as a believer in me, shall never die'. Jesus is presented as the pledge and agent of both resurrection and immortality./61/ He raises the dead and gives them life. Now these two characteristics of the Son of God correspond precisely to two that are mentioned in Jn 5: 21-29. 'For as the Father raises the dead and gives them life, so also the Son [raises the dead (*cf.* 5:25, 28-29) and] gives life to whom he will' (5:21). This earlier passage in the Gospel anticipates chapter 11 also in emphasizing that 'the dead ... will live' as a result of hearing the voice (φωνή) of the Son of God (5:25, 28).

John 5, then, presents Jesus as 'the resurrection', the one who raises the dead by his command, and as 'the life', the one who dispenses life to anyone he chooses. John 11 affords a concrete and dramatic illustration of the truth of these claims. Just as the teaching of John 5:21-29 precedes the summary statement of John 11:25-26, so these latter verses provide an advance interpretation of the event described in John 11:43-44. When Jesus cried out in a loud voice (φωνῇ μεγάλῃ ἐκραύγασεν, 11:43; *cf.*5:25, 28), Lazarus, who had been dead in the tomb (ἐν τῷ μνημείῳ, 11:17; *cf.* 5:28) for four days, came out (ἐξῆλθεν, 11:44; *cf.* 5:29a).

But the raising of Lazarus did more than dramatise and validate the claims of Jesus. It also pictured the destiny of the followers of Jesus. As surely as the dead Lazarus responded to the command of the earthly Jesus and rose from the dead, so whoever believes in Jesus, though he die, will hear the voice of the exalted Son of God and come to life. Physical death remains real (11:14, 17, 21, 25, 32, 37, 39, 44) but does not have the final word. Almost certainly, however, the author intends his readers to recognise, along with this similarity, a stark contrast between the reanimation of Lazarus and the resurrection of believers. His was a revivification on the fourth day (Jn 11:17, 39), leading merely to renewed mortal life. Our next glimpse of Lazarus is of a person sitting at a meal-table (Jn 12:1-2), a potent reminder of the materiality of his restored life. And the subsequent plot to kill him (Jn 12:10) underlines this renewed mortality. On the other hand, theirs will be a resurrection on the last day (Jn 6:39, 40, 44, 54), leading to eternal life (Jn 5:29). There is also an implicit contrast between the circumstances of the revival of Lazarus and those of Jesus' resurrection. Both died, Lazarus as a result of illness (Jn 11:1-4), Jesus at his own volition (Jn 10:18). In each instance a stone sealed the tomb, but in one case it was removed by natural means (Jn 11:38-41), in the other, by supernatural (Jn 20:1, by implication). Both were bound in graveclothes when buried, but whereas Lazarus needed others to unbind him when he emerged from the tomb (Jn 11:44), Jesus left his own burial cloths intact in his grave as a sign of his resurrection (Jn 20:5-7)./62/ Both rose from the dead, Lazarus with a new lease of physical life (Jn 12:2, 10), Jesus as the possessor of transformed somatic life (Jn 20:17, 19-20, 26).

There is pathos in the fact that when Jesus is proving his sovereignty over death by restoring physical life to Lazarus, he himself stands under the ever-encroaching shadow of death. It was precisely the 'sign' of Lazarus's raising (Jn 12:18) that precipitated the Sanhedrin's decision to investigate possible ways of having Jesus killed (Jn 11:45-53). And the next incident the Evangelist relates is the anointing of Jesus by Mary, already intimated in John 11:2 and now described as 'for the day of my embalming' (Jn 12:7). Between the raising of Lazarus to renewed mortality and the resurrection of Jesus and of believers to immortality there lay, of necessity, Jesus' death.

As well as symbolising future resurrection, this miracle is portrayed as a revelation of God's glory. Lazarus's illness would not ultimately issue in death (πρὸς θάνατον) but would promote God's glory by leading to the Son's glorification (Jn 11:4). It was not that people would be led simply to declare that a great prophet had arisen in their midst (*cf.* Lk 7:16) but rather some would glorify God by believing in Jesus (Jn 11:45) and the incident would culminate in the death of Jesus (Jn 11:50-51, 53), the first stage in his being glorified by crucifixion - resurrection - ascension (Jn 12:23-24; 17:1). In addition, the miracle is depicted as a stimulus to faith. While the reanimation of a corpse would not and could not compel belief (Jn 11:46-48, 53), as the parable of the rich man and Lazarus had shown (Lk 16:19-31), this miracle was designed to engender and strengthen faith (Jn 11:15). By witnessing her brother's revivification, Martha would be encouraged to believe that Jesus was the resurrection and the life (Jn 11:26b, 40). Such faith would forestall that display of inconsolable grief which had so deeply aroused Jesus' emotions (Jn 11:19, 31, 33),/63/ and would offer true comfort to the bereaved (*cf.* 1 Thess 4:13-18).

IV CONCLUDING OBSERVATIONS

A. *The Problem of Historicity*

Accounts of reanimation are found in three strands of the Gospels - Mark (5:21-43, and the parallels in Matthew and Luke), the special Lukan source L (Lk 7:11-17), and John (11:1-44). There are also allusions to the raising of the dead in Q (Mt 11:5 // Lk 7:22) and Matthew's special source, M (Mt 10:8). These records of or references to the restoration of the dead to life cannot therefore be dismissed as belonging to a distinctive strand of Gospel tradition that has a penchant for the spectacularly miraculous. Each major strand of the Gospels affords evidence of this theme.

We have seen that in each of the four Gospels Jesus' action in raising the dead is described as a historical fact. This does not, of course, establish the historicity of these miracles but it does mean that those who contest their rootage in history must account adequately for the rise of this uniform and startling belief among the Evangelists that on occasion Jesus of Nazareth actually raised the dead. At least to this present writer it seems to accommodate more of the data to suppose that in this matter the Evangelists give us a transcript of what actually happened than that they knowingly converted a providential rescue from premature burial or a 'miracle' of medical insight or a piece of parabolic teaching or tenet of doctrine into an actual miracle of reanimation (in which case they cannot be exonerated from a charge of duplicity) or that they failed to recognise in their source material that what appeared to be cases of revivification were in fact merely instances of the revival of comatose persons or the product of a well-orchestrated conspiracy between Jesus' disciples and certain subjects along with their relatives to pass Jesus off (with his connivance) as the wonder-worker *par excellence*./64/

B. The Miracles of Revivification as Dramatised Theology

The three specific instances of Jesus' raising the dead recorded in the Gospels point to and illustrate theological truths, all of which relate to the person of Jesus.

1. They pointed to the messiahship of Jesus

Because they met with unbelief as well as belief, these miracles were not in themselves 'proofs' of Jesus' messiahship, but they were indicators of the presence of the messianic kingdom and so of the Messiah (Mt 11:2, 5; Lk 7:18-19, 22). In the Fourth Gospel, 'signs' that have reference to Jesus (such as the raising of Lazarus) are miraculous occurrences that to the eye of faith point beyond themselves to Jesus' glory (Jn 2:11; 11:40, 45; 12:18) as the messianic Son of God (Jn 20:30-31).

2. They demonstrated the power of Jesus

In each instance there is an emphasis on the 'deadness' of the person whom Jesus raises to life,/65/ an emphasis that highlights the sheer potency of his spoken word which is always the sole means by which the miracle is performed: 'Young man, I say to you, get up!' (Lk 7:14); 'Little girl, I say to you, stand up!' (Mk 5:41); 'Lazarus, come out!' (Jn 11:43). Also noteworthy is the fact that on each occasion health and strength were regained as well as life restored. Whatever the cause of their death and whether or not bodily decomposition had set in, the subjects returned (so the texts imply) to life as they had known it before their death, illness or injury apart. It was a case of reanimation (breath returned, Lk 8:55) with healing but not transformation; Lazarus did not become a νεανίσκος, nor did the twelve-year old daughter of Jairus (a κοράσιον) become a γυνή. The raisings were instantaneous, and proof of the miracle was afforded by the subject's speaking (Lk 7:15), walking about (Mk 5:42) and eating (Mk 5:43; Lk 8:55).

3. They illustrated the compassion of Jesus

Those who were restored to life are not depicted merely as a man, a young man, and a little girl, but principally as an only brother, an only son, and an only daughter whose deaths aroused Jesus' compassion and prompted his action. This shows his sensitive understanding of the strength of human and family ties and the sorrow of bereavement./66/ Through Jesus the God of all comfort was comforting the downcast (*cf.* 2 Cor 1:3-4; 7:6). The tender concern of Jesus is also seen in the fact that at Nain the miracle was unsolicited, prompted by a providentially timed meeting, and no reference is made to the mother's faith: it was sheer compassion, especially since Jesus contracted ceremonial defilement by touching the bier (Lk 7:14; *cf.* 8:54). In all three instances, also, Jesus graciously cared for the physical or emotional needs of those raised (Mk 5:43; Lk 7:15; Jn 11:44).

4. They pictured the conquest of Jesus over death

In our three stories death is seen to be not only real but also universal, striking both child and adult, both male and female, and severing the most cherished of ties, whether parent-child, or brother-sister. But equally clearly there is shown the total sovereignty of Jesus over all death, wherever it is found. Moreover this full mastery is demonstrated by his raising one person from a death-bed, another from his funeral bier, and another from the grave. Because he is able to rob death of its prey, for his followers death is a 'falling asleep' (κοιμᾶσθαι, Jn 11:11) or 'sleep' (καθεύδειν, Mk 5:39), and despair in the face of death is illegitimate (Mt 9:23-24; Lk 8:52; Jn 11:33) although grief is natural (Jn 11:35; *cf.* 1 Thess 4:13).

5. They prefigured the resurrection of Jesus and of all people

How are the 'raisings' linked to 'resurrection'? In the Synoptics the link is forged by the ambiguity of the verbs ἐγείρειν and ἀνιστάναι, which may mean 'get up' from a reclining or lying position, or 'arise' from the dead. So when Jesus addresses the young man at Nain with the word ἐγέρθητι (Lk 7:14) and Jairus's daughter with the word ἔγειρε (Mk 5:41), both forms meaning 'Up you get!', the

Christian reader thinks of the coming resurrection day when the same command will be issued, 'Arise!' (*cf.* Eph 5:14). When, in response to the command of Jesus, it is said that the little girl 'got up' (ἠγέρθη, Mt 9:25; ἀνέστη, Mk 5:42; Lk 8:55), the reader would have recalled that exactly the same forms were traditionally used of the resurrection of Jesus (*e.g.*, Mk 16:6 and 1 Thess 4:14, respectively) and the same verbs of the resurrection of Christians (*e.g.*, 1 Cor 15:52 and Mt 12:41, respectively).

As for John's Gospel, the link is effected by means of concept rather than by terminology. Just as Lazarus in his tomb was raised at the command of Jesus and came out (Jn 11:43-44), so all the dead who are in the tombs will hear the voice of the Son of God and come forth (Jn 5:25, 28-29). Also we have already noted the implied contrasts in John 11:38-44 between the raising of Lazarus and the resurrection of Jesus.

'Once a man is slain (by death) ... there is no resurrection (ἀνάστασις)'. From a Christian viewpoint, according to which resurrection involves transformation as well as reanimation, these words of Aeschylus remained true until the resurrection of Jesus. They were true until then, for Jesus was 'the first to rise from the dead' (Acts 26:23) in a true resurrection, a rising to immortality (Rom 6:9). Earlier 'raisings' were merely cases of revivification, a waking (ἔγερσις) that issued in renewed mortal life, but they pointed forward to the decisive resurrection of Jesus after which believers in him are destined to share in 'a resurrection that issues in eternal life' (ἀνάστασις ζωῆς, Jn 5:29). Between the three instances of the awaking of the dead (what we might term ἔγερσις νεκρῶν) that are described in detail in the Gospels, and the resurrection of the Christian dead (ἀνάστασις νεκρῶν or ἀνάστασις δικαίων), there lay the epoch-making resurrection of Jesus. Before Jesus' resurrection, it could be said only that 'the dead are restored to life' (νεκροὶ ἐγείρονται, Mt 11:5; Lk 7:22). After his resurrection, it can be said that 'the dead will be raised immortal' (οἱ νεκροὶ ἐγερθήσονται ἄφθαρτοι, 1 Cor 15:52).

Notes

/1/ E. E. Ellis (*The Gospel of Luke* [London: Nelson, 1966] 31-32, 98-99) suggests that the Galilean ministry (4:31-9:50 on his division) is depicted in some 24 episodes arranged in four groups of six, which conclude the first section of the Gospel. For an alternative, less schematic division, see I. H. Marshall, *The Gospel of Luke* (Exeter: Paternoster, 1978) 7-8.
/2/ D. F. Payne, 'Nain', in *The New Bible Dictionary*, ed. J. D. Douglas *et al.* (Leicester: IVP, 1982[2]) 810.
/3/ On Jewish mourning customs, see A. Edersheim, *The Life and Times of Jesus the Messiah* (Grand Rapids: Eerdmans, 1971 repr. of 1886 ed.) 1.555-556; *Sketches of Jewish Social Life* (London: Religious Tract Society, 1876) 169-170; *SB* 1.521-523.
/4/ *Pace* J. Drury, *Tradition and Design in Luke's Gospel* (London: Darton, Longman & Todd, 1976) 71.
/5/ On this use of κύριος, see Marshall, *Luke*, 285-286; and I. de la Potterie, 'Le Titre ΚΥΡΙΟΣ appliqué à Jésus dans l'évangile de Luc', in *Mélanges bibliques en hommage au R. P. Béda Rigaux*, ed. A. Descamps (Gembloux: Duculot, 1970) 117-146, who, however, stresses the messianic overtones of κύριος in Lk 7:13, 19, pointing to the Lukan conjunction of χριστός and κύριος in Lk 2:11 and Acts 2:36 (pp. 125-126).
/6/ So also F. Gils, *Jésus prophète d'après les Évangiles synoptiques* (Louvain: Publications Universitaires, 1957) 26-27, 45, 164; J. A. Fitzmyer, *The Gospel according to Luke I-IX* (Garden City, New York: Doubleday, 1981) 215, 656, 659-660.
/7/ A similar conclusion is reached by G. Friedrich, 'προφήτης', *TDNT* 6.846. See also n.5 above.
/8/ Edersheim, *Life* 1.555-556.
/9/ While Shunem, where Elisha raised an only son (2 Kgs 4:18-37), and Nain are located near one another, this fact would hardly provide a sufficient genesis for the whole Nain episode. Even less convincing is the proposal that the site of the miracle was actually Shunem (שונם) which was corrupted to *nēm* (נם) and then confused with Nain (Ναΐν).
/10/ The other three accounts are Lk 8:40-42, 49-56; Acts 9: 36-43; 20:7-12.
/11/ 'La figure d'Elie dans la perspective lucanienne', *RHPR* 53 (1973) 167-173.
/12/ The LXX has the plural τέκνα in 1 Kgs 17:12-13, possibly under the influence of τέκνα (= MT בית, household) in v. 15.
/13/ The strange LXX expression [Ηλιου] ἐκοίμισεν αὐτὸν ἐπὶ τῆς κλίνης (1 Kgs 17:19) must mean, in the context (v. 17), not

'[Elijah] put him to sleep on the bed' but '[Elijah] laid him, in his sleep of death, on the bed'.
/14/ But in 1 Kgs 17:22 (LXX) J. A. Montgomery prefers the reading ἀνεβίωσεν ('he revived') to ἀνεβόησεν ('he cried out') (*A Critical and Exegetical Commentary on The Books of Kings*, ed. H. S. Gehman [Edinburgh: T. & T. Clark, 1951] 297-298).
/15/ Similarly Gils, *Jésus* 26, 43, 45, 164; A. George, 'Le miracle dans l'oeuvre de Luc', in *Les miracles de Jésus*, ed. X. Léon-Dufour (Paris: du Seuil, 1977) 252-253.
/16/ Scarcely less radical is the suggestion of R. H. Fuller that what was originally a popular tale, comparable to the miracle attributed to Apollonius of Tyana (see below), has been 'Christianised' by the addition of several traits deliberately chosen to recall the Elijah-Elisha miracles of revivification (*Interpreting the Miracles* [London: SCM, 1963] 64).
/17/ 'Αφανῶς here seems to mean 'secretly', although J. A. Fitzmyer proposes the rendering 'indistinctly' (*The Gospel according to Luke I-IX* [Garden City, New York: Doubleday, 1981] 657, 659).
/18/ See J. S. Phillimore, *Philostratus. In Honour of Apollonius of Tyana* (Oxford: Clarendon, 1912) I.lxxvi, citing nine passages listed in K. L. Kayser's 1870-1871 edition of Philostratus.
/19/ On Philostratus's scepticism as 'der aufgeklärte wissenschaftliche Sophist', see G. Petzke, 'Historizität und Bedeutsamkeit von Wunderberichten', in *Neues Testament und christliche Existenz*, ed. H. D. Betz and L. Schottroff (Tübingen: Mohr, 1973) 375-376, 383.
/20/ For a defence of this assessment, see B. F. Harris, 'Apollonius of Tyana: Fact and Fiction', *The Journal of Religious History* 5 (1968-69) 189-199, especially pp. 190, 198-199. On the history of Christian interpretation of the Apollonius traditions, see G. Petzke, *Die Traditionen über Apollonius von Tyana und das Neue Testament* (Leiden: Brill, 1970) 5-16.
/21/ Just as there is no reason to question Apollonius's presence in Rome (*Life* 4.39 ff.), so there is no reason to deny that he might have displayed exceptional medical insight in recognizing certain signs of life in the young bride and have acted accordingly.
/22/ Similarly Petzke, *Traditionen* 130 n.1, 137, although G. Theissen avers that Luke's account 'could be modelled on similar ancient miracle stories', citing Philostratus, *Vita Apoll.* 4.45 and Apuleius, *Florida* 19 (*The Miracle Stories of the Early Christian Tradition*, ed. J. Riches [Edinburgh:

T.& T.Clark, 1983] 277).

/23/ Many scholars believe that the two stories were originally independent, with Mark inheriting a tradition in which the stories were already combined (so R. Bultmann, *The History of the Synoptic Tradition* [Oxford: Blackwell, 1968[2]] 214) or himself combining the stories which were already associated in his *Vorlage*, in a manner characteristic of his use of traditional material (thus P. J. Achtemeier, 'Toward the Isolation of Pre-Markan Miracle Catenae', *JBL* 89 [1970] 276-279). But there seems to be no compelling reason for denying that this 'intercalation' of narratives was not a literary device employed by Mark or his predecessors but reflected the actual sequence of events (so also, *inter alios*, V. Taylor, *The Gospel according to St Mark* [London: Macmillan, 1966[2]] 289).

/24/ See the useful discussion of D. A. Carson, 'Matthew' in *The Expositor's Bible Commentary*, 8, ed. F.E.Gaebelein (Grand Rapids: Zondervan, 1984) 221, 229. On this view Jairus entered Matthew's house in order to make his request (*cf.* Mt 9:10, 18) and Jesus 'got up' (ἐγερθείς) from the meal and followed Jairus (Mt 9:19).

/25/ *Cf.* W. Schrage, 'ἀρχισυνάγωγος', *TDNT* 7.844-847; Bernadette J. Brooten, *Women Leaders in the Ancient Synagogue* (Chico, California: Scholars, 1982) 15-16, 27, 29-30.

/26/ Edersheim, *Life*, 1.619.

/27/ Against the proposal of R. Bultmann (*History*, 215) that the name Ἰάϊρος was introduced into the Markan text from Luke, see R. Pesch, 'Jaïrus (Mk 5,22/Lk 8,41)', *BZ* 14(1970) 252-256.

/28/ *The Gospel according to Saint Mark* (Cambridge: CUP, 1959) 183.

/29/ So Pesch, 'Jaïrus', 255.

/30/ The minimum requirement, even for a poor family, was two flute players and one wailing woman (b Ketub 46b).

/31/ Similarly R.C. Trench, *Notes on the Miracles of our Lord* (London: Kegan Paul, 1908) 197.

/32/ For an opposite view see M. Wilcox, 'ΤΑΛΙΘΑ ΚΟΥΜ(Ι) in Mk 5,41', in *Logia. Les paroles de Jésus. Mémorial Joseph Coppens*, ed. J. Delobel (Leuven: University Press, 1982) 469-476.

/33/ While it is not impossible that in 1 Thess 5:10 γρηγορεῖν refers to being awake and καθεύδειν to being asleep (perhaps in a proverbial expression), it is far more likely, given the fact that γρηγορεῖν in reference to physical life would be a *hapax legomenon* in the Greek Bible, that these two verbs specify the two categories of believers at the Parousia. In that case, within a single paragraph Paul uses καθεύδειν in three distinct senses - of moral lethargy or insensibility (v.6), of physical sleep (v.7), and of the sleep of death (v.10).

/34/ If this is so, καὶ ζήσεται (Mt 9:18) will mean 'and she will come to life', while ἵνα σωθῇ καὶ ζήσῃ (Mk 5:23) has the sense 'that she may get well and go on living'. This explanation of the problem posed by the Matthean record of Jairus's statement is preferable to the suggestion that the Evangelist is reporting what was in Jairus's mind rather than what he actually said, or that Jairus made two separate appeals, the second being after his daughter's death.
/35/ Wilcox, however, has proposed that Ταλιθα is a transliterated proper name ('ΤΑΛΙΘΑ', in *Logia*, 473-476).
/36/ *Viz.* Mk 3:17; 7:11, 34; 10: 46; 14:36; 15:22, 34. In 11:9-10 there is no translation.
/37/ There is nothing in the Aramaic that corresponds to σοὶ λέγω (but *cf.* Mk 2:11; Lk 5:24; 7:14).
/38/ Cranfield, *Mark*, 190.
/39/ *Cf.* T. Schramm, *Der Markus - Stoff bei Lukas* (Cambridge: CUP, 1971) 126-127.
/40/ Thus Marshall, *Luke*, 348.
/41/ The LXX has ψυχή, not πνεῦμα, with ἐπιστρέφειν.
/42/ Similarly H. van der Loos, *The Miracles of Jesus* (Leiden: Brill, 1968) 571.
/43/ Cranfield, *Mark*, 191. For alternative explanations of the injunctions to silence or secrecy found here and elsewhere in Mark, see C. Tuckett (ed.), *The Messianic Secret* (London: SPCK, 1983).
/44/ Wilcox, for example, believes that the Markan version in its original form, presented Jesus as 'the Great Physician: the Doctor who outclasses all other doctors'. After bringing the girl out of a deep coma that was perhaps due to a severe drop in her blood-sugar level, Jesus perceptively orders that she be given food (Mk 5:43) to prevent a relapse - wholly appropriate advice for a patient suffering from hypoglycaemia ('ΤΑΛΙΘΑ', in *Logia*, 469, 476 and n.39).
/45/ Edersheim, *Sketches*, 166-167.
/46/ This argument must, however, be used with caution, since, as E. P. Sanders has shown (*The Tendencies of the Synoptic Tradition* [Cambridge: CUP, 1969] 139-140, 145, 186, 275), the apocryphal gospels display a tendency to add circumstantial detail in their recording of gospel traditions.
/47/ See, *e.g.*, R. E. Brown, *The Gospel according to John (i - xii)* cxxxviii - cxliv.
/48/ See, *e.g.*, W. Wilckens, 'Die Erweckung des Lazarus', *TZ* 15 (1959) 22-39; R. T. Fortna, *The Gospel of Signs* (Cambridge: CUP, 1970) 74-87.
/49/ *Historical Tradition in the Fourth Gospel* (Cambridge: CUP, 1963) 230; *cf.* 232.

/50/ *Miracles*, 576.
/51/ Thus L. Morris, *The Gospel According to John* (Grand Rapids: Eerdmans, 1971) 534-535, who notes that Peter is not mentioned in John between 6:68 and 13:6, in Matthew between 19:27 and 26:33, in Luke between 18:28 and 22:8, and in Mark between 10:28 and 11:21; and that Thomas, not Peter, is the spokesman for the Twelve in John 11:16.
/52/ J. N. Sanders, *The Gospel according to St John*, ed. and completed by B. A. Mastin (London: A. & C. Black, 1968) 276.
/53/ See, *e.g.*, J. A. T. Robinson, *The Priority of John* (London: SCM, 1985), especially pp. 123-295 and the literature cited there.
/54/ On the geographical point, see Brown, *John*, 1.441.
/55/ R. Dunkerley aptly comments: 'We must not speak as though Jesus would not have been in peril if he had not done this thing [the raising of Lazarus]; the authorities may have regarded it as the last straw, but they still had to wait for the right opportunity, and this came of course with the Entry and the purging of the Temple' ('Lazarus', *NTS* 5 [1958-59] 326).
/56/ Similarly S. S. Smalley, *John: Evangelist and Interpreter* (Exeter: Paternoster, 1978) 182.
/57/ E. Rénan, *The Life of Jesus* (London: Trübner, 1867) 251-252.
/58/ See, *e.g.*, D. F. Strauss, *The Life of Jesus Critically Examined* (London: SCM, 1973 ed. of the fourth German ed. of 1840) 480-495, especially 495.
/59/ J. P. Martin, 'History and Eschatology in the Lazarus Narrative. John 11:1-44', *SJT* 17 (1964) 338; *cf*. 333.
/60/ Observing that full exegetical justice is done to Johannine narratives only when the dual context of the historical and the symbolic-didactic is taken into account, L. Sabourin affirms that symbolism and historical reality are not incompatible since the former presupposes and rests on the latter ('Resurrectio Lazari (Jo 11, 1-44)', *Verbum Domini* 46 [1968] 339-350, especially 339, 341; *cf*. his *The Divine Miracles Discussed and Defended* [Rome: Catholic Book Agency, 1977] 124-128). Many commentators, however, prefer to see the Fourth Evangelist as inheriting traditional historical material and augmenting it creatively to achieve his theological purposes.
/61/ For a defence of this exegesis, see M. J. Harris, *Raised Immortal* (London: Marshall, Morgan & Scott, 1983) 211-214.
/62/ See the discussion of this point in two articles in the *Heythrop Journal*: W. E. Reiser, 'The Case of the Tidy Tomb: The Place of the Napkins of John 11:44 and 20:7', *HJ* 14 (1973) 47-57; B. Osborne, 'A Folded Napkin in an Empty Tomb: John 11:44 and 20:7 Again', *HJ* 14 (1973) 437-440.

/63/ On the meaning of the phrase ἐνεβριμήσατο τῷ πνεύματι (Jn 11:33), see Morris, *John*, 555-558.
/64/ On various criteria for establishing the historicity of the gospel miracles, see Sabourin, *Miracles*, 68-70; *cf.* 54.
/65/ Lk 7:12, 15 (the widow of Nain's son); Mk 5:35; Lk 8:49, 53, 55 (the daughter of Jairus); Jn 11:13, 14, 16, 21, 32, 37, 39, 44 (Lazarus).
/66/ A. Plummer makes the interesting observation that nearly all of the instances of raising the dead recorded in the Bible were performed for women - 1 Kgs 17:23; 2 Kgs 4:36; Lk 7:12-13, 15; Jn 11:21, 32; Acts 9:41; Heb 11:35 (*A Critical and Exegetical Commentary on the Gospel according to S. Luke* [Edinburgh: T. & T. Clark, 1896] 198). The exceptions are the cases of Jairus's daughter (Mk 5:22-23, 40-42) and Eutychus (Acts 20:12), yet even here women were among the beneficiaries.

THE MIRACLES AS PARABLES

Craig L. Blomberg
Palm Beach Atlantic College
1101 S. Olive Avenue
West Palm Beach, FL 33401

The parables of the Synoptic gospels reflect the authentic voice of the historical Jesus more certainly than any of the other gospel 'forms'. If modern biblical scholarship has reached a consensus on anything, it is that Jesus spoke in parables which revealed the in-breaking kingdom of God./1/ Christianity began as a 'new age' religion, as its founder combined beliefs about the presence and future of God's reign into a concept which has been increasingly referred to as 'inaugurated eschatology'./2/

On the other hand, the gospel miracle stories have undoubtedly suffered more criticism and ridicule than any other form of gospel pericope, since many modern men reject the possibility of the historicity of a narrative of anything miraculous./3/ And even where many now admit the possibility of psychosomatic processes effecting healings and even exorcisms, the nature miracles seem to remain as unbelievable as ever./4/ Yet despite being at opposite poles of a spectrum of historical credibility, the nature miracles and the parables attributed to Jesus in the New Testament strikingly parallel each other both in their overall function in the gospels and in many specific details of their contents. Perhaps one of the reasons the miracle stories have so often been found incredible is because these parallels have been overlooked, and the events have therefore not been interpreted as they were originally intended to be.

Why do the four evangelists describe Jesus stilling a storm and walking on water, feeding the multitudes and changing water into wine, or withering a fig tree but guiding the disciples to a phenomenal catch of fish, to cite the six stories to be examined here? Is there any reason for believing in some kind of historical events underlying these narratives, especially since the rise of *Religionsgeschichte*, which has uncovered extra-canonical parallels whose historicity is seldom accepted even by the most conservative scholars?/5/ The prevailing view of this century would reply negatively, viewing canonical and non-canonical traditions alike as varying attempts to present Jesus as a thaumaturge *par excellence*, often referred to as a θεῖος ἀνήρ, in keeping with Hellenistic fashions of the day./6/ David Tiede has thoroughly surveyed this trend and concludes that there exists no uniform picture of the divine man in pre-Christian sources but agrees that the miracle stories served for early Christians to authenticate Jesus' charismatic status *vis-à-vis* stories which present him as a sufferer, teacher, or revealer./7/ Tiede, moreover, seems no more open to historicity than does the consensus which he critiques. M. E. Glasswell finds the main point of the group of miracles beginning at Mark 4:35 in the nature and necessity of faith,/8/ but this holds true more consistently for the healing miracles and exorcisms than for the nature miracles. Even more conservative commentators often end up spiritualizing these stories, so that Christians today are enjoined to hope merely for the deliverance from the 'storms' of life or for provisions of 'daily bread'. The language differs, but the concepts remarkably parallel the demythologizing program of more 'liberal' existentialists,/9/ against which conservatives otherwise loudly protest!/10/

On a popular level, Christians have often underlined the apologetic value of the more spectacular miracles as proofs of Jesus' deity, but they have not always grappled with the apparently contradictory approach attributed to Jesus, in which he refuses to work miracles when asked for 'signs' (e.g. Mark 8:11-13 par., Matt. 12:38-42)./11/ G. Klein thus goes so far as to argue that Mark and John emphatically warn their readers against belief in miracles,/12/ to which G. Theissen rightly replies that Mark's inclusion of sixteen miracle stories seems a rather 'clumsy' way to accomplish this./13/ Some kind of mediating position seems more likely to explain the gospel writers' purposes. Such a position should emphasize that although the miracle stories encourage belief in a transcendent power, the origin of that power, as the Pharisees' reaction to Jesus in Mark 3:22 pars. indicates, can be drastically misinterpreted. For Mark, at least, even the disciples lacked insight into the miracles in a manner remarkably parallel to their (and others') confusion over Jesus' parables (cf. further Mark 6:52 and 8:21 with 4:13 and 7:18, respectively). The words ascribed to Jesus after the two feeding miracles (Mark 8:18) hark back to the same Old Testament quotation (Isa. 6:9 10) which he cited after the parable of the sower--'seeing but not perceiving. . .hearing but not understanding'. Although the locations of these sayings have been argued to be redactional, a good case can be made for seeing them as in their original contexts, reflecting Jesus' own intentions./14/

These parallels prove even closer still. Just as parables both concealed and revealed,/15/ Jesus' miracles, especially those over powers of the natural world, not only triggered misunderstanding but also revealed the in-breaking of the power of God's reign. A description of the function of the gospel miracle stories better than all of those surveyed above and accepted by a growing number of scholars ties these narratives very closely to the parables. Thus H. van der Loos, in the most detailed study of Jesus' miracles in this generation, comments that 'we do not regard miracles primarily as signs, seals, additions, attendant phenomena, or however they are described, but. . .as a function sui generis of the kingdom of God.'/16/ More specifically, 'miracles happen if the kingdom of God proceeds to function in deeds, just as parables "happen" if it functions in words.'/17/ B. Bron echoes these thoughts: 'Die Wunder Jesu sind im Neuen Testament durchgehend als messianische Zeichen verstanden in denen das in Erfüllung geht, was für die Heilszeit geweissagt ist, lässt deshalb durch die leiblichen Wunder konstitutive Elemente der einbrechenden Herrschaft Gottes sein.'/18/ Or as Kallas concludes, 'The message of Jesus concentrated on the announcement of the kingdom of God. . .and the miracles showed what the kingdom of God would be like.'/19/

This catena of citations comes primarily from studies often more interested in interpreting the miracle stories at a redactional level than in assessing their historicity. When historical questions are raised, the traditional scepticism often reappears./20/ It is the thesis of this article, however, that if the functions of both parable and miracle are so similar then perhaps it is not entirely logical to come to such diametrically opposite conclusions regarding historicity for these forms. Of course if one excludes miracle *a priori* as impossible, further discussion is useless. But thoroughgoing rationalism is not held with the virtual unanimity that it once commanded in philosophical circles./21/ On the other hand, if one is open to the possibility of the gospel miracle stories as factual, a criterion presents itself whereby one is not subsequently compelled to believe in the truth of every other wondrous narrative from antiquity (though it is unnecessary to argue for the unreliability of all apocryphal material!/22/). Jesus' authentic miracles distinguished themselves in that they corresponded to and cohered with the fundamental message of his teaching--teaching illustrated nowhere more dramatically than in his parables--the announcement and depiction of the inauguration of God's reign. This thesis now requires exegetical corroboration from the six main nature miracle stories of the four gospels./23/ In each case we will seek to establish the earliest meaning(s) of the miracle that is still discernible from a study of the gospel texts as we now have them, and then we will ask if any barriers prohibit moving back to Jesus himself as the original performer of the events described when interpreted in light of those meanings.

The Withered Fig Tree (Mark 11:12-14, 20-25, Matt. 21:18-22)

The nature miracle which links most closely with one of Jesus' parables also proves perhaps the most perplexing to interpret. Can one seriously believe in the historicity of this solitary example of a miracle used to curse and destroy a barren fig tree, especially when Mark specifically states (11:13) that it was not the season for figs?/24/ Yet one of Jesus' parables also threatens the destruction of a fruitless fig tree (Luke 13:6-9) in a context where it is clear that the tree symbolizes the nation of Israel (or perhaps, more specifically, her leaders)./25/ This symbolism stems from a rich Old Testament and intertestamental background of texts on fig trees,/26/ leaving a metaphorical interpretation of the significance of the later fig tree which Jesus curses overwhelmingly likely, at least at the early stages of the tradition. In fact, commentators have often sought the literary origin of the cursing story in the earlier parable,/27/ but this overlooks the substantial verbal differences between the two./28/ The major problem with taking the withered fig tree as a symbol for impending judgment upon Israel is that the passage's conclusion speaks instead of the power of faith to move mountains. The vast majority of scholars therefore argues that Mark 11:23-25 and Matt. 21:21-22 represent the redactional activity of the evangelists, who link these independent sayings of Jesus with the miracle narrative to give it new meaning. On the other hand if one argues for a traditional connection of any or all of these sayings on faith and prayer with the preceding material, one seems forced to reject the symbolic interpretation./29/ To complicate matters further, Mark narrates the story of the fig tree in two stages, covering two successive days (11:12-14 and 20-22), thereby framing the cleansing of the temple (vv. 15-19). Matthew is quite different, placing the latter story earlier (21:12-17) and recounting the former afterwards as if it occurred all at one time (vv. 18-20).

It is difficult to decide which account is more chronological and which is more topical. Markan scholars generally find the framing device redactional and the Matthean form more original,/30/ while commentators on Matthew usually assume that Matthew has simplified and 'telescoped' the more complex and original Markan narrative./31/ Both approaches can cite similar activity by Matthew and Mark elsewhere. For Markan framing, compare especially the interpolation of Jesus' trial before the Sanhedrin into the Petrine denial narrative (Mark 14:53-72), followed by Matthew (26:57-75) but not Luke (22:54-71); for Matthean telescoping, compare especially the combination of the sendings of the twelve and seventy in Matthew 10./32/ In this instance, it seems more plausible that Mark has preserved the more original chronology, since his topical arrangements elsewhere do not usually preserve the detailed references to time and sequence found in 11:11b, 12, 20, and 27 (cf. e.g. the deliberately vague introductions to pericopae in his topical grouping of pronouncement stories in 2:13, 18, 23, 3:1). Moreover, only Mark specifically mentions Peter by name, as the one who marveled over the withered tree, perhaps reflecting a Petrine reminiscence./33/ This Markan distinction is not as likely a redactional invention, since it is Matthew who much more frequently introduces Peter's name into a narrative when Mark makes no mention of him./34/

If Mark's account is thus more original, what is its meaning in his context, and is this miracle comprehensible as a genuine action of the historical Jesus? In addition to the apparent shift of topic in vv. 23-25, at least two other incongruities appear. Vv. 20-21 depict a withered tree, whereas v. 14 relates only that Jesus condemned it to eternal fruitlessness./35/ More seriously, the last clause of v. 13 seems to render Jesus' action highly irrational or arbitrary; was he unaware of the time of year when he could expect ripe figs? A myriad of explanations have been offered: the clause is a gloss/36/ or should have been punctuated as a question,/37/ the narrative originally belonged to the context of the Feast of Booths (Tabernacles),/38/ Jesus believed that the Messianic Age had begun and expected all trees to bear fruit at once,/39/ or the tree was prematurely ripe since the presence of leaves indicated that figs should have been found as well./40/ But there is no textual evidence whatever for a gloss or displacement or punctuation variant, and the last two theories still fail to explain why Mark apparently goes out of his way to emphasize that Jesus had no reason to expect figs even on this particular tree. The best explanation finds Jesus' action deliberately incongruous in order to alert his disciples to a metaphorical or symbolical meaning./41/ The parallels with Old Testament passages like Micah 7:1-6 and Jer. 8:13 are too striking (the latter especially, since it follows the 'den of robbers' saying in Jer. 7:11 quoted by Jesus in Mark 11:17b/42/) to avoid the conclusion that Jesus intended to depict the impending eschatological destruction of Israel if she did not repent. Precisely because God's kingdom had come, because Jesus was ushering in the new age, the time for ultimate blessing or judgment for Israel was at hand.

The intervening account of Jesus' cleansing the temple makes this interpretation virtually certain and foreshadows even more specifically the coming destruction of the temple cult./43/ This is true even if the Markan 'sandwiching' of these events is redactional, since both Matthew and Mark agree on their temporal proximity in any case. H. Giesen nicely epitomizes this miracle both for Jesus and for the evangelists as a 'symbolische Handlung. . .als eschatologische Zeichen der hereinbrechenden Gottesherrschaft.'/44/ The implications of the withered fig tree closely match those of its twin parable. As Jesus concludes in Luke 13:9, 'if it bears fruit. . .but if not, cut it down.' Or again, in the same chapter (v. 35), 'Behold, your house is left to you desolate, and I say to you, you shall not see me until the time comes when you say, "Blessed is he who comes in the name of the Lord."' These words were undoubtedly fresh in the disciples' minds, whether they were originally spoken in any close connection with the fig tree parable or not, since the crowds had just repeated a portion of them on the previous day's triumphal entry. Jesus, though, knew the superficiality of the acclamation. The new age had dawned, but only incipiently (*pace* the above view requiring all trees to bear fruit at once), and the fulfilment of Luke 13:35 would not precede his more imminent rejection in Israel.

It is possible that part or all of Mark 11:20-25 was relocated here secondarily, especially in light of the parallels to vv. 23-25 in other Synoptic contexts (Luke 17:6, Matt. 17:20, 6:14-15). But the symbolic significance of Jesus' curse suggests a way in which all could also be in their original context. The withering of vv. 20-21 no longer poses a problem when viewed as an enacted parable. Since a curse of mere fruitlessness would not have visibly distinguished the tree from its previous condition, more was needed to create an intelligible object lesson. The saying on faith which moves '*this* mountain' (vv. 22-23) follows logically as an allusion to either of the two mountains visible from the Bethany road. Zech. 14:4 prophesies the upheaval of the Mount of Olives in the Day of the Lord, while a reference to Mount Zion would fit well with the cleansing of the temple. The generalizations on the power of prayer (vv. 24-25) follow with almost equal ease, but Jesus' original point in introducing them would likely have been fairly specific. Harrington's suggestion that 'faith and prayer, not temple cult, are now the way to God,'/45/ may not miss the mark by much. The 'parallels' in Matthew and Luke may well reflect similar sayings in variant forms from other occasions in Jesus' ministry./46/

Concern over the fate of the actual tree misses the symbolism involved and reflects a more sentimental attitude toward non-human life than Scripture warrants. In a milieu which could view even those creatures made in God's image as clay in the hands of a potter (see esp. Rom. 9:19-22 with its OT parallels), few questions would arise over the destruction of one solitary fig tree. Regardless of the original context of vv. 23-25, the historicity of vv. 12-14 and 20-22 as a genuine miracle of Jesus remains fully plausible. If such a *Strafwunder* is admitted to be at all possible, then the coherence of its significance in this context with the core of Jesus' authentic teaching elsewhere makes it very probable.

Water into Wine (John 2:1-11)

The parallelism between this miracle and one of Jesus' parables strikes the reader almost as forcefully as with the previous example. What again seems at first glance as an extravagant outpouring of miraculous power for at best frivolous and at worst very destructive purposes (the complete drunkenness of the Cana wedding party!) takes on profound symbolism when compared with Jesus' parable of the wineskins (Mark 2:18-22 pars.). Again this close parallelism has given rise to theories of parables turned into miracles. Dodd and Lindars have both suggested that a short parable with a wedding feast setting formed the traditional nucleus of this passage, and that the parable likely concluded with a 'pregnant saying' like that of John 2:10b--'you have kept the good wine until now.' This parable then became combined with a pagan miracle story in the pre-Johannine tradition./47/ F. E. Williams traces the origin to an expansion of the Lucan form of the parable of the wineskins, since it alone contains the conclusion, 'And no one after drinking old wine desires new, for he says, "the old is good",' which closely resembles John 2:10./48/ Stephen Smalley, partially following B. Olsson, turns these approaches upside down, claiming that 'John has not created a miracle out of a parable, but a parable out of a miracle.'/49/ In other words, for Smalley, an apparently genuine miracle has received additional symbolism through its traditio-critical development.

The fact that the passage can lead to such diametrically opposite views suggests that neither extreme has captured the entire traditio-historical picture and that a mediating view may be more appropriate. If, as most of the views agree, the parallels with Mark 2:18-22 pars. are close enough to provide insight into a historically plausible interpretation for John 2:1-11 in a *Sitz im Leben Jesu*, whether or not John knew the canonical form of Mark, then perhaps this passage is neither a transformation of a parable into a miracle or vice-versa, but a miracle as (enacted) parable./50/ The Synoptic 'parallels' prove all the more significant since this miracle itself occurs only in John, and questions of historicity in the fourth gospel are notoriously complex./51/

Not surprisingly, exceedingly diverse interpretations of the Cana miracle abound. Commentators have claimed that it merely teaches about the conversion of sinners,/52/ Jesus' positive attitude to human life,/53/ or his blessing on the institution of marriage./54/ Others view it as a retrospective meditation on Pentecost,/55/ anti-Baptist polemic,/56/ or the reflection of God's power and love in meeting human needs./57/ J. D. M. Derrett adopts a specially innovative approach, seeing Jesus' miracle as his literal wedding gift to compensate for having arrived without one./58/ But all of these views overlook key features of the text which point to a richer symbolism involved. From John's point of view (v. 11) the miracle is a sign (even if he has adopted it from a 'signs-source,' he has done so approvingly/59/), and more specifically a manifestation of the glory of Jesus, causing his disciples to deepen their belief in him. Schnackenburg rightly remarks, 'The most important *[thought]* for the evangelist is the revelation of Jesus' glory. . .and any interpretation which departs from this Christological perspective loses sight of the central issue.'/60/ Other characteristic Johannine themes appear, especially the interest in Jesus' relationship with his mother and the timing of his 'hour' (v. 4). But John's emphases do not likely reflect Jesus' original primary intention (if a historical core for this narrative exists), in light of his refusal to work miracles as signs in the Synoptics. That is not to say that John's interpretation is false, for miracles that Jesus performed for other reasons could still have had the results which John assigns to them (and even John is not unequivocally positive toward miracles as signs--cf. esp. 20:29). It is to say, though, that one must probe more deeply to discover the original significance of the miracle story at the earliest traditio-critical stage.

Two basic alternatives remain. The first rejects the historicity of the Cana miracle and attributes the pre-Johannine form to a Hellenistic milieu. Bultmann, for example, pointed to parallels with the Dionysus legends (see esp. Euripides, *Bacchae*, ll. 704-7; Athenaeus, *Deipnosophistae* I. 61.34a; Pausanius, *Description of Greece*, 6.26,1f.) and argued that John inherited a slightly modified pagan myth applied to Jesus./61/ E. Linnemann identifies a similar background but believes that the tradition presented Jesus in this way not to serve but to oppose Hellenistic categories./62/ Nevertheless the amount of parallelism with these myths has regularly been exaggerated; none of the sources cited describes the transformation of water into wine but only the appearance of wine in locations where usually only water (or no liquid at all) was found./63/ The most famous 'parallel' involves the story of empty caldrons once a year appearing filled with wine after sitting in the Dionysiac temple overnight behind locked doors, yet even in ancient Greece many sceptics suspected that temple priests had secret access to the appropriate chambers in order to perform the 'miracle'. This is a far cry from the fourth gospel's narrative which stresses the presence of the servants (v. 9) who could give eyewitness testimony to full jugs of water turned into wine in an instant and without opportunity for subterfuge./64/

The other alternative, following a resurgence of interest in Jewish origins for the fourth gospel, is to interpret the miracle as a vivid illustration of the transformation of the old 'water' of Mosaic religion into the new 'wine' of the kingdom. The otherwise unnecessary reference to the water jars as 'for the Jewish rites of purification' (v. 6) reinforces this interpretation. The otherwise remarkable sparsity of detail in the narrative makes an aside like this all the more striking and suggests that more is involved than mere justification of the presence of water jars for a Hellenistic audience unfamiliar with Jewish customs./65/ In Mark, before

Jesus' Galilean ministry can get underway with its call for new wineskins (Mark 2:22), Jesus must provide the new wine which will necessitate them. Before he can point to the appropriate celebration which his presence as bridegroom requires (Mark 2:19) he must illustrate the proper festivity for the weddings of others. The similarities between the Cana miracle and Mark's narrative are thus not limited to vv. 21-22 but also involve the preceding dialogue on fasting and weddings (vv. 18-20). This in turn calls to mind the rich antecedent symbolism of marriages and marriage feasts in Jewish literature as foreshadowings of the coming eschatological banquet. Again the parables reinforce this interpretation, as one notices how often Jesus uses a banquet to represent the new age he is inaugurating (cf. esp. Matt. 22:1-10, Luke 14:7-24, Matt. 25:1-13/66/). The most plausible purpose for Jesus turning the water into wine at this celebration was to show that 'the final "wedding feast" between God and his people [had] begun.'/67/ But this feast could not go on within traditional Jewish confines; Old Testament religion had to be 'purified and transformed in order to find its fulfillment in Christ.'/68/ Or as Breuss nicely summarizes: 'Jesus erweist sich als der welcher das Wasser des Alten Testament in den Wein des Neuen Bundes verwandelt.'/69/ It is also possible that eucharistic foreshadowings present themselves here,/70/ but these would have arisen more naturally in later reflection on the miracle story after Jesus' last supper. If additional significance must be sought, the Old Testament and intertestamental background of wine as one of the abundant blessings of the Messianic age (see esp. Isa. 55:1, Joel 3:18, Amos 9:13) would appear more likely to have been influential./71/

As with the cursing of the fig tree, contemporary ethical reservations about this miracle seem anachronistic. John 2:10 does not say that the crowd was drunk, and modern teetotalers do not reflect ancient Jewish views on drinking wine discreetly (cf. Sirach 31:27-28--'Wine is like life to men, if you drink it in moderation. . .it has been created to make men glad. Wine drunk in season and temperately is rejoicing of heart and gladness of soul;' for canonical parallels cf. Psa. 104:15 and Jdgs. 9:13). Jesus himself came 'eating and drinking,' so that his opponents never characterized him as an ascetic but offered a caricature of him as 'a glutton and a drunkard' (Luke 7:34 par.). The early church would scarcely have invented these characterizations which grew increasingly embarrassing as 'early catholicism' developed, and the awkwardness of Jesus' supplying an already festive wedding party with further large quantities of alcohol argues equally strongly for the historicity of the miracle. No obstacle remains, therefore, to accepting the Johannine account as depicting one of the *ureigene Taten* of Jesus, with parabolic significance. The new age had dawned, the true bridegroom had appeared, and his followers were to rejoice and make merry.

Feeding the Multitudes (Mark 6:32-44, Matt. 14:13-21, Luke 9:10b-17, John 6:1-15)

Like the provision of wine, the feeding of the five thousand, at the very least, depicts Jesus working a miracle to provide abundantly for the physical appetites of the multitudes. Both Mark and Matthew narrate a further feeding miracle involving four thousand (Mark 8:1-10, Matt. 15:32-39), which is regularly interpreted as a secondary doublet./72/ However, the differences in geography, numbers, and terminology (esp. the distinction between words for 'basket'--κόφινος vs. σπυρίς, a distinction significantly preserved in Mark 8:19-20) show that the two stories are not as similar as a superficial glance might suggest. Both are historically plausible as separate events in the ministry of Jesus; the five thousand are primarily Jews and the four thousand more likely Gentiles./73/ Mark 8:14-21 par., moreover, describes a later dialogue between Jesus and the disciples which views the events as separate, and the form and structure of this dialogue points to its substantial authenticity (E. E. Lemcio, e.g., identifies four characteristic features of tradition: an oracular, ambiguous utterance; misunderstanding by the audience; a surprised, critical rejoinder; and final explanation./74/)

The severest problem for viewing the feeding of the four thousand as a separate event, however, comes in Mark 8:4 when the disciples ask how the provision of food for so many is possible. Surely they would never have inquired in this way if they had already seen Jesus perform a similar, previous wonder. Yet Matthew rewords the disciples' question with the first person plural--'Where are we to get bread. . . ?' (15:33), placing the pronoun ἡμῖν in a strongly emphatic position in the sentence. It is not impossible that he rightly interpreted the meaning of their question as an admission of their inability to resolve the problem without doubting the power of their master to deal with it./75/ Regardless of the probability of this hypothesis, however, the meanings of the two accounts seem similar enough not to demand separate treatment here for each. Even as reflecting separate events, the second account remains shorter, most likely being abbreviated and omitting unnecessarily repetitive details. It seems best to focus primarily on the feeding of the five thousand in a quest for the original meaning of the miracle(s).

A second preliminary problem surfaces, since both John and the Synoptics include versions of this miracle. The literary relationship between the fourth gospel and its predecessors remains far from established, and good arguments arise on behalf of John's version as the most primitive here./76/ Yet even in John, eschatological and Messianic overtones recur, even if not as clearly as in the Synoptic versions. Schnackenburg, for example, identifies Johannine elements in the Passover setting (John 6:4), the naming of disciples (Philip, Andrew, and Simon Peter in vv. 5-8), the emphasis on 'losing nothing' (v. 12), and the reaction of the crowd (v. 14), but he still finds the pre-Johannine form presenting Jesus as the eschatological prophet, especially in light of the parallel with Elisha's feeding miracle in 2 Kgs. 4:42-44./77/ Because of the uncertainty of the age of the Johannine version, however, subsequent discussion will be focused exclusively on the Synoptics.

The dialogue about the leaven of the Pharisees (Mark 8:14), which refers back to the two feedings, suggests a link with the parable of the leaven (Matt. 13:33/Luke 13:20-21). In the latter, of course, the yeast symbolizes the positive influence and growth of God's kingdom, while in the former it refers to the opposition to Jesus by the leaders of Israel. But the metaphor functions identically in each instance--the subtle and persistent permeation of a large area by a small substance. The significance of feeding the multitudes fits this usage of the leaven metaphor remarkably well. In an undescribed (and apparently imperceptible) way,/78/ Jesus enables his disciples to distribute bread and fish for the crowds when originally there was seemingly far too little. Although not as obviously parallel to one of Jesus' parables as the previous miracles considered, and even apart from the validity of such speculative parallelism, a view of the feeding as an enacted parable of growth and blessings of the imminent kingdom of God makes excellent sense. The imagery of the bread reappears in the parable of the friend at midnight (Luke 11: 5-8), in which Jesus compares God (by *a fortiori* logic) to the awakened man who provides food in an equally unexpected setting. Finally, one might also compare the banquet parable of Luke 14:16-24, notably the replacement of the invited guests by the outcasts, with the repetition of the feeding miracle for both Jews and Gentiles./79/ The multiple attestation of these motifs in Mark, Q, and L (or at least in the three gospel strata conventionally so designated) argues strongly for their authenticity.

In fact, a large number of commentators do favor an eschatological interpretation for the feeding of the multitudes. Although some still speak only more generally of divine provision for human need,/80/ of a pure *Wundergeschichte* told for its own sake,/81/ or of the simple, creative power of God,/82/ and a few still resort to rationalizations of a previous century, /83/ too many details compel a more specific and supernatural interpretation. The setting is the wilderness, bringing to mind Moses and the wandering Israelites. Jesus views the crowds as 'sheep without a shepherd' (Mark 6:34), echoing language from Ezekiel's prophecy (Ezek. 34:5). He commands them to sit down 'by companies' (συμπόσια συμπόσια) on the 'green' grass (Mark 6:39). The former phrase is a striking Semitism and a military allusion with close parallels in the description of Qumran's preparation for the eschatological conflagration;/84/ the latter harks back again to Ezekiel 34 (vv. 26-29)./85/ The miracle itself recalls the provision of manna in the wilderness, along with Elisha's feeding miracle noted above, as well as pointing forward to the heavenly banquet to come. Some sort of prophetic typology seems unavoidable.

Of course Matthew and Luke emphasize these elements less, but this probably stems from either stylistic or theological redaction. Both evangelists consistently abbreviate Mark elsewhere, especially when drawing from this section of his gospel on the 'Galilean' ministry. It is also possible that the more exclusive focus on the words and actions of Jesus (blessing, breaking, and distributing the bread) serves to heighten a eucharistic interpretation which Matthew and Luke want to stress, /86/ although Luke in part compensates for his abbreviation by expressly adding that Jesus spoke to them of the kingdom of God (Luke 9:11). That a eucharistic interpretation again competes with strictly eschatological symbolism suggests that even in Mark's version the former is more redactional and the latter more traditional. Mark has also undoubtedly highlighted the disciples' misunderstanding (6:37), as he does consistently elsewhere. But the pre-Markan tradition seems clearly to preserve a portrayal of Jesus as the Messiah, the eschatological prophet and shepherd of Israel. Pesch, for example, traces this theme all the way back to the early Palestinian Jewish-Christian community, and Gnilka even finds a historical meal from Jesus' own ministry at the core of the pericope. Neither will assign the miracle itself to a *Sitz im Leben Jesu*, believing it to have been constructed out of the Elisha parallel./87/ But this is a *non sequitur*; the Old Testament background enhances the case for authenticity. As Taylor observes, 'that Jesus should have anticipated the Messianic feast is in harmony with His teaching concerning the Kingdom with God *and with Jewish customs*' (italics mine)./88/

The feeding narratives, *pace* Caird, have therefore not turned 'an impressive act of prophetic symbolism'/89/ into a miracle; rather they most likely present an original miracle with impressive prophetic symbolism. As P. G. Ziener characterizes it, 'Wie Moses einst das *eine* Gottesvolk aufteilte und jeder Gruppe ihren Vorsteher gab, so teilt auch der Hirte des neutestamentlichen Gottesvolkes als neuer Moses [and one should add, as a New Elisha] seine Herde in Einzelgemeinden auf und gibt ihnen Vorsteher, welche den Gemeinden das vom Herrn bereitet Brot austeilen.'/90/ Or more concisely, with Albright and Mann, 'Jesus, who feeds them now in token of the impending Kingdom and the Messianic Feast, will never fail to feed them. There is enough and to spare.'/91/ Such exegesis coheres so fundamentally with Jesus' undeniably authentic teaching elsewhere (in addition to previously cited passages, cf. esp. Matt. 6:11 par., 7:7-9 par., and the close relation between 'daily bread' and the coming of the kingdom/92/), that a verdict in favor of the historicity of this miracle can be denied only via philosophical prejudices.

Stilling the Storm (Mark 4:35-41, Matt. 8:23-27, Luke 8:22-25)

Here the focus of attention turns somewhat away from the blessings or curses of the new age to the herald of that new age himself. Mark again has the fullest of the three Synoptic versions. Matthew and Luke retain no reference to the enigmatic extra boats of Mark 4:36b/93/, they do not describe Jesus' words to the wind and sea ('Peace, be still'), nor do they include the disciples' address to the sleeping Jesus as bluntly, substituting also their favorite words for 'teacher'./94/ Matthew also employs σεισμός rather than λαῖλαψ to describe the storm./95/ All of these changes make good sense as Matthean and Lucan redaction, but Mark's resulting distinctives do not contribute materially to the meaning of the miracle. The one difference between gospels which may affect the meaning comes with Matthew's (or Mark's) inversion of the sequence of Jesus' miracle and question for the disciples.

Ever since Bornkamm's and Held's pioneering redaction-critical work, many have argued that Matthew stresses the positive side of the disciples much more so than Mark./96/ Here Jesus' rebuke precedes his miracle; afterwards the disciples exhibit no fear or doubt. Ὀλιγόπιστοι (Matt. 8:26) substantially tones down Mark's οὔπω ἔχετε πίστιν; (Mark 4:40b). Similarly Luke altogether omits Mark's τί δειλοί ἐστε; (Mark 4:40a). Yet Mark consistently emphasizes the disciples' misunderstanding at least as strongly as Matthew does their faith, so it is not as obvious that a decision here is that clear cut. Despite protests to the contrary,/97/ it is hard to see how Matthew's 'O men of little faith' is any less harsh than Mark's 'Have you no faith (still)?' One could even just barely argue the reverse, that Matthew's declarative form leaves no room for the possibility that Mark's interrogative might in part be answered positively!/98/ Moreover, Matthew's rebuke seems less justified coming before Jesus' display of power rather than after, and Matthew uses a more chronological transition than does Mark (τότε--Matt. 8:26 vs. καί--Mark 4:39).

Either way, it is not surprising that the issue of discipleship has been regularly viewed as the central thrust of the miracle story./99/ But regardless of which direction redactional activity has taken, discipleship and misunderstanding more likely represent the primary concerns of the evangelists and played less explicit a role in the original event, since both themes are distinctive and characteristic of their respective gospels. Possible parallels in Jesus' parables (e.g. the story of the two builders in Matt. 7:24-27 par.) are less significant here. The traditional form of the story falls into the genre of *Rettungswundergeschichte* and more specifically *Seenotrettungswunder*./100/ While a few still cling to a *religionsgeschichtlich* origin in pagan traditions,/101/ most current commentators recognize the more substantial biblical parallels, especially in Jonah and Acts 27 (for influential shorter verses, see e.g. Psa. 104:7, 107:23-24; and from Qumran, 1QH 6:19ff./102/) The climax of the miracle story, on which all three Synoptists agree, calls the reader, like the disciples, to consider the question, 'Who then is this, that even wind and sea obey him?' (Mark 4:41). Jesus' power over nature mirrors the divine sovereignty and prerogative of Yahweh himself,/103/ but it also discloses the compassion of one who saves and redeems his people./104/ Jesus makes no Christological affirmation, nor does the miracle unambiguously compel faith and understanding. Rather it arouses awe, creates a certain confusion, and sets the disciples thinking about who this man is.

To this extent, the miracle functions exactly like Jesus' teaching on the kingdom. It is 'another mode of language (more dramatic certainly, but in its own way more ambivalent) communicating like parabolic teaching the mystery of God's action in the world, a mystery that discloses itself only to faith.'/105/ Ought the miracle therefore not be anchored in a *Sitz im Leben Jesu*? Koch's objection that the linchpin of the narrative (Mark 4:38b) does not fit a sterotypic 'Hilferuf an der Wundertäter' /106/ does not render the remainder of the account secondary; it is equally likely that such an apparently non-theological deviation from standard 'form' would reflect a stage of tradition *prior* to the onset of stereotyping. Even Bultmann rejects his customary appeal to Hellenistic parallels and finds an early Palestinian origin for this miracle./107/ It should be merely a logical corollary to agree with what Schille calls 'die erstaunliche Tatsache,' that the core of the miracle story 'als Bericht vom Irdischen und nicht als nachösterliche Erzählung entstanden ist.'/108/

Walking on Water (Mark 6:45-52, Matt. 14:22-33, John 6:16-21)

The other sea-rescue miracle in the gospels combines elements of the stilling of the storm with an epiphany of Jesus apparently mastering the power of gravity. Matthew, Mark, and John all agree that it occurred the evening of the day on which Jesus fed the five thousand, although the geographical details of the journey across the Sea of Galilee are not altogether clear./109/ Mark 6:52 creates an additional link with the feeding by attributing the disciples' astonishment to their lack of understanding ἐπὶ τοῖς ἄρτοις. Quentin Quesnel has devoted an entire monograph to the significance of this verse and concludes that it provides a redactional connection with Mark's eucharistic interpretation of the feeding miracle and his emphasis on the mystery of faith. The walking on the water then becomes a displaced narrative of a resurrection appearance of the type which were regularly accompanied by the celebration of the eucharist./110/ But there is not the remotest hint of a meal anywhere in the story of the walking on the water, *per se*, so this cannot be the key to interpreting the *original* meaning of the miracle now before us (and this much Quesnel readily concedes). Lane makes much better sense, even if his interpretation is more general; the disciples failed to grasp in the feeding miracle the secret to Jesus' identity which would have enabled them to understand his self-revelation on the lake. /111/ No parallelism with any individual parable of Jesus emerges here, but the parallelism with the twin functions of parables--to reveal and to conceal--appears as strong as ever. Mark's concluding explanation 'indicates that some events in Jesus' ministry are 'parabolic' in that they provide the key to other events.' /112/

Can this view of Jesus' miracle here be applied to its earliest form? Among the three canonical versions, all have elements which could point to a primitive stage of the tradition. Most find Mark earlier than Matthew, due to Mark's less positive view of the disciples. Matthew's distinctives closely resemble those in his account of the storm-stilling, especially in the wording of Peter's cry, κύριε σῶσόν με (Matt. 14:30), Jesus' use of ὀλιγόπιστε in reply (v. 31), and the disciples'climactic confession which turns doubt into belief (v. 33). The addition of the four verses on Peter's attempt to imitate Jesus' miracle (vv. 28-31) are also usually assigned to Matthew,/113/ although some find their origin in an oral cycle of Petrine tradition,/114/ and a few are even willing to argue for their authenticity./115/ Again, though, the difference in perspective between Matthew and Mark can easily be overstated. John Heil has recently examined the three versions of this miracle in great detail and shows that the similarities in function both in tradition and in redaction far outweigh their differences. On the point at hand, Heil stresses that the 'little faith' of Matthew's disciples, while not the complete lack seemingly implied in Mark, nevertheless functions just as negatively, as that which prevents the disciples (and here, specifically, Peter) from doing what Christ commands./116/ The conclusions of Mark and Matthew do seem at first glance to contradict each other, but here Heil argues that Mark deliberately delays the confession of Jesus as God's Son until the end of his gospel (15:39) to create a continuous progression of growing Christological awareness./117/ The title 'Son of God' is not uniquely Matthean,/118/ despite its centrality in Matthew's Christology, since both Mark and John open and close their gospels with programmatic declarations of Jesus as ὁ υἱὸς τοῦ θεοῦ (Mark 1:1, 15:29; John 1:34, 51, 20:31). Even though Mark has no immediate counterpart to Matt. 14:33, Pesch can nevertheless conclude that Mark presents Jesus 'als der mit Jahwes Kraft und Vollmacht ausgerüstete "Sohn Gottes" epiphan'./119/

Turning to the fourth gospel, many Johannine scholars argue that this version is the most primitive of the three./120/ It is certainly the shortest and simplest and seems to contain no trace of the storm-stilling motif which Markan studies regularly ascribe to redactional (though possibly pre-Markan) activity./121/

Here Heil again dissents, noting the need for some situation of danger to precipitate Jesus' manifestation in this manner,/122/ and Kertelge rightly observes that glimpses of this context remain even in John/123/ (6:18 is explicit and v. 21b makes best sense as a compression of the details about the change in weather and the resulting brevity of the completion of the journey).

All three accounts agree, therefore, that Jesus both revealed his dominance over the sea and made it crossable for the disciples,/124/ the identical accomplishments of Jesus' storm-stilling miracle. Both functions have Old Testament parallels (see esp. Job 9:8 and Psa. 77:20) which again suggest that Jesus is exercising the power and authority of Yahweh himself. The two *cruces interpretum* are Mark's ἤθελεν παρελθεῖν αὐτούς (6:48--hardly redactional due to its highly enigmatic character) and Jesus' revelation, identical in all versions--ἐγώ εἰμι· μὴ φοβεῖσθε. Παρέρχομαι, like the English 'pass by,' can mean both 'avoid' and 'draw near'; while most commentators choose one over the other,/125/ perhaps something of both meanings is intended./126/ Again, as with his parables, Jesus' miracle reveals and yet conceals, pointing to his divine origin and yet transcending conventional categories. Jesus ushers in the kingdom and yet leaves its later consummation to fulfill and to explain all of God's promises. The ἐγώ εἰμι may well function identically. The parallel with the theophany to Moses and revelation of the divine name has escaped few commentators' attention, and yet as Morris rightly reminds us, 'here it is primarily a means of self-identification. What else would he say?'/127/

A certain reserve and dignity thus distinguishes Jesus' walking on the water from pagan parallels (which include some from even as far away as Buddhist India/128/), and a background of targumic and Qumranic teaching on God's lordship over the sea /129/ should make one perfectly content with a Palestinian Jewish-Christian origin of the story. It is not that great a step from here to the conclusion that Jesus himself must have performed some feat closely resembling that described in these narratives to give rise to such an early belief in the miracle. Naturalistic explanations again fail to convince;/130/ the parallelism of ἐπὶ τῆς θαλάσσης (Mark 6:48) with ἐπὶ τῆς γῆς (v. 47) demands a translation of 'on the sea' and not 'by the sea'./131/ Similarities with the other nature miracles and even exorcisms (cf. the triple tradition juxtaposition of Jesus' stilling the storm and exorcising the Gerasene demoniac--Mark 4:35-5:20 pars.) makes the theory of a dislocated resurrection appearance highly improbable./132/ As R. H. Fuller properly points out, the story 'in the last resort echoes the proclamation of Jesus; "The Reign of God has drawn nigh."' Thus Fuller's accompanying conclusion that 'this story has been constructed by the early church'/133/ does not follow; the criteria of authenticity almost require one to accept that which coheres so closely with the core of Jesus' authentic teaching.

The Great Catch of Fish (Luke 5:1-11)

This final nature miracle differs from the preceding five in at least two important ways. First, strictly speaking, nothing transcends the natural course of events here, except for Jesus' timing and insight. The Sea of Galilee regularly provided large catches for its fishermen. This time Peter and his companions had toiled all night and took nothing (Luke 5:5), but Jesus was able to direct them immediately to a great shoal of fish. Second, a post-resurrection appearance of Jesus offers some striking parallels (John 21:1-11), leading many to assume that Luke has read this narrative back into the earthly life of Jesus and conflated it with the Markan story of the call of Peter, James, and John (Mark 1:16-20 par.)./134/ On the other hand, the story describes Jesus providing bountifully to meet physical needs, exactly as with the 'gift miracles' of the wine and of the bread and fish. Moreover, the manner in which Jesus supplied those other provisions, though apparently more miraculous, remains equally unobtrusive and unexpressed. The similarities are close enough to warrant the narrative's inclusion as this final example of Jesus' parabolic nature miracles. A specific parable, that of the dragnet (Matt. 13:47-50), again offers parallel imagery, though with somewhat different significance--the separation of good and bad fish (= people). The accompanying nature parables of the sower and mustard seed more closely resemble the miracle of the catch, in meaning if not in exact imagery, as they depict the overabundant harvest of the kingdom of God.

Direct literary relationship with the Johannine narrative seems unlikely, since the only two words of any consequence shared by the two accounts are ἰχθύς and δίκτυον./135/ J. Bailey, however, argues that Luke does depend on a pre-Johannine form of the resurrection appearance, since (a) Luke 5:8 fits better after Peter's threefold denial of Jesus, (b) Σίμων Πέτρος is the fourth gospel's name for this disciple and not Luke's, and (c) the miracle story is easily detachable from its context./136/ On the other hand, Plummer finds two completely independent events here. Luke describes Peter's call and John his recall./137/ Perhaps an intermediate view best solves the problem. Bailey's argument (b) is his best (John uses the double name 17X; Luke only here and in a way in 6:14--Σίμωνα ὃν καὶ ὠνόμασεν Πέτρον), but it scarcely affects the entire narrative. Point (c) is borne out by Mark's and Matthew's versions which show no knowledge of the miracle but must be balanced by the tight structural coherence that Delorme has demonstrated for Luke 5:1-11./138/ Against (a), I. H. Marshall comments: 'What Simon expressed was a sense of unworthiness (Mt. 8:8; Job 42:5f.) and fear (Jdg. 6:22, 13:22, 1 Ki. 17:18, Is. 6:5) which men should feel in the presence of the divine. . . a post-resurrection setting is not required.'/139/ Most likely two independent stories have influenced each other slightly in oral transmission but nevertheless refer back to two originally distinct events./140/

Luke's parallelism with Mark proves more significant. It is not impossible that Jesus called Peter twice, with the second occasion leading to a more decisive initiation into his discipleship though still preceding the official naming of twelve (Mark 3:13-19, Luke 6:12-16)./141/ But the identity of the climactic statements in Mark 1:17 and Luke 5:10, on becoming fishers of men, weighs heavily against this hypothesis. Most likely, Luke has transposed the Markan version just as he probably did his preceding account of Jesus preaching in Nazareth (Luke 4:16-30; cf. Mark 6:1-6a par.)/142/ These two stories may even serve as foils for each other--Peter's obedient faith sharply contrasting with the rejection and unbelief of Jesus' hometown acquaintances./143/ But both passages also contain substantially unparalleled material which nevertheless seems historical and in an entirely plausible *Sitz im Leben Jesu*. Pesch has exhaustively demonstrated the pre-Lucan style and vocabulary of the account of the great catch of fish,/144/ but concludes that it was still purely legendary since it neither met a need nor had symbolic value./145/ The former criticism is possible, although Luke 5:5 suggests at the very least that Jesus' action compensated for a physically exhausting and emotionally defeating experience. The latter comment is incomprehensible; even without the explicit Markan framework, the miracle presents a 'zeichenhaften Handlung' as a 'Selbstoffenbarung Jesu als der machtvollwirkende Kyrios'./146/

Redactional studies may speculate on the narrative's function for Luke--underlining apostolic activity and dignity, /147/ the unity of the church (in the unbroken net and the help from other boats--v. 7) under Peter's leadership,/148/ or the urgency of mission (v. 11)./149/ Having stripped away these elements, however, the resulting *Wundergeschichte* conveys the identical impression as repeatedly above. Jesus displays the power and blessings of God's in-breaking kingdom with a lavish gift which symbolizes a coming sphere of existence in which luxury will become commonplace. As with the other feeding miracles, 'the parabolic strain surely continues.'/150/

Conclusion

The logic of our argument remains quite simple and can be expressed by the following propositions: (1) A large consensus of scholars from a wide cross-section of the theological spectrum agrees that a basic criterion of authenticity to be applied to the Jesus-tradition is the criterion of coherence: that which is fully consistent with material authenticated by the other recognized criteria may be accepted as authentic as well. (2) Jesus' teaching about the in-breaking kingdom of God, especially in his parables, is by these criteria the most demonstrably authentic core of historical information about Jesus in the gospels. (3) The narratives of the nature miracles when examined in their earliest forms recoverable from the gospel texts depict in symbol the identical in-breaking kingdom, often with striking parallels in both imagery and significance to specific parables of Jesus. In short, the nature miracles and the parables closely cohere with each other. From these three propositions it therefore follows that the earliest forms of these miracle stories should be recognized as most probably historical (that is to say factual accounts of deeds from the life of Christ). A very similar argument has been used to defend the reliability of the narratives of Jesus' healings and exorcism/151/; no longer need the nature miracles be categorized separately in this respect.

Only a few would question propositions (1) and (2) in this summary; the most recent studies of the miracles lean more and more toward accepting (3)/152/. Consequently, only philosophical bias (i.e. a commitment to anti-supernaturalism) stands in the way of upholding the conclusion/153/. If the nature miracles are admitted to be *possible* on philosophical grounds, then the reliability of these six narratives becomes very *probable* on historical grounds. Of course, the criterion of coherence is not foolproof; it is conceivable that the gospel authors (or tradents of the traditions they inherited) went out of their way to invent detailed and subtle parallels between fantasy and fact much like modern examples of 'historical fiction'. If this is the case, then *as historians* we have little hope of separating the two and must rest content only with our concusions about the parabolic significance of the texts (cf. Bruce Chilton's very balanced conclusions in his essay on exorcism elsewhere in this volume/154/). But I have elsewhere argued against such an approach to the genre of the gospel material as a whole /155/ and more recent studies on the topic have not dissuaded me./156/ The more limited scope of this essay, however, merely permits me to highlight some often overlooked parallels between the miracles and the parables and to suggest that the former make very good sense when viewed as genuine, symbolic enactments of the dawning new age by its harbinger, Jesus. Caird correctly concludes, 'The miracles of Jesus were all "miracles of the kingdom," evidence that God's sovereignty was breaking in with a new effectiveness, upon the confusion of a rebellious world. The question of his disciples --"Who then is this?"--admitted of only one answer: this is the man to whom God has entrusted the authority of his kingdom.'/157/ This quotation applies almost certainly to the earliest stages of the gospel tradition and ought to be taken seriously as a summary of the significance of actions of the historical Jesus as well.

Notes

/1/ On the parables, see esp. J. Jeremias, *The Parables of Jesus* (London: SCM, 1972); and H. Weder, *Die Gleichnisse Jesu als Metaphern* (Göttingen: Vandenhoeck & Ruprecht, 1978). This consensus does not extend to every detail of every parable, but few of the allegedly inauthentic parts need be taken as such; see my 'Tradition History of the Parables Peculiar to Luke's Central Section' (Ph.D. Diss.: Aberdeen, 1982); and more briefly P. B. Payne, 'The Authenticity of the Parables of Jesus,' in *Gospel Perspectives*, II (ed. R. T. France and D. Wenham; Sheffield: JSOT, 1981) 329-44. The three major exceptions to this consensus in recent study have been J. Drury, M. Goulder, & G. Sellin, whose arguments are exceptionally weak; see in detail my 'Tradition History,' 240-52, 364-72. Drury's new *The Parables in the Gospels* (London: SPCK, 1985) furthers his radical scepticism but with little discussion of the traditional arguments for authenticity and without any reference to publications on the parables since 1975! On the kingdom, see esp. B. D. Chilton, *God in Strength: Jesus' Announcement of the Kingdom* (Freistadt: F. Plöchl, 1979).
/2/ See esp. G. E. Ladd, *The Presence of the Future* (Grand

Rapids: Eerdmans, 1974); W. G. Kümmel, *Promise and Fulfilment* (London: SCM, 1957).

/3/ For the programmatic exposition of this position, see R. Bultmann, *Jesus and the Word* (London: Ivor Nicholson & Watson, 1935); *Jesus Christ and Mythology* (London: SCM, 1960). Cf. also R. H. Fuller, *Interpreting the Miracles* (London: SCM, 1963) 37-39. To read a recent survey text such as J. Tyson, *The New Testament and Early Christianity* (New York: Macmillan, 1984) 38, one might imagine that no one had ever challenged Bultmann on this issue! Note also the tenacity of this view in the literature surveyed by G. Maier, 'Zur neutestamentliche Wunderexegese im 19. und 20. Jahrhundert,' elsewhere in this volume.

/4/ On this distinction, see K. Tagawa, *Miracles et Évangile* (Paris: Presses Universitaires, 1966) 14; S. Légasse, 'L'historien en quête de l'événement,' in *Les miracles de Jésus selon le Nouveau Testament* (ed. X. Léon-Dufour; Paris: Editions du Seuil, 1977) 118-29; R. Pesch, *Jesu ureigene Taten?* (Freiburg: Herder, 1970) 17; D. Aune, 'Magic in Early Christianity,' in *Aufstieg und Niedergang der römischen Welt*, II 23.2 (ed. W. Haase; Berlin: de Gruyter, 1980) 1524. On 1538 Aune says of the nature miracles that 'most. . .are creations out of whole cloth by the early communities,' though from the grammar of the sentence it is not clear if he means just 'magical folkloristic motifs' in them.

/5/ Few conservatives have recognized the full weight of this observation; one who has is L. Sabourin, *The Divine Miracles Discussed and Defended* (Rome: Catholic Book Agency, 1977) 54-55, who points to some crucial distinctions between the two *corpora* of miracles.

/6/ See B. Blackburn, '"Miracle Working Θεῖοι Ἄνδρες" in Hellenism (and Hellenistic Judaism),' elsewhere in this volume (who offers important correctives to this notion), and the literature there cited.

/7/ D. L. Tiede, *The Charismatic Figure as Miracle Worker* (Missoula: SBL, 1972). Equally critical of this trend but with different conclusions are E. Best, 'The Miracles in Mark,' *Rev Exp* 75 (1978) 539-54; and D. Aune, 'The Problem of the Genre of the Gospels,' in *Gospel Perspectives*, II, 9-60.

/8/ M. E. Glasswell, 'The Use of Miracles in the Marcan Gospel,' in *Miracles* (ed. C. F. D. Moule; London: Mowbray, 1965) 151-62.

/9/ An extremely lucid example is the 'exegesis' of E. & M.-L. Keller, *Miracles in Dispute* (London: SCM, 1969) 226-50.

/10/ A tendency sometimes characterizing the otherwise fine study of A. Richardson, *The Miracle Stories of the Gospels* (London: SCM, 1941); and even more so in W. Neil, 'The Nature

Miracles,' *ExpT* 67 (1955-56) 369-72. On a more popular level the approach is much clearer. See e.g. H. Lockyer, *All the Miracles of the Bible* (Grand Rapids: Zondervan, 1961) 248-49, 284, 307-9, 313.
/11/ E.g. Lockyer, *Miracles,* 15-17. C. Brown, *Miracles and the Critical Mind* (Grand Rapids: Eerdmans, 1984) 197-235, nicely surveys recent discussion by Christian apologists, a number of which subscribe to this evidentialism to one degree or another.
/12/ G. Klein, *Ärgernisse* (München: Kaiser, 1970) 56.
/13/ G. Theissen, *The Miracle Stories of the Early Christian Tradition* (Philadelphia: Fortress, 1983) 294.
/14/ See esp. J. R. Kirkland, 'The Earliest Understanding of Jesus' Use of Parables: Mark 4:10-12 in Context,' *NovT* 19 (1977) 1-21.
/15/ See esp. R. H. Stein, *An Introduction to the Parables of Jesus* (Philadelphia: Westminster, 1981) 27-35; H.-J. Klauck, *Allegorie und Allegorese in synoptischen Gleichnistexten* (Münster: Aschendorff, 1978) 251; C. A. Evans, 'The Function of Isaiah 6:9-10 in Mark and John,' *NovT* 24 (1982) 124-38.
/16/ H. van der Loos, *The Miracles of Jesus* (Leiden: Brill, 1965) 250-51.
/17/ Ibid., 701-2. For a similar statement of a generation ago, cf. D. S. Cairns, *The Faith That Rebels* (London: SCM, 1929) 67.
/18/ B. Bron, *Das Wunder* (Göttingen: Vandenhoeck & Ruprecht, 1975) 239. Cf. O. Betz & W. Grimm, *Wesen und Wirklichkeit der Wunder Jesu* (Frankfurt: P. Lang, 1977) 54; R. Kratz, *Rettungswunder* (Frankfurt: P. Lang, 1979) 543.
/19/ J. Kallas, *The Significance of the Synoptic Miracles* (London: SPCK, 1961) 77.
/20/ E.g. K. Kertelge, *Die Wunder Jesu im Markusevangelium* (München: Kösel, 1970) 201-2, agrees with the previous interpretation for the nature miracles, but argues that Mark was the first to so view them. Theissen, *Miracle Stories*, utilizes form criticism more than redaction criticism to trace this approach to an early stage of the tradition, but avoids the question of authenticity on ideological and methodological grounds (pp. 30-40). H. C. Kee, *Miracle in the Early Christian World* (New Haven: Yale, 1983) is very similar to Theissen in this respect.
/21/ See esp. R. Swinburne, *The Concept of Miracle* (London: SCM, 1970). Brown, *Miracles*, 174-95, summarizes the views of several other recent philosophers who follow suit. Cf. now also K. Yandell, *Christianity and Philosophy* (Grand Rapids: Eerdmans, 1984).
/22/ Cf. the approach of the early church, which accepted the truth of at least some reports of parallel prodigies, often

attributing them to other supernatural powers, both angelic and demonic. See esp. H. Remus, *Pagan-Christian Conflict over Miracle in the Second Century* (Cambridge, MA: Philadelphia Patristic Foundation, 1983).

/23/ An apparent nature miracle left untouched here is Matt. 17:27--the coin in the fish's mouth. Its purpose, though, is so markedly different and its narrative so tantalizingly brief, that it seems more likely that only a metaphorical statement of some type is intended. See for more detail my 'The New Testament Miracles and Higher Criticism: Climbing Up the Slippery Slope,' *Journal of the Evangelical Theological Society* 27 (1984) 425 -38. For a different approach, see R. Bauckham, 'The Coin in the Fish's Mouth,' elsewhere in this volume, but note his admission of the uniqueness of the form remaining largely unexplained.

/24/ T. W. Manson, e.g., in 'The Cleansing of the Temple,' *BJRL* 33 (1951) 279, finds the story as it stands 'simply incredible'.

/25/ Cf. K. E. Bailey, *Through Peasant Eyes: More Lucan Parables* (Grand Rapids: Eerdmans, 1980) 80-87. J. Gnilka, *Das Evangelium nach Markus*, II (Neukirchen-Vluyn: Neukirchener; Zurich: Benziger, 1979) 125, strikes a sane balance between these two alternatives: 'Damit ist kein Urteil über den einzelnen Israeliten gefällt, aber im heilsgeschichtlichen Sinn ein Schlussstrich unter die Geschichte Gottes mit seinem Volk gezogen.'

/26/ One of the fullest summaries of these texts appears in M. Trautmann, *Zeichenhafte Handlungen Jesu* (Würzburg: Echter, 1980) 335.

/27/ E.g. H. Anderson, *The Gospel of Mark* (London: Marshall, Morgan & Scott, 1976) 263; V. Taylor, *The Gospel according to St. Mark* (London: Macmillan, 1952); D. E. Nineham, *St. Mark* (Harmondsworth: Penguin, 1963) 299. J. C. Fenton, *St. Matthew* (Harmondsworth: Penguin, 1963) 336, postulates an origin from a saying of John the Baptist *à la* Matt. 3:10.

/28/ See esp. Trautmann, *Handlungen*, 329.

/29/ Thus R. Pesch, *Das Markusevangelium*, II (Freiburg: Herder, 1977) 190-97, finds at least Mark 11:23 linked with vv. 12-14 and 20-22 at a pre-Markan, pre-passion narrative stage, but he also finds the main point of the miracle to be the power of faith.

/30/ E.g. E. Schweizer, *The Good News according to Mark* (Atlanta: John Knox, 1970) 230; Nineham, *Mark*, 298; Gnilka, *Markus*, II, 133.

/31/ E.g. A. W. Argyle, *The Gospel according to Matthew* (Cambridge: University Press, 1963) 159; R. H. Gundry, *Matthew: A Commentary on His Literary and Theological Art* (Grand Rapids:

Eerdmans, 1982) 415-16; D. A. Carson, 'Matthew,' in *Expositor's Bible Commentary*, VIII (ed. F. E. Gaebelein; Grand Rapids: Zondervan, 1984) 444.

/32/ For the details of this conflation see R. E. Morosco, 'Redaction Criticism and the Evangelical: Matthew 10 A Test Case,' *Journal of the Evangelical Theological Society* 22 (1979) 323-31; for an alternate explanation, D. Wenham, *The Rediscovery of Jesus' Eschatological Discourse: Gospel Perspectives*, IV (Sheffield: JSOT, 1984) 219-51.

/33/ W. L. Lane, *The Gospel according to Mark* (Grand Rapids: Eerdmans, 1974) 409.

/34/ Gundry, *Matthew*, 299.

/35/ Emphasized by G. Münderlein, 'Die Verfluchung des Feigenbaums (Mk. xi. 12-14),' *NTS* 10 (1963) 103-4.

/36/ More popular a generation ago, but re-argued vigorously by Trautmann, *Handlungen*, 343-44.

/37/ K. Romaniuk, '"Car ce n'é tait pas la saison de figues. . ." (Mk 11, 12-14 parr.),' *ZNW* 66 (1975) 275-78.

/38/ See esp. C. W. F. Smith, 'No Time for Figs,' *JBL* 79 (1960) 315-27.

/39/ E.g. R. H. Hiers, '"Not the Season for Figs",' *JBL* 87 (1968) 400; H.-W. Bartsch, 'Die "Verfluchung" des Feigenbaums,' *ZNW* 53 (1962) 256-60.

/40/ E.g. A. Plummer, *An Exegetical Commentary on the Gospel according to St. Matthew* (London: Robert Scott, 1915) 291; D. Hill, *The Gospel of Matthew* (London: Oliphants, 1972) 294.

/41/ E.g. C. E. B. Cranfield, *The Gospel according to St. Mark* (Cambridge: University Press, 1977) 356; Lane, *Mark*, 409.

/42/ See esp. J. W. Doeve, 'Purification du Temple et dessèchement du figuier,' *NTS* 1 (1954-55) 297-308.

/43/ Cf. the conclusions of the recent, exhaustive study of the history of and issues in the interpretation of this passage by W. R. Telford, *The Barren Temple and the Withered Tree* (Sheffield: JSOT, 1980) 238-39; and those of W. Harrington, *Mark* (Wilmington: Glazier, 1979) 179: 'a prophetic gesture symbolizing the end of the temple and its worship'. See also A. Cole, *The Gospel according to St. Mark* (London: Tyndale, 1961) 177: 'Like tree, like temple, like nation, the parallel is exact.'

/44/ H. Giesen, 'Der verdorrte Feigenbaum--Eine symbolische Aussage? Zu Mk 11, 12-14.20f,' *BZ* 20 (1976) 103.

/45/ Harrington, *Mark*, 181.

/46/ Cole, *Mark*, 181.

/47/ C. H. Dodd, *Historical Tradition in the Fourth Gospel* (Cambridge: University Press, 1963) 227; B. Lindars, 'Two Parables in John,' *NTS* 16 (1970) 318-22. Lindars differs from

Dodd in assuming that some (non-miraculous) historical event in Jesus' life trigerred this addition and embellishment, where Dodd sees none.

/48/ F. E. Williams, 'Fourth Gospel and Synoptic Tradition: Two Johannine Passages,' *JBL* 86 (1967) 311-16.

/49/ S. Smalley, *John: Evangelist and Theologian* (Exeter: Paternoster, 1978) 178; cf. B. Olsson, *Structure and Meaning in the Fourth Gospel* (Lund: Gleerup, 1974) 285, who speaks of 'desymbolization'.

/50/ So J. N. Sanders and B. A. Mastin, *A Commentary on the Gospel according to St. John* (London: Black, 1968) 114-15.

/51/ But not as insoluble as some think; see D. A. Carson, 'Historical Tradition in the Fourth Gospel: After Dodd, What?' in *Gospel Perspectives*, II, 83-145.

/52/ M. C. Tenney, 'John,' in *The Expositor's Bible Commentary*, IX, 43.

/53/ van der Loos, *Miracles*, 615.

/54/ C. Armerding, 'The Marriage in Cana,' *BSac* 118 (1961) 320-26.

/55/ J.A. Grassi, 'The Wedding at Cana (John 2:1-11): A Pentecostal Meditation?' *NovT* 14 (1972) 131-36.

/56/ A. Geyser, 'The Semeion at Cana of the Galilee,' in *Studies in John* (n. ed.; Leiden: Brill, 1970) 10-21.

/57/ B. F. Westcott, *The Gospel according to St. John* (London: John Murray, 1886) 39.

/58/ J. D. M. Derrett, 'Water into Wine,' in *Law in the New Testament* (London: Darton, Longman & Todd, 1970) 228-46.

/59/ On such a signs source, see esp. R. T. Fortna, *The Gospel of Signs* (Cambridge: University Press, 1970) 29-38.

/60/ R. Schnackenburg, *The Gospel according to St. John*, I (London: Burns & Oates, 1968) 337.

/61/ R. Bultmann, *The Gospel of John* (Philadelphia: Westminster, 1971) 118.

/62/ E. Linnemann, 'Die Hochzeit zu Kana und Dionysius,' *NTS* 20 (1974) 408-18.

/63/ Rightly stressed by E. Haenchen, *Das Johannesevangelium* (ed. U. Busse; Tübingen: Mohr, 1980) 195-96; *pace* C. K. Barrett, *The Gospel according to St. John* (Philadelphia: Westminster, 1978) 188; B. Lindars, *The Gospel of John* (London: Marshall, Morgan & Scott, 1972) 127; Sanders & Mastin, *John*, 114.

/64/ Cf. further I. Broer, 'Noch einmal: Zur religionsgeschichtlichen "Ableitung" von Jo 2, 1-11,' *SNTU* 8 (1983) 103-23.

/65/ See esp. Olsson, *Structure*, 100-1; *pace* Bultmann, *John*, 117.

/66/ Significant portions of these parables, of course, have often been seen as secondary, but often precisely because they

do not readily cohere with this interpretation of their indisputably authentic cores (classically Jeremias, *Parables*, 63-69, 176-80, 206-10). For similar exposition which finds less incoherence and thus less inauthenticity, see S. Kistemaker, *The Parables of Jesus* (Grand Rapids: Baker, 1980) 99-106, 146-57, 193-201.
/67/ W. Nicol, *The Semēia in the Fourth Gospel* (Leiden: Brill, 1972) 54.
/68/ Richardson, *Miracle Stories*, 121.
/69/ J. Breuss, *Das Kanawunder* (Fribourg: Schweizerisches Katholisches Bibelwerk, 1976) 30. So also Betz & Grimm, *Wunder*, 128-30; R. H. Lightfoot, *St. John's Gospel: A Commentary* (ed. C. F. Evans; Oxford: Clarendon, 1956) 100; R. Brown, *The Gospel according to John, I-XII* (Garden City: Doubleday, 1966) 105.
/70/ J. Marsh, *The Gospel of St. John* (Harmondsworth: Penguin, 1968) goes too far in demanding this symbolism (p. 147). Cf. R. Kysar, *The Fourth Evangelist and His Gospel* (Minneapolis: Augsburg, 1975) 250: 'The only basis for finding a sacramental insinuation in this passage is the role of the wine, and it seems quite unnecessary to assign it that referent.'
/71/ Cf. R. J. Dillon, 'Wisdom Tradition and Sacramental Retrospect in the Cana Account,' *CBQ* 24 (1962) 287-88; J. McPolin, *John* (Wilmington: Glazier, 1979) 23.
/72/ An important exception is R. M. Fowler, *Loaves and Fishes* (Chico: Scholars, 1980) 37, who concludes that Mark 6:32-44 is a secondary expansion of 8:1-10.
/73/ N. A. Beck, 'Reclaiming a Biblical Text: The Mark 8:14-21 Discussion about Bread in the Boat,' *CBQ* 43 (1981) 52, n. 15; S. Masuda, 'The Good News of the Miracle of the Bread: The Tradition and Its Markan Redaction,' *NTS* 28 (1982) 211-12; H. Kruse, 'Jesu Seefahrten und die Stellungen von Joh. 6,' *NTS* 30 (1984) 521-22.
/74/ E. E. Lemcio, 'External Evidence for the Structure and Function of Mark iv. 1-20, vii. 14-23 and viii. 14-21,' *JTS* 29 (1978) 323-38.
/75/ See esp. J. Knackstedt, 'Die beiden Brotvermehrungen im Evangelium,' *NTS* 10 (1963-64) 315-16. For additional, incisive comments on this problem, see Carson, 'Matthew,' 358.
/76/ Brown, *John, I-XII*, 236-50, gives a very detailed discussion. Cf. now P. W. Barnett, 'The Feeding of the Multitude in Mark 6/John 6,' elsewhere in this volume.
/77/ Schnackenburg, *John*, II (New York: Seabury, 1980) 16-22.
/78/ See the emphasis of Theissen, *Miracle Stories*, 103-6, on the unobtrusiveness of this and other 'gift miracles'.
/79/ On the authenticity of this often allegedly secondary motif in Luke 14:23, see esp. K. E. Bailey, *Through Peasant Eyes: More*

Lucan Parables (Grand Rapids: Eerdmans, 1980) 101-9.
/80/ Schweizer, *Mark*, 139; Cole, *Mark*, 115.
/81/ B. van Iersel, 'Die wunderbare Speisung und das Abendmahl in der synoptischen Tradition,' *NovT* 7 (1964) 167-94 (with a eucharistic interpretation overlaid); D. A. Koch, *Die Bedeutung der Wundererzählungen für die Christologie des Markusevangeliums* (Berlin: de Gruyter, 1975) 102.
/82/ Anderson, *Mark*, 176; J. Schmid, *The Gospel according to Mark* (New York: Alba House, 1968) 129-30.
/83/ Richardson, *Miracle Stories*, 96-97; Hill, *Matthew*, 245.
/84/ See esp. E. Stauffer, "Zum apokalyptischen Festmahl in Mc 6, 34ff.' *ZNW* 46 (1955) 264-66.
/85/ Lane, *Mark*, 229.
/86/ See esp. Gundry, *Matthew*, 291-94; I. H. Marshall, *The Gospel of Luke* (Grand Rapids: Eerdmans, 1978) 357-58, who also highlights Luke's enhanced Christological stress. For an innovative view of eucharistic significance, concerning the fish, see J.-M. van Cangh, 'Le thème des poissons dans les récits évangéliques de la multiplication des pains,' *RB* 78 (1971) 71-83.
/87/ Pesch, *Markusevangelium*, I (1976) 354-56; Gnilka, *Markus*, I (1978) 263.
/88/ Taylor, *Mark*, 321.
/89/ G. B. Caird, *St. Luke* (Harmondsworth: Penguin, 1963) 127.
/90/ P. G. Ziener, 'Die Brotwunder im Markusevangelium,' *BZ* 4 (1960) 284.
/91/ W. F. Albright and C. S. Mann, *Matthew* (Garden City: Doubleday, 1971) 177. Cf. similar statements by W. Grundmann, *Das Evangelium nach Lukas* (Berlin: Evangelische Verlagsanstalt, 1966) 134; L. Morris, *The Gospel according to John* (Grand Rapids: Eerdmans, 1971) 340-41. The overtly political interpretation of H. Montefiore, 'Revolt in the Desert? (Mark vi. 30ff.),' *NTS* 8 (1962) 135-41, has gained few adherents.
/92/ Esp. if ἄρτος ἐπιούσιος is interpreted eschatologically as 'bread for the morrow'. Cf. C. Hemer, 'ἐπιούσιος,' *JSNT* 22 (1984) 81-94.
/93/ Of all the explanations perhaps that which views this as an incidental eyewitness detail, and therefore a Petrine reminiscence, still remains the best. See Cranfield, *Mark*, 173; Lane, *Mark*, 175.
/94/ Ἐπιστάτης occurs 6X in Luke and nowhere else in the NT. The vocative κύριε occurs 30X in Matthew compared with only 2X in Mark (although it reappears 24X in Luke).
/95/ E. Schweizer, *The Good News according to Matthew* (Atlanta: John Knox, 1975) 221, thinks this clarifies a link with the signs of the coming kingdom.

/96/ G. Bornkamm, G. Barth, & H. J. Held, *Tradition and Interpretation in Matthew* (Philadelphia: Westminster, 1963).
/97/ Esp. by Gundry, *Matthew*, 625-26, who identifies the difference between Matthew and Mark here as one of the least harmonizable contradictions among the gospels!
/98/ See Theissen, *Miracle Stories*, 137-38.
/99/ See the survey of this line of interpretation in Gnilka, *Markus*, I, 198.
/100/ Kratz, *Rettungswunder*, 201.
/101/ Kertelge, *Wunder*, 97.
/102/ This last citation is especially stressed by W. Grundmann, *Das Evangelium nach Markus* (Berlin: Evangelische Verlagsanstalt, 1959) 103.
/103/ Kratz, *Rettungswunder*, 217; P. J. Achtemeier, 'Person and Deed: Jesus and the Storm Tossed Sea,' *Int* 16 (1962) 169-76; Harrington, *Mark*, 65.
/104/ Betz & Grimm, *Wunder*, 82-83. Van der Loos, *Miracles*, 648, unjustifiably pits the latter point against the former.
/105/ Anderson, *Mark*, 143.
/106/ Koch, *Wundererzählungen*, 96.
/107/ R. Bultmann, *The History of the Synoptic Tradition* (Oxford: Blackwell, 1963) 240.
/108/ G. Schille, 'Die Seesturmerzählung Markus 4, 35-41 als Beispiel neutestamentlicher Aktualisierung,' *ZNW* 56 (1965) 40.
/109/ Mark says that they left for Bethsaida; John, for Capernaum. But both agree Jesus had been across the Jordan and that he now headed for the other side of the lake, so some type of harmonization seems in order, perhaps even text-critically (note the omission of εἰς τὸ περάν from Mark 6:45 in W λ q sy^{s} and conjecturally p^{45}).
/110/ Q. Quesnel, *The Mind of Mark: Interpretation and Method through the Exegesis of Mark 6:52* (Rome: PBI, 1969) esp. 261-67.
/111/ Lane, *Mark*, 237-38.
/112/ Ibid., 238. Cf. A.-M. Denis, 'La marche de Jésus sur les eaux,' in *De Jésus aux Évangiles* (ed. I. de la Potterie; Gembloux: Duculot, 1967) 238: 'pour Marc. . .ont un sens de mystère, et les trois synoptiques paraissent l'attribuer aux paraboles du royaume,' and 244: 'Dans la marche sur les eaux, réservée aux Douze, le Seigneur du royaume en mystère. . .sauve aussi la communauté (la barque) des dangers de la mer par un pouvoir supraterrestre. . .'
/113/ Perhaps specifically as a 'preacher's elaboration' (Fenton, *Matthew*, 246) or 'haggadic midrash' (Gundry, *Matthew*, 300) on discipleship.
/114/ G. D. Kilpatrick, *The Origins of the Gospel according to St. Matthew* (Oxford: Clarendon, 1946) 38-44; Schweizer, *Matthew*,

319.
/115/ Plummer, *Matthew*, 207, e.g., notes that the episode is 'so exactly in harmony with his *[Peter's]* character, that invention is unlikely,' and cf. p. 209; Argyle, *Matthew*, 115.
/116/ J. Heil, *Jesus Walking on the Sea* (Rome: PBI, 1981) 63, & 64, n. 83. Cf. Albright & Mann, *Matthew*, 181, who maintain that Matthew shows 'no hesitation in recording Peter's weakness under the strain of testing'.
/117/ Heil, *Sea*, 75.
/118/ *Pace* Gundry, *Matthew*, 301; Held, in *Tradition*, 206.
/119/ Pesch, *Markusevangelium*, I, 359.
/120/ E.g. Schnackenburg, *John*, II, 25-28; Lindars, *John*, 238.
/121/ E.g. Schweizer, *Mark*, 141; Nineham, *Mark*, 180-81; Gnilka, *Markus*, I, 266; Koch, *Wundererzählungen*, 104-5.
/122/ Heil, *Sea*, 95.
/123/ Kertelge, *Wunder*, 147.
/124/ See esp. the emphasis on these two features in Heil, *Sea*, 56.
/125/ On the former, see e.g. Cole, *Mark*, 116; on the latter, van der Loos, *Miracles*, 652-53.
/126/ See esp. T. Snoy, 'La rédaction marcienne de la marche sur les eaux (Mc., VI, 45-52),' *ETL* 44 (1968) 205-41; H. Fleddermann, '"And He Wanted to Pass by Them" (Mark 6:48c),' *CBQ* 45 (1983) 389-95.
/127/ Morris, *John*, 350, n. 43.
/128/ R. Stehly, 'Bouddhisme et Nouveau Testament à propos de la marche de Pierre sur l'eau (Matthieu 14.28s),' *RHPR* 57 (1977) 433-37.
/129/ See Heil, *Sea*, 17-30, 42-57.
/130/ *Pace* Taylor, *Mark*, 327; J. D. M. Derrett, 'Why and How Jesus Walked on the Sea,' *NovT* 23 (1981) 330-48.
/131/ Cranfield, *Mark*, 226.
/132/ Rightly Kertelge, *Wunder*, 148-49.
/133/ Fuller, *Miracles*, 59.
/134/ E.g. Bultmann, *John*, 704; Grundmann, *Lukas*, 127; A. R. C. Leaney, 'Jesus and Peter: The Call and Post-Resurrection Appearances (Luke v. 1-11 and xxiv. 34),' *ExpT* 65 (1954) 381-82; D. Losada, 'El relato de la pesca milagrosa,' *Revista bíblica* 40 (1978) 22.
/135/ J. A. Bailey, *The Traditions Common to the Gospels of Luke and John* (Leiden: Brill, 1963) 12.
/136/ Ibid., 14.
/137/ A. Plummer, *A Critical and Exegetical Commentary on the Gospel according to St. Luke* (Edinburgh: T & T Clark, 1896) 142. So also N. Geldenhuys, *Commentary on the Gospel of Luke* (London: Marshall, Morgan & Scott, 1950) 181; Morris, *John*, 860, n. 4.

/138/ J. Delorme, 'Luc v. 1-11: Analyse structurale et histoire de la rédaction,' *NTS* 18 (1972) 331-50.
/139/ Marshall, *Luke*, 204-5.
/140/ Ibid., 200; Caird, *Luke*, 91.
/141/ So e.g. Geldenhuys, *Luke*, 183; L. Morris, *The Gospel according to St. Luke* (London: IVP, 1974) 112.
/142/ J. A. Fitzmyer, *The Gospel according to Luke*, I (Garden City: Doubleday, 1981) 560.
/143/ H. Conzelmann, *The Theology of St. Luke* (London: Faber & Faber, 1960) 42.
/144/ R. Pesch, *Der reiche Fischfang* (Düsseldorf: Patmos, 1969) 53-84; and for a reconstruction, see 109-10. Cf. G. Schneider, *Das Evangelium nach Lukas*, I (Würzburg: Echter, 1977) 122.
/145/ Pesch, *Fischfang*, 128.
/146/ J. Ernst, *Das Evangelium nach Lukas* (Regensburg: Pustet, 1977) 185.
/147/ H. Schürmann, *Das Lukasevangelium*, I (Freiburg: Herder, 1969) 265; Betz & Grimm, *Wunder*, 82.
/148/ E. C. Hoskyns, *The Fourth Gospel* (ed. F. N. Davey; London: Faber & Faber, 1947) 554; K. Zillessen, 'Das Schiff des Petrus und die Gefährten vom andern Schiff (Zur Exegese von Luc 5:1-11),' *ZNW* 57 (1966) 137-39.
/149/ Marshall, *Luke*, 206; McPolin, *John*, 226.
/150/ Marsh, *John*, 662, though without necessarily accepting his strongly eucharistic interpretation in each instance.
/151/ See esp. R. Latourelle, 'Authenticité historique des miracles de Jésus: Essai de critériologie,' *Greg* 54 (1973) 225-61; L. Sabourin, *Miracles*, 57-120. Cf. R. G. Gruenler's deduction of explicit Christology from the implicit Christology of the undeniably authentic sayings of Jesus in his *New Approaches to Jesus and the Gospels* (Grand Rapids: Baker, 1982) 11-131.
/152/ See now also the survey by H. Weder, 'Wunder Jesu und Wundergeschichten,' *VF* 29 (1984) 26-49.
/153/ Cf. ibid., 32: 'Diese relativ ausführliche Behandlung der Wunder Jesu könnte der Eindruck erwecken, der historische Tatsachenbezug fände eine entsprechende Beachtung in der besprochenen Literatur. Dies ist nicht der Fall. . . . Die Frage mag erlaubt sein: welche grundlegende theologische. . . Orientierung sprecht in dieser durchgehenden Gewichtung aus?'
/154/ B. Chilton, 'Exorcism and History: Mark 1:21-28.'
/155/ With S. C. Goetz in 'The Burden of Proof,' *JSNT* 11 (1981) 48-51.
/156/ For similar assessments, see L. Cantwell, 'The Gospels as Biographies,' *SJT* 34 (1981) 193-200; H. Kraft, 'Die Evangelien und die Geschichte Jesu,' *TZ* 37 (1981) 321-41; R. Guelich, 'The

Gospel Genre,' in *Das Evangelium und die Evangelien* (ed. P. Stuhlmacher; Tübingen: Mohr, 1983) 183-219. More specifically apposite to this discussion, G. Maier, 'Wunderexegese,' elsewhere in this volume, demonstrates that a sizable portion of even that scholarship which rejects the historicity of the nature miracles acknowledges that the gospel writers originally intended to pass their stories off as historical fact.
/157/ Caird, *Luke*, 121.

'ΕΙ ΔΕ. . . ΕΓΩ ΕΚΒΑΛΛΩ ΤΑ ΔΑΙΜΟΝΙΑ. . .'

Graham H. Twelftree
The Manse
Main Road
Houghton 5131
South Australia

Answers to three sets of interrelated questions are sought in this paper.

1. Was the historical Jesus an exorcist or did this aspect of the Jesus tradition have its origin in the early Church's shaping of the tradition to conform to the perspective of its own theology or perhaps those of contemporary charismatic figures?

2. If it can be shown that Jesus was an exorcist, what can we discover from the Gospel records about Jesus as an exorcist? Further, how would he have appeared in comparison with his contemporaries? Would he in any way have appeared to be distinctive or even unique in his exorcistic activities? For example, does the following view of Leon Morris adequately describe Jesus' technique?

> In His conflict with the demons Jesus did not behave like a typical exorcist. Such a man would have techniques, spells, incantations, and the like. The Gospel writers do not picture Jesus as just another of this type. . .our Gospel writers do not think of Jesus as in a position anything like that of the magicians. He stood in a place all His own. He was uniquely the object of Satanic opposition. He was unique in the methods He used to defeat it. And He was unique in the completeness of His victory./1/

With this can be compared a statement by William Everts. 'A greater contrast cannot be conceived than that between the foolish notions, and the superstitious practices, of the Jewish exorcists and the simple, direct command of our Lord as he cast them out [the demons].'/2/

Or, on the other hand, are statements like those by Geza Vermes more adequate in describing Jesus as an exorcist?

> The representation of Jesus in the Gospels as a man whose supernatural abilities derived, not from secret powers, but from immediate contact with God, proves him to be a genuine charismatic, the true heir of an age-old prophetic religious line. But can other contemporary figures be defined in the same way?
>
> The answer is yes. . .the person of Jesus is to be seen as part of first-century charismatic Judaism and as the paramount example of the early Hasidim or Devout.'/3/

With this can be compared the statement by C. K. Barrett: '. . . the therapeutic methods employed by Jesus did not differ in form from those of magicians.'/4/

3. How did Jesus understand his exorcisms? In particular, if exorcism was part of Jesus' ministry, how important was it in the context of his wider ministry? Is Kenneth Grayston correct when he says of Jesus: 'The problems of demon possession in Galilee were marginal to his work'?/5/ Or is Harvey Cox correct? 'Though it frequently embarrasses us today, Jesus was viewed by his own age as a great exorcist. His power to cast out demons was central to his ministry. It focused all his various roles.' /6/ We will also ask, what is the origin of the eschatological understanding of the exorcisms of Jesus?

However there is a difficulty which prevents us from immediately proceeding to answer these three sets of questions. That is, it is not agreed that exorcism is a distinct form of healing or healing story in the Gospels./7/ For example, O. Böcher blurs the distinction between exorcism and healing by being very inclusive in what he considers to be demonic./8/ For example he says that Jesus' address to Peter, 'Get behind me, Satan!' (Mark 8:33/Matt. 16:23), is an exorcism formula and that all the reports of the healing of the paralytic (Mark 2:1-12) bear witness to it being an exorcism not least because of the reference to the opening of the roof./9/ He concludes: 'Dass die neutestamentlichen Autoren Krankheiten als dämonengewirkt und Krankenheilungen als Exorzismen verstanden haben, ist nach dem oben Gesagten kaum noch zu bezweifeln.'/10/

But when we look at the NT, it can be shown that Mark, for example, recognizes a clear distinction between exorcism and other healings. In 1:32 he says that they brought to Jesus τοὺς κακῶς ἔχοντας and τοὺς δαιμονιζομένους. And in v. 34 Mark maintains the distinction between Jesus healing πολλοὺς κακῶς ἔχοντας ποικίλαις νόσοις and his action, δαιμόνια πολλὰ ἐξέβαλεν (cf. 3:10-11). The same can be said of 6:13 where καὶ δαιμόνια πολλὰ ἐξέβαλλον is distinguished from ἤλειφον ἐλαίῳ πολλοὺς ἀρρώστους καὶ ἐθεράπευον. It is not that the καί connecting these two clauses needs to be taken as an adversative. Rather in listing sicknesses Mark considers demon-possession and exorcism to be sufficiently different from other sicknesses and healings to mention them separately. Although Luke does occasionally blur the distinction between exorcism and other healings (e.g. Acts 10:38) he otherwise takes up (cf. Mark 3:9-11/Luke 6:17-18; Luke 9:1-2/Matt. 10:6-7) and continues this distinction (Luke 7:21; 13:32; Acts 5:16; 8:7), as does Matthew (cf. e.g. 4:24; 8:16/Mark 1:32; 10:6-7/Mark 6:7, 12; Luke 9:1-2). Thus we can see that the Synoptic Evangelists drew a distinction between exorcisms and other healings.

We can go further and say something about the fundamental characteristic of an exorcism story. From the phrase καὶ δαιμόνια πολλὰ ἐξέβαλεν (Mark 1:34; cf. Luke 4:41--ἐξήρχετο δὲ καὶ δαιμόνια ἀπὸ πολλῶν) we may expect that an exorcism story would involve the expelling or casting out of an evil spiritual being (δαιμόνιον, πνεῦμα ἀκαθάρτον/κακόν). As we will see, the Synoptic Gospel traditions do contain such stories (see the list in part one below). Having identified the fundamental characteristic of an exorcism story, at this stage of our investigations we do not need to set out other possible characteristics/11/ for they will emerge in the course of our study. We can now proceed to answer our three sets of questions.

I. Was Jesus an Exorcist?

Ἐξορκιστής--used only at Acts 19:13--is not an epithet accorded to Jesus in the NT. And, judging from such 'lives' of Jesus in the New Quest as Günther Bornkamm's *Jesus of Nazareth* /12/ or, more recently, John Marsh's *Jesus in His Lifetime*/13/ as well as Leonhard Goppelt's *Theology of the New Testament* I, /14/ exorcism, if part of Jesus' ministry, was of almost no significance. On the other hand, if, as we have just argued, exorcism is the expelling of evil spiritual beings from people then the evidence from the NT, at first sight at least, is overwhelmingly in support of an affirmative answer to our question. Our task is now to collect and examine this evidence.

We have a number of areas from which we can gather evidence to discover whether or not Jesus was an exorcist. *First* are the exorcism *stories* related to Jesus in the Gospel traditions.

Of these stories Mark provides four--1:21-28 (the Demoniac in the Capernaum Synagogue), 5:1-20 (the Gadarene Demoniac), 7:24-30 (the Syrophoenician Woman's Daughter) and 9:14-29 (the Epileptic Boy). There are only nine other healing stories in Mark. In 1:29-31 there is the story of the healing of Peter's mother-in-law from fever, 1:40-45 is of a leper being cleansed, in 2:1-12 a paralytic is healed and forgiven, 3:1-6 tells of the healing of a man with a withered hand, 5:21-43 contains the stories of Jairus' daughter being raised from death and a woman's haemorrhaging being healed, in 7:31-37 a deaf-mute is healed and in 8:22-26 and 10:46-52 Jesus heals a blind man. This makes exorcism the most dominant and largest single category of healing story in the oldest Gospel./15/ Q provides the only other very brief exorcism story in the Gospel traditions (Matt. 9:32-33/12:22-24/Luke 11:14--the Dumb Demoniac).

With regard to the historicity of these stories, elsewhere I have argued that the evidence demands that we place the origin of at least the core of these Markan exorcism stories, and the one in Q, in the ministry of the historical Jesus./16/ Luke's version of the healing of Simon's mother-in-law (Luke 4:38-39) suggests that he may have viewed this as an exorcism, but there is no hint of this in his Markan source (Mark 1:29-31)./17/ So also Luke 13:10-17 refers to an 'evil' spirit's causing an illness, but no exorcism is performed./18/ Nevertheless, even without these two stories from Luke, we still have four stories of Jesus as an exorcist which most probably have their origin in the ministry of the historical Jesus.

Second, the Synoptic Gospels contain *sayings* of Jesus that presume his ministry of exorcism. In the pericopes Mark 3:22-27, Matt. 9:32-34, 12:22-30, Luke 11:14-15 and 17-23, the Synoptic Evangelists and Q have brought together some sayings which form what is often called the Beelzebul controversy. Luke 13:32, the warning to Herod, also needs to be considered. These sayings have all been discussed in recent literature./19/ We need only to touch on those discussions with particular reference to the origin of the sayings.

(a) Both Q and Mark contain the charge that Jesus cast out demons by Beelzebul, the Prince of Demons (Matt. 12:24/Luke 11:15 and Mark 3:22). Such a charge belongs to the bedrock of historical material, since such offensive material could have originated only in a *Sitz im Leben Jesu*./20/

(b) The saying that Jesus exorcised by the Spirit/finger of God (Matt. 12:28/Luke 11:20, cf. section three below) is also generally agreed to be authentic because it conforms to the theme of Jesus' call in relation to the present nearness of the kingdom of God./21/ Its authenticity is also affirmed by the fact that Jesus' source of power-authority is revealed; but the early Church, as we will see, does not pick up this point in its portrayal of Jesus as an exorcist.

(c) The parable of the Strong Man is preserved in Mark (3:27, followed by Matt. 12:29), Luke (11:21-22, possibly following Q/22/) and the Gospel of Thomas (35). The comparison of a possessed person to the house of a demon is still common in the East./23/ Thus, by its multiple attestation and Semitic nature, this parable which refers to exorcism and the defeat of Satan/24/ probably belongs to the authentic sayings of Jesus.

(d) Jesus' warning to Herod which mentions exorcism--'Go tell that fox, 'Behold, I cast out demons and perform cures today and tomorrow, and the third day I finish my course. . .' (Luke 13:32)--is peculiar to Luke. Recent redactional studies have attributed the pericope (13:31-33) to Luke./25/ But Bultmann, while questioning the origin of v. 33, thought it would be difficult to imagine how the situation in vv. 31 and 32a (the Pharisees warning Jesus of Herod's death threat) could have been constructed and that we have here, in the strict sense, a piece of biographical material./26/

Thus the Gospel traditions contain a number of most probably authentic sayings of Jesus which assume that he was an exorcist.

Third, in the Synoptic Gospels and Acts there are brief generalizing summaries of Jesus' ministry. The *Sammelberichten* at Mark 1:32-34/27/ (Matt. 8:16-17/Luke 4:40-41), 1:39 (Matt. 4:24/Luke 4:44) and 3:7-12 (Matt. 4:24-25; 12:15-16/Luke 6:16-19; 4:41) mention the casting out of demons by Jesus. To this list we can add Luke 7:21 and Acts 10:38. These brief reports are particularly important not simply in indicating that Jesus was an exorcist but that exorcism was a key feature of his ministry. Even if all this material cannot be shown conclusively to have originated in the life of the historical Jesus, at the very least, what these *Sammelberichten* do show is that the early Church remembered Jesus as an exorcist.

Fourth, in the NT era the names of exorcists with high

reputations were used by other exorcists in their healing incantations. For example, in this period Solomon was considered to have been a great exorcist. Evidence for this is seen, for example, in Pseudo-Philo (*LAB* 60) and Josephus (*Ant.* 8:46-49). In the latter story Eleazar is said to have performed an exorcism using the name of Solomon. The NT carries a number of reports of this happening in relation to Jesus. If these reports that Jesus' name was being used by other exorcists can be shown to be historically reliable the NT writers inadvertently give further evidence that Jesus was believed to have been an exorcist with a high reputation. In Mark 9:38 (Luke 9:49) John comes to Jesus and says, 'Teacher we saw a man casting out demons in your name. . .' It is often asserted that this report arose in the early Church./28/ But a number of factors point to the historical reliability of the report.

(a) Those who argue for the late origin of this saying consider it unlikely that exorcism in the name of Jesus would be practised before Easter. However in Acts 19:13 the sons of Sceva include reference to Paul in their incantation, thus showing how quickly names may have been taken up into incantations.

(b) For Bultmann, a point against the historicity of the passage is the fact that 'the subject of v. 38 is not following Jesus but association with the Apostles.'/29/ On the other hand, consider the fact that in Mark 9:38 John says that he had prevented the man from casting out demons in Jesus' name '*because he was not following us*' (ὅτι οὐκ ἠκολούθει/30/ ἡμῖν). Luke (9:49) alters this to read, 'because he does not (present tense) follow *with us*' (μεθ' ἡμῶν). Similarly, in 9:50 Luke has altered Mark's καθ' ἡμῶν (9:40) to καθ' ὑμῶν. Thus Luke probably understood the story to refer to a pre-Easter setting and what he has done in changing the imperfect to the present tense is to apply the story to his post-Easter readers./31/

(c) The use of the word ἀκολουθεῖν in the NT weighs in favour of the historicity of the report. Kittel summarizes the position:

> . . .the connection of the word with the concrete processes of the history of Jesus is so strongly felt and retained that no noun ever came into use corresponding to the concept of discipleship. The NT simply has the active term, because what it is seeking to express is an action and not a concept. On this basis it is no accident that the word

ἀκολουθεῖν is used only in the Gospels,/32/ that there is agreement as to its use in all four Gospels, and that they restrict the relationship signified by it to the historical Jesus. In the Epistles other expressions are used (σύν, ἐν) in which the emphasis falls on relationship to the exalted κύριος and His πνεῦμα./33/

(d) Matthew Black has shown that an Aramaic source probably lies behind Mark 9:38 and the accompanying group of sayings./34/

We can take it then that this story of the so-called Strange Exorcist is an historically reliable report from the pre-Easter ministry of Jesus. Even if this story arose in the early Church we would still have evidence that the early Church considered that Jesus was an exorcist. However we have taken the time to discuss the issue of the historicity of the story because our particular conclusions mean not only that we have evidence of Jesus being considered an exorcist, but--in light of the speed with which Jesus' name was taken up--that Jesus was an exorcist of considerable repute. If Luke 10:17 and Acts 16:18 are historical, they add further evidence for this, but even if they are not they demonstrate that the Christian community believed in the name of Jesus as a key ingredient in exorcism. Then in Acts 19:13-16 Luke says that some peripatetic 'Jewish exorcists undertook to pronounce the name of the Lord Jesus over those who had evil spirits saying, "I adjure you by the Jesus whom Paul preaches." Seven sons of a Jewish high priest named Sceva were doing this' (13-15). Even Haenchen considers this to be a piece of pre-Lukan tradition./35/ But even if, as some claim, it is not historically reliable, this pericope still shows us that Christians believed others were using the name of Jesus the exorcist as a power-authority for their own exorcisms.

So far we have been collecting evidence from the NT to show that Jesus was an exorcist. The *fifth* area from which we can gather evidence comes from outside the NT. For example the magical papyri have the now famous incantation intended for use by exoricsts--'I adjure you by the God of the Hebrews, Jesu, . . .' (PGM IV:3019-30, cf. 1233). Also, in that the use of Jesus' name for healing was censured by the Jews, we probably have further evidence that Jesus was at least considered a powerful healer by them (*t. Hul*. 2:22-23; *y. Sabb*. 14:4:14d; *y. Abod. Zar*. 2:2:40d-41a; *b. Abod. Zar*. 27b)./36/

Conclusions

The question being addressed in this section is: Was the historical Jesus an exorcist or did this aspect of the Jesus tradition have its origin in the early Church's shaping of the tradition to conform to its own theological perspective or the perspectives of contemporary charismatic figures? We have found more than sufficient evidence for the historian to be able to say not only that exorcism was an assured aspect of the ministry of the historical Jesus but also that Jesus had a reputation, from very early, of being an extremely successful exorcist. The corollary of this conclusion is that this aspect of the tradition did not have its origin in the early Church's wish to portray Jesus as conforming to its theological perspectives or perhaps those of contemporary charismatic figures.

II. Jesus as an Exorcist

The second set of questions on our agenda is: if it can be shown that Jesus was an exorcist, what can we discover from the Gospel records about Jesus as an exorcist? How would he have appeared in comparison with his contemporaries? Would he in any way have appeared to be distinctive or even unique in his exorcistic techniques? That the Gospel writers understood Jesus to have had contemporaries who were also exorcists is quite clear from the report of the Strange Exorcist (Mark 9:38-41/Luke 9:49-50) and from Matthew 12:27/Luke 11:19--'. . .by whom do your sons cast them out?' So, on having witnessed Jesus perform an exorcism, what would his audience have reported to have seen and heard? What kind of exorcist was he? What techniques did he use?

Despite the relative importance of exorcism both to Jesus and the Gospel writers, we have, in contrast to a number of references and sayings on exorcism, only four longer exorcism stories of Jesus in the Gospels: Mark 1:21-28, 5:1-20, 7:24-30 and 9:14-29. Then just before the so-called Beelzebul controversy pericope there is a very brief report of an exorcism (Matt. 9:32-34/12:22/Luke 11:14).

If, as most scholars agree, Mark is the earliest of the three Synoptic Gospels and Matthew and Luke have used Mark as one of their sources, then it is in Mark that the earliest version of the major exorcism stories have been preserved. Therefore we will need to concentrate our attention primarily on Mark as we answer the set of questions at the beginning of this section.

When we compare Matthew and Luke with Mark it is obvious that they have made alterations and additions to this tradition. For example, looking at some of the material related to our subject we can note that Matthew does not report the story of the demoniac at Capernaum (cf. Mark 1:21-28)/37/ and Luke does not tell his readers about the Syrophoenician woman's sick girl (cf. Mark 7:24-30)./38/ Also, if we look more closely at one of the stories, say Mark 5:1-20, we see that when Luke uses it he does not mention the demoniac being chained hand and foot at the beginning of the story, but further on (cf. Mark 5:4 and Luke 8:29). In his use of the same story Matthew adds that there were two demoniacs (cf. Mark 5:8 and Matt. 8:29) and he leaves out Jesus' request for the demon's name and the healed man's request to be with Jesus (cf. Mark 5:18-20) and Matt. 8:34). Like Luke, Matthew also leaves out mention of the demoniac being bound; he simply says that 'they were so violent that no one could pass that way' (cf. Mark 5:4 and Matt. 8:28)./39/ It may well be that Matthew and Luke were influenced in some of their alterations of Mark by other early traditions with which they were familiar, but other alterations probably reflect the fact that they did not woodenly or slavishly transmit the stories of Jesus but, as authors, were creatively involved in handing on the traditions. If this is so, we ought to allow as a strong probability that, before them, Mark also acted as an author rather than a copyist relaying the Jesus story to his particular readers.

However, the great difficulty in identifying Mark's creativity in any particular pericope is that we no longer possess the sources he used: so far as it is possible they can generally only be reconstructed from what we now find in Mark. In the study which follows we shall be heavily dependent on those who have done considerable work on the methodology for ascertaining the hand of Mark in the second Gospel./40/

As well as isolating Markan from pre-Markan material we will need to check the latter material to see if it is likely to belong to the reliable historical traditions about Jesus as an exorcist. The criteria for identifying the authentic *sayings* or words of Jesus are well known and often debated. Recently, a most thorough list has been given and discussed by R. H. Stein in a previous volume of *Gospel Perspectives*. His list is as follows: (1) The criterion of multiple attestation or the cross-section approach. (2) The criterion of multiple forms. (3) The criterion of Aramaic linguistic phenomena. (4) The criterion of Palestinian environmental phenomena. (5) The criterion of the tendencies of the developing tradition. (6) The criterion of dissimilarity or discontinuity. (7) The criterion of modification by Jewish Christianity. (8) The criterion of divergent patterns from the redaction. (9) The criterion of environmental contradiction. (10) The criterion of contradiction of authentic sayings. (11) The criterion of coherence (or consistency)./41/

Our primary concern here is not with the sayings but with the activities of Jesus. However in relation to the activities or *works* of Jesus very much less work has been done on criteria for testing authenticity./42/ With due regard for the differences between sayings and reports or narrative material the same criteria can be used. But other criteria can also be utilized. I would suggest that the following might be helpful.

(1) If a class or category of sayings has been established as belonging to the bedrock of historical material, then reported activities which cohere with this sayings material, while not in turn automatically established as authentic without further discussion, can at least be given the benefit of the doubt in relation to historicity. For example, in relation to our theme, if some or all of the sayings that are now found in the Beelzebul controversy can be shown probably to come from the historical Jesus then we are predisposed to consider more favourably the historicity of an exorcism story than if we were unable to find an authentic saying of Jesus that assumed that he was an exorcist. So we have a criterion of *coherence with reliable sayings material*. (2) If an activity of Jesus is referred to indirectly or incidentally we may have a pointer to historical data, that is, we have a criterion of *incidental transmission*. Again, for example, if the parable of the Strong Man in the Beelzebul controversy can be shown to be authentic we have an incidental reference to Jesus being an exorcist. (3) *The witness of extra-canonical material* can, with care, be used to help test the historicity of events behind the Gospel narratives. Thus, for example, Jesus' choosing disciples is supported by Jewish traditions (*b. Sanh.* 43a)./43/ (4) Finally, we can takes as historically reliable those *reports*, like the baptism or the crucifixion of Jesus, *which,* at least early in the transmission of the tradition, *would have been embarrassing for the Church to transmit*.

We need now to turn our attention to an historical examination of the exorcism stories in Mark (see the list above). This will provide a basis for helping to gain a picture of Jesus as an exorcist. We will conduct our inquiry under a number of headings./44/

1. Initial Dramatic Confrontation

All four exorcism stories report an initial dramatic confrontation between Jesus and the central figure in the story, that is, the demoniac--save in Mark 7:25 where it was the sufferer's mother who encountered Jesus. On meeting Jesus in Mark 1:23 the demoniac cried out (ἀνέκραξεν); in Mark 5:6-7, on seeing Jesus, the Gadarene Demoniac ran, fell on his knees in front of Jesus (προσεκύνησεν αὐτῷ) and shouted out (κράξας φωνῇ μεγάλῃ); in Mark 7:25 the Syrophoenician Woman came and fell at Jesus' feet (προσέπεσεν πρὸς τοὺς πόδας αὐτοῦ) and in Mark 9:20, on seeing Jesus, the demon threw the boy into a convulsion (καὶ ἰδὼν αὐτὸν τὸ πνεῦμα εὐθὺς συνεσπάραξεν αὐτόν, καὶ πεσὼν ἐπὶ τῆς γῆς ἐκυλίετο ἀφρίζων). How reliable is this element of the reports? Each of the verses in question, not surprisingly, bears the stamp of Mark's authorship. In 1:23 εὐθύς is distinctively Markan (42 of the 56 occurrences in the NT are in Mark) and πνεύματι ἀκαθάρτῳ may be characteristic of Mark./45/ The remaining bulk of the verse does not exhibit strong Markan characteristics./46/ In 5:6-7 only ἀπὸ μακρόθεν /47/ appears to be characteristic of Mark's hand. In 7:25 Mark's hand is particularly evident through his use of ἀλλά,/48/ εὐθύς (see above), θυγάτριον,/49/ and πνεῦμα ἀκάθαρτον (see above). In 9:20 φέρω /50/ and εὐθύς (see above) are particularly revealing of Mark's hand. This evidence for Mark's hand is probably not sufficient to indicate that these verses are the creation of the Evangelist. On the other hand the use of προσκυνέω in Mark 5:6 (and 15:19) has to do with worship and reverence. When προσκυνέω is used in the NT 'the object is always something--truly or supposedly--divine.'/51/ Προσπίπτω, used by Luke in 5:8 to denote worship, is used in 7:25 as part of the description of the dramatic confrontation. Mark uses it only here, in 3:11 (where demons fall down or worship Jesus the Son of God) and in 5:33--both often considered to be redactional. /52/ Thus it is possible that the early Church, either Mark or his predecessors, may have introduced at least the 'worship' interpretation into the dramatic confrontation. But we must still ask if, on meeting Jesus, the demoniacs were so disturbed that they 'fell down' (i.e., πίπτω, Mark 9:20) and cried out. A history of religions parallel will help us answer this question in the affirmative. In *Life* 4:20 Philostratus says that the gaze of Apollonius causes a demon to cry out with a scream. Thus, as an exorcist of his time it is likely that Jesus also would have been expected to cause consternation in the demoniacs.

We can go further than this and suggest that it is probable that this consternation is part of the authentic historical tradition for two reasons at least.

First, Matthew is reticent about Jesus being an ordinary exorcist. For example, in the healing of the Gadarene Demoniac in Mark 5:7 the demoniac attempts to put a supernatural restriction on Jesus (see below) by crying out, 'I adjure/bind (ὁρκίζω) you by God. . .' However Matthew removes ὁρκίζω--the idea of the demon trying to put a spell on Jesus. Also Matthew severely abbreviates the dialogue (Mark 5:5-10/Matt. 8:29)./53/ The dialogue was (see below) thought to be part of the healing technique. However this has been reduced so that all that remains is Jesus' simple authoritative command 'Go'. The impression we gain is that from Matthew's perspective the Son of God (8:29; cf. Mark 5:7) does not need to use such involved techniques. Yet while Matthew prunes the stories to suit his purposes he does not see himself able to obliterate entirely this aspect of an exorcism story about Jesus (cf. Mark 5:7 and Matt. 8:29 and Mark 9:20 and Matt. 17:17-18). In other words, Matthew recognized consternation as an essential element in an exorcism story.

Second, if Mark, for example, had introduced this idea of consternation then we might expect some consistency in his portrayal of this element. However he shows no such consistency in either his vocabulary or use of this motif--see Mark 1:23, 3:11, 5:6 (33) and 9:20. Luke also shows no consistency in his reporting here--see 4:33, 41; 8:28; 9:42.

As other exorcists of the time were involved in dramatic confrontations with demoniacs and as the early Church was not consistent in the attention it paid to this element in the stories we can conclude that Jesus probably did cause consternation in the demoniacs he met, resulting in a dramatic confrontation.

2. *The Words of the Demons*

In Mark 7 a mother speaks for her daughter and in chapter 9 a father speaks for his son. In the other two stories, set at Capernaum and Gadara, where Jesus is said to deal directly with the demoniacs, the consternation felt by the demoniacs in the initial dramatic confrontation is vocalized.

> What have we to do with you, Jesus of Nazareth? Have you come to destroy us? I know who you are, the Holy One of God! (Mark 1:24).

and

> What have I to do with you, Jesus, son of the Most High God? I adjure you by God not to torment me (Mark 5:7).

Is this material historically reliable? To some extent an answer to this question depends on the meaning of the words of the demon. It is sometimes thought that the demons had supernatural knowledge of Jesus' (true) identity and were declaring this and their defeat to the world./54/ If this were the case, many scholars would conclude that the early Church had been responsible for the 'confessions'. But why should those responsible for transmitting the Gospel traditions, particularly Mark, choose demons to play such an important part in declaring Jesus' messiahship when they 'might have called on kings or other great persons such as philosophers, or angels, or inspired persons, or infants or persons raised from the dead'?/55/ In any case, as S. V. McCasland also says, this 'theory is weak because it shows no motive why demons should be anxious to bear testimony to one whom they recognize to be their enemy'./56/ Thus far we are tending to affirm the historicity of this element in the exorcism stories. We can go further only if we can find reasonable meaning to the words of the demons. So, why did the demons or demoniacs vocalize their distress and speak in this way?

In both Mark 1:24 and 5:7 the reported words of the demons begin in the same way--τί ἡμῖν (5:7 has ἐμοί) καὶ σοί;. What does this question mean? Hugh Anderson says that, although in classical Greek it would mean 'What have we in common?', in Mark 1:24 it probably corresponds to Hebrew usage and means: 'Why are you bothering us?'/57/ J. D. M. Derrett has examined the question--with a view to understanding John 2:4--and says that the phrase is a 'protestation that there is not, or should not be, a difference of viewpoint, still less a dispute, between the two personalities.'/58/ Others take the question to be the demon's defence against Jesus the exorcist./59/

The question in Mark has parallels in the NT era in John 2:4, in the OT/60/ and in Philo (see below). In the rabbinic literature Strack and Billerbeck (II, 401) cite only *Pesiqta Rabbati* 5.

Two examples from the OT will help us to elucidate its

meaning. In 2 Samuel 19:16-23 Shimei asks David for forgiveness for cursing and throwing stones at him (2 Sam. 16:5-14). But Abishai suggested that Shimei be put to death. David replies: 'What have I to do with you?', giving the impression that he is asking not be interfered with. Josephus shows that in the NT era the phrase in question was understood as a rebuttal or counter-attack. In his rewriting of this story he has David reply: οὐ παύσεσθ'. . .; (*Ant.* VII:265). In 1 Kings 17 a widow is providing food and water for Elijah and her son becomes seriously ill.

> καὶ εἶπεν πρὸς Ηλίου, τί ἐμοὶ καὶ σοί, ἄνθρωπε τοῦ θεοῦ; εἰσῆλθες πρός με τοῦ ἀναμνῆσαι τὰς ἀδικίας μου καὶ θανατῶσαι τὸν υἱόν μου (1 Kings [LXX 3 Kings] 17:18).

In this story the widow connects her son's illness with the arrival of Elijah, a man of God. What the woman attempts to do in these words is to defend her household by a kind of warding off of Elijah from the situation. Also in Judges 11:12 Jephthah sent messengers to the King of Ammon in an attempt to avert war. The messengers were to say:

> τί ἐμοὶ καὶ σοί, ὅτι ἥκεις πρός με σύ πολεμησαί με ἐν τῇ γῇ μου;

With this we need to compare Philo *Quod Deus immutabilis sit*, 138.

> λέγει δὲ πρὸς τὸν προφήτην πᾶσα διάνοια χήρα καὶ ἐρήμη κακῶν μέλλουσα γίνεσθαι· ἄνθρωπε τοῦ θεοῦ, εἰσῆλθες πρός μὲ ἀναμνῆσαι τὸ ἀδίκημά μου καὶ τὸ ἁμάρτημά μου.

In view of these parallels it seems best to adopt the view of Bauernfeind and those who have followed him, that the words of the demons were most likely defence mechanisms against Jesus the exorcist./61/

Two other elements in these words of the demons confirm the idea that in them the demons were seeking to defend themselves.

First, in Mark 1:24 the man with an unclean spirit cried out οἶδά σε τίς εἶ. The magical papyri furnish us with a number of parallels to this formula. For example, 'I know your name which was received in heaven, I know you and your forms. . .' (PGM VIII:6-7) and 'I know you Hermes, who you are and whence you came and which is your city' (PGM VIII:13). These parallels from the magical papyri are, by the very nature of the material --here incantations for exorcists--words to gain control by the exorcist not the demons. Apart from perhaps Acts 19:15 we do not have any precise parallels to the words of the demons in question in Mark 1:24./62/ Nevertheless the evidence from the magical papyri show that the οἶδα language is used in an attempt to gain control over a 'spiritual' enemy.

A *second* element in these initial words of the demons which shows that they are defence mechanisms against Jesus are the words in Mark 5:7, 'I adjure you by God. . .' To adjure (ὁρκίζειν) someone was thought to bind, or even to put a curse upon a person to do or say something. In 1 Kings (LXX 3 Kings) 22:16 Ahab says to the prophet Micaiah 'How many times shall I adjure you that you speak to me nothing but the truth in the name of the Lord?' (cf. 2 Chr. 18:15). Joshua cursed (ὁρκίζειν) or put an oath on the people of Jericho against their rebuilding the city (Josh. 6:26 [LXX]). But the closest parallels to these words of the demons are again found in the magical material. The following two quotations are typical of the use of 'I adjure' to bind a spiritual enemy.

> I adjure you by the God of the Hebrews. . .(PGM IV:3019)

and

> I adjure you, demonic spirit, who rests here. . .by the God of Abraan. . ./63/

Not only do these incantations illustrate the user 'binding' an adversary but they show that the adversary is bound by a third party./64/ In Matthew 26:63 we see this same form of 'binding' by a third party where the High Priest says to Jesus 'I bind you by the living God, tell us if you are the Christ...' While one may be able to suggest that ὁρκίζω would have been understood 'rationally', along the lines of the High Priest attempting to make Jesus declare himself by (implicitly) threatening him with divine sanctions, the preternatural context of Mark 5:7 and the parallels just quoted incline us to think that ὁρκίζω would have been considered directly performative. Returning to the words of the demons and their meaning in Mark 5:7, we see that the demon is attempting to bind Jesus by God, trying to prevent Jesus the exorcist from tormenting him./65/

We have not completely shown that the words of the demons are defences rather than supernatural knowledge leading to a messianic confession, for the view depends to a large extent on what is to be made of the way the demons address Jesus. In Mark 1:24 the demoniac addresses Jesus as 'Jesus of Nazareth' and 'the Holy One of God'. In Mark 5:7 the demoniac addresses Jesus as 'Jesus, Son of the Most High God'. In other words, does the use of these particular titles or addresses indicate that the demons had a supernatural knowledge of Jesus, or should we look in the area of preternatural defence for the explanation of the use of the titles?

From what we see in the magical papyri it seems that it was important to know the name or identity of the enemy to be overpowered: to know the name or identity of an adversary was to score a point over him. Part of that identity was the origin of the one over whom power was sought (cf. PGM VIII:13 quoted above). In the light of this it is not surprising that the demons should identify Jesus as from Nazareth.

What then are we to make of the designations 'the Holy One of God' (Mark 1:24) and 'Jesus, son of the Most High God'? The phrase or title 'the Holy One of God' is used of Jesus only here (Mark 1:24/Luke 4:34) and in John 6:69 (cf. Acts 3:14; 4:27, 30; 1 John 2:20; Rev. 3:7). Although the early Christians understood this phrase to refer to Jesus' messiahship, as John 6:69 makes clear, we must not too quickly identify what the demoniacs intended by the designation with early Christian understanding of the phrase.

In Psalm 106 (LXX 105):16 Aaron is called 'the Holy One of the Lord'. In one of the texts of the LXX at Judges 16:17 (B) Samson says 'I am a Holy One of God from my birth' (see also Jud. 16:7, LXX[B]); Sirach 45:6 'And he exalted Aaron a holy one like him. . .' (see also [LXX] Wis 11:1; Isa. 62:12; Dan. 7:27; and then later by the Christians, e.g. Acts 3:21; 1 Cor. 7:14; Heb. 3:1; 1 Pet. 1:16; 2 Pet. 3:2; Eph. 3:5 and 1 Clem. 8:3; Barn. 14:16)./66/ These texts show that to call someone 'holy' or 'a Holy One of God' need mean nothing more than that individual had a special relationship with God.

The rabbinic material also shows that demons were thought to recognize the Palestinian ḥasidim as having a special relationship with God. For example the story goes that Ḥanina ben Dosa, from Galilee at the turn of the first and second centuries A.D., was out walking one evening when he was met by Agrath, the queen of the demons. She said--'Had they not made an announcement concerning you in heaven, "Take heed of Ḥanina and his learning," I would have put you in danger.' Ḥanina replies--'If I am of account in heaven, I order you never to pass through settled regions' (*b. Pesaḥ*. 112b).

In any case 'holy' or 'Holy One of God' had no tradition as a messianic title in the early Church. That is, before Mark the word or phrase was not understood as referring to the messiah. Thus what the demon(iac) in Mark 1:24 is saying is probably no more than that he considered Jesus to have a special relationship with God.

The demons also called Jesus 'Son (of the Most High God)' (Mark 5:7). In relation to Jesus 'Son' is of such special interest to Mark (cf. 1:1 (?), 11; 3:11; 9:7; 15:37) that he may have added it to these words. But, as we have found in the preceding paragraphs, it can be shown that in first century Palestine the view was current that 'son' was used to indicate a special relationship with God./67/ According to Rab, the great Babylonian teacher and collector of Galilean traditions, the following comment was heard day after day during the life of Ḥanina ben Dosa:

> The whole universe is sustained on account of my son Ḥanina; but my son Ḥanina is satisfied with one kab of carob from one Sabbath eve to another (*b. Ta'an.* 24b; *b. Ber.* 17b; *b. Ḥul.* 86a).

With this can be compared a prayer of Honi the Circle-Drawer.

> Lord of the universe, thy sons have turned to me because I am a son of the house before thee (*m. Ta'an.* 3:8)./68/

In short the presence of the appellation 'son' (of God) does not necessarily indicate either a messianic confession for the demoniacs or that Mark has introduced the word. Indeed the rest of this phrase '. . .of the Most High God' can readily be accepted and understood as coming from the demon(iac) rather than having been introduced by the early Christians who made only very sparing use of the title--usually quoting or alluding to the OT (cf. Matt. 21:9/Luke 19:38 [=Ps. 118:26]; Luke 1:32 [=Isa. 9:6 and 7]). In fact, apart from Hebrews 7:1, a quotation of Genesis 14:18, the precise phrase or title, τοῦ θεοῦ τοῦ ὑψίστου, occurs only on the lips of the demoniacs in the NT (Mark 5:7/ Luke 8:28 and Acts 16:17).

For the Greeks the title 'Most High' was predicated of the great god Zeus (e.g. Pindar *Nemea* 1:60, 11:2 and Aeschylus *Eumenides* 28; Sophocles *Philoctetes* 1289). The Jews also attributed his name (*elion*--the Highest) to their God (e.g. Gen. 14:18-22, Num. 24:16, Deut. 32:8, 2 Sam. 22:14). And 'quantitatively and qualitatively ὑψίστος as a divine name is on the margin of the NT tradition.'/69/ Then, important for our study, the appellation occurs in the magical papyri where it is used in incantations where victory is sought over an adversary (cf. PGM IV: 1068, V:46). Thus in the demoniac's attempt to disarm and score a point over Jesus it is not surprising that the name 'of the Most High God' should be used.

In this section (*2.*), a case has been made to show that what the demon(iac)s said in their consternation as they confronted Jesus was not necessarily the result of supernatural knowledge but what any demon(iac) might have said when facing a well known, powerful, Jewish exorcist. In other words, what the demon(iac)s were doing--despite how it was understood later, even by Mark--was not necessarily intentionally declaring Jesus' messiahship. Instead they were, through naming and attempting to bind Jesus, trying to defend themselves by disarming their adversary.

3. The Words of Exorcism

It is often said that what set Jesus apart from his contemporary exorcists was his simple 'non-magical' healings--he only had to command the demons and they would depart./70/ How correct is such a view in relation to what Jesus said to the demons?

Looking at the three stories in which Jesus addressed the demoniacs--he does not meet the demoniac in Mark 7:24-30--there are four elements of the words of exorcism that demand our attention.

First, in Mark 1:25 Jesus says to the demon 'Be quiet. . .' (RSV). But this translation does not give the full sense of the word φιμόω. This word is strongly related to 'incantation-restriction', rather than simply to talking, and its use puts someone in a position where they are unable to operate. Thus P. Oslo 1:161-62 has 'a remedy to prevent the wrath of a person. . . *bind* the mouths which speak against me. . .' And there are examples of φιμοῦν and καταδεῖν being used as equivalents (P. Lond. 121:396, 967; PGM IX:9; XXXVI: 164/71/).

It is most probable that not even Mark understood φιμώθητι as 'Be silent!' for Mark goes on to say that the demon caused the man to cry out in a loud voice. Thus it would be better to understand the words of Jesus, closely paralleled in the magical material, as 'Be bound' or 'Be restricted'.

Second, in all three stories Jesus is reported as saying 'Come out (ἐξέλθε) of (him)' (Mark 1:25, 5:8, 9:25). This command is found in the stories of other exorcists of the period. It was used in Lucian (*Philops*. 11 and 16), by two rabbis (*b. Me*ʿ*il*. 17b), and a similar expression, ἀπαλλαττέσθαι ('to quit'), is used by Apollonius (*Life* 4:20). Importantly, it is also used in the magical papyri (e.g. PGM IV:1243-45). In fact, the command to the demons to 'come out' is the basic command found regardless of whether or not we would categorize them as 'magical'.

Third, in Mark 5:9 Jesus asks the demon 'What is your name?'. Verses 7-10 have been seen as confused dialogue, not least because of the puzzling phrase in v. 8 ἔλεγεν γὰρ αὐτῷ. Klostermann solves the problem by considering the verse a later insertion./72/ Others have suggested that the extant text of Mark 5:1-20 is an amalgamation of two previously independent stories./73/ There is an alternative solution which has the advantage of leaving the extant text intact. On meeting Jesus and recognizing him as a threat the demoniac defends himself with the formula 'What have you to do with me, Jesus, Son of the Most High God?' (v. 7a). Jesus responds by seeking to cast out what he recognizes as an unclean spirit with the address 'Come out of the man, unclean spirit!' (v. 8). However the demoniac retaliates with a binding spell, 'I bind you by God, do not torment me' (v. 7b). Therefore, in this spiritual battle Jesus counter-attacks with 'What is your name?' (v. 9) in order to gain the upper hand. The demoniac gives his name and the battle is all but over.

Although some may find it distasteful even to consider that Jesus may not have been initially or immediately successful in a healing, the story of the two-part cure of the blind man in Mark 8:22-26 is evidence that the early Church could contemplate such an idea. My suggestion is that Mark 5:8-9 is a similar case. When Jesus asks the demon's name, he has already commanded the demon to come out of the man; but the demon, instead of submitting, tries to fend off Jesus' attack. So Jesus comes at the problem of overcoming the demon in another way by asking its name.

The magical papyri offer further support to the idea that to know the name of an adversary was an essential element in gaining control over an enemy./74/ To quote Bietenhard:

> The magical papyri are full of expressions showing belief in the power and efficacy of names. Expressed here is the primitive belief that knowledge of names gives power over their bearers, that the simple utterance of a name puts a spell on its owner and brings him under the power of the speaker./75/

The Testament of Solomon reveals a similar perspective. Solomon is confronted by a demon--'I, Solomon, got up from my throne and saw the demon shuddering and trembling with fear. I said to him, "Who are you? What is your name?"' (2:1; cf. e.g. 3:6; 4:3, 4; 5:1). The magical papyri have specific instructions to wrest name and nature from silent spirits (e.g. PGM V:247-303). In PGM IV:1017-19 a god reveals its name and nature: 'My name is Bairchoaoch. I am he that sprang from heaven, my name is Balsames.'

In the minds of those of the period, name and nature were inextricably bound toether. It is into this category--the need to know one's adversary--that we should place Mark 9:21-22 where Jesus asks about the history of the young lad's illness (cf. Philostratus *Life* 4:20). In the ancient world it was thought that demons inhabited fire and water/76/ and so the father's reply to Jesus' question also shows that the dialogue had to do with discovering the nature of the demon. So, to conclude this point, in asking for the name of the demon in Mark 5:9 Jesus was then making a second attempt at overpowering this stubborn adversary. That Jesus was thought to be successful is shown not only by the demon's surrendering his name and nature but also by the desperate plea not to be sent out of the region (v. 10)--a fate which every demon feared.

The *fourth* and final element of Jesus' words of commmand to the demons which we need to explore briefly in relation to their so-called 'magical' character and understanding is the injunction καὶ μηκέτι εἰσελθῇς εἰς αὐτόν (Mark 9:25). The idea of demons returning to a person is extremely old. In a Babylonian text, perhaps seven hundred to a thousand years B.C., there is an incantation--'that the evil spirit. . .may stand aside, and a kindly spirit. . .be present.'/77/ This is obviously a precaution against the evil spirit's return. And in the NT Jesus mentions an unclean spirit, having roamed through waterless places, returning to a man accompanied by seven more evil spirits (Matt. 12:43-45/Luke 11:24-26). The words of Jesus to the demon not to return are paralleled, in some cases exactly, in a number of pieces of literature. In the story of Eleazar, Josephus says that the exorcist 'adjured the demon never to come back into him. . .' (*Ant.* 8:46-49). In a story Philostratus tells of Apollonius, the demon 'swore that he would leave the young man alone and never take possession of any man again' (*Life* 4:20). In the magical papyri there is a Jewish prescription after the demon has left (PGM IV:1254) as well as an incantation to catch a demon 'on the loose'--'Let your angel descend. . .and let him draw into captivity the demon as he flies around this creature. . .' (PGM IV:3024-25). Thus Jesus' command to the demons is again very closely paralleled in the repertoire of other exorcistic, 'magical' literature.

These four words of Jesus to the demons are indeed simple and straightforward. They are reported as, and we have established them as being, 'Be bound, and come out of him' (Mark 1:25; cf. 5:7, 9:25), 'What is your name?' (Mark 5:9) and 'Come out of him and no longer enter into him' (Mark 9:25). Just what we can conclude from the fact that in every case these words are paralleled in stories of other exorcists or the healers' recipes in the magical papyri, or both, we will mention in the conclusion to this section. However, at the very least, we can say that the simple word of command used by Jesus does not set him over against his contemporary exorcists.

4. The Demons' Plea

In Mark 5:10-12, where they are reported to have been overpowered by Jesus, the demons plead for leniency. In stories in the NT period of battles between holy individuals and demons, demons are said to make pleas for mercy on realizing their impending defeat. The earliest example is in Ethiopic Enoch 12-14. Azazel and his cohorts are seized with fear and trembling on hearing of their impending doom. Azazel asks Enoch to plead their case before the Lord of heaven. However the petition is not granted. Another example is in Jubilees 10 where Mastema, the chief of the evil spirits, makes a plea for mercy, but this time the request is granted.

With these parallels in mind and in view of the non-theological nature of the plea in our earliest story (contrast Matt. 8:29, Luke 8:31) we can see no motivation for Mark or his predecessors adding this element to the story. Also the plea by the demon in Mark 5 to stay in the area rests on the notion, paralleled in Tobit 8:3, that demons were especially associated with particular regions and on defeat were sent out of the area. So, here, rather than being sent out of the region the demons are allowed to enter the herd of pigs which was grazing nearby. Although Matthew and Luke give a theological understanding of the pleas, Mark does not, which in view of the history of religions parallels means that this is probably an authentic element of the Jesus tradition (cf. Matt. 8:29, Luke 8:31).

It is not immediately clear what was thought to have

drowned, the pigs only, or the demons as well as the pigs. That is, were the demons considered to have been destroyed or simply transferred from the man into the herd of pigs? In Matthew, going into the sea is seen as an alternative to eschatological torment (cf. Matt. 8:29 and 31). Also in Luke, entering the pigs is seen as an alternative to being sent into the abyss (ἄβυσσος)--thought to be the place of final destruction for evil (cf. Luke 8:31-32; see also Rom. 10:7; Rev. 9:1, 2, 11; 11:7, 17:8; 20:1, 3). And Luke uses the singular '*it* drowned' rather than the ambiguous plural '*they* drowned' showing that he thought that it was the herd (of pigs) that perished. That Mark also thinks that just the pigs drowned is suggested by 5:13 which mentions the drowning in close connection with the pigs rushing down the bank. Not only does a look at the text show that all the Gospel writers understood only the pigs to have been drowned, but so also does a glance at an aspect of ancient demonology. As water was thought to be one of the habitats of demons,/78/ then for the demons--via the pigs--to enter the water would hardly have been considered to be the cause of their death. Rather it was probably understood that the demons had been transferred from one habitat to another.

This leads us on to consider the idea, sometimes expressed by scholars, that the destruction of the pigs was proof of Jesus' success in the exorcism./79/ However, consider the following three points. (1) As we have just seen, the demons were probably thought to have been transferred from the man to the pigs and then to the sea. (2) In antiquity, to effect a cure it was sometimes thought appropriate to transfer the demons from the sufferer to some object like a pebble or piece of wood or a pot or some water. These objects, thought to contain the demons, were thrown away or destroyed to effect and perhaps signify the demon's departure from the situation./80/ (3) The proof of the cure in the story in Mark 5 is not the destruction of the pigs but the people seeing the cured man 'sitting there, clothed and in his right mind' (v. 15b). Thus rather than as a proof of cure, the pigs episode was probably understood as an integral part of the cure.

5. *The Violent Cure*

The destruction of the pigs, just mentioned, is the best example in the Jesus tradition of the violence accompanying an exorcism, but it is also found in Mark 1:26, where the demon is said to convulse the man and in Mark 9:26 where the demon also apparently convulses the boy. In stories outside the NT the demon cast out by Eleazar upset a bowl of water (*Ant.* 8:49), and the demon Apollonius exorcised destroyed a statue (*Life* 4:20). That this violence has not been added to, but was already part of the authentic Jesus tradition, is indicated by Mark's showing no consistent use of, or interest in, this violence. That is, in 1:26 the convulsion is said to occur only as the demon leaves, while in chapter 9 the whole story is couched in violence, in the encounter as well as in the healing.

6. *The Uniqueness of Jesus*

So far we have been trying to identify those elements that were part of the historical Jesus' technique of exorcism. And when we set Jesus the exorcist within his own milieu it becomes obvious that there are certain aspects of ancient techniques of which Jesus did not avail himself.

(a) Jesus does not seem to have used any material or mechanical devices in his exorcisms. In contrast to this we can note that in Tobit 8:3 incense is burnt to expel the demon; in Jubilees 10:10 and 12 'medicines' are used; in the Genesis Apocryphon 20 Abraham lays hands on the Pharaoh; Eleazar uses a finger ring and a bowl of water; in the Babylonian Talmud, amulets, palm tree prickles, wood chips, ashes, pitch, cummin, dog's hair, thread and trumpets are used; Lucian tells of the use of iron rings, and the magical papyri of amulets, olive branches, marjoram and special sounds were used by the exorcists.

How different the techniques of Jesus seem with the straightforward formulae like 'Be bound, and come out of him' (Mark 1:25)! The only thing resembling a mechanical aid was the use of the herd of pigs. However the pigs are not used to exorcise the demons but to provide a habitat for the expelled demons./81/

But it cannot be claimed that Jesus stood alone in not using any technical aids in exorcism. Even among the rabbis--those most like Jesus--he cannot be said to be alone in his simple verbal cures. Even if using only the tone of his voice and a gaze, Apollonius used his words alone to expel the offending demon (in *Life* 4:20). Nevertheless, despite these two parallels, an outstanding characteristic of Jesus' technique was probably considered to be his unaided words of command to the demons. And this is not a characteristic of Jesus' healing method which the early Church either added or sought to cultivate. For example, it quite happily transmitted the stories in which Jesus is said to use spittle which is also part of the recipes in the magical papyri (cf. Mark 7:33, 8:23, John 9:6 and PGM III:420).

Is there an explanation for Jesus not using mechanical aids in his exorcism? On the one hand the use of aids in our period seems to have been by the anonymous or unknown exorcists who appealed to an outside power-authority for success. On the other hand what Jesus, Apollonius, and some of the rabbis have in common is not only their success without 'aids' but a reliance on their own personal force for success.

(b) Jesus did not use any 'proofs' to indicate the success of his cures. The truth of this statement depends on how Jesus understood the destruction of the pigs at Gadara (Mark 5:11-12). We have tried to show that those who reported this story, as well as Jesus himself as a man of his time (in that he used many of the techniques of healing familiar in the first century), would have understood the pigs episode as part of the cure--a providing of an alternative habitat for the demons--rather than as a proof. It would have considerably enhanced Jesus' reputation to be able to report 'proofs of cure' and so it is unlikely that the early Church would have excised any such proofs that were in the Jesus tradition. It is, then, reasonable to conclude that proofs were not part of Jesus' technique as an exorcist.

(c) Unlike even some of the Jewish holy men Jesus is not reported as praying when he performed an exorcism. Even though Ḥanina ben Dosa did not use traditional formulae, he, like the Abraham of the Qumran Scrolls, prayed to remove the demon (*b. Ber.* 34b; cf. *Ta'an.* 24b, 1 QapGen 20). Although the early Church, particularly Luke, was keen to accentuate the prayer life of Jesus (e.g. προσεύχομαι occurs 15 times in Matt., 11 in Mark and 18 in Luke),/82/ at no point does the tradition seek to attach the practice of prayer to Jesus' exorcistic technique. Thus like Apollonius (*Life* 4:20) and some of the rabbis (*b. Meʿil.* 17b), rather than pray, Jesus used simple, recognizable verbal formulae, relying on his own resources to defeat the offending demons.

(d) Related to the previous point, it seems that in his exorcisms Jesus did not call up or invoke any power-authority. In the magical papyri one of the preliminary steps in an exorcism was to invoke the aid of some god as the power-authority for the ensuing conflict. One frequent source of power-authority was found in the use of powerful names. The name of Solomon seems to have been frequently used (e.g. *Ant.* 8:47) and in Acts 19:13 the sons of Sceva try using Jesus' name as does the Strange Exorcist in Mark 9:38-40 (Luke 9:49-50). In Matthew 12:28 (Luke 11:20) Jesus declares his source of power-authority to be the Spirit (Luke has 'finger'/83/) of God. We might then expect that in his exorcisms he would call on the Spirit or finger of God to aid him. But he does not. In view of the early Church being anxious to show that Jesus was endowed with the eschatological Spirit it is unlikely that those who preserved the Jesus-tradition would have excised this aspect of Jesus' technique from the tradition had it been present. Jesus is not the only exorcist of his time not to have appeared to call up any source of power-authority. Rabbis Simeon ben Yohai and Eleazar ben Yose exorcised a demon from the Emperor's daughter without declaring any source of power-authority (*b. Me'il.* 17b). Also Apollonius mentions no outside aid in his healings (*Life* 4:20). Once again we see that Jesus is an exorcist, like others of his time, who relied not on outside aids but on his own charismatic personal force to subdue and expel the demon.

(e) It does not seem that Jesus used the formula 'I bind you' (Aramaic = *shb'*). From the discussion above it was established that this word, used by the demoniac in Mark 5:7 and frequently in the magical papyri (e.g. PGM IV:3019), meant to 'charge', 'adjure' or 'bind' someone by another power-authority.

For example Mark 5:7 has 'I bind you *by* God, do not torment me.' Acts 19:13 reads 'I bind you *by* the Jesus whom Paul preaches,' and 1 Thessalonians 5:27 has 'I bind you *by* the Lord that this letter be read to all the brethren' (cf. Matt. 26:63). As 'bind' is closely associated with exorcism and found in the exorcists' incantations, and from its use in 1 Thess. 5:27 showing that the early Church was not averse to using it, it is perhaps surprising either that Jesus did not use the word or that the early Church did not attribute it to the tradition. As 'I bind' is found in conjunction with the power-authority being used to perform the exorcism and the early Church recognized that Jesus relied on the Spirit/finger of God, the tradition is probably faithful in recording that Jesus did not use the word. Thus again, like Apollonius and some of the rabbis, Jesus apparently neither acknowledged the use of a source of power-authority nor used the accompanying 'I bind (you by. . .)' formula.

In the light of this it is important to recall Jesus' use

of the emphatic 'I' (Aramaic = *ana*) in Mark 9:25. I can find no parallel to this emphatic use of 'I' in any other incantation or exorcism story in the ancient world. Thus along *with no declaration of his source of power-authority Jesus deliberately draws attention to himself and his own resources in his ability to expel the demon.*

Conclusions

In this section we have been examining the techniques Jesus used in his exorcisms--or at least what his audience reportedly saw and heard. In many ways Jesus seems to have been a man of his time in that he used readily recognizable techinques, and what was reported of other exorcists was also reported of Jesus' exorcisms. There was the vocalized distress on the part of the demon(iac) as he was confronted by Jesus, the then familiar though brief verbal formulae from Jesus, the demon's desperate plea for leniency, the usual violence accompanying the healing. Then, as with some others of his time, Jesus' technique was so simple that it contained no mechanical aids, no prayers, no invoking of a power-authority, and no 'proofs'--save the cured demoniac.

Despite this simplicity of method we cannot, as we have seen, say that in this he was unique among his contemporaries. Nor, also, can it be concluded that Jesus stood over against those exorcists who used traditional stock phrases or verbal formulae (incantations?) to effect a cure.

Yet having said this we should not rush to the conclusion that Jesus was considered to be a magician. Even if his use of traditional exorcistic formulae might be technically categorized in twentieth-century sociological terms as 'magical', there is no reliable evidence to support a case that Jesus' *contemporaries* considered him to be a magician.

We must also keep in mind that we have seen that in drawing attention to his own authority in his ability to subdue the demons--even though he acknowledged that his power-authority was the Holy Spirit--Jesus' technique appears to be unique. This point probably reveals an important aspect of Jesus' technique. That is, an exorcism performed by Jesus was a confrontation between the demon and Jesus. The uncluttered verbal formulae, the absence of calling upon the aid of a third party, the absence of all mechanical or physical aids and especially the use of the emphatic 'I' all point to *Jesus being successful because of who he was and the demon being forced to confront*

Jesus. Even Jesus' asking the demon's name (Mark 5:9) fits this idea of a demand that the demons confront Jesus.

III. How Did Jesus Understand His Exorcisms?

As well as answering this question, with particular reference to the origin of the eschatological understanding of Jesus' exorcisms, we need to address the subsidiary question on our agenda: how important was exorcism to Jesus in the context of his wider ministry?

1. Matthew 12:28/Luke 11:20, to which we will turn in a moment, is probably important in providing material to help answer this question. Although this verse places exorcism in the centre of Jesus' ministry we should not conclude that in exorcism the whole of Jesus' ministry was summed up, whether for himself or for the early Church.

The clearest evidence that, despite the central importance Jesus may have given to exorcism, he considered his ministry wider than exorcism is in his answer to John the Baptist.

Matthew 11:2-6

2 "Now when John heard in
prison about the deeds of
the Christ,
he sent word by his
disciples 3 and said to him,
'Are you he who is to come,
or shall we look for another?'

4 And Jesus answered them,
'Go and tell John what you
hear and see 5 the blind receive their sight and the lame
walk, lepers are cleansed and
the deaf hear, and the dead
are raised up, and the poor
have good news preached to

Luke 7:18-23

18 "The disciples of John told
him of all these things. 19 And
John, calling to him two of
his disciples, sent them to
the Lord saying,
'Are you he who is to come,
or shall we look for another?'
20 *And* when the men *had come to*
him, *they* said, 'John the Baptist
has sent us *to* you, saying, "Are
you he who is to come, or shall
we look for another?"' 21 *In that*
hour he cured many *of diseases*
and plagues and *evil spirits*,
and on many that were blind he
bestowed sight. 22 And he
answered them, 'Go and tell John
what you have seen and heard:
the blind receive their sight,
the lame walk, lepers are
cleansed, and the deaf hear, the
dead are raised up, the poor
have good news preached to

them. 6 And blessed is he who takes no offence at me.'"	them. 23 And blessed is he who takes no offence at me.'"

In vv. 20-21, Luke says exorcism formed part of the new state of affairs attending Jesus' ministry. However the vocabulary and style (in italics above) and the awkward addition of v. 21 into the context probably mean that Luke has added this reference to exorcism to Q, his source. It is Matthew then who more nearly reproduces the Q tradition. That this tradition goes back to the earliest reports of the historical Jesus is probable because the dialogue fits so well into the life situation of Jesus. In particular Jesus' reply is unlikely to have been composed after Easter and the tradition is unlikely to have invented the notion of John the Baptist, a major witness to Jesus, questioning the status and ministry of Jesus./84/

Therefore in this pericope we probably have a description originating from Jesus of the new state of affairs attending his ministry--yet there is no mention of exorcism. Here it is not healings that are most significant. In fact the climax of Jesus' reply draws attention to his preaching. Thus we cannot claim that exorcism was *the* key to his ministry, but with Matthew 12:28/Luke 11:20 in mind, we may claim that exorcism was at least one of the important functions or aspects of his ministry.

2. It is in the collection of sayings now found in what is usually called the Beelzebul controversy that we may find out most about how Jesus understood his ministry of exorcism (Mark 3:22-27 and Matt. 9:32-34/12:22-30/Luke 11:14-23). Within these sayings the 'Spirit/finger' saying of Matthew 12:28/Luke 11:20 is in turn of considerable significance. Recently E. P. Sanders has discussed this passage as an example of the exegetical efforts of scholars of the last decades proving negative. Sanders has shown that we have come to this verse with a predetermined agenda and sought to derive more from it than it can probably bear./85/ We are reminded to proceed with caution!

It is, as we have noted in section one above, most probably an authentic Jesus saying. Jesus says 'If it is by the Spirit (Luke has 'finger') of God that I cast out demons then the Kingdom of God has come upon you.' From this saying we learn a number of things about how Jesus viewed his exorcisms.

First, Jesus says he was casting out demons by the Spirit/

finger of God./86/ Many scholars take 'finger' to be more original. However James Dunn has shown that 'Spirit' is more likely to represent the original./87/ In the NT period other Jews were using God as the source of power-authority (e.g. PGM IV:3019). But significantly Jesus says he is operating by the Spirit of God. The Jews believed that when the special individual--the Messiah--came from God he would be especially endowed with the Spirit of God (see e.g. Isa. 61:1, Luke 4:18, Acts 2:33). Here Jesus claims to be authorized by that very Spirit. This then is one of the clearest indications that Jesus was aware of his special relationship with, and status before, God.

Second, not only is Jesus' mention of 'Spirit' important here, but so also is the emphatic 'I'/88/ about which we have already spoken. If we take this into account Jesus was not simply saying that because the Spirit had come then the Kingdom had arrived but that because the Spirit had come upon him, and he was casting out demons, then the Kingdom of God had come. Sanders' comment on ἔφθασεν is pertinent here. He says '. . .it seems to me obviously dubious to lean so heavily on the meaning of the verb *ephthasen*. How can we know that the Greek verb accurately captures not only something which Jesus said but also the nuance which he intended to convey? Clearly we cannot.'/89/ Of course, in the nature of historical enquiry, we cannot finally know whether or not the Greek ἔφθασεν reflects what Jesus said or a nuance he intended. However ἔφθασεν (and probably ἤγγικεν, Mark 1:15) is most likely to be a translation of *mt'* which means 'to come' or 'to arrive'./90/ So at the very least we can say that Jesus understood his exorcisms to have something to do with the coming of the Kingdom of God whether that 'coming' was imminent or realized. Thus, in turn, we can suggest that Jesus believed that *where the Spirit was operating in him there was the coming of the Kingdom of God*.

Thus, *third*, it is clear that Jesus understood his exorcisms not to be preparatory to the Kingdom,/91/ nor signs of the Kingdom,/92/ nor indications that the Kingdom had arrived, /93/ nor even illustrations of the Kingdom, but actually the *Kingdom of God itself in operation*; the coming of the Kingdom--God's reign itself in operation in the defeat of Satan in people's lives./94/

Within the Beelzebul controversy pericope there is a parable which helps elucidate Jesus' understanding of his exorcisms. In Matthew 12:29/Mark 3:27/Luke 11:21-22 Jesus likens his exorcisms to someone entering a strong man's house, binding him and plundering his house. Thus in exorcism Jesus sees himself as binding Satan in order to plunder his property--those hitherto held by Satan. The view that Satan was thought to be defeated at the Temptation/95/ is untenable not least because of the pericope we are discussing along with the fact that Mark views the Temptation as continuing during Jesus' subsequent ministry (cf. e.g. Mark 1:12-13 with 14-15). If Mark, or indeed the other Evangelists, understood Satan's final defeat to have taken place in the Temptation then we would expect a more obvious reference to the fact. Evidence from the Testaments of the Twelve Patriarchs is sometimes cited as indicating that in the NT era the Messiah was expected to defeat Satan and his minions through exorcism./96/ However an examination of this material shows either that it comes from a Christian hand or, as in the Assumption of Moses 10:1 and 3, that there is only a general reference to Satan's being no more in the New Age./97/ In short we can conclude that *Jesus is the first one to make a specific connection between the relatively ordinary events of exorcism and the defeat of Satan, between exorcism and eschatology.*/98/

But here we meet a difficulty. If Jesus understood his exorcisms as the defeat of Satan, how are we to explain the sayings of Jesus which assume the continued existence and operation of Satan (cf. e.g. Luke 10;17-18 and 22:31)? If Satan was thought to be defeated in Jesus' ministry why did the early Church so readily accept the reality of Satan's existence and power? And if Jesus' exorcistic ministry was the defeat of Satan, why does material like 2 Peter 2:4-10, Jude 6 and Revelation 20:1-3 see Satan's defeat as taking place at the final judgment? Or, put another way, if Jesus' ministry marks the defeat of Satan then why did the early Church engage in exorcism? Can we answer all these questions in Barrett's words: 'The devil is defeated, but he is not destroyed. The Church was too well acquainted with his devices to suppose that Satan had died'?/99/

It is possible that, while Jesus may have viewed his exorcisms as the defeat of Satan, the early Church was still confronted with the reality of evil and so inserted secondary material into the tradition to account for this tension as well as its own experience. The material in the Jesus tradition that assumes the continuing reality of Satan or evil to the end of the age is not extensive. It includes the commission in the longer ending of Mark (Mark 16:17), the parable of the Wheat and the Weeds (Matt. 13:24-30), the explanation of the parable of the Wheat and the Weeds (13:36-43), the parable of the Net and its explanation (13:47-50), and the parable of the Sheep and Goats (25:31-46).

Scholars suspect that some, if not most, of this material is probably secondary and cannot, with confidence, be traced back to the historical Jesus. The ending of Mark (16:9-20), which includes the commission (v. 17), is not in many of the best manuscripts (e.g. Codices Sinaiticus and Vaticanus) and therefore probably does not convey authentic Jesus tradition. Views vary on the authenticity of the parable of the Wheat and the Weeds. Some regard the core, Matt. 13:24b-26, 30b, as authentic,/100/ while others, notably Jeremias, have argued convincingly that the whole parable faithfully reflects the words and views of Jesus./101/ Importantly, this means that we can conclude that the reference to the destruction of the enemy's work in the eschaton probably goes back to Jesus, even though the authenticity of the parables' interpretation is often rejected./102/ We can leave aside from consideration the parable of the Net and its explanation, for, while the parable could have referred to the last judgment, no clear reference is made to Satan or his works. The parable of the Sheep and the Goats is generally agreed to contain at least significant traces of authentic Jesus tradition--especially in Matt. 25:35-40 and 42-45./103/ However v. 41 ('Then he will say to those at his left hand, 'Depart from me, you cursed, into the *eternal fire* prepared for *the devil and his angels*. . ."') and v. 46 ('And they will go away into *eternal punishment*, but *the righteous* into *eternal* life') show by the Matthean traits (in italics) that they have probably come from the Evangelist's hand./104/ In conclusion, this means that the tradition which Matthew has used here in chapter 25 was probably free of the notion of Satan's defeat or destruction in the eternal fire.

From this very brief investigation of the Gospel material where Jesus is said to have associated the defeat of Satan and evil with the last judgment, the parable of the Wheat and the Weeds is the most secure evidence. *Nevertheless*, even with this small amount of material we have evidence that *Jesus believed that his exorcisms were the defeat of Satan and yet that Satan's activity would also continue until the final judgment*. How then can we explain this apparent tension? Does Jesus assume two defeats of Satan?

In Isaiah 24:21-22 and Ethiopic Enoch 10:4-6 (see also 10:12-13, 18:14-19:2, 21:6-7, 90:23-25, Jubilees 5:5-10, 10:5-9) the view is that the defeat of Satan or evil is to take place in two stages. Isaiah 24:22 puts it simply--'they will be shut up in a prison, and after many days they will be punished.' Ethiopic Enoch 10:4-6 develops this simple picture clarifying how the first century mind probably understood the nature of each stage of the defeat.

> The Lord said to Raphael: 'Bind Azazel hand and foot, and cast him into the darkness. . .and let him abide there forever. . . . And on the day of the great judgment he shall be cast into the fire' (note also vv. 11-13).

Ethiopic Enoch 19:1 is even more explicit about the second stage:

> . . .here [in a deep abyss of heavenly fire] shall they stand until the day of judgment in which they shall be judged till they are made an end of.

What is in mind seems to be a first or preliminary stage in which evil or Satan is bound or constrained for an extended period until the second and final destruction of Satan and his minions. From what we see reflected in the authentic Jesus-tradition this is how Jesus understood the destruction of Satan. His exorcisms were the first stage of binding Satan (Mark 3:23-25/Matt. 12:25-26/Luke 11:17-18; cf. Matt. 12:28/Luke 11:20) but the final defeat would take place in the final judgment (Matt.13:30).

So far in this section we have been attempting to shed light on Jesus' understanding of the 'cosmic' significance of his exorcisms. But is it possible to say something about what he thought he was doing for the individual concerned?

The material in the Beelzebul controversy pericope, particularly the parable of the Strong Man (Matt. 12:29/Mark 3:27/Luke 11:21-23) indicates that Jesus thought that in exorcism he was releasing the individual from Satan's grip (cf. Luke 13:16). This pericope (note Matt. 12:28/Luke 11:20) as well as the parable of the seven other returning evil spirits (Matt. 12:43/Luke 11:24-26) shows that Jesus also thought that the destruction of Satan's kingdom in an individual was only part of the ministry of exorcism. There needed to follow the coming of the Holy Spirit to the individual's life. Thus the person whom Jesus healed became part of the coming of the Kingdom and was the action of the Kingdom of God in microcosm (cf. Matt. 12:28/Luke 11:20).

Conclusions

In the first part of this paper it was concluded that there

is more than sufficient evidence to affirm that Jesus was an extremely successful exorcist. In the second section it was shown, in relation to his ministry of exorcism, that in many ways Jesus seems to have been a man of his time in that he used readily recognizable techniques. He can be seen, as Vermes suggests (see note 3 above), as standing in the tradition of first-century charismatic Judaism. His uniqueness *as an exorcist* may be as simple, though as profound, as his seeing his exorcisms as empowered by God, through the eschatological Spirit, yet depending on his own personal resources. Jesus' method of exorcism can be summed up as a confrontation between the divine and the demonic in which the demonic is defeated. He was successful because of who he was and because the demons were forced to confront him.

While we can agree that exorcism played a large part in his ministry,/105/ from the final section of this paper, we cannot conclude that Jesus understood his exorcisms to sum up the whole of his ministry. Nevertheless he saw exorcism as of central importance as it was the first of a two-stage defeat of Satan. Being empowered by the eschatological Spirit, he believed that where the Spirit was operating through him--not least in his exorcisms--there was the Kingdom of God. This understanding was unique. Jesus was the first to believe that in the ordinary events of exorcism Satan was being destroyed and the Kingdom of God was arriving./106/

Notes

/1/ L. Morris, *The Cross in the New Testament* (Exeter: Paternoster, 1965) 56-57. Cf. V. Taylor, *The Gospel according to St. Mark* (London: Macmillan, 1952) 171.
/2/ W. Everts, 'Jesus Christ, No Exorcist,' *BSac* 81 (1924) 357.
/3/ G. Vermes, *Jesus the Jew* (Glasgow: Fontana, 1976) 69, 79; cf. 223.
/4/ C. K. Barrett, *The Holy Spirit and the Gospel Tradition* (London: SPCK, 1966) 61.
/5/ K. Grayston, 'Exorcism in the New Testament,' *Epworth Review* 2 (1975) 94.
/6/ H. Cox, *The Secular City* (London: SCM, 1965) 149.
/7/ See G. Theissen, *Miracle Stories of the Early Christian Tradition* (Edinburgh: T & T Clark, 1983) 85-90.
/8/ O. Böcher, *Christus Exorcista* (Stuttgart: Kohlhammer, 1972) 77-80. Cf. F. Fenner, *Die Krankheit im Neuen Testament* (Leipzig: Hinrichs, 1930) 21-26.
/9/ Böcher, *Christus Exorcista*, 78.

/10/ Ibid., 80.
/11/ Cf. Theissen, *Miracle Stories*, 87-90, who lists: a) The person must be in the power of the demons; b) The battle between the demon and the exorcist and c) The destructive activity of the demon in nature, as characteristics specific to the genre exorcism story.
/12/ (London: Hodder & Stoughton, 1960).
/13/ (London: Sidgwick & Jackson, 1981).
/14/ (Grand Rapids: Eerdmans, 1981).
/15/ Cf. P. W. Hollenbach, 'Jesus, Demoniacs, and Public Authorities,' *JAAR* 49 (1981) 568.
/16/ Graham H. Twelftree, *Jesus the Exorcist* (forthcoming).
/17/ Luke says that Jesus 'stood over her' (4:39) when he healed the woman. It is possible that Luke says this simply because the woman was on a pallet on the ground (I. H. Marshall, *The Gospel of Luke* [Exeter: Paternoster, 1978] 195). However it is arguable that by this phrase Luke is indicating the technique of an exorcist. The practice of an exorcist standing over a patient has its roots in ancient Babylonian healings (R. C. Thompson, *The Devils and Evil Spirits of Babylonia* [London: Luzac, 1903] vol. 1, 103, 119-21). In the NT period it is directly paralleled in the magical papyri (e.g. PGM IV:745, 1229, 2735) where the focus of attention in healing was often directed towards the head. Further evidence that Luke may intend this report to be understood as an exorcism is his use of ἐπιτιμάω (4:39). This word is used in the Gospels apart from reference to exorcism (Matt. 8:26/Mark 4:39/Luke 8:24; Matt. 16:20/Mark 8:30/Luke 9:21; Matt. 16:22/Mark 8:32; Matt. 19:13/ Mark 10:13/Luke 18:15; Matt. 20:31/Mark 10:48/Luke 18:39; Mark 8:33; Luke 9:55; 17:3; 19:39; 23:40). However it is also used in reports describing the action of an exorcist (Matt. 17:18/Mark 9:25/Luke 9:42; Mark 1:25/Luke 4:35, [39]; cf. Matt. 12:16/Mark 3:12; Mark 1:34/Luke 4:41) and carries the idea 'of command by which God's agent defeats his enemies, thus preparing for the coming of God's kingdom' (H. C. Kee, 'The Terminology of Mark's Exorcism Stories,' *NTS* 14 [1967-68] 244; cf. 243).
/18/ The story is also so different from the traditional exorcism stories (cf. n. 11 above) that Luke is unlikely to have regarded this as an exorcism story. Rather this is probably another example of the blurring of the distinction between healing and exorcism stories.
/19/ See the literature listed in R. Pesch, *Das Markusevangelium*, vol. 1 (Freiburg: Herder, 1977) 220-21 and in Marshall, *Luke*, 570.
/20/ See J. Jeremias, *New Testament Theology* (London: SCM, 1971) 91.

/21/ J. M. Robinson, *A New Quest of the Historical Jesus* (London: SCM, 1959) 121 (cf. N. Perrin, *The Kingdom of God in the Teaching of Jesus* [London: SCM, 1963] 74-76); J. D. G. Dunn, *Jesus and the Spirit* (London: SCM, 1975) 44 and n. 18. See also below.
/22/ J. M. Creed, *The Gospel according to St. Luke* (London: Macmillan, 1930) 161. On the view that Luke is elaborating Mark see B. Lindars, *New Testament Apologetic* (London: SCM, 1961) 84-85; and S. Légasse, 'L'homme fort de Luc 11:21-22,' *NovT* 5 (1962) 5-9. This is unlikely for Luke does not usually rewrite Mark so extensively. See Marshall, *Luke*, 477.
/23/ P. Joüon, cited by J. Jeremias, *The Parables of Jesus* (London: SCM, 1972) 197.
/24/ See further Twelftree, *Jesus, passim.*
/25/ See A. Denaux, 'L'hypocrisie des Pharisiens et le dessein de Dieu. Analyse de Lc., xiii, 31-33,' in F. Neirynck, ed., *L'évangile de Luc* (Gembloux: Duculot, 1973) 245-85; and M. Rese, 'Einige Überlegungen zu Lukas xiii, 31-33,' in J. Dupont, et al., *Jésus aux origenes de la christologie* (Gembloux: Duculot, 1975) 201-25.
/26/ R. Bultmann, *History of the Synoptic Tradition* (New York: Harper & Row, 1963) 35; cf. 56. V. Taylor (*Jesus and His Sacrifice* [London: Macmillan, 1937] 167-71) further pointed to the irony, sense of urgency and mission, and the roughness of the saying as indications of its authenticity. See also H. W. Hoehner, *Herod Antipas* (Grand Rapids: Zondervan, 1980) 214-24.
/27/ The objection of Taylor that this pericope is not a summary statement like 3:7-12 because it is connected with a particular time and place need not detain us and only holds in part, for the healings are only summarised (v. 34) (*The Gospel according to St. Mark* [London: Macmillan, 1959] 180.
/28/ E.g. Bultmann, *History*, 25; Creed, *Luke*, 138-39; Taylor, *Mark*, 407; S. E. Johnson, *The Gospel according to St Mark* (London: A & C Black, 1960) 165; E. Haenchen, *Der Weg Jesu* (Berlin: Töpelmann, 1966) 327; E. Schweizer, *The Good News according to Mark* (London: SPCK, 1971) 194; H. C. Kee, *Community of the New Age* (London: SCM, 1977) 43.
/29/ Wellhausen, cited by Bultmann, *History*, 25.
/30/ Note the imperfect tense indicating a linear or protracted activity in the past.
/31/ Further see Graham H. Twelftree, *Christ Triumphant: Exorcism Then and Now* (London: Hodder & Stoughton, 1985) 114-15.
/32/ G. Kittel ('ἀκολουθέω,' *TDNT*, I, 214) later on the same page notes Rev. 14:4 as an exception to this. (John 11:31 is the only instance in the Gospels of ἀκολουθέω being used without Jesus as the object.)

/33/ Ibid.
/34/ M. Black, *An Aramaic Approach to the Gospels and Acts* (Oxford: Clarendon, 1967[3]) 71, 169-71.
/35/ E. Haenchen, *The Acts of the Apostles* (Oxford: Blackwell, 1972) 566.
/36/ On the use of Jesus' name by Jewish exorcists, see D. Chwolson, cited by A. Fridrichsen, *The Problem of Miracle in Primitive Christianity* (Minneapolis: Augsburg, 1972) 170, n. 29.
/37/ J. M. Hull (*Hellenistic Magic and the Synoptic Tradition* [London: SCM, 1974] 137-38) says that Matthew's omission of the story is not difficult to understand in the light of his reticence about exorcism. While it is not until 8:28-34 that he gives his readers an exorcism story and there is an apparent distance from Mark in giving exorcism a low status, Matthew is very clear about the importance of exorcism in revealing the significance of Jesus as well as the role of exorcism in Jesus' ministry (Matt. 12:22-32, see further Twelftree, *Christ*, 123-27). E. Schweizer (*The Good News according to Matthew* [London: SPCK, 1976] 73) suggests Matthew's omission is because he invariably cites only one instance of each type of miracle (cf. 8:28-34). It may also be that Matthew felt it more appropriate to illustrate the motif of Jesus' authoritative teaching (Mark 1:22/ Matt. 7:29) more directly and fully with the Sermon on the Mount (5:1-7:27).
/38/ This is part of Luke's so-called Great Omission of material where Mark (6:45-8:26) has Jesus in Gentile territory. Luke is most probably 'motivated by his historical convictions that the mission to the gentiles is not yet.' John Drury, *Tradition and Design in Luke's Gospel* (London: DLT, 1976) 101; cf. 96-102.
/39/ For fuller treatment of these stories, see Twelftree, *Jesus*, chap. 3. On the Synoptic Evangelists' perspectives of Jesus as an exorcist, see Twelftree, *Christ*, chap. 4.
/40/ E.g. R. H. Stein, 'What is Redaktionsgeschichte?' *JBL* 88 (1969) 45-56; idem, 'The "Redaktionsgeschichtlich" Investigation of a Markan Seam (Mc 1:21f.),' *ZNW* 61 (1970) 70-94; idem, 'The Proper Methodology for Ascertaining a Markan Redaction History,' *NovT* 13 (1971) 181-98; S. S. Smalley, 'Redaction Criticism,' in I. H. Marshall, ed., *New Testament Interpretation* (Exeter: Paternoster, 1977) 181-95.
/41/ R. H. Stein, 'The "Criteria" for Authenticity,' in R. T. France & D. Wenham, eds., *Gospel Perspectives*, vol. 1 (Sheffield: JSOT, 1980) 225-63. See also R. Bultmann, 'The Study of the Synoptic Gospels,' in R. Bultmann & K. Kundsin, *Form Criticism* (New York: Harper & Row, 1962) chap. 4; C. E. Carlston, 'A "Positive" Criterion of Authenticity?' *BibRes* 7 (1962) 33-44;

H. K. McArthur, 'A Survey of Recent Gospel Research' *Int* 18 (1964) 47-51; E. P. Sanders, *The Tendencies of the Synoptic Tradition* (Cambridge: Cambridge University, 1969); J. K. Elliott, 'The Synoptic Problem and the Laws of Tradition: A Cautionary Note,' *ExpTim* 82 (1970-71) 148-52; D. G. A. Calvert, 'An Examination of the Criteria for Distinguishing the Authentic Words of Jesus,' *NTS* 18 (1971-72) 209-19; R. S. Barbour, *Traditio-Historical Criticism of the Gospels* (London: SPCK, 1972) part 1; N. Perrin, *Rediscovering the Teaching of Jesus* (New York: Harper & Row, 1967) 15-53; R. H. Fuller, 'The Criterion of Dissimilarity: The Wrong Tool?' in R. F. Berkey & S. A. Edwards, eds., *Christological Perspectives* (New York: Pilgrim, 1982) 42-48.

/42/ Though see F. Mussner, *The Miracles of Jesus* (Shannon: Ecclesia Press, 1970) 27-39; idem, 'Ipsissima facta Jesu?' *ThRv* 68 (1972) cols. 177-85.

/43/ See Graham H. Twelftree, 'Jesus in Jewish Traditions' in D. Wenham, ed., *Gospel Perspectives*, vol. 5 (1985) 322.

/44/ For a more thorough historical examination of the exorcism stories, see Twelftree, *Jesus*, chap. 3.

/45/ See Taylor, *Mark*, 173; cf. J. Hawkins, *Horae Synopticae* (Oxford: Clarendon, 1899) 10.

/46/ E. J. Pryke, *Redactional Style in the Marcan Gospel* (Cambridge: Cambridge University, 1978) 139, identifies συναγωγή as a Markan feature of the verse. However Pryke's method of attempting to break new ground in identifying redactional passages in Mark by a consensus of scholars (10-24), thereby identifying Markan style, is circular. Συναγωγή occurs 8 times in Mark, 9 times in Matthew and 15 times in Luke--hardly figures that enable us to think that Mark had a predilection for the word.

/47/ Taylor, *Mark*, 44.

/48/ Mark = 43, Matthew = 37, Luke = 35. Cf. Taylor, *Mark*, 44; C. H. Turner, 'Markan Usage,' *JTS* 29 (1928) 279.

/49/ The significance of θυγάτριον occurring at 5:23 and 7:25 in the NT is increased in view of Mark's predilection towards diminutives. Turner, 'Usage,' 349; Taylor, *Mark*, 45.

/50/ Mark = 15; Matthew = 6, Luke = 4. Taylor, *Mark*, 44.

/51/ H. Greeven, 'προσκυνέω,' *TDNT*, VI, 763.

/52/ See those listed by Pryke, *Redactional Style*, 14.

/53/ On Matthew abbreviating the miracle stories, see H. J. Held, 'Matthew as Interpreter of the Miracle Stories,' in G. Bornkamm, G. Barth, & H. J. Held, *Tradition and Interpretation in Matthew* (London: SCM, 1963) 165-299.

/54/ E.g. see H. Seesemann, 'οἶδα,' *TDNT*, V, 117-18.

/55/ S. V. McCasland, 'The Demonic "Confessions" of Jesus,' *JR* 24 (1944) 33.
/56/ Ibid.
/57/ H. Anderson, *Mark* (London: Marshall, Morgan & Scott, 1976) 91.
/58/ J. D. M. Derrett, *Law in the New Testament* (London: DLT, 1970) 241.
/59/ O. Bauernfeind, *Die Worte der Dämonen im Markusevangelium* (Stuttgart: Kohlhammer, 1927) 3-28.
/60/ See 2 Sam. (LXX 2 Kings) 16:10, 19:22, 2 Kings (LXX 4 Kings) 3:13, 2 Chr. 35:21.
/61/ Bauernfeind, *Worte der Dämonen*, 3-28.
/62/ Cf. Bultmann, *History*, 209, n. 1.
/63/ A lead tablet in A. Deissmann, *Bible Studies* (Edinburgh: T & T Clark, 1903) 275-82.
/64/ From the second example just given where an evil spirit is being adjured or bound by the god of Abraan, we can, because of the misspelling, probably conclude that non-Jews were taking up Jewish material in their exorcistic incantations, just as non-Christian exorcists attempted to take up the name of Jesus in their healings (cf. Acts 19:13).
/65/ Matthew (8:29) and Luke (8:28) do not seem to accept the idea that a demon(iac) was attempting to put a preternatural restriction or spell on Jesus, and, respectively, alter the words to 'Have you come before time to torment us?' and 'I beg you, do not torment me.' See also the incorrect NIV translation of ὁρκίζω, 'Swear to God that you won't torment me!'
/66/ For other examples of ἅγιος being used of people close to God, see BAGD, s.v.
/67/ Cf. Vermes, *Jesus*, 206-10.
/68/ On the phrase 'son of the house' see A. Büchler, *Types of Jewish-Palestinian Piety* (New York: KTAV, 1968 [repr. of 1922]) 203.
/69/ G. Bertram, 'ὕψιστος,' *TDNT*, VIII, 620. A little further on he says 'Apart from liturgical use this term for God, which is essentially controlled by the OT, found little place in the religious consciousness of early Christianity.'
/70/ E.g. Morris, *Cross*, 56-57; and Taylor, *Mark*, 171.
/71/ S. Eitrem, *Some Notes on the Demonology in the New Testament* (Oslo: A. W. Brøgger, 1950) 30-1.
/72/ E. Klostermann, *Das Markusevangelium* (Tübingen: Mohr, 1950) 49.
/73/ E.g. C. G. Montefiore, *The Synoptic Gospels* (London: Macmillan, 1927) vol. 1, 11; M. Dibelius, *From Tradition to Gospel* (London: James Clarke, 1971) 88; W. E. Bundy, *Jesus and*

the First Three Gospels (Cambridge: Harvard University, 1955) 243; D. L. Bartlett, *Exorcism Stories in the Gospel of Mark* (Unpublished Ph.D. thesis: Yale, 1972) 136-38.
/74/ E.g. PGM VIII:6-7, 13 quoted above.
/75/ H. Bietenhard, 'ὄνομα,' *TDNT*, V, 250.
/76/ Böcher, *Christus Exorcista*, 20-32.
/77/ Thompson, *Devils*, vol. 2 (1904) 109; cf. 19-21; vol. 1, 103, 119, 151.
/78/ See n. 76 above.
/79/ See e.g. Bultmann, *History*, 225; Dibelius, *Tradition*, 87-88.
/80/ Count d'Alviella (E. Goblet), *Lectures on the Origin and Growth of the Conception of God* (London: Williams & Norgate, 1892) 88-89; M. P. Nilson, *A History of Greek Religion* (Oxford: Clarendon, 1949) 85-86.
/81/ Although there is no evidence for it, it is possible that the pigs episode offered evidence to the demoniac that his cure was complete.
/82/ See P. T. O'Brien, 'Prayer in Luke-Acts,' *TynB* 24 (1973) 111-27.
/83/ On the discussion of whether 'Spirit' or 'finger' is the earlier term, see below.
/84/ For more detail on the tradition going back to the historical Jesus, see Dunn, *Jesus*, 55-60.
/85/ E. P. Sanders, *Jesus and Judaism* (London: SCM, 1985) 133-40.
/86/ Cf. '. . .the mighty hand of God shall bring down [the army of Satan, and all] the angels of his kingdom, and all the members [of his company]. . .' (1 QM 1:15; cf. 15:12-14). This paper is not the place to discuss the ontological existence of demons. However see my discussion in *Christ*, chap. 5.
/87/ Dunn, *Jesus*, 46.
/88/ See also ibid., 48-49.
/89/ Sanders, *Jesus*, 134.
/90/ Cf. W. G. Kümmel, *Promise and Fulfilment* (London: SCM, 1961) 106, n. 6.
/91/ As thought by, e.g., O. Betz, 'Jesu Heiliger Krieg,' *NovT* 2 (1958) 115-37; R. H. Hiers, *The Kingdom of God in the Synoptic Tradition* (Gainesville: University of Florida, 1970).
/92/ E.g. A. Richardson, *The Miracle Stories of the Gospels* (London: SCM, 1941) 45-50; H. C. Kee, *Miracle in the Early Christian World* (New Haven: Yale University, 1983) 155.
/93/ E.g. C. L. Mitton, *Your Kingdom Come* (London: Mowbray, 1978) 37. R. H. Fuller (*Interpreting the Miracles* [London: SCM, 1963] 40) also misrepresents Jesus' understanding of his miracles when he says they 'foreshadow. . .the establishment of his [God' [God's] Reign in the last days'. Cf. idem, *The Mission and*

Achievement of Jesus (London: SCM, 1954) 37-38.
/94/ Cf. L. Goppelt, *Theology of the New Testament* (Grand Rapids: Eerdmans, 1981) vol. 1, 147.
/95/ E.g. E. Best, *Temptation and Passion* (Cambridge: Cambridge University, 1965) 13. For further reply, see Twelftree, *Jesus*, chap. 3.
/96/ E.g. Barrett, *Spirit*, 57-59. Cf. Sanders, *Jesus*, 134-35 and nn. 54-55.
/97/ In more detail, see Twelftree, *Jesus, passim.*
/98/ Cf. M. Trautmann, *Zeichenhafte Handlungen Jesu* (Würzburg: Echter, 1980) 265.
/99/ Barrett, *Spirit*, 52.
/100/ E.g. J. D. Kingsbury, *The Parables of Jesus in Matthew 13* (London: SPCK, 1969) 65.
/101/ E.g. J. Jeremias, *The Parables of Jesus* (London: SCM, 1972) 224-25.
/102/ Cf. R. H. Stein, *An Introduction to the Parables of Jesus* (Philadelphia: Westminster, 1981) 143--'The great majority of scholars argue for the view that the interpretation is essentially a Matthean creation, and for many Jeremias' analysis of this passage makes it "impossible to avoid the conclusion that the interpretation of the parable of the Tares is the work of Matthew himself." *[*quoting Jeremias, *Parables*, 84-85*]* Others have attempted to find in the interpretation a pre-Matthean layer of tradition, *[*citing J. D. Crossan, 'The Seed Parables of Jesus,' *JBL* 92 (1973) 260-61*]* but in essence the interpretation is still seen as being primarily the work of Matthew.'
/103/ See, e.g., J. A. T. Robinson, 'The "Parable" of the Sheep and the Goats,' *NTS* 2 (1956) 225-37, reprinted in idem, *Twelve New Testament Studies* (London: SCM, 1962) 76-93.
/104/ See further ibid., 85.
/105/ Hollenbach, 'Jesus,' 568-69.
/106/ An earlier, more popular version of some of the material in this article appeared in chapter three of my *Christ Triumphant.*

APOLOGETIC AND APOCALYPTIC:
THE MIRACULOUS IN THE *GOSPEL OF PETER*

David F. Wright
Department of Ecclesiastical History
New College
Edinburgh EH1 2LU

Bold reassessments and a newly discovered papyrus have conspired to focus fresh attention on the apocryphal *Gospel of Peter* (hereafter *EvP*), that is to say, on the gospel fragment found in a manuscript at Akhmîm in Egypt near the end of the last century and almost universally identified with the Docetists' gospel exposed by bishop Serapion of Antioch shortly before A.D. 200 (Eusebius, *H. E.* 6:12). In Pap. Oxy. 2949, of c. 200, published in 1972, we now have two scraps of a text of *EvP* some five or six centuries older than the Akhmîm manuscript and sufficiently divergent from it to raise questions about the relationship between the latter and the work unmasked by Serapion./1/ The Docetic character of *EvP* is by no means as obvious to contemporary students as it was to most (but by no means all) commentators in the 1890's./2/ Furthermore, the earlier hypotheses of Harnack and others, that made *EvP* earlier than the canonical Gospels, have found a modern counterpart in the views of Helmut Koester in particular, which discern in *EvP* an independent witness to pre-canonical forms of both the passion narrative and an epiphany resurrection story./3/ Most recently, John Dominic Crossan has argued that most of *EvP*, which he calls the Passion-Resurrection Source, is independent of the canonical Gospels and was used by all four of them, but that the final integrated form of *EvP* incorporates some material derived directly from the canonical Gospels./4/

The present study is not concerned to address directly this renewed debate about the relation of *EvP* to the gospel tradition. (I have elsewhere tested Koester's theory against one section of *EvP* and found it wanting./5/) Its interest lies instead in the prominent miraculous element in the work. According to the author of the fullest commentary on the text, its account of the resurrection 'relève de la fantasmagorie'. Yet the same scholar acknowledges that, taken overall, *EvP* is less marked by a delight in wonders ('toujours plus ou moins amusant, parfois grotesque. Ce n'est pas du miracle, c'est de la féerie pour les enfants') than other apocryphal gospels./6/ Nevertheless the undeniable obtrusiveness of the supernatural in the resurrection narrative has tended to colour interpretations of the whole fragment, which extends from Pilate's washing his hands to the beginning of an appearance of the risen Christ at the lakeside at Tiberias. The aim of this paper is to assess the prevalence of miracles in *EvP*, and to characterize the nature of any special interest in miracles that *EvP* may display. It may thereby contribute to the reassessment of the significance of the extra-canonical, including post-canonical, gospel traditions for which Richard Bauckham pled in his epilogue to the previous volume of *Gospel Perspectives*./7/ He argues convincingly that the study of the canonical Gospels cannot logically be detached from enquiry into the fortunes of the broader gospel tradition, pointing out in particular that those whose concern lies with the historical reliability of the canonical Gospels do not have a vested interest in the unreliability of the rest.

I. The Passion Narrative

At the point of transition from the passion account to the resurrection, Ps-Peter makes 'all the people' say, 'If at his death these very great signs (ταῦτα τὰ μέγιστα σημεῖα) have come to pass, see how righteous he was!' (8:28). But *EvP* has so far recorded hardly anything exceptionally miraculous when compared with the canonical accounts. The following list includes, for completeness, some features which most probably do not belong to the category of miracle at all.

1. The Silence on the Cross--'as if he experienced no pain' (ὡς μηδὲν πόνον ἔχων, 4:10)

This translation/8/ 'says explicitly neither that [Jesus] did nor that he did not suffer pain'./9/ But if the verse is not clear evidence of *EvP*'s Docetism, it exemplifies the kind of material that could have made the work congenial to Docetists. For even if its inspiration is Isaiah 53:7 (although there is no verbal link),/10/ this silence *on the cross* is much more suggestive of the supernatural character of 'the Lord' (*EvP*'s unvarying designation for Jesus) than the refusal to reply while on trial which the canonical Gospels records. It may be comparable with the similar achievement of the early Christian martyrs,/11/ but their silence may also attest special supernatural intervention. So it is not entirely correct to suppose that the translation given above removes the issue from the realm of theology (divine impassibility) to that of asceticism (endurance of suffering),/12/ for there is no evidence that Ps-Peter's Christ was vulnerable to pain.

The non-Docetic interpretation advanced by J. W. McCant goes too far in claiming that not only is it 'clearly implied' by 4:10 that Jesus did experience pain, but 'suffering is integral to the "Petrine" passion narrative, and silence is a pronounced feature of this narrative, with the Lord speaking only once'./13/ This reading fails to give due weight to the absence from *EvP*, largely through the continuing silence of 'the Lord', of any indication that what was done to him actually caused him suffering. The distinctive form of its sole word from the cross, a parallel to the synoptic cry of dereliction, confirms this impression (see below). *EvP* is not crudely Docetic, for 'the Lord' can be manhandled, buffeted, scourged and crucified (cf. 1 Cor. 2:8, the nearest NT parallel to *EvP* 4:10a), but it nowhere discloses that such treatment impinged upon him in a painfully human way. In failing to break his legs, it was his executioners' intention that he should die in torments (4:14), but Ps-Peter does not assure us that he did./14/ Freedom from pain is therefore a more likely explanation of his silence than heroic conquest of it. Such impassibility belongs to *EvP*'s presentation of 'the Lord', whether it be viewed as divine/15/ or angelic/16/ impassibility.

2. *The Cry of Departure* (Ἡ δύναμίς μου, ἡ δύναμις, κατέλειψάς με, 5:19)

This is the sole utterance from the cross in *EvP*, and is ascribed to 'the Lord'. Its interpretation cannot be wholly separated from its immediate sequel, καὶ εἰπὼν ἀνελήφθη. The differences from the synoptic cry of dereliction (Mk 15:35, Mt 27:46) are obvious enough: δύναμις instead of θεός, indicative rather than interrogative 'why?', and a verbal form different from the ἐγκατέλιπες provided by Ps 21:2 (22:1) LXX. But if it is correct not to seek an explanation for these differences in a full-blooded Docetisation of the tradition, suggesting that the divine power of Christ left the human Jesus before the moment of death, it remains difficult to choose between the various possible sources or inspirations for *EvP*'s version./17/

The indicative assertion instead of the synoptics' questioning plaint may remove the implication of distress on the speaker's part./18/ *EvP*'s κατέλειψας should therefore probably be translated neutrally ('left') rather than pejoratively ('abandoned'). Furthermore, the cry and the death of Jesus are more closely related in *EvP* than in Matthew and Mark, where, after the cry, Jesus is given vinegar to drink by bystanders before breathing his last with another loud cry. The connexion between the two in *EvP* must be an important clue to their interpretation. In particular, it weakens the force of suggestions that δύναμις reflects a Jewish circumlocution for God, or another translation, such as Aquila's, of Ps 21:2 (22:1), or a confused misunderstanding of the Hebrew of the Psalm verse. Such explanations tend to fasten upon a comparison between the synoptic and Ps-Petrine forms of the cry, instead of setting the cry in its context in *EvP*./19/ It can reasonably be maintained that *EvP* does not suggest God-forsakenness on the part of Christ.

But what is the relation between the departure of the δύναμις and the 'taking up' of the Lord? Does the cry tell us that the precondition for the ἀνάλημψις of the Lord has now occurred? Does the departure of the δύναμις actually bring about, rather than allow for, the taking up? Does Ps-Peter present us with two happenings, even two ascensions, or with two aspects of a single event, even two ways of describing a single event? More precisely still, should the cry be read as explaining wherein the taking up consisted?

One effect of the immediate juxtaposition of the two statements in *EvP* is to imply a Christological or anthropological reference more obviously than do the synoptic accounts. Was the Lord's δύναμις his natural life-force, or the indwelling power of God that overshadowed him from his conception (cf. Lk 1:35) and enabled him to work miracles (cf. Lk 5:17, 7:19)? What is the significance of *EvP*'s subsequent references to 'the Lord' within the passion narrative after his taking up in 5:19? Nails are withdrawn from 'the hands of the Lord' (6:21), while it is 'the Lord' himself (not the body of the Lord) that Joseph washed prior to burial (6:24).

Before bringing into this enquiry the question of the meaning of ἀνελήφθη, note must be taken of the ease with which Ps-Peter's cry of departure could have been read in a Docetic fashion. A gnosticizing interpretation lay only too readily to hand, especially if attention was focussed narrowly on 5:19 alone--or rather on the first part of the verse alone, for ἀνελήφθη does not at first sight seem an appropriate description of the death of a Christ-less human Jesus (on the assumption, which will shortly be questioned, that the two parts of 5:19 are to be taken in strict consequence, so that the subject of ἀνελήφθη must be Christ minus his δύναμις).

3. The 'Taking Up' of the Lord (ἀνελήφθη, 5:19)

This single Greek word is clearly a critical one in the interpretation of *EvP*. Does it denote the death of the Lord, albeit perhaps euphemistically, or his ascension, or some combination of the two, such as death-as-ascension or ascension via death? Its difference from the words used by the canonical Gospels (ἐξέπνευσεν, Mk 15:37, Lk 23:46; ἀφῆκεν τὸ πνεῦμα, Mt 27:50; παρέδωκεν τὸ πνεῦμα, Jn 19:30) may suggest that the emission of Christ's πνεῦμα, of which all four speak in their various ways, has already transpired, or at least has already been spoken of, in *EvP*'s cry of departure. If it is a euphemistic avoidance of ἀπέθανεν, the latter is a term which none of the canonical accounts uses in this context, and in any case Ps-Peter elsewhere talks unambiguously of the Lord's 'death' (8:28).

Commentators have found it difficult to be dogmatic about the meaning of the verb. McCant insists that it is not Docetic, but will not go beyond affirming that, if it denotes ascension, this meaning does not preclude that of death./20/ The noun in Lk 9:51 (τὰς ἡμέρας τῆς ἀναλήμψεως αὐτοῦ) suggests on the contrary a primary emphasis on death together with a secondary allusion to ascension./21/ Mara's interpretation hinges on his rapprochement between Ps-Peter's cry of departure and Lk 23:46: the cry records not the abandonment of the Lord by the δύναμις but its ascension, as the Lord yields up his spirit into the hands of the Father./22/ The result of this is the glorification of the Lord denoted by ἀνελήφθη./23/

There are obvious difficulties in the way of this interpretation. It presents an ascension of the δύναμις followed by, and resulting in, the elevation to glory of the Lord himself (for the Lord must be the subject of ἀνελήφθη). This twofold ascension is awkward, to say the least, and compounds the difficulty of explaining what the δύναμις is--a question to which no clear answer emerges from Mara's discussion. A more substantial objection is offered by the continuation of *EvP*'s narrative, in which follow deposition, burial, descent into the realm of the dead and resurrection. It is after these events that the angel tells the women that the Lord ἀνέστη. . . καὶ ἀπῆλθεν ἐκεῖ ὅθεν ἀπεστάλη (13:56). Mara nevertheless holds that ἀνελήφθη announces 'l'acte final' of the ascension, while 'l'exigence du récit' has not allowed Ps-Peter to anticipate the resurrection.

If we are justified in seeking to make unified sense of the passion and resurrection sections of *EvP*, then the presumption exists that 5:19 refers only to the death of the Lord--to the θάνατος that the scribes, Pharisees and elders look back to in 8:28./24/ Furthermore, it is likely that the cry of departure and ἀνελήφθη do not signify separate happenings. More plausibly the cry interprets ἀνελήφθη by anticipation--or ἀνελήφθη may, vice versa, disclose the significance of the departure of the δύναμις. Either way, the death of the Lord could be spoken of both as the departure of his δύναμις and, euphemistically no doubt, as his being taken up./25/ In this way Ps-Peter gives expression once again to the *Christologia gloriae* which informs his whole narrative./26/ His Christ is always 'the Lord', who suffers no pain, experiences no thirst, and is not forsaken by God, whether in reality or in agony.

The precise meaning of δύναμις becomes on this interpretation of lesser importance. It is sufficient to establish that Ps-Peter is not affirming a dichotomist Christology, of a Docetic or any other kind. *EvP* will go on to talk about the deposition and burial of 'the Lord' (6:21, 24), and to declare that it was 'the one who was crucified' who rose and departed thither whence he had been sent (13:56). If δύναμις denotes the Lord's divine power, its departure means that in death 'the Lord' is accepted of God rather than that the humanity of Christ is abandoned or that Christ dies under divine displeasure. That is to say, *EvP*'s form of the cry of departure is concerned to exclude precisely what the synoptic cry of dereliction appears to suggest, that Christ dies in weakness, accursed and forsaken by God.

The outcome of this discussion is that no miraculous ascension or translation of 'the Lord' is recorded in *EvP* 5:19. The author's theological or, more strictly, Christological apologetic has occasioned an account of the Lord's passion which tends towards the Docetic, or at least could only too easily be read as Docetic, but this is a *Tendenz* that is seen more clearly elsewhere in the passion account. Here it has contrived merely to rob the death of Christ of its agony and its sting. The Lord was taken from us in triumphant peace. The contrast is, of course, most marked with Matthew and Mark, for Luke and John do not record the cry of dereliction.

4. *The 'Very Great Signs' Accompanying the Lord's Death* (5:20-7:27; cf. 8:28)

The summary statement of 8:28 presumably refers to the

following features of the passion narrative:

(i) *darkness and sunshine* (5:15, 6:22)
The darkness envelopping the whole of Judaea at mid-day is paralleled in all the synoptic accounts, but some noteworthy differences appear in Ps-Peter. The darkness is intensified by 5:18, 'Many went around with lamps, thinking it was night, and tripped over.' Ps-Peter's special interest in the preternatural darkness arises from the Jewish concern that the body should not remain on the cross after sunset (5:15, citing Dt 21:23). The reappearance of the sun at what is found to be mid-afternoon (6:22, ninth hour), after the deposition of the body from the cross (6:21), evokes Jewish rejoicing (6:23), presumably because this concern had been met. Although the synoptics all limit the darkness to the three hours from noon to 3 P.M., they are in different ways imprecise about the temporal relation between the end of the darkness and the moment of the death of Christ. More significantly, all four canonical accounts place the taking down of the body considerably later, such that, despite Jn 19:31, a Judaeo-Christian reader could not be certain from any of these accounts that Dt 21:23 had been observed. Ps-Peter puts the matter beyond doubt. The body is removed from the cross before 3 P.M., when the sun shines out again (a point without canonical parallel, although Lk 23:45 ascribes the darkness to the sun's failing), demonstrating that the darkness had not been night as many supposed.

Although these differences only marginally enhance the miraculous element in *EvP* when compared with the canonical Gospels, they provide further illustration of the miraculous serving the cause of Christological apologetic. In this case the ending of the abnormal darkness is correlated to the success in avoiding an infringement of Dt 21:23. In *EvP* the dying Christ is neither accursed of God (cf. above, on 5:19) nor the cause of defilement for the land.

There may be a further significance in the renewed sunshine of 6:22, which will be discussed below in connexion with the earthquake of 6:21.

(ii) *rending of the temple curtain* (5:20)
As in the synoptics, this is immediately contiguous to the expiry of Jesus. *EvP* agrees with Mt 27:51 and Mk 15:38 against Lk 23:45 in placing the death first. It also strengthens the implied causal connexion between the two happenings by stressing that the rending took place 'at the very moment' of the Lord's

death. But at the same time it lacks the phrase 'from top to bottom' found in Matthew and Mark. At first sight this appears to make the supernatural character of the incident less marked than in the two synoptics. But in Ps-Peter divine power belongs to 'the Lord' even in and after his death, as the next happening to be considered makes clear, and he may have envisaged the rending of the curtain as the work not so much of God from heaven (as 'from top to bottom' implies) but of 'the Lord' himself on earth.

(iii) *earthquake* (6:21)

Ps-Peter's affinities with Matthew's *Sondergut* are obvious at this point, but whereas in Matthew the earthquake is mentioned immediately after the rending of the curtain in a coordinate clause (27:51), in *EvP* it is separated from the rending by the deposition from the cross. *EvP* also stresses that ἡ γῆ πᾶσα (Mt simply ἡ γῆ) was shaken, and seems to relate the tremor causally to the laying of the body on the ground (ἐπὶ τῆς γῆς). If this connexion is accepted, there may be implications for Ps-Peter's Christology. It is from 'the hands of the Lord' that the nails were drawn, and it is the Lord (αὐτόν) whom they placed on the ground. Mara comments that the body of the Lord even bereft of his δύναμις creates the effects of a theophany when it touches the earth./27/ This verse has been an embarrassment to a thoroughgoing Docetic interpretation of *EvP*, to the extent that it has been seen by some as an interpolation. Vaganay views it as evidence of the 'naive and popular' character of Ps-Peter's Docetism./28/ One could more confidently conclude that it counts against the allegedly Docetic character of *EvP*, and also against interpretations of 5:19 which treat the departure of the δύναμις as a happening which leaves Christ a merely human corpse.

According to Crossan, the earthquake is 'more original' in Ps-Peter than in Matthew./29/ His sole ground for this conclusion is its better integration into *EvP*, as the earth's reaction to the deposition of Jesus, whereas Matthew records it and other eschatological phenomena as though they had no effect on anyone. This patently ignores Mt 27:54, as well as resting on a questionable criterion of greater originality. The closer integration may well betray a more deliberate *Tendenz*!

It is possible that the reappearance of the sun (6:22), which immediately follows the earthquake with its attendant φόβος μέγας, should also be seen as an effect of the body's contact with the earth. It seems more probable, however, that its significance lies in the chronological realm, as explained above.

Ps-Peter has no parallel to the splitting of the rocks and the resurrection of the saints found in Matthew's account (27:51-53). Yet if in this respect *EvP* may appear more restrained than the canonical Gospel with which it has most affinity, it nevertheless betrays a *Tendenz* which heightens the supernatural dimension of the passion,

(a) by stressing the Lord's impassibility,
(b) by its distinctive form of the cry of departure,
(c) by depicting the Lord's death as an ἀνάλημψις, and
(d) by ascribing an earthquake to the deposition of the Lord's body on the ground.

This *Tendenz* is not strictly Docetic, but may validly be described as proto-Docetic. It belongs to Ps-Peter's presentation of Christ as 'the Lord' throughout his passion. It has led not to the recording of miraculous events unparalleled in the canonical versions, but to a more sharply nuanced presentation effected by modifications of the tradition, whether or not *EvP* is here dependent on one or more of the four Gospels. These modifications include relocation (of the Lord's silence) and reordering (in the new connexion between the earthquake and the Lord's body touching the ground), as well as a radically recast form of the cry from the cross, making it express almost the opposite of the synoptics' dereliction.

EvP 8:28 confirms the importance for the author of the miraculous features of the passion story. It is τὰ μέγιστα σημεῖα accompanying the Lord's death which have convinced the people of his righteousness. Comparison with the synoptics is again revealing. In Mark the manner of Christ's dying evokes the centurion's confession (15:39). In Matthew the centurion and his men are impelled to the same confession by observing the earthquake and τὰ γινόμενα (27:54). Luke's centurion makes the same confession as the crowd in *EvP*, and in addition the crowds at the spectacle, θεωρήσαντες τὰ γενόμενα, went away beating their breasts (23:47-48). Ps-Peter goes further than them all in pinpointing both the impact of the miraculous signs on ὁ λαός ἅπας and the recognition of this impact by the scribes, Pharisees and elders.

Whether Ps-Peter's *Christologia gloriae* is angelomorphic /30/ or more Johannine in its 'compénétration'/31/ of different moments in the passage of the Lord through suffering and death to resurrection and exaltation cannot be established from the passion narrative alone. It is certainly compatible with the devotion to an exaggeratedly divine Christ to which popular Christianity has inclined in every age.

II. The Resurrection Narrative

The miraculous is far more evident in Ps-Peter's account of the resurrection than in the preceding part of the fragment. *EvP* comes very close to recounting the actual moment of resurrection. It stops short of describing what happened in the tomb itself, but this minimal limitation may itself have been dictated by its unmistakable apologetic interest. For everything that it does record is presented as heard or seen by those guarding or observing the tomb--a company which in *EvP* includes Jews (elders, 10:38; by implication, elders and scribes, 8:31; perhaps even scribes, Pharisees and elders, 8:28) as well as Romans (the centurion Petronius and his soldiers, 8:31), and even a crowd from Jerusalem (9:34). Ps-Peter is intent on showing that the resurrection took place in full view of the watching world. In due course we must clarify more precisely the apologetic concern that has motivated this presentation.

But if *EvP* chooses not to tell its readers what transpired within the tomb itself, it has plenty of wonders for those outside to marvel at:

1. The Opening of the Tomb (9:35-37)

The miraculous features here are three in number:

(i) a loud voice heard from heaven (9:35),

(ii) the opening of the heavens and the descent to the tomb of two (young) men envelopped in light (9:36),

(iii) the stone rolling back of its own accord (ἀφ' ἑαυτοῦ, 9:37)./32/

The only canonical parallel is Mt 28:2-3, part of the visit to the tomb by the two Mary's, but there is little in common between the two texts. *EvP*'s loud heavenly voice may conceivably be a counterpart to Matthew's great earthquake, but in Matthew a single 'angel of the Lord' descended, in the sight of the two Mary's alone, rolled back the stone and sat on it. *EvP* will in fact narrate the visit of Mary of Magdala and her friends to the tomb later in its account (12:50 ff.; cf. 11:44, 13:55 for a further parallel to Mt 28:2-3).

Mara is surely right in regarding Ps-Peter's portrayal of the resurrection as drawn in the lines and colours of apocalyptic. /33/ The parallels he adduces between this passage and the

Johannine Apocalypse alone are impressive enough, starting with ἡ κυριακή (9:35; Rev 1:10). The presence in *EvP* of this name for the first day of the week may perhaps be thought to be due to Ps-Peter's unvarying focus on ὁ κύριος. But in fact he never uses this designation for Christ throughout the central section of the resurrection narrative, i.e., between 6:24 (washing and burial) and 12:50, where *EvP*'s account again becomes parallel to the canonical accounts with the visit to 'the tomb of the Lord' by Mary of Magdala, 'the disciple of the Lord'. Since other elements here belong to the world of apocalyptic--μεγάλη φωνή (cf. Rev 1:10, 11:11-15, 12:10), the opening of the heavens (cf. Rev 4:1, 11:9f.), the heavenly visitors full of light, identified in 9:37 as νεανίσκοι, a frequent term for angels in early Christian literature (cf. Mk 16:5), ἡ κυριακή may also be derived from the same quarter.

The most unusual feature here is the stone's rolling back of its own accord. In Matthew this is the work of the angel, while in Mk 16:4 and Lk 24:2 the stone is found already rolled back. A rationale for *EvP*'s version is elusive. Is it simply an example of 'un merveilleux facile'?/34/ Perhaps his two angelic visitants were intended for quite another role (!) (see below). The only clue we might discern in the text is Ps-Peter's emphasis in this verse that the self-rolling stone was ἐκεῖνος ὁ βεβλημένος ἐπὶ τῇ θύρᾳ--i.e., the stone set in place jointly by the centurion, his troops and 'all those who were there', including the elders and scribes, and sealed by them seven times (8:32-33). But to frustrate such a combined effort a self-rolling stone is not much more remarkable than one rolled by angelic strength.

But perhaps this stone only appeared to roll of its own accord. Perhaps we are meant to understand that 'the Lord' rolled it back, just as, it was tentatively suggested, 'the Lord' rent the temple curtain, and the body of 'the Lord', removed from the cross, shook the ground.

2. The Exit from the Tomb (10:38-42)

Still in the full view and hearing of the assorted guardians and spectators, another series of extraordinary events took place.

(i) the emergence from the tomb of three men (ἄνδρας), two bearing up (ὑπορθοῦντας) or leading (χειραγωγουμένου) the third (10:39-40),

(ii) the cross followed them out (10:39),

(iii) the two were as tall as the heavens, while the third

was taller still (10:40),

(iv) a heavenly voice asked whether he (it?) had preached to the dead (10:41),

(v) the cross replied in the affirmative (10:42).

Again it is evident that in these verses Ps-Peter belongs to the realm of early Judaeo-Christian apocalyptic, whose elements he uses to give expression to his *Christologia gloriae* in a resurrection that is also an ascension. The only possible discordant note is the need for the third man, i.e., the Christ figure, to be held upright or led by the hand by the other two. This has been explained as the consequence of the abandonment of Christ by his δύναμις, which is also why the cross and not he answers the heavenly question./35/ It is much more likely, however, that the two angels are escorting the third in triumph rather than compensating for his weakness. The rare word ὑπορθοῦντας would then mean bear up almost in the sense of bear aloft. In the *Ascension of Isaiah* 3:16-17 Christ comes forth from the sepulchre sitting on the shoulders of the angel of the Holy Spirit and the archangel Michael./36/

This interpretation accords with the transformation of the cross into a symbol of victory and glory, and its personification in the process./37/ The cross answers the voice from heaven because it has accompanied Christ on his *descensus ad inferos*. It is now raised and exalted with him, and in works like the *Apocalypse of Peter* 1 (Eth.) and *Epistle of the Apostles* 16 it will precede Christ at his parousia. Even if it provides no precise parallel to the cross speaking, a range of early Christian literature illustrates the speculation on the living and active cross which here finds a voice.

The immense height of Christ is another feature of early Christian works influenced by Jewish apocalyptic-angelic theology./38/ It serves to declare his transcendent majesty. The *descensus ad inferos* to preach 'to those who sleep' also belongs to primitive Jewish Christianity, for the sleeping ones are almost certainly the Old Testament saints./39/ Ps-Peter may here betray a further contact with Matthew's special material. His question and answer about Christ's preaching τοῖς κοιμωμένοις attest the deliverance which Mt 27:52 (cf. τῶν κεκοιμημένων ἁγίων) dramatizes.

EvP's apologetic concern is still evident in this passage. It was while the soldiers were reporting the opening of the tomb that they, and presumably the others present, beheld (πάλιν ὁρῶσιν, 10:39) the next happenings. Ps-Peter repeats that they heard (ἤκουον, 10:41) the heavenly voice, and the reply from the cross was heard (ἠκούετο). But the nature of Ps-Peter's apologetic interest must not be misunderstood. W. L. Craig has compared Matthew's story of the guard at the tomb with *EvP*'s 'apologetic legend'. The latter is 'a failsafe apologetic. . . By contrast in Matthew's story the guard is something of an afterthought'./40/ But this may be to compare stories of a rather different character, for *EvP*'s apologetic is theological rather than historical in emphasis. Mara points out that, apart from 8:30 (the elders' expression of concern to Pilate that the disciples of Jesus might steal the body, parallel to Mt 27:64), Ps-Peter is relatively uninterested in the empty tomb (but cf. later 13:56). The attention he gives to the co-operation of Jews and Romans in closing and sealing the tomb and witnessing its subsequent opening and the resurrection is directed, not to proving that the body was not stolen and that the tomb was found empty because Christ was raised on the third day, but to manifesting the glory of the Lord. Even while the tomb was shut, Christ with his cross had been announcing salvation to the sleeping saints of Israel. The opening of the tomb demonstrated that not even its sevenfold sealing by an alliance of Jewish religious leaders and a Roman militia could contain the power of the rising and ascending Lord.

3. Another Angelic Descent (11:44, 13:55)

While the guard and the Jewish representatives were preparing to report all to Pilate, a further figure (ἄνθρωπός τις) descended from the re-opened heavens and entered the tomb, in full view of the assembled company (ταῦτα ἰδόντες, 11:45). Here *EvP* seems to link up again with the synoptic tradition (cf. Mt 28:2), as it paves the way for the visit of the women to the tomb (12:50ff.)./41/ *EvP*'s account is in part closer to Mark (16:5, brilliant angelic raiment; 16:8, flight of women in fear) than to Matthew and Luke, but differs significantly from all three in declaring what has happened to Christ. Whereas they say only that Christ οὐκ ἔστιν ὧδε and ἠγέρθη (in Lk 24:7 the women are also reminded of his prediction that he must ἀναστῆναι on the third day), Ps-Peter's νεανίσκος states twice that the Lord ἀνέστη καὶ ἀπῆλθεν, adding the second time ἐκεῖ ὅθεν ἀπεστάλη (11:56, 57). The synoptics direct the women to earthly duties--telling the disciples, awaiting Christ in Galilee--whereas *EvP* has no such reference, for the one who was crucified is no longer on earth. There may possibly be some significance in the difference between *EvP*'s τὸν σταυρωθέντα and τὸν ἐσταυρωμένον of Mt 28:5 and Mk 16:6. Was Ps-Peter more inclined to regard the crucifixion as a merely past event, with the cross itself transfigured into an emblem of power and victory?

Apart from the merging of resurrection and ascension/42/ in the angelic message to the women, *EvP* here is not obviously a more miracle-weighted account than its canonical counterparts. The running together of resurrection and exaltation could be viewed as Johannine, but no more than in John, if we may judge from the incomplete sequel in *EvP* 14:55-60, did it exclude appearances of the risen Lord. In default of the rest of *EvP* beyond what looks like the beginning of an appearance to the disciples on the shore of Galilee, we cannot argue too confidently from the angelic message to how Ps-Peter might have presented, if at all, the final exaltation of the Lord to heaven. Vaganay reminds us that quite orthodox writers in the early Church could speak in terms very similar to the angel here in *EvP*./43/

According to Daniélou, Ps-Peter's 'characteristic feature is to make use of apocalyptic symbolism in presenting the events of the life of Christ with a view to bringing out their theological import'./44/ But as we have seen, a distinction probably has to be drawn between those parts of *EvP* where the author remains firmly in contact with the canonical gospel tradition (whether he had access to it in the form of our actual Gospels or not), and those where he seems considerably freer of the control of this tradition./45/ The latter comprise the core of his resurrection narrative, including 9:34-10:42. In the passion story and the last part of the resurrection account (12:50-14:60, and probably 11:43-49 also), despite numerous modifications of various kinds, the shape of the canonical tradition remains clearly recognizable. Ps-Peter has enhanced its miraculous content, as we concluded above, only marginally, and in the interests of his consistent presentation of Christ as the Lord. Its strong apologetic thread, which is built up largely out of the ingredients of an originally historical apologetic, is now directed to this theological purpose. In so far as the miraculous dimension has undergone elaboration, the chief causative factor has been the desire to depict Christ, even on the cross and after death before the resurrection, as the Lord.

But in the central section of the resurrection story, apocalyptic has taken over, and *EvP* has more the colour of the apocalyptic literature of primitive Christianity. The Akhmîm manuscript contained also, it must be remembered, a fragment of the *Apocalypse of Peter* and parts of *1 Enoch*. It is consistent with the heavily apocalypticized character of 9:34-10:42 that here, where one might have expected it most in *EvP*, Christ is not called ὁ κύριος. The passage betrays the oblique symbolic approach typical of apocalyptic.

The relevance of such an evaluation of the work to the question of its sources is not the concern of this study, but it obviously raises the possibility of an influence upon the central description of the resurrection quite different from the broadly canonical gospel tradition which may account for the rest of the fragment./46/ If, however, the dazzling colour of that description is to be ascribed to Ps-Peter himself (since for some of its most noteworthy features no earlier witnesses are known),/47/ the relative restraint of the rest of his work is the more impressive. It is not too far from sustaining the conclusion that 'There is nothing docetic about the Lord of the apocryphal "Petrine" gospel fragment'./48/ By contrast, the claim that Ps-Peter's resurrection narrative is basically a very early miraculous epiphany story antedating the canonical accounts and partly reflected in them seems the more hazardous./49/ To argue this for a narrative including the self-rolling stone, the heavenly height of the risen Christ and his escorting angels and the walking cross,/50/ is certainly to champion a case burdened by improbability.

Notes

/1/ Cf. the present writer's 'Apocryphal Gospels: The "Unknown Gospel" (Pap. Egerton 2) and the *Gospel of Peter*,' in *Gospel Perspectives*, vol. 5, ed. D. Wenham (Sheffield: JSOT, 1985) 222-25. Cf. R. Bauckham, 'The Study of Gospel Traditions Outside the Canonical Gospels: Problems and Prospects,' in ibid., 401, n. 41 (where, however, the papyrus is wrongly numbered).
/2/ J. W. McCant, 'The Gospel of Peter: Docetism Reconsidered,' *NTS* 30 (1984) 258-73.
/3/ H. Koester, 'Apocryphal and Canonical Gospels,' *HTR* 73 (1980) 105-40, esp. 126-30.
/4/ *Four Other Gospels* (Minneapolis: Winston, 1985) esp. 132-34. See my review forthcoming in *Themelios*. Crossan regards the section in Pap.Oxy. 2949 as part of the integrated composition, but fails to consider the significance of its textual divergence from the Akhmîm MS.
/5/ See n. 1 above.
/6/ L. Vaganay, *L'Évangile de Pierre* (Paris: Gabalda, 1930) 127-28; cf. P. Vielhauer, *Geschichte der urchristlichen*

Literatur (Berlin: de Gruyter, 1975) 648.
/7/ Bauckham, 'Problems and Prospects,' 369-403, esp. 370-77.
/8/ Accepted by Vaganay, *Pierre*, 236; and M. G. Mara, *Évangile de Pierre* (Paris: Cerf, 1973) 106-7. It is confirmed by a similar ὡς + participle clause in 7:26. Mara's text of *EvP* is followed in this study.
/9/ McCant, 'Peter,' 261.
/10/ The formulation may reflect Is 53:4 LXX. Cf. J. Denker, *Die theologiegeschichtliche Stellung des Petrusevangeliums* (Bern: Lang, 1975) 69.
/11/ Cf. Vaganay, *Pierre*, 236; Mara, *Pierre*, 110-11; Denker, *Petrusevangeliums*, 120-22. Closely similar is *Ascension of Isaiah* 5:14, 'When Isaiah was being sawn in sunder, he neither cried aloud nor wept' (ed. R. H. Charles, 42).
/12/ Mara, *Pierre*, 107.
/13/ McCant, 'Peter,' 261. (Crossan, *Four Other Gospels*, 131, accepts McCant's evaluation.)
/14/ Cf. McCant, 'Peter,' 262: 'There is every indication of pain and humiliation. . .Left to die in torments, he maintains his Lordly dignity to the end.' Crossan, *Four Other Gospels*, 143f., reads the text differently, attributing the unbroken legs to the good criminal of 4:13 (cf. Lk 23:40-41), not to Jesus. Such a reading makes 4:14 pointless (cf. Mara, *Pierre*, 121), contrary to Crossan's general picture of Ps-Peter as an author and redactor. *EvP*'s concern in 4:13 is not with the penitent malefactor himself, but with his confession about Jesus.
/15/ Mara, *Pierre*, 111.
/16/ Denker, *Petrusevangeliums*, 120-22.
/17/ Vaganay, *Pierre*, 255-56; Mara, *Pierre*, 133-38; Denker, *Petrusevangeliums*, 118-20; McCant, 'Peter,' 262-65.
/18/ Vaganay, *Pierre*, 248--the question gives 'un caractère douloureux' to the cry.
/19/ It is a particular weakness of McCant, 'Peter,' that he fails to relate the cry to its sequel in the text.
/20/ Ibid., 265-67, 270. McCant (272, n. 50) has misread Bauer's *Lexicon*, which gives take up (to heaven) as the meaning here.
/21/ Cf. I. H. Marshall, *The Gospel of Luke* (Exeter: Paternoster, 1978) 405.
/22/ Mara, *Pierre*, 135-36.
/23/ Ibid., 138-40.
/24/ C. Maurer takes ἀνελήφθη of the death, in 'The Gospel of Peter,' in *New Testament Apocrypha*, vol. 1, ed. E. Hennecke and W. Schneemelcher (London: Lutterworth, 1963) 181.
/25/ This is in effect Denker's interpretation, *Petrusevangeliums*, 74, 118-20.

/26/ Cf. J. Daniélou, *The Theology of Jewish Christianity* (London: Darton, Longman & Todd, 1964) 21: 'This *theologia gloriae* is one of the marks of Jewish Christian theology'.
/27/ Mara, *Pierre*, 142-43.
/28/ Vaganay, *Pierre*, 39, 260.
/29/ Crossan, *Four Other Gospels*, 142.
/30/ With Denker, *Petrusevangeliums*, 102-6, 111-18.
/31/ Mara's word, *Pierre*, 220. Cf. his commentary, *passim*.
/32/ Crossan, *Four Other Gospels*, 157ff., believes that the equation of 'men' and '*young* men' in 9:37-10:39 and the descent of the 'man' in 11:44 are 'redactional preparations' made by Ps-Peter for his incorporation of 12:50-13:57 in the second stage of the compilation of *EvP*. These insertions, which, like 12:50-13:57, reflect dependence upon Mark, into material which is independent of Mark and the other Gospels (9:35-11:49), prepare the reader to find a '*young* man' in the tomb in 13:55. On this occasion careful integration is for Crossan an index of later redaction, not greater originality. The same scholar regards the *Ascension of Isaiah* and Codex Bobiensis as two further witnesses, independent of the Gospels and of each other, to a similar account of the resurrection of Jesus aided by two angelic men (167-72). He forgets, however, that Bobiensis does not specify their number--unless it is emended to agree with *EvP*!
/33/ Mara, *Pierre*, 177-79, 182-83; Daniélou, *Jewish Christianity*, 21.
/34/ Vaganay, *Pierre*, 290. Crossan, *Four Other Gospels*, 166, makes Matthew dependent on Ps-Peter, and appears to base this judgment on the direct causality present in the former but not the latter. He does not discuss why Matthew preserves no more than a 'minor reminiscence'.
/35/ Cf. Mara, *Pierre*, 185; Vaganay, *Pierre*, 297-98, for references.
/36/ Cf. Daniélou, *Jewish Christianity*, 249-51.
/37/ Ibid., 266-68; Vaganay, *Pierre*, 299.
/38/ Ibid., 300; Daniélou, *Jewish Christianity*, 21, 65, 121; Mara, *Pierre*, 185.
/39/ Daniélou, *Jewish Christianity*, 233-35; Vaganay, *Pierre*, 300-1.
/40/ 'The Guard at the Tomb,' *NTS* 30 (1984) 278.
/41/ Crossan, *Four Other Gospels*, 157f., holds that *EvP* 12:50-13:57 is dependent on the canonical Gospels, essentially Mark.
/42/ Not confusion but synthesis, according to Mara, *Pierre*, 175-76, citing various Fathers who did likewise. But cf. Daniélou, *Jewish Christianity* 21, 249-50, who interprets *EvP* as *identifying* the resurrection with the ascension.
/43/ Vaganay, *Pierre*, 329-30.

/44/ Daniélou, *Jewish Christianity*, 20-21. (Cf. Mara, *Pierre*, 176-80, for details.) He quotes Vaganay, *Pierre*, 119--*EvP*'s purpose is 'rehausser la figure du Christ, faire ressortir le caractère divin de sa personne'.
/45/ Maurer, 'Peter,' 181, fails to differentiate both in claiming that 'the author. . .deliberately purposes to keep to the line of the hitherto existing Gospels' and in asserting that passion as well as resurrection are released from the *terra firma* of history and transferred to the realm of legend and myth. Mara, *Pierre*, 173, distinguishes between the extraordinary phenomena 'd'ordre naturel' which accompany the crucifixion and those 'd'ordre surnaturel' which attend the resurrection. Vaganay, *Pierre*, 133 (cf. 288, 291), ascribes the difference to Ps-Peter's purpose, which focusses on the resurrection. For the passion he is content to reproduce the community's catechesis.
/46/ Crossan, *Four Other Gospels*, 180-81, draws attention to the fact that Denker's analysis (*Petrusevangeliums*) of *EvP* finds only the passion narrative to be closely undergirded by Old Testament texts. Denker's work was the basis of Koester's characterization ('Apocryphal and Canonical Gospels') of the passion narrative in terms quite different from the resurrection.
/47/ Daniélou, *Jewish Christianity*, 234-35, 266. The starting-point for the speculative development about the cross is probably Mt 24:30.
/48/ McCant, 'Peter,' 270.
/49/ Koester, 'Apocryphal and Canonical Gospels,' 128-29.
/50/ Ibid., 128, n. 73, excludes the heavenly question about the preaching to the dead and the answering cross from his ancient resurrection epiphany, but they seem integral to the story, and are so in Crossan's account (*Four Other Gospels*, 165-72).

THE MIRACLE AT CANA: A PHILOSOPHER'S PERSPECTIVE

Stephen T. Davis
Philosophy Department
Claremont McKenna College
Claremont, California 91711

> On the third day there was a marriage at Cana in Galilee, and the mother of Jesus was there; Jesus also was invited to the marriage, with his disciples. When the wine failed, the mother of Jesus said to him, 'They have no wine.' And Jesus said to her, 'O woman, what have you to do with me? My hour has not yet come.' His mother said to the servants, 'Do whatever he tells you.' Now six stone jars were standing there, for the Jewish rites of purification, each holding twenty or thirty gallons. Jesus said to them, 'Fill the jars with water.' And they filled them up to the brim. He said to them, 'Now draw some out, and take it to the steward of the feast.' So they took it. When the steward of the feast tasted the water now become wine, and did not know where it came from (though the servants who had drawn the water knew), the steward of the feast called to the bridegroom and said to him, 'Every man serves the good wine first; and when men have drunk freely, then the poor wine; but you have kept the good wine until now.' This, the first of his signs, Jesus did at Cana in Galilee, and manifested his glory; and his disciples believed in him. (John 2:1-11; RSV)

I

This brief and arresting story has captured the attention of Christians throughout the history of the church. Interestingly, most Christians have considered it a *true* story. That is, they have believed that Jesus really did, as claimed, turn water into wine. My aim in this paper is to ask whether this belief is a *rational* belief, i.e., whether those who hold it are justified in doing so. Some will claim that such a belief is *irrational*, i.e., that it cannot rationally be defended and ought to be given up.

Equally interestingly, recent and contemporary commentators seem sharply divided over the historical accuracy of John 2:1-11. Three main stances can be found. (1) Some boldly argue that the story is not historically reliable. W. F. Howard, for example, offers a rationalistic explanation--what happened was that Jesus simply ordered that the wine be diluted with water./1/ Rudolf Bultmann suggests that the story was taken over by Christians from pagan water-into-wine tales./2/ Barnabas Lindars says that the story was created by the evangelist out of a submerged parable of Jesus./3/ And Robert Fortna agrees that a paradigmatic saying or parable told *by* Jesus has become a story *about* Jesus; a form critical study of the text, he says, 'suggests that the pericope is not a true tale.'/4/

(2) Other scholars either defend the view that the Cana story reports an actual event in the life of Jesus that includes the miracle, or else at least strongly oppose skeptical arguments like those mentioned above. J. D. M. Derrett,/5/ Richard J. Dillon,/6/ Stephen Smalley,/7/ and Leon Morris/8/ could be mentioned. (3) But an apparent majority of contemporary commentators either believe it impossible to decide to what degree the story is historically reliable or else simply do not seriously raise the question of its historical reliability. Raymond Brown sums up this position as follows: 'Theological themes and innuendo so dominate the Cana narrative that it is very difficult to reconstruct a convincing picture of what is thought to have happened and the motivation of the dramatis personae.'/9/ Others who fit in this group (some of whom seem nevertheless to have serious doubts about the reliability of the story) are C. K. Barrett,/10/ Rudolf Schnackenburg,/11/ and Alan Richardson./12/

Before proceeding, it should be noted that I am a philosopher rather than a New Testament scholar. Originally I envisioned writing a purely philosophical paper about the water-into-wine story, but as I wrote found I could not do so. Questions that belong properly in the field of New Testament studies kept cropping up, and had to be dealt with. There are, however, several critical issues in Johannine scholarship about which I say little, despite their relevance to the issue at hand./13/ Some I ignore for lack of space; some, for lack of competence.

It will help if I distinguish between a question that I am

asking and a nearby question that I am not asking. The issue I wish to address is *not* this: can it be established with certainty that the Cana story is historical, that it occurred as (or nearly as) described? Or conversely, can it be shown that the skeptical positions mentioned above are wholly irrational or indefensible? The answer to both of these questions is probably no. In addition to the fact that historical inquiry deals in probabilities rather than certainties, two problems especially plague a defense of the historicity of an excerpt from John's Gospel. (1) Uncertainty about the dating of the Gospel of John and its various hypothetical sources makes it difficult to argue with assurance that Johannine distinctives stem from reliable traditions. (2) The striking differences between John and the Synoptics lead many scholars to doubt the general historical reliability of the Fourth Gospel even apart from questions of dating and sources. Both of these points have undoubtedly been exaggerated; recent scholarship generally favors an earlier date for John and views his traditions as divergent largely due to his independence from the Synoptics./14/ But the type of detailed discussion required to defend this shift in scholarship lies outside the scope of this essay.

The question I *do* wish to ask in this paper, then, is this: can it be shown that Christians who hold that the Cana story is a true story or is based upon a true story that includes the miracle are justified or rational? That is, can a case be made on scholarly grounds--a case that can be defended against criticism--for acceptance of *this* miracle story? I argue that the answer to this question is yes.

In the course of this paper it will be necessary to trek across much diverse territory, from New Testament scholarship to science to philosophy. Accordingly, let me provide a brief road map of where we will be going. First, we will look in a preliminary way at the more obvious characteristics of the story itself. Second, we will look at the historical-critical arguments that can be presented both for and against the claim that the story is a true story. Third, I will reply to some of the historical-critical objections to the story and suggest considerations which in my view support rational belief in its historicity. Fourth, I will explain and discuss Humean and neo-Humean general objections to belief in miracles. Fifth, I will argue that the rationality or irrationality of belief in this miracle depends on the epistemological context with which one approaches the story. Finally, I will discuss some difficulties raised by the argument of this paper, and will conclude that belief in the truth of the story is rational.

II

Let us then begin by noting some of the main characteristics of the story--characteristics any careful reader might notice. The *first* is an insistence that something extraordinary has occurred. The evangelist clearly wants us to understand that Jesus miraculously changed a quantity of water into a quantity of wine. As noted, there have been attempts to interpret the story in such a way as not to entail the occurrence of anything miraculous. The water was poured into jars already filled with the dregs of wine, it is said, and the resulting mixture tasted wonderful. Or: Jesus' presence so graced and entertained the guests that they later concluded, 'It was almost as if we had been drinking fine wine.' But all such attempts seem at least at first glance (i.e., before considering the scholarly arguments that might be presented on their behalf) slightly ridiculous. It is hard to see how events like these could have led anyone to believe that they constituted 'the first of his signs,' nor how they could have 'manifested his glory,' even postulating a complex tradition history for the passage. A rationalizing explanation of this miracle is highly improbable./15/

The *second* thing we notice about the story is apparent verisimilitude. The account has much to commend itself to us. Notice the realistic detail and local color, for example. The story fits well with what we know of first century Jewish weddings and ceremonial obligations./16/ Notice the eye for detail the evangelist shows--e.g., the 'awkward' saying of Jesus to his mother, and the exact number of jars and their sizes are both recorded. But most of all, the story seems to fit with what we know of human nature. For example, there is the slightly strained relationship between the mother and the son. How typical it is for a parent to make a declarative statement ('They have no wine') that is actually a request or even a demand for action (cf. 'Your room is a mess' or 'The rubbish needs to be taken out'). Notice too how well the mother seems to know the son. 'Do whatever he tells you,' she says to the servants, confident he can solve the problem. And notice the way Jesus speaks rather harshly to his mother ('What have you to do with me?'),/17/ but proceeds to do what she wants anyway. Notice finally the pleasantry of the ignorant but jolly steward of the feast ('Every man serves the good wine first, then the poor wine; but you have kept the good wine until now'). This seems just the sort of statement an affable man who is enjoying himself might make in the described context.

But despite the realism of the story, the *third* thing we notice is its terseness. We conclude a reading of it full of questions that the text does not want to answer. (1) If, as he claimed, Jesus' hour had not yet come, why did he proceed to change the water into wine? (2) *How* did he perform the miracle, i.e., precisely what did he do or say? (3) If this was indeed his first sign, why was his mother so confident of his ability to solve the problem, almost as if she knew things about him that nobody else did? Did she know he had the power to change water into wine, or did she simply expect him to solve the problem by more mundane means? (4) Did *all* the water in the six jars turn to wine, i.e., were there in the end some 120 to 180 gallons of wine, or just that which was drawn by the servants? (5) Did the servants who knew where the wine had come from become believers in Jesus too? (6) How did the bride and groom react? (7) How widely did the story of the miracle spread--no further than the servants and the disciples? throughout the wedding party? throughout Cana? throughout the surrounding countryside? throughout all Israel? On these and many other matters, the text is silent.

III

But let us return to the question raised earlier. Could these events, so vividly described for us by the evangelist, really have occurred? Is there any good reason for us to believe that Jesus really did, as claimed, change water into wine? Can we rationally hold that the story of the miracle at Cana is a *true* story? Suppose we first look at what might be said for and against the claim that the event really occurred. Such a glance offers tentative support for the historicity of the passage, but whether one does or does not believe that Jesus changed water into wine at Cana ultimately will be decided on the basis of deeper considerations, which will be discussed below.

Let us look at the positive evidence first. (1) One point is that the evangelist presents the story as if it were a true story. There is not even a hint, let alone decisive evidence, that it is intended as a parable, fable, or myth. (Note the author's own cross-reference to the story in 4:46.)

(2) As mentioned above, the verisimilitude of the story

itself argues for its veracity. Ignoring the miracle for a moment, the rest of the story has about it the ring of truth. It seems an event that could well have happened as described. Beside the points already made (local color, detail, psychological realism, etc.), notice the understated, matter-of-fact way the miracle itself is described. Nothing whatever is said about the mechanics of the miracle, and the performer of the deed remains curiously unobtrusive in the story.

(3) Finally, on behalf of the miracle itself it should be noted that if the other parts of the story are all true, we would be hard pressed to see why the disciples believed in Jesus if he achieved nothing extraordinary at Cana. Doubtless this argument will not take us very far--the other parts of the story being true constitutes a very big 'if' in the light of Johannine scholarship. I mention it only because the history of the exegesis of the Cana passage shows a decided tendency on the part of some commentators to reject the miracle but accept as much of the rest of the story as possible. And that (I argue) seems at least vaguely inconsistent./18/ The evangelist clearly wants us to understand that the glory Jesus manifested at Cana (see 1:14) through the miracle was the basis of the disciples' faith in him.

But points can also be made against the veracity of the story. (1) Verisimilitude by itself is not convincing. Any skilled literary artist can write a miracle story that 'rings true'. Some biblical scholars have even argued that realistic detail betrays an attempt to make fiction look like history./19/ (2) The Fourth Gospel is the only gospel in which this miracle is recorded; furthermore (with the exception of the raising of Lazarus), this is the only one of the seven 'signs' recorded by the fourth evangelist with no parallel in the Synoptics. This is odd because the miracle at Cana seems the sort of event that would have caused a huge public stir. (3) Why would Jesus perform a miracle, let alone his first, on such a trivial occasion? What was at stake in Cana was merely social embarrassment--nobody's life or health was in danger. What we have here, then, is a 'miracle of luxury'/20/ entirely out of character with the other miracles Jesus performs in the gospels. Moreover, why so much wine (assuming all the water became wine)? 180 gallons seems far more than would have been required at the feast. Surely this aspect of the story makes us believe the evangelist is making a theological rather than historical point here--something, perhaps, about the inexhaustible abundance of the grace of God.

(4) Perhaps the water-into-wine motif was simply borrowed by the evangelist from pagan sources. It is known, for example, that worshippers of Dionysus, the god of wine and of prophetic inspiration, were inspired by intoxication. Ancient myths suggest that on the day of his feast the god filled empty jars with wine at feasts in his honor at Elis, and sprayed wine out of water fountains at Andros and Teos./21/ (5) In any case, the main point the evangelist appears to be making in our text concerns the superiority of the religion of Jesus to Judaism. Perhaps, then, the story ought to be regarded as an allegory, with Mary representing the best of Judaism, the empty ceremonial water jars and the lack of wine at a Jewish wedding representing the inadequacy of the old religion of law, and the new wine created by Jesus representing the superiority of the new religion of the Spirit (see John 15:1).

(6) Finally, the alleged miracle itself must be mentioned; it is doubtless the factor that argues most strongly against the veracity of the story. (Had the story been told without the miracle, one suspects that few would doubt its truth.) This factor will take up much of our attention in the pages ahead. Is it ever rational for us to believe any account which suggests that somebody changed water into wine? For it surely must be admitted that the act of instantly changing water into wine is so improbable as to be virtually impossible; here surely is an event (if it occurred as described) that present science has no way of understanding, let alone predicting or controlling.

To change water into wine instantaneously would involve the sudden creation of substances like ethanol (ethyl alcohol) and the many trace substances that give wine its taste, color, smell, etc. It would have to be done not just by chemical but by nuclear means, i.e., it would involve the creation, e.g., of carbon atoms not present in water. Now the sun certainly creates carbon atoms (possibly thermonuclear devices do too), but the energies involved there are not available elsewhere and are not minutely controllable by human beings. The upshot is that there is no natural means (where 'natural' means in accordance with our present beliefs about the way nature works) of instantaneously changing water into wine.

With the advent of twentieth-century physics, few scientists seem willing to rule out any logically possible event as scientifically impossible. The physicists I know, at any rate, seem more open to the possibility of scientifically inexplicable events than many of the biblical scholars I know./22/ Given Heisenberg's indeterminacy principle, virtually any event is theoretically possible. However, there is little comfort here for defenders of the biblical miracles. The switch from classical to quantum mechanics does nothing to make the water-into-wine miracle more believable. It is true that such an event is consistent with the statistical laws of quantum mechanics, but the event as described by the evangelist is so highly improbable as to constitute (if the event were confirmed) excellent reason for giving up those laws, or at least some of them. Newtonian physics still works exceedingly well for events on the macro-level.

IV

Again, what I wish to argue is that while the story cannot be proved with mathematical certainty to be true, those who believe it is a true story, i.e., that Jesus really did change water into wine at Cana, are fully rational and hold a defensible position. The six reasons just discussed for denying the miracle fall into two categories. The first five reasons are *historical* arguments for denying that the story in John 2:1-11 is an authentic part of the earliest Christian tradition. On historical-critical grounds, so it is argued, it can be shown that no such event occurred in the life of Jesus; the story was invented by later Christians (or an actual but scientifically ordinary event in the life of Jesus was embellished by them). The story is a 'legendary accretion' told to further the theological ends of the Church.

The sixth reason is a *philosophical* argument for denying the miracle (which can even be combined with an admission that the story is, so far as we can tell, part of the earliest Christian tradition). This argument simply insists on scientific grounds or on the grounds of common sense that such an event just cannot (or at least did not) happen. No matter what the Bible says, no matter how early in the first century the story was written, nobody has ever had the power instantaneously to change water into wine.

The philosophical way of denying this particular miracle seems to me stronger than the historical ways. In fact, several of the historical arguments against the veracity of this story are based on the persistently held but false dichotomy between history and theology. Unquestionably the four gospels, and especially John, reflect the understanding of Jesus of a generation removed from his lifetime. But it does not follow from this, as so many argue, that the events recorded in the gospels are unreliable accounts of what Jesus himself said and did. Historical events can be perceived to have symbolic and theological significance as easily as can fictitious narratives. A comparison of gospel parallels makes it clear that we do in places have to try to differentiate between tradition and redaction. But this does not imply the evangelists' accounts are largely unreliable portraits of what the historical Jesus said and did./23/

The point can be generalized. In reading the work of any historian writing about any period or person in history, we certainly do come in contact with the consciousness of the historian at the time the work was written. But if the historian has done a worthwhile job of writing history we also in the book come in contact with the period or person written about. *All* history, after all, is interpreted history. Though I do not claim that the gospels are entirely or even primarily works of history, I believe that these books can bring us in contact with the redemptive events themselves. Furthermore, I have never seen a convincing argument to the effect that the water-into-wine story is a later addition, invented or embellished by the church. There is no doubt that the evangelist interpreted and shaped it—note the typical Johannine themes of ὥρα, δόξα, and interest in the relationship between Jesus and his mother. But again I fail to see how this entails that the event he describes is not historical.

Thus before proceeding to the sixth objection, let me say some things about the other five. As to the *first*, it is quite correct that verisimilitude by itself does not suffice to show that a story is a true story; other convincing reasons will have to be adduced if we are to make a case for rational belief that the event occurred as described. At times the boundary between fiction and non-fiction is not easy to draw; nevertheless, unless authors give some indication of their intention they remain open to charges of deception of a nature somewhat inconsistent with the Fourth Gospel's emphasis on truthtelling. /24/ As to the *second*, there may be good reasons why the Synoptic Gospels do not mention this miracle; it may be that the Synoptic evangelists never heard of the marriage at Cana./25/ At any rate single attestation is not a valid criterion for dismissing the story. Historians regularly accept information from sources which cannot be corroborated./26/ (Of course, the fact that John alone mentions this story may well constitute a telling objection to it in combination with *other* arguments; my point here is simply that this objection *by itself* gives us no good reason to disbelieve the story.) As to the *third*, it is true that nobody's life or health was in danger here and that we are talking about a huge amount of wine. (The latter point depends on the assumption--which the text does not require, incidentally--that *all* the water in the jars became wine.) But it is again hard to see why these facts argue against the veracity of the story. Perhaps the Lord had good reason--a reason having to do with the wedding context itself, or with his understanding of his own mission--to perform a miracle at Cana which was in some ways unlike most of his others. The overabundance of wine does not make this miracle unique--after the feeding of the multitudes large basketfuls were left over, and in the miraculous catches of fish the nets were strained to the breaking point. Furthermore, in a fascinating look at the moral and legal implications of the story, Derrett argues that far more than embarrassment was involved for a wedding host who failed to provide sufficient wine for the celebration. Incurring a financial obligation to unsatisfied guests was a real possibility./27/

As to the *fourth* objection, the pagan myths which critics have cited all seem to be of a different character than the miracle at Cana. They are annual, cultic events rather than one-time-only deeds; they involve fountains or empty jars magically filling with wine rather than water being changed into wine; they involve the act of a distant and unseen divinity (Dionysus) rather than a flesh-and-blood person. I do not want to stress this point, however, because any early Christian who wanted to use the Dionysian myth and apply it to Jesus would naturally have had to make some changes in it. Two other points seem more telling. First, nowhere else in the Johannine literature do we see evidence of any influence of the cult of Dionysus. There is no sign of any 'borrowing' from this particular pagan source./28/ Why could not the story be true even if there are certain similarities with apparently mythical stories in other religions? Unless the parallels are close enough to prove direct borrowing, very little can be proved about historicity./29/ And as to the *fifth* objection, it may well be true that the evangelist is making a theological point about the superiority of the religion of Jesus to Judaism. I strongly suspect he is. But this brings us back to the issue of history and theology. Although it is surely possible to make a theological point by means of a fictional story, it is also possible to tell a true story and in telling it make a theological point. (That the second is what is being done here is the burden of the historical sections of this paper.)

But neutralization of objections is one thing; presenting positive evidence is another. Accordingly, let me now present three reasons why one can rationally hold that the water-into-wine story is historical or at least has a historical core that includes the miracle. The arguments are all rather modest in character--none is compelling by itself. But taken together, and taken in conjunction with the three more provisional points made earlier (that the story is told as if it were to be taken as true, that the story has the 'ring of truth,' and that the other parts of the story require the miracle if they are to be believed), they do constitute an impressive cumulative case.

First, we notice in the gospels that during his lifetime Jesus was apparently charged with being a 'glutton and a drunkard' (see, e.g., Matt. 11:19; Luke 7:33-34). Thus it would seem odd indeed for the early church to invent a story that might be taken as reinforcing this caricature. The fact that a story like this one was used attests to its authenticity. Second, the rather harsh statement Jesus makes to his mother seems to me evidence of authenticity. Perhaps with ingenuity the saying can be interpreted as a theological embellishment--Jesus' divine sonship is underscored because his actions will be determined by God his father not Mary his mother. But it is surely cleaner simply to admit that what we have here is an awkward saying (notice how commentators throughout Christian history have struggled to interpret it) that argues for authenticity. (Furthermore, the apparent uneasy relationship between Jesus and his mother that we see depicted here seems to be confirmed by the Synoptics--see Mark 3:31, Luke 2:49, 11:27-28.) Third, if the water-into-wine story is a theological construct of the evangelist, told for the purpose of proving Jesus' divine sonship, we can wonder (1) why the Lord remains so unobtrusive in the story, and (2) why no use is made of the story to introduce a discourse of Jesus or an 'I am'saying./30/ All things considered, it seems much more plausible to say that the evangelist is reporting an early 'sign' tradition he received.

But suppose the story *does* reflect an early tradition. Critics can still doubt its truth on the simple grounds that nobody can turn water into wine. So the crucial issue appears to be the miracle. There are two questions here. First, is it ever rational for a person to believe that *any* miracle has occurred? Second, is it rational for a person to believe that *this* miracle occurred?

V

Virtually all modern discussion of the first question revolves around David Hume's famous argument in Section X of *An Enquiry Concerning Human Understanding*./31/ There Hume makes two main points. The first is that the evidence against the occurrence of any purported miracle is apt to be far weightier than the evidence for it. Miracles, by definition, are events so extraordinary that (as Hume says) 'the unanimous testimony of mankind' is against them. So any claim that a miracle has occurred is in automatic conflict with the fact that such an event has never occurred before. What a rational person does in such cases is 'accept the lesser miracle,' i.e., the more probable event. So if (as it normally will be) the probability that the miracle actually occurred is lower than the probability that the people who testify to it are wrong, we should doubt the miracle.

Hume's second point is that while it might be theoretically possible for the evidence for a miracle to outweigh the evidence against it, in fact this never occurs. No miracle has ever been sufficiently attested by a sufficient number of people of 'unquestioned good-sense, education, learning, and integrity.' Testimony is often mistaken, people who claim that miracles have occurred sometimes have ulterior motives, miracles are mainly testified to in what Hume calls 'ignorant and barbarous nations,' and miracles are testified to in incompatible religions. In short, it is never rational to believe that a miracle has occurred.

But I believe it has now been recognized by most philosopers that Hume's argument, at least as it stands, is unconvincing./32/ Events quite contrary to our past experience fairly frequently occur. These events (new inventions, trips to the moon, etc.) do not perhaps typically involve violations of natural laws, but we can imagine cases where the evidence in favor of such a violation (the levitation of a building, for example) is so strong as to outweigh the evidence against it. So we cannot *a priori* rule out the possibility of miracles or of rational belief in their occurrence.

Hume is both right and wrong, I believe. He is surely

right (1) that rational expectation of what *will* occur ought to be based on our knowledge of what *has* occurred, (2) that rational people ought to accept the epistemological principle of always believing the lesser miracle, and (3) that rational people ought to require very strong evidence indeed before they will ever believe that a miracle has occurred. But Hume is wrong (1) that our past experience of the normal course of events by itself settles the question whether a miracle can occur, (2) that the purported miraculous deed is always a 'greater miracle' than the testifiers to it being mistaken, and (3) that it can accordingly never be rational to believe that a miracle has occurred.

However, defenders of Hume still abound in philosophical circles. Antony Flew, for example, offers three Hume-like arguments against belief in miracles./33/ Let me briefly describe and respond to each argument.

(1) Flew first points out that believers in miracles typically offer historical or probabilistic arguments in favor of the miracles they believe in. But this makes their position inconsistent, for their arguments always presuppose the very regularity of nature and the reliability of nature's laws that they are arguing against. Much of what Flew says here is correct. Believers in miracles do indeed presuppose regular workings of nature in order to argue that certain irregularities (i.e. miracles) occur. But how does this make their position inconsistent? Is it not possible that nature, so to speak, acts regularly and predictably most but not all of the time? If this is possible, then miracle-believers will naturally argue for certain irregularities in nature on the basis of regularities seen elsewhere.

(2) Second, Flew asks what control we have over the explanations of events that are offered once violations of natural law are allowed. For example (this is my example, not Flew's), why not say that the bridegroom and the steward of the feast, unbeknownst to the other revelers, purchased a huge quantity of fine wine and secretly brought it to the feast, but were later quite unable to falsify the miracle claim because for some psychologically inexplicable reason they completely forgot what they had done? Why prefer any other explanation to this one, once miracles are allowed (Flew would ask)? But surely Flew's argument is exaggerated. The only control we either have or need over proposed explanations of events, once miracles are allowed, is the same control we have, quite apart from miracles,

over proposed explanations in science and history in general. We simply accept the most plausible explanations we can find and reject all the others. That is, we try to discover (just as we do in ordinary cases of attempts to determine what happened) which explanation is more consistent with all that we know. The question is whether it is more plausible to believe that the bridegroom and the steward forgot what they had done or that Jesus changed water into wine. When phrased this way, it is easy to see why rationalistic explanations were abandoned in favor of mythological ones. But if both of these approaches now seem lacking, then we are thrust back to a supernatural interpretation as actually the most probable.

(3) Finally, Flew asks how we could ever be sure it is *God* who is responsible for a given violation of a natural law (once we allow such violations)? Since in the tradition God is said to be incorporeal and thus unobservable, the problem seems insurmountable. Furthermore, Flew says, when theists talk about certain theological problems, notably the problem of evil, they stress our inability to comprehend God or fathom God's ways. How then could we ever have rational expectations about what God is likely to do in certain situations? Flew is surely correct that it seems impossible ever to prove that a given event was caused by God. But suppose an event occurs that (a) seems scientifically inexplicable and (b) fits well with a given view of God and God's aims. Then it can surely be rational for those who hold that view of God and of the divine purposes to believe that the event was brought about by God. If there is a good reason ahead of time to believe that a God exists who is likely in certain circumstances (say after prayers or as aspects of epiphanies or incarnations) to bring about events like this one, it seems reasonable to hold (though we cannot prove) that God brought about this event .

But surely (so a critic might respond) I am ignoring something here--the Humean point about miracles occuring mainly in 'ignorant and barbarous nations'. The fact is--so it will be said--that the water-into-wine story is dubious because people in first century Palestine were far more superstitious and gullible than we are today. Thus Chester M. Quimby says: 'The problem of natural law versus miracles was unknown in John's day. Miracles were considered to be as possible as daily sunshine, or mighty starshine.'/34/

But it is surprising (at least to me) that this argument is so frequently cited against the biblical miracles, for it is quite unconvincing. Its only strong point is the sociological claim that the percentage of miracle-believers in the general population is lower now than then. This claim may well be true, though one need not look far to discover that superstition and gullibility abound today. Nevertheless, Quimby's main point is completely wrong. If first century folk believed that miracles occurred at the drop of a hat, why was this particular miracle taken to be so significant? Why was it said to reveal Jesus' glory? Why was it said to have caused the disciples to believe in him? Surely first century Palestinians believed no less firmly than we do that one can't instantaneously change water into wine!

VI

Let us then turn to the second question mentioned earlier, viz., is it rational for a person to believe that this particular miracle occurred (i.e. as described in John 2)? The point I wish to make is that the *context* of the story makes all the difference. Suppose for a moment that John 2:1-11 were a story from antiquity that appeared on its own about a deed performed by some unknown miracle-worker from the first century. If this were the case, I frankly would be no more inclined to believe the story than the hundreds of other ancient miracle stories (including Christian ones) that we know about. As impressive as the story is (verisimilitude, local color, detail, etc.) most Christians would not be inclined to believe it were it an isolated story about some long-forgotten character. In fact, most Greco-Roman 'parallels,' like the apocryphal miracle-stories throughout the church's history, have far less historical evidence supporting them, so that the comparison is not entirely fair. And Christians of many theological traditions have acknowledged that miracles have occurred in addition to those narrated in Scripture. But the miracles of Jesus still retain a unique following.

Why then do I believe the story? What is the context within which Christians throughout history have believed it? Near the beginning of this paper, I mentioned that a glance at the evidence for and against the veracity of the story itself would turn out not to be entirely conclusive, that deeper considerations would have to be looked at. The two main 'deeper considerations' I had in mind can be summed up in the following two questions: (1) Does God exist? and (2) Is Jesus Lord? (The second question contains Pauline rather than Johannine terminology--we could have chosen to ask: is Jesus divine? or is Jesus the Son of God?). Here finally we can see the ultimate reasons Christians believe that Jesus turned water into wine--because they believe in God and because they believe that Jesus is Lord.

Let me now define two terms. *Naturalism*, I will say, is the belief that (1) nature alone exists (where 'nature' is the sum total of all that could in principle be observed by human beings or studied by methods analogous to those used in the natural sciences); (2) nature is uniform, regular, continuous (there are no non-natural events like, e.g., miracles); and (3) every macro-event is in principle explicable and predictable via methods analogous to those used in the natural sciences. *Supernaturalism*, I will say, is the belief that (1) something else besides nature exists, viz. God; (2) nature depends for its existence on God; (3) the regularity of nature can be and sometimes is interrupted by miraculous acts of God; and (4) such events are scientifically quite unpredictable and inexplicable.

All human beings interpret their experience by means of a certain philosophical framework. The philosophical assumptions held by many people exclude God's existence and the possibility of miracles. Such people, naturalists, ultimately deny that Jesus turned water into wine not because the historical evidence for the veracity of the story is weak. As mentioned earlier, if the story contained no miracle, surely few people would take the trouble to doubt that it really occurred. They reject the miracle because it does not fit with their naturalistic world view.

Others, supernaturalists, are much more inclined to accept the possibility that miracles occur because they believe that God created the laws of nature and is perfectly capable of setting them aside. Of course not all supernaturalists are Christians; some supernaturalists are suspicious of alleged miracles reported in the Christian tradition. But for supernaturalists who are also Christians, the water-into-wine account in the Fourth Gospel is rationally believable. This, then, is the context of which I was speaking earlier. So far as I can tell, apart from Christian supernaturalsim, there is no wholly compelling reason to believe that Jesus turned water into wine, however suggestive the historical arguments may prove. Only the fact that the story is about Jesus Christ, whom Christians acknowledge as Lord, only the fact that the story appears in Scripture and in the context of the entire Christian tradition, renders the story credible. It is true that many of the historical arguments I raised earlier in support of the believability of John 2:1-11 do not presuppose supernaturalism; nevertheless such arguments can always be deemphasized by committed naturalists. Such people can always say something like: 'Yes, it appears that a case can be made for the historical integrity of the Cana story--still, it is certain that no one can turn water into wine.'

Is it then rational to believe that the story of the miracle at Cana is a true story? The conclusion of our efforts in this paper appears to be as follows: *no matter what the historical evidence in favor of the truth of the story, belief in its truth is not rational for naturalists*. A naturalist can always say: I do not know what happened at Cana, but I am quite sure that nobody instantaneously turned water into wine. Naturalism seems to me a consistent (though mistaken) position. /35/ The discussion of Hume and Flew earlier was designed not to refute naturalism but rather to refute the attempt of some naturalists to disprove supernaturalism. Those naturalists are mistaken; supernaturalism too is a consistent position. Accordingly, another conclusion also follows: *assuming the historical evidence in favor of the truth of the story is strong (and I have been arguing that it is), belief in its truth is rational for supernaturalist Christians*.

In an odd way, this conclusion confirms at least one aspect of what Hume was saying. What one can rationally believe, he argues, is in part a function of what one has experienced. In this, as noted above, Hume is surely correct. But theists can accordingly argue that miracles are congruous with and in continuity with *their* experience. Of course not all theists personally experience miracles, but many of them experience a spectrum of realities (answered prayers, visions, mystical experiences) to which miracles are not alien.

From a supernaturalist perspective, then, what happened at Cana was that God miraculously set aside those natural laws which normally preclude people from changing water into wine. What natural laws do, we might then say, is to describe the ways in which God ordains that things ordinarily behave; miracles describe the ways in which God ordains that things extraordinarily behave. The beauty of this perspective (contrary to what is often charged) is that it allows science to stand. Since natural laws describe not whatever happens but whatever happens regularly and predictably (ignoring unpredictable quantum events), the miracle at Cana did nothing to abrogate or negate or nullify those natural laws which entail that we cannot instantaneously change water into wine. Those laws still stand, as does science.

VII

At the end of the text we are considering, the evangelist calls the miracle a 'sign' (σημεῖον). It is one of seven such 'signs' Jesus performs in the Fourth Gospel. This is a significant term for the evangelist; a 'sign' in this Gospel is a miraculous deed that contains a deep meaning that can be detected by the eye of faith. Here, of course, the deep meaning is what the water-into-wine sign tells us about the doer of the deed. In this sign, we are told, Jesus' glory (τὴν δόξαν αὐτοῦ) is revealed and the disciples are moved to believe in him. *Jesus is Lord.* That is the ultimate meaning of the miracle at Cana.

A full discussion of the question of the relationship of *signs* to *faith* in the Fourth Gospel cannot be undertaken here. Briefly, however, it is undeniable that the Johannine tradition sends what seem like mixed signals./36/ On the one hand, we have stories and sayings like the water-into-wine story where miraculous signs performed by Jesus are seen as legitimate avenues to faith. The healed blind man is quoted as saying of Jesus: 'If this man were not from God, he could do nothing' (9:33). And on two occasions Jesus himself is quoted as expressing sentiments like these: 'Believe me that I am in the Father and the Father in me; or else believe me for the sake of the works themselves' (14:11; cf. also 10:38, 20:30-31). In short, we are to believe in Jesus' divine sonship because Jesus has the power to change water into wine, restore sight, raise the dead, etc.

On the other hand, it also seems that the Fourth Evangelist wishes to deemphasize miracles as avenues to faith. The evangelist quotes Jesus as commenting negatively to an official in Capernaum: 'Unless you see signs and wonders you will not believe' (4:48). The evangelist says of the crowd: 'Though he had done so many signs before them, yet they did not believe in him' (12:37). And, classically, the apostle Thomas is criticized and unfavorably compared with 'those who have not seen and yet believe' (20:29). How do we explain these apparent mixed signals?

We might conjecture that some came to believe in Jesus during his lifetime because of his miracles and that others came to believe after his lifetime because of convincing accounts of his miracles. But naturally many who observed the miracles or heard accounts of them failed to believe (in the Synoptics the classic example is the Beelzebul controversy). And perhaps some who believed (or at least apparently believed) because of such 'signs' fell away after the crucifixion, and perhaps some who believed (or apparently believed) afterward because of miracle stories also fell away. Thus the evangelist was moved to suggest other, perhaps superior, avenues to faith. Miracles may be a fine stepping-stone to faith and should indeed, in some cases, move us to faith--so the evangelist seems to say--but are not the best or most secure basis for it. The δόξα of the Lord includes far more than his ability to perform signs.

If this is indeed what the evangelist is saying, then I believe he is right. Christian faith does involve, in my opinion, belief in the power of the Lord to perform miracles. Some of Jesus' miracles quite apparently were intended to call forth faith from those who witnessed them. And there are some even today who come to believe because of miracles--the biblical miracles of Jesus, or alleged miracles in their own experience. But miracles are surely not a secure foundation for Christian faith or apologetics. No matter how spectacular the deed, a skeptic can always find room for doubt ('It was all done with mirrors'). Miracles can strengthen and even in cases engender faith, but never compel it or form its permanent foundation. So if someone today comes to believe because of an experienced miracle, that is perfectly acceptable, though ultimately there had better be other reasons as well. But defenders of Christian belief run serious risks, in my opinion, if they base their argument primarily on miracles. Belief in the miracles of our Lord (and in divine miracles of today) ought typically to be a product rather than cause of faith.

VIII

Let me close by discussing two difficulties my argument raises. First, there is an apparent logical circularity entailed by my argument. I have been arguing that *context is what ultimately makes the water-into-wine story believable*. And by the term 'context,' I mean the fact that the story is about Jesus, occurs in Scripture, and is part of the Christian tradition. But surely something like the reverse is true as well: *the water-into-wine story, with its historical-critical integrity, helps to make the context believable*. That is, this particular story, along with many others, forms the context.

What we call 'the Christian tradition' is to a great extent based upon this story and a whole series of others. Christians see themselves as standing in the Christian tradition in large part precisely because they accept the historical and theological truth of these stories.

This is circularity, to be sure, but not *vicious* circularity. Most Christians wouldn't believe the story if it were from outside the Christian tradition; most Christians see themselves as within the Christian tradition in part because they deem believable the stories about Jesus of which it largely consists. These are facts; I see no serious difficulty here. Perhaps the circularity described is true of those committed to any large belief-system. (Only Marxists are likely to hold the vast majority of the statements in *Das Kapital* true; what makes a person a Marxist is largely acceptance of the vast majority of those statements.) In any case, what we have here is not an instance of the fallacy of circular reasoning where one both believes that a proposition p is true because one believes that q is true *and* believes that q is true because one believes that p is true. The 'context' of the water-into-wine story is reliable not merely because of the integrity of the story itself but due to the integrity of the other items which also comprise the context.

The second difficulty also involves apparent circularity. It has probably not gone without notice that the logical strategy of the evangelist in John 2:1-11 is slightly different from mine in the present paper. The evangelist appears to be arguing as follows: *since Jesus turned water into wine, we can rationally believe that Jesus is Lord*. My related but quite different argument is: (assuming a case can be made that the evangelist's account is historically reliable, then) *if Jesus is Lord, we can rationally believe that Jesus turned water into wine*./37/ An astute critic may well try to turn this into an objection: isn't there something circular in holding that Jesus is Lord because he turned water into wine *and* holding that Jesus truly turned water into wine because he is Lord?

But I see no difficulty here. Let me explain. Suppose one is trying to get people to believe two propositions. Naturally, there are various strategies that might be used to try to convince them. Which strategy is adopted will depend on various factors, e.g., (1) what the people one is trying to convince already believe (perhaps they are already prepared to accept one of the two propositions); (2) which proposition one is surest of or can make the best case for; (3) what logical relationships if any obtain between the two propositions (e.g. perhaps one entails but is not entailed by the other). So in certain circumstances or with a certain audience one may well adopt one strategy and in other circumstances or with a different audience quite another.

As I interpret the passage we have been discussing, the evangelist is trying to convince readers of the two propositions that *Jesus turned water into wine* and that *Jesus is Lord* (although again the second is admittedly not Johannine terminology). And I too confess to a strong hope that people accept both propositions. The evangelist's argument (since Jesus turned water into wine, then Jesus is Lord) appears to be an argument aimed at those who either already believe that Jesus turned water into wine at Cana or else are prepared to believe the evangelist's claim that he did so. My argument (if Jesus is Lord and if a convincing case can be made for the general credibility of the evangelist's account, then we can rationally believe that Jesus turned water into wine) is an argument aimed at those who already believe that Jesus is Lord but who wonder whether it can ever be rational to believe that somebody instantaneously turned water into wine.

My answer is this: if the somebody one is talking about is the Lord of all creation (as a Christian I assume this, and have argued for it in other contexts/38/), and if the testimony that he turned water into wine seems otherwise credible (as I have been arguing here), then one can rationally believe that he turned water into wine. A rational and defensible case can be made, then, on both historical and philosophical grounds, for the conclusion that John 2:1-11 records an event in the life of Jesus that occurred as described./39/

Notes

/1/ W. F. Howard, *The Fourth Gospel* (London: Epworth, 1955) 190.
/2/ R. Bultmann, *The Gospel of John: A Commentary* (Oxford: Basil Blackwell, 1971) 113-21. 'There can be no doubt that the story has been taken over from heathen legend and ascribed to Jesus' (118).
/3/ B. Lindars, *The Gospel of John* (London: Oliphants, 1972) 123-33.
/4/ R. Fortna, *The Gospel of Signs* (Cambridge: CUP, 1970) 29-38.
/5/ J. D. M. Derrett, 'Water into Wine,' *BZ* 7 (1963) 80-97. The argument of Derrett's paper, he says, 'leaves the door open for the miracle's being genuine'(97).

/6/ R. J. Dillon, 'Wisdom Tradition and Sacramental Retrospect in the Cana Account (Jn 2:1-11),' *CBQ* 24 (1962) 286-95.
/7/ S. S. Smalley, *John: Evangelist and Interpreter* (Grand Rapids: Zondervan, 1978) 174-78.
/8/ L. Morris, *The Gospel according to John* (Grand Rapids: Eerdmans, 1971) 174-86.
/9/ R. E. Brown, *The Gospel according to John I-XII* (Garden City: Doubleday, 1966) 101.
/10/ C. K. Barrett, *The Gospel according to John* (Philadelphia: Westminster, 1978[2]) 188-94.
/11/ R. Schnackenburg, *The Gospel according to St. John*, vol. 1 (Montreal: Palm, 1968) 323-40.
/12/ A. Richardson, *The Gospel according to Saint John* (London: SCM, 1959) 58-61. See also idem, *The Miracle Stories of the Gospels* (London: SCM, 1941) 116-17, 121, 127.
/13/ For example, I will not discuss the general historical reliability of the Fourth Gospel, the first century setting of the Cana story, or the form history of the story.
/14/ The fullest survey of modern critical study of John is R. Kysar, *The Fourth Evangelist and His Gospel* (Minneapolis: Augsburg, 1975). More briefly, but more recently, cf. D. A. Carson, 'Recent Literature on the Fourth Gospel: Some Reflections,' *Themelios* 9 (1983) 8-18. For a striking defense of the historicity of much of the Fourth Gospel, see now J. A. T. Robinson, *The Priority of John* (London: SCM, 1985).
/15/ Cf. the historical surveys of this movement in the articles by W. L. Craig and G. Maier elsewhere in this volume.
/16/ As well as Derrett, 'Water into Wine,' see S. Safrai and M. Stern, eds., *The Jewish People in the First Century*, vol. 2 (Philadelphia: Fortress, 1976) 752-60. See also H. Granquist, 'Marriage Customs in a Palestinian Village,' in *Commentationes Humanarum Litterarum*, III, 8 and VI, 8 (Helsingfors, 1931, 1935).
/17/ A. H. Maynard, 'ΤΙ ΕΜΟΙ ΚΑΙ ΣΟΙ (John 2:4),' *NTS* 31 (1985) 582-86.
/18/ Even Lindars, who as noted has grave doubts about the historicity of the story, concedes as much: 'But if the narrative is accepted as substantially historical, it is essential to accept the miraculous element along with it, and to assume that Jesus could and did perform the miracle as it is described.' (*John*, 131)
/19/ Perhaps no one has done this as dramatically as F. Kermode, *The Genesis of Secrecy* (Cambridge, MA: Harvard, 1979). For an unpersuasive attempt to reconcile John's testimony to truth-telling with fictional writing, see pp. 101-23.
/20/ D. F. Strauss, *The Life of Jesus Critically Examined*

(London: SCM, 1973) 519-27.
/21/ See C. H. Dodd, *Historical Tradition in the Fourth Gospel* (Cambridge: CUP, 1963) 224-25.
/22/ Historically this has often been the case. Cf. esp. C. A. Russell, *Crosscurrents: Interactions between Science and Faith* (Leicester: IVP, 1985).
/23/ The general point being made here is argued convincingly by D. A. Carson in 'Historical Tradition in the Fourth Gospel: After Dodd, What?' in *Gospel Perspectives*, vol. 2, ed. R. T. France and D. Wenham (Sheffield: JSOT, 1981) 104-7. See also I. H. Marshall, *I Believe in the Historical Jesus* (Grand Rapids: Eerdmans, 1977) esp. chaps. 4, 8, 9 and 10.
/24/ Cf. e.g. T. J. Roberts, *When Is Something Fiction?* (Carbondale: Southern Illinois University, 1972) 21.
/25/ An implication of the entire Gospel may be that the news did not spread far at all. Perhaps 4:43-45 shows that Galileans in general were not particularly impressed by Jesus until his later deeds in Jerusalem. If the miracle were not as well-known as those recorded in the Synoptics, this may explain at least in part why only John's Gospel includes it.
/26/ Cf. D. Fischer, *Historians' Fallacies* (London: Routledge & Kegan Paul, 1971) 62-63; J. Lange, 'The Argument from Silence,' *History and Theory* 5 (1966) 288-301.
/27/ Derrett, 'Water into Wine,' 94.
/28/ Bultmann of course would strenuously deny this point. But see the definitive refutation by H. Noetzel, 'Christos und Dionysos,' *Arbeiten zur Theologie* 1 (1960) 5-59.
/29/ It could be argued, e.g., that the Cana miracle was designed to refute Dionysiac teaching--cf. E. Linnemann, 'Die Hochzeit zu Kana und Dionysios,' *NTS* 20 (1974) 408-18; or to point to the reality behind its false god--cf. C. S. Lewis, *Miracles: A Preliminary Study* (New York: Macmillan, 1947) 141.
/30/ The second and third of these arguments are used by Smalley, *John*, 176.
/31/ D. Hume, *An Enquiry concerning Human Understanding* (LaSalle, IL: Open Court, 1946).
/32/ Cf. C. D. Broad, 'Hume's Theory of the Credibility of Miracles,' in *Human Understanding*, ed. A. Sesonske & N. Fleming (Belmont, CA: Wadsworth, 1965). Cf. the survey of recent philosophical opinion on this issue by C. Brown, *Miracles and the Critical Mind* (Grand Rapids: Eerdmans, 1984) 171-95.
/33/ A. Flew, *God and Philosophy* (New York: Delta Books, 1966) 148-52.
/34/ C. M. Quimby, *John: The Universal Gospel* (New York: Macmillan, 1947) 110. One suspects a misprint here; Quimby's text says 'mighty starshine,' but perhaps 'nightly starshine'

was intended?
/35/ In recent years, certain Christian philosophers--among them, Richard Purtill, Norman Geisler, Stuart Hackett--have argued that naturalism is an inconsistent position. Although I find some of their arguments promising, I do not find any of them convincing. Unfortunately I do not have space to discuss these matters here.
/36/ For more detail, see, e.g., R. Kysar, *John: The Maverick Gospel* (Atlanta: John Knox, 1976) 67-73.
/37/ I am assuming that if Jesus is Lord (or indeed if *anybody* is Lord), supernaturalism is true.
/38/ S. T. Davis, *Logic and the Nature of God* (London: Macmillan, 1983). See also idem, *Encountering Jesus: Live Options in Christology* (Atlanta: John Knox, 1986).
/39/ I would like to thank my friends Jim Brashler, Tony Fucaloro, Robert Gundry, Tom Helliwell, John Roth, and Joseph Runzo for helpful comments on an earlier draft of this paper. I should also thank the editors and other contributors to this volume for their many criticisms and suggestions.

CONCLUDING REFLECTIONS ON MIRACLES AND *GOSPEL PERSPECTIVES*

Craig L. Blomberg
Tyndale House
36 Selwyn Gardens
Cambridge CB3 9BA

I. Final Thoughts on Volume 6 (Miracles)

Are the gospel miracle stories credible? Do they narrate genuine historical events, however literarily stylized and theologically interpreted they may be? Negative answers to these questions may be reduced to three major objections related to scientific, philosophical, and historical methodology. For some, the principles of modern physics simply preclude miracles. For others, epistemology makes the identification of any event as miraculous impossible. A final group finds these narratives lacking adequate historical criteria of authenticity, quite apart from the distinctive problems created by the concept of miracles itself. And of course many combine more than one of these objections in their views.

It is interesting to see the relative priorities given to these objections by different writers. For Stephen Davis, one of the philosophers to contribute to this volume, the philosophical problems are much greater than the historical or the scientific. According to Gerhard Maier's survey, many of the most recent studies of miracle by biblical scholars find the historical questions the most perplexing. For many scientists today, the laws of the physical world remain most intractable./1/ It is perhaps natural that professionals in each field should understand most comprehensively the problems bound up with their own disciplines and assume that those outside their areas of expertise can be dealt with more easily. But there is also a sizeable body of scholarship in each of the three broad categories which argues that the problems are soluble; this volume has attempted in some small ways to further the debate from that perspective. It may prove worthwhile to reflect for a moment on how successful that attempt has been.

1. The Scientific Problems

The volume has had no representatives of the natural sciences as contributors. But the philosophical articles have noted the revolution in modern physics, especially associated with Heisenberg's indeterminacy principle, while rightly recognising the extremely limited value of this revolution for offering direct corroboration of the possibility of miracles such as the gospels narrate. On the other hand, current scientific understanding precludes the absolutism of a previous era which could claim logically to reject the supernatural as impossible by definition. As Colin Russell's balanced survey of the 'crisis in Newtonian physics' concludes:

> The demolition of the old mechanistic, deterministic view of nature has prompted some misguidedly to announce that science can now permit miracles or can attribute free will to Heisenberg uncertainty. However neither miracles nor free will depend for their credibility on particular scientific models of reality, and it is unwise to put one's trust in the changing theories of science.
>
> But for those whose faith was already in the Word made flesh as revealed in Scripture, the swift currents of modern physics posed no problems and actually swept away the last props of Victorian scientific naturalism which had for so long concealed the ways of God from man./2/

This volume has therefore rightly focussed on the philosophical and historical issues.

2. The Philosophical Problems

The essays by Davis and William Craig have briefly but adequately responded to the classic challenges of Spinoza, Hume, and Troeltsch, and, more recently, Flew. If we realise how much of the modern debate was anticipated in the 'eighteenth-century crucible' (and Maier's article significantly contributes to this recognition as well), we may be released from the tyranny of the present--the illusion that only the latest discussions are the most thorough and informed, and therefore most correct. There has been a dramatic paradigm shift in the last generation of German scholarship--from dogmatic antisupernaturalism to the claim of insufficient historical evidence as the primary objection to the miracle stories. This should prevent us from continuing to respond to a philosophical concern that is no longer the main problem. Yet the fact that nature miracles continue to be the most doubted of the wonders ascribed to Jesus, even when healings and exorcisms are regularly admitted, makes us question whether or not the spectre of uniformitarianism has really vanished. The history-of-religions parallels, for example, are less abundant or convincing for the nature miracles than for the rest, so reconstruction of Jesus as a wonder-worker on the analogy of various other ancient figures should actually find the historical case strongest for these narratives, even if such miracles are less explicable philosophically or scientifically.

One issue which was touched on only briefly (most notably in Edwin Yamauchi's concluding section) was the argument from contemporary experience. This may provide a helpful counter-balance to the attack on uniformitarianism which dwells too much on the demonstrable differences between the past and present. No doubt history has seen many events without analogy in the present, but it is not clear that all the biblical miracles should be lumped under this heading. Especially with healings and exorcisms, the evidence is overwhelming that naturally unexplainable events do occur today in religious contexts and with meaningful patterns which prevent our dismissing them as merely paranormal. Here Craig's distinction between miracles as the violation of nature and that which is naturally (but not logically) impossible is quite helpful.

Perhaps the most important point raised by our philosophers involves the theistic (or at least deistic) framework which such discussion requires. If God exists then one can logically defend the possibility of miracles. But today this premise is widely doubted. It is quite appropriate that both Craig and Davis can therefore refer back to full-length, technical monographs which they have authored in defence of the reality and attributes of God as conceived by Christians./3/ Such discussions will of course vary along a continuum from evidentialism to presuppositionalism, but, like Davis's two-pronged attack on the questions of the lordship of Jesus and the credibility of the miracle at Cana, both would seem to have their place./4/ Similarly, Davis's mediating view in which the miracles offer suggestive but not unambiguous testimony to the nature and identity of Jesus seems convincingly argued and thoroughly biblical.

3. The Historical Problems

Here lies the burden of this book. If the possibility of miracles cannot be disproved by either science or philosophy, then the trustworthiness of the stories in question must be decided based on the criteria involved in assessing any purportedly historical narrative. At least two types of consideration come into play here: (a) arguments for or against the reliability of the gospel tradition more generally and (b) arguments appropriate to the miracle stories in particular. The discussion further below of the entire *Gospel Perspectives* series will consider some aspects of (a) not already treated in one of the six volumes; here attention will be concentrated on (b).

Graham Twelftree's rehearsal of Robert Stein's criteria of authenticity from volume one/5/ along with Twelftree's additional criteria peculiar to miracle stories provide a convenient checklist to guide us in our analysis. Six primary lines of inquiry seem most fruitful.

(1) *Multiple Attestation*. Miracles, including nature miracles, appear in every layer and putative source of the canonical gospel tradition. They appear in different forms and are referred to in the sayings tradition and in the primitive kerygma (usually as 'signs and wonders') as reflected in Acts. The nineteenth-century liberal quest for a miracle-free layer of Christian tradition has been all but abandoned. The positive consequences for historicity should be acknowledged just as readily. The historical reliability of the Fourth Gospel has been the most doubted of these various layers; hence the importance of Paul Barnett's discussion of the Johannine account of the feeding of the 5000--the only miracle attested in all four gospels. The strength of Barnett's study lies in the careful and detailed comparison of parallels; many studies deal with the dependence or independence of apparent parallels merely with unsubstantiated summary statements concerning the relative weights of similarities and differences. But the limitations of any such comparison, however detailed, must also be acknowledged. It is arguable, for example, that John's diversity of language, greater than either Matthew or Luke *vis-à-vis* Mark, merely points to a freer use of his source. Nor must any dependence of John on Mark be viewed as detrimental to the case for the passage's authenticity. Multiple attestation enhances the case but single attestation in and of itself does not detract./6/ Nevertheless Barnett has the weight of current Johannine scholarship on his side.

(2) *Palestinian Environment*. Although dealing primarily with Hellenistic parallels, Barry Blackburn's catalogue of Jewish miracle stories with similarities to the gospel accounts amply justifies his carefully phrased conclusion: 'certainly

with all other things equal the case for historicity is enhanced if the features and stories in question are conceivable in a Jewish, Aramaic-speaking milieu' (p. 206). I have tried to make the same point repeatedly in my examination of the nature miracles.

(3) *Incidental Details and Tendencies of the Tradition.* Murray Harris's defence of the historicity of the reanimation narratives rests largely on the restrained, unadorned nature of the accounts along with their incidental, true-to-life details. This is a type of argument to which classicists (of which Harris is one) and historians often give greater priority/7/ than do biblical scholars without rigorous training in historiography. One must be careful neither to underestimate nor to overestimate the value of such an approach. Among literary critics, Erich Auerbach's sharp distinction between the straightforward style of the apparently factual biblical histories and the more elaborate stylization of what today would be called pure historical fiction is countered by the other extreme of Northrop Frye's attempt to view all the canonical writings as subtle interplays of metaphor and myth./8/ Yet surely both hypotheses are too sweeping. Much more nuanced study of the gospels from a literary perspective is needed, especially in light of styles of fiction and history in the ancient world. Too many of the new literary studies of biblical texts focus only on synchronic at the expense of diachronic methods and thus run the risk of anachronistically interpreting ancient texts in light of later categories and methods./9/

(4) *Internal and External Coherence.* In my discussion of the nature miracles, I rely heavily on the argument from consistency, or coherence, in this case with the authentic parables of Jesus. Richard Bauckham dispenses with one of the most serious obstacles to belief in the miracle of the coin in the fish's mouth (its apparently uniquely trivial and self-serving nature) by showing its coherence with other 'gift miracles', while nevertheless acknowledging that its unique form (an imperative rather than a narrative) still poses a puzzle, leading some to prefer a metaphorical interpretation. And Twelftree in volume 5 discussed the non-Christian testimony to Jesus' wonder-working, in both Josephus and the Talmud./10/ Thus Bauckham and I have appealed to internal coherence and Twelftree to external coherence in support of the historicity of the gospel miracles. Once again such argumentation has its limits. Testimony can seem to cohere even when all of it is not true. But this observation cuts two ways. To the extent that a

given scholar should choose to minimise the significance of arguments for historicity based on criteria of coherence, it is logically necessary that he minimise to an equal extent arguments against historicity based on seemingly inconsistent or incoherent testimony. Appearances may be just as deceiving in either case.

(5) *Divergent Patterns from Redaction.* Twelftree's article is clearly the most rigorous redaction-critical study in the volume; Bruce Chilton's and mine also employ redactional methods but in conjunction with other considerations. The dictional analysis which confidently assigns solitary words and phrases to either tradition or redaction is the least secure aspect of much redaction criticism,/11/ especially when trying to determine pre-Markan or pre-Johannine material. With broader themes and concepts one is on more solid ground. Either way, Twelftree's positive conclusions, after generous concessions to the evangelists' redactional activity (perhaps in the case of the testimony to Satan's ongoing activity too generous?), are, because of his critical caution, that much more worthy of note. The historical Jesus was an exorcist who viewed his ministry in a uniquely eschatological light. Yet even here disagreement reappears with the parallel case of the nature miracles. The symbolism concerning the in-breaking kingdom which I attribute to a traditional stage (following the most recent commentators) Bauckham would sometimes label secondary.

(6) *Dissimilarity.* No doubt the most crucial issue in the historical study of the gospel miracles involves the question of their relationship to apparent parallels in the ancient world. Even if Jesus did not work anything like the wondrous feats ascribed to him in the New Testament, one must still account for the rise of the narratives which claim that he did. The four sources most often appealed to in the attempt to do precisely this, in order of increasing frequency of appeal, are the apocryphal gospels, stories of Graeco-Roman heroes of various kinds, descriptions of magic and magicians in antiquity, and the ancient Jewish references to 'charismatic' holy men of Palestine.

The apocryphal gospels recount remarkable prodigies of Jesus as a child (largely to fill in the 'gaps' in his 'biography') and heighten the miraculous elements surrounding his death and resurrection. It is easy to extrapolate backwards and suppose that the canonical texts have similarly embellished their traditions, but in fact there is little evidence to commend this hypothesis. Most of the apocryphal accounts are obviously too late and too fanciful to be taken seriously, and many were probably never intended to be read as historical. The Gospel of Peter is a possible exception since it follows portions of the canonical passion narrative fairly closely, but David Wright's study is an example of the type of careful, even-handed analysis that such texts require, even if the results are less exciting than the daring but largely unsubstantiated generalizations by those who would find authentic, pre-Synoptic traditions permeating the apocrypha. The remarkable feature of this body of literature, given the apparent *carte blanche* provided for them by John 20:30 and 21:25, is that only a few miracles of Jesus' adult ministry unparalleled in the canonical texts are ever described at all. And the ones which are paralleled are usually referred to only in summary or abbreviated form. To the extent that tendencies of second- and third-century works may permit one to postulate first-century trends, the evidence is substantial that the early church was not interested in inventing or embellishing miracle stories of Jesus./12/

Accounts of Hellenistic miracle workers have also held scholars' fascination as possible analogies to the gospel portraits of Jesus. In a previous generation, the legends surrounding Alexander the Great, Asclepius, Dionysus, or Apollonius were often appealed to as the closest parallels. More recently these have largely given way to the 'divine-man' hypothesis, but J. D. Kingsbury argues that the growing disfavour with this theory also marks the end of an era./13/ Blackburn's research/14/ should close the door once and for all to the view that the early church created an unhistorical picture of Jesus as a miracle-working divine-man after a common, uniform, and stereotyped pattern of the day.

Yamauchi's thorough study should close another door--to the claim that Jesus was a magician, unless, as the study notes, the definition of magic employed becomes so broad as to be relatively useless in differentiating categories of miracle-working. With regard to Yamauchi's other principal thesis about the general distinction between disease and demon possession in the ancient world, his encyclopedic catalogue of relevant evidence goes a long way to establishing his point, even if some questions could do with further exploration and elucidation. We may conclude that Jesus was both a healer and an exorcist, but that for the most part those two titles should not be confused.

Due to the tenuous nature of explaining the gospel miracle-stories in light of later apocrypha, Hellenistic heroes, or ancient magic, it is not surprising that many of the trajectories in current research converge upon the charismatic, Jewish wonder-workers like Ḥanina ben Dosa or Honi the Rain-Maker. Here *Gospel Perspectives* VI has the least to say. Part of this lacuna stems from the non-existence of the critical tools needed for Rabbinic research in general in the areas of source, tradition, and redaction criticism;/15/ part, from the lack of familiarity with the field by most Christian scholars. In both of these areas, the comprehensive compilations of ancient miracle-stories currently underway in the SBL seminar on that topic will go a long way toward meeting a major need./16/ But to the extent that Old Testament or other early Jewish parallels prove closest to Jesus' miracles, the logic of Blackburn's conclusion (that consonance with a Jewish, Aramaic-speaking milieu enhances the case for historicity) must not be ignored. At the same time, the similarities are not so slavish as to suggest direct dependence. A. E. Harvey's analysis, from his 1980 Bampton Lectures, is so incisive that it merits extended citation.

> The most common miracle attributed to holy men of [Jesus'] time and culture was that of procuring rainfall--an important and welcome feat in a country absolutely dependent on seasonal rain. But this is something never credited to Jesus. Again Jewish miracle-workers certainly succeeded in curing diseases, but there is a notable absence of reports of the curing of any kind of lameness or paralysis. . . . Above all, Jesus is credited with three instances of a very notable miracle indeed: that of raising a dead person to life. The frequently alleged parallels to this are highly questionable. The Jewish tradition knows of no actual instances of such a feat: it merely suggests that a rabbi of exceptional holiness might in theory be capable of it. . . .stories of miraculous deeds are mainly confined to a small group of men whom it has been customary to call 'charismatics' and whom rabbinic sources themselves call, significantly, 'men of deed'. These men--Honi the Rain-maker and Hanina ben Dosa are the only two of whom we have any detailed knowledge--have a very clear frame of reference for their miraculous feats. They were men of prayer, and the degree of intimacy which they gained with their heavenly father afforded them an almost physical guarantee that their prayers would be answered. . . .there is a notable humorousness--almost a flippancy--about the way they were narrated which suggests that these 'deeds' were by no means regarded as the most significant thing about them./17/

Significantly, E. P. Sanders's new study of *Jesus and Judaism*/18/ engages in a running dispute with much of Harvey's work, especially with his treatment of Jesus' miracles, but the excerpts quoted above seem to have escaped unscathed. Harvey nicely summarizes the result of the application of the criterion of dissimilarity to Jesus' miracles: 'the style of the "Charismatic" is not the one chosen by Jesus' and 'we have come to the remarkable conclusion that the miraculous activity of Jesus conforms to no known pattern'./19/ The closest pattern may in fact be the Elijah-Elisha cycles in the Old Testament (another area of study noticeably absent from this volume) but the implications in favour of historicity are still noteworthy.

From very different angles both the articles by Chilton and by Maier stress that the historical argument can take one only so far. Even if the scientific and philosophical objections can be met, literary criticism will stress the verisimilitude in much of fiction, while the sociology of religion (a newly burgeoning field) will point out possible ahistorical motives for the narration of miracle stories. But to the extent that historical arguments can either support or undermine the case for the credibility of the gospel miracles, the balance of evidence tips to the positive side.

II. Final Thoughts on the *Gospel Perspectives* Series

Any anthology of studies appearing over a period of seven years on as wide-ranging a group of topics and organised as loosely as *Gospel Perspectives* is bound to have sizeable gaps. We do not pretend to have covered all of the major issues relating to gospel historicity, nor to have given equal treatment to those we have broached. Important works have appeared with which the series has been unable to deal. In a more popular work designed to address the types of issues with which this series has been concerned and to disseminate the results of these essays along with other recent scholarship on the trustworthiness of the gospels, I have attempted to fill in some of these gaps./20/ Five stand out in my mind as all worthy of more serious examination.

To begin with, several weighty monographs have appeared on the nature of the oral tradition behind the gospels. Werner Kelber's bold thesis, which pits the written gospels against the oral tradition, contains brilliant insights as well as major gaffes./21/ An example of each may be seen in his handling of the work of A. B. Lord on oral transmission in traditional eastern European folk epics. On the one hand, Kelber rightly stresses Lord's discovery of the decisive difference that the fixity of writing can create for an otherwise flexible oral tradition. On the other hand, he fails to stress Lord's caveat that such a difference occurs only when the written text gains authoritative status and the oral traditions no longer circulate as an equally viable alternative. /22/ Such a situation did not prevail in early Christianity until at least the middle of the second century, so the value of Kelber's sweeping hypotheses for the formation of the New Testament 50-100 years earlier is rather diminished. More deserving of serious attention is a trio of German theses which all build on the so-called Scandinavian school or 'guarded tradition' model, while trying to avoid the previously committed error of reading later Rabbinic data back into a first-century context./23/ Of the three, the most significant comes from Rainer Riesner, who provided us with an excerpt in volume 1./24/ It is hard to imagine how any future reconstructions of the history of the gospel tradition which fail to interact with at least one of these studies can be considered complete.

When we turn from historical to literary methods, much reflection on the structuralist and poststructuralist movements remains to be done. Reader-response criticism, a term unknown in biblical circles until just a few years ago, may turn out to be the literary method most widely applied to the study of the gospels./25/ And while literary and historical critics often view their methods as rivals, it is becoming progressively clearer (as Chilton's article in this volume explicitly notes) that each is indispensable for the other. The question of form also becomes crucial; if apparently historical narratives turn out in fact to represent a different genre--be it a certain kind of midrash, romance, dramatic comedy, or whatever--then supporters of their historicity, however well-intentioned, will be wasting their energy. The same of course applies to the converse error.

Third, the gauntlet thrown down by Robert Banks in volume 2 has yet to be taken up./26/ The whole field of the social-scientific study of religions is increasingly impinging on gospel research and questions of historical reliability, but with marked ambiguity. Gerd Theissen, one of its most noted practitioners, illustrates this in the introduction to his sociology of early Palestinian Christianity. In the same breath he can affirm both that the movement 'transcends the dispute of both "conservative" and "critical" exegetes over the authenticity and historicity of the tradition. . .unaffected by the dilemmas of the quest for the historical Jesus' and yet also that 'it does make a contribution toward solving these problems. . . .we should assume a continuity between Jesus and the Jesus movement and in so doing [open] up the possibility of transferring insights into the Jesus movement to Jesus himself'. /27/ Further clarity on these questions is crucial.

Fourth, apart from David Wenham's detailed monograph on the eschatological discourse,/28/ only a handful of the *Gospel Perspectives* articles have dealt with a detailed comparison of Synoptic parallels. One can discuss general methodology only so long; ultimately the true test of one's theory is its application to the most difficult texts for gospel harmonisation. Methodologically, for some, *any* attempt at reconciling apparent discrepancies is anathema, but this flies in the face of almost every historiographical precedent. Nevertheless, bad attempts at resolving seeming contradictions understandably bring the whole project into disrepute; much additional study on 'the legitimacy and limits of harmonization'/29/ is needed, especially in the context of the exegesis of specific texts and their parallels.

Finally, these six volumes of studies have been decidedly topheavy with scrutiny of the Synoptics at the expense of John. This imbalance is characteristic of conservative scholarship in general in recent years, perhaps because the issues seem so much more complex in the Fourth Gospel. In this light, John Robinson's posthumously published work is especially welcome./30/ There is a danger that his book will be quickly dismissed by critics who find his views so different from their own, but this would be a pity. He has not, of course, spoken the last word on the historicity of the Fourth Gospel, but he has raised serious questions about the approach and conclusions of those who discount the historical value of John and presented evidence and arguments which go a long way toward showing that John, as well as the Synoptics, are firmly rooted in history. The fact that Robinson does so, while nevertheless distancing himself theologically from most who would attempt similar defences, makes his study that much more remarkable.

In short, the question of gospel historicity can hardly be said to have been decisively settled by the six books in our series. But we do believe that we have given quite a wide range of issues detailed coverage. Reviews of earlier volumes have been encouraging, especially where praise has been meted out for even-handed and non-polemical discussions. We hope that volume

6 has upheld the standard set by the previous five, and that all six can contribute to the reduction of the scholarly polarisation which has so often characterised debate on such topics and often confused the true issues involved. We take heart in the recent Tübingen symposium which has seemed to fulfil this same objective in a very eirenic spirit./31/ And as with that gathering, a diversity of perspectives is reflected among our contributors, sometimes even within the same volume on the same topic, but we feel that it is a healthy diversity.

In response to some of the most radically sceptical of recent works on the historical Jesus, widely disseminated by a 1984 London Weekend Television series, J. D. G. Dunn gave a series of four semi-popular lectures in Durham which have now been published with the title, *The Evidence for Jesus*./32/ While perhaps sometimes conceding to his opponents more than the evidence requires, the general thrust of Dunn's work is very positive and sides with those who would defend the historical trustworthiness of the gospels. C. S. Rodd, in his review of Dunn's little book, suggests that the television series was 'extreme and unrepresentative' and finds Dunn's work the ideal antidote./33/ We have aimed for a similar goal at a more technical level with *Gospel Perspectives*--challenging the extremes of scholarship and even the critical consensus where we believe it has neglected significant portions of the evidence. The quest for the historical Jesus has made remarkable strides in recovering ground lost during the years in which Bultmann proclaimed its demise. We believe that the recovery is not yet complete and offer these volumes as yet one more expedition in reclaiming territory that need never have been abandoned./34/

Notes

/1/ E.g. P. Medawar's celebrated *The Limits of Science* (Oxford: OUP, 1985). In his last two chapters, however, it would seem that Medawar shifts his position to one in which the problem of evil is the biggest obstacle to belief for him.
/2/ C. A. Russell, *Cross-currents: Interactions Between Science and Faith* (Leicester: IVP, 1985) 222. Cf. W. Schaafs, *Theology, Physics, and Miracles* (Washington: Canon, 1974) 61, 67. For a similar perspective in astronomy by an avowed agnostic, see R. Jastrow, *God and the Astronomers* (London: Norton, 1978).
/3/ W. L. Craig, *The Kalam Cosmological Argument* (London: Macmillan, 1979); S. T. Davis, *Logic and the Nature of God* (London: Macmillan, 1983).
/4/ Thus e.g. K. E. Yandell, *Christianity and Philosophy*

(Leicester: IVP, 1984) 48-94, believes that the traditional 'proofs' for God's existence demonstrate only the coherence of theism, while C. S. Evans, *Philosophy of Religion* (Leicester: IVP, 1985) 45-76, affirms that they also show its reasonableness.
/5/ R. H. Stein, 'The "Criteria" for Authenticity,' in *Gospel Perspectives*, vol. 1, ed. R. T. France and D. Wenham (Sheffield: JSOT, 1980) 225-63.
/6/ Cf. L.-E. Halkin, *Initiation à la critique historique* (Paris: Librairie Armand Colin, 1973) 65: 'L'adage juridique *testis unus, testis nullus* n'a pas sa place en historie.' So also D. Fischer, *Historians' Fallacies* (London: Routledge & Kegan Paul, 1971) 62.
/7/ E.g. M. Bloch, *The Historian's Craft* (Manchester: University Press, 1954) 60-61.
/8/ E. Auerbach, *Mimesis: The Representation of Reality in Western Literature* (Princeton: University Press, 1953); N. Frye, *The Great Code: The Bible and Literature* (New York: Harcourt, Brace, Jovanovich, 1982).
/9/ For an introduction to this problem in the *Gospel Perspectives* series, see D. S. Greenwood, 'Poststructuralism and Biblical Studies: Frank Kermode's, *The Genesis of Secrecy*,' in vol. 3, ed. R. T. France and D. Wenham (Sheffield: JSOT, 1983) 263-88.
/10/ G. Twelftree, 'Jesus in Jewish Traditions,' in *Gospel Perspectives*, vol. 5, ed. D. Wenham (Sheffield: JSOT, 1985) 289-341.
/11/ The most valid statistical analysis of this problem is L. Gaston, *Horae Synopticae Electronicae* (Missoula: SBL, 1973).
/12/ An important, too little-known article, which agrees with most of the assertions of this paragraph is P. J. Achtemeier, 'Jesus and the Disciples as Miracle Workers in the Apocryphal New Testament,' in *Aspects of Religious Propaganda in Judaism and Early Christianity*, ed. E. S. Fiorenza (Notre Dame: University Press, 1976) 149-86.
/13/ J. D. Kingsbury, 'The "Divine Man" as the Key to Mark's Christology--The End of an Era?' *Int* 35 (1981) 243-57.
/14/ The article reflects only a small portion of Blackburn's Aberdeen thesis.
/15/ Ten years ago, J. Neusner could lament: 'We have at hand scarcely any critical work comparing various versions of a story appearing in successive compilations' ('The History of Earlier Rabbinic Judaism,' *HistRel* 16 *[*1976-77*]* 222). Despite the prodigious output of works from Neusner and his students in the decade since, there is still nothing like a systematic synopsis of parallel traditions for any sizeable portion of the Rabbinic literature. One study very relevant to the issue at hand,

however, has just appeared (B. M. Bokser, 'Wonder-working and the Rabbinic Tradition: The Case of Hanina ben Dosa,' *JSJ* 16 (1985) 42-92, but it does not inspire confidence in our ability to know much about these first-century figures apart from the substantial modifications of traditions several centuries later.

/16/ The seminar is chaired by Prof. A. C. Wire, of San Francisco Theological Seminary, who kindly alerted me to the existence of the project.

/17/ A. E. Harvey, *Jesus and the Constraints of History* (London: Duckworth, 1982) 100, 104.

/18/ (London: SCM, 1985).

/19/ Harvey, *Jesus*, 107, 113.

/20/ C. L. Blomberg, *Are the Gospels Reliable History?* (forthcoming).

/21/ W. Kelber, *The Oral and the Written Gospel* (Philadelphia: Fortress, 1983). Cf. the response and critique of J. G. Williams, *Gospel against Parable* (Sheffield: Almond, 1985).

/22/ A. B. Lord, *The Singer of Tales* (Cambridge, MA: Harvard, 1960) esp. 128, 137.

/23/ R. Riesner, *Jesus als Lehrer* (Tübingen: Mohr, 1981); P.-G. Müller, *Traditionsprozess im Neuen Testament* (Freiburg: Herder, 1982); A. F. Zimmermann, *Die urchristliche Lehrer* (Tübingen: Mohr, 1984).

/24/ R. Riesner, 'Jüdische Elementarbildung und Evangelienüberlieferung,' in *Gospel Perspectives*, vol. 1, 209-23.

/25/ A good introduction appears in J. L. Resseguie, 'Reader-Response Criticism and the Synoptic Gospels,' *JAAR* 52 (1984) 322. For a preliminary but incisive critique, cf. A. C. Thiselton, 'Reader-Response Hermeneutics, Action Models, and the Parables of Jesus,' in *The Responsibility of Hermeneutics*, with R. Lundin and C. Walhout (Exeter: Paternoster, 1985) 79-113.

/26/ R. J. Banks, 'Setting the "Quest for the Historical Jesus" in a Broader Framework,' in *Gospel Perspectives*, vol. 2, ed. R. T. France and D. Wenham (Sheffield: JSOT, 1981) 61-82. Cf. the excellent little introduction of D. Tidball, *An Introduction to the Sociology of the New Testament* (Exeter: Paternoster, 1983).

/27/ G. Theissen, *The First Followers of Jesus* (London: SCM, 1978) 4. The same ambiguity characterises Theissen's more recent *The Miracle Stories of the Early Christian Tradition* (Edinburgh: T & T Clark, 1983).

/28/ D. Wenham, *The Rediscovery of Jesus' Eschatological Discourse [Gospel Perspectives*, vol. 4*]* (Sheffield: JSOT, 1984).

/29/ I have attempted an initial foray into this field in an article so entitled in *Hermeneutics, Authority, and Canon*, ed. D. A. Carson and J. Woodbridge (Grand Rapids: Zondervan, 1986) forthcoming.

/30/ J. A. T. Robinson, *The Priority of John* (London: SCM, 1985).
/31/ *Das Evangelium und die Evangelien*, ed. P. Stuhlmacher (Tübingen: Mohr, 1983).
/32/ (London: SCM, 1985).
/33/ *ExpT* 97 (1986) 131-32.
/34/ I would like to thank Prof. E. Miller of Boulder, CO; Dr. R. T. France of London; Mr. S. Porter of Sheffield; and Dr. M. J. Harris and Mr. M. Bockmuehl of Cambridge, for valuable assistance with my portions of the editorial responsibilities for this volume.